college accounting
9TH EDITION

A. B. Carson, PhD, CPA

Professor of Accounting
University of California, Los Angeles

Arthur E. Carlson, PhD

Professor of Accounting
Washington University, St. Louis

Clem Boling

A80

Published by

SOUTH-WESTERN PUBLISHING CO.

Cincinnati   West Chicago, Ill.   Dallas   New Rochelle, N.Y.
Palo Alto, Calif.   Brighton, England

preface

College Accounting is for students of accounting, business administration, and secretarial science. An understanding of the principles of business accounting is essential for anyone who aspires to a successful career in business, in many of the professions, and in numerous branches of government. Those who manage or operate a business, its owners, its prospective owners, its present and prospective creditors, governmental taxing authorities, and other government agencies have need for various types of information. Accounting systems are designed to fill such needs. The particular practices followed are tailored to meet the requirements and the circumstances in each case. However, the same accounting principles underlie the practices — just as the same principles of structural engineering apply to the construction of a one-car frame garage and of a fifty-story steel and concrete office building.

This ninth edition of *College Accounting* continues the pattern of earlier editions — explanations of principles with examples of practices. Numerous forms and documents are illustrated. Because the terminology of accounting is undergoing gradual change, the currently preferred terms are used throughout the textbook. Diagrams and color are used both to facilitate understanding and, in the case of many of the color illustrations, to conform to practice. Because the discussion of accounting practices involves several references to computers, an appendix entitled "Computer-Based Accounting Systems — Design and Use" is included.

The textbook is organized to facilitate the use of various supplementary learning aids. Each chapter consists of one or more study assignments. Workbooks containing correlated practice assignments are available. Each

parts 1/2/3

workbook *report* includes an exercise on principles and one or more problems bearing on the material discussed in the related section of the textbook. Additional accounting problems to be used for either supplementary or remedial work are included following Chapters 5, 10, 15, 20, 25, and 30. In addition to the workbooks, four practice sets (one of which is completely new) are available: the first involves the accounting records of a professional man (Howard C. Miller, an architect), the second involves the accounting records of a retail appliance store (The Adams Appliance Store), the third involves the accounting records of a wholesale paint and varnish business (the partnership of Holling & Renz), and the fourth involves the accounting records of a manufacturing business (The B. J. Patrick Manufacturing Co.). These sets provide realistic work designed to test the student's ability to apply his knowledge of the principles of accounting which he has gained from studying the textbook and completing the workbook assignments.

A comprehensive testing program is provided. Tests are available for use following completion of Chapters 2, 5, 10, 15, 20, 25, and 30. Upon completion of each practice set, a test is provided to determine the student's ability to interpret intelligently the records and financial statements of the enterprise.

The authors acknowledge their indebtedness and express their appreciation to the considerable number of accounting instructors, business executives, accountants, and other professional people whose suggestions contributed to the preparation of this textbook.

A. B. C.
A. E. C.
C. B.

contents

parts 1/2/3

contents

chapter 1

the nature of business accounting

The purpose of business accounting is to provide information about the financial affairs and operations of an enterprise to the individuals, agencies, and organizations who have the need and the right to be so informed. These interested parties normally include the following:

(a) The owners of the business — both existing and prospective.

(b) The managers of the business. (Often, but not always, the owners and the managers are the same persons.)

(c) The creditors of the business — both existing and prospective. (*Creditors* are those who furnish or supply products and services "on credit" — meaning that payment need not be made immediately. The creditor category also includes banks and individuals who lend money to the business.)

(d) Government agencies — local, state, and national. (For purposes of either regulation or taxation — sometimes both — various governmental agencies must be given certain financial information.)

The preceding list of four classes of users of information applies to virtually every business enterprise. In connection with many businesses, some or all of the following also make use of relevant information: customers or clients, labor unions, competitors, trade associations, stock exchanges, commodity exchanges, financial analysts, and financial journalists.

The information needed by all of the users is not identical, though most want data regarding either results of operations — net income or loss — for a recent period, or financial status as of a recent date, or both. In addition to these requirements, a variety of other information may be wanted. The exact requirement depends upon who wants it and for what purpose. As might be expected, the demand for the most and greatest variety of information comes from the managers of the business. They constantly need up-to-the-minute information about many things.

The accountant has the task of accumulating and dispensing needed financial information. Since his activities touch upon nearly every phase of business operation and financial information is communicated in accounting terms, accounting is said to be the "language of business." Anyone intending to engage in any type of business activity is well advised to learn this language.

Since accounting relates to so many phases of business, it is not surprising that there are several fields of specialization in accounting. Some major fields are tax work, cost accounting, information systems design and installation, and budget preparation. Many accountants have but one employer; whereas, others become qualified as public accountants and offer their services as independent contractors or consultants. Some states license individuals as *Public Accountants* or *Registered Accountants.* All states grant the designation *Certified Public Accountant* (CPA) to those who meet various prescribed requirements, including the passing of a uniform examination prepared by the American Institute of Certified Public Accountants. Public accountants perform various functions. One of their major activities is *auditing.* This involves testing and checking the records of an enterprise to be certain that acceptable policies and practices have been consistently followed. In recent years, public accountants have been extending their activities into what is called "management services" — a term that covers a variety of specialized consulting assignments. Specialization is common among members of the accounting profession. Tax work is one important example of specialization.

All of the foregoing comments have related to accounting and accountants in connection with profit-seeking organizations. Since there are thousands of nonprofit organizations (such as governments, educational institutions, churches, and hospitals) that also need to accumulate information, thousands of accountants are in their employ. These organizations also engage public accountants. While the "rules of the game" are somewhat different for nonprofit organizations, much of the record keeping is identical with that found in business.

The accounting process

Business accounting may be defined as the art of analyzing and recording financial transactions and certain business-related economic events in a manner that facilitates classifying and summarizing the information, and reporting and interpreting the results.

Analysis is the first step. There may be more than one way of looking at something that has happened. The accountant must determine the fundamental significance to the business of each transaction or event in order to record it properly.

Recording traditionally has meant writing something by hand. Much of the record keeping in accounting still is manual, but for years typewriters and many varieties of so-called "bookkeeping machines" (which typically combine the major attributes of typewriters and adding machines or desk calculators) have been in use. Today the recording sometimes takes the form of holes punched in certain places on a card or a paper tape, or of invisible magnetized spots on a special type of tape used to feed information into an electronic computer.

Classifying relates to the process of sorting or grouping like things together rather than merely keeping a simple, diary-like narrative record of numerous and varied transactions and events.

Summarizing is the process of bringing together various items of information to determine or explain a result.

Reporting refers to the process of attempting to communicate the results. In accounting, it is common to use tabular arrangements rather than narrative-type reports. Sometimes, a combination of the two is used.

Interpreting refers to the steps taken to direct attention to the significance of various matters and relationships. Percentage analyses and ratios often are used to help explain the meaning of certain related bits of information.

Accounting and bookkeeping

Accounting involves forms and records design, policy making, data analysis, report preparation, and report interpretation. A person involved with or responsible for these functions may be referred to as an accountant. Bookkeeping is the recording phase of the accounting process. The person who records the information in the books of account may be referred to as a bookkeeper. Sometimes the accountant also serves as the bookkeeper—an experience that may be of great value to him.

3

Accounting elements

If complete accounting records are to be maintained, all transactions and events that affect the basic accounting elements must be recorded. The basic accounting elements are *assets*, *liabilities*, and *owner's equity*.

Assets. Properties of value that are owned by a business are called assets. Properties such as money, accounts receivable, notes receivable, merchandise, furniture, fixtures, machinery, buildings, and land are common examples of business assets. *Accounts receivable* are unwritten promises by customers to pay at a later date for goods purchased or for services rendered. *Notes receivable* are formal written promises by debtors to pay specified sums of money at some future time.

It is possible to conduct a business or a professional practice with very few assets. A dentist, for example, may have relatively few assets, such as money, instruments, laboratory equipment, and office equipment. But in many cases, a variety of assets is necessary. A merchant must have merchandise to sell and store equipment on which to display the merchandise, in addition to other assets. A manufacturer must have materials, tools, and various sorts of machinery, in addition to other assets.

Liabilities. An obligation of a business to pay a debt is a business liability. The most common liabilities are accounts payable and notes payable. *Accounts payable* are unwritten promises to pay creditors for property, such as merchandise, supplies, and equipment, purchased on credit or for services rendered. *Notes payable* are formal written promises to pay creditors or lenders specified sums of money at some future time. A business also may have one or more types of *taxes payable*.

Owner's Equity. The amount by which the business assets exceed the business liabilities is termed the owner's equity in the business. The word "equity" used in this sense means "interest in" or "claim of." It would be quite reasonable to call liabilities "creditors' equity," but this is not customary. The terms *proprietorship, net worth,* or *capital* are sometimes used as synonyms for owner's equity. If there are no business liabilities, the owner's equity in the business is equal to the total amount of the assets of the business.

In visualizing a business that is owned and operated by one person (traditionally called the proprietor), it is essential to realize that a distinction must be made between his *business* assets and liabilities and any *non-business* assets and liabilities that he may have. The proprietor will certainly have various types of personal property, such as clothing; it is probable that he will have a home, furniture, and a car. He may own a wide variety of other valuable properties quite apart from his business. Like-

4

wise, the proprietor may owe money for reasons that do not pertain to his business. Amounts owed to merchants from whom food and clothing have been purchased and amounts owed to doctors and dentists for services received are common examples. Legally there is no distinction between his business and nonbusiness assets nor between his business and nonbusiness liabilities; but since it is to be expected that the formal accounting records for the enterprise will relate to the business only, any nonbusiness assets and liabilities should be excluded. While the term "owner's equity" can be used in a very broad sense, its use in accounting is nearly always limited to the meaning: business assets minus business liabilities.

Frequent reference will be made to the owner's investing money or other property in the business, or to his withdrawal of money or other property from the business. All that is involved in either case is that some property is changed from the category of a nonbusiness asset to a business asset or vice versa. It should be apparent that these distinctions are important if the owner is to be able to judge the financial condition and results of the operations of his business apart from his nonbusiness affairs.

The accounting equation

The relationship between the three basic accounting elements can be expressed in the form of a simple equation:

ASSETS = LIABILITIES + OWNER'S EQUITY

When the amounts of any two of these elements are known, the third can always be calculated. For example, R. M. Williams has business assets on December 31 in the sum of $25,600. His business debts on that date consist of $500 owed for supplies purchased on account and $800 owed to a bank on a note. The owner's equity element of his business may be calculated by subtraction ($25,600 − $1,300 = $24,300). These facts about his business can be expressed in equation form as follows:

ASSETS = LIABILITIES + OWNER'S EQUITY
$25,600 $1,300 $24,300

In order to increase his equity in the business, Mr. Williams must either increase the assets without increasing the liabilities, or decrease the liabilities without decreasing the assets. In order to increase the assets and owner's equity without investing more money or other property in the business, he will have to operate the business at a profit.

For example, if one year later the assets amount to $39,700 and the liabilities to $1,600, the status of the business would be as follows:

ASSETS = LIABILITIES + OWNER'S EQUITY
$39,700 $1,600 $38,100

However, the fact that Mr. Williams' equity in the business had increased by $13,800 (from $24,300 to $38,100) does not prove that he had made a profit (often called *net income*) equal to the increase. He might have invested additional money or other property in the business. Suppose, for example, that he invested additional money during the year in the amount of $5,000. In that event the remainder of the increase in his equity ($8,800) would have been due to profit (net income).

Another possibility could be that he had a very profitable year and withdrew assets in an amount less than the amount of profit. For example, his equity might have been increased by $20,000 as a result of profitable operation; and during the year he might have withdrawn a total of $6,200 in cash for personal use. This series of events could account for the $13,800 increase. It is essential that the business records show the extent to which the change in owner's equity is due to the regular operation of the business and the extent to which increases and decreases in owner's equity are due to the owner's investing and withdrawing assets.

Transactions

Any activity of an enterprise which involves the exchange of values is usually referred to as a *transaction.* These values are expressed in terms of money. Buying and selling property and services are common transactions. The following typical transactions are analyzed to show that each one represents an exchange of values.

TYPICAL TRANSACTIONS	ANALYSIS OF TRANSACTIONS
(a) Purchased equipment for cash, $850.	Money was exchanged for equipment.
(b) Received cash in payment of professional fees, $200.	Professional service was rendered in exchange for money.
(c) Paid office rent, $150.	Money was exchanged for the right to use property.
(d) Paid an amount owed to a creditor, $500.	Money was given in settlement of a debt that may have resulted from the purchase of property on account or from services rendered by a creditor.
(e) Paid wages in cash, $110.	Money was exchanged for services rendered.
(f) Borrowed $2,000 at a bank giving a 7 percent interest-bearing note due in 30 days.	A liability known as a note payable was incurred in exchange for money.
(g) Purchased office equipment on account, $300.	A liability known as an account payable was incurred in exchange for office equipment.

Effect of transactions on the accounting equation

Each transaction affects one or more of the three basic accounting elements. For example, the purchase of equipment for cash represents both an increase and a decrease in assets. The assets increased because equipment was acquired; the assets decreased because cash was disbursed. If the equipment had been purchased on account, thereby incurring a liability, the transaction would result in an increase in assets (equipment) with a corresponding increase in liabilities (accounts payable). Neither of these transactions has any effect upon the owner's equity element of the equation.

The effect of any transaction on the basic accounting elements may be indicated by addition and subtraction. To illustrate: assume that Frank Smith, an engineer, decided to go into business for himself. During the first month of this venture (May, 1972), the following transactions relating to his business took place:

An Increase in an Asset Offset by an Increase in Owner's Equity

Transaction (a). Mr. Smith opened a bank account with a deposit of $5,000. This transaction caused his new business to receive the asset cash; and since no business liabilities were involved, the owner's equity element was increased by the same amount. As a result of this transaction, the equation for the business would appear as follows:

$$
\left.\begin{array}{c} \text{ASSETS} \\ \text{Cash} \\ \text{(a) } 5{,}000 \end{array}\right\} = \left\{\begin{array}{c} \text{LIABILITIES} + \text{OWNER'S EQUITY} \\ \text{Frank Smith, Capital} \\ 5{,}000 \end{array}\right.
$$

An Increase in an Asset Offset by an Increase in a Liability

Transaction (b). Mr. Smith purchased office equipment (desk, chairs, file cabinet, etc.) for $3,100 on 30 days' credit. This transaction caused the asset office equipment to increase by $3,100 and resulted in an equal increase in the liability accounts payable. Updating the foregoing equation by this (b) transaction gives the following result:

ASSETS			LIABILITIES	+ OWNER'S EQUITY
Cash +	Office Equipment		Accounts Payable	Frank Smith, Capital
Bal. 5,000				5,000
(b) ⎯⎯	+3,100	=	+3,100	⎯⎯
Bal. 5,000	3,100		3,100	5,000

An Increase in One Asset Offset by a Decrease in Another Asset

Transaction (c). Mr. Smith purchased office supplies (stationery, carbon paper, pencils, etc.) for cash, $420. This transaction caused a $420 increase in the asset office supplies that exactly offset the $420 decrease in the asset cash. The effect on the equation is as follows:

ASSETS				LIABILITIES +	OWNER'S EQUITY
		Office	Office	Accounts	Frank Smith,
	Cash +	Equipment +	Supplies	Payable	Capital
Bal.	5,000	3,100		3,100	5,000
(c)	−420		+420		
Bal.	4,580	3,100	420	3,100	5,000

A Decrease in an Asset Offset by a Decrease in a Liability

Transaction (d). Mr. Smith paid $1,500 on account to the company from which the office equipment was purchased. (See Transaction (b).) This payment caused the asset cash and the liability accounts payable both to decrease $1,500. The effect on the equation is as follows:

ASSETS				LIABILITIES +	OWNER'S EQUITY
		Office	Office	Accounts	Frank Smith,
	Cash +	Equipment +	Supplies	Payable	Capital
Bal.	4,580	3,100	420	3,100	5,000
(d)	−1,500			−1,500	
Bal.	3,080	3,100	420	1,600	5,000

8

An Increase in an Asset Offset by an Increase in Owner's Equity Resulting from Revenue

Transaction (e). Mr. Smith received $1,000 cash from a client for professional services. This transaction caused the asset cash to increase $1,000, and since the liabilities were not affected, the owner's equity increased by the same amount. The effect on the equation is as follows:

ASSETS				LIABILITIES +	OWNER'S EQUITY
		Office	Office	Accounts	Frank Smith,
	Cash +	Equipment +	Supplies	Payable	Capital
Bal.	3,080	3,100	420	1,600	5,000
(e)	+1,000				+1,000
Bal.	4,080	3,100	420	1,600	6,000

A Decrease in an Asset Offset by a Decrease in Owner's Equity Resulting from Expense

Transaction (f). Mr. Smith paid $250 for office rent for May. This transaction caused the asset cash to be reduced by $250 with an equal reduction in owner's equity. The effect on the equation is as follows:

ASSETS				LIABILITIES + OWNER'S EQUITY	
	Office	Office		Accounts	Frank Smith,
Cash +	Equipment +	Supplies		Payable	Capital
Bal. 4,080	3,100	420	=	1,600	6,000
(f) −250					−250
Bal. 3,830	3,100	420		1,600	5,750

Transaction (g). Mr. Smith paid a bill for telephone service, $28. This transaction, like the previous one, caused a decrease in the asset cash with an equal decrease in the owner's equity. The effect on the equation is as follows:

ASSETS				LIABILITIES + OWNER'S EQUITY	
	Office	Office		Accounts	Frank Smith,
Cash +	Equipment +	Supplies		Payable	Capital
Bal. 3,830	3,100	420	=	1,600	5,750
(g) − 28					− 28
Bal. 3,802	3,100	420		1,600	5,722

The financial statements

A set of accounting records is maintained to fill a variety of needs. Foremost is its use as source data in preparing various reports including those referred to as _financial statements_. The two most important of these are the _income statement_ and the _balance sheet_.

The Income Statement. The income statement, sometimes called a _profit and loss statement_ or _operating statement_, shows the _net income_ (_net profit_) or _net loss_ for a specified period of time and how it was calculated. A very simple income statement relating to the business of Frank Smith for the first month's operation, May, 1972, is shown below. The information it contains was obtained by analysis of the changes in the owner's equity element of the business for the month. This element went from zero to $5,722. Part of this increase, $5,000, was due to the investment of Mr. Smith. The remainder of the increase, $722, must have been due to net income, since Mr. Smith had made no withdrawals. Transaction (e) involved revenue of $1,000; transactions (f) and (g) involved expenses of $250 and $28, respectively. Taken together, these three transactions explain the net income of $722.

FRANK SMITH, ENGINEER
Income Statement
For the Month of May, 1972

Professional fees......................		$1,000
Expenses:		
Rent expense.....................	$250	
Telephone expense................	28	278
Net income for month..................		$ 722

The Balance Sheet. The balance sheet, sometimes called a *statement of financial condition* or *statement of financial position,* shows the assets, liabilities, and owner's equity of a business at a specified date. A balance sheet for Mr. Smith's business as of May 31, 1972, is shown below. The information it contains was obtained from the accounting equation after the last transaction (g).

FRANK SMITH, ENGINEER
Balance Sheet
May 31, 1972

Assets		Liabilities	
Cash.....................	$3,802	Accounts payable..........	$1,600
Office supplies............	420		
Office equipment.........	3,100	Owner's Equity	
		Frank Smith, capital........	5,722
	$7,322		$7,322

NOTE: In order to keep the illustrations of transaction analysis, the income statement, and the balance sheet as simple as possible at this point, two expenses were ignored; namely, office supplies used and depreciation of office equipment.

10

Report No. 1-1

A workbook is provided for use with this textbook. Each practice assignment in the workbook is referred to as a report. The work involved in completing Report No. 1-1 requires a knowledge of the principles developed in the preceding study assignment. Before proceeding with the following assignment, complete Report No. 1-1 in accordance with the instructions given in the workbook.

The double-entry mechanism

The meanings of the terms asset, liability, and owner's equity were explained in the preceding pages. Examples were given to show how each business transaction causes a change in one or more of the three basic accounting elements. The first transaction (a) shown on page 7 involved an increase in an asset with a corresponding increase in owner's equity. In the second transaction (b), an increase in an asset caused an equal increase in a liability. In the third transaction (c), an increase in one asset was offset by a decrease in another. In each of the transactions illustrated, there was this *dual effect*. This is always true. A change (increase or decrease) in any asset, any liability, or in owner's equity is always accompanied by an offsetting change within the basic accounting elements.

The fact that each transaction has two aspects — a dual effect upon the accounting elements — provides the basis for what is called *double-entry bookkeeping*. This phrase describes a recording system that involves the making of a record of each of the two aspects that are involved in every transaction. Double entry does not mean that a transaction is recorded twice; instead, it means that both of the two aspects of each transaction are recorded.

The technique of double entry is described and illustrated in the following pages. This method of recording transactions is not new. Double entry is known to have been practiced for at least 500 years. This long popularity is easily explained since the method has several virtues. It is orderly, fairly simple, and very flexible. There is no transaction that cannot be recorded in a double-entry manner. Double entry promotes accuracy. Its use makes it impossible for certain types of errors to remain undetected for very long. For example, if one aspect of a transaction is properly recorded but the other part is overlooked, it will soon be found that the records are "out of balance." The bookkeeper then knows that something is wrong and can check his work to discover the trouble and can make the needed correction.

The account

It has been explained previously that the assets of a business may consist of a number of items, such as money, accounts receivable, notes receivable, merchandise, equipment, buildings, and land. The liabilities may consist of one or more items, such as accounts payable and notes payable. A separate record should be kept of each asset and of each liability. Later it will be shown that a separate record should also be kept of the increases and decreases in owner's equity. The form of record kept for each item is known as an *account*. There are many types of account forms in general use. They may be ruled on sheets of paper and bound in book form or kept in a loose-leaf binder, or they may be ruled on cards and kept in a file of some sort. Following is an illustration of a standard form of account that is widely used:

ACCOUNT   ACCOUNT NO.

DATE	ITEM	POST. REF.	DEBIT	DATE	ITEM	POST. REF.	CREDIT

Standard Form of Account

This account form is designed to facilitate the recording of the essential information regarding each transaction that affects the account. Before any entries are recorded in an account, the title and number of the account should be written on the horizontal line at the top of the form. Each account should be given an appropriate title that will indicate whether it is an asset, a liability, or an owner's equity account. The standard account form is divided into two equal parts or sections which are ruled identically to facilitate recording increases and decreases. The left side is called the debit side, while the right side is called the credit side. The columnar arrangement and headings of the columns on both sides are the same except that the amount column on the left is headed "Debit" while that on the right is headed "Credit." The Date columns are used for recording the dates of transactions. The Item columns may be used for writing a brief description of a transaction when deemed necessary. The Posting Reference columns will be discussed later. The Debit and Credit columns are used for recording the amounts of transactions.

The three major parts of the standard account form are **(1)** the title (and, usually, the account number), **(2)** the debit side, and **(3)** the credit side. To determine the balance of an account at any time, it is necessary only to total the amounts in the Debit and Credit columns, and calculate the difference between the two totals. To save time, a "T" form of account is commonly used for instructional purposes. It consists of a two-line drawing resembling the capital letter T and is sometimes referred to as a skeleton form of account.

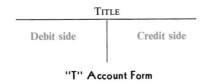

"T" Account Form

Debits and credits

To debit an account means to record an amount on the left or debit side of the account. To credit an account means to record an amount on the right or credit side of the account. The abbreviation for debit is Dr. and for credit Cr. (based on the Latin terms *debere* and *credere*). Sometimes the word *charge* is used as a substitute for debit. Increases in assets are recorded on the left side of the accounts; increases in liabilities and in owner's equity are recorded on the right side of the accounts. Decreases in assets are recorded on the right side of the accounts; decreases in liabilities and in owner's equity are recorded on the left side of the accounts. Recording increases and decreases in the accounts in this manner will reflect the basic equality of assets to liabilities plus owner's equity; at the same time it will maintain equality between the total amounts debited to all accounts and the total amounts credited to all accounts. These basic relationships may be illustrated in the following manner:

13

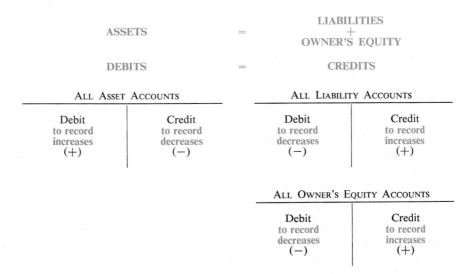

Use of asset, liability, and owner's equity accounts

To illustrate the application of the double-entry process, the transactions discussed on pages 7-9 will be analyzed and their effect on the accounting elements will be indicated by showing the proper entries in "T" accounts. As before, the transactions are identified by letters; dates are omitted intentionally.

An Increase in an Asset Offset by an Increase in Owner's Equity

Transaction (a). Frank Smith, an engineer, started a business of his own and invested $5,000 in cash.

CASH		FRANK SMITH, CAPITAL	
(a) 5,000			(a) 5,000

Analysis: As a result of this transaction the business acquired an asset, cash. The amount of money invested by Mr. Smith represents his equity in the business; thus the amount of the asset cash is equal to the owner's equity in the business. Separate accounts are kept for the asset cash and for the owner. To record the transaction properly, the cash account was debited and Frank Smith's capital account was credited for $5,000.

An Increase in an Asset Offset by an Increase in a Liability

Transaction (b). Purchased office equipment (desk, chairs, file cabinet, etc.) for $3,100 on 30 days' credit.

OFFICE EQUIPMENT		ACCOUNTS PAYABLE	
(b) 3,100			(b) 3,100

Analysis: As a result of this transaction the business acquired a new asset, office equipment. The debt incurred as a result of purchasing the office equipment on 30 days' credit is a liability, accounts payable. Separate accounts are kept for office equipment and for accounts payable. The purchase of office equipment caused an increase in the assets of the business. Therefore, the asset account Office Equipment was debited for $3,100. The purchase also caused an increase in a liability. Therefore, the liability account Accounts Payable was credited for $3,100.

An Increase in One Asset Offset by a Decrease in Another Asset

Transaction (c). Purchased office and drawing supplies (stationery, carbon paper, pencils, etc.) for cash, $420.

CASH				OFFICE SUPPLIES	
(a)	5,000	(c)	420	(c)	420

Analysis: As a result of this transaction the business acquired a new asset, office supplies. However, the addition of this asset was offset by a decrease in the asset cash. To record the transaction properly, Office Supplies was debited and Cash was credited for $420. (It will be noted that this is the second entry in the cash account; the account was previously debited for $5,000 when Transaction (a) was recorded.)

It is proper to record office supplies as an asset at time of purchase even though they will become an expense when consumed. (The procedure in accounting for supplies consumed will be discussed later.)

A Decrease in an Asset Offset by a Decrease in a Liability

Transaction (d). Paid $1,500 "on account" to the company from which the office equipment was purchased. (See Transaction (b).)

CASH				ACCOUNTS PAYABLE			
(a)	5,000	(c)	420	(d)	1,500	(b)	3,100
		(d)	1,500				

Analysis: This transaction resulted in a decrease in the liability accounts payable with a corresponding decrease in the asset cash; hence, it was recorded by debiting Accounts Payable and by crediting Cash for $1,500. (It will be noted that this is the second entry in the accounts payable account and the third entry in the cash account.)

Revenue and expense

The owner's equity element of a business or professional enterprise may be increased in two ways as follows:

(a) The owner may invest additional money or other property in the enterprise. Such investments result in an increase both in the assets of the enterprise and in the owner's equity, but they do not further enrich the owner; he merely has more property invested in the enterprise and less property outside of the enterprise.

(b) Revenue may be derived from sales of goods or services, or from other sources.

As used in accounting, the term *revenue* refers to an increase in the owner's equity in a business resulting from transactions of any kind except the investment of assets in the business by its owner. In most cases, the increase in owner's equity due to revenue results from an addition to the assets without any change in the liabilities. Often it is cash that is increased. However, an increase in cash and other assets can occur in connection with several types of transactions that do not involve revenue. For this reason, revenue is defined in terms of the change in owner's equity rather than the change in assets. Any transaction that causes owner's equity to increase, except investments in the business by its owner, involves revenue.

The owner's equity element of a business or professional enterprise may be decreased in two ways as follows:

(a) The owner may withdraw assets (cash or other property) from the enterprise.

(b) Expenses may be incurred in operating the enterprise.

As used in accounting, the term *expense* means a decrease in the owner's equity in a business caused by a transaction other than a withdrawal by the owner. When an expense is incurred, either the assets are reduced or the liabilities are increased. In either event, owner's equity is reduced. If the transaction causing the reduction was not a withdrawal of assets by the owner, an expense was incurred. Common examples of expense are rent of office or store, salaries of employees, telephone service, supplies consumed, and many types of taxes.

If, during a specified period of time, the total increases in owner's equity resulting from revenue exceed the total decreases resulting from expenses, it may be said that the excess represents the *net income* or net profit for the period. On the other hand, if the expenses of the period exceed the revenue, such excess represents a *net loss* for the period. The time interval used in the measurement of net income or net loss can be chosen by the owner. It may be a month, a quarter (three months), a year, or some other period of time. If the accounting period is a year, it is usually referred to as a *fiscal year*. The fiscal year frequently coincides with the *calendar year*.

Transactions involving revenue and expense always cause a change in the owner's equity element of an enterprise. Such changes could be recorded by debiting the owner's equity account for expenses and crediting it for revenue. If this practice were followed, however, the credit side of the owner's equity account would contain a mixture of increases due to revenue and to the investment of assets in the business by the owner, while the debit side would contain a mixture of decreases due to expenses and to the withdrawal of assets from the business by the owner. In order to calculate the net income or the net loss for each accounting period, a careful analysis of the owner's equity account would be required. It is, therefore, better practice to record revenue and expenses in separate accounts. These are called *temporary* owner's equity accounts because it is customary to close them at the end of each accounting period by transferring their balances to a *summary* account. The balance of this summary account then represents the net income or net loss for the period. The summary account is also a temporary account which is closed by transferring its balance to the owner's equity account.

A separate account should be kept for each type of revenue and for each type of expense. When a transaction produces revenue, the amount of the revenue should be credited to an appropriate revenue account. When a transaction involves expense, the amount of the expense should be debited to an appropriate expense account. The relationship of these temporary accounts to the owner's equity account and the application of the debit and credit theory to the accounts are indicated in the following diagram:

ALL OWNER'S EQUITY ACCOUNTS

Debit	Credit
to record decreases (−)	to record increases (+)

ALL EXPENSE ACCOUNTS		ALL REVENUE ACCOUNTS	
Debit	Credit	Debit	Credit
to record increases (+)	to record decreases (−)	to record decreases (−)	to record increases (+)

It is important to recognize that the credit side of each revenue account is serving temporarily as a part of the credit side of the owner's equity account. Increases in owner's equity are recorded as credits. Thus, increases in owner's equity resulting from revenue should be credited to revenue accounts. The debit side of each expense account is serving temporarily as a part of the debit side of the owner's equity account. Decreases in owner's equity are recorded as debits. Thus, decreases in owner's equity resulting from expense should be debited to expense accounts.

Use of revenue and expense accounts

To illustrate the application of the double-entry process in recording transactions that affect revenue and expense accounts, the transactions that follow will be analyzed and their effect on the accounting elements will be indicated by showing the proper entries in "T" accounts. These transactions represent a continuation of the transactions completed by Frank Smith, an engineer, in the conduct of his business. (See pages 14 and 15 for Transactions (a) to (d).)

An Increase in an Asset Offset by an Increase in Owner's Equity Resulting from Revenue

Transaction (e). Received $1,000 in cash from a client for professional services rendered.

CASH			PROFESSIONAL FEES	
(a) 5,000	(c) 420			(e) 1,000
(e) 1,000	(d) 1,500			

Analysis: This transaction resulted in an increase in the asset cash with a corresponding increase in owner's equity because of revenue from professional fees. To record the transaction properly, Cash was debited and an appropriate account for the revenue was credited for $1,000. Accounts should always be given a descriptive title that will aid in classifying them in relation to the accounting elements. In this case the revenue account was given the title Professional Fees. (It will be noted that this is the fourth entry in the cash account and the first entry in the account Professional Fees.)

A Decrease in an Asset Offset by a Decrease in Owner's Equity Resulting from Expense

Transaction (f). Paid $250 for office rent for one month.

CASH			RENT EXPENSE	
(a) 5,000	(c) 420	(f)	250	
(e) 1,000	(d) 1,500			
	(f) 250			

Analysis: This transaction resulted in a decrease in the asset cash with a corresponding decrease in owner's equity because of expense. To record the transaction properly, Rent Expense was debited and Cash was credited for $250. (This is the first entry in the rent expense account and the fifth entry in the cash account.)

18

Transaction (g). Paid bill for telephone service, $28.

	CASH					TELEPHONE EXPENSE	
(a)	5,000	(c)	420		(g)	28	
(e)	1,000	(d)	1,500				
		(f)	250				
		(g)	28				

Analysis: This transaction is identical with the previous one except that telephone expense rather than rent expense was the reason for the decrease in owner's equity. To record the transaction properly, Telephone Expense was debited and Cash was credited for $28.

The trial balance

It is a fundamental principle of double-entry bookkeeping that the amount of the assets is always equal to the sum of the liabilities and owner's equity. In order to maintain this equality in recording transactions, the sum of the debit entries must always be equal to the sum of the credit entries. To determine whether this equality has been maintained, it is customary to take a trial balance periodically. A *trial balance* is a list of all of the accounts showing the title and balance of each account. The balance of any account is the amount of difference between the total debits and the total credits to the account. Preliminary to taking a trial balance, the debit and credit amounts in each account should be totaled. This is called *footing* the amount columns. If there is only one item entered in a column, no footing is necessary. To find the balance of an account it is necessary only to determine the difference between the footings by subtraction. Since asset and expense accounts are debited for increases, these accounts normally have *debit balances*. Since liability, owner's equity, and revenue accounts are credited to record increases, these accounts normally have *credit balances*. The balance of an account should be entered on the side of the account that has the larger total. The footings and balances of accounts should be written in small figures just below the last entry. A pencil is generally used for this purpose. If the footings of an account are equal in amount the account is said to be *in balance*.

The accounts of Frank Smith are reproduced on page 20. To show the relationship to the fundamental accounting equation, the accounts are arranged in three columns under the headings of Assets, Liabilities, and Owner's Equity. It will be noted that the cash account has been footed and the balance inserted on the left side. The two debits totaled $6,000; the four credits totaled $2,198. Thus, the debit balance was $3,802. The

19

footings and the balance are printed in italics. It was not necessary to foot any of the other accounts because none of them contained more than one entry on either side. The balance of the accounts payable account is shown on the credit side in italics. It was not necessary to enter the balances of the other accounts because there were entries on only one side of those accounts.

ASSETS	=	LIABILITIES	+	OWNER'S EQUITY

CASH

(a)	5,000	(c)	420
(e)	1,000	(d)	1,500
3,802		(f)	250
	6,000	(g)	28
			2,198

ACCOUNTS PAYABLE

| (d) | 1,500 | (b) | 3,100 |
| | | *1,600* | |

FRANK SMITH, CAPITAL

| | | (a) | 5,000 |

OFFICE SUPPLIES

| (c) | 420 |

PROFESSIONAL FEES

| | | (e) | 1,000 |

OFFICE EQUIPMENT

| (b) | 3,100 |

RENT EXPENSE

| (f) | 250 |

TELEPHONE EXPENSE

| (g) | 28 |

20 A trial balance of Frank Smith's accounts is shown below. The trial balance was taken on May 31, 1972; therefore, this date is shown in the third line of the heading. The trial balance reveals that the debit and credit totals are equal in amount. This is proof that in recording Transactions (a) to (g) inclusive the total of the debits was equal to the total of the credits.

Frank Smith, Engineer
Trial Balance
May 31, 1972

Account	Dr. Balance	Cr. Balance
Cash	3802 00	
Office Supplies	420 00	
Office Equipment	3100 00	
Accounts Payable		1600 00
Frank Smith, Capital		5000 00
Professional Fees		1000 00
Rent Expense	250 00	
Telephone Expense	28 00	
	7600 00	7600 00

Frank M. Smith's Trial Balance

A trial balance is not a formal statement or report. Normally, it is never seen by anyone except the accountant or bookkeeper. It is used to aid in preparing the income statement and the balance sheet. If the trial balance on the preceding page is studied in conjunction with the income statement and balance sheet shown on pages 9 and 10, it will be seen that those statements could have been prepared quite easily from the information that this trial balance provides.

Report No. 1-2

Refer to the workbook and complete Report No. 1-2 in accordance with the instructions given therein. The work involved in completing the assignment requires a knowledge of the principles developed in the preceding discussion. Any difficulty experienced in completing the report will indicate a lack of understanding of these principles. In such event further study should be helpful. After completing the report, you may continue with the textbook discussion in Chapter 2 until the next report is required.

21

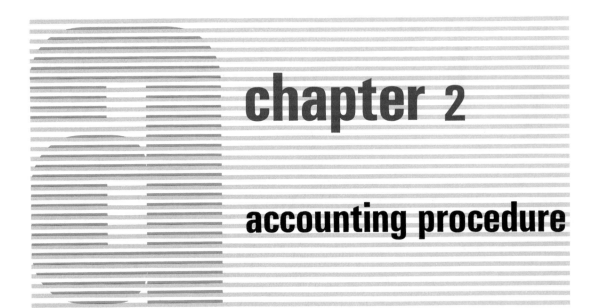

chapter 2

accounting procedure

The principles of double-entry bookkeeping were explained and illustrated in the preceding pages. To avoid distraction from the fundamentals, the mechanics of collecting and classifying information about business transactions were ignored. In actual practice the first record of a transaction (sometimes called the "source document") is made in the form of a business paper, such as a check stub, receipt, cash register tape, sales ticket, or purchase invoice. The information supplied by source documents is an aid in analyzing transactions to determine their effect upon the accounts.

Journalizing transactions

The first formal double-entry record of a transaction is usually made in a record called a *journal* (frequently in book form). The act of recording transactions in a journal is called *journalizing*. It is necessary to analyze each transaction before it can be journalized properly. The purpose of the journal entries is to provide a chronological record of all transactions completed showing the date of each transaction, titles of accounts to be debited and credited, and amounts of the debits and credits. The journal then provides all the information needed to record the debits and credits in the proper accounts. The flow of data concerning transactions can be illustrated in the following manner:

Transactions are evidenced
by various
SOURCE DOCUMENTS────→The source documents provide the information needed to record the transactions in a
JOURNAL────────────→The journal provides the information needed to record the debits and credits in the accounts which collectively comprise a
LEDGER

Source documents

The term source document covers a wide variety of forms and papers. Almost any document that provides information about a business transaction can be called a source document.

SOURCE DOCUMENTS

Examples:	Provide information about:
(a) Check stubs or carbon copies of checks	Cash disbursements
(b) Receipt stubs, or carbon copies of receipts, cash register tapes, or memos of cash register totals	Cash receipts
(c) Copies of sales tickets or sales invoices issued to customers or clients	Sales of goods or services
(d) Purchase invoices received from vendors	Purchases of goods or services

23

The journal

While the original record of a transaction usually is a source document as explained above, the first formal double-entry record of a transaction is made in a journal. For this reason a journal is commonly referred to as a *book of original entry*. The ruling of the pages of a journal varies with the type and size of an enterprise and the nature of its operations. The simplest form of journal is a two-column journal. A standard form of such a journal is illustrated on page 24. It is referred to as a two-column journal because it has only two amount columns, one for debits and one for credits. In the illustration the columns have been numbered as a means of identification in connection with the following discussion.

	DATE	DESCRIPTION	POST. REF.	DEBIT	CREDIT	
1						1
2						2
3						3
4	①	②	③	④	⑤	4
5						5
6						6
7						7
8						8
9						9
10						10

Standard Two-Column Journal

Column No. 1 is a date column. The year should be written in small figures at the top of the column immediately below the column heading and need only be repeated at the top of each new page unless an entry for a new year is made farther down on the page. The date column is a double column, the perpendicular single rule being used to separate the month from the day. Thus in writing June 20, the name of the month should be written to the left of the single line and the number designating the day of the month should be written to the right of this line. The name of the month need only be shown for the first entry on a page unless an entry for a new month is made farther down on the page.

Column No. 2 is generally referred to as a description or an explanation column. It is used to record the titles of the accounts affected by each transaction, together with a description of the transaction. Two or more accounts are affected by each transaction, and the titles of all accounts affected must be recorded. Normally the titles of the accounts debited are written first and then the titles of the accounts credited. A separate line should be used for each account title. The titles of the accounts to be debited are generally written at the extreme left of the column, while the titles of the accounts to be credited are usually indented about one-half inch. The description should be written immediately following the credit entry, and usually is indented an additional one-half inch. Reference to the journal reproduced on pages 31 and 32 will help to visualize the arrangement of the copy in the Description column. An orderly arrangement is desirable.

Column No. 3 is a posting reference column — sometimes referred to as a folio column. No entries are made in this column at the time of journalizing the transactions; such entries are made only at the time of posting (which is the process of entering the debits and credits in the proper accounts in the ledger). This procedure will be explained in detail later in this chapter.

Column No. 4 is an amount column in which the amount that is to be debited to any account should be written on the line on which the title of the account appears. In other words, the name of the account to be debited should be written in the Description column and the amount of the debit entry should be written on the same line in the Debit column.

Column No. 5 is an amount column in which the amount that is to be credited to any account should be written on the line on which the title of the account appears. In other words, the name of the account to be credited should be written in the Description column and the amount of the credit entry should be written on the same line in the Credit column.

Journalizing

Journalizing involves recording the significant information concerning each transaction either **(1)** at the time the transaction occurs or **(2)** subsequently, but in the chronological order in which the transactions occurred. For every transaction the entry should record the date, the title of each account affected, the amount, and a brief description. The only effect a transaction can have on any account is either to increase or to decrease the balance of the account. Before a transaction can be recorded properly, therefore, it must be analyzed in order to determine:

    (a) Which accounts are affected by the transaction.
    (b) What effect the transaction has upon each of the accounts involved; that is, whether the balance of each affected account is increased or decreased.

The chart of accounts

In analyzing a transaction preparatory to journalizing it, the accountant or bookkeeper must know which accounts are being kept. When an accounting system is being established for a new business, the first step is to decide which accounts are required. The accounts used will depend upon the information needed or desired. Ordinarily it will be found desirable to keep a separate account for each type of asset and each type of liability, since it is certain that information will be desired in regard to what is owned and what is owed. A permanent owner's equity or capital account should be kept in order that information may be available as to the owner's interest or equity in the business. Furthermore, it is advisable to keep separate accounts for each type of revenue and each kind of expense. The revenue and expense accounts are the temporary accounts that are used in recording increases and decreases in owner's equity apart from changes caused by the owner's investments and withdrawals. The specific accounts to be kept for recording the increases and the decreases in owner's equity depend upon the nature and the sources of the revenue and the nature of the expenses incurred in earning the revenue.

A professional man or an individual engaged in operating a small enterprise may need to keep relatively few accounts. On the other hand, a large manufacturing enterprise, a public utility, or any large business may need to keep a great many accounts in order that the information required or desired may be available. Regardless of the number of accounts kept, they can be segregated into the three major classes and should be grouped according to these classes in the ledger. The usual custom is to place the asset accounts first, the liability accounts second, and the owner's equity accounts, including the revenue and the expense accounts, last. It is common practice to prepare a list of the accounts that are to be kept. This list, often in the form of an outline, is called a *chart of accounts.* It has become a general practice to give each account a number and to keep the accounts in numerical order. The numbering usually follows a consistent pattern and becomes a *code.* For example, asset accounts may be assigned numbers that always start with "1," liability accounts with "2," owner's equity accounts with "3," revenue accounts with "4," and expense accounts with "5."

To illustrate: Suppose that on November 30, 1972, W. F. Brown engages in the advertising business under the name of The Brown Advertising Agency. He decides to keep his accounts on the calendar year basis; therefore, his first accounting period will be for one month only, that is, the month of December. It is decided that a two-column journal and a ledger with the standard form of account will be used. Mr. Brown realizes that he will not need many accounts at present because the business is new. He also realizes that additional accounts may be added as the need arises. Following is a chart of the accounts to be kept at the start:

THE BROWN ADVERTISING AGENCY

CHART OF ACCOUNTS

*Assets**
111 Cash
112 Office Supplies
121 Office Equipment

Liabilities
211 Accounts Payable

Owner's Equity
311 W. F. Brown, Capital
312 W. F. Brown, Drawing

Revenue
411 Advertising Fees

Expenses
511 Rent Expense
512 Salary Expense
513 Traveling Expense
514 Telephone Expense
515 Office Supplies Expense
516 Miscellaneous Expense

Words in italics represent headings and not account titles.

Journalizing procedure illustrated

To illustrate journalizing procedure, the transactions completed by The Brown Advertising Agency through December 31, 1972, will be journalized. A *narrative* of the transactions follows. It provides all of the information that is needed in journalizing the transactions. Some of the transactions are analyzed to explain their effect upon the accounts, with the journal entry immediately following the explanation of the entry. The journal of The Brown Advertising Agency with all of the entries recorded is reproduced on pages 31 and 32.

THE BROWN ADVERTISING AGENCY

NARRATIVE OF TRANSACTIONS

Thursday, November 30, 1972

Mr. Brown invested $2,000 cash in a business enterprise to be known as The Brown Advertising Agency.

> As a result of this transaction, the business acquired the asset cash in the amount of $2,000. Since neither a decrease in any other asset nor an increase in any liability was involved, the transaction caused an increase of $2,000 in owner's equity. Accordingly, the entry to record the transaction is a debit to Cash and a credit to W. F. Brown, Capital, for $2,000.

JOURNAL   PAGE *1*   **27**

	DATE	DESCRIPTION	POST. REF.	DEBIT	CREDIT	
1	*1972* Nov. 30	Cash		2000.00		1
2		W. F. Brown, Capital			2000.00	2
3		Original investment in				3
4		advertising agency.				4

Note that the following steps were involved:

(a) Since this was the first entry on the journal page, the year was written at the top of the Date column.

(b) The month and day were written on the first line in the Date column.

(c) The title of the account to be debited, Cash, was written on the first line at the extreme left of the Description column. The amount of the debit, $2,000, was written on the same line in the Debit column.

(d) The title of the account to be credited, W. F. Brown, Capital, was written on the second line indented one half inch from the left side of the Description column. The amount of the credit, $2,000, was written on the same line in the Credit column.

(e) The explanation of the entry was started on the next line indented an additional one-half inch. The second line of the explanation was also indented the same distance as the first.

Friday, December 1

Paid office rent for December in advance, $300.

This transaction resulted in a decrease in owner's equity because of expense, with a corresponding decrease in the asset cash. The transaction is recorded by debiting Rent Expense and by crediting Cash for $300.

5	Dec. 1	Rent Expense	300 00	
6		Cash		300 00
7		Paid December rent.		

Note: Mr. Brown ordered several pieces of office equipment. Since the dealer did not have in stock what Mr. Brown wanted, the articles were ordered from the factory. Delivery is not expected until the latter part of the month. Pending their arrival, the dealer loaned Mr. Brown some used office equipment. No entry is required until the new equipment is received.

Monday, December 4

Purchased office supplies from the Business Supply Co. on account, $216.14.

In this transaction the business acquired a new asset which represented an increase in the total assets. A liability was also incurred because of the purchase on account. The transaction is recorded by debiting Office Supplies and by crediting Accounts Payable for $216.14. As these supplies are consumed, the amount will become an expense of the business.

8	4	Office Supplies	216 14	
9		Accounts Payable		216 14
10		Business Supply Co.		

Tuesday, December 5

Paid the Central Telephone Co. $27.50 covering the cost of installing a telephone in the office, together with the first month's service charges payable in advance.

This transaction caused a decrease in owner's equity because of expense and a corresponding decrease in the asset cash. The transaction is recorded by debiting Telephone Expense and by crediting Cash for $27.50.

11	5	Telephone Expense	27 50	
12		Cash		27 50
13		Paid telephone bill.		

Wednesday, December 6

Paid $7 for a subscription to a trade journal.

This transaction resulted in a decrease in owner's equity due to expense and a corresponding decrease in the asset cash. The transaction is recorded by debiting Miscellaneous Expense and by crediting Cash for $7.

14	6	Miscellaneous Expense		7 00			14
15		Cash			7 00		15
16		Trade journal subscription.					16

Thursday, December 7

Received $150 from the Century Hardware Co. for services rendered.

This transaction resulted in an increase in the asset cash with a corresponding increase in owner's equity because of revenue from advertising fees. The transaction is recorded by debiting Cash and by crediting Advertising Fees for $150. In keeping his accounts Mr. Brown follows the practice of not recording revenue until it is received in cash. This practice is common to professional and personal service enterprises.

17	7	Cash		1 50 00			17
18		Advertising Fees			1 50 00		18
19		Century Hardware Co.					19

Monday, December 11

Paid the Whitman Travel Service $153.40 for an airplane ticket to be used the next week for a business trip.

20	11	Traveling Expense		1 53 40			20
21		Cash			1 53 40		21
22		Airplane fare—business trip.					22

29

Friday, December 15

Paid Esther Johnson $195 covering her salary for the first half of the month.

Miss Johnson is employed by Mr. Brown as his secretary and bookkeeper at a salary of $390 a month. The transaction resulted in a decrease in owner's equity because of salary expense with a corresponding decrease in the asset cash. The transaction is recorded by debiting Salary Expense and by crediting Cash for $195. (The matter of payroll taxes is purposely ignored at this point. These taxes will be discussed in detail in Chapter 4.)

23	15	Salary Expense		1 95 00			23
24		Cash			1 95 00		24
25		Paid secretary's salary.					25

Note: The Posting Reference column has been left blank in the eight foregoing journal entry illustrations. This is because the column is not used until the amounts are posted to the accounts in the ledger, a process to be described starting on page 33. Account numbers are shown in the Posting Reference column of the journal illustrated on pages 31–32, since the illustration shows how the journal appears *after* the posting has been completed.

The journal entries for the following transactions (as well as for those to this point) are illustrated on pages 31–32.

Monday, December 18

Received $465 from The Drew Manufacturing Co. in payment for services rendered.

Wednesday, December 20

Mr. Brown withdrew $500 for personal use.

> Amounts of cash withdrawn for personal use by the owner of a business enterprise represent a decrease in owner's equity. Although amounts withdrawn might be recorded as debits to the owner's capital account, it is better practice to record withdrawals in a separate account. Doing it in this way makes it a little easier to summarize the decreases in owner's equity caused by the owner's withdrawals. This transaction is recorded in the journal by debiting W. F. Brown, Drawing, and by crediting Cash for $500.

Friday, December 22

Received $640 from Spencer Sales Co. for services rendered.

Tuesday, December 26

Paid $35 membership dues in the American Association of Advertising Agencies.

Wednesday, December 27

Received the office equipment ordered December 1. These items were purchased on account from the Young Office Equipment Co. Cost: $2,794.18. The dealer removed the used equipment that had been loaned to Mr. Brown.

Thursday, December 28

Paid the Business Supply Co. $216.14 for the office supplies purchased on December 4.

> This transaction caused a decrease in the liability accounts payable with a corresponding decrease in the asset cash. The transaction was recorded by debiting Accounts Payable and by crediting Cash for $216.14.

Received $400 from Benson Davis for services rendered.

Friday, December 29

Paid Esther Johnson $195 covering her salary for the second half of the month. (Paid this day since it is the last working day of the month.)

Office supplies used during the month, $30.

> By referring to the transaction of December 4 it will be noted that office supplies amounting to $216.14 were purchased and were recorded as an asset. By taking an inventory, counting the supplies in stock at the end of the month, Mr. Brown was able to determine that the cost of supplies used during the month amounted to $30. The expenses for the month of December would not be reflected properly in the accounts if the supplies used during the month were not taken into consideration. Therefore, the cost of supplies used was recorded by debiting the expense account, Office Supplies Expense, and by crediting the asset account, Office Supplies, for $30.

30

	DATE		DESCRIPTION	POST. REF.	DEBIT	CREDIT	
1	1972 Nov.	30	Cash	111	2000 00		1
2			W. F. Brown, Capital	311		2000 00	2
3			Original investment in				3
4			advertising agency.				4
5	Dec.	1	Rent Expense	511	300 00		5
6			Cash	111		300 00	6
7			Paid December rent.				7
8		4	Office Supplies	112	216 14		8
9			Accounts Payable	211		216 14	9
10			Business Supply Co.				10
11		5	Telephone Expense	514	27 50		11
12			Cash	111		27 50	12
13			Paid telephone bill.				13
14		6	Miscellaneous Expense	516	7 00		14
15			Cash	111		7 00	15
16			Trade journal subscription.				16
17		7	Cash	111	150 00		17
18			Advertising Fees	411		150 00	18
19			Century Hardware Co.				19
20		11	Traveling Expense	513	153 40		20
21			Cash	111		153 40	21
22			Airplane fare-business trip.				22
23		15	Salary Expense	512	195 00		23
24			Cash	111		195 00	24
25			Paid secretary's salary.				25
26		18	Cash	111	465 00		26
27			Advertising Fees	411		465 00	27
28			The Drew Mfg. Co.				28
29		20	W. F. Brown, Drawing	312	500 00		29
30			Cash	111		500 00	30
31			Withdrawn for personal use.				31
32		22	Cash	111	640 00		32
33			Advertising Fees	411		640 00	33
34			Spencer Sales Co.				34
35		26	Miscellaneous Expense	516	35 00		35
36			Cash	111		35 00	36
37			A.A.A.A. dues.				37
38		27	Office Equipment	121	2794 18		38
39			Accounts Payable	211		2794 18	39
40			Young Office Equipment Co.		7483 22	7483 22	40

31

The Brown Advertising Agency Journal
(continued on next page)

	DATE	DESCRIPTION	POST. REF.	DEBIT	CREDIT	
1	1972 Dec. 28	Accounts Payable	211	216 14		1
2		Cash	111		216 14	2
3		Business Supply Co.				3
4	28	Cash	111	400 00		4
5		Advertising Fees	411		400 00	5
6		Benson Davis.				6
7	29	Salary Expense	512	195 00		7
8		Cash	111		195 00	8
9		Paid secretary's salary.				9
10	29	Office Supplies Expense	515	30 00		10
11		Office Supplies	112		30 00	11
12		Cost of supplies used				12
13		during December.		841 14	841 14	13

The Brown Advertising Agency Journal (*concluded*)

Note: Some bookkeepers leave a blank line after the explanation of each entry. This practice is acceptable though not recommended.

Proving the journal

32

Because a double entry is made for each transaction, the equality of debit and credit entries on each page of the journal may be proved merely by totaling the amount columns. The total of each column is usually entered as a footing immediately under the last entry. When a page of the journal is filled, the footings may be entered just under the last single horizontal ruled line at the bottom of the page as shown in the illustration on page 31. When the page is not filled, the footings should be entered immediately under the last entry as shown in the illustration above.

Report No. 2-1

Refer to the workbook and complete Report No. 2-1. To complete this assignment correctly, the principles developed in the preceding discussion must be understood. Review the text assignment if necessary. After completing the report, continue with the following study assignment until the next report is required.

Posting to the ledger;
the trial balance

The purpose of a journal is to provide a chronological record of financial transactions expressed as debits and credits to accounts. These accounts are kept to supply desired information. Collectively the accounts are described as the *general ledger* or, often, simply as "the ledger." (Frequently, so-called "subsidiary" ledgers are also used. These will be explained and illustrated in Chapter 8.) The account forms may be on sheets of paper or on cards. When on sheets of paper, the sheets may be bound in book form or they may be kept in a loose-leaf binder. Usually a separate page or card is used for each account. The accounts should be classified properly in the ledger; that is, the asset accounts should be grouped together, the liability accounts together, and the owner's equity accounts together. A proper grouping of the accounts in the ledger is an aid in preparing the various reports desired by the owner. Mr. Brown decided to keep all of the accounts for The Brown Advertising Agency in a loose-leaf ledger. The numbers shown in the agency's chart of accounts on page 26 were used as a guide in arranging the accounts in the ledger. The ledger of The Brown Advertising Agency is reproduced on pages 35–37. Note that the accounts are in numerical order.

33

Since Mr. Brown makes few purchases on account, he does not keep a separate account for each creditor. When invoices are received for items purchased on account, the invoices are checked and recorded in the journal by debiting the proper accounts and by crediting Accounts Payable. The credit balance of Accounts Payable indicates the total amount owed to creditors. After each invoice is recorded, it is filed in an unpaid invoice file, where it remains until it is paid in full. When an invoice is paid in full, it is removed from the unpaid invoice file and is then filed under the name of the creditor for future reference. The balance of the accounts payable account may be proved at any time by determining the total of the unpaid amounts of the invoices.

Posting

The process of recording (often called "entering") information in the ledger from the journal is known as *posting*. All amounts entered in the journal should be posted to the accounts kept in the ledger in order to summarize the results. Such posting may be done daily or at frequent intervals. The ledger is not a reliable source of information until all of the transactions recorded in the journal have been posted.

Since the accounts provide the information needed in preparing financial statements, a posting procedure that will insure accuracy in maintaining the accounts must necessarily be followed. Posting from the journal to the ledger involves recording the following information in the accounts:

(a) The date of each transaction.
(b) The amount of each transaction.
(c) The page of the journal from which each transaction is posted.

As each amount in the journal is posted to the proper account in the ledger, the number of that account should be entered in the Posting Reference column in the journal so as to provide a cross-reference between the journal and the ledger. The first entry to be posted from the journal (a segment of which is reproduced below) required a debit to Cash of $2,000. This was accomplished by entering the year, "1972," the month, abbreviated "Nov.," and the day, "30," in the Date column of the cash account (reproduced below); the number "1" in the Posting Reference column (since the posting came from Page 1 of the journal); and the amount, "$2,000.00" in the Debit column. Inasmuch as the number of the cash account is 111, that number was entered in the Posting Reference column of the journal on the same line as the debit of $2,000.00 that was just posted to Cash. The same pattern was followed in posting the credit part of the entry — $2,000 to W. F. Brown, Capital, Account No. 311 (reproduced below).

34

JOURNAL   PAGE   1

	DATE		DESCRIPTION	POST. REF.	DEBIT	CREDIT	
1	1972 Nov. 30	Cash		111	2000 00		1
2		W. F. Brown, Capital		311		2000 00	2
3		Original investment in					3
4		advertising agency.					4

ACCOUNT Cash   ACCOUNT NO. 111

DATE	ITEM	POST. REF.	DEBIT	DATE	ITEM	POST. REF.	CREDIT
1972 Nov. 30		1	2000 00				

ACCOUNT W. F. Brown, Capital   ACCOUNT NO. 311

DATE	ITEM	POST. REF.	DEBIT	DATE	ITEM	POST. REF.	CREDIT
				1972 Nov. 30		1	2000 00

Reference to the journal of The Brown Advertising Agency (reproduced on pages 31 and 32) and its ledger (reproduced below and on pages 36 and 37) will indicate that a similar procedure was followed in posting every amount from the journal. Note also that in the ledger, the year "1972" was entered only at the top of each Date column, and that (with the exception of the first posting to Cash and the first posting to W. F. Brown, Capital, where the month "Nov." was entered) the month "Dec." was entered only with the first posting to an account.

ACCOUNT *Cash* ACCOUNT NO. *111*

DATE	ITEM	POST. REF.	DEBIT	DATE	ITEM	POST. REF.	CREDIT
1972 Nov. 30		1	2000 00	1972 Dec. 1		1	300 00
Dec. 7		1	150 00	5		1	27 50
18		1	465 00	6		1	7 00
22		1	640 00	11		1	153 40
28		2	400 00	15		1	195 00
	2025.96		3655 00	20		1	500 00
				26		1	35 00
				28		2	216 14
				29		2	195 00
							1629 04

35

ACCOUNT *Office Supplies* ACCOUNT NO. *112*

DATE	ITEM	POST. REF.	DEBIT	DATE	ITEM	POST. REF.	CREDIT
1972 Dec. 4		1	216 14	1972 Dec. 29		2	30 00
	186.14						

ACCOUNT *Office Equipment* ACCOUNT NO. *121*

DATE	ITEM	POST. REF.	DEBIT	DATE	ITEM	POST. REF.	CREDIT
1972 Dec. 27		1	2794 18				

ACCOUNT *Accounts Payable* ACCOUNT NO. *211*

DATE	ITEM	POST. REF.	DEBIT	DATE	ITEM	POST. REF.	CREDIT
1972 Dec. 28		2	216 14	1972 Dec. 4		1	216 14
				27		1	2794 18
					2794.18		3010 32

The Brown Advertising Agency Ledger
(*continued on next page*)

ACCOUNT _W. F. Brown, Capital_   ACCOUNT NO. 311

DATE	ITEM	POST. REF.	DEBIT	DATE	ITEM	POST. REF.	CREDIT
				1972 Nov. 30		1	2000 00

ACCOUNT _W. F. Brown, Drawing_   ACCOUNT NO. 312

DATE	ITEM	POST. REF.	DEBIT	DATE	ITEM	POST. REF.	CREDIT
1972 Dec. 20		1	500 00				

ACCOUNT _Advertising Fees_   ACCOUNT NO. 411

DATE	ITEM	POST. REF.	DEBIT	DATE	ITEM	POST. REF.	CREDIT
				1972 Dec. 7		1	150 00
				18		1	465 00
				22		1	640 00
				28		2	400 00
							1 655 00

ACCOUNT _Rent Expense_   ACCOUNT NO. 511

DATE	ITEM	POST. REF.	DEBIT	DATE	ITEM	POST. REF.	CREDIT
1972 Dec. 1		1	300 00				

ACCOUNT _Salary Expense_   ACCOUNT NO. 512

DATE	ITEM	POST. REF.	DEBIT	DATE	ITEM	POST. REF.	CREDIT
1972 Dec. 15		1	195 00				
29		2	195 00				
			390 00				

ACCOUNT _Traveling Expense_   ACCOUNT NO. 513

DATE	ITEM	POST. REF.	DEBIT	DATE	ITEM	POST. REF.	CREDIT
1972 Dec. 11		1	153 40				

The Brown Advertising Agency Ledger (_continued_)

ACCOUNT *Telephone Expense*   ACCOUNT NO. 514

DATE	ITEM	POST REF	DEBIT	DATE	ITEM	POST REF.	CREDIT
1972 Dec. 5		1	27 50				

ACCOUNT *Office Supplies Expense*   ACCOUNT NO. 515

DATE	ITEM	POST REF	DEBIT	DATE	ITEM	POST REF.	CREDIT
1972 Dec. 29		2	30 00				

ACCOUNT *Miscellaneous Expense*   ACCOUNT NO. 516

DATE	ITEM	POST REF	DEBIT	DATE	ITEM	POST REF.	CREDIT
1972 Dec. 6		1	7 00				
26		1	35 00				
			42 00				

The Brown Advertising Agency Ledger (*concluded*)

It will be seen from the foregoing discussion that there are four steps involved in posting — three involving information to be recorded in the ledger and one involving information to be recorded in the journal. The date, the amount, and the effect of each transaction are first recorded in the journal. The same information is later posted to the ledger. Posting does not involve an analysis of each transaction to determine its effect upon the accounts. Such an analysis is made at the time of recording the transaction in the journal, and posting is merely transcribing the same information in the ledger. In posting, care should be used to record each debit and each credit entry in the proper columns so that the entries will reflect correctly the effects of the transactions on the accounts.

When the posting is completed, the same information is provided in both the journal and the ledger as to the date, the amount, and the effect of each transaction. A cross-reference from each book to the other book is also provided. This cross-reference makes it possible to trace the entry of November 30 on the debit side of cash account in the ledger to the journal by referring to the page indicated in the Posting Reference column. The entry of November 30 on the credit side of the account for W. F. Brown, Capital, may also be traced to the journal by referring to the page indicated in the Posting Reference column. Each entry in the journal may be traced to the ledger by referring to the account numbers indicated in the Posting Reference column of the journal. By referring to pages 31 and 32, it will be seen that the account numbers were inserted in the Posting Reference column. This was done as the posting was completed.

The trial balance

The purpose of a trial balance is to prove that the totals of the debit and credit balances in the ledger are equal. In double-entry bookkeeping, equality of debit and credit balances in the ledger must be maintained. A trial balance may be taken daily, weekly, monthly, or whenever desired. Before taking a trial balance, all transactions previously completed should be journalized and the posting should be completed in order that the effect of all transactions will be reflected in the ledger accounts.

Footing Accounts. When an account form similar to the one illustrated on page 36 is used, it is necessary to foot or add the amounts recorded in each account preparatory to taking a trial balance. The footings should be recorded immediately below the last item in both the debit and credit amount columns of the account. The footings should be written in small figures close to the preceding line so that they will not interfere with the recording of an item on the next ruled line. At the same time, the balance, the difference between the footings, should be computed and recorded in small figures in the Item column of the account on the side with the larger footing. In other words, if an account has a debit balance, the balance should be written in the Item column on the debit or left side of the account. If the account has a credit balance, the balance should be written in the Item column on the credit or right side of the account. The balance or difference between the footings should be recorded in the Item column just below the line on which the last regular entry appears and in line with the footing.

Reference to the accounts kept in the ledger shown on pages 35–37 will reveal that the accounts have been footed and will show how the footings and the balances are recorded. When only one item has been posted to an account, regardless of whether it is a debit or a credit amount, no footing is necessary.

Care should be used in computing the balances of the accounts. If an error is made in adding the columns or in determining the difference between the footings, the error will be carried to the trial balance; and considerable time may be required to locate the mistake. Most accounting errors result from carelessness. For example, a careless bookkeeper may write an account balance on the wrong side of an account or may enter figures so illegibly that they may be misread later. Neatness in writing the amounts is just as important as accuracy in determining the footings and the balances.

Preparing the Trial Balance. It is important that the following procedure be followed in preparing a trial balance:

(a) Head the trial balance, being certain to show the name of the individual, firm, or organization, the title, "Trial Balance," and the date. (The date shown is the day of the last transaction that is included in the accounts — usually the last day of a month. Actually, the trial balance might be prepared on January 3, but if the accounts reflected only transactions through December 31, this is the date that should be used.)

(b) List the account titles in order, showing each account number.

(c) Record the account balances in parallel columns, entering debit balances in the left amount column and credit balances in the right amount column.

(d) Add the columns and record the totals, ruling a single line across the amount columns above the totals and a double line below the totals in the manner shown in the illustration below.

A trial balance is usually prepared on ruled paper (though it can be typewritten on plain paper if desired). An illustration of the trial balance, as of December 31, 1972, of the ledger of The Brown Advertising Agency is shown below.

Even though the trial balance indicates that the ledger is in balance, there still may be errors in the ledger. For example, if a journal entry has

The Brown Advertising Agency
Trial Balance
December 31, 1972

Account	Acct. No.	Dr. Balance	Cr. Balance
Cash	111	2025 96	
Office Supplies	112	186 14	
Office Equipment	121	2794 18	
Accounts Payable	211		2794 18
W. F. Brown, Capital	311		2000 00
W. F. Brown, Drawing	312	500 00	
Advertising Fees	411		1655 00
Rent Expense	511	300 00	
Salary Expense	512	390 00	
Traveling Expense	513	153 40	
Telephone Expense	514	27 50	
Office Supplies Expense	515	30 00	
Miscellaneous Expense	516	42 00	
		6449 18	6449 18

Model Trial Balance

been made in which the wrong accounts are debited or credited, or if an item has been posted to the wrong account, the ledger will still be in balance. It is important, therefore, that extreme care be used in preparing the journal entries and in posting them to the ledger accounts.

Report No. 2-2

Refer to the workbook and complete Report No. 2-2. To complete this assignment correctly, the principles developed in the preceding discussion must be understood. Review the text assignment if necessary. After completing the report, continue with the following study assignment until the next report is required.

40

The financial statements

The transactions completed by The Brown Advertising Agency during the month of December were recorded in a two-column journal (see pages 31 and 32). The debits and credits were subsequently posted to the proper accounts in a ledger (see pages 35–37). At the end of the month a trial balance was taken as a means of proving that the equality of debits and credits had been maintained throughout the journalizing and posting procedures (see page 39).

Although a trial balance may provide much of the information that the owner of a business may desire, it is primarily a device used by the bookkeeper for the purpose of proving the equality of the debit and credit account balances. Although the trial balance of The Brown Advertising Agency taken as of December 31 contains a list of all of the accounts showing the amounts of the debit and credit balances, it does not clearly present all of the information that Mr. Brown may need or desire regarding either the results of operations during the month or the status of his business at the end of the month. To meet these needs it is customary to prepare two types of *financial statements*. One is known as an income statement and the other as a balance sheet or statement of financial position.

The income statement

The purpose of an *income statement* is to provide information regarding the results of operations *during a specified period of time.* It is an itemized statement of the changes in owner's equity resulting from the revenue and expenses of the period. Such changes are recorded in temporary owner's equity accounts known as revenue and expense accounts. Changes in owner's equity resulting from investments or withdrawals of assets by the owner are not included in the income statement as they involve neither revenue nor expense.

A model income statement for The Brown Advertising Agency showing the results of operations for the month ended December 31, 1972, is reproduced below. The heading of an income statement consists of the following:

(a) The name of the business.
(b) The title of the statement — Income Statement.
(c) The period of time covered by the statement.

The Brown Advertising Agency
Income Statement
For the Month Ended December 31, 1972

Revenue:		
Advertising fees		$165500
Expenses:		
Rent expense	$30000	
Salary expense	39000	
Traveling expense	15340	
Telephone expense	2750	
Office supplies expense	3000	
Miscellaneous expense	4200	
Total expenses		94290
Net income		$71210

Model Income Statement

The body of an income statement consists of **(1)** an itemized list of the sources and amounts of revenue received during the period and **(2)** an itemized list of the various expenses incurred during the period. It is said that the "heart" of income measurement is the process of *matching* on a *periodic basis* the revenue and expenses of a business. The income statement carries out this matching concept.

The financial statements usually are prepared first on ruled paper. Such handwritten copies may then be typed so that a number of copies will be available for those who are interested in examining the statements. Since the typewritten copies are not on ruled paper, dollar signs are included in the handwritten copy so that the typist will understand just where they are to be inserted. Note that a dollar sign is placed beside the first amount in each column and the first amount below a ruling in each column. The income statement illustrated below is shown on two-column ruled paper; however, the columns do not have any debit-credit significance.

In the case of The Brown Advertising Agency the only source of revenue was advertising fees that amounted to $1,655. The total expenses for the month amounted to $942.90. The revenue exceeded the expenses by $712.10. This represents the amount of the net income for the month. If the total expenses had exceeded the total revenue, the excess would have represented a net loss for the month.

The trial balance supplied the information needed in preparing the income statement. However, it can be seen readily that the income statement provides more information concerning the results of the month's operations than is supplied by the trial balance.

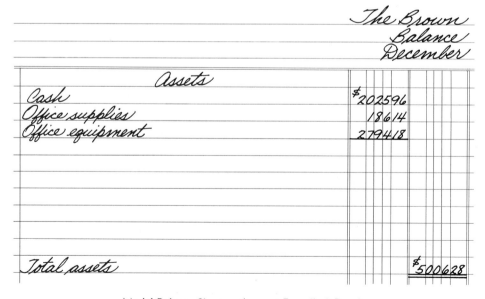

Model Balance Sheet — Account Form (Left Page)

The balance sheet

The purpose of a *balance sheet* is to provide information regarding the status of assets, liabilities and owner's equity of a business enterprise *as of a specified time or date.* It is an itemized statement of the respective amounts of these basic accounting elements at the close of business on the date indicated in the heading.

A model balance sheet for The Brown Advertising Agency showing the status of the business as of December 31, 1972, is reproduced below and on page 42. The heading of a balance sheet contains the following:

(a) The name of the business.
(b) The title of the statement — Balance Sheet.
(c) The date of the statement.

The body of a balance sheet consists of an itemized list of the assets, the liabilities, and the owner's equity, the latter being the difference between the total amount of the assets and the total amount of the liabilities. The balance sheet illustrated is arranged in account form. Note the similarity of this form of balance sheet to the standard account form illustrated on page 12. The assets are listed on the left side and the liabilities and owner's equity are listed on the right side. The information provided by the balance sheet of The Brown Advertising Agency may be summarized in equation form as follows:

ASSETS = LIABILITIES + OWNER'S EQUITY
$5,006.28 $2,794.18 $2,212.10

Advertising Agency
Sheet
31, 1972

Liabilities		
Accounts payable	$2794.18	
Total liabilities		$2794.18
Owner's Equity		
W. F. Brown, capital		
Capital, Nov. 30, 1972	$2000.00	
Net income	$712.10	
Less withdrawals	500.00	
Net increase	212.10	
Capital, Dec. 31, 1972		2212.10
Total liabilities and owner's equity		$5006.28

Model Balance Sheet — Account Form (Right Page)

43

The trial balance was the source of the information needed in listing the assets and liabilities in the balance sheet. The amount of the owner's equity may be calculated by subtracting the total liabilities from the total assets. Thus, Mr. Brown's equity as of December 31, 1972, is as follows:

Total assets	$5,006.28
Less total liabilities	2,794.18
Owner's equity	$2,212.10

Proof of the amount of the owner's equity as calculated above may be determined by taking into consideration the following factors:

(a) The amount invested in the enterprise by Mr. Brown on November 30 as shown by his capital account.

(b) The amount of the net income of The Brown Advertising Agency for December as shown by the income statement.

(c) The total amount withdrawn for personal use during December as shown by Mr. Brown's drawing account.

The trial balance on page 39 shows that Mr. Brown's equity in The Brown Advertising Agency on November 30 amounted to $2,000. This is indicated by the credit balance of his capital account. The income statement on page 41 shows that the net income of The Brown Advertising Agency for December amounted to $712.10. The trial balance shows that the amount withdrawn by Mr. Brown for personal use during the month amounted to $500. This is indicated by the debit balance of his drawing account. On the basis of this information, Mr. Brown's equity in The Brown Advertising Agency as of December 31, 1972, is as follows:

Amount of capital November 30		$2,000.00
Net income for December	$712.10	
Less amount withdrawn for personal use during the month	500.00	212.10
Capital at end of December		$2,212.10

Report No. 2-3

Refer to the workbook and complete Report No. 2-3. This assignment provides a test of your ability to apply the principles developed in Chapters 1 and 2 of this textbook. The textbook and the workbook go hand in hand, each serving a definite purpose in the learning process. Inability to solve correctly any problem included in the report indicates that you have failed to master the principles developed in the textbook. After completing the report, you may proceed with Chapter 3 until the next report is required.

chapter 3

accounting for cash

45

In the preceding chapters the purpose and nature of business accounting, transaction analysis, and the mechanics of double-entry bookkeeping were introduced. Explanations and illustrations were given of **(1)** *journalizing* (recording transactions in a *general journal* — a "book of original entry"), **(2)** *posting* (transcribing the entries to the accounts that, all together, comprise the *general ledger*), **(3)** taking a *trial balance*, and **(4)** using the latter to prepare an *income statement* and a *balance sheet* (two basic and important *financial statements*). This chapter is devoted to a discussion of the handling of and accounting for cash receipts and disbursements, including various considerations that are involved when cash is kept in a commercial bank. (The use of bank "checking accounts" is a near-universal business practice.)

Records of cash receipts and disbursements; petty cash

The term *cash* has several different, though not totally dissimilar, meanings. In a very narrow sense, cash means currency and coin. In a broader sense, cash includes <u>checks, drafts, and money orders.</u> All of these, as well as currency and coin, are sometimes called "cash items." Usually any reference to the *cash receipts* of a business relates to the receipt of checks, drafts, and money orders payable to the business, as well as to the receipt of currency and coin. The amount of the balance of the cash account, as well as the amount shown for cash in a balance sheet, normally includes cash and cash items on hand plus the amount on deposit in a bank checking account. In some cases the balance sheet figure for cash includes amounts on deposit in more than one bank. In accounting for cash, it is rather rare to make a distinction between "cash on hand" and "cash in bank," but sometimes this is done.

The cash account

This account is debited when cash is increased and credited when cash is decreased. This means that the cash account has a debit balance unless the business has no cash. In the latter case, the account will be *in balance* — meaning that the account has no balance since the total of the debits is equal to the total of the credits.

Cash Receipts. It is vital that an accurate and timely record be kept of cash receipts. When the volume of the receipts is large in both number and amount, a practice designed to reduce the danger of mistake and embezzlement may be followed. In order to segregate the functions of (1) handling money and cash items and (2) keeping the records, some one other than the bookkeeper prepares, in duplicate, a list of all receipts. One copy is kept with the receipts until a deposit ticket has been prepared and checked against the actual receipts. The other copy goes to the bookkeeper for recording purposes. An example of such a list is as follows:

DATE	FROM WHOM RECEIVED	NATURE OF REMITTANCE	AMOUNT
1972			
Jan. 3	James Albert	Check	$ 31.18
	Harry Dawson	Postal Money Order	57.92
	Arthur Finch	Currency	40.00
	Mrs. Charles Monroe	Express Money Order	52.61
	Frank Quincy	Check	34.70
	William Tucker	Cashier's Check	39.25
Total cash receipts...			$255.66

When numerous cash receipts are involved, the amounts received are usually recorded in a cash register. The cash register tape provides a list of the receipts. If a cash register is not used, some form of receipt in duplicate should be used for each cash transaction. The customer should be given one copy and the other copy should be retained for accounting purposes. Under such a plan the bookkeeper does not actually handle any cash; instead he records cash receipts from lists prepared by other persons. The procedure of having transactions involving cash handled by two or more persons reduces the danger of fraud and is one of the important features of a system of internal control.

Cash Disbursements. Disbursements may be made in cash or by bank check. When a disbursement is made in cash, a receipt or a receipted voucher should be obtained as evidence of the payment. When a disbursement is made by bank check, it is not necessary to obtain a receipt since the canceled check that is returned by the bank serves as a receipt.

Recording Cash Receipts and Disbursements. In the preceding chapter, transactions involving the receipt and disbursement of cash were recorded in a two-column general journal along with other transactions. If the number of cash transactions is relatively small, the manner of recording that was illustrated is quite satisfactory. If, however, the number of such transactions is large, the repetition entailed in making numerous debit postings or credit postings to the cash account is time-consuming, tedious, and burdensome. Reference to the cash account in the ledger on page 35 discloses that even the brief illustration presented in that chapter involved fourteen postings to Cash (five debits and nine credits) out of a total of thirty-four postings required to record the seventeen transactions. It clearly would be more efficient to reduce the number of postings to the debit side of the cash account by summarizing the cash receipts for the month and posting the total. A similar observation applies to the transactions that involve cash disbursements.

The Multi-Column Journal. One means of reducing the number of postings as well as conserving space, time, and effort in journalizing is to use a journal with special columns. If, for example, there are numerous entries involving cash receipts and disbursements, it may be advantageous to use a four-column journal. That is, a journal with one column in which to place all debits to cash, and another column in which to place all credits to cash, as well as a general debit and a general credit column. An illustration of this form is shown below. Note that it is the same as the journal

JOURNAL   PAGE

| CASH | | DATE | DESCRIPTION | POST. REF. | GENERAL | |
DEBIT	CREDIT				DEBIT	CREDIT

Four-Column Journal

used in the preceding chapter except that two additional amount columns have been added. (In this case the additional columns are placed at the left of the date column; however, such placement is not essential.) The two amount columns at the left are used exclusively for debits and credits to Cash; the two amount columns at the right, headed "General," are used for the amounts to be debited or credited to all other accounts. The Description column is used primarily to record the titles of the accounts that are to be debited or credited with the amount entered in one of the columns at the right. Sometimes, a brief explanatory note is also included in the Description column.

Journalizing Procedure Illustrated. To illustrate the use of the four-column journal and to contrast it with the two-column type, the transactions of The Brown Advertising Agency that were given in Chapter 2 (starting on page 27) are recorded in a four-column journal reproduced on page 49. Several features of this journal should be noted:

(a) In the case of each entry that involves either a debit or a credit to Cash, the title of the account to receive the related credit or debit is written starting at the extreme left of the Description column. No indentation is made. However, in the case of any entry that does not involve cash, the title of the account to be debited is written at the extreme left, and the title of the account to be credited is indented about one-half inch. Note the entries of December 4 and 27, and the second entry of December 29. These entries appear just as they did in the two-column journal.

(b) Usually a separate line is not used for an explanation of each entry. While this could be done, it is not customary because it is desirable to save space. Furthermore, in most instances, the entries explain themselves. Consider the first entry: It is evident that Mr. Brown invested $2,000 in the business. In other cases, an appropriate notation is made following the title of the account. For example, when a debit or a credit to Accounts Payable is involved, the name of the creditor is noted. (See entries of December 4, 27, and 28.) In all entries involving a credit to Advertising Fees, the name of the client is noted. (See entries of December 7, 18, 22, and 28.) A word or two of explanation should be given whenever appropriate. (Note the entries of December 15 and 29 where the word "[Secretary]" was included.) Occasionally an explanation will be of such a length that an additional line will be required. When a cash disbursement is made by check, the check number should be noted. It is quite common to have a narrow column headed "Check Number" placed next to the Cash Credit column to use in noting the number of each check issued. (In Chapter 2, no mention was made of the manner of cash payments; therefore, no check numbers were given and there is no need for a check number column in the illustration.)

(c) The numbers shown in the Posting Reference column were not entered at the time of journalizing the transactions; they were entered later when the amounts were posted to the accounts in the ledger.

CASH DEBIT	CASH CREDIT	DATE	DESCRIPTION	POST. REF.	GENERAL DEBIT	GENERAL CREDIT	
2000 00		1972 Nov. 30	W. F. Brown, Capital	311		2000 00	1
	300 00	Dec. 1	Rent Expense	511	300 00		2
		4	Office Supplies	112	216 14		3
			Accts. Pay. (Business Supply Co.)	211		216 14	4
	27 50	5	Telephone Expense	514	27 50		5
	7 00	6	Miscellaneous Expense	516	7 00		6
150 00		7	Advertising Fees (Cent. Hard. Co.)	441		150 00	7
	153 40	11	Traveling Expense	513	153 40		8
	195 00	15	Salary Expense (Secretary)	512	195 00		9
465 00		18	Advertising Fees (Drew Mfg Co.)	441		465 00	10
	500 00	20	W. F. Brown, Drawing	312	500 00		11
640 00		22	Advertising Fees (Spencer Sales Co.)	441		640 00	12
	35 00	26	Miscellaneous Expense	516	35 00		13
		27	Office Equipment	121	2794 18		14
			Accts. Pay. (Young Office Equip Co.)	211		2794 18	15
	216 14	28	Accounts Pay. (Business Supply Co.)	211	216 14		16
400 00		28	Advertising Fees (Benson Davis)	441		400 00	17
	195 00	29	Salary Expense (Secretary)	512	195 00		18
		29	Office Supplies Expense	515	30 00		19
			Office Supplies	112		30 00	20
3 655 00	1 629 04		2,025.96		4 669 36	6 695 32	21
3 655 00	1 629 04				4 669 36	6 695 32	
(111)	(111)				(✓)	(✓)	22
							23

49

The Brown Advertising Agency Four-Column Journal

Proving the Four-Column Journal. In order to be sure that the debits recorded in the journal are equal to the credits, the journal must be *proved*. Each amount column should be footed and the sum of the footings of the debit columns and the sum of the footings of the credit columns compared. The footings should be recorded in small pencil figures immediately below the last regular entry. If these sums are not the same, the journal entries must be checked to discover and correct any errors that are found. The footings should be proved frequently; when the transactions are numerous, it may be advisable to prove the footings daily. The footings must be proved when a page of the journal is filled to be sure that no error is carried forward to a new page. Proof of the footings is essential at the end of the month before the journal is ruled or any column totals are posted. At the top of the next page is a proof of the footings of the four-column journal of The Brown Advertising Agency at the end of December. (Note that, as is common practice, the footings were proved using an adding machine.)

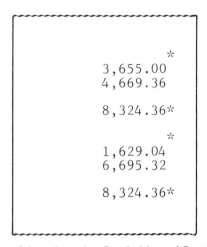

```
                              *
                    3,655.00
                    4,669.36

                    8,324.36*

                              *
                    1,629.04
                    6,695.32

                    8,324.36*
```

Four-Column Journal — Proof of Journal Footings

Footing and Ruling the Four-Column Journal. Normally, the journal should be footed and ruled at the end of each month. (In the illustration of The Brown Advertising Agency, the business was started on November 30, and the single transaction on that date was included with the entries for December.) As previously stated, the footings should be recorded in small pencil figures immediately below the last regular entry. After being proved, the figures should be recorded in ink on the next horizontal line. A single rule should be drawn across all of the amount columns just above the totals, and a double rule should be drawn across all of the columns except the Description column just below the totals. A practice often followed when journals of this type are used is to make a notation of the cash balance at the end of the month. This amount should be equal to the balance at the end of the previous month, plus the receipts and minus the disbursements of the month just ended. This balance may be noted in small figures (in pencil, if preferred) in the Description column just below the line on which the last regular entry was made. It is common practice to start the entries for a new month on a fresh page. When this practice is followed, the cash balance at the start of the month (the balance at the end of the month just past) is entered in small figures in the Description column at the top of the new page.

When it is necessary to use more than one journal page for the transactions of a month, no regular entry should be made on the last line of a page. That line is used to show the column totals. These should not be recorded in ink until the equality of the footings has been proved. The words "Carried Forward" should be written in the Description column on the last line. The amount-column totals then are entered on the top line of the new page with the words "Amounts Forwarded" written in the Description column.

Posting the Four-Column Journal. Posting from a four-column journal involves both individual posting and summary (column total) posting. The individual amounts in the two General columns are posted. This may be done daily or as often as convenient, but it should be done by the end of each month. The totals of the Cash Debit and Cash Credit columns cannot be posted until the end of the month when the journal has been proved and the column totals recorded. As the individual amounts in the General columns are posted, the numbers of the accounts to which the postings were made are entered in the Posting Reference column of the journal. (Entering the journal page from which an amount has come is a part of the process of posting to the ledger.) When the totals of the Cash Debit and Cash Credit columns are posted, the number of the cash account (No. 111 in the illustration) is shown in parentheses just below the column totals. In order to indicate that the totals of the General Debit and General Credit columns are not to be posted, a check mark is shown in parentheses (√) below each of those totals.

The general ledger of The Brown Advertising Agency after completion of postings from the two-column journal is illustrated on pages 35–37. If these postings had come from the four-column journal instead, the ledger accounts would appear exactly the same except for the fact that some of the postings came from page 2 of the two-column journal, whereas all of the postings came from page 1 of the four-column journal. Furthermore, the cash account, instead of containing five debits and nine credits, would contain only one debit and one credit as illustrated below.

ACCOUNT *Cash*   ACCOUNT NO. *111*

DATE	ITEM	POST. REF.	DEBIT	DATE	ITEM	POST. REF.	CREDIT
1972 Dec. 31		/	3655 00	1972 Dec. 31		/	1629 04
	2025.96						

Comparison of the two-column journal illustrated on pages 31 and 32 and the four-column journal shown on page 49 reveals that the former required thirty-four postings, while the latter needed only twenty-two. If there had been 100 transactions, of which ninety involved either a debit or a credit to Cash, 200 postings would have been required if the transactions had been recorded in a two-column journal. If the same transactions had been recorded in a four-column journal of the type illustrated, only 112 postings would have been required. These savings in the number of postings roughly reflect comparable savings in space required, words and figures to be written, and time needed.

The four-column journal discussed and illustrated might be called a "junior version" of a book of original entry known as a *combined cash journal*. This designation arises from the fact that such a book combines the features of a two-column general journal and a *cashbook* — the latter being a book in which only transactions involving cash receipts and disbursements are recorded. The fundamental characteristics of a combined cash journal are that it provides columns for debits to cash, credits to cash, debits and credits to be posted individually ("general" columns), and as many other "special" columns as circumstances require. These "special" columns are used to record like debits or credits so that the totals of amounts destined for the same place can be summary posted. Thus, in addition to the four columns whose uses have already been explained and illustrated, there may be one, two, three, or even a dozen other "special" columns if needed. The Brown Advertising Agency example included four transactions requiring a credit to Advertising Fees, Account No. 411. This circumstance suggests that a special column for "Advertising Fees Credit" would have been in order. The use of combined cash journals is explained and illustrated in Chapters 5, 6, and 8.

Other Types of Cash Journals. In many businesses, transactions involving the receipt or the disbursement of cash are so numerous that it is desirable to keep the original journal record of such transactions separate from the record of noncash transactions. When a separate original record is kept of cash receipts, it is usually referred to as a *cash receipts journal*. When a separate original record is kept of cash payments or disbursements, it is usually referred to as a *cash payments journal* or a *cash disbursements journal*. When all disbursements are made by check, the journal is sometimes called a *check register*. When cash receipts and cash payments are both recorded in the same book of account, the book is usually referred to as a cashbook. This type of record typically has a facing-page arrangement. Receipts are recorded on the left-hand page; disbursements on the right-hand page.

All original entry books (journals) relating to cash have the same characteristics regardless of whether there are separate books for receipts and disbursements or whether they are combined and called a cashbook. For cash receipts, there is one debit column in which the amounts of all receipts are recorded. At the end of a month, the total of this column is posted as a debit to Cash. Some or all of the individual credit amounts are separately posted as credits to the proper accounts. If there are numerous credits to the same account, a column may be provided in which to record the amounts of these credits so that their sum can be posted at the end of the month. Within limits, there may be as many "special" columns as needed. A comparable set of observations relates to the cash disbursements: The major column in this case, of course, is the credit column that assembles all of the decreases in cash so that one summary credit to Cash can be posted each month. The debits may all be posted individually or, if needed, special columns may be used to reduce the number of postings.

In each instance, all of the fundamental qualities of <u>any journal</u> are present: **(1)** space is provided to show <u>the date</u> of the transaction, **(2)** provision is made to indicate <u>the titles of the accounts</u> that are affected, **(3)** space is provided for any needed <u>explanation or description,</u> **(4)** the <u>amount of each transaction</u> is shown, and **(5)** space is provided to indicate <u>the number of the account to which each posting was made</u>. If cash disbursements are made by check, the cash disbursements record will probably have a column in which to note the check numbers. It is not uncommon for there to be a memo column in which to note the bank balance after each deposit and each check written. It is possible to "prove" any of these journals at any time by determining whether the total debits recorded are equal to the total credits.

It must be understood that cash journals do not completely eliminate the need for a general journal, unless every transaction of the business involves cash — an unlikely circumstance. At later points in the text, a few other varieties of "special journals" will be introduced. In almost every business, however, there is need for a general journal — either separate or combined with another journal — in which to record unusual, infrequent transactions.

53

Proving Cash. <u>The process of determining whether the amount of cash</u> (on hand and in the bank) <u>is the amount that should be there according to</u> <u>the records is called</u> *proving cash.* Cash should be proved at least once a week and, perhaps, more often if the volume of cash transactions is large. The first step is to determine from the records what amount of cash should be on hand. The cash balance should be calculated by adding the total of the receipts to the opening balance and subtracting the total of the payments. The result should be equal to the amount of cash on deposit in the bank plus the total of currency, coins, checks, and money orders on hand. Normally, an up-to-date record of cash in bank is maintained — often by using stubs in a checkbook for this purpose. There is space provided on the stubs to show deposits as well as the record of checks drawn, and the resulting balance after each deposit made or check drawn. (See check stubs illustrated on page 67.) The amount of cash and cash items on hand must be determined by actual count.

Cash Short and Over. If the effort to prove cash is not successful, it means that either **(1)** the records of receipts, disbursements, and cash on deposit contain one or more errors, **(2)** the count of cash and cash items was incorrect, or **(3)** a "shortage" or an "overage" exists. If a verification of the records and the cash count does not uncover any error, it is evident that due to some mistake in handling cash, either not enough or too much cash is on hand.

Finding that cash is slightly short or over is not unusual. If there are numerous cash transactions, it is difficult to avoid occasional errors in making change. (There is always the danger of shortages due to dishonesty, but most discrepancies are the result of mistakes.) Many businesses have a ledger account entitled *Cash Short and Over*. If, in the effort to prove cash, it is found that a shortage exists, its amount is treated as a cash disbursement transaction involving a debit to Cash Short and Over. Any overage discovered is regarded as a cash receipt transaction involving a credit to Cash Short and Over. By the end of the fiscal year it is likely that the cash short and over account will have both debits and credits. If the total of the debits exceeds the total of the credits, the balance represents an expense or loss; if the reverse is the case, the balance represents revenue.

The petty cash fund

A good policy for a business enterprise to adopt is one which requires that all cash and cash items which it receives shall be deposited in a bank. When this is done, its total cash receipts will equal its total deposits in the bank. It is also a good policy to make arrangements with the bank so that all checks and other cash items received by the business from customers or others in the usual course of business will be accepted by the bank for deposit only. This will cause the records of cash receipts and disbursements of the business to agree exactly with the bank's record of deposits and withdrawals.

When all cash and cash items received are deposited in a bank, an office fund or *petty cash fund* may be established for paying small items. ("Petty" means small or little.) Such a fund eliminates the necessity of writing checks for small amounts.

Operating a Petty Cash Fund. To establish a petty cash fund, a check should be drawn for the amount that is to be set aside in the fund. The amount may be $25, $50, $100, or any amount considered necessary. The check is usually made payable to "Cash," "Petty Cash," or "Office Fund." When the check is cashed by the bank, the money is placed in a cash drawer, a cash register, or a safe at the depositor's place of business; and a designated individual in the office is authorized to make payments from the fund. The one who is responsible for the fund should be able to account for the full amount of the fund at any time. Disbursements from the fund should not be made without obtaining a voucher or a receipt.

PETTY CASH VOUCHER

No. _6_   Date _December 12, 1972_

Paid To _C. D. Mason_   Amount

For _Red Cross_   _10 | 00_

Charge To _Donations Expense_

Payment Received:

C. D. Mason   Approved By _Miller Stevens_

Petty Cash Voucher

A form of petty cash voucher is shown above. Such a voucher should be used for each expenditure unless a receipt or receipted invoice is obtained.

The check drawn to establish the petty cash fund may be recorded in the journal by debiting Petty Cash Fund and by crediting Cash. When it is necessary to replenish the fund, the petty cashier usually prepares a statement of the expenditures, properly classified. A check is then drawn for the exact amount of the total expenditures. This check is recorded in the journal by debiting the proper accounts indicated in the statement and by crediting Cash.

The petty cash fund is a revolving fund that does not change in amount unless the fund is increased or decreased. The actual amount of cash in the fund plus the total of the petty cash vouchers or receipts should always be equal to the amount originally charged to the petty cash fund.

This method of handling a petty cash fund is sometimes referred to as the *imprest method.* It is the method most commonly used.

Petty Cash Disbursements Record. When a petty cash fund is maintained, it is good practice to keep a formal record of all disbursements from the fund. Various types of records have been designed for this purpose. One of the standard forms is illustrated on pages 56 and 57. The headings of the Distribution columns may vary with each enterprise, depending upon the desired classification of the expenditures. It should be remembered that the headings represent accounts that eventually are to be charged for the expenditures. The desired headings may either be printed on the form or they may be written in. Often the account numbers instead of account titles are used in the headings to indicate the accounts to be charged.

The petty cashier should have a document for each disbursement made from the petty cash fund. Unless a receipt or receipted invoice is obtained, the petty cashier should prepare a voucher. The vouchers should be numbered consecutively.

55

A model petty cash disbursements record is reproduced below and on page 57. It is a part of the records of Miller Stevens, a business consultant. Since Mr. Stevens is out of the office much of the time, he considers it advisable to provide a petty cash fund from which his secretary is authorized to make petty cash disbursements not to exceed $20 each. A narrative of the petty cash transactions completed by Mr. Stevens' secretary during the month of December follows:

MILLER STEVENS
Narrative of Petty Cash Transactions

Dec. 1. Issued check for $100 payable to Petty Cash, cashed the check, and placed the proceeds in a petty cash fund.

This transaction was recorded in the journal by debiting Petty Cash Fund and by crediting Cash. A memorandum entry was also made in the Description column of the petty cash disbursements record reproduced below and on page 57.

During the month of December the following disbursements were made from the petty cash fund:

5. Gave Mr. Stevens $11.50 to reimburse him for the amount spent in having his automobile serviced. Petty Cash Voucher No. 1.

PAGE 1   PETTY CASH DISBURSEMENTS

	DAY	DESCRIPTION	VOU. NO.	TOTAL AMOUNT	Tr. & T. Exp.	Auto Exp.	
1		AMOUNTS FORWARDED					1
2	1	Received in fund 100.00	✓				2
3	5	Automobile repairs	1	11 50		11 50	3
4	6	Client luncheon	2	8 00			4
5	7	Messenger	3	5 00			5
6	11	Advertising expense	4	4 25			6
7	11	Miller Stevens, personal use	5	20 00			7
8	12	Red Cross	6	10 00			8
9	15	Typewriter repairs	7	7 50			9
10	18	Traveling expense	8	4 80			10
11	19	Washing automobile	9	1 75		1 75	11
12	22	Collect telegram	10	1 25	1 25		12
13	23	Salvation Army	11	5 00			13
14	26	Postage stamps	12	8 00			14
15	27	Long distance call	13	3 20	3 20		15
16				90 25	4 45	13 25	16
				90 25	4 45	13 25	
17	29	Balance 9.75					17
18	29	Received in fund 90.25					18
19		Total 100.00					19

Miller Stevens' Petty Cash Disbursements Record (Left Page)

6. Gave Mr. Stevens $8 to reimburse him for the amount spent in entertaining a client at lunch. Petty Cash Voucher No. 2.
7. Paid $5 for messenger fees. Petty Cash Voucher No. 3.
11. Paid $4.25 for an ad in local newspaper. Petty Cash Voucher No. 4.
11. Gave Mr. Stevens $20 for personal use. Petty Cash Voucher No. 5.

This item was entered in the Amount column provided at the extreme right of the petty cash disbursements record since no special distribution column had been provided for recording amounts withdrawn by the owner for personal use.

12. Gave the Red Cross a $10 donation. Petty Cash Voucher No. 6.
15. Paid $7.50 for typewriter repairs. Petty Cash Voucher No. 7.
18. Gave Mr. Stevens $4.80 to reimburse him for traveling expenses. Petty Cash Voucher No. 8.
19. Gave Mr. Stevens $1.75 to reimburse him for the amount spent in having his automobile washed. Petty Cash Voucher No. 9.
22. Paid $1.25 for collect telegram. Petty Cash Voucher No. 10.
23. Donated $5 to the Salvation Army. Petty Cash Voucher No. 11.
26. Paid $8 for postage stamps. Petty Cash Voucher No. 12.
27. Gave Mr. Stevens $3.20 to reimburse him for a long distance telephone call made from a booth. Petty Cash Voucher No. 13.
29. Issued check for $90.25 to replenish the petty cash fund.

This transaction was recorded in the journal by debiting the proper accounts and by crediting Cash for the total amount of the expenditures.

FOR MONTH OF *December* 19 72   PAGE *1*

	Post. Exp.	Don. Exp.	Adv. Exp.	Travel Exp.	Misc. Exp.	ACCOUNT	AMOUNT	
1								1
2								2
3								3
4					8 00			4
5					5 00			5
6			4 25					6
7						Miller Stevens, Draw.	20 00	7
8		10 00						8
9					7 50			9
10				4 80				10
11								11
12								12
13		5 00						13
14	8 00							14
15								15
16	8 00	15 00	4 25	4 80	20 50		20 00	16
16	8 00	15 00	4 25	4 80	20 50		20 00	16
17								17
18								18
19								19

DISTRIBUTION OF CHARGES

Miller Stevens' Petty Cash Disbursements Record (Right Page)

Proving the Petty Cash Disbursements Record. To prove the petty cash disbursements record, it is first necessary to foot all of the amount columns. The sum of the footings of the Distribution columns should equal the footing of the Total Amount column. After proving the footings, the totals should be recorded and the record should be ruled as shown in the illustration. The illustration shows that a total of $90.25 was paid out during December. Since it was desired to replenish the petty cash fund at this time, the following statement of the disbursements for December was prepared:

STATEMENT OF PETTY CASH DISBURSEMENTS
For December

Telephone and telegraph expense.............................	$ 4.45
Automobile expense...	13.25
Postage expense..	8.00
Donations expense..	15.00
Advertising expense..	4.25
Traveling expense..	4.80
Miscellaneous expense......................................	20.50
Miller Stevens, drawing....................................	20.00
Total disbursements......................................	$90.25

58

The statement of petty cash disbursements provides the information for the issuance of a check for $90.25 to replenish the petty cash fund. After footing and ruling the petty cash disbursements record, the balance in the fund and the amount received to replenish the fund may be recorded in the Description column below the ruling as shown in the illustration. It is customary to carry the balance forward to the top of a new page before recording any of the transactions for the following month.

The petty cash disbursements record reproduced on pages 56 and 57 is an *auxiliary record* that supplements the regular accounting records. No posting is done from this auxiliary record. The total amount of the expenditures from the petty cash fund is entered in the journal at the time of replenishing the fund by debiting the proper accounts and by crediting Cash. A *compound entry* (one that affects more than two accounts, though the sum of the debits is equal to the sum of the credits) is usually required. The statement of petty cash disbursements provides the information needed in recording the check issued to replenish the petty cash fund. The entry is posted from the journal.

The method of recording the check issued by Miller Stevens on December 29 to replenish the fund is illustrated at the top of the next page. It is assumed that Mr. Stevens uses a four-column journal similar to the one on page 49.

CASH		DATE	DESCRIPTION	POST. REF.	GENERAL		
DEBIT	CREDIT				DEBIT	CREDIT	
	90 25	*1972* Dec. 29	Telephone & Telegraph Expense		4 45		1
			Automobile Expense		13 25		2
			Postage Expense		8 00		3
			Donations Expense		15 00		4
			Advertising Expense		4 25		5
			Traveling Expense		4 80		6
			Miscellaneous Expense		20 50		7
			Miller Stevens, Drawing		20 00		8
							9
							10

Miller Stevens' Four-Column Journal

Report No. 3-1

Refer to the workbook and complete Report No. 3-1. After completing
the report, proceed with the textbook discussion until the next report is
required.

59

Banking procedure

A bank is a financial institution that receives deposits, lends money,
makes collections, and renders other services, such as providing vaults
for the safekeeping of valuables and handling trust funds for its customers.
Most banks offer facilities for both checking accounts and savings accounts.

Checking account

A checking account is sometimes referred to as a commercial account.
Important factors in connection with a checking account are **(1)** opening
the account, **(2)** making deposits, **(3)** making withdrawals, and **(4)** reconciling the bank statement.

Opening a Checking Account. To open a checking account with a bank, it is necessary to obtain the approval of an official of the bank and to make an initial deposit. Money, checks, bank drafts, money orders, and other cash items usually will be accepted for deposit. Cash is accepted for deposit subject to verification as to its amount and validity. Cash items are accepted for deposit subject to their being paid by the makers when presented for payment by the bank or its agent.

Signature Card. Banks usually require a new depositor to sign his name on a card or form as an aid in verifying the depositor's signature on checks that he may issue, on cash items that he may indorse for deposit, and on other business papers that he may present to the bank. The form a depositor signs to give the bank a sample of his signature is called a *signature card*. If desired, a depositor may authorize others to sign his name to checks and to other business forms. Each person who is so authorized is required to sign the depositor's name along with his own signature on a signature card. A signature card is one of the safeguards that a bank uses to protect its own interests as well as the interests of its depositors.

Deposit Ticket. Banks provide depositors with a printed form to use for a detailed listing of items being deposited. This form is called a *deposit ticket*. A model filled-in deposit ticket is reproduced on page 61. This illustration is typical of the type of ticket that most banks provide. Note that the number of the depositor's account is preprinted at the bottom in so-called "MICR" numbers (meaning *magnetic ink character recognition*) that can be "read" by a type of electronic equipment used by banks. This series of digits (which also is preprinted at the bottom of all of the depositor's checks) is actually a code used in sorting and routing deposit slips and checks. In the first set of digits, 0420-0003, the "4" indicates that the bank is in the Fourth Federal Reserve District. The "20" following is what is called a "routing" number. The "3" is a number assigned to the Liberty National Bank. This numbering method was established by the American Bankers Association (ABA). The second set of digits, 136-92146, is the number assigned by the Liberty National Bank to the Donley Company's account.

It is very common practice to prepare deposit tickets in duplicate so that one copy, when receipted by the bank teller, may be retained by the depositor. In preparing a deposit ticket, the date should be written in the space provided. Currency (paper money) should be arranged in the order of the denominations, the smaller denominations being placed on top. The bills should all be faced up and top up. Coins (pennies, nickels, dimes, quarters, and half dollars) that are to be deposited in considerable quantities should be wrapped in coin wrappers, which the bank will provide. The name and account number of the depositor should be written

Deposit Ticket

on the outside of each coin wrapper as a means of identification in the event that a mistake has been made in counting the coins. The amounts of cash represented by currency and by coins should be entered in the amount column of the deposit ticket on the lines provided for these items.

Each additional item to be deposited should be listed on a separate line of the deposit ticket as shown in the illustration above. In listing checks on the deposit ticket, the instructions of the bank should be observed in describing the checks for identification purposes. It was once common practice to list local checks by name and bank and out-of-town checks by name of city. Another practice widely followed at one time was to show the name of the maker (drawer) of each check being deposited. Still another procedure that is used by some depositors is to attach to the deposit slip an adding machine tape listing of the checks that merely shows the amount of each one (and their total). For many years, banks preferred to have the checks identified on the deposit slip by showing the ABA "transit number" of each check (the numerator of a fraction-type bank identification that was, and almost always still is, printed on each check). Today, banks ask their depositors to identify checks being deposited by showing the numbers contained in the first set of MICR digits that appears to the left at the bottom of each check. Any zeros ("0") that lie to the left of a group of digits may be omitted. For example, in the illustration, the first check (for $141.50) shows the number "420-1." On that check, the MICR numbers were actually 0420-0001.

61

Indorsements. The signature or stamp of a depositor on the back of a check is called an *indorsement*. Negotiable instruments (checks, notes, and drafts) made payable to the depositor either directly or by prior indorsement, must be indorsed by him before a bank will accept them for deposit. One purpose of such indorsement is to transfer the title of the instrument to the bank. By means of his indorsement the depositor also guarantees the payment of the instrument. Checks and other items submitted for deposit that require indorsements on the bank may be indorsed as shown in the illustration below. In indorsing a check, the name of the payee should be written exactly as it appears on the face of the check. Note that the indorsement is written near the left end of the check. <u>An indorsement that limits the holder of the check as to the use to be made of the amount collected is known as a *restrictive indorsement.*</u> The check reproduced below has a restrictive indorsement. This type of indorsement makes it unlikely that the check will be cashed by anyone other than the bank or person to whom it is indorsed. Businesses commonly use a rubber stamp to indorse checks for deposit.

62

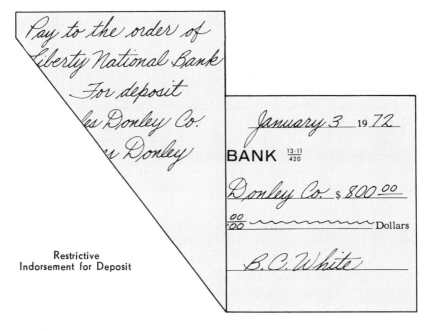

Restrictive
Indorsement for Deposit

The total of the cash and other items deposited should be entered on the deposit tickets. The deposit tickets, prepared in duplicate, together with the cash and the other items to be deposited, should be delivered to the receiving teller of the bank. The teller receipts the duplicate copy and returns it to the depositor.

Instead of preparing deposit slips in duplicate, another practice — very widely followed at one time, and still often used — is for the bank to provide the depositor with a *passbook* in which the bank teller enters the date and amount of each deposit together with his initial. This gives the depositor a receipt for the deposit; a duplicate deposit slip is not needed. Of course, the passbook must be brought in (or sent in) to the bank with each deposit.

Instead of providing the depositor with either duplicate deposit tickets or a passbook, the bank may provide him with a machine-printed receipt for each deposit. Some banks use *automatic teller machines* in preparing the receipts. The use of such machines saves the time required to make manual entries in a passbook and eliminates the need for making duplicate copies of deposit tickets. Such machines are not only timesaving, but they also promote accuracy in the handling of deposits. The deposits handled by each teller during the day may be accumulated so that at the end of the day the total amount of the deposits received by a teller is automatically recorded by the machine. This amount may be proved by counting the cash and cash items accepted by a teller for deposit during the day.

Dishonored Checks. A check that a bank refuses to pay is described as a *dishonored check*. A depositor guarantees all items that he deposits and is liable to the bank for the amount involved if, for any reason, any item is not honored when presented for payment. When a check or other cash item is deposited with a bank and is not honored upon presentation to the bank upon which it is drawn, the depositor's bank may charge the amount of the dishonored item to the depositor's account or may present it to the depositor for reimbursement. It is not uncommon for checks that have been deposited to be returned to the depositor for various reasons, as indicated on the debit advice reproduced below. The most common reason for checks being returned unpaid is "not sufficient funds" (NSF).

63

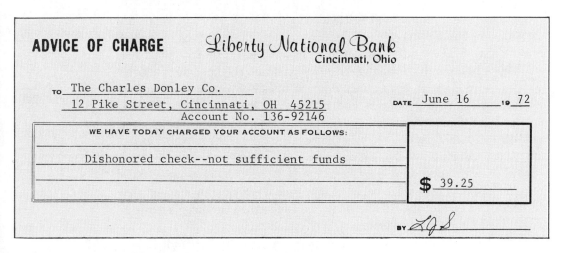

Debit Advice

Under the laws of most states, it is illegal for anyone to issue a check on a bank without having sufficient funds on deposit with that bank to cover the check when it is presented for payment. When a dishonored check is charged to the depositor's account, the depositor should deduct the amount from the balance shown on his checkbook stub.

Postdated Checks. Checks dated subsequent to the date of issue are known as *postdated checks*. For example, a check that is issued on March 1 may be dated March 15. The recipient of a postdated check should not deposit it before the date specified on the check. One reason for issuing a postdated check may be that the maker does not have sufficient funds in his bank at the time of issuance to pay it, but he may expect to have a sufficient amount on deposit by the time the check is presented for payment on or after the date of the check. When a postdated check is presented to the bank on which it is drawn and payment is not made, it is handled by the bank in the same manner as any other dishonored check and the payee should treat it as a dishonored check. Generally, it is not considered good practice to issue postdated checks.

Making Deposits by Mail. Bank deposits may be made either over the counter or by mail. The over-the-counter method of making deposits is generally used. It may not always be convenient, however, for a depositor to make his deposits over the counter, especially if he lives at a great distance from the bank. In such a case it may be more convenient for him to make his deposits by mail. When a depositor makes his deposits by mail, the bank may provide him with a special form of deposit ticket, and a form for him to self address which is subsequently returned to him with a receipt for his deposit.

Night Deposits. Some banks provide night deposit service. While all banks do not handle this in the same way, a common practice is for the bank to have a night safe with an opening on the exterior of the bank building. Upon signing a night depository contract, the bank supplies the depositor with a key to the outside door of the safe, together with a bag that has an identifying number and in which valuables may be placed, and two keys to the bag itself. Once the depositor places his bag in the night deposit safe it cannot be retrieved because it moves to a vault in the bank that is accessible to bank employees only. Since only the depositor is provided with keys to his bag, he or his authorized representative must go to the bank to unlock the bag. At that time the depositor may or may not deposit in his account in the bank the funds that he had placed previously in the night deposit safe.

Night deposit banking service is especially valuable to those individuals and concerns that do not have safe facilities in their own places of business and that accumulate cash and other cash items which they cannot take to the bank during regular banking hours.

Making Withdrawals. The amount deposited in a bank checking account may be withdrawn either by the depositor himself or by any other person who has been properly authorized to make withdrawals from the depositor's account. Such withdrawals are accomplished by the use of checks signed by the depositor or by others having the authority to sign checks drawn on the account.

Checkbook. Banks provide printed forms known as checks for the convenience of their depositors. Such checks are used by depositors to authorize the bank to pay out specified amounts from the funds credited to their accounts. Special forms of checks may be used for payrolls, dividends, or other purposes. It is estimated that roughly 90 percent of all money payments in the United States are made by check.

Blank checks are often bound in a book with one or more checks to a page. Each check usually contains spaces for recording the following information:

(a) The number of the check (if not already printed on each check).
(b) The date of the check.
(c) The name of the payee.
(d) The amount the bank is authorized to pay the payee.
(e) The signature of the drawer — the depositor or his authorized agent.

Very often, each blank check is attached (usually along its left side) to what is called a *check stub*. The stubs usually contain blank spaces for recording the same information as is recorded on the checks so that the completed stubs will provide the depositor with a complete record of all checks issued. Sometimes space is also provided on the stub for recording what the check is for or the title of the account to be debited. In any event, sufficient data should be entered on the stub of each check to provide all information needed for recording purposes. Sometimes, instead of stubs, the depositor is provided with a checkbook that includes a type of register in which to record the data about each check and to show the date and amount of each deposit as well as the bank balance after each deposit and check.

Most banks supply their depositors (sometimes for a charge) with checks that have the depositor's name and address printed on them as well as the MICR numbers at the bottom. It is probable that the checks are pre-numbered — commonly in the upper right corner. Some firms prepare carbon copies of checks instead of using check stubs. The copy itself is not a check; very often it is only a blank sheet except for the carbon-paper imprint of the check number, name of payee, amount, and any

65

notations that were made on the check as to what it pays. Checks with carbon copies usually are prepared on a typewriter.

Writing a Check. If the check has a stub, the latter should be filled in at the time the check is written. If, instead of a stub, a checkbook register is used, an entry for the check should be made therein. This plan insures that the drawer will retain a record of each check issued.

When a depositor withdraws funds personally, the payee of the check is usually "Cash." If the money is to go into a petty cash fund, the check may be made payable to "Petty Cash."

When a depositor desires the bank to pay the money to a third party, he writes the name of that party, referred to as the payee, on the stub or in the register and on the check. When the payee presents the check to the bank for payment, he may be required by the bank to identify himself.

The purpose for which a check is drawn is often noted in some appropriate area of the check itself. Indicating the purpose on the check provides information for the benefit of the payee and provides a specific receipt for the drawer.

The amount of the check is stated on the check in both figures and words. If the amount shown on the check in figures does not agree with the amount shown in words, the bank usually will contact the drawer for the correct amount or will return the check unpaid.

66

Care must be used in writing the amount on the check in order to avoid any possibility that the payee or a subsequent holder may change the amount. If the instructions given below are followed in the preparation of a check, it will be difficult to change the amount.

(a) The amount shown in figures should be written so that there is no space between the dollar sign and the first digit of the amount.

(b) The amount stated in words should be written beginning at the extreme left on the line provided for this information. The cents should be written in the form of a common fraction; if the check is for an even number of dollars, use two ciphers or the word "no" as the numerator of the fraction. If a vacant space remains, a line should be drawn from the amount stated in words to the word "Dollars" on the same line with it, as illustrated at the top of the next page.

A machine frequently used to write the amount of a check in figures and in words is known as a *checkwriter*. The use of a checkwriter is desirable because it practically eliminates the possibility of a change in the amount of a check.

Each check issued by a depositor will be returned to him by the bank on which it is drawn after the check has been paid. Canceled checks are returned to the depositor with the bank statement, which is usually rendered each month. Canceled checks will have been indorsed by the payee

NO. 65	THE CHARLES DONLEY COMPANY	No. 65	13-3 / 420
DATE April 3 1972	12 Pike Street		
TO Baker Bros.	Cincinnati, Ohio 45215	April 3 19 72
FOR April rent		
ACCT. Rent Expense	Pay to the order of Baker Bros.	$125.00
	One hundred twenty-five 00/100 ———— Dollars

	DOLLARS	CENTS
BAL. BRO'T FOR'D	2,126	34
AMT. DEPOSITED		
TOTAL		
AMT. THIS CHECK	125	00
BAL. CAR'D FOR'D	2,001	34

Liberty National Bank   By Charles Donley

⑆0420⑉0003⑆ 136⑈92146⑈

NO. 66	THE CHARLES DONLEY COMPANY	No. 66	13-3 / 420
DATE April 5 1972	12 Pike Street		
TO Patrick Mfg. Co.	Cincinnati, Ohio 45215	April 5 19 72
FOR Inv. March 31		
ACCT. Accounts Payable	Pay to the order of Patrick Manufacturing Co.	$642.18
	Six hundred forty-two 18/100 ———— Dollars

	DOLLARS	CENTS
BAL. BRO'T FOR'D	2,001	34
AMT. DEPOSITED	893	50
TOTAL	2,894	84
AMT. THIS CHECK	642	18
BAL. CAR'D FOR'D	2,252	66

Liberty National Bank   By Charles Donley

⑆0420⑉0003⑆ 136⑈92146⑈

Checks and Stubs

and any subsequent holders. They constitute receipts that the depositor should retain for future reference. They may be attached to the stubs from which they were removed originally or they may be filed.

Overdraft. As stated previously, it is illegal in most states for a depositor to issue a check against a bank in excess of the amount on deposit. However, it may happen that through an oversight or an error in calculation a depositor will overdraw his checking account. Should this happen the bank may refuse to honor the check or it may honor the check and notify the depositor by mail that he has overdrawn his account. Sometimes an official of the bank will telephone the depositor instead of notifying him by mail. Overdrawing a bank checking account is considered a serious matter, and the depositor is expected to make the necessary adjustment without delay. Some banks impose a small charge against a depositor who has overdrawn his account.

Electronic Processing of Checks. It has already been mentioned that nearly all banks furnish their depositors with a special type of check that can be processed by MICR (magnetic ink character recognition) equipment. The unique characteristic of such checks is that there is imprinted in magnetic ink along the lower margin of the check a series of numbers or digits in the form of a code that indicates **(1)** the identity of the Federal Reserve District in which the bank is located and a routing number, **(2)** the identity of the bank, and **(3)** the account number assigned to the depositor. In processing checks with electronic equipment, the first bank that handles a check will imprint its amount in magnetic ink characters to further aid in the processing of the check. The amount will be printed directly below the signature line in the lower right-hand corner of the check.

Checks imprinted with the bank's number and the depositor's number can be fed into MICR machines which will "read" the numbers and cause the checks to be sorted in the desired fashion. If the amounts of the checks are printed thereon in magnetic ink, such amounts can be totaled, and each check can be posted electronically to the customer's account. This process can be carried on at extremely high speed with almost no danger of error.

The two checks reproduced at the top of the preceding page illustrate the appearance of the magnetic ink characters that have been printed at the bottom, as well as check stubs properly completed. (For a further discussion of electronic processing of checks, see Appendix, pages A-12 and A-13.)

68

Recording Bank Transactions. A depositor should keep a record of the transactions he completes with his bank. The usual plan is to keep this record on the checkbook stubs as shown in the illustration on page 67. It will be noted that the record consists of detailed information concerning each check written and an amount column in which should be recorded **(1)** the balance brought forward or carried down, **(2)** the amount of deposits to be added, and **(3)** the amount of checks to be subtracted. The purpose is to keep a detailed record of deposits made and checks issued and to indicate the balance in the checking account after each check is drawn.

As the amount of each check is recorded in the journal, a check mark may be placed immediately after the account title written on the stub to indicate that it has been recorded. When the canceled check is subsequently received from the bank, the amount shown on the stub may be checked to indicate that the canceled check has been received.

Records Kept by a Bank. The usual transactions completed by a bank with a depositor are:

  (a) Accepting deposits made by the depositor.
  (b) Paying checks issued by the depositor.
  (c) Lending money to the depositor.

(d) Discounting commercial paper for the depositor (another type of lending).

(e) Collecting the amounts of various kinds of commercial paper, such as notes and drafts, for the account of the depositor.

The bank keeps an account for each depositor. Each transaction affecting a depositor's account is recorded by debiting or crediting his account, depending upon the effect of the transaction. When a bank accepts a deposit, the account of the depositor is credited for the amount of the deposit. The deposit increases the bank's liability to the depositor.

When the bank pays a check that has been drawn on the bank, it debits the account of the depositor for the amount of the check. If the bank makes a collection for a depositor, the net amount of the collection is credited to his account. At the same time the bank notifies the depositor on a form similar to the one shown below that the collection has been made.

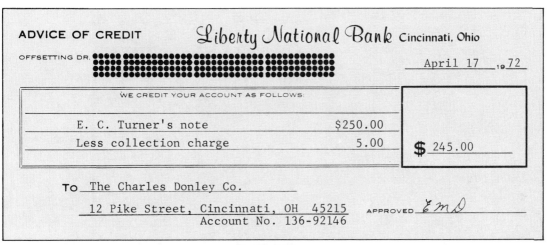

69

Credit Advice

Bank Statement. Once each month a bank renders a statement of account to each depositor. An illustration of a widely used form of bank statement is shown on the next page. It may be mentioned that some banks provide statements that also present information about savings accounts, loan accounts, etc., for those depositors that have such additional accounts. Very commonly, however, a separate statement is furnished for each type of account.

The statement illustrated is for a checking account. It is a report showing **(1)** the balance on deposit at the beginning of the period, **(2)** the amounts of deposits made during the period, **(3)** the amounts of checks honored during the period, **(4)** other items charged to the depositor's account during the period, and **(5)** the balance on deposit at the end of the period. With his bank statement, the depositor also receives all checks

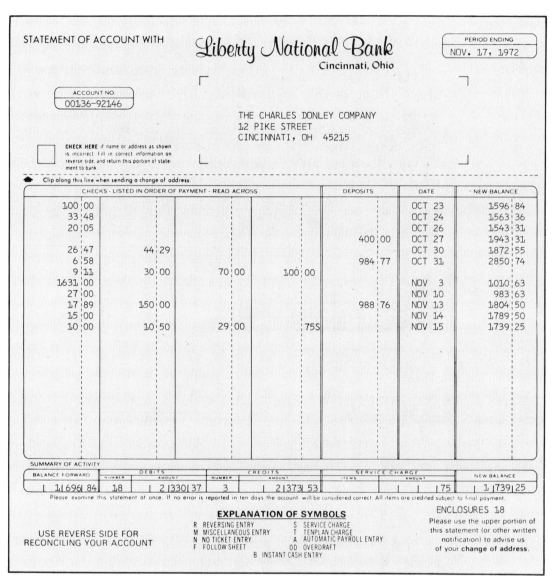

CHECKS - LISTED IN ORDER OF PAYMENT - READ ACROSS				DEPOSITS	DATE	NEW BALANCE
100 00					OCT 23	1,596 84
33 48					OCT 24	1,563 36
20 05					OCT 26	1,543 31
				400 00	OCT 27	1,943 31
26 47	44 29				OCT 30	1,872 55
6 58				984 77	OCT 31	2,850 74
9 11	30 00	70 00	100 00			
1,631 00					NOV 3	1,010 63
27 00					NOV 10	983 63
17 89	150 00			988 76	NOV 13	1,804 50
15 00					NOV 14	1,789 50
10 00	10 50	29 00	75S		NOV 15	1,739 25

SUMMARY OF ACTIVITY

BALANCE FORWARD	DEBITS		CREDITS		SERVICE CHARGE		NEW BALANCE
	NUMBER	AMOUNT	NUMBER	AMOUNT	ITEMS	AMOUNT	
1 696 84	18	2 330 37	3	2 373 53		75	1 739 25

Please examine this statement at once. If no error is reported in ten days the account will be considered correct. All items are credited subject to final payment.

EXPLANATION OF SYMBOLS

R	REVERSING ENTRY	S	SERVICE CHARGE
M	MISCELLANEOUS ENTRY	T	TENPLAN CHARGE
N	NO TICKET ENTRY	A	AUTOMATIC PAYROLL ENTRY
F	FOLLOW SHEET	OD	OVERDRAFT
		B	INSTANT CASH ENTRY

USE REVERSE SIDE FOR RECONCILING YOUR ACCOUNT

ENCLOSURES 18

Please use the upper portion of this statement (or other written notification) to advise us of your **change of address**.

STATEMENT OF ACCOUNT WITH

Liberty National Bank
Cincinnati, Ohio

PERIOD ENDING
NOV. 17, 1972

ACCOUNT NO.
0036-92146

THE CHARLES DONLEY COMPANY
12 PIKE STREET
CINCINNATI, OH 45215

CHECK HERE if name or address as shown is incorrect. Fill in correct information on reverse side, and return this portion of statement to bank.

Clip along this line when sending a change of address.

Bank Statement

paid by the bank during the period, together with any other vouchers representing items charged to his account.

Reconciling the Bank Statement. When a bank statement is received, the depositor should check it immediately with the bank balance record kept on his check stubs. This procedure is known as *reconciling the bank statement.* The balance shown on the bank statement may not be the same as the amount shown on the check stubs for one or more of the following reasons:

(a) Some of the checks issued during the period may not have been presented to the bank for payment before the statement was prepared. These are known as *outstanding checks*.

(b) Deposits made by mail may have been in transit, or a deposit placed in the night depository may not have been recorded by the bank until the day following the date of the statement.

(c) Service charges or other charges may appear on the bank statement that the depositor has not recorded on his check stubs.

(d) The depositor may have erred in keeping his bank record.

(e) The bank may have erred in keeping its account with the depositor.

If a depositor is unable to reconcile his bank statement, he should report the matter to his bank immediately.

A suggested procedure in reconciling the bank statement is enumerated below:

(a) The amount of each deposit recorded on the bank statement should be checked with the amount recorded on the check stubs.

(b) The amount of each canceled check should be compared both with the amount recorded on the bank statement and with the amount recorded on the depositor's check stubs. When making this comparison it is a good plan to place a check mark by the amount recorded on each check stub to indicate that the canceled check has been returned by the bank and its amount verified.

(c) The amounts of any items listed on a bank statement that represent charges to a depositor's account which have not been entered on the check stubs should be deducted from the balance on the check stubs and should be recorded in the journal that is being used to record cash disbursements.

71

(d) A list of the outstanding checks should be prepared. The information needed for this list may be obtained by examining the check stubs and noting the amounts that have not been check marked.

After completing the foregoing steps, the balance shown on the check stubs should equal the balance shown in the bank statement less the total amount of the checks outstanding.

At the top of page 72 is a reconciliation of the bank balance shown in the statement reproduced on page 70. In making this reconciliation it was assumed that the depositor's check stub indicated a balance of $1,825.65 on November 17, that Checks Nos. 312, 315 and 317 had not been presented for payment and thus were not returned with the bank statement, and that a deposit of $358.21 placed in the night depository on November 17 is not shown on the statement. In matching the canceled checks that were returned with the bank statement against the check stubs, an error on the stub for Check No. 294 was discovered. That check was for $17.98. On its stub, the amount was shown as $17.89. This is called a *transposition* error. The "9" and the "8" were transposed (order reversed).

THE CHARLES DONLEY CO.
Reconciliation of Bank Statement
November 17, 1972

Balance, November 17, per bank statement.....		$1,739.25
Add: Deposit, November 17................		358.21
		$2,097.46
Less checks outstanding, November 17:		
No. 312.............................	$ 85.00	
No. 315.............................	17.40	
No. 317.............................	170.25	272.65
Corrected bank balance, November 17........		$1,824.81
Check stub balance, November 17............		$1,825.65
Less: Bank service charge...................	$ .75	
Error on stub for Check No. 294.........	.09	.84
Corrected check stub balance, November 17....		$1,824.81

On Stub No. 294 and the others that followed, the bank balance shown
was 9 cents too large. The correct amount, $17.98, should be shown on
Stub No. 294, and the bank balance shown on the stub of the last check
used should be reduced $.09. If Check No. 294 was in payment of, say, a
telephone bill, an entry should be made debiting Telephone and Telegraph
Expense and crediting Cash. (Alternatively, since such a small amount
was involved, the debit might be made to Miscellaneous Expense.)

Service Charges. A service charge may be made by a bank for the
handling of checks and other items. The basis and the amount of such
charges vary with different banks in different localities.

When a bank statement indicates that a service charge has been made,
the depositor should record the amount of the service charge by debiting
an expense account, such as Miscellaneous Expense, and by crediting Cash.
He should also deduct the amount of such charges from the check stub
balance.

Keeping a Ledger Account with the Bank. As explained previously, a
memorandum account with the bank may be kept on the depositor's
checkbook stub. The depositor may also keep a ledger account with the
bank if desired. The title of such an account usually is the name of the
bank. Sometimes more than one account is kept with a bank in which case
each account should be correctly labeled. Such terms as "commercial,"
"executive," and "payroll" are used to identify the accounts.

The bank account should be debited for the amount of each deposit
and should be credited for the amount of each check written. The account
should also be credited for any other items that may be charged to the
account by the bank, including service charges.

When both a cash account and a bank account are kept in the ledger, the following procedure should be observed in recording transactions affecting these accounts:

Cash		Liberty National Bank	
Debit	Credit	Debit	Credit
For all receipts of cash and cash items.	(a) For all payments in cash. (b) For all bank deposits.	For all deposits.	(a) For all checks written. (b) For all service charges. (c) For all other charges, such as for dishonored checks.

Under this method of accounting for cash and banking transactions, the cash account will be in balance when all cash on hand has been deposited in the bank. To prove the balance of the cash account at any time, it is necessary only to count the cash and cash items on hand and to compare the total with the cash account balance. To prove the bank account balance, it will be necessary to reconcile the bank balance in the same manner in which it is reconciled when only a memorandum record of bank transactions is kept on the check stubs.

The cash account can be dispensed with when a bank account is kept in the ledger and all cash receipts are deposited in the bank. When this is done, all disbursements (except small expenditures made from a petty cash fund) are made by check.

Under this method of accounting, the Cash Debit and the Cash Credit columns of the journal may be headed as follows:

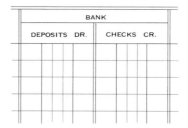

BANK	
DEPOSITS DR.	CHECKS CR.

When this form of journal is used, all cash receipts should be entered in the Bank Deposits Debit column and all checks issued should be entered in the Bank Checks Credit column. Daily, or at frequent intervals, the receipts are deposited in the bank. If all cash received during the month has been deposited before the books are closed at the end of the month, the total amount of the bank deposits will equal the total cash receipts for the month. If all disbursements during the month are made by check, the total amount of checks issued will be the total disbursements for the month.

73

Savings account

When a savings account is opened in a bank, a signature card must be signed by the depositor. He is then given a passbook that he must present at the bank when making deposits or when making withdrawals. By signing the signature card, the depositor agrees to abide by the rules and the regulations of the bank. These rules and regulations vary with different banks and may be altered and amended from time to time. The principal differences between a savings account and a checking account are that interest is paid by the bank on a savings account and withdrawals from a savings account may be made at the bank or by mail by the depositor or his authorized agent. Interest usually is computed on a quarterly basis. The passbook must be presented or mailed along with a withdrawal slip when money is drawn from the account. Banks do not pay interest on the balances in checking accounts. Depositors use checking accounts primarily as a convenient means of making payments, while savings accounts are used primarily as a means of accumulating funds with interest.

Savings accounts are not common for businesses. If the assets of a business include money in a bank savings account, there should be a separate account in the ledger with a title and a number that indicate the nature of the deposit. Sometimes the name of the bank is in the title, as, for example, "Liberty National Bank — Savings Account." When the bank credits interest to the account, the depositor should record the amount in his accounts by a debit to the savings account and by a credit to Interest Earned. The interest is revenue whether withdrawn or not.

Report No. 3-2

Refer to the workbook and complete Report No. 3-2. This assignment provides a test of your ability to apply the principles developed in the first three chapters of the textbook. After completing the report, you may proceed with the textbook discussion in Chapter 4 until the next report is required.

chapter 4

payroll accounting

Employers need to maintain detailed and accurate payroll accounting records. Accurate accounting for employees' earnings preserves the legal and moral right of each employee to be paid according to his employment contract and the laws governing such contracts.

Payroll accounting records also provide information useful in the analysis and classification of labor costs. At the same time, payroll accounting information is invaluable in contract discussions with labor unions, in the settlement of company-union grievances, and in other forms of collective bargaining. Clearly, there is virtually no margin for error in payroll accounting.

Earnings and deductions

The first step in determining the amount to be paid to an employee is to calculate the amount of his total or gross earnings for the pay period. The second step is to determine the amounts of any deductions that are required either by law or by agreement. Depending upon a variety of circumstances, either or both of these steps may be relatively simple or quite complicated. An examination of the factors that are involved follows.

Employer-employee relationships

Not every individual who performs services for a business is considered to be an employee. A public accountant, lawyer, or management consultant who sells his services to a business does not become its employee. Neither does a plumber nor an electrician who is hired to make specific repairs or installations on business property. These people are told what to do, but not how to do it, and the compensation that they receive for their services is called a *fee*. Any person who agrees to perform a service for a fee and is not subject to the control of those whom he serves is called an *independent contractor*.

In contrast, an employee is one who is under the control and direction of his employer with regard to the performance of services. The difference between an independent contractor and an employee is an important legal distinction. The nature and extent of the responsibilities of a contractor and a client to each other and to third parties are quite different from the mutual obligations of an employer and his employee.

Types of compensation

Compensation for managerial or administrative services usually is called *salary*. A salary normally is expressed in terms of a month or a year. Compensation either for skilled or for unskilled labor usually is referred to as *wages*. Wages ordinarily are expressed in terms of hours, weeks, or pieces of accomplishment. The terms salaries and wages often are used interchangeably in practice.

Supplements to basic salaries or wages of employees include bonuses, commissions, cost-of-living adjustments, pensions, and profit sharing plans. Compensation also may take the form of goods, lodging, meals, or other property, and as such is measured by the fair value of the property or service given in payment for the employee's efforts.

Determination of total earnings

An employee's earnings commonly are based on the time worked during the payroll period. Sometimes earnings are based on units of output or of sales during the period. Compensation based on time requires a record of the time worked by each employee. Where there are only a few employees, a record of times worked kept in a memorandum book may suffice.

Where there are many employees, time clocks commonly are used to record time spent on the job each day. With time clocks, a clock card is provided for each employee and the clock is used to record arrival and departure times. Alternatively, plastic cards or badges with holes punched in them for basic employee data are now being used in computer-based time-keeping systems. Whatever method is used, the total time worked during the payroll period must be computed.

Employees often are entitled to compensation at more than their regular rate of pay for work during certain hours or on certain days. If the employer is engaged in Interstate Commerce, the Federal Fair Labor Standards Act (commonly known as the Wages and Hours Law) provides that all employees covered by the Act must be paid one and one-half times the regular rate for all hours worked over 40 per week. Labor-management agreements often require extra pay for certain hours or days. In such cases, hours worked in excess of eight per day or work on Sundays and specified holidays may be paid for at higher rates.

To illustrate, assume that the company which employs Cyril Ling pays time and a half for all hours worked in excess of 40 per week and double time for work on Sunday. Ling's regular rate is $5 per hour; and during the week ended April 13, he worked nine hours each day Monday through Friday, six hours on Saturday, and four on Sunday. Ling's total earnings for the week ended April 13 would be computed as follows:

40 hours @ $5.00..	$200.00
11 hours @ $7.50..	82.50
(Ling worked 9 hours each day Monday through Friday and 6 hours on Saturday — a total of 51 hours. Forty hours would be paid for at the regular rate and 11 hours at time and a half.)	
4 hours (on Sunday) @ $10.00....................................	40.00
Total earnings for the week....................................	$322.50

An employee who is paid a regular salary may be entitled to premium pay for any overtime. If this is the case, it is necessary to compute the regular hourly rate of pay before computing the overtime rate. To illustrate, assume that Ronald Slone receives a regular salary of $800 a month. Slone is entitled to overtime pay at the rate of one and one-half times his regular hourly rate for any time worked in excess of 40 hours per week. His overtime pay may be computed as follows:

$800 × 12 months = $9,600 annual pay
$9,600 ÷ 52 weeks = $184.62 per week
$184.62 ÷ 40 hours = $4.62 per regular hour
$4.62 × 1½ = $6.93 per overtime hour

Deductions from total earnings

With few exceptions, employers are required to withhold portions of each employee's total earnings both for federal income tax and for social security taxes. Certain states and cities also require income or earnings tax withholding on the part of employers. Besides these deductions, an agreement between the employer and the employee may call for amounts to be withheld for any one or more of the following reasons:

(a) To purchase United States savings bonds for the employee.
(b) To pay a life, accident, or health insurance premium for the employee.
(c) To pay the employee's union dues.
(d) To add to a pension fund or profit sharing fund.
(e) To pay to some charitable organization.
(f) To repay a loan from the company or from the company credit union.

Social security and tax account number

Each employee is required to have a social security account and tax account number for payroll accounting purposes. A completed Form SS-5, the official form to be used in applying for an account number, follows:

Completed Application for Social Security and Tax Account Number (Form SS-5)

Employees' income tax withheld

Under federal law, employers are required to withhold certain amounts from the total earnings of each employee to be applied toward the payment of the employee's federal income tax. The amount to be withheld is governed by (1) the total earnings of the employee, (2) the number of *withholding exemptions and allowances* claimed by the employee, (3) the marital status of the employee, and (4) the length of the employee's pay period.

Each federal income taxpayer is entitled to one exemption for himself or for herself and one each for certain other qualified relatives whom he or she supports. The law specifies the relationship that must exist, the extent of support required, and how much the *dependent* may earn in order that an exemption may be claimed. Beginning in 1972, each single taxpayer, or each married taxpayer whose spouse is not also employed, is entitled to one *special withholding allowance*. A taxpayer and spouse each get an extra exemption for age over 65 years and still another exemption for blindness.

An employed taxpayer must furnish his employer with an Employee's Withholding Exemption Certificate, Form W-4, showing the number of exemptions and allowances, if any, claimed. The exemption certificate completed by Phillip Theodore May, Jr. is shown below.

Form **W-4**	Department of the Treasury—Internal Revenue Service
(Rev. Dec. 1971)	**Employee's Withholding Exemption Certificate**

Type or print full name	Social security number
Phillip Theodore May, Jr.	388-32-0538

Home address (Number and street or rural route)	City or town, State and ZIP code
545 Florence	St. Louis, Missouri 63119

Marital status—check one (if married but legally separated, or spouse is a nonresident alien, check "Single"): ☐ Single ☒ Married

If you expect to owe more tax than will be withheld, you may either claim fewer or zero exemptions or ask for additional withholding on line 8.

1 Personal exemption for yourself. Write "1" if claimed 1
2 If married, personal exemption for your wife (or husband) if not separately claimed by her (or him). Write "1" if claimed 1
3 Special withholding allowance.¹ (See instruction 2.) Write "1" if claimed 0
4 Exemptions for age and blindness (applicable only to you and your wife but not to dependents):
    (a) If you or your wife will be 65 years of age or older at the end of the year, and you claim this exemption, write "1"; if both will be 65 or
    older, and you claim both of these exemptions, write "2" . . . .
    (b) If you or your wife are blind and you claim this exemption, write "1"; if both are blind, and you claim both exemptions, write "2" . . . .
5 Exemptions for dependents. (Do not claim an exemption for a dependent unless you are qualified under instruction 5.) 2
6 Additional withholding allowances for itemized deductions. See table on reverse 0
7 Add the exemptions and allowances (if any) which you have claimed above and enter total . . . . $ 4
8 Additional withholding per pay period under agreement with employer . . . . $

Under the penalties of perjury, I certify that the number of withholding exemptions and allowances claimed on this certificate does not exceed the number to which I am entitled.

(Date) January 3 , 19 72 (Signed) *Phillip Theodore May, Jr.*

Completed Withholding Exemption Certificate (Form W-4)

Employees with large itemized deductions are permitted to claim additional withholding exemptions called *withholding allowances*. Each withholding allowance will give the taxpayer an additional exemption.

Any employee desiring to claim one or more withholding allowances must estimate his expected total earnings and itemized deductions for the coming year. Generally, the amount of these itemized deductions cannot exceed the amount of itemized deductions (or standard deduction) claimed on the income tax return filed for the preceding year.

The instructions provided for completing Form W-4 include a table, illustrated at the top of the next page, from which the taxpayer can determine the number of withholding allowances to which he is entitled. As shown on Line 6 of the W-4 illustrated above, Mr. May's estimated earnings and deductions did not qualify him for any withholding allowances.

Most employers use the *wage-bracket method* of determining the amount of tax to be withheld. This method involves the use of income tax withholding tables provided by the Internal Revenue Service. Such tables

Estimated salaries and wages	Number of additional withholding allowances for the amount of itemized deductions shown in the appropriate column (See Line 6 on other side)												
	0	1		2		3		4		5		6	
						PART I: SINGLE EMPLOYEES							
	Under	At least	But less than	At least	But less than	At least	But less than	At least	But less than	At least	But less than	At least	But less than
						PART II: MARRIED EMPLOYEES (WHEN SPOUSE IS NOT EMPLOYED)							
Under $8,000	1,700	1,700– 2,450		2,450– 3,200		3,200– 3,950		3,950– 4,700		4,700– 5,450		5,450– 6,200	
8,000–10,000	1,800	1,800– 2,550		2,550– 3,300		3,300– 4,050		4,050– 4,800		4,800– 5,550		5,550– 6,300	
10,000–12,000	2,200	2,200– 2,950		2,950– 3,700		3,700– 4,450		4,450– 5,200		5,200– 5,950		5,950– 6,700	
12,000–35,000	2,400	2,400– 3,150		3,150– 3,900		3,900– 4,650		4,650– 5,400		5,400– 6,150		6,150– 6,900	

Portion of Table for Determining Number of Withholding Allowances Based on Itemized Deductions

cover monthly, semimonthly, biweekly, weekly, and daily or miscellaneous periods. There are two types of tables: (1) single persons and unmarried heads of households, and (2) married persons. Copies may be obtained from any District Director of Internal Revenue. A portion of a weekly income tax wage-bracket withholding table for married persons is illustrated below. As an example of the use of this table, assume that Phillip Theodore May, Jr. (who claims 4 exemptions) had gross earnings of $215 for the week ending December 15, 1972. On the line showing the tax on wages of "at least $210, but less than $220," in the column headed "4 withholding exemptions," $23.10 is given as the amount to be withheld.

80

Weekly PAYROLL PERIOD   *Married* PERSONS*

WAGES: $100 – $530 and over

Wages are		Number of withholding exemptions claimed										
At least	Less than	0	1	2	3	4	5	6	7	8	9	10 or more
		Amount of income tax to be withheld										
$100	$105	$13.10	$11.10	$9.10	$7.00	$4.80	$2.80	$1.00				
105	110	13.90	11.90	9.90	7.80	5.70	3.60	1.70				
110	115	14.70	12.70	10.70	8.70	6.50	4.40	2.40	$ .70			
115	120	15.50	13.50	11.50	9.50	7.40	5.30	3.10	1.40			
120	125	16.30	14.30	12.30	10.30	8.20	6.10	4.00	2.10	$ .30		
125	130	17.10	15.10	13.10	11.10	9.10	7.00	4.80	2.80	1.00		
130	135	17.90	15.90	13.90	11.90	9.90	7.80	5.70	3.60	1.70		
135	140	18.70	16.70	14.70	12.70	10.70	8.70	6.50	4.40	2.40	$ .70	
140	145	19.50	17.50	15.50	13.50	11.50	9.50	7.40	5.30	3.10	1.40	
145	150	20.30	18.30	16.30	14.30	12.30	10.30	8.20	6.10	4.00	2.10	$ .30
150	160	21.50	19.50	17.50	15.50	13.50	11.50	9.50	7.40	5.30	3.10	1.40
160	170	23.10	21.10	19.10	17.10	15.10	13.10	11.10	9.10	7.00	4.80	2.80
170	180	25.00	22.70	20.70	18.70	16.70	14.70	12.70	10.70	8.70	6.50	4.40
180	190	26.90	24.50	22.30	20.30	18.30	16.30	14.30	12.30	10.30	8.20	6.10
190	200	28.80	26.40	24.10	21.90	19.90	17.90	15.90	13.90	11.90	9.90	7.80
200	210	30.70	28.30	26.00	23.60	21.50	19.50	17.50	15.50	13.50	11.50	9.50
210	220	32.60	30.20	27.90	25.50	23.10	21.10	19.10	17.10	15.10	13.10	11.10
220	230	34.50	32.10	29.80	27.40	25.00	22.70	20.70	18.70	16.70	14.70	12.70
230	240	36.40	34.00	31.70	29.30	26.90	24.50	22.30	20.30	18.30	16.30	14.30
240	250	38.30	35.90	33.60	31.20	28.80	26.40	24.10	21.90	19.90	17.90	15.90

*As of the date of printing, the above Weekly Federal Income Tax Withholding Table is the most current available.

Portion of Weekly Federal Income Tax Withholding Table for Married Persons

Whether the wage-bracket method or some other method is used in computing the amount of tax to be withheld, the employee is given full benefit for all exemptions claimed plus a standard deduction of approximately 14 percent (15 percent for 1973 and thereafter). In any event, the sum of the taxes withheld from an employee's wages only approximates the tax on his actual income derived solely from wages. An employee may be liable for a tax larger than the amount withheld. On the other hand, the amount of the taxes withheld by the employer may be greater than the employee's actual tax liability. In such an event, the employee will be entitled to a refund of the excess taxes withheld, or he may elect to apply the excess to his tax liability for the following year.

Several of the states have adopted state income tax withholding procedures. Some of these states supply employers with withholding exemption certificate forms and income tax withholding tables that are similar in appearance to those used by the federal Internal Revenue Service. Note, however, that each state that has an income tax law uses the specific tax rates and dollar amounts for exemptions as required by its law. Some states determine the amount to be withheld merely by applying a fixed percentage to the federal withholding amount.

Employees' FICA tax withheld   81

Payroll taxes are imposed on almost all employers and employees for old-age, survivors, and disability insurance (OASDI) benefits and health insurance benefits for the aged (HIP) — both under the Federal Insurance Contributions Act (FICA). The base of the tax and the tax rate have been changed several times since the law was first enacted and are subject to change by Congress at any time in the future. For purposes of this chapter, the rate is assumed to be 4.8 percent of the taxable wages paid during the calendar year for OASDI and 0.7 percent for HIP. Only the first $9,000 of the wages paid to each employee in any calendar year is taxable. Any amount of compensation paid in excess of $9,000 is assumed to be exempt from the tax. The employees' portion of the FICA tax must be withheld from their wages by the employer. Although it is true that the base and rate of the tax may be changed at the pleasure of Congress, the accounting principles or methods of recording payroll transactions are not affected.

A few states require employers to withhold a percentage of the employees' wages for unemployment compensation benefits or for disability benefits. In some states and cities, employers are required to withhold a percentage of the employees' wages for other types of payroll taxes. The withholding of income taxes at the state and city level has already been mentioned. Despite the number of withholdings required, each employer must comply with the proper laws in withholding any taxes based on payrolls and in keeping his payroll accounting records.

Payroll records

The needs of management and the requirements of various federal and state laws make it necessary for employers to keep records that will provide the following information:

(a) The name, address, and social security number of each employee.
(b) The gross amount of each employee's earnings, the date of payment, and the period of employment covered by each payroll.
(c) The total amount of gross earnings accumulated since the first of the year.
(d) The amount of any taxes or other items withheld from each employee's earnings.

Regardless of the number of employees or type of business, three types of payroll records usually need to be prepared for or by the employer. They are: **(1)** the payroll register or payroll journal; **(2)** the payroll check with earnings statement attached; and **(3)** the earnings record of the individual employee (on a weekly, monthly, quarterly, or annual basis). These records can be prepared either by *manual* or by *automated* methods.

Payroll Register. A manually prepared payroll register used by Central States Diversified, Inc. for the payroll period ended December 15, 1972, is illustrated below and on page 83. The usual source of information for preparing a payroll register is the time memorandum book, the time clock cards, or a computer print-out. Central States Diversified, Inc. has eight employees, as the illustration shows. Regular deductions are made from

82

PAYROLL REGISTER

	NAME	EMPLOYEE NO.	NO. OF EXEMP.	MARITAL STATUS	EARNINGS				TAXABLE EARNINGS		
					REGULAR	OVER-TIME	TOTAL	CUMULATIVE TOTAL	UNEM-PLOY. COMP.	FICA	
1	Abernathy, David J.	1	2	m	160 00		160 00	8,200 00		160 00	1
2	Blank, Alan C.	2	3	m	175 00	50 00	225 00	9,250 00			2
3	Fritzshall, Susan	3	1	s	135 00		135 00	6,850 00		135 00	3
4	May, Phillip J. Jr.	4	4	m	175 00	40 00	215 00	9,497 00			4
5	Morrison, Thomas K.	5	3	m	170 00	35 00	205 00	8,780 00		205 00	5
6	Oakley, Jack D.	6	3	m	145 00		145 00	7,500 00		145 00	6
7	Pratzel, Robert M.	7	2	m	155 00	20 00	175 00	8,050 00		175 00	7
8	Ryan, Ronald J.	8	1	s	140 00		140 00	7,200 00		140 00	8
9					1,255 00	145 00	1,400 00	65,327 00		960 00	
					1,255 00	145 00	1,400 00	65,327 00		960 00	9

Payroll Register — Manually Prepared (Left Page)

the earnings of employees for FICA tax, federal income tax, and city earnings tax. In addition, for the pay period ending nearest to the middle of the month, deductions are made for life insurance, private hospital insurance, the company credit union, and (if desired) for the purchase of United States savings bonds.

Alan C. Blank and Phillip T. May, Jr. have each authorized Central States Diversified, Inc. to withhold $10 on the payday nearest to the middle of each month for United States savings bonds. When the amount withheld reaches or exceeds the sum of $37.50, a $50 Series E, United States savings bond is purchased at the bank for each of the two employees and delivered to them.

Only the first $9,000 of earnings received in any calendar year is subject to FICA tax. Mr. May's earnings for the week ending December 15 are exempt from the FICA tax because he has already been taxed on earnings totaling $9,000.

After the payroll register has been completed the amount columns should be footed and the footings proved as follows:

Regular earnings.....................................		$1,255.00
Overtime earnings.....................................		145.00
Gross earnings..		$1,400.00
Deductions:		
FICA tax...	$ 52.82	
Federal income tax.................................	167.70	
City earnings tax..................................	28.00	
Life insurance premiums............................	25.00	
Private hospital insurance premiums................	13.00	
Credit union......................................	15.00	
United States savings bonds........................	20.00	321.52
Net amount of payroll...............................		$1,078.48

FOR PERIOD ENDED *December 15*   19 72

	FICA TAX	FEDERAL INC. TAX	CITY TAX	LIFE INS.	PRIV. HOSP. INS.	CREDIT UNION	OTHER		TOTAL	DATE	NET PAY	CK. NO.	
1	8 80	19 10	3 20	5 00		3 00			39 10	12/15/72	120 90	201	1
2		27 40	4 50			3 00	Sav. Bonds	10 00	44 90	12/15/72	180 10	202	2
3	7 43	19 30	2 70		3 00				32 43	12/15/72	102 57	203	3
4		23 10	4 30	6 00	3 50	3 00	Sav. Bonds	10 00	49 90	12/15/72	165 10	204	4
5	11 28	23 60	4 10	6 00	3 50	3 00			51 48	12/15/72	153 52	205	5
6	7 98	14 30	2 90	4 00					29 18	12/15/72	115 82	206	6
7	9 63	20 70	3 50			3 00			36 83	12/15/72	138 17	207	7
8	7 70	20 20	2 80	4 00	3 00				37 70	12/15/72	102 30	208	8
9	52 82	167 70	28 00	25 00	13 00	15 00		20 00	321 52		1,078 48		9

Payroll Register — Manually Prepared (Right Page)

OFFICE PAYROLL

eSD CENTRAL STATES DIVERSIFIED, INC.

5221 NATURAL BRIDGE ST. LOUIS, MO. 63115

PLANTS: ST. LOUIS - PALATKA, FLA.

NUMBER

204

4-97
810

	DATE	NAME	DOLLARS	CENTS
PAY TO THE ORDER OF	12-15-72	Phillip Theodore May, Jr.	$ 165 ~~	A 10 N D 100

CENTRAL STATES DIVERSIFIED, INC.

MOUND CITY TRUST CO.
ST. LOUIS, MO.

BY William C. Bouchein

1:08 10 ... 0097 1:   49 053 2 11 .

Completed Paycheck — Manually Prepared

After proving the footings, the totals should be entered in ink and the record should be ruled with single and double lines as shown in the illustration. Employees may be paid in cash or by check. Many businesses prepare a check for the net amount of the payroll and deposit it in a special Payroll Bank Account. Individual paychecks are then drawn on that account for the amount due each employee. The employer usually furnishes a statement of payroll deductions to the employee along with each wage payment. Paychecks with detachable stubs, like the one for Phillip T. May, Jr., illustrated above, are widely used. The stub should be detached before the check is cashed, and the stub should be retained by the employee as a permanent record of his earnings and payroll deductions.

Employee's Earnings Record. An auxiliary record of each employee's earnings usually is kept in order to provide the information needed in preparing the various federal, state, and local reports required of employers. A manually prepared employee's earnings record used by Central States Diversified, Inc. for Phillip Theodore May, Jr., during the last two quarters of the current calendar year is illustrated on pages 86 and 87. This record may be kept on separate sheets or on cards, which may be filed alphabetically or numerically for ready reference. The information recorded on this form is taken from the payroll register.

Phillip May Jr.'s earnings for the last half of the year up to December 15 are shown on this form. The entry for the pay period ended December 15 is posted from the payroll register illustrated on pages 82 and 83. It can be

CENTRAL STATES DIVERSIFIED, INC.

ST. LOUIS, MO.

STATEMENT OF EARNINGS

MISC.	HOSPITAL	BONDS	INSURANCE	CR. UNION	PARK	CHARITY	CHECK NO.	DATE
	3.50	10.00	6.00	3.00			204	12-15-72

175.00	40.00		23.10		4.30		49.90	165.10
REGULAR	O'TIME	OTHER	WH. TAX	FICA	CITY	STATE	TOTAL DEDUCTIONS	NET PAY
	EARNINGS			TAXES				

NON-NEGOTIABLE

and Deduction Stub

seen from Mr. May's earnings record that his cumulative earnings passed the $9,000 mark during the week ended December 1. Although his total earnings for that week amounted to $175, only $68 of such wages was subject to the combined FICA tax of 5.5 percent, hence only $3.74 was withheld from his wages for that week. For the remainder of the current calendar year, his entire earnings will be exempt from further FICA tax withholding.

The payroll register is a summary of the earnings of all employees for each pay period, while the earnings record is a summary of the annual earnings of each employee. The earnings record illustrated on pages 86 and 87 is designed so that a record of the earnings of the employee for the first half of the year may be kept on one side of the form and a record of the earnings for the last half of the year may be kept on the reverse side of the form. Thus, at the end of the year, the form provides a complete record of the earnings of the employee for the year. It also provides a record of the employee's earnings for each calendar quarter needed by the employer in the preparation of his quarterly returns. These returns will be discussed later in this chapter.

Automated payroll systems

Automated payroll systems may involve the use of small-capacity bookkeeping machines, large-capacity (often electronic) bookkeeping machines,

EMPLOYEE'S EARNINGS RECORD

1972 PERIOD ENDING	EARNINGS				TAXABLE EARNINGS		DEDUCTIONS	
	REGULAR	OVER-TIME	TOTAL	CUMULATIVE TOTAL	UNEMPLOY. COMP.	FICA	FICA TAX	FEDERAL INC. TAX
1 7/7	175 00		175 00	5,075 00		175 00	9 63	16 70
2 7/14	175 00	35 00	210 00	5,285 00		210 00	11 55	23 10
3 7/21	175 00		175 00	5,460 00		175 00	9 63	16 70
4 7/28	175 00	45 00	220 00	5,680 00		220 00	12 10	25 00
5 8/4	175 00		175 00	5,855 00		175 00	9 63	16 70
6 8/11	175 00		175 00	6,030 00		175 00	9 63	16 70
7 8/18	175 00	40 00	215 00	6,245 00		215 00	11 83	23 10
8 8/25	175 00		175 00	6,420 00		175 00	9 63	16 70
9 9/1	175 00		175 00	6,595 00		175 00	9 63	16 70
10 9/8	175 00	35 00	210 00	6,805 00		210 00	11 55	23 10
11 9/15	175 00		175 00	6,980 00		175 00	9 63	16 70
12 9/22	175 00	40 00	215 00	7,195 00		215 00	11 83	23 10
13 9/29	175 00		175 00	7,370 00		175 00	9 63	16 70
THIRD QUARTER	2,275 00	195 00	2,470 00			2470 00	135 90	25 00
1 10/6	175 00		175 00	7,545 00		175 00	9 63	16 70
2 10/13	175 00	37 00	212 00	7,757 00		212 00	11 66	23 10
3 10/20	175 00	30 00	205 00	7,962 00		205 00	11 28	21 50
4 10/27	175 00		175 00	8,137 00		175 00	9 63	16 70
5 11/3	175 00		175 00	8,312 00		175 00	9 63	16 70
6 11/10	175 00	30 00	205 00	8,517 00		205 00	11 28	21 50
7 11/17	175 00	35 00	210 00	8,727 00		210 00	11 55	23 10
8 11/24	175 00	30 00	205 00	8,932 00		205 00	11 28	21 50
9 12/1	175 00		175 00	9,107 00		68 00	3 74	16 70
10 12/8	175 00		175 00	9,282 00				16 70
11 12/15	175 00	40 00	215 00	9,497 00				23 10
12								
13								
FOURTH QUARTER								
YEARLY TOTAL								

SEX	DEPARTMENT	OCCUPATION	SOCIAL SECURITY NO.	MARITAL STATUS	EXEMP-TIONS
M ✓ F	Maintenance	Service	388-32-0538	M	4

Employee's Earnings Record — Manually Prepared (Left Page)

86

or electronic data processing equipment. Both bookkeeping machine payroll systems and electronic payroll systems make it possible to prepare a payroll check with deduction stub, an earnings record, and a payroll register simultaneously. This is an application of the *write-it-once principle*, which recognizes that each time the same information is recopied there is another chance for an error.

	CITY TAX	LIFE INS.	PRIVATE HOSP. INS.	CREDIT UNION	OTHER		TOTAL	CK. NO.	AMOUNT	
1	3 50						29 83	20	145 17	1
2	4 20	6 00	3 50	3 00	Savings Bond 10 00		61 35	28	148 65	2
3	3 50						29 83	36	145 17	3
4	4 40						41 50	44	178 50	4
5	3 50						29 83	52	145 17	5
6	3 50						29 83	60	145 17	6
7	4 30	6 00	3 50	3 00	Savings Bond 10 00		61 73	68	153 27	7
8	3 50						29 83	76	145 17	8
9	3 50						29 83	84	145 17	9
10	4 20						38 85	92	171 15	10
11	3 50	6 00	3 50	3 00	Savings Bond 10 00		52 33	100	122 67	11
12	4 30						39 23	108	175 77	12
13	3 50						29 83	116	145 17	13
	49 40	18 00	10 50	9 00		30 00	503 80		1,966 20	
1	3 50						29 83	124	145 17	1
2	4 24	6 00	3 50	3 00	Savings Bond 10 00		61 50	132	150 50	2
3	4 10						36 88	140	168 12	3
4	3 50						29 83	148	145 17	4
5	3 50						29 83	156	145 17	5
6	4 10						36 88	164	168 12	6
7	4 20	6 00	3 50	3 00	Savings Bond 10 00		61 35	172	148 65	7
8	4 10						36 88	180	168 12	8
9	3 50						23 94	188	151 06	9
10	3 50						20 20	196	154 80	10
11	4 30	6 00	3 50	3 00	Savings Bond 10 00		49 90	204	165 10	11
12										12
13										13

87

PAY RATE	DATE OF BIRTH	DATE EMPLOYED	NAME - LAST	FIRST	MIDDLE	EMP. NO.
$175 wk	3-2-49	1-3-72	May, Phillip		Theodore Jr.	4

Employee's Earnings Record — Manually Prepared (Right Page)

Service Bureaus and Payroll Accounting. The development of automated accounting methods and electronic data processing equipment have led to the establishment of a large number of *service bureaus.* Service bureaus are business organizations engaged in data processing on a contract basis for other businesses of small and medium size. They either are independently operated or are owned and operated by the major business machine manufacturers, banks, or other financial institutions. In any case, their employees are trained in accounting and systems work and can set up and operate effective payroll systems for customers.

When payroll accounting is done for a business by a service bureau, the preliminary work that the business needs to do usually is quite limited. One or more cards are punched for each employee for each payroll period, with the aid of a key-punch machine and these cards contain necessary information such as:

(a) Employee name
(b) Employee address
(c) Employee social security number
(d) Regular earnings
(e) Overtime earnings

(f) Federal income tax withheld
(g) FICA (OASDI and HIP) tax withheld
(h) Other deductions

These punched cards are picked up by the service bureau at regular intervals, and the payroll records desired by the business customer are prepared.

A recent development in payroll accounting is the use of *time sharing*. Several small-to-medium-sized businesses may own or rent time on a computer jointly. These businesses contact the computer by telephone over leased lines and carry on their payroll accounting through a typewriter-printer console.

In a manual payroll system, the payroll register normally is prepared first and serves as a journal. The employee earnings records, checks, and stubs are then prepared from the payroll register information. However, in an automated payroll system all three records are prepared simultane-

PAYROLL

NAME	EMPLOYEE NUMBER	NUMBER OF EXEMP.	MARITAL STATUS	EARNINGS				TAXABLE EARNINGS	
				REGULAR	OVERTIME	TOTAL	CUMULATIVE TOTAL	UNEMPLOY- MENT COMP.	FICA
Abernathy, David T.	1	2	M	160.00		160.00	8,200.00		160.00
Blank, Alan C.	2	3	M	175.00	50.00	225.00	9,250.00		
Fritzshall, Susan	3	1	S	135.00		135.00	6,850.00		135.00
May, Phillip T. Jr.	4	4	M	175.00	40.00	215.00	9,497.00		
Morrison, Thomas K.	5	3	M	170.00	35.00	205.00	8,780.00		205.00
Oakley, Jack G.	6	3	M	145.00		145.00	7,500.00		145.00
Pratzel, Robert M.	7	2	M	155.00	20.00	175.00	8,050.00		175.00
Ryan, Ronald J.	8	1	S	140.00		140.00	7,200.00		140.00
				1,255.00	145.00	1,400.00	65,327.00		960.00

Payroll Register — Machine Prepared (Left Page)

ously. Because of this, the order of their preparation is not of any concern to the accountant.

Employer-Operated Payroll Systems. A payroll check with deduction stub, earnings record, and payroll register entry prepared simultaneously on a bookkeeping machine are illustrated below and on the following pages. Assume that these records were prepared by Central States Diversified, Inc. for its employee, Phillip T. May, Jr., for the same pay period as the manual records previously illustrated on pages 82 to 87, inclusive. Contrast the two types of payroll systems. The primary advantage of the machine system is the saving of time and labor.

In addition to the *write-it-once* features of modern bookkeeping machines, electronic payroll systems can also provide speed and storage as well as needed adding and multiplying ability. Through the use of electronic equipment, adding and multiplying of payrolls can be speeded up, and information such as wage rates and withholding table amounts can be stored inside the equipment. As one would expect, the cost of electronic payroll equipment is noticeably higher than the cost of more conventional bookkeeping machines. The type of electronic data processing system well suited, among other things, to payroll accounting is described and illustrated in the appendix to this textbook.

Much of the work usually required to figure employees' gross earnings, deductions, and net pay may be eliminated if the equipment provides sufficient automation, storage capacity, and electronic calculation capability. When conventional electric bookkeeping machines are used, gross earnings

REGISTER

				DEDUCTIONS						
FICA TAX	FEDERAL INC. TAX	CITY TAX	LIFE INS.	PRIVATE HOSP. INS.	CREDIT UNION	U.S. SAVINGS BONDS	TOTAL	DATE	NET PAY	CK. NO.
8.80	19.10	3.20	5.00		3.00		39.10	Dec. 15, '72	120.90	201
	27.40	4.50			3.00	10.00	44.90	Dec. 15, '72	180.10	202
7.43	19.30	2.70		3.00			32.43	Dec. 15, '72	102.57	203
	23.10	4.30	6.00	3.50	3.00	10.00	49.90	Dec. 15, '72	165.10	204
11.28	23.60	4.10	6.00	3.50	3.00		51.48	Dec. 15, '72	153.52	205
7.98	14.30	2.90	4.00				29.18	Dec. 15, '72	115.82	206
9.63	20.70	3.50			3.00		36.83	Dec. 15, '72	138.17	207
7.70	20.20	2.80	4.00	3.00			37.70	Dec. 15, '72	102.30	208
52.82	167.70	28.00	25.00	13.00	15.00	20.00	321.52		1,078.48	

Payroll Register — Machine Prepared (Right Page)

are often computed separately on a calculator, and withholding and other tax amounts are either read from tables or worked out manually.

An electronic payroll accounting system completes all of the major payroll records at once, just as do modern electric bookkeeping machines. Also, an electronic payroll accounting system determines automatically:

(a) The presence of the proper earnings record.
(b) The next available posting line.

NAME	PHILLIP THEODORE MAY, JR.
ADDRESS	545 FLORENCE
CITY	ST. LOUIS, MISSOURI 63119
SEX	Male
MARITAL STATUS	Married

NUMBER OF EXEMPTIONS 4

	EARNINGS				TAXABLE EARNINGS	
REGULAR	OVERTIME	TOTAL	CUMULATIVE TOTAL	UNEMPLOY-MENT COMP.	FICA	
175.00		175.00	5,075.00		175.00	
175.00	35.00	210.00	5,285.00		210.00	
175.00		175.00	5,460.00		175.00	
175.00	45.00	220.00	5,680.00		220.00	
175.00		175.00	5,855.00		175.00	
175.00		175.00	6,030.00		175.00	
175.00	40.00	215.00	6,245.00		215.00	
175.00		175.00	6,420.00		175.00	
175.00		175.00	6,595.00		175.00	
175.00	35.00	210.00	6,805.00		210.00	
175.00		175.00	6,980.00		175.00	
175.00	40.00	215.00	7,195.00		215.00	
175.00		175.00	7,370.00		175.00	
THIRD QUARTER						
2,275.00	195.00	2,470.00			2,470.00	
175.00		175.00	7,545.00		175.00	
175.00	37.00	212.00	7,757.00		212.00	
175.00	30.00	205.00	7,962.00		205.00	
175.00		175.00	8,137.00		175.00	
175.00		175.00	8,312.00		175.00	
175.00	30.00	205.00	8,517.00		205.00	
175.00	35.00	210.00	8,727.00		210.00	
175.00	30.00	205.00	8,932.00		205.00	
175.00		175.00	9,107.00		68.00	
175.00		175.00	9,282.00			
175.00	40.00	215.00	9,497.00			
FOURTH QUARTER						
YEARLY TOTAL						

Employee's Earnings Record — Machine Prepared (Left Page)

90

(c) Whether overtime earnings are due.

(d) Whether there are other earnings.

(e) Whether the FICA limit has been reached.

(f) What tax deductions should be made.

(g) Whether insurance premiums should be deducted.

(h) Whether there are any other deductions to be made.

(i) Whether there are any delinquent deductions to be made.

(j) Whether there is anything else to be done.

EARNINGS RECORD

DEPARTMENT	Maintenance	SOCIAL SECURITY NUMBER	388-32-0538
OCCUPATION	Service	DATE OF BIRTH	March 2, 1949
PAY RATE	$175 Weekly	DATE EMPLOYED	January 3, 1972
EMPLOYEE NO.	4	DATE EMPLOYMENT TERMINATED	

FICA TAX	FEDERAL INC. TAX	CITY TAX	LIFE INS.	PRIVATE HOSP. INS.	CREDIT UNION	U.S. SAVINGS BONDS	TOTAL	DATE	NET PAY
9.63	16.70	3.50					29.83	July 7, '72	145.17
11.55	23.10	4.20	6.00	3.50	3.00	10.00	61.35	July 14, '72	148.65
9.63	16.70	3.50					29.83	July 21, '72	145.17
12.10	25.00	4.40					41.50	July 28, '72	178.50
9.63	16.70	3.50					29.83	Aug. 4, '72	145.17
9.63	16.70	3.50					29.83	Aug. 11, '72	145.17
11.83	23.10	4.30	6.00	3.50	3.00	10.00	61.73	Aug. 18, '72	153.27
9.63	16.70	3.50					29.83	Aug. 25, '72	145.17
9.63	16.70	3.50					29.83	Sept. 1, '72	145.17
11.55	23.10	4.20					38.85	Sept. 8, '72	171.15
9.63	16.70	3.50	6.00	3.50	3.00	10.00	52.33	Sept. 15, '72	122.67
11.83	23.10	4.30					39.23	Sept. 22, '72	175.77
9.63	16.70	3.50					29.83	Sept. 29, '72	145.17
135.90	251.00	49.40	18.00	10.50	9.00	30.00	503.80		1,966.20
9.63	16.70	3.50					29.83	Oct. 6, '72	145.17
11.66	23.10	4.24	6.00	3.50	3.00	10.00	61.50	Oct. 13, '72	150.50
11.28	21.50	4.10					36.88	Oct. 20, '72	168.12
9.63	16.70	3.50					29.83	Oct. 27, '72	145.17
9.63	16.70	3.50					29.83	Nov. 3, '72	145.17
11.28	21.50	4.10					36.88	Nov. 10, '72	168.12
11.55	23.10	4.20	6.00	3.50	3.00	10.00	61.35	Nov. 17, '72	148.65
11.28	21.50	4.10					36.88	Nov. 24, '72	168.12
3.74	16.70	3.50					23.94	Dec. 1, '72	151.06
	16.70	3.50					20.20	Dec. 8, '72	154.80
	23.10	4.30	6.00	3.50	3.00	10.00	49.90	Dec. 15, '72	165.10

Employee's Earnings Record — Machine Prepared (Right Page)

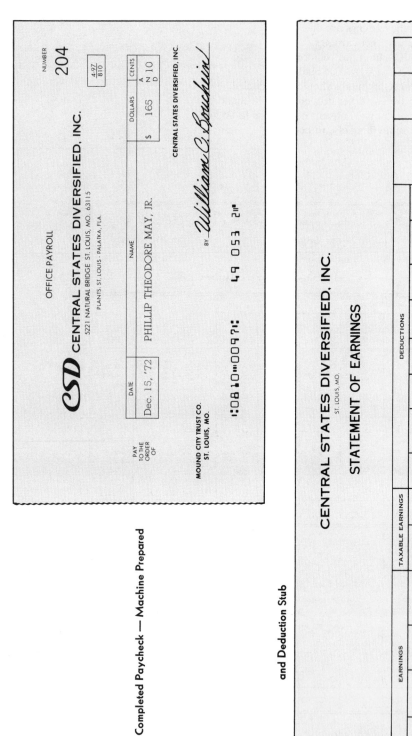

Completed Paycheck — Machine Prepared

and Deduction Stub

Once this system is properly set up, the operator is relieved of manual figuring and of looking up amounts in tables. The primary job is one of feeding in blank payroll accounting record forms and getting these forms back as completed payroll accounting records. (For a further discussion of automated accounting systems and procedures, see Appendix, page A-1.)

Wage and tax statement

Not later than January 31 of each year the law requires employers to furnish each employee from whom income taxes have been withheld the Wage and Tax Statement, Form W-2, showing the total amount of wages paid and the amount of such tax withheld during the preceding calendar year. This statement should be issued 30 days after the last wage payment to a terminating employee. If the employee's wages were subject to FICA tax as well as federal, state, or local income tax, the employer must report total wages paid and the amounts deducted both for income tax and for FICA tax. Information for this purpose should be provided by the employee's earnings record. A completed form W-2 is illustrated below.

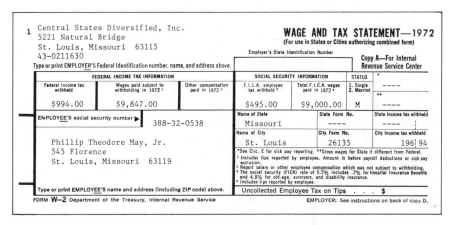

Completed Wage and Tax Statement (Form W-2)

The number appearing on the Wage and Tax Statement below the name and address of the employer is an *identification number* assigned to the employer by the Social Security Administration. Every employer of even one person receiving taxable wages must get an identification number within a week of the beginning of such employment. This number must be shown on all reports required of Central States Diversified, Inc. under the Federal Insurance Contributions Act.

Wage and Tax Statements must be prepared in quadruplicate (four copies). Copy A goes to the District Director of Internal Revenue with the employer's return of taxes withheld for the fourth quarter of the calendar year. Copies B and C are furnished to the employee, so that he can send Copy B in with his federal income tax return as required and keep Copy C for his files. Copy D is kept by the employer for his records. In states or cities which have state or city income tax withholding laws, two more copies are furnished to the employee. Copy 1 is sent in by the employer to the appropriate state or city tax department, and Copy 2 is sent in by the employee with his state or city income tax return.

Accounting for wages and wage deductions

In accounting for wages and wage deductions it is desirable to keep separate accounts for (1) wages earned and (2) wage deductions. Various account titles are used in recording wages, such as Wages Expense, Salaries Expense, and Salaries and Commissions Expense. The accounts needed in recording wage deductions depend upon what deductions are involved. A separate account should be kept for recording the liability incurred for each type of deduction, such as FICA tax, employees income tax, and savings bond deductions.

Wages Expense. This is an expense account which should be debited for the total amount of the gross earnings of all employees for each pay period. Sometimes separate

WAGES EXPENSE	
Debit	
to record gross earnings of employees for each pay period.	

wage accounts are kept for the employees of different departments. Thus, separate accounts might be kept for Office Salaries Expense, Sales Salaries Expense, and Factory Wages Expense.

FICA Tax Payable. This is a liability account which should be credited for (1) the FICA tax withheld from employees' wages and (2) the FICA tax imposed on the employer. The account should be debited for amounts paid to apply on

FICA TAX PAYABLE	
Debit	Credit
to record payment of FICA tax.	to record FICA taxes (a) withheld from employees' wages and (b) imposed on the employer.

such taxes. When all of the FICA taxes have been paid, the account should be in balance.

Employees Income Tax Payable. This is a liability account which should be credited for the total income tax withheld from employees' wages. The account should be

EMPLOYEES INCOME TAX PAYABLE	
Debit	Credit
to record payment of income tax withheld.	to record income tax withheld from employees' wages.

debited for amounts paid to apply on such taxes. When all of the income taxes withheld have been paid, the account will be in balance. A city or state earnings tax payable account is used in a similar manner.

Life Insurance Premiums Payable. This is a liability account which should be credited with amounts withheld from employees' wages for the future payment of life insurance premiums. The account should be debited for the subsequent payment

LIFE INSURANCE PREMIUMS PAYABLE	
Debit	Credit
to record the payment of life insurance premiums withheld.	to record amounts withheld for the future payment of life insurance premiums.

of these premiums to the life insurance company. Accounts for private hospital insurance premiums payable, credit union contributions payable, and savings bond deductions payable are similarly used.

Journalizing Payroll Transactions. The payroll register should provide the information needed in recording wages paid. The payroll register illustrated on pages 88 and 89 provided the information needed in drafting the following general journal entry to record the wages paid on December 15:

```
Dec. 15. Wages Expense................................  1,400.00
            FICA Tax Payable...........................             52.82
            Employees Income Tax Payable ...............            167.70
            City Earnings Tax Payable..................             28.00
            Life Insurance Premiums Payable.............            25.00
            Private Hospital Insurance Premiums Payable.....         13.00
            Credit Union Contributions Payable............          15.00
            Savings Bond Deductions Payable..............           20.00
            Cash.......................................          1,078.48
                Payroll for week ended December 15.
```

95

It will be noted that the foregoing journal entry involves one debit and eight credits. Regardless of the number of debits and credits needed to record a transaction, the total amount debited must be equal to the total amount credited.

Report No. 4-1

Complete Report No. 4-1 in the workbook and submit your working papers to the instructor for approval. After completing the report, continue with the following study assignment until the next report is required.

Payroll taxes imposed
on the employer

The employer is liable to the government for the taxes which he is required by law to withhold from the wages of his employees. These taxes include the federal income tax and the FICA tax which must be withheld from wages paid to employees. Such taxes are not an expense of the employer; nevertheless, the employer is required by law to collect the taxes and he is liable for the taxes until payment is made.

Certain taxes are also imposed on the employer for various purposes, such as old-age, survivors, and disability insurance benefits; hospital insurance benefits for the aged; and unemployment, relief, and welfare. Most employers are subject to payroll taxes imposed under the Federal Insurance Contributions Act (FICA) and the Federal Unemployment Tax Act (FUTA). An employer may also be subject to the payroll tax imposed under the unemployment compensation laws of one or more states. These commonly are called "State Unemployment Tax."

Payroll taxes expense

All of the payroll taxes imposed on an employer under federal and state social security laws are an expense of the employer. In accounting for such taxes at least one expense account should be maintained. This account may be entitled Payroll Taxes Expense. It is an expense account which should be debited for all taxes imposed on the employer under federal and state social security laws. Sometimes separate expense accounts are kept for (1) FICA Tax Expense,

PAYROLL TAXES EXPENSE	
Debit	
to record FICA, FUTA, and State Unemployment Taxes imposed on the employer.	

(2) FUTA Tax Expense, and (3) State Unemployment Tax Expense. In small business enterprises it is usually considered satisfactory to keep a single expense account for all federal and state social security taxes imposed on the employer.

Employer's FICA tax

The taxes imposed under the Federal Insurance Contributions Act apply equally to employers and to employees. As explained on page 81, both the rate and base of the tax may be changed by Congress at any time. In this discussion it is assumed that the combined rate is 5.5 percent which applies both to the employer and to his employees (a total of 11 percent) with respect to taxable wages. Only the first $9,000 of the wages paid to each employee in any calendar year constitutes taxable wages. Any amount of wages paid to an employee during a year in excess of $9,000 is exempt from FICA tax. While the employer is liable to the government both for the tax withheld from his employees' wages and for the tax imposed on the business, only the latter constitutes an expense of the business.

Employer's FUTA tax

Under the Federal Unemployment Tax Act, a payroll tax is levied on employers for the purpose of implementing more uniform administration of the various state unemployment compensation laws. Employers who employ one or more individuals for at least 20 calendar weeks in the calendar year, *or* who pay wages of $1,500 or more in any calendar quarter, are subject to this tax. The federal law imposes a specific rate of tax but allows a substantial credit against this levy if the state in which the employer is located has an unemployment compensation law that meets certain requirements. Since all states have such laws, the rate actually paid by most employers is much less than the maximum legal rate. As in the case of the FICA tax, Congress can and does change the rate from time to time. For the purpose of this discussion, a rate of 3.2 percent with a credit of 2.7 percent available to most employers is used. The difference, 0.5 percent (3.2 — 2.7) is, then, the effective rate. This is applied to the first $4,200 of compensation paid to each employee during the calendar year. It is important to note this limitation in contrast to the $9,000 limit in the case of the FICA tax. It is also important to note that all of the payroll taxes relate to gross wages paid — not to wages earned. Sometimes wages are earned in one quarter or year, but not paid until the following period.

97

FUTA tax payable

In recording the federal unemployment tax, it is customary to keep a separate liability account entitled FUTA Tax Payable. This is a liability account which should be credited for the tax imposed on employers under the Federal Unemployment Tax Act. The account should be debited for amounts paid to apply on such taxes. When all of the FUTA taxes have been paid, the account should be in balance.

FUTA Tax Payable	
Debit	Credit
to record payment of FUTA tax.	to record FUTA tax imposed on the employer with respect to wages paid.

State unemployment tax

All of the states and the District of Columbia have enacted unemployment compensation laws providing for the payment of benefits to qualified unemployed workers. The cost of administering the state unemployment compensation laws is borne by the federal government. Under the federal law an appropriation is made for each year by the Congress from which grants are made to the states to meet the proper administrative costs of their unemployment compensation laws. As a result of this provision, the entire amount paid into the state funds may be used for the payment of benefits to qualified workers. While in general there is considerable uniformity in the provisions of the state laws, there are many variations in coverage, rates of tax imposed, and benefits payable to qualified workers. Not all employers covered by the Federal Unemployment Tax Act are covered by the unemployment compensation laws of the states in which they have employees. But most employers of one or more individuals are covered by the federal law.

The minimum number of employees specified under state laws varies from 1 to 4. However, in many of the states an employer who is covered by the federal law and has one or more individuals employed within the state is also covered by the state law. Furthermore, under the laws of most states an employer who is covered by the federal law may elect voluntary coverage in states where he has one or more employees, even though he may have less than the number of employees specified by the law in that particular state. In any event, it is necessary for each employer to be familiar with the unemployment compensation laws of all the states in which he has one or more employees, and if such employees are covered, he must keep such records and pay such taxes for unemployment compensation purposes as are prescribed by those laws.

In most states the unemployment benefit plan is financed entirely by taxes imposed on employers. However, in a few states employees are also required to contribute, and the amount of the tax imposed on the employees must be withheld from their wages.

In most states the maximum tax imposed upon employers is 2.7 percent of the first $4,200 of wages paid to each employee in any calendar year. However, under the laws of most states there is a *merit-rating* system which provides a tax-saving incentive to employers to stabilize employment. Under this system an employer's rate may be considerably less than the maximum rate if he provides steady work for his employees.

There are frequent changes in the state laws with respect to coverage, rates of contributions required, eligibility to receive benefits, and amounts of benefits payable. In this discussion, it is assumed that the state tax rate is 2.7 percent of the first $4,200 of wages paid each employee each year.

State unemployment tax payable

In recording the tax imposed under state unemployment compensation laws, it is customary to keep a separate liability account entitled State Unemployment Tax Payable. This is a liability account which should be credited for the tax imposed on employers under the state unemployment compensation laws. The account should be debited for the amount paid to apply on such taxes. When all of the state taxes have been paid, the account should be in balance. Some employers who are subject to taxes imposed under the laws of several states keep a separate liability account for the tax imposed by each state.

STATE UNEMPLOYMENT TAX PAYABLE	
Debit	Credit
to record state unemployment tax paid.	to record liability for state unemployment tax required of employers.

Journalizing employer's payroll taxes

The payroll taxes imposed on employers may be recorded periodically, such as monthly or quarterly. It is more common to record such taxes at the time that wages are paid so that the employer's liability for such taxes and related expenses may be recorded in the same period as the wages on which the taxes are based. The payroll register illustrated on pages 88 and 89 provides the information needed in recording the FICA tax imposed on Central States Diversified, Inc. with respect to wages paid on December 15. The FICA taxable earnings for the pay period involved amounted to $960.00. Assuming that the combined rate of the tax imposed on the employer was 5.5 percent, which is the same as the rate of the tax imposed on the employees, the tax would amount to $52.80. (This amount will not necessarily be the same as that calculated by multiplying the tax rate times total taxable earnings due to the rounding up of amounts in calculating the tax deduction for each employee.) If only $672.00 of the earnings for the period had been subject to unemployment taxes (none actually were), the federal and state taxes would have been computed as follows:

State unemployment tax, 2.7% of $672.00	$18.14
FUTA tax, 0.5% of $672.00	3.36
Total unemployment taxes	$21.50

The following general journal entry may be made to record the payroll taxes imposed on the employer with respect to the wages paid on December 15:

Dec. 15. Payroll Taxes Expense	74.30	
FICA Tax Payable		52.80
FUTA Tax Payable		3.36
State Unemployment Tax Payable		18.14
Payroll taxes imposed on employer with respect to wages paid December 15.		

Filing returns and paying the payroll taxes

When the cumulative amount withheld from employees' wages for income tax and FICA tax purposes plus the amount of the FICA tax imposed on the employer during the first or second month of any quarter is more than $200, the total must be deposited at a District Federal Reserve Bank or some other United States depositary by the 15th of the following month. If the $200 minimum limitation is reached in the last month of a calendar quarter, the liability must be paid to the District Director of Internal Revenue at the time of filing the quarterly return on or before the last day of the following month. If the total amount of the taxes for the quarter is less than $200, the total taxes must be paid at the time of filing the quarterly return.

When the cumulative amount of income and FICA tax is over $200 but under $2,000, the total is required to be deposited by the 15th day of the next month. If this $200–$2,000 limitation is reached in the third month of any quarter, no deposit need be made until the last day of the month following the quarter.

When the cumulative amount is $2,000 or more by the 7th, 15th, 22d, or last day of any month, a deposit must be made within three banking days after that quarter-monthly period.

A completed copy of the Federal Tax Deposit — Withheld Income and FICA Taxes, Form 501, is shown below. The stub is detached by the bank on payment of the taxes due and is the employer's record of the deposit.

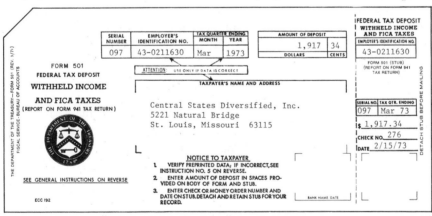

Completed Federal Tax Deposit Form (Form 501)

To illustrate the accounting procedure in recording the payment of employees' income tax and FICA tax withheld, it will be assumed that on February 15 Central States Diversified, Inc. issued a check in payment of the following taxes imposed with respect to wages paid during the month of January:

Employees' income tax withheld from wages...............		$1,295.20
FICA tax:		
Withheld from employees' wages.......................	$311.07	
Imposed on employer................................	311.07	622.14
Amount of check......................................		$1,917.34

A check for this amount accompanied by the Federal Tax Deposit form, Form 501, was sent to a bank that is qualified as a depositary for federal taxes. (All national banks are qualified.) This transaction may be recorded as indicated by the following general journal entry:

```
Feb. 15.  FICA Tax Payable............................    622.14
          Employees Income Tax Payable ................. 1,295.20
          Cash.......................................              1,917.34
               Remitted $1,917.34 in payment of taxes.
```

Further assume that on March 15, $1,933.66 was deposited. This covered income tax withholdings of $1,306.60 during February and the employer's and employees' FICA tax of $627.06 for February. The proper entry was made to record the payment of $1,933.66. Also assume that during March, income tax withholdings amounted to $1,318.30 and FICA tax (employer's and employees'), $632.46 – a total of $1,950.76. Finally assume that on April 15, the quarterly return, Form 941, illustrated on page 102 was sent to the nearest office of the District Director of Internal Revenue, accompanied by a check for $1,950.76. The proper entry was made to record the payment of $1,950.76 to the Internal Revenue **101** Service.

The amount on lines 2 and 4 of the quarterly tax return illustration, $3,920.10, is the sum of the employees' income tax withheld in January ($1,295.20), February ($1,306.60), and March ($1,318.30). The amount on line 5 of this return comes from the total of wages reported on line 21 (the total taxable FICA wages reported on Schedule A) times 11 percent (the combined FICA tax rate for employer and employee). The adjusted total of FICA tax on line 9 is added to the adjusted total of income tax withheld, line 4, to give the amount on line 10, which is the total income tax and FICA tax due to the federal government.

The amount on line 11 of the Form 941 illustration, $3,851.00, is the sum of the tax deposits for February 15 ($1,917.34) and March 15 ($1,933.66). The amount on line 12a, $1,950.76, is the balance due to the Internal Revenue Service for which the check was written and sent to the nearest District Director's office with the return.

The amount of the tax imposed on employers under the state unemployment compensation laws must be remitted to the proper state office during the month following the close of the calendar quarter. Each state provides an official form to be used in making a return of the taxes due. Assuming that a check for $316.27 was issued on April 30 in payment of state unemployment compensation tax on wages paid during the preceding

FORM 941
(Rev. Apr. 1971)
Department of the Treasury
Internal Revenue Service

**Employer's
Quarterly
Federal
Tax
Return**

1. TOTAL WAGES AND TIPS SUBJECT TO WITHHOLDING PLUS OTHER COMPENSATION . . . . . ➙	17,106	00
2. AMOUNT OF INCOME TAX WITHHELD FROM WAGES, TIPS, ANNUITIES, etc. (See instructions)	3,920	10
3. ADJUSTMENT FOR PRECEDING QUARTERS OF CALENDAR YEAR	---	
4. ADJUSTED TOTAL OF INCOME TAX WITHHELD . . . . ➙	3,920	10
5. TAXABLE FICA WAGES PAID (Item 21) . . $17,106.00 ____ multiplied by 11.0% = TAX	1,881	66
6. TAXABLE TIPS REPORTED (Item 22) . . . $ ____ multiplied by 5.5% = TAX	---	
7. TOTAL FICA TAXES (Item 5 plus Item 6) . . . . ➙	1,881	66
8. ADJUSTMENT (See instructions)	---	
9. ADJUSTED TOTAL OF FICA TAXES . . . . ➙	1,881	66
10. TOTAL TAXES (Item 4 plus Item 9)	5,801	76
11. TOTAL DEPOSITS FOR QUARTER (INCLUDING FINAL DEPOSIT MADE FOR QUARTER) AND OVERPAYMENT FROM PREVIOUS QUARTER. LIST IN SCHEDULE B. (See instructions on page 4)	3,851	00

Note: If undeposited taxes due at the end of the quarter are $200 or more, the entire balance must be deposited. This deposit must be entered in Schedule B and included in item 11.

12a. UNDEPOSITED TAXES DUE (ITEM 10 LESS ITEM 11—THIS SHOULD BE LESS THAN $200). PAY TO INTERNAL REVENUE SERVICE AND ENTER HERE . . . . ➙	1,950	76

12b. IF ITEM 11 IS MORE THAN ITEM 10, ENTER EXCESS HERE ➙ $ ____ AND CHECK IF TO BE: ☐ APPLIED TO NEXT RETURN, OR ☐ REFUNDED.

13. If not liable for returns in succeeding quarters write "FINAL" here ➙ ____ and enter date of final payment of taxable wages here ➙

Under penalties of perjury, I declare that I have examined this return, including accompanying schedules and statements, and to the best of my knowledge and belief it is true, correct, and complete.

Date 4-15-73   Signature *William C. Bouchein*   Title (Owner, etc.)   Treasurer

	T	
	FF	
	FD	
	FP	
	I	
	T	

Employer's name, address, employer identification number, and calendar quarter. (If not correct, please change)

Name (as distinguished from trade name)   Date quarter ended
Central States Diversified, Inc.   3-31-73
Trade name, if any   Employer Identification No.
► Central States   43-0211630
Address and ZIP code
5221 Natural Bridge, St. Louis, Missouri 63115
-------------------- Entries must be made both above and below this line --------------------
Name (as distinguished from trade name)   Date quarter ended
Central States Diversified, Inc.   3-31-73
Trade name, if any   Employer Identification No.
► Central States   43-0211630
Address and ZIP code
5221 Natural Bridge, St. Louis, Missouri 63115

**SCHEDULE A—QUARTERLY REPORT OF WAGES TAXABLE UNDER THE FEDERAL INSURANCE CONTRIBUTIONS ACT
(FOR SOCIAL SECURITY)
IF WAGES WERE NOT TAXABLE UNDER FICA MAKE NO ENTRIES BELOW**

14. (First quarter only) Number of employees (except household) employed in the pay period including March 12th. 8	15. Total pages of this return including this page and any pages of Form 941a. 2	16. Total number of employees listed. 8

List for each nonagricultural employee the WAGES taxable under FICA which were paid during the quarter. If you pay an employee more than $9,000 in a calendar year, report only the first $9,000 of such wages. In the case of "Tip Income," see instructions on Page 4.

Please be sure to report each employee's name and number exactly as shown on his Social Security card.

17. EMPLOYEE'S SOCIAL SECURITY NUMBER (If number is unknown, see Circular E) 00C 00 0000	18. NAME OF EMPLOYEE (Please type or print)	19. TAXABLE FICA WAGES Paid to Employee in Quarter (Before deductions) ▼ Dollars Cents	20. TAXABLE TIPS REPORTED (See page 4) If amounts in this column are not tips check here ☐ Dollars Cents
258-05-3753	David T. Abernathy	2,080.00	
504-38-8340	Alan C. Blank	2,600.00	
810-04-1629	Susan Fritzshall	1,756.00	
388-32-0538	Phillip T. May, Jr.	2,350.00	
258-08-8221	Thomas K. Morrison	2,470.00	
472-04-2335	Jack G. Oakley	1,885.00	
521-08-6503	Robert M. Pratzel	2,145.00	
269-07-1132	Ronald J. Ryan	1,820.00	

If you need more space for listing employees, use Schedule A continuation sheets, Form 941a.
Totals for this page—Wage total in column 19 and tip total in column 20 ➙   17,106.00

21. **TOTAL WAGES** TAXABLE UNDER FICA PAID DURING QUARTER.
(Total of column 19 on this page and continuation sheets.) Enter here and in Item 5 above . . $ 17,106.00

22. **TOTAL TAXABLE TIPS** REPORTED UNDER FICA DURING QUARTER. (If no tips reported, write "None.")
(Total of column 20 on this page and continuation sheets.) Enter here and in Item 6 above . . . . ➙ $ None

SEE "WHERE TO FILE" ON PAGE 2.

Employer's Quarterly Federal Tax Return and Quarterly Report, Schedule A (Form 941)

quarter ended March 31, the transaction may be recorded as indicated by the following journal entry:

Apr. 30.	State Unemployment Tax Payable...................	316.27	
	Cash..		316.27
	Paid state unemployment tax.		

Federal unemployment tax must be computed on a quarterly basis. If the amount of the employer's liability under the Federal Unemployment Tax Act during any quarter is more than $100, the total must be paid to the District Federal Reserve Bank or some other United States depositary on or before the last day of the first month following the close of the quarter. If the amount is $100 or less, no deposit is necessary, but this amount must be added to the amount subject to deposit for the next quarter.

When paying FUTA tax, it is necessary to complete the Federal Tax Deposit form, Form 508, and to send or take it to the bank with the remittance. This form is not illustrated here, but it is similar in nature to Form 501, previously illustrated on page 100.

The amount of the tax on employers under the Federal Unemployment Tax Act for the entire year must be paid to the District Director of Internal Revenue by the end of the month following the close of the calendar year. An official form (Form 940) is provided to the employer for use in making a report of the taxes due. This form is not illustrated here.

Assuming that a check for $105.40 was issued on January 31 in payment of the tax imposed under the Federal Unemployment Tax Act with respect to wages paid during the preceding year ended December 31, the transaction may be recorded as indicated by the following journal entry:

Jan. 31.	FUTA Tax Payable...............................	105.40	
	Cash..		105.40
	Paid federal unemployment tax.		

Report No. 4-2

Complete Report No. 4-2 in the workbook and submit your working papers to the instructor for approval. After completing the report, you may continue with the textbook discussion in Chapter 5 until the next report is required.

chapter 5

accounting for a personal service enterprise

104

A personal service enterprise is one in which the principal source of revenue is compensation for personal services rendered. There are two types of personal service enterprises:

(a) Business enterprises
(b) Professional enterprises

Business enterprises of the personal service type include real estate, insurance, advertising, transportation, storage, entertainment, brokerage, and various others in which the revenue is derived chiefly from personal services rendered. Mercantile enterprises are not classified as personal service enterprises for the reason that their principal source of revenue is from the sale of merchandise rather than from compensation received for services provided.

Professional enterprises include law, medicine, dentistry, public accounting, engineering, architecture, art, and education. The principal source of revenue for individuals engaged in such professions is usually the compensation received for the personal services rendered.

The cash basis of accounting for a personal service enterprise

Accounting for revenue on a cash basis means that, in most cases, no record of revenue is made in the accounts until cash is received for the services performed. This may mean that the services are rendered in one period, and the revenue is accounted for in the succeeding period. The business or professional man may well take the view that, in most cases, he has had no revenue until it is received in such form that it can be spent. He cannot "spend" the promise of a customer or client to pay him some money.

The cash basis of accounting for the revenue of a personal service enterprise is widely used. It is acceptable for federal and state income tax purposes. Not only is the receipt of cash accounted for as revenue under this basis; many other types of transactions are accounted for similarly. Any property or service that is accepted in place of cash for services is treated as revenue to the extent of its fair market value at the time received. Revenue is said to be *constructively received* if it is credited to a depositor's account or set apart so that he can draw upon it. For example, when interest on a savings account is credited to the depositor's account, such interest is considered to be revenue to the depositor even though it is not actually received in cash or is not immediately withdrawn.

Accounting for expenses on the cash basis generally means that expenses are not recorded in the accounts until paid in cash. An expense may be incurred in one period and recorded in the accounts in the succeeding period. In the case of many expenses of a recurring nature, however, this set of circumstances is regarded as a minor objection. If, for example, twelve monthly telephone bills of about the same amount must be paid during each year, little importance is attached to the fact that the bill that is paid and recorded as an expense in January was really for service received in December.

An exception to the cash basis of accounting for expenses is made in connection with most long-lived assets. For example, it would be unreasonable to consider the entire cost of a building or of most equipment to be an expense of the period in which such assets were purchased. If it is expected that an asset will serve for a number of years, its cost (less expected scrap or salvage value, if any) is prorated over its estimated life. The share of cost assigned to each period is described as *depreciation expense*. Such expense cannot be calculated with precise accuracy. Still, an allocation that eventually turns out to have been somewhat in error results in a far more equitable periodic net income (profit) or loss measurement than simply considering the cost of such assets to be entirely an expense of the period in which they were purchased.

105

Another exception to the cash basis of accounting for expenses is sometimes made in connection with supplies purchased and used. If the amount of money involved is substantial and the end of the accounting period finds a considerable quantity of expensive supplies still on hand, an effort is made to determine the cost of those items which are on hand, so that only the cost of the supplies used will be treated as an expense of the period. If both the quantity and the cost of the items on hand at the end of a period are small, the usual practice is to ignore them and to consider the total cost of all items purchased during that accounting period to be an expense of that period.

Accounting procedure

As an aid in applying the principles involved in keeping the accounts of a personal service enterprise on the cash basis, a system of accounts for Howard C. Miller, an architect, will be described. While certain distinctive problems may arise in keeping the accounts of any specific enterprise, it will be found that the principles are generally the same; hence, the system of accounts used by Mr. Miller may readily be adapted to the needs of any personal service enterprise regardless of whether it is of a professional or a business nature.

Chart of accounts

Mr. Miller's chart of accounts is reproduced on page 107. Note that all account numbers beginning with 1 relate to assets; 2, liabilities; 3, owner's equity; 4, revenue; and 5, expenses. Account numbers beginning with 0 represent *contra accounts* (meaning "opposite" or "offsetting" accounts) used to show the decrease in the related element. This system of account numbering permits the addition of new accounts as they may be needed without disturbing the numerical order of the existing accounts.

Most of the accounts in the foregoing list have been discussed and their use illustrated in the preceding chapters. Three notable exceptions are: Accumulated Depreciation — Office Equipment (No. 013), Depreciation Expense (No. 517), and Expense and Revenue Summary (No. 321). Each of these will be explained and its use illustrated as the need for the account arises in the narrative of transactions later in the chapter. Except for Depreciation Expense (No. 517), every debit to an expense account arises in connection with a cash disbursement. The cost of all blueprints and supplies purchased is debited (charged) to Account No. 515. The amount of

CHART OF ACCOUNTS

*Assets**
111 First National Bank
112 Petty Cash Fund
131 Office Equipment
013 Accumulated Depreciation—
Office Equipment

Liabilities
211 Employees Income Tax Payable
212 FICA Tax Payable

Owner's Equity
311 Howard C. Miller, Capital
031 Howard C. Miller, Drawing
321 Expense and Revenue Summary

Revenue
411 Professional Fees

Expenses
511 Salary Expense
512 Payroll Taxes Expense
513 Rent Expense
514 Telephone and Telegraph Expense
515 Blueprints and Supplies Expense
516 Automobile Expense
517 Depreciation Expense
518 Insurance Expense
519 Travel and Entertainment Expense
521 Charitable Contributions Expense
522 Miscellaneous Expense

Words in italics represent headings and not account titles.

any unused supplies that may be on hand at the end of the year is ignored because such quantities normally are very small. (Note that there is no asset account for supplies.) The car that Mr. Miller uses for business purposes is leased. The monthly car rental and the cost of gasoline, oil, lubrication, washing, and automobile insurance are charged to Automobile Expense, Account No. 516. The cost of all other types of insurance that relate to the enterprise, such as workmen's compensation, "errors and omissions" insurance (normally carried by architects), and fire insurance on the office equipment and contents, is charged to Insurance Expense, Account No. 518, when the premiums on the policies are paid.

107

Books of account

Mr. Miller uses the following books of account:

(a) General books
    (1) Combined cash journal
    (2) General ledger
(b) Auxiliary records
    (1) Petty cash disbursements record
    (2) Employees' earnings records
    (3) Copies of statements rendered to clients (billings for fees) with collections noted thereon

Combined Cash Journal. Mr. Miller uses only one book of original entry — a combined cash journal. This journal, reproduced on pages 112–115, has eight amount columns, two at the left and six at the right of the Description column. The headings of the amount columns (as they read from left to right on the journal page) are as follows:

First National Bank
Deposits 111 Dr.
Checks 111 Cr.

General
  Debit
  Credit

Professional Fees 411 Cr.

Salary Expense 511 Dr.

Wage Deductions
  Employees Income Tax Payable 211 Cr.
  FICA Tax Payable 212 Cr.

The account numbers in the headings are an aid in completing the summary posting at the end of each month. Comparison of this combined cash journal and the four-column journal illustrated in Chapter 3 (page 47) will reveal two differences: **(1)** the presence of a Check Number column just to the right of the Checks 111 Cr. column, and **(2)** the four special columns to the right of the pair of General columns. Each of these four special columns is justified because there are enough transactions requiring entries in the accounts indicated by the column headings to warrant this arrangement which will save time and labor in the bookkeeping process. A narrative of transactions completed by Mr. Miller during the month of December, 19--, is given on pages 109–116. These transactions are recorded in the combined cash journal on pages 112–115. Attention is called to the fact that before any transactions were recorded in this journal, the bank balance at the start of the month, $2,468.15, was entered in the Description column just above the words "Amounts Forwarded."

General Ledger. The standard form of account is used in the general ledger of Mr. Miller's enterprise. The ledger is reproduced on pages 116–119. In each instance, the balance of the account as of December 1 has been entered. Two accounts are omitted: Expense and Revenue Summary (No. 321) and Depreciation Expense (No. 517). They are not included because neither had a balance on December 1, and neither received any debits or credits as a result of the cash receipt and disbursement transactions in December. These accounts are not used until the end-of-year process of adjusting and closing the accounts takes place. This procedure will be explained and illustrated on pages 124–130.

Auxiliary Records. The auxiliary records included in Mr. Miller's system of accounts are not reproduced in this chapter. The petty cash disbursements record that is used is almost identical in form to the one illustrated in Chapter 3 on pages 56 and 57. However, the combined cash journal entry to record the reimbursement of the petty cash fund at the end of December is shown (see the first entry of December 29 on pages 114 and 115). Mr. Miller has two employees: Mr. John Davis, a full-time draftsman, and Miss Sally Wilson, a part-time secretary. An employee's earnings record, similar to the one illustrated in Chapter 4 on pages 86 and 87, is maintained for each employee. Mr. Miller keeps a file for each client which includes, among other things, a copy of the contract or agreement with the client. This agreement stipulates the fee for the assignment and the time of payment (or payments, if the fee is to be paid in installments — which is the usual case). A carbon copy of each statement or billing for fees earned is placed in each client's file. When money is received from a client, the date and amount are noted on the copy of the billing in addition to the formal record made in the combined cash journal.

HOWARD C. MILLER, ARCHITECT
NARRATIVE OF TRANSACTIONS

Friday, December 1

Issued Check No. 311 for $174.90 to John Davis, draftsman, in payment of his salary for week: $200 less income tax withholding, $25.10. (Note: Mr. Davis has been employed since the start of the year. His gross earnings reached $9,000 during the week of November 5. Since that time, no FICA tax has been withheld.)

> Since individual posting of this entry was not required, a check mark was placed in the Posting Reference column of the combined cash journal at the time the transaction was recorded.

Issued Check No. 312 for $50.30 to Sally Wilson, secretary (part-time), in payment of her salary for week: $60 less income tax withholding, $6.40, and FICA tax withholding, $3.30.

Issued Check No. 313 for $240 to C. A. Peters for December office rent.

Monday, December 4

Received a check for $700 from R. J. Monroe, a client.

> Note that the client's name was written in the Description column and that a check mark was placed in the Posting Reference column.

Wednesday, December 6

Issued Check No. 314 for $36.40 to Lloyd G. Hild, an insurance agent, in payment of the one-year premium on a fire insurance policy covering Mr. Miller's office equipment and contents.

Friday, December 8

Issued Check No. 315 for $174.90 to John Davis and Check No. 316 for $50.30 to Sally Wilson in payment of salaries for the week. (See explanation relating to Checks Nos. 311 and 312 issued on December 1.)

END-OF-THE-WEEK WORK

(1) Proved the footings of the combined cash journal as follows:

Column	Dr.	Cr.
First National Bank	$ 700.00	$ 726.80
General	276.40	
Professional Fees		700.00
Salary Expense	520.00	
Employees Income Tax Payable		63.00
FICA Tax Payable		6.60
	$1,496.40	$1,496.40

(2) Deposited the $700 check from R. J. Monroe in the bank, proved the bank balance ($2,441.35), and entered the new balance in the Description column following the second transaction of December 8. **(3)** Posted each entry individually from the General Debit column of the combined cash journal to the proper general ledger accounts. (Note that there were two such postings and that their respective account numbers, 513 and 518, were entered in the Posting Reference column.)

Monday, December 11

Issued Check No. 317 for $63.19 to Superior Blue Print Co. in payment for prints.

Received a check for $1.80 from Lloyd G. Hild, the insurance agent to whom Mr. Miller had sent a check (No. 314) a few days earlier in the amount of $36.40 in payment of the premium on a fire insurance policy on his office equipment and contents. The check for $1.80 was accompanied by a letter from Mr. Hild explaining that a clerk in his office had made an error in preparing the invoice for the policy. The correct amount was $34.60 — not $36.40. Mr. Miller's check for $36.40 had been deposited before the mistake was discovered. Accordingly, Mr. Hild sent his check for $1.80 as a refund of the excess premium.

> This insurance premium refund check was recorded in the combined cash journal by a debit to First National Bank, Account No. 111, and a credit to Insurance Expense, Account No. 518, in the amount of $1.80. Since the entry to record Check No. 314 had already been posted as a debit to Insurance Expense, this manner of handling was required. (The trouble resulted from the fact that the clerk in Mr. Hild's office had made a *transposition* error — a mistake well known to bookkeepers and accountants. The intention was to write or type "$34.60," but $36.40" was written instead. The "4" and the "6" were placed in the wrong order — they were *transposed.*)

Tuesday, December 12

Received a check for $775 from M. C. Watson, a client.

Issued Check No. 318 for $152.40 to the First National Bank, a United States depositary, in payment of the following taxes:

Employees' income tax withheld during November..............		$126.00
FICA tax imposed —		
On employees (withheld during November).................	$13.20	
On the employer......................................	13.20	26.40
Total...		$152.40

This disbursement involved three factors (in addition to the decrease in the bank balance): **(1)** payment of the recorded liability, Employees Income Tax Payable, Account No. 211, of $126.00; **(2)** payment of the recorded liability, FICA Tax Payable, Account No. 212, of $13.20; and **(3)** payment of the unrecorded liability of $13.20, the employer's FICA tax relating to the taxable earnings paid in November. To record the transaction correctly, the first two amounts were debited to the proper liability accounts, and the third amount was debited to Payroll Taxes Expense, Account No. 512. Note that three lines were needed in the combined cash journal.

(The checks from Mr. Watson and Mr. Hild were deposited in the bank, and the check for $152.40, together with a Tax Deposit Form, was presented at the bank in payment of the taxes. The stub attached to the form was filled out and retained as a record of the deposit.)

Wednesday, December 13

Issued Check No. 319 for $1,000 to Mr. Miller for personal use.

Thursday, December 14

Issued Check No. 320 for $72.30 to the Executive Car Leasing Co. in payment of one month's rent of the leased automobile used by Mr. Miller for business purposes.

This disbursement was recorded by a debit to Automobile Expense, Account No. 516.

Friday, December 15

Issued Check No. 321 for $174.90 to John Davis and Check No. 322 for $50.30 to Sally Wilson in payment of salaries for week. (See explanation relating to Checks Nos. 311 and 312 issued on December 1.)

Issued Check No. 323 for $50 to American Red Cross.

END-OF-THE-WEEK WORK

(1) Proved the footings of the combined cash journal. **(2)** Proved the bank balance ($1,655.06). **(3)** Posted each entry individually from the General Debit and General Credit columns of the combined cash journal to the proper general ledger accounts. When the entry of December 12 relating to Check No. 318 was posted, debits were made to Employees Income Tax Payable, Account No. 211, and FICA Tax Payable, Account No. 212, which caused those accounts to be in balance. Each of those two accounts was ruled with a double line as illustrated on page 117.

Monday, December 18

Issued Check No. 324 for $28.17 to Wally's Service Station in payment of charges for gasoline, oil, and lubrication purchased on credit during the past month. (All of these purchases related to the leased car used for business purposes.)

Issued Check No. 325 for $9.50 to Acme Typewriter Service in payment of charges for cleaning and repairing office typewriter.

The amount of this check was charged to Miscellaneous Expense, Account No. 522.

Tuesday, December 19

Issued Check No. 326 for $36.45 to Southwestern Telephone Co. in payment of statement just received showing charges for local service, long

112

PAGE 36   COMBINED CASH JOURNAL

	FIRST NATIONAL BANK		CK. NO.	DAY	DESCRIPTION	POST. REF.	
	DEPOSITS 111 DR.	CHECKS 111 CR.					
1					AMOUNTS FORWARDED Balance 2,468.15		1
2		174 90	311	1	John Davis	✓	2
3		50 30	312	1	Sally Wilson	✓	3
4		240 00	313	1	Rent Expense	513	4
5	700 00			4	R. J. Monroe	✓	5
6		36 40	314	6	Insurance Expense	518	6
7		174 90	315	8	John Davis	✓	7
8	700 00	50 30	316	8	Sally Wilson	✓	8
9		726 80 63 19	317	11	Blueprints and Supplies Expense 2,441.35	515	9
10	1 80			11	Insurance Expense	518	10
11	775 00			12	M. C. Watson	✓	11
12		152 40	318	12	Employees Income Tax Payable	211	12
13					FICA Tax Payable	212	13
14					Payroll Taxes Expense	512	14
15		1000 00	319	13	Howard C. Miller, Drawing	031	15
16		72 30	320	14	Automobile Expense	516	16
17		174 90	321	15	John Davis	✓	17
18		50 30	322	15	Sally Wilson	✓	18
19		50 00	323	15	Charitable Contributions Expense 1,655.06	521	19
20	1476 80	2289 89 28 17	324	18	Automobile Expense	516	20
21		9 50	325	18	Miscellaneous Expense	522	21
22		36 45	326	19	Telephone and Telegraph Expense	514	22
23	1050 00			20	Mrs. James Hinman	✓	23
24		72 18	327	21	Blueprints and Supplies Expense	515	24
25		174 90	328	22	John Davis	✓	25
26		50 30	329	22	Sally Wilson	✓	26
27	2526 80 2526 80	2661 39 2661 39		22	Carried Forward 2,333.56		27

Howard C. Miller, Architect — Combined Cash Journal (Left Page)

distance calls, and telegrams during the past month. (This telephone bill related exclusively to the phone in Mr. Miller's office.)

Wednesday, December 20

Received a check for $1,050 from Mrs. James Hinman, a client.

Thursday, December 21

Issued Check No. 327 for $72.18 to Architects Supply Co. in payment for supplies purchased.

FOR MONTH OF *December* 19 —— PAGE 36

Line	GENERAL DEBIT	GENERAL CREDIT	PROFESSIONAL FEES 411 CR.	SALARY EXPENSE 511 DR.	EMP. INC. TAX PAY. 211 CR.	FICA TAX PAY. 212 CR.	Line
1							1
2				200 00	25 10		2
3				60 00	6 40	3 30	3
4	240 00						4
5			700 00				5
6	36 40						6
7				200 00	25 10		7
8	276 40		700 00	520 00	63 00	6 60	8
9	63 19						9
10		1 80					10
11			775 00				11
12	126 00						12
13	13 20						13
14	13 20						14
15	1000 00						15
16	72 30						16
17				200 00	25 10		17
18				60 00	6 40	3 30	18
19	50 00						19
20	1614 29 / 28 17	1 80	1475 00	780 00	94 50	9 90	20
21	9 50						21
22	36 45						22
23			1050 00				23
24	72 18						24
25				200 00	25 10		25
26				60 00	6 40	3 30	26
27	1760 59 / 1760 59	1 80 / 1 80	2525 00 / 2525 00	1040 00 / 1040 00	126 00 / 126 00	13 20 / 13 20	27

Howard C. Miller, Architect — Combined Cash Journal (Right Page)

113

Friday, December 22

Issued Check No. 328 for $174.90 to John Davis and Check No. 329 for $50.30 to Sally Wilson in payment of salaries for week. (See explanation relating to Checks Nos. 311 and 312 issued on December 1.)

END-OF-THE-WEEK WORK

(1) Proved the footings of the combined cash journal. **(2)** Deposited the $1,050 check from Mrs. Hinman and proved the bank balance ($2,333.56). **(3)** Posted each entry individually from the General Debit column of the combined cash journal.

> Because a page of the combined cash journal was filled after Check No. 329 was recorded, the footings of the columns were proved, these footings were recorded as totals on the last line of the page, and the words "Carried Forward" were written in the Description column. The totals were entered in the appropriate columns on the top line of the next page. The bank balance was entered in the Description column of the new page just above the words "Amounts Forwarded."

Wednesday, December 27

Issued Check No. 330 for $87.90 to Rolling Hills Country Club in payment of food and beverage charges for one month.

> The amount of this check was charged to Travel and Entertainment Expense, Account No. 519. Mr. Miller uses the facilities of the club to entertain prospective clients.

114

PAGE *37* COMBINED CASH JOURNAL

FIRST NATIONAL BANK		CK. NO.	DAY	DESCRIPTION	POST. REF.	
DEPOSITS 111 DR.	CHECKS 111 CR.					
2526 80	266 39		22	AMOUNTS FORWARDED *Balance 2,333.56*	✓	1
	87 90	330	27	Travel and Entertainment Expense	519	2
600 00			28	Frank Poulson	✓	3
	53 33	331	29	Howard C. Miller, Drawing	031	4
				Telephone and Telegraph Expense	514	5
				Blueprints and Supplies Expense	515	6
				Automobile Expense	516	7
				Travel and Entertainment Expense	519	8
				Charitable Contributions Expense	521	9
				Miscellaneous Expense	522	10
	174 90	332	29	John Davis	✓	11
	50 30	333	29	Sally Wilson 2,567.13	✓	12
3126 80	3027 82					13
3126 80	3027 82					13
(111)	(111)					14
						15

Howard C. Miller, Architect — Combined Cash Journal (Left Page)
(concluded)

Thursday, December 28

Received a check for $600 from Frank Poulson, a client.

Friday, December 29

Issued Check No. 331 for $53.33 to replenish the petty cash fund. Following is a summary of the petty cash disbursements for the month of December prepared from the Petty Cash Disbursements Record:

Howard C. Miller, drawing	$10.00
Telephone and telegraph expense	1.10
Blueprints and supplies expense	7.85
Automobile expense	3.40
Travel and entertainment expense	21.90
Charitable contributions expense	5.00
Miscellaneous expense	4.08
Total disbursements	$53.33

Issued Check No. 332 for $174.90 to John Davis and Check No. 333 for $50.30 to Sally Wilson in payment of salaries for week. (See explanation relating to Checks Nos. 311 and 312 issued on December 1.)

115

FOR MONTH OF *December* 19 —— PAGE *37*

	GENERAL		PROFESSIONAL FEES 411 CR.	SALARY EXPENSE 511 DR.	WAGE DEDUCTIONS		
	DEBIT	CREDIT			EMP. INC. TAX PAY. 211 CR.	FICA TAX PAY. 212 CR.	
1	1760.59	1.80	2525.00	1040.00	126.00	13.20	1
2	87.90						2
3				600.00			3
4	10.00						4
5	1.10						5
6	7.85						6
7	3.40						7
8	21.90						8
9	5.00						9
10	4.08						10
11				200.00	25.10		11
12				60.00	6.40	3.30	12
12	1901.82	1.80	3125.00	1300.00	157.50	16.50	
13	1901.82	1.80	3125.00	1300.00	157.50	16.50	13
14	(✓)	(✓)	(411)	(511)	(211)	(212)	14
15							15

Howard C. Miller, Architect — Combined Cash Journal (Right Page)
(concluded)

Chapter 5 / Accounting for a Personal Service Enterprise

ROUTINE END-OF-THE-MONTH WORK

(1) Proved the footings and entered the totals in the combined cash journal. **(2)** Deposited the $600 check from Mr. Poulson and proved the bank balance ($2,567.13). **(3)** Completed the individual posting from the General Debit column of the combined cash journal. **(4)** Completed the summary posting of the column totals of the combined cash journal and ruled the journal as illustrated on pages 114 and 115. (Note that the number of the account to which the total was posted was written in parentheses just below the total, and that check marks were placed below the General Debit and General Credit column totals in parentheses to indicate that these amounts were not posted.) **(5)** Footed the ledger accounts and noted the account balances where necessary, as illustrated below and on pages 117–119. **(6)** Prepared a trial balance of the ledger accounts.

> Usually a trial balance at the end of a month is prepared using two-column paper. However, because Mr. Miller has chosen the calendar year for his fiscal year (a common, but by no means universal, practice), the trial balance at the end of December is put in the first two amount columns of a page known as a *work sheet*. The purpose and manner of preparation of a work sheet is explained and illustrated on pages 120–123.

116

ACCOUNT *First National Bank*   ACCOUNT NO. *111*

DATE	ITEM	POST. REF.	DEBIT	DATE	ITEM	POST. REF.	CREDIT
19— Dec. 1	Balance	✓	2468 15	19— Dec. 29		CJ37	3027 82
29	2567.13	CJ37	3126 80				
			5594 95				

ACCOUNT *Petty Cash Fund*   ACCOUNT NO. *112*

DATE	ITEM	POST. REF.	DEBIT	DATE	ITEM	POST. REF.	CREDIT
19— Dec. 1	Balance	✓	75 00				

ACCOUNT *Office Equipment*   ACCOUNT NO. *131*

DATE	ITEM	POST. REF.	DEBIT	DATE	ITEM	POST. REF.	CREDIT
19— Dec. 1	Balance	✓	4115 95				

ACCOUNT *Accumulated Depreciation-Office Equipment*   ACCOUNT NO. *013*

DATE	ITEM	POST. REF.	DEBIT	DATE	ITEM	POST. REF.	CREDIT
				19— Dec. 1	Balance	✓	1334 78

Howard C. Miller, Architect — General Ledger

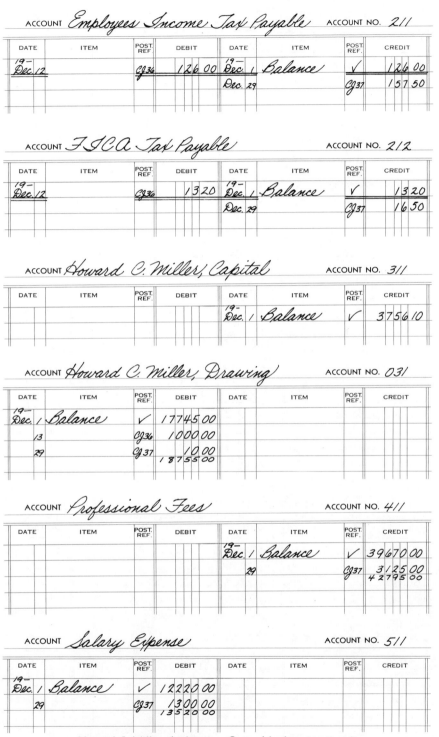

ACCOUNT *Employees Income Tax Payable* ACCOUNT NO. 211

DATE	ITEM	POST. REF.	DEBIT	DATE	ITEM	POST. REF.	CREDIT
19— Dec. 12		CJ36	126 00	19— Dec. 1	Balance	✓	126 00
				Dec. 29		CJ37	157 50

ACCOUNT *FICA Tax Payable* ACCOUNT NO. 212

DATE	ITEM	POST. REF.	DEBIT	DATE	ITEM	POST. REF.	CREDIT
19— Dec. 12		CJ36	13 20	19— Dec. 1	Balance	✓	13 20
				Dec. 29		CJ37	16 50

ACCOUNT *Howard C. Miller, Capital* ACCOUNT NO. 311

DATE	ITEM	POST. REF.	DEBIT	DATE	ITEM	POST. REF.	CREDIT
				19— Dec. 1	Balance	✓	3756 10

ACCOUNT *Howard C. Miller, Drawing* ACCOUNT NO. 031

DATE	ITEM	POST. REF.	DEBIT	DATE	ITEM	POST. REF.	CREDIT
19— Dec. 1	Balance	✓	17745 00				
13		CJ36	1000 00				
29		CJ37	10 00				
			18755 00				

ACCOUNT *Professional Fees* ACCOUNT NO. 411

DATE	ITEM	POST. REF.	DEBIT	DATE	ITEM	POST. REF.	CREDIT
				19— Dec. 1	Balance	✓	39670 00
				29		CJ37	3125 00
							42795 00

ACCOUNT *Salary Expense* ACCOUNT NO. 511

DATE	ITEM	POST. REF.	DEBIT	DATE	ITEM	POST. REF.	CREDIT
19— Dec. 1	Balance	✓	12220 00				
29		CJ37	1300 00				
			13520 00				

Howard C. Miller, Architect — General Ledger (*continued*)

117

ACCOUNT *Payroll Taxes Expense* ACCOUNT NO. 512

DATE	ITEM	POST. REF.	DEBIT	DATE	ITEM	POST. REF.	CREDIT
19— Dec. 1	Balance	✓	887 64				
12		CG36	13 20				
			900 84				

ACCOUNT *Rent Expense* ACCOUNT NO. 513

DATE	ITEM	POST. REF.	DEBIT	DATE	ITEM	POST. REF.	CREDIT
19— Dec. 1	Balance	✓	2640 00				
1		CG36	240 00				
			2880 00				

ACCOUNT *Telephone and Telegraph Expense* ACCOUNT NO. 514

DATE	ITEM	POST. REF.	DEBIT	DATE	ITEM	POST. REF.	CREDIT
19— Dec. 1	Balance	✓	356 20				
19		CG36	36 45				
29		CG37	1 10				
			393 75				

ACCOUNT *Blueprints and Supplies Expense* ACCOUNT NO. 515

DATE	ITEM	POST. REF.	DEBIT	DATE	ITEM	POST. REF.	CREDIT
19— Dec. 1	Balance	✓	1281 06				
11		CG36	63 19				
21		CG36	72 18				
29		CG37	7 85				
			1424 28				

ACCOUNT *Automobile Expense* ACCOUNT NO. 516

DATE	ITEM	POST. REF.	DEBIT	DATE	ITEM	POST. REF.	CREDIT
19— Dec. 1	Balance	✓	1157 20				
14		CG36	72 30				
18		CG36	28 17				
29		CG37	3 40				
			1261 07				

ACCOUNT *Insurance Expense* ACCOUNT NO. 518

DATE	ITEM	POST. REF.	DEBIT	DATE	ITEM	POST. REF.	CREDIT
19— Dec. 1	Balance	✓	137 86	19— Dec. 11		CG36	1 80
6	172.46	CG36	36 40				
			174 26				

Howard C. Miller, Architect — General Ledger (*continued*)

ACCOUNT *Travel and Entertainment Expense* ACCOUNT NO. *519*

DATE		ITEM	POST. REF.	DEBIT	DATE	ITEM	POST. REF.	CREDIT
19— Dec.	1	Balance	✓	1308 74				
	27		CJ37	87 90				
	29		CJ37	21 90				
				1418 54				

ACCOUNT *Charitable Contributions Expense* ACCOUNT NO. *521*

DATE		ITEM	POST. REF.	DEBIT	DATE	ITEM	POST. REF.	CREDIT
19— Dec.	1	Balance	✓	373 00				
	15		CJ36	50 00				
	29		CJ37	5 00				
				428 00				

ACCOUNT *Miscellaneous Expense* ACCOUNT NO. *522*

DATE		ITEM	POST. REF.	DEBIT	DATE	ITEM	POST. REF.	CREDIT
19— Dec.	1	Balance	✓	134 28				
	18		CJ36	9 50				
	29		CJ37	4 08				
				147 86				

Howard C. Miller, Architect — General Ledger (*concluded*)

Work at close of the fiscal period

As soon as possible after the end of the fiscal period, the owner (or owners) of an enterprise wants to be provided with (1) an income statement covering the period just ended, and (2) a balance sheet as of the last day of the period. In order to provide these statements, the accountant must consider certain matters that will not have been recorded in routine fashion. (Depreciation of Office Equipment for the past year is the one such matter in the case of Mr. Miller's enterprise.) Furthermore, the revenue accounts, the expense accounts, and the account showing the owner's withdrawals will have performed their function for the period just ended (in this case, the year) and need to be made ready to receive the entries of the new period. In the language of accountants and bookkeepers, "the books must be adjusted and closed." Actually, it is only the temporary owner's equity accounts — those for revenue, expense, and the owner's drawings — that are closed, but the remark quoted is widely used to describe what takes place at this time.

Howard C. Miller, Architect
Work Sheet
For the Year Ended December 31, 19—

Account	Acct. No.	Trial Balance Debit	Trial Balance Credit	Adjustments Debit	Adjustments Credit	Income Statement Debit	Income Statement Credit	Balance Sheet Debit	Balance Sheet Credit	
First National Bank	111	256713						256713		1
Petty Cash Fund	112	7500						7500		2
Office Equipment	131	411595						411595		3
Accum. Deprec.-Office Equip.	013		133478		41160				174638	4
Employees Income Tax Pay.	211		15750						15750	5
FICA Tax Payable	212		1650						1650	6
Howard C. Miller, Capital	311		375610						375610	7
Howard C. Miller, Drawing	031	1875500						1875500		8
Professional Fees	411		4279500				4279500			9
Salary Expense	511	1352000				1352000				10
Payroll Taxes Expense	512	90084				90084				11
Rent Expense	513	288000				288000				12
Telephone-Telegraph Exp.	514	39375				39375				13
Blueprints + Supplies Exp.	515	142428				142428				14
Automobile Expense	516	126107				126107				15
Depreciation Expense	517			41160		41160				16
Insurance Expense	518	17246				17246				17
Travel+Entertainment Exp.	519	141854				141854				18
Charitable Contributions Exp.	521	42800				42800				19
Miscellaneous Expense	522	14786				14786				20
		4805988	4805988	41160	41160	2295840	4279500	2551308	567648	21
Net Income						1983660			1983660	22
						4279500	4279500	2551308	2551308	23

Howard C. Miller, Architect — End-of-Period Work Sheet

The End-of-Period Work Sheet. To facilitate **(1)** the preparing of the financial statements, **(2)** the making of needed adjustments in the accounts, and **(3)** the closing of the temporary owner's equity accounts, it is common practice to prepare what is known as a *work sheet*. Because that term is used to describe a variety of schedules and computations that accountants may prepare, the specific type to be discussed here is commonly called an *end-of-period work sheet*. Various forms of this device are used. Because of the nature of Mr. Miller's enterprise, an eight-column work sheet is adequate. This form is illustrated on page 120. Note that the heading states that it is for the year ended December 31, 19--. The fact that December 29 was the last working day is not important. The income statement will relate to the full year, and the balance sheet will show the financial position as of the last day of the fiscal period.

The first pair of columns of the work sheet was used to show the trial balance taken after the routine posting for the month of December had been completed. Note that the account, Depreciation Expense, No. 517, was included in the list of accounts and account numbers even though that account had no balance at this point. The second pair of columns, headed "Adjustments," was used to show the manner in which the expense of estimated depreciation of office equipment for the year affects the accounts. The trial balance shows that the account, Office Equipment (No. 131) had a balance of $4,115.95, and that the balance of the account, Accumulated Depreciation — Office Equipment (No. 013) was $1,334.78. No new equipment was purchased during the year and there were no sales or retirements of such property during the year. Accordingly, the balances of these two accounts had not changed during the year. The two accounts are closely related: the debit balance of the office equipment account indicates the cost of such assets, and the credit balance of the accumulated depreciation account indicates the amount of such cost that has been charged off as depreciation in past years — that is, to January 1 of the current year. The amount of the difference between the two balances, $2,781.17, is described as the *undepreciated cost* of the office equipment. The amount may also be called the *book value* of the equipment. A better description of the difference is "cost yet to be charged to expense."

Since the year had just ended, it was necessary to record as an expense the estimated depreciation for that year. Mr. Miller estimates that the various items of office equipment have average useful lives of ten years and that any scrap or salvage value at the end of that time is likely to be so small that it can be ignored. Accordingly, estimated depreciation expense for the year was calculated to be $411.60 (10 percent of $4,115.95). This expense was due to be recorded in the ledger accounts, but that had to wait. The immediate need was to get the expense entered on the work sheet so that it would be considered when the financial statements were prepared.

121

The record was made on the work sheet as follows: $411.60 was written in the Adjustments Debit column on the line for Depreciation Expense, and the same amount was written in the Adjustments Credit column on the line for Accumulated Depreciation — Office Equipment. The Adjustments Debit and Credit columns were totaled.

The next step was to combine each amount in the Trial Balance columns with the amount, if any, in the Adjustments columns and to extend the total into the Income Statement or Balance Sheet columns. Revenue and expense account balances are extended to the Income Statement columns and balance sheet account balances to the Balance Sheet columns. Note that the new amount for Accumulated Depreciation — Office Equipment, $1,746.38 ($1,334.78 + $411.60), appears in the Balance Sheet Credit column, and that the depreciation expense of $411.60 appears, along with all other expenses, in the Income Statement Debit column. The last four columns were totaled. The total of the Income Statement Credit column exceeded the total of the Income Statement Debit column by $19,836.60 — the calculated net income for the year. That amount, so designated, was placed in the Income Statement Debit column to bring the pair of Income Statement columns into balance. When the same amount ($19,836.60) was placed in the Balance Sheet Credit column, the last pair of columns was brought into balance. The final totals of the last four columns were recorded at the bottom of the work sheet.

The fact that adding the net income for the year, $19,836.60, to the Balance Sheet Credit column caused its total to equal the total of the Balance Sheet Debit column is explained as follows. The amounts for the assets and liabilities in the last pair of columns were up-to-date. The difference between total assets and total liabilities, $4,837.70, was Mr. Miller's equity in the enterprise at the year's end. The balance of his capital account was $3,756.10 — the amount of his equity at the start of the year (since he had made no additional investments during the year). His withdrawals during the year, according to the balance in the account Howard C. Miller, Drawing, were $18,755.00. How could he start the year with an owner's equity of $3,756.10, make no additional investments, withdraw $18,755.00, and end the year with an owner's equity of $4,837.70? The explanation is that there had been profitable operations during the year that caused the owner's equity element to increase $19,836.60. This can be expressed in the form of the following equation:

OWNER'S EQUITY AT START OF PERIOD	+	NET INCOME FOR THE PERIOD	+	INVESTMENTS	−	WITHDRAWALS	=	OWNER'S EQUITY AT END OF PERIOD
$3,756.10	+	$19,836.60	+	0	−	$18,755.00	=	$4,837.70

Since the correct amounts for assets and liabilities and two of the three factors (owner's equity at start of period and withdrawals) needed to deter-

122

mine the correct amount of the owner's equity as of December 31 were already in the Balance Sheet columns, only the amount of the third factor — the net income for the year — had to be included in order that those columns would reflect the basic equation: Assets = Liabilities + Owner's Equity.

The Financial Statements. The work sheet supplied all of the information needed to prepare an income statement and a balance sheet. These statements for Mr. Miller's enterprise are shown below and on page 124.

Three features of the following balance sheet should be noted: **(1)** It is in so-called "report form" — the liabilities and the owner's equity sections are shown below the assets section. An alternative is the so-called "account form" — the assets are at the left, and the liabilities and the owner's equity sections are at the right. (See the balance sheet of The Brown Advertising Agency on pages 42 and 43.) **(2)** The assets are classified on the basis of whether they are *current* or *long-lived.* Current assets include cash and any other assets that will be converted into cash within the *normal operating cycle* of the business. This cycle is often a year in length. Mr. Miller's enterprise does not take into account any current assets other than cash. (The amount shown includes both cash in bank and petty cash.) The long-lived assets are those which are expected to serve for many years. **(3)** All of the liabilities are classified as current, since they must be paid in the near future. Certain types of obligations are classified as long-term, but Mr. Miller had no debts of this type.

HOWARD C. MILLER, ARCHITECT
Income Statement
For the Year Ended December 31, 19--

Professional fees.............................		$42,795.00
Professional expenses:		
Salary expense.............................	$13,520.00	
Payroll taxes expense........................	900.84	
Rent expense...............................	2,880.00	
Telephone and telegraph expense.............	393.75	
Blueprints and supplies expense................	1,424.28	
Automobile expense..........................	1,261.07	
Depreciation expense........................	411.60	
Insurance expense...........................	172.46	
Travel and entertainment expense..............	1,418.54	
Charitable contributions expense................	428.00	
Miscellaneous expense........................	147.86	
Total professional expenses.................		22,958.40
Net income....................................		$19,836.60

Howard C. Miller, Architect — Income Statement

HOWARD C. MILLER, ARCHITECT
Balance Sheet
December 31, 19--

Assets

Current assets:		
Cash............................		$2,642.13
Long-lived assets:		
Office equipment..................	$4,115.95	
Less accumulated depreciation......	1,746.38	2,369.57
Total assets........................		$5,011.70

Liabilities

Current liabilities:		
Employees income tax payable	$ 157.50	
FICA tax payable..................	16.50	
Total current liabilities...............		$ 174.00

Owner's Equity

Howard C. Miller, capital:			
Capital, January 1, 19--...........		$3,756.10	
Net income for year...............	$19,836.60		
Less withdrawals.................	18,755.00	1,081.60	
Capital, December 31, 19--........			4,837.70
Total liabilities and owner's equity......			$5,011.70

124

Howard C. Miller, Architect — Balance Sheet

Adjusting Entries for a Personal Service Enterprise. The financial statements must agree with the ledger accounts. To speed up the preparation of the statements, a work sheet was used with the one needed adjustment included. Subsequently this adjustment had to be formally recorded in the accounts. This was accomplished by posting the first journal entry at the top of page 125. The two accounts affected by the entry, Depreciation Expense, No. 517 and Accumulated Depreciation — Office Equipment, No. 013, are reproduced at the bottom of page 125 as they appeared after the entry was posted. After this posting was completed, the balances of all asset and liability accounts agreed exactly with the amounts shown in the balance sheet.

Closing Entries for a Personal Service Enterprise. The revenue and expense accounts and the account for Howard C. Miller, Drawing (No. 031) had served their purpose for the year 19-- and the balance of each of these accounts needed to be reduced to zero in order to make the accounts ready for entries in the following year. Since the means of closing a ledger account under the double-entry procedure is to add the amount of the account's balance to the side of the account having the smaller total (so that

DAY	DESCRIPTION	POST. REF.	GENERAL DEBIT	GENERAL CREDIT	
	AMOUNTS FORWARDED				1
31	*Adjusting Entry*				2
	Depreciation Expense	517	41160		3
	Accumulated Deprec.-Office Equip.	013		41160	4
					5
31	*Closing Entries*				6
	Professional Fees	411	4279500		7
	Expense and Revenue Summary	321		4279500	8
	Expense and Revenue Summary	321	2295840		9
	Salary Expense	511		1352000	10
	Payroll Taxes Expense	512		90084	11
	Rent Expense	513		288000	12
	Telephone and Telegraph Expense	514		39375	13
	Blueprints and Supplies Expense	515		142428	14
	Automobile Expense	516		126107	15
	Depreciation Expense	517		41160	16
	Insurance Expense	518		17246	17
	Travel & Entertainment Expense	519		141854	18
	Charitable Contributions Expense	521		42800	19
	Miscellaneous Expense	522		14786	20
	Expense and Revenue Summary	321	1983660		21
	Howard C. Miller, Capital	311		1983660	22
	Howard C. Miller, Capital	311	1875500		23
	Howard C. Miller, Drawing	031		1875500	24
			10475660	10475660	25
					26

Adjusting and Closing Entries

ACCOUNT *Depreciation Expense*   ACCOUNT NO. *517*

DATE	ITEM	POST. REF.	DEBIT	DATE	ITEM	POST. REF.	CREDIT
19— Dec 31		CJ38	411 60				

ACCOUNT *Accumulated Depreciation-Office Equipment* ACCOUNT NO. *013*

DATE	ITEM	POST. REF.	DEBIT	DATE	ITEM	POST. REF.	CREDIT
				19— Dec 1	Balance	✓	1334 78
				31		CJ38	411 60
							1746 38

Ledger Accounts After Posting Adjusting Entries

125

the account will have no balance), each of the temporary owner's equity accounts was closed in this way. The net effect was an increase in the credit balance of the account for Howard C. Miller, Capital (No. 311) of $1,081.60 — the excess of his net income for the year, $19,836.60, over his withdrawals for the year, $18,755. However, this result was accomplished by means of four entries illustrated in the combined cash journal shown on page 125:

(a) The $42,795 credit balance of Professional Fees, Account No. 411, was closed to (transferred to the credit side of) Expense and Revenue Summary, Account No. 321.

(b) The debit balances of all eleven expense accounts (Nos. 511 through 519 and 521 and 522) which, in total, amounted to $22,958.40, were closed to (transferred to the debit side of) Expense and Revenue Summary (No. 321). Some accountants favor showing and identifying each amount that is being closed to the summary account. This procedure, called *posting in detail*, is followed in the illustration on page 127.

(c) The result of entries (a) and (b) was a credit balance of $19,836.60 — the net income for the year — in Expense and Revenue Summary (No. 321). This was closed to Howard C. Miller, Capital, Account No. 311.

(d) The $18,755 debit balance of Howard C. Miller, Drawing, Account No. 031, was closed to Howard C. Miller, Capital (No. 311).

126   As in the case of the adjusting entry, these closing entries were made as of December 31. It should be noted that the work sheet provided all of the data needed to prepare the adjusting and closing entries. The purpose and use of Expense and Revenue Summary, Account No. 321, should be apparent from this illustration. As its name indicates, the account is used to summarize the amounts of expense and revenue which are *reasons* for changes in owner's equity that were *not* the result of investments and withdrawals by the owner.

Ruling the Closed Accounts. After posting the closing entries, all of the temporary owner's equity accounts were in balance (closed), and they were ruled in the manner illustrated on pages 127–129.

The following procedures were used:

(a) Where two or more amounts had been posted to either side of an account, the amount columns were footed to be sure that the total debits were equal to the total credits.

(b) A single line was ruled across the debit and credit amount columns immediately below the last amount on the side with the most entries.

(c) The totals of the debit and credit amount columns were entered on the next line in ink.

(d) Double lines were ruled just below the totals. These rulings extended through all but the Item columns.

ACCOUNT *Howard C. Miller, Drawing* ACCOUNT NO. 031

DATE	ITEM	POST. REF.	DEBIT	DATE	ITEM	POST. REF.	CREDIT
19— Dec. 1	Balance	✓	17745 00	19— Dec. 31		CJ38	18 755 00
13		CJ36	1 000 00				
29		CJ37	10 00				
			18 755 00 18 755 00				18 755 00

ACCOUNT *Expense and Revenue Summary* ACCOUNT NO. 321

DATE	ITEM	POST. REF.	DEBIT	DATE	ITEM	POST. REF.	CREDIT
19— Dec. 31	Salary Exp.	CJ38	13520 00	19— Dec. 31	Prof. Fees	CJ38	42795 00
	Pay. Tax Exp.	CJ38	900 84				
	Rent Exp.	CJ38	2880 00				
	Tel. + Tel. Exp.	CJ38	393 75				
	Blprts + Sup. Exp.	CJ38	1424 28				
	Auto Exp.	CJ38	1261 07				
	Deprec. Exp.	CJ38	411 60				
	Ins. Exp.	CJ38	172 46				
	Trav. + Ent. Exp.	CJ38	1418 54				
	Char. Cont. Exp.	CJ38	428 00				
	Misc. Exp.	CJ38	147 86				
	H. C. Miller, Cap.	CJ38	19836 60 42795 00 42795 00				42795 00

ACCOUNT *Professional Fees* ACCOUNT NO. 411

DATE	ITEM	POST. REF.	DEBIT	DATE	ITEM	POST. REF.	CREDIT
19— Dec. 31		CJ38	42795 00	19— Dec. 1	Balance	✓	39670 00
				29		CJ37	3125 00 42795 00
			42795 00				42795 00

ACCOUNT *Salary Expense* ACCOUNT NO. 511

DATE	ITEM	POST. REF.	DEBIT	DATE	ITEM	POST. REF.	CREDIT
19— Dec. 1	Balance	✓	12220 00	19— Dec. 31		CJ38	13520 00
29		CJ37	1300 00 13520 00 13520 00				13520 00

Howard C. Miller, Architect — Partial General Ledger
(*continued on next page*)

ACCOUNT _Payroll Taxes Expense_   ACCOUNT NO. _512_

DATE	ITEM	POST. REF.	DEBIT	DATE	ITEM	POST. REF.	CREDIT
19— Dec. 1	Balance	✓	887 64	19— Dec. 31		CJ38	900 84
12		CJ36	13 20				
			900 84				
			900 84				900 84

ACCOUNT _Rent Expense_   ACCOUNT NO. _513_

DATE	ITEM	POST. REF.	DEBIT	DATE	ITEM	POST. REF.	CREDIT
19— Dec. 1	Balance	✓	2640 00	19— Dec. 31		CJ38	2880 00
1		CJ36	240 00				
			2880 00				
			2880 00				2880 00

ACCOUNT _Telephone and Telegraph Expense_   ACCOUNT NO. _514_

DATE	ITEM	POST. REF.	DEBIT	DATE	ITEM	POST. REF.	CREDIT
19— Dec. 1	Balance	✓	356 20	19— Dec. 31		CJ38	393 75
19		CJ36	36 45				
29		CJ37	1 10				
			393 75				
			393 75				393 75

128

ACCOUNT _Blueprints and Supplies Expense_   ACCOUNT NO. _515_

DATE	ITEM	POST. REF.	DEBIT	DATE	ITEM	POST. REF.	CREDIT
19— Dec. 1	Balance	✓	1281 06	19— Dec. 31		CJ38	1424 28
11		CJ36	63 19				
21		CJ36	72 18				
29		CJ37	7 85				
			1424 28				
			1424 28				1424 28

ACCOUNT _Automobile Expense_   ACCOUNT NO. _516_

DATE	ITEM	POST. REF.	DEBIT	DATE	ITEM	POST. REF.	CREDIT
19— Dec. 1	Balance	✓	1157 20	19— Dec. 31		CJ38	1261 07
14		CJ36	72 30				
18		CJ36	28 17				
29		CJ37	3 40				
			1261 07				
			1261 07				1261 07

Howard C. Miller, Architect — Partial General Ledger (*continued*)

ACCOUNT *Depreciation Expense* ACCOUNT NO. 517

DATE	ITEM	POST. REF.	DEBIT	DATE	ITEM	POST. REF.	CREDIT
19— Dec. 31		CJ38	411 60	19— Dec. 31		CJ38	411 60

ACCOUNT *Insurance Expense* ACCOUNT NO. 518

DATE	ITEM	POST. REF.	DEBIT	DATE	ITEM	POST. REF.	CREDIT
19— Dec. 1	Balance	✓	137 86	19— Dec. 11		CJ36	1 80
6	172.46	CJ36	36 40	31		CJ38	172 46
			174 26				174 26
			174 26				174 26

ACCOUNT *Travel and Entertainment Expense* ACCOUNT NO. 519

DATE	ITEM	POST. REF.	DEBIT	DATE	ITEM	POST. REF.	CREDIT
19— Dec. 1	Balance	✓	1308 74	19— Dec. 31		CJ38	1418 54
27		CJ37	87 90				
29		CJ37	21 90				
			1418 54				1418 54
			1418 54				

129

ACCOUNT *Charitable Contributions Expense* ACCOUNT NO. 521

DATE	ITEM	POST. REF.	DEBIT	DATE	ITEM	POST. REF.	CREDIT
19— Dec. 1	Balance	✓	373 00	19— Dec. 31		CJ38	428 00
15		CJ36	50 00				
29		CJ37	5 00				
			428 00				428 00
			428 00				

ACCOUNT *Miscellaneous Expense* ACCOUNT NO. 522

DATE	ITEM	POST. REF.	DEBIT	DATE	ITEM	POST. REF.	CREDIT
19— Dec. 1	Balance	✓	134 28	19— Dec. 31		CJ38	147 86
18		CJ36	9 50				
29		CJ37	4 08				
			147 86				147 86
			147 86				

Howard C. Miller, Architect — Partial General Ledger (*concluded*)

If an account had only one item on each side, only the double ruling was made. (Note the ruling for Depreciation Expense, Account No. 517.) If an account page is not filled, it may be used for recording the transactions of the following period.

Balancing and Ruling Open Accounts. After the temporary owner's equity accounts were closed, the open accounts (those for assets, liabilities, and Howard C. Miller, Capital) were balanced and ruled, where necessary, to prepare them to receive entries in the next fiscal period. Only two of Mr. Miller's ledger accounts needed to be balanced and ruled: First National Bank, Account No. 111, and Howard C. Miller, Capital, Account No. 311. These two accounts are shown at the top of page 131. The procedure in each case was as follows:

(a) The amount of the balance of the account was entered on the side having the smaller total to equalize total debits and total credits. The word "Balance" was written in the Item column.

(b) The columns were footed to prove the equality of the debits and credits.

(c) A single line was ruled across the debit and credit amount columns immediately below the line with the last amount. (This line would have been below the last amount on the side with the most entries, if the number of entries on each side had not been the same.)

(d) The totals of the debit and credit amount columns were entered on the next line in ink.

(e) Double lines were ruled just below the totals extending through all but the Item column.

(f) An entry was made on the next line under date of January 1, with the amount of the balance — so labeled in the Item column — entered in the amount column on the proper side (the debit side for the asset account and the credit side for the owner's equity account). If the account page had been filled, the balance would have been entered at the top of a new account page.

No balancing and ruling was needed in the cases of Petty Cash Fund, Account No. 112, or Office Equipment, Account No. 131, since each of these accounts had only one entry. (These two accounts remained just as illustrated on page 116.) Accumulated Depreciation — Office Equipment, Account No. 013, needed no further attention since it had only two entries, both on the same side. (This account remains as illustrated on page 125.) The two liability accounts, Employees Income Tax Payable (No. 211) and FICA Tax Payable (No. 212) remain as illustrated on page 117, inasmuch as each has had only one entry since previously ruled.

Post-Closing Trial Balance. After posting the closing entries, it is advisable to take a *post-closing trial balance* to prove the equality of the debit and credit balances in the general ledger accounts. The post-closing trial balance of Mr. Miller's ledger is shown at the bottom of page 131.

ACCOUNT **First National Bank**   ACCOUNT NO. **111**

DATE	ITEM	POST. REF.	DEBIT	DATE	ITEM	POST. REF.	CREDIT
19— Dec. 1	Balance	✓	2468 15	19— Dec. 29		CJ37	3027 82
29	*2567.13*	CJ37	3126 80	31	Balance	✓	2567 13
			5594 95				5594 95
			5594 95				5594 95
19— Jan. 1	Balance	✓	2567 13				

ACCOUNT **Howard C. Miller, Capital**   ACCOUNT NO. **311**

DATE	ITEM	POST. REF.	DEBIT	DATE	ITEM	POST. REF.	CREDIT
19— Dec. 31		CJ38	18755 00	19— Dec. 1	Balance	✓	3756 10
31	Balance	✓	4837 70	31		CJ38	19836 60
			23592 70				23592 70
			23592 70				23592 70
				19— Jan. 1	Balance	✓	4837 70

Balancing and Ruling Open Accounts

Howard C. Miller, Architect
Post-Closing Trial Balance
December 31, 19—

Account	Acct. No.	Dr. Balance	Cr. Balance
First National Bank	111	2567 13	
Petty Cash Fund	112	75 00	
Office Equipment	131	4115 95	
Accumulated Depreciation—Office Equip.	013		1746 38
Employees Income Tax Payable	211		157 50
FICA Tax Payable	212		16 50
Howard C. Miller, Capital	311		4837 70
		6758 08	6758 08

Howard C. Miller, Architect — Post-Closing Trial Balance

The accounting cycle

The steps involved in handling all of the transactions and events completed during an accounting period, beginning with recording in a book of original entry and ending with a post-closing trial balance, are referred to collectively as the *accounting cycle*. This chapter has illustrated a complete accounting cycle. A brief summary of the various steps follows:

(a) Journalizing the transactions.
(b) Posting to the ledger accounts.
(c) Taking a trial balance.
(d) Determining the needed adjustments.
(e) Completing an end-of-period work sheet.
(f) Preparing an income statement and a balance sheet.
(g) Journalizing and posting the adjusting and closing entries.
(h) Ruling the closed accounts and balancing and ruling the open accounts.
(i) Taking a post-closing trial balance.

In visualizing the accounting cycle, it is important to realize that steps (c) through (i) in the foregoing list are performed *as of the last day of the accounting period*. This does not mean that they necessarily are done *on* the last day. The accountant or bookkeeper may not be able to do any of these things until the first few days (sometimes weeks) of the next period. Nevertheless, the work sheet, statements, and entries are prepared or recorded as of the closing date. While the journalizing of transactions in the new period proceeds in regular fashion, it is not usual to post to the general ledger any entries relating to the new period until the steps relating to the period just ended have been completed.

Report No. 5-1

Complete Report No. 5-1 in the workbook and submit your working papers to the instructor for approval. After completing the report you will then be given instructions as to the work to be done next.

chapters 1-5

practical accounting problems

The following problems supplement those in Reports 1-1 through 5-1 of the Part 1 Workbook. These problems are numbered to indicate the chapter of the textbook with which they correlate. For example, Problem 1-A and Problem 1-B correlate with Chapter 1. Loose-leaf stationery should be used in solving these problems. The paper required includes plain ruled paper, two-column and four-column journal paper, two-column and three-column statement paper, cash journal paper, ledger paper, and work sheet paper.

Problem 1-A

R. A. Hamilton is a practicing attorney. As of December 31 he owned the following property that related to his business: Cash, $1,291, office equipment, $2,250; and an automobile, $3,240. At the same time he owed business creditors $960.

REQUIRED: (1) On the basis of the above information, compute the amounts of the accounting elements and show them in equation form. (2) Assume that during the following year there is an increase in Mr. Hamilton's business assets of $2,200 and a decrease in his business liabilities of $125. Indicate the changes in the accounting elements by showing them in equation form after the changes have occurred.

Problem 1-B

H. L. Wood, a CPA who has been employed by a large national firm of certified public accountants, decides to go into business for himself. His business transactions for the first month of operations were as follows:

(a) Mr. Wood invested $10,000 cash in the business.
(b) Paid office rent for one month, $200.
(c) Purchased office equipment from the Ponser Office Supply Co., $2,260 on account.
(d) Paid telephone bill, $22.
(e) Received $800 for services rendered to John J. Lang & Co.
(f) Paid $1,000 to the Ponser Office Supply Co. on account.
(g) Received $650 for services rendered to the Stewart Garage.
(h) Paid $400 salary to office secretary.

REQUIRED: (1) On a plain sheet of paper rule eight "T" accounts and enter the following titles: Cash, Office Equipment, Accounts Payable, H. L. Wood, Capital, Professional Fees, Rent Expense, Telephone Expense, and Salary Expense. (2) Record the foregoing transactions directly in the accounts. (3) Foot the accounts and enter the balances where necessary. (4) Prepare a trial balance of the accounts, using a sheet of two-column journal paper.

Problem 2-A

Following is a narrative of the transactions completed by B. H. Sirkin, a management consultant, during the first month of his business operations:

Oct. 1. Mr. Sirkin invested $5,000 cash in the business.
     1. Paid office rent, $150.
     2. Purchased office furniture for $1,250 cash.
     3. Paid $18.65 for installation of telephone and for one month's service.
     4. Received $325 from The Morris Linen Service for consulting services rendered.
     5. Purchased stationery and supplies on account from Will Ecker & Co., $226.94.
     6. Paid $8 for subscription to a professional management magazine. (Charge Miscellaneous Expense.)
     8. Paid $45 to Dr. Robert Harris, a dentist, for dental service performed for Mrs. Sirkin.
          (Note: This is equivalent to a withdrawal of $45 by Mr. Sirkin for personal use. Charge to his drawing account.)
     9. Received $100 from Dolphin Pool Service & Supply Co. for professional services rendered.
    12. Paid $55.82 for an airplane ticket for a business trip.
    14. Paid other traveling expenses, $47.20.
    19. Paid account of Will Ecker & Co. in full, $226.94.
    20. Received $325 from Century Electric Co. for professional services rendered.
    31. Paid $350 monthly salary to secretary.

REQUIRED: Journalize the foregoing transactions, using a sheet of two-column journal paper. Number the pages and use both sides of the sheet, if necessary. Select the account titles from the following chart of accounts:

CHART OF ACCOUNTS

Assets
111 Cash
112 Stationery and Supplies
121 Office Furniture

Liabilities
211 Accounts Payable

Owner's Equity
311 B. H. Sirkin, Capital
312 B. H. Sirkin, Drawing

Revenue
411 Professional Fees

Expenses
511 Rent Expense
512 Telephone Expense
513 Traveling Expense
514 Salary Expense
515 Miscellaneous Expense

After journalizing the transactions, prove the equality of the debits and credits by footing the amount columns. Enter the footings in pencil immediately under the line on which the last entry appears.

Problem 2-B

M. J. Rosen is a certified public accountant engaged in practice on his own account. Following is the trial balance of his business taken as of June 30, 19—.

135

M. J. ROSEN, CERTIFIED PUBLIC ACCOUNTANT

Trial Balance

June 30, 19—

Cash	111	1,884.62	
Office Equipment	121	1,050.00	
Automobile	122	4,400.00	
Accounts Payable	211		624.72
M. J. Rosen, Capital	311		5,024.00
M. J. Rosen, Drawing	312	3,600.00	
Professional Fees	411		8,000.00
Rent Expense	511	1,500.00	
Telephone Expense	512	175.50	
Electric Expense	513	120.00	
Automobile Expense	514	435.80	
Charitable Contributions Expense	515	320.00	
Miscellaneous Expense	516	162.80	
		13,648.72	13,648.72

A narrative of the transactions completed by Mr. Rosen during the month of July follows on the next page.

July 1. (Thursday) Paid one month's rent, $250.
      2. Paid telephone bill, $18.70.
      2. Paid electric bill, $12.15.
      5. Received $350 from General Grocers for services rendered.
      7. Paid a garage bill, $28.40.
      9. Received $200 from the Hilton International Hotels for services rendered.
     12. Paid Target Department Store, $34.20. (Charge to Mr. Rosen's drawing account.)
     15. Mr. Rosen withdrew $300 for personal use.
     16. Paid Royal-McBee, Inc. $120 on account.
     19. Received $150 from National Food Stores for services rendered.
     23. Gave the American Red Cross $25.
     26. Paid the American Institute of Certified Public Accountants $60 for annual membership dues and fees.
     29. Received $75.20 from Yates Motor Sales Co. for professional services.
     30. Mr. Rosen withdrew $300 for personal use.

REQUIRED: **(1)** Journalize the July transactions, using a sheet of two-column journal paper. Number the pages and use both sides of the sheet, if necessary. Foot the amount columns. **(2)** Open the necessary accounts, using the standard account form of ledger paper. Allow one page for each account. Record the July 1 balances as shown in the June 30 trial balance and post the journal entries for July. **(3)** Foot the ledger accounts, enter the balances, and prove the balances by taking a trial balance as of July 31. Use a sheet of two-column journal paper for the trial balance.

136

Problem 2-C

THE R. G. SETTLAGE AGENCY
Trial Balance
January 31, 19—

Cash	111	5,792.82	
Stationery and Supplies	112	1,125.52	
Office Furniture	121	3,684.00	
Notes Payable	211		1,800.00
Accounts Payable	212		1,286.58
R. G. Settlage, Capital	311		7,033.76
R. G. Settlage, Drawing	312	1,260.80	
Professional Fees	411		3,374.40
Rent Expense	511	300.00	
Telephone Expense	512	43.20	
Salary Expense	513	560.00	
Traveling Expense	514	633.04	
Stationery and Supplies Expense	515	36.86	
Miscellaneous Expense	516	58.50	
		13,494.74	13,494.74

REQUIRED: (1) Prepare an income statement for The R. G. Settlage Agency showing the results of operations for the month of January. (2) Prepare a balance sheet in account form showing the financial condition of the agency as of January 31. Use a sheet of two-column journal paper for the income statement. Two sheets of two-column journal paper may be used for the balance sheet. List the assets on one sheet and the liabilities and owner's equity on the other sheet.

Problem 3-A

M. L. Bell is an advertising counselor. The only book of original entry for his business is a four-column journal. He uses the standard account form of general ledger. Following is the trial balance of his business taken as of November 30:

M. L. BELL, ADVERTISING COUNSELOR
Trial Balance
November 30, 19—

Cash.................................	111	3,346.82	
Office Equipment........................	112	700.00	
Accounts Payable.......................	211		151.94
M. L. Bell, Capital......................	311		6,250.00
M. L. Bell, Drawing.....................	312	4,750.00	
Advertising Fees.......................	411		8,480.00
Rent Expense..........................	511	1,760.00	
Telephone Expense......................	512	210.40	
Electric Expense........................	513	134.90	
Salary Expense.........................	514	3,573.00	
Charitable Contributions Expense............	515	302.00	
Miscellaneous Expense...................	516	104.82	
		14,881.94	14,881.94

137

NARRATIVE OF TRANSACTIONS FOR DECEMBER

Dec. 1. (Friday) Paid December office rent in advance, $160.
    1. Paid electric bill, $9.76.
    4. Paid telephone bill, $12.25.
    4. Received a check from Emerson Electric Co. for $300 for services rendered.
    4. Received $350 from West Foods Co. for services rendered.
    7. Donated $20 to the American Red Cross.
    7. Paid $6.75 for cleaning office.
    8. Received check for $350 from Concordia Publishing House for advertising counsel.

11. Mr. Bell withdrew $300 for personal use.
15. Paid secretary's salary for the half month, $175.
18. Purchased office furniture on credit from Fish Furniture Co., $500.
19. Paid $4 for having the office windows washed.
20. Received $175 from Associated Grocery Co. for services rendered.
22. Paid traveling expenses while on business, $27.50.
25. Donated $25 to the United Fund.
26. Paid Fish Furniture Co. $100 on account.
28. Mr. Bell withdrew $125 for personal use.
29. Paid secretary's salary for the half month, $175.

REQUIRED: (1) Journalize the December transactions. For the journal use one sheet of four-column journal paper and number the page. (2) Open the necessary ledger accounts. Allow one page for each account and number the accounts. Record the December 1 balances and post the four-column journal entries. Foot and rule the four-column journal and enter the new cash balance. (3) Take a trial balance.

Problem 3-B

Thomas J. Hall, a plumber, completed the following transactions with the Citizens Trust and Savings Bank during the month of October:

Oct.	2. (Monday) Balance in bank per record kept on check stubs..........	$5,000.00	Oct.	11. Check No. 118..	160.00
				11. Check No. 119..	91.80
				13. Check No. 120..	895.50
	2. Deposit........	3,000.00		14. Check No. 121..	83.60
	2. Check No. 108..	576.40		14. Check No. 122..	494.64
	3. Check No. 109..	60.00		14. Deposit........	762.86
	4. Check No. 110..	950.00		16. Check No. 123..	250.00
	4. Check No. 111..	220.00		18. Check No. 124..	530.02
	5. Check No. 112..	250.00		21. Check No. 125..	194.90
	6. Check No. 113..	180.00		21. Deposit........	1,942.00
	7. Check No. 114..	311.20		24. Check No. 126..	262.84
	7. Check No. 115..	100.00		25. Check No. 127..	216.76
	7. Check No. 116..	92.00		27. Check No. 128..	555.94
	7. Deposit........	536.90		28. Check No. 129..	166.00
	10. Check No. 117..	908.64		30. Check No. 130..	1,095.26
				30. Deposit........	1,650.28

REQUIRED: (1) A record of the bank account as it would appear on the check stubs. (2) A reconciliation of the bank statement for October which indicated a balance of $5,861.74 on October 31, with Checks Nos. 116, 126, 129, and 130 outstanding, and a service charge of 90 cents.

Problem 3-C

I. E. Millstone, a general contractor, had a balance of $100 in his petty cash fund as of June 1. During June the following petty cash transactions were completed:

June 2. (Friday) Paid $2.25 for typewriter repairs. Petty Cash Voucher No. 22.
  6. Paid for telegram, $3.50. Petty Cash Voucher No. 23.
  8. Gave $15 to the United Fund. Petty Cash Voucher No. 24.
  9. Paid garage for washing car, $2.25. Petty Cash Voucher No. 25.
  12. Gave Mr. Millstone's son $4. (Charge I. E. Millstone, Drawing.) Petty Cash Voucher No. 26,
  14. Paid for postage stamps, $5. Petty Cash Voucher No. 27.
  19. Paid for newspaper for month, $2.40. Petty Cash Voucher No. 28.
  22. Paid for window washing, $3.25. Petty Cash Voucher No. 29.
  27. Paid $3 to the Parent-Teachers Association for dues. (Charge I. E. Millstone, Drawing.) Petty Cash Voucher No. 30.
  28. Paid for car lubrication, $2.50. Petty Cash Voucher No. 31.
  29. Donated $20 to the American Red Cross. Petty Cash Voucher No. 32.
  30. Rendered report of petty cash expenditures for month and received the amount needed to replenish the petty cash fund.

REQUIRED: (1) Record the foregoing transactions in a petty cash disbursements record, distributing the expenditures as follows:

I. E. Millstone, Drawing	Charitable Contributions Expense
Automobile Expense	Miscellaneous Expense
Telephone and Telegraph Expense	

(2) Prove the petty cash disbursements record by footing the amount columns and proving the totals. Enter the totals and rule the amount columns with single and double lines. (3) Prepare a statement of the petty cash disbursements for June. (4) Bring down the balance in the petty cash fund below the ruling in the Description column. Enter the amount received to replenish the fund and record the total.

Problem 4-A

Following is a summary of the hours worked, rates of pay, and other relevant information concerning the employees of The Simpson Machine Tool Co., A. G. Simpson, Owner, for the week ended Saturday, November 4. Employees are paid at the rate of time and one half for all hours worked in excess of 8 in any day or 40 in any week.

No.	NAME	EXEMPTIONS CLAIMED	M	T	W	T	F	S	REGULAR HOURLY RATE	CUMULATIVE EARNINGS JAN. 1–OCT. 28
1	Bohl, George E..........	3	8	8	8	8	8	6	$2.50	$6,010
2	Hawley, Walter J........	4	8	9	8	8	8	4	2.70	6,955
3	Meyer, Wayne T........	3	8	8	8	8	8	0	2.60	6,825
4	Read, Brooks R.........	1	8	8	8	9	8	4	2.40	4,021
5	Slack, Frank X..........	2	8	8	8	8	8	4	2.65	4,769
6	Watts, John R..........	1	8	8	8	8	4	0	2.90	5,580

139

Bohl and Read each have $3.50 withheld this payday for group life insurance. Hawley and Watts each have $3 withheld this payday for private hospital insurance. Slack has $8 withheld this payday as a contribution to the United Fund.

REQUIRED: (1) Using plain ruled paper size 8½″ by 11″, rule a payroll register form similar to that reproduced on pages 82 and 83 and insert the necessary columnar headings. Enter on this form the payroll for the week ended Saturday, November 4. Refer to the Weekly Income Tax Table on page 80 to determine the amounts to be withheld from the wages of each worker for income tax purposes. All of Simpson's employees are married. Five and one-half percent of the taxable wages of each employee should be withheld for FICA tax. Checks Nos. 511 through 516 were issued to the employees. Complete the payroll record by footing the amount columns, proving the footings, entering the totals, and ruling. (2) Assuming that the wages were paid on November 8, record the payment on a sheet of two-column general journal paper.

Problem 4-B

140   The Crestwood Store employs twelve people. They are paid by checks on the 15th and last day of each month. The entry to record each payroll includes the liabilities for the amounts withheld. The expense and liabilities arising from the employer's payroll taxes are recorded on each payday.

Following is a narrative of the transactions completed during the month of January that relate to payrolls and payroll taxes:

Jan. 15. Payroll for first half of month:

Total salaries...........................		$3,360.00
Less amounts withheld:		
FICA tax............................	$184.80	
Employees' income tax.................	370.80	555.60
Net amount paid.......................		$2,804.40

15. Social security taxes imposed on employer:
   FICA tax, 5.5%
   State unemployment tax, 2%
   FUTA tax, 0.5%

28. Paid $1,264.50 for December's payroll taxes:
   FICA tax, $439.20.
   Employees' income tax withheld, $825.30.

28. Paid State unemployment tax for quarter ended December 31, $272.60.

28. Paid balance due on FUTA tax for last half of year ended December 31, $136.98.

31. Payroll for last half of month:
    Total salaries............................. $3,400.00
    Less amounts withheld:
       FICA tax............................. $187.00
       Employees' income tax.................. 372.60   559.60
    Net amount paid........................ $2,840.40

31. Social security taxes imposed on employer:
    All salaries taxable; rates same as on January 15.

REQUIRED: (1) Journalize the foregoing transactions, using two-column general journal paper. (2) Foot the debit and credit amount columns as a means of proof.

Problem 5-A

Kim Obata is an architect engaged in professional practice on his own account. Since his revenue consists entirely of compensation for personal services rendered, he keeps his accounts on the cash basis. His trial balance for the current year ending December 31 appears below.

KIM OBATA, ARCHITECT
Trial Balance
December 31, 19—

		Debit	Credit
Cash...............................	111	7,670.12	
Office Equipment......................	131	3,840.00	
Accumulated Depreciation — Office Equipment.	013		384.00
Automobiles...........................	141	7,280.00	
Accumulated Depreciation — Automobiles.....	014		910.00
Accounts Payable......................	211		1,514.04
Employees Income Tax Payable	212		170.40
FICA Tax Payable.......................	213		175.00
Kim Obata, Capital.....................	311		11,456.80
Kim Obata, Drawing.....................	031	17,000.00	
Professional Fees.......................	411		39,837.96
Rent Expense..........................	511	4,800.00	
Salary Expense.........................	512	11,200.00	
Automobile Expense.....................	513	812.00	
Depreciation Expense....................	514		
Payroll Taxes Expense	515	750.00	
Charitable Contributions Expense...........	516	480.00	
Miscellaneous Expense...................	517	616.08	
		54,448.20	54,448.20

REQUIRED: (1) Prepare an eight-column work sheet making the necessary entries in the Adjustments columns to record the depreciation of the assets listed at the top of the next page.

Office equipment, 10%, $384
Automobiles, 25%, $1,820

(2) Prepare the following financial statements:

    (a) An income statement for the year ended December 31.
    (b) A balance sheet in report form as of December 31.

Problem 5-B

Frank Tippitt operates an airline charter service, specializing in all weather passenger and freight service. A trial balance of his general ledger accounts is reproduced below.

FRANK TIPPITT AIR SERVICE

Trial Balance

December 31, 19—

Cash.................................	111	23,928.92	
Office Equipment.....................	131	5,000.00	
Accumulated Depreciation — Office Equip...	031		1,000.00
Air Service Equipment.................	141	238,400.00	
Accumulated Depr. — Air Service Equip....	014		95,360.00
Accounts Payable.....................	211		10,682.00
Employees Income Tax Payable	212		540.00
FICA Tax Payable.....................	213		500.00
Frank Tippitt, Capital.................	311		86,000.00
Frank Tippitt, Drawing.................	031	16,800.00	
Traffic Revenue.......................	411		171,125.04
Rent Expense.........................	511	12,000.00	
Salary Expense........................	512	32,000.00	
Office Expense........................	513	2,480.00	
Air Service Expense...................	514	31,876.52	
Depreciation Expense..................	515		
Payroll Taxes Expense	516	2,144.00	
Charitable Contributions Expense..........	517	400.00	
Miscellaneous Expense.................	518	177.60	
		365,207.04	365,207.04

REQUIRED: **(1)** Prepare an eight-column work sheet making the necessary adjustments to record the depreciation of long-lived assets as shown below.

PROPERTY	RATE OF DEPRECIATION	AMOUNT OF DEPRECIATION
Office equipment...............................	10%	$ 500
Air service equipment..........................	20	47,680

(2) Prepare an income statement for the year ended December 31. **(3)** Prepare a balance sheet in report form as of December 31. **(4)** Using two-column journal paper, prepare the entries required:

(a) To adjust the general ledger accounts so that they will be in agreement with the financial statements

(b) To close the temporary owner's equity accounts on December 31.

Foot the amount columns as a means of proof.

Problem 5-C

Ralph Chapman is the sole proprietor of a dry cleaning establishment called Chapman Cleaners. Since revenue consists of compensation for services rendered, he keeps his accounts on the cash basis. He does not extend credit to customers but operates on a cash-on-delivery basis. The Trial Balance columns of his work sheet for the current year ended December 31 are reproduced below.

CHAPMAN CLEANERS
Work Sheet
For the Year Ended December 31, 19—

Account	Acct. No.	Trial Balance	
		Debit	Credit
Fidelity National Bank....................	111	12,625.60	
Office Equipment........................	131	2,000.00	
Accumulated Depreciation — Office Equip . . .	013		200.00
Cleaning Equipment......................	141	7,200.00	
Accumulated Depreciation — Cleaning Equip.	014		576.00
Delivery Trucks.........................	151	3,680.00	
Accumulated Depreciation — Delivery Trucks.	015		1,104.00
Accounts Payable.......................	211		646.16
Employees Income Tax Payable	212		428.24
FICA Tax Payable.......................	213		257.04
Ralph Chapman, Capital..................	311		15,232.88
Ralph Chapman, Drawing.................	031	12,649.80	
Dry Cleaning Revenue....................	411		37,235.40
Pressing Revenue........................	412		15,958.04
Rent Expense...........................	511	8,320.00	
Heat, Light, and Power Expense............	512	5,214.68	
Salary Expense..........................	513	16,450.00	
Delivery Expense........................	514	1,657.72	
Depreciation Expense....................	515		
Payroll Taxes Expense	516	1,102.15	
Miscellaneous Expense...................	517	737.81	
		71,637.76	71,637.76

REQUIRED: **(1)** Complete the work sheet making the necessary adjusting entries to record the depreciation of long-lived assets as follows:

> Office equipment, 10% a year, $200
> Cleaning equipment, 8% a year, $576
> Delivery trucks, 30% a year, $1,104

(2) Prepare an income statement for the year ended December 31. **(3)** Prepare a balance sheet as of December 31 in report form. **(4)** Using two-column general journal paper, prepare the entries required to adjust and close the ledger. Foot the amount columns as a means of proof.

144

chapter 6

accounting for merchandise

In the preceding chapter, accounting and bookkeeping practices suitable for a personal service enterprise were discussed and illustrated. The calculation of net income for the year was made on the so-called "cash basis" except for the matter of depreciation expense. Revenue was not recorded until money was received for the service performed, even though the service may have been performed in a prior period. Similarly, most expenses were not recorded until cash was disbursed for them, even though many of the payments were for things of value received and consumed in a prior period or for things to be received and consumed in a later period. An exception to this practice was made in the matter of depreciation since it would be unrealistic to consider the entire cost of an asset such as an article of office equipment (expected to be used for many years) to be an expense only of the month or year of purchase. The cost of such long-lived assets is spread as expense over their expected useful lives.

The cash basis, even when slightly modified, is not technically perfect; but it has the virtues of simplicity and ease of understanding. This basis has proved to be quite satisfactory for most personal service enterprises. In the case of business enterprises whose major activity is the purchase and sale of merchandise, however, the cash basis of periodic income calculation usually does not give a meaningful or useful measure of net income or net loss. There are two reasons why this is true: **(1)** Merchandising businesses commonly purchase and often sell merchandise "on account" or "on credit" — meaning that payment is postponed a few days or weeks. The amount of cash paid or collected in any accounting period is almost never the same as the amount of purchases and sales of that period. **(2)** Merchandising businesses normally start and end each period with some goods on hand (commonly called *merchandise inventory*), but the dollar amount is not likely to be the same at both points of time. When either or both of these circumstances exist, the *accrual basis* of accounting must be used.

In the calculation of periodic income under the accrual basis, the focus of the effort is to try to match the *realized revenue* of a period against the expenses reasonably assignable to that period. ("Realized revenue" nearly always means the receipt of cash or a collectible claim to cash arising in return for something of value given up — commonly goods.) In the case of merchants, the process starts with the calculation of what is called *gross margin* (also known as *gross profit*). This is the difference between *net sales* and *cost of goods sold*. Net sales is simply the gross amount of revenue from sales less the sales price of any goods returned by customers because the merchandise turned out to be unsatisfactory or unwanted for some reason. (Maybe the goods were found to be defective or the wrong color or size.) Sometimes a reduction in the price — an *allowance* — is given to the customer rather than having the goods returned. Cost of goods sold (really *expense* of goods sold) is most simply defined by the following formula:

$$\text{COST OF GOODS SOLD} = \text{MERCHANDISE INVENTORY, BEGINNING OF PERIOD} + \text{NET PURCHASES} - \text{MERCHANDISE INVENTORY, END OF PERIOD}$$

Net purchases is the difference between the cost of goods purchased and the total of (1) the cost of goods returned to suppliers and (2) the amount of any allowances made by suppliers. To illustrate, consider the following circumstances:

Cost of merchandise (goods) on hand, beginning of period	$10,000
Cost of merchandise purchased during the period	72,000
Cost of goods returned to the supplier for some reason (not ordered, unsatisfactory for some reason, etc.)	3,000
Cash disbursements during the period for goods purchased both in prior periods and the current period	60,000
Sales price of all goods sold and delivered to customers during the current period	90,000
Sales price of goods returned by customers	4,000
Cash received from customers during the period in payment for sales both of prior periods and the current period	75,000
Cost of merchandise (goods) on hand, end of period	14,000

If the *relevant* information in the foregoing array of data is assembled in the proper fashion, the gross margin for the period is calculated to be $21,000. The conventional means of exhibiting the pertinent amounts is as follows:

Sales...			$90,000
Less sales returns and allowances...................			4,000
Net sales.....................................			$86,000
Cost of goods sold:			
Merchandise inventory, beginning of period........		$10,000	
Add: Purchases.............................	$72,000		
Less purchases returns and allowances	3,000		
Net purchases...............................		69,000	
Cost of goods available for sale...................		$79,000	
Less merchandise inventory, end of period.........		14,000	
Cost of goods sold............................			65,000
Gross margin on sales			$21,000

Note that the movement of cash in both directions (to suppliers and from customers) was ignored as being irrelevant. (It should be mentioned that the manner of accounting for depreciation illustrated in the last chapter was in accordance with the accrual basis of accounting.) Because accrual accounting is widely used, and because one of its major applications relates to the accounting for merchandise transactions, this subject will be examined in some detail.

In recording transactions concerned with merchandising, it is desirable to keep at least the following accounts:

147

(a) Purchases
(b) Purchases Returns and Allowances
(c) Sales
(d) Sales Returns and Allowances
(e) Merchandise Inventory

Purchases and the purchases journal

The word *purchase* can refer to the act of buying almost anything or, if used as a noun, to the thing that is bought. In connection with the accounting for a merchandising business, however, the term usually refers to merchandise. A reference to "purchases for the year," unless qualified in some way, would relate to the merchandise (*stock in trade*) that had been bought.

Purchases account

The purchases account is a temporary owner's equity account in which the cost of merchandise purchased is recorded. The account should be debited for the cost of all merchandise purchased during the accounting period. If the purchase was for cash, the cash account should be credited; if on account, Accounts Payable should be credited. The purchases account may also be debited for any transportation charges, such as freight, express, and parcel post charges, that increase the cost of the merchandise purchased.

PURCHASES	
Debit to record the cost of merchandise purchased.	

Purchases returns and allowances account

This account is a temporary owner's equity account in which purchases returns and allowances are recorded. The account should be credited for the cost of any merchandise returned to creditors or suppliers and for any allowances received from creditors that decrease the cost of the merchandise purchased. The offsetting debit is to Accounts Payable if the goods were purchased on account, or to Cash if a refund is received because the purchase was originally for cash. Allowances may be received from creditors for merchandise delivered in poor condition or for merchandise that does not meet specifications as to quality, weight, size, color, grade, or style.

PURCHASES RETURNS AND ALLOWANCES	
	Credit to record returns and allowances.

Although purchases returns and allowances might be credited directly to Purchases, it is better to credit Purchases Returns and Allowances. The accounts will then show both the amount of gross purchases and the amount of returns and allowances. If returns and allowances are large in proportion to gross purchases, a weakness in the purchasing operations is indicated. It may be that better sources of supply should be sought or that purchase specifications should be stated more clearly.

Purchase invoice

A document received by the buyer from the seller that provides information for recording a purchase transaction is known as a *purchase invoice*. An invoice includes the supplier's invoice number, the purchaser's order number, the dates of shipment and billing, the terms of sale, a description of the goods, the quantities shipped, the unit prices, and the total amount of the purchase. A variety of forms and sizes of purchase invoices is in common use.

When both the goods and the invoice have been received, it is customary for the purchaser to assign the incoming invoice a number. (Note that the invoice below was marked "#37.") Someone must check to see that the invoice is correct as to quantities and unit prices, and that the extensions and total are correct. ("Extensions" are the amounts resulting from multiplying the quantity times the price of each item purchased.) It is common practice for the purchaser to imprint a form on the face of the invoice by means of a rubber stamp. This form provides spaces for the initials of the persons who have verified that the goods were received, and that the prices, extensions, and total are correct. Sometimes there is space to show the number of the account to be debited — Purchases, if the invoice relates to merchandise bought for resale. If everything is found to be in order, the invoice will be paid at the proper time.

Below is a reproduction of a purchase invoice as it would appear after the various aspects of the transaction have been verified and approved.

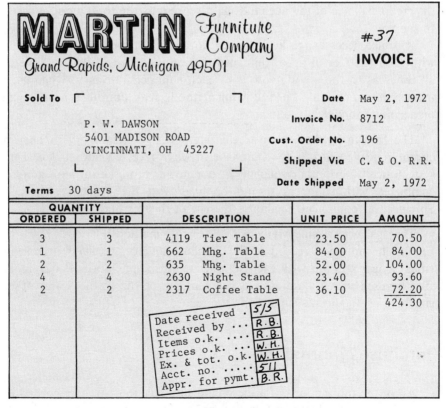

Purchase Invoice

Merchandise may be bought for cash or on account. When merchandise is bought for cash, the transaction results in an increase in purchases and a decrease in the asset cash; hence, it should be recorded by debiting Purchases and by crediting Cash. When merchandise is bought on account, the transaction results in an increase in purchases with a corresponding increase in the liability accounts payable; hence, it should be recorded by debiting Purchases and by crediting Accounts Payable.

Accounts payable

In order that the owner or manager may know the total amount owed to his suppliers (sometimes referred to as "creditors"), it is advisable to keep a summary ledger account for Accounts Payable. This is a liability account. The credit balance of the account at the beginning of the period represents the total amount owed to suppliers. During the period, the account should be credited for the amount of any transactions involving increases and should be debited for the amount of any transactions involving decreases in the amount owed to suppliers. At the end of the period, the credit balance of the account again represents the total amount owed to suppliers.

150 It is also necessary to keep some record of the transactions completed with each supplier in order that information may be readily available at all times as to the amount owed to each supplier and as to when each invoice should be paid. The following methods of accounting for purchases on account are widely used:

The Invoice Method. Under this method it is customary to keep a chronological record of the purchase invoices received and to file them systematically. All other vouchers or documents representing transactions completed with suppliers should be filed with the purchase invoices. Special filing equipment facilitates the use of this method.

The Ledger Account Method. Under this method it is customary to keep a chronological record of the purchase invoices received. An individual ledger account with each supplier is also kept. Special equipment may be used in maintaining a permanent file of the invoices and other vouchers or documents supporting the records.

Purchases journal

All of the transactions of a merchandising business can be recorded in an ordinary two-column general journal or in a combined cash journal.

However, in many such enterprises purchase transactions occur frequently. If most of the purchases are made on account, such transactions may be recorded advantageously in a special journal called a *purchases journal*. One form of a purchases journal is illustrated below.

It will be noted that in recording each purchase, the following information is entered in the purchases journal:

(a) Date on which the invoice is received.
(b) Number of the invoice (i.e., the number assigned by the buyer).
(c) From whom purchased (the supplier).
(d) Amount of the invoice.

PURCHASES JOURNAL   PAGE 9

	DATE	INVOICE NO.	FROM WHOM PURCHASED	POST. REF.	AMOUNT	
1	1972 May 5	37	Martin Furniture Company	✓	424 30	1
2	6	38	J. G. Paterson Company	✓	819 36	2
3	12	39	Stanton Manufacturing Co.	✓	1427 90	3
4	29	40	Monroe Brothers	✓	1562 11	4
5	31		Purchases Dr.—Accounts Payable Cr.	51/231	4233 67	5
6						6
7						7

Model Purchases Journal

151

When the invoice method of accounting is used for purchases on account, it is not necessary to record the address of the supplier in the purchases journal; neither is it necessary to record the terms in the purchases journal. With this form of purchases journal, each transaction can be recorded on one horizontal line.

If an individual ledger account is not kept with each supplier, the purchase invoices should be filed immediately after they have been recorded in the purchases journal. It is preferable that they be filed according to due date in an unpaid invoice file.

If a partial payment is made on an invoice, a notation of the payment should be made on the invoice, and it should be retained in the unpaid invoice file until it is paid in full. It is generally considered a better policy to pay each invoice in full. Paying specific invoices in full simplifies record keeping for both the buyer and the seller. If credit is received because of returns or allowances, a notation of the amount of the credit should also be made on the invoice so that the balance due will be indicated.

When an invoice is paid in full, the payment should be noted on the invoice, which should be transferred from the unpaid invoice file to a paid invoice file.

The unpaid invoice file is usually arranged with a division for each month with folders numbered 1 to 31 in each division. This makes it possible to file the unpaid invoices according to the date they will become due, which facilitates payment of the invoices on or before their due dates. Since certain invoices may be subject to discounts if paid within a specified time, it is important that they be handled in such a manner that payment in time to get the benefit of the discounts will not be overlooked.

The folders in the paid invoice file are usually arranged in alphabetic order, according to the names of suppliers. This facilitates the filing of all paid invoices, and all other vouchers or documents representing transactions with suppliers, in such a manner that a complete history of the business done with each supplier is maintained.

Posting from the Purchases Journal. Under the invoice method of accounting for purchases on account, individual posting from the purchases journal is not required. When this plan is followed, it is customary to place a check mark in the Posting Reference column of the purchases journal at the time of entering each invoice.

At the end of the month the Amount column of the purchases journal should be totaled and the ruling completed as illustrated. The total of the purchases on account for the month should then be posted as a debit to Purchases and as a credit to Accounts Payable. A proper cross-reference should be provided by entering the page of the purchases journal preceded by the initial "P" in the Posting Reference column of the ledger and by entering the account number in the Posting Reference column of the purchases journal. The titles of both accounts and the posting references may be entered on one horizontal line of the purchases journal as shown in the illustration. Posting the total in this manner usually is referred to as *summary posting*.

The proper method of completing the summary posting from P. W. Dawson's purchases journal on May 31 is shown in the following illustration of the accounts affected.

ACCOUNT *Accounts Payable*   ACCOUNT NO. *231*

DATE	ITEM	POST. REF.	DEBIT	DATE	ITEM	POST. REF.	CREDIT
				1972 May 31		P9	4233 67

ACCOUNT *Purchases*   ACCOUNT NO. *511*

DATE	ITEM	POST. REF.	DEBIT	DATE	ITEM	POST. REF.	CREDIT
1972 May 31		P9	4233 67				

General Ledger Accounts After Posting from Purchases Journal

The Ledger Account Method. If an individual ledger account is kept for each supplier, all transactions representing either increases or decreases in the amount owed to each supplier should be posted individually to the proper account. The posting may be done by hand, or posting machines may be used. If the posting is done by hand, it may be completed either directly from the purchase invoices and other vouchers or documents representing the transactions, or it may be completed from the books of original entry. If the posting is done with the aid of posting machines, it will usually be completed directly from the purchase invoices and other vouchers or documents. The ledger account method of accounting for accounts payable is explained in detail in Chapter 8.

Report No. 6-1

Refer to the workbook and complete Report No. 6-1. After completing the report, continue with the following study assignment until the next report is required.

153

Sales and the sales journal

On page 147 reference was made to the fact that in recording transactions arising from merchandising activities it is desirable to keep certain accounts, including accounts for sales and for sales returns and allowances. A discussion of these accounts, together with a discussion of the sales journal, follows.

Sales account

The sales account is a temporary owner's equity account in which the revenue resulting from sales of merchandise is recorded. The account should be credited for the selling price of all merchandise sold during the accounting period. If sales are for cash, the credit to Sales is offset by a debit to Cash; if the sales are on account, the debit is made to an asset account, Accounts Receivable.

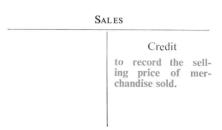

SALES	
	Credit
	to record the selling price of merchandise sold.

Sales returns and allowances account

This account is a temporary owner's equity account in which sales returns and allowances are recorded. The account should be debited for the selling price of any merchandise returned by customers or for any allowances made to customers that decrease the selling price of the merchandise sold. The offsetting credit is to Accounts Receivable if the goods were sold on account, or to Cash if a refund was made because the sale was originally for cash. Such allowances may be granted to customers for merchandise delivered in poor condition or for merchandise that does not meet specifications as to quality, weight, size, color, grade, or style.

SALES RETURNS AND ALLOWANCES	
Debit	
to record returns and allowances.	

While sales returns and allowances could be debited directly to Sales, it is better to debit Sales Returns and Allowances. The accounts will then show both the amount of gross sales and the amount of returns and allowances. If returns and allowances are large in proportion to gross sales, a weakness in the merchandising operations is indicated; and the trouble should be determined and corrected.

Retail sales tax

A tax imposed upon the sale of tangible personal property at retail is known as a *retail sales tax*. The tax is usually measured by the gross sales price or the gross receipts from sales. Retail sales taxes are imposed by most states and by many cities. Retail sales taxes may also include taxes imposed upon persons engaged in furnishing services at retail, in which case they are measured by the gross receipts for furnishing such services. The rates of the tax vary considerably but usually range from 1 percent to 5 percent. In most states the tax is a general sales tax. However, in some states the tax is imposed only on specific items, such as automobiles, cosmetics, radios, and playing cards.

To avoid fractions of cents and to simplify the determination of the tax, it is customary to use a sales tax table or schedule. For example, where the rate is 5 percent the tax may be calculated as shown in the following schedule:

AMOUNT OF SALE	AMOUNT OF TAX
1¢ to 10¢	None
11¢ to 27¢	1¢
28¢ to 47¢	2¢
48¢ to 68¢	3¢
69¢ to 89¢	4¢
90¢ to $1.09	5¢

and so on

The amount of the tax imposed under the schedule approximates the legal rate. Retail sales tax reports accompanied by remittances for the amounts due must be filed periodically, usually monthly or quarterly, depending upon the law of the state or city in which the business is located.

In the case of a retail store operated in a city or state where a sales tax is imposed on merchandise sold for cash or on account, it is advisable to keep an account for Sales Tax Payable. This is a liability account which should be credited for the amount of the tax collected or imposed on sales. The account should be debited for the amount of the tax paid to the proper taxing authority. A credit balance in the account at any time indicates the amount of the merchant's liability for taxes collected or imposed.

SALES TAX PAYABLE

Debit	Credit
to record payment of tax to the proper taxing authority or for tax on merchandise returned by customers.	to record tax imposed on sales.

155

Sales tax accounting may be complicated by such factors as (1) sales returns and allowances and (2) exempt sales. If the tax is recorded at the time the sale is recorded, it will be necessary to adjust for the tax when recording sales returns and allowances. If some sales are exempt from the tax, it will be necessary to distinguish between the taxable and the nontaxable sales. A common example of nontaxable sales is sales to out-of-state customers.

Sales ticket

The first written record of a sales transaction is called a *sales ticket*. Whether merchandise is sold for cash or on account, a sales ticket should be prepared. When the sale is for cash, the ticket may be printed by the cash register at the time that the sale is rung up. However, some stores prefer to use handwritten sales tickets no matter whether the sale is for cash or on account. Regardless of the method used in recording cash sales,

Sales Ticket

it is necessary to prepare a handwritten sales ticket or charge slip for every sale on account. Such sales tickets are usually prepared in duplicate or in triplicate. The original copy is for the bookkeeping department. A carbon copy is given to the customer. Where more than one salesperson is employed, each is usually provided with his own pad of sales tickets. Each pad bears a different number that identifies the clerk. The individual sales tickets are also numbered consecutively. This facilitates sorting the tickets by clerks if it is desired to compute the amount of goods sold by each clerk. Reference to the sales ticket above will show the type of information usually recorded.

When merchandise is sold for cash in a state or a city which has a retail sales tax, the transaction results in an increase in the asset cash offset by an increase in sales revenue and an increase in the liability sales tax payable. Such transactions should be recorded by debiting Cash for the amount received and by crediting Sales for the sales price of the merchandise and crediting Sales Tax Payable for the amount of the tax collected. When merchandise is sold on account in such a state or city, the transaction results in an increase in the asset accounts receivable offset by an increase in sales revenue and an increase in the liability sales tax payable. Such transactions should be recorded by debiting Accounts Receivable for the total amount charged to the customer and by crediting Sales for the amount of the sale and crediting Sales Tax Payable for the amount of the tax imposed.

An alternative procedure that is permissible under some sales tax laws is to credit the total of both the sales and the tax to the sales account in the first place. Periodically — usually at the end of each month — a calculation is made to determine how much of the balance of the sales account is presumed to be tax, and an entry is made to remove this amount from the sales account and to transfer it to the sales tax payable account. Suppose, for example, that the tax rate is 4 percent, and that the sales account includes the tax collected or charged, along with the amount of the sales. In this event, 100/104 of the balance of the account is presumed to be the amount of the sales, and 4/104 of the balance is the amount of the tax. If the sales account had a balance of $10,400, the tax portion would be $400 (4/104 of $10,400). A debit to Sales of $400 would remove this tax portion; the credit would be to Sales Tax Payable.

Bank credit card sales

The use of bank credit cards in connection with the retail sales of certain types of goods and service is a growing practice. The two most widely used credit cards of this type in the United States are the "Bank-Americard" and the "Master Charge" card. The former was started by the Bank of America in California. That bank now franchises numerous banks in other localities to offer the program. Likewise, several thousand banks participate in the Master Charge program. The two systems have much in common.

Participating banks encourage their depositors and other customers to obtain the cards by supplying the necessary information to establish their credit reliability. When this has been accomplished, a small (approximately 2″ x 3″) plastic card containing (in raised characters so that the card may be used for imprinting) the cardholder's name and an identifying number is issued to the applicant.

Merchants and other businesses are invited to participate in the program. If certain conditions are met, the bank will accept for deposit completed copies of the prescribed form of sales invoices (also sometimes called "tickets," "drafts" or "vouchers") for goods sold or services rendered to cardholders and evidenced by the invoices bearing the card imprints and the buyers' signatures. The bank, in effect, either "buys" the tickets at a discount (amounting to from 1 percent to 5 percent, depending upon various factors) immediately, or gives the merchant immediate credit for the full face amount of the tickets, and, once a month, charges the merchant's account with the total amount of the discount at the agreed rate.

For the merchant, bank credit card sales are nearly the equivalent of cash sales. The service is performed or the goods are sold; and the money is secured. It is then up to the bank to collect from the buyer or to bear the loss, if the account proves to be uncollectible.

In most respects, the accounting for bank credit card sales is very much the same as the accounting for regular cash sales. Very often a regular sales ticket is prepared as well as the credit card form of invoice. The transactions may be accounted for either as cash sales for the net amount to be secured from the bank, or as sales for the full price with the amount of the discount being treated as an expense.

It will be apparent that bank credit card sales are similar in many respects to the sales made by certain types of businesses that use other forms of retail credit cards — notably those of petroleum companies, and businesses participating in the "Diners Club," "Carte Blanche" and American Express programs.

158

Accounts receivable

In order that the owner or manager of an enterprise may know the total amount due from charge customers at any time, it is advisable to keep a summary ledger account with Accounts Receivable. This is an asset account. The debit balance of the account at the beginning of the period represents the total amount due from customers. During the period, the account should be debited for the amount of any transactions involving increases and should be credited for the amount of any transactions involving decreases in the amount due from customers. At the end of the period, the debit balance of the account again represents the total amount due from charge customers.

It is also necessary to keep some record of the transactions completed with each customer in order that information may be readily available at all times as to the amount due from each customer. The following methods of accounting for charge sales are widely used:

The Sales Ticket Method. Under this method it is customary to file the charge sales tickets systematically. All other related vouchers or documents representing transactions with customers should be filed with the appropriate sales tickets. Special filing equipment facilitates the use of this method. In some cases a chronological record of the charge sales tickets is kept as a means of control.

The Ledger Account Method. Under this method it is customary to keep a chronological record of the charge sales tickets. An individual ledger account with each customer is also kept. Special equipment may be used in maintaining a permanent file of the charge sales tickets and other vouchers or documents supporting the records.

Under either of these methods of accounting for transactions with charge customers, it is necessary that a sales ticket or charge slip be made for each sale on account. In making a charge sales ticket the date, the name and address of the customer, the quantity, a description of the items sold, the unit prices, the total amount of the sale, and the amount of the sales tax should be recorded.

Sales journal

Transactions involving the sale of merchandise on account can be recorded in an ordinary two-column general journal or in a combined cash journal. However, in many merchandising businesses sales transactions occur frequently, and if it is the policy to sell merchandise on account, such transactions may be recorded advantageously in a special journal. If the business is operated in an area where no sales taxes are imposed, all sales on account can be recorded in a *sales journal* with only one amount column as illustrated below.

159

	DATE	SALE NO.	TO WHOM SOLD	POST. REF.	AMOUNT	
1						1
2						2
3						3
4						4
5						5
6						6

SALES JOURNAL   PAGE

Sales Journal Without Sales Taxes

At the end of the month, the total of the amount column should be posted as a debit to Accounts Receivable and as a credit to Sales.

The second model sales journal illustrated on page 160 provides three amount columns. This format is most appropriate for use in an area where a sales tax is imposed. The transactions recorded in the journal were completed by P. W. Dawson, a retail merchant, during the month of May.

	DATE	SALE NO.	TO WHOM SOLD	POST. REF.	ACCOUNTS RECEIVABLE DR.	SALES CR.	SALES TAX PAYABLE CR.	
1	1972 May 5	240	Melvin Williams	✓	258 51	246 20	12 31	1
2	5	241	G. H. Johnson	✓	1 638 42	1 560 40	78 02	2
3	11	242	A. J. Payton	✓	504 95	480 90	24 05	3
4	15	243	S. M. Maxwell	✓	1 439 34	1 370 80	68 54	4
5	22	244	V. F. French	✓	884 36	842 25	42 11	5
6	26	245	C. B. Cooper	✓	1 412 46	1 345 20	67 26	6
7					6 138 04 / 6 138 04	5 845 75 / 5 845 75	292 29 / 292 29	7
8					(123)	(411)	(241)	8
9								9
10								10

Sales Journal With Sales Taxes

His store is located in a state that imposes a tax of 5 percent on the retail sale of all merchandise whether sold for cash or on account.

It will be noted that the following information regarding each charge sales ticket is recorded in the sales journal:

(a) Date.
(b) Number of the sales ticket.
(c) To whom sold (the customer).
(d) Amount charged to customer.
(e) Amount of sale.
(f) Amount of sales tax.

160

With this form of sales journal, each transaction can be recorded on one horizontal line. The sales ticket should provide all the information needed in recording each sale.

If an individual ledger account is not kept with each customer, the charge sales tickets should be filed immediately after they have been recorded in the sales journal. They are usually filed under the name of the customer. There are numerous types of trays, cabinets, and files on the market that are designed to facilitate the filing of charge sales tickets by customer name. Such devices are designed to save time, to promote accuracy, and to provide a safe means of keeping a record of the transactions with each charge customer.

When a customer makes a partial payment on his account, the amount of the payment should be noted on the most recent charge sales ticket and the new balance should be indicated. Sales tickets paid in full should be receipted and may either be given to the customer or may be transferred to another file for future reference. If a customer is given credit for merchandise returned or because of allowances, a notation of the amount of credit should be made on the most recent charge sales ticket and the new balance should be indicated. If a credit memorandum is issued to a customer, it should be prepared in duplicate and the carbon copy should be attached to the sales ticket on which the amount is noted.

Posting from the Sales Journal. Under the sales ticket method of accounting for sales on account, individual posting from the sales journal is not required. When this plan is followed, it is customary to place a check mark in the Posting Reference column of the sales journal at the time of entering each sale.

At the end of the month the amount columns of the sales journal should be footed in small figures. On a separate sheet of paper the total of the credit columns should then be added. The sum of the totals of the credit columns should equal the total of the debit column. If it does, the totals should be entered in ink and the ruling completed as illustrated. The totals should be posted to the general ledger accounts indicated in the column headings. This summary posting should be completed in the following order:

(a) Post the total of the Accounts Receivable Dr. column to the debit of Accounts Receivable.
(b) Post the total of the Sales Cr. column to the credit of Sales.
(c) Post the total of the Sales Tax Payable Cr. column to the credit of Sales Tax Payable.

A proper cross-reference should be provided by entering the page of the sales journal preceded by the initial "S" in the Posting Reference column of the ledger and by entering the account number immediately below the column total of the sales journal. The proper method of completing the summary posting from P. W. Dawson's sales journal on May 31 is shown in the accounts affected as illustrated below.

ACCOUNT *Accounts Receivable* ACCOUNT NO. *123*

DATE	ITEM	POST. REF.	DEBIT	DATE	ITEM	POST. REF.	CREDIT
1972 May 31		S14	6138.04				

ACCOUNT *Sales Tax Payable* ACCOUNT NO. *241*

DATE	ITEM	POST. REF.	DEBIT	DATE	ITEM	POST. REF.	CREDIT
				1972 May 31		S14	292.29

ACCOUNT *Sales* ACCOUNT NO. *411*

DATE	ITEM	POST. REF.	DEBIT	DATE	ITEM	POST. REF.	CREDIT
				1972 May 31		S14	5845.75

General Ledger Accounts After Posting from Sales Journal

The Ledger Account Method. If an individual ledger account is kept for each customer, all transactions representing either increases or decreases in the amount due from each customer should be posted individually to the proper account. The posting may be done by hand or posting machines may be used. If the posting is done by hand, it may be completed either directly from the charge sales tickets and other vouchers or documents representing the transactions, or it may be completed from the books of original entry. If the posting is done with posting machines, it will usually be completed directly from the charge sales tickets and other vouchers or documents.

Report No. 6-2

Refer to the workbook and complete Report No. 6-2. After completing the report, continue with the following study assignment until the next report is required.

162

Accounting procedure

The accounting procedure in recording the transactions of a merchandising business is, in general, the same as that involved in recording the transactions of any other enterprise. In a small merchandising business where the number of transactions is not large and all the bookkeeping may be done by one person, a standard two-column general journal or a combined cash journal may be used as the only book of original entry. However, if desired, a purchases journal and a sales journal may be used also. The purchases journal may be used for keeping a chronological record of purchases of merchandise on account, and the sales journal may be used for keeping a chronological record of sales of merchandise on account. All of the accounts may be kept in one general ledger, which may be either a bound book, a loose-leaf book, or a card file. The posting from a general journal or from the "General" columns of a combined cash journal may be completed daily or periodically; summary posting from the purchases and sales journals and from the special columns of a combined cash journal is done at the end of the month.

A trial balance should be taken at the end of each month as a means of proving the equality of the debit and credit account balances. The balance of the summary account for Accounts Receivable should be proved periodically, or at least at the end of each month. This may be done by determining the total of the unpaid sales tickets or charge slips that are kept in a customer's file. Likewise, the balance of the summary account for Accounts Payable should be proved periodically, or at least at the end of each month. This may be done by determining the total of the unpaid invoices that are kept in an unpaid invoice file.

This procedure will be illustrated **(1)** by recording a narrative of certain transactions for one month in a purchases journal, a sales journal, and a combined cash journal, **(2)** by posting to the ledger accounts, **(3)** by preparing a schedule of accounts receivable to reconcile the balance of the summary account for Accounts Receivable, and **(4)** by preparing a schedule of accounts payable to reconcile the balance of the summary account for Accounts Payable. (The end-of-month trial balance is not shown since the illustration does not involve all of the accounts in the general ledger.)

Arthur Phillips is the owner of a small retail business operated under the name of "The Phillips Store." A purchases journal, a sales journal, and a combined cash journal are used as books of original entry. All of the accounts are kept in a general ledger. Individual ledger accounts with customers and suppliers are not kept; instead, the purchase invoices and the charge sales tickets are filed in the manner previously described. All sales are subject to a retail sales tax of 5 percent, whether for cash or on account. All sales on account are payable by the tenth of the following month unless otherwise agreed. A partial chart of accounts is reproduced below. It includes only the accounts needed to record certain transactions completed during March 1972, the first month that Mr. Phillips has owned and operated the business.

163

THE PHILLIPS STORE

PARTIAL CHART OF ACCOUNTS

*Assets**

111 Cash
123 Accounts Receivable
181 Store Equipment

Revenue from Sales

411 Sales
041 Sales Returns and Allowances

Liabilities

231 Accounts Payable
241 Sales Tax Payable

Cost of Goods Sold

511 Purchases
051 Purchases Returns and Allowances

Words in italics represent headings and not account titles.

THE PHILLIPS STORE

PARTIAL NARRATIVE OF TRANSACTIONS

Thursday, March 2

Purchased store equipment on account from the City Store Equipment Co., 103 E. Jasper St., $1,462.80.

Since this transaction involved a purchase of store equipment, it was recorded in the combined cash journal. (The purchases journal is used only for recording purchases of merchandise on account.)

Friday, March 3

Received invoice dated March 1 from Dunn's, 920 Iris Ave., for merchandise purchased, $185.10. Terms, 30 days net. (Assigned number "1" to this invoice.)

Saturday, March 4

Sold merchandise on account to Peter C. Vance, 206 Elm St., $31.40, tax $1.57. Sale No. 1-1.

Sundry cash sales per cash register tape, $54, tax $2.70.

Each Saturday the store's total cash sales for the week and related tax are recorded, using the cash register tape as the source of the amounts. This transaction was recorded in the combined cash journal by debiting Cash for the total amount received and by crediting Sales for the selling price of the merchandise and crediting Sales Tax Payable for the amount of the tax imposed on cash sales. This was recorded in the combined cash journal since only sales on account are entered in the sales journal. A check mark was entered in the Posting Reference column to indicate that no individual posting is required.

Monday, March 6

Purchased merchandise from Minton Company, 1001 Garfield Ave., for cash, $92. Check No. 4.

This transaction was recorded in the combined cash journal since only purchases of merchandise on account are recorded in the purchases journal.

Tuesday, March 7

Sold merchandise on account to A. A. Wright, 908 High St., $36, tax $1.80. Sale No. 1-2.

Wednesday, March 8

Gave A. A. Wright credit for merchandise returned, $11, tax 55 cents.

This transaction increased sales returns and allowances and decreased sales tax payable and accounts receivable. It was recorded in the combined cash journal by debiting Sales Returns and Allowances for the amount of the merchandise returned, by debiting Sales Tax Payable for the amount of the sales tax, and by crediting Accounts Receivable for the total amount of the credit allowed Mr. Wright.

Thursday, March 9

Received invoice (No. 2) dated March 8 from Dunn's for merchandise purchased, $345. Terms, 30 days net.

Friday, March 10

Sold merchandise on account to Charles F. Joseph, 13 Wallace Ave., $16.60, tax 83 cents. Sale No. 2-1.

Saturday, March 11

Sundry cash sales for week, $192.20, tax $9.61.

Received a check for $32.97 from Peter C. Vance for merchandise sold to him March 4.

Monday, March 13

Received credit for $23.40 from Dunn's for merchandise returned by agreement.

> The credit applies to Invoice No. 2, dated March 8. This transaction had the effect of increasing purchases returns and allowances and decreasing accounts payable. It was recorded in the combined cash journal by debiting Accounts Payable and by crediting Purchases Returns and Allowances for the amount of the credit received from Dunn's.

Tuesday, March 14

Paid Transit, Inc., freight and drayage on merchandise purchased, $18.60. Check No. 5.

> In the simple set of accounts maintained for The Phillips Store, no separate account is used to record the cost of freight on merchandise purchases. Instead, the amount is debited to the purchases account. This treatment is acceptable since freight on purchases is really a part of the cost of goods purchased.

Wednesday, March 15

Received invoice (No. 3) dated March 13 from Alex A. Carlton & Son, Dayton, for merchandise purchased, $44. Terms, 60 days net.

Thursday, March 16

Paid Dunn's $185.10 in settlement of Invoice No. 1 dated March 1. Check No. 6.

Friday, March 17

Received $26.25 from A. A. Wright for merchandise sold March 7 less merchandise returned March 8.

Saturday, March 18

Sundry cash sales for week, $92.05, tax $4.60.

Monday, March 20

Paid City Store Equipment Co. $700 on account. Check No. 7.

Tuesday, March 21

Sold merchandise on account to Charles F. Joseph, $36, tax $1.80. Sale No. 1-3.

Wednesday, March 22

Received invoice (No. 4) dated March 20 from Alex A. Carlton & Son for merchandise purchased, $73.20. Terms, 30 days net.

Thursday, March 23

Sold merchandise on account to Peter C. Vance, $42, tax $2.10. Sale No. 2-2.

Saturday, March 25

Sundry cash sales for week, $92.80, tax $4.64.

Monday, March 27

Sold merchandise on account to A. A. Wright, $31.95, tax $1.60. Sale No. 2-3.

Friday, March 31

Sundry cash sales, $56.20, tax $2.81.

Since this is the last day of the month, the amount of cash sales since March 25, including tax, was recorded.

Journalizing

The transactions completed by The Phillips Store during the month of March were recorded in the combined cash journal reproduced on pages 168 and 169, the purchases journal reproduced on page 167, and the sales journal reproduced on page 167. (The footings of the combined cash journal reflect the amounts of more transactions than are actually recorded. The footings of the purchases journal and of the sales journal reflect only the amounts of the transactions recorded.)

Posting

The accounts affected by the transactions narrated are reproduced on pages 170 and 171. The posting was completed from the books of original

PURCHASES JOURNAL

	DATE	INVOICE NO.	FROM WHOM PURCHASED	POST. REF.	AMOUNT	
1	1972 Mar. 3	1	Dunn's	✓	18510	1
2	9	2	Dunn's	✓	34500	2
3	15	3	Alex A. Carlton & Son	✓	4400	3
4	22	4	Alex A. Carlton & Son	✓	7320	4
5	31		Purchases Dr. – Accounts Payable Cr.	511 231	64730	5
6						6
7						7
8						8
9						9
10						10
11						11
12						12
13						13

The Phillips Store — Purchases Journal

SALES JOURNAL

	DATE	SALE NO.	TO WHOM SOLD	POST. REF.	ACCOUNTS RECEIVABLE DR.	SALES CR.	SALES TAX PAYABLE CR.	
1	1972 Mar. 4	1-1	Peter C. Vance	✓	3297	3140	157	1
2	7	1-2	A. A. Wright	✓	3780	3600	180	2
3	10	2-1	Charles F. Joseph	✓	1743	1660	83	3
4	21	1-3	Charles F. Joseph	✓	3780	3600	180	4
5	23	2-2	Peter C. Vance	✓	4410	4200	210	5
6	27	2-3	A. A. Wright	✓	3355	3195	160	6
7					20365 20365	19395 19395	970 970	7
8					(123)	(411)	(241)	8
9								9
10								10
11								11
12								12
13								13

The Phillips Store — Sales Journal

entry in the following order; first, the combined cash journal; second, the purchases journal; and third, the sales journal. After the columns of the combined cash journal were footed and the footings were proved, the totals were entered and the rulings were made as illustrated. Each entry in the General Debit and General Credit columns was posted individually

CASH		CK. NO.	DAY	DESCRIPTION	POST. REF.	
RECEIPTS 111 DR.	DISBURSEMENTS 111 CR.					
				AMOUNTS FORWARDED		
			2	Store Equipment	181	4
				Accts. Payable - City Store Equip. Co.	231	5
56 70			4	Cash Sales	✓	10
	92 00	4	6	Purchases	511	11
			8	Sales Ret. + Allow. (A.A. Wright)	041	12
				Sales Tax Payable	241	13
201 81			11	Cash Sales	✓	14
32 97			11	Peter C. Vance (on acct.)	✓	15
			13	Purchases Ret. + Allow. (Dunn's)	051	16
	18 60	5	14	Purchases (freight)	511	17
	185 10	6	16	Dunn's	✓	18
26 25			17	A.A. Wright (on acct.)	✓	19
96 65			18	Cash sales	✓	20
	700 00	7	20	City Store Equipment Co.	✓	21
97 44			25	Cash sales	✓	22
59 01			31	Cash sales	✓	31
2 47 2 48	1 48 0 99				9 31.49	32
2 41 2 48	1 48 0 99					32
(111)	(111)					33

The Phillips Store — Combined Cash Journal (Left Page)

to the proper account. The total of each of the six special columns was posted to the account indicated by the column heading. The number of the account to which the posting was made was written below the total. Since the totals of the General Debit and General Credit columns were not posted, a check mark ($\sqrt{}$) was made under each of these columns to so indicate. The total of the single column in the purchases journal was posted as a debit to Purchases and also as a credit to Accounts Payable. The number of each of these accounts was noted in the Posting Reference column beside the total of the Amount column. After the three amount columns of the sales journal were footed and the footings were proved, the totals were entered and the rulings were made as illustrated. Each total was posted to the account indicated by the column heading, and the account number was shown below that total.

When more than one book of original entry is used, it is advisable to identify each book by means of an initial (or initials) preceding the page

	GENERAL		ACCOUNTS PAYABLE 231 DR.	ACCOUNTS RECEIVABLE 123 CR.	SALES 411 CR.	SALES TAX PAYABLE 241 CR.	
	DEBIT	CREDIT					
4	146280						4
5		146280					5
10					5400	270	10
11	9200						11
12	1100						12
13	55			1155			13
14					19220	961	14
15				3297			15
16		2340	2340				16
17	1860						17
18			18510				18
19				2625			19
20					9205	460	20
21			70000				21
22					9280	464	22
31	259258	385019	90850	7077	5620 / 48725	281 / 2436	31
32	259258	385019	90850	7077	48725	2436	32
33	(✓)	(✓)	(231)	(123)	(411)	(241)	33

The Phillips Store — Combined Cash Journal (Right Page)

number. The following code was used in conjunction with the page number to indicate the source of each entry in the ledger accounts:

CJ = Combined cash journal
P = Purchases journal
S = Sales journal

Trial balance

After the posting was completed, the accounts in the general ledger were footed where necessary, and the balances were entered in the Item column on the proper side. Usually a trial balance then would be prepared to prove the equality of the debit and credit account balances. However, since the illustration did not involve all of the general ledger accounts nor all of the transactions for the month, a trial balance of the general ledger of The Phillips Store as of March 31, 1972, is not reproduced.

ACCOUNT Cash — ACCOUNT NO. 111

DATE	ITEM	POST. REF.	DEBIT	DATE	ITEM	POST. REF.	CREDIT
1972 Mar. 31	931.49	CJ1	2412 48	1972 Mar. 31		CJ1	1480 99

ACCOUNT Accounts Receivable — ACCOUNT NO. 123

DATE	ITEM	POST. REF.	DEBIT	DATE	ITEM	POST. REF.	CREDIT
1972 Mar. 31	132.88	S1	203 65	1972 Mar. 31		CJ1	70 77

ACCOUNT Store Equipment — ACCOUNT NO. 181

DATE	ITEM	POST. REF.	DEBIT	DATE	ITEM	POST. REF.	CREDIT
1972 Mar. 2		CJ1	1462 80				

ACCOUNT Accounts Payable — ACCOUNT NO. 231

DATE	ITEM	POST. REF.	DEBIT	DATE	ITEM	POST. REF.	CREDIT
1972 Mar. 31		CJ1	908 50	1972 Mar. 2		CJ1	1462 80
				31	1,201.60	P1	647 30
							2110 10

ACCOUNT Sales Tax Payable — ACCOUNT NO. 241

DATE	ITEM	POST. REF.	DEBIT	DATE	ITEM	POST. REF.	CREDIT
1972 Mar. 8		CJ1	55	1972 Mar. 31		CJ1	24 36
				31	33.51	S1	9 70
							34 06

ACCOUNT Sales — ACCOUNT NO. 411

DATE	ITEM	POST. REF.	DEBIT	DATE	ITEM	POST. REF.	CREDIT
				1972 Mar. 31		CJ1	487 25
				31		S1	193 95
							681 20

ACCOUNT Sales Returns and Allowances — ACCOUNT NO. 041

DATE	ITEM	POST. REF.	DEBIT	DATE	ITEM	POST. REF.	CREDIT
1972 Mar. 8		CJ1	11 00				

The Phillips Store — General Ledger Accounts

ACCOUNT *Purchases*   ACCOUNT NO. 511

DATE	ITEM	POST. REF.	DEBIT	DATE	ITEM	POST. REF.	CREDIT
1972 Mar. 6		CJ1	92 00				
14		CJ1	18 60				
31		P1	647 30				
			757 90				

ACCOUNT *Purchases Returns and Allowances* ACCOUNT NO. 051

DATE	ITEM	POST. REF.	DEBIT	DATE	ITEM	POST. REF.	CREDIT
				1972 Mar. 13		CJ1	23 40

The Phillips Store — General Ledger Accounts (*concluded*)

Schedule of accounts receivable

A list of customers showing the amount due from each one as of a specified date is known as a *schedule of accounts receivable*. It is usually advisable to prepare such a schedule at the end of each month. An example for The Phillips Store as of March 31, 1972, is provided below. Such a schedule can be prepared easily by going through the customers' file and listing the names of the customers and the amount due from each. Should the total not be in agreement with the balance of the summary accounts receivable account, the error may be in either the file or the ledger account. The file may be incorrect in that either one or more sales tickets on which collection has been made have not been removed or that one or more uncollected ones are missing. Another possibility is that a memorandum of a partial collection was overlooked in preparing the list. The accounts receivable account could be incorrect, also, because of an error in posting or because of an error in a journal from which the totals were posted. In any event, the postings, journals, and sales tickets must be checked until the reason for the discrepancy is found so that the necessary correction can be made.

171

The Phillips Store
Schedule of Accounts Receivable
March 31, 1972

Charles F. Joseph	55 23
Peter C. Vance	44 10
A. A. Wright	33 55
	132 88

The Phillips Store — Schedule of Accounts Receivable

Schedule of accounts payable

A list of suppliers showing the amount due to each one as of a specified date is known as a *schedule of accounts payable*. It is usually advisable to prepare such a schedule at the end of each month. An example for The Phillips Store as of March 31, 1972, is provided below. Such a schedule can be prepared easily by going through the unpaid invoice file and listing the names of the suppliers and the amount due to each. Should the total of the schedule not be in agreement with the balance of the summary accounts payable account, the error may be in either the file or the ledger account. The file may be incorrect in that either one or more paid invoices have not been removed or in that one or more unpaid ones are missing. Another possibility is that a memorandum of a partial payment was overlooked in preparing the list. The accounts payable account could be incorrect, also, because of an error in posting or because of an error in a journal from which the total purchases was posted. In any event, the postings, journals, and invoices must be checked until the reason for the discrepancy is found so that the necessary correction can be made.

The Phillips Store
Schedule of Accounts Payable
March 31, 1972

Alex A. Carlton & Son	117 20
City Store Equipment Co.	762 80
Dunn's	321 60
	1201 60

The Phillips Store — Schedule of Accounts Payable

Merchandise inventory

Apart from the fact that the foregoing illustration did not include any transactions or information about various operating expenses, Mr. Phillips could not calculate his net income or net loss for the month because the amount of the merchandise inventory at March 31 was not determined. Lacking this information, cost of goods sold could not be calculated. Since there was no inventory at the first of the month, the amount of the month's purchases of merchandise, $757.90, less the amount of purchases returns and allowances, $23.40, is the cost of the goods that were *available* for sale, $734.50. To calculate the cost of goods *sold*, however, the cost of the goods that remained on hand on March 31 would have to be deducted. The first step would have been to count the items of merchandise in the store at the end of that day. Next, these goods would have to have been assigned a reasonable share of the total purchases cost. Since Mr. Phillips does not expect to calculate monthly net income (or net loss), he will not "take inventory" until the end of the year. This may be December 31, if he plans to keep his records on a calendar year basis, or it might be February 28 (or 29), if he wants to use a fiscal year that ends on the last day of February. Whatever the period chosen, a crucial step in the calculation of the periodic net income (or net loss) of a merchandising business under the accrual basis of accounting is the determination of the merchandise inventory at the end of the fiscal period — a point in time that is also the beginning of the next fiscal period.

When the end of the fiscal period does arrive and the cost to be assigned to the merchandise on hand at that time is calculated, the amount of this calculation will have to be recorded in an asset account. The title of the account usually used is "Merchandise Inventory." This account will be debited; the related credit is made to an account with the title "Expense and Revenue Summary" — a temporary owner's equity account used in summarizing the accounts whose balances enter into the determination of the net income (or loss) for a period. The manner of using the expense and revenue summary account in the end-of-period process of adjusting and closing the books of a retail merchandising business will be explained and illustrated in Chapters 9 and 10.

173

Report No. 6-3

Refer to the workbook and complete Report No. 6-3. After completing the report, you may proceed with the textbook discussion in Chapter 7 until the next report is required.

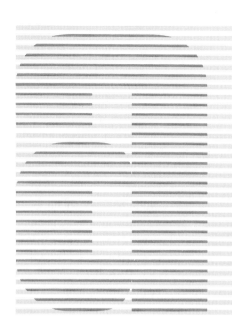

chapter 7

accounting for notes and interest

174

A major characteristic of modern business is the extensive use of credit. Each day hundreds of millions of transactions occur that involve the sale of goods or services in return for promises to pay at a later date for what has been received. Sales of this type are said to be "on credit" or "on account"; they are often described as "charge sales." To facilitate such transactions, the use of *credit cards* has become commonplace. The majority of credit transactions do not involve a written promise to pay a specified amount of money. Often the buyer signs a sales slip or sales ticket, but this is done as an acknowledgment of the receipt of the merchandise or service. When "opening an account" the prospective customer may sign a form or document that obligates him to pay for all purchases that he (and, often, members of his family) may make, but this is a general promise to pay if and when something is purchased.

While not nearly so commonplace as transactions that involve "open account" credit, the use of *promissory notes* (usually just called *notes*) is an important business practice. A promise to repay a loan of money nearly always takes the form of a note. The extension of credit for periods of more than 60 days, or when large amounts of money are involved, usually entails the use of notes. Such notes nearly always have certain legal characteristics that cause them to be *negotiable instruments*. In order to be considered a negotiable instrument, a promissory note must evidence the following:

(a) Be in writing and signed by the person or persons agreeing to make payment.
(b) Be an unconditional promise to pay a certain amount of money.
(c) Be payable to the order of a specified person or firm, or to bearer.
(d) Be payable either on demand or at a definite time.

A promissory note is illustrated below. It will be observed that this note has all of the characteristics listed above. It should also be understood that to Charles Martin it is a *note payable*, while to John Thomas it is a *note receivable*. Charles Martin is known as the *maker* of the note because he is the one who promises to pay. John Thomas is called the *payee* of the note because he is the one who is to receive the specified amount of money.

The note illustrated is interest bearing. This is often, though not always, the case. Sometimes no rate of interest is specified, but it is likely that a transaction in which a nominally non-interest-bearing note is involved will entail some interest. For example, a borrower might give a $1,000 note payable in 60 days to a bank in return for a loan of $987.50. The $12.50 difference between the amount received and the amount that must be repaid when the note matures will become, in reality, interest expense at maturity. Such a difference is described as *prepaid interest* until the date that the note matures. When a bank is involved in such a transaction, the difference between the amount received and the amount to be repaid may be referred to as *bank discount*.

175

$ 465.75   Atlanta, Georgia _____ May 5 ____ 19 72 __

Ninety days _____ AFTER DATE ____ I ____ PROMISE TO PAY TO

THE ORDER OF John Thomas _____

PAYABLE AT **citizens savings bank**

Four hundred sixty-five 75/100 -- DOLLARS

VALUE RECEIVED WITH INTEREST AT 7% _____

No. 5 ____ DUE August 3, 1972

                                   Charles Martin

Model Filled-In Promissory Note

Calculating interest

In calculating interest on notes, it is necessary to take the following factors into consideration:

(a) The principal of the note.
(b) The rate of interest.
(c) The time.

The principal is the face amount of the note — the amount that the maker promises to pay at maturity, apart from any specified interest. The principal is the base on which the interest is calculated.

The rate of interest is usually expressed in the form of a percentage, such as 6 percent or 7 percent. Ordinarily the rate is an annual percentage rate, but in some cases the rate is quoted on a monthly basis, such as 1½ percent a month. A rate of 1½ percent a month is equivalent to a rate of 18 percent a year payable monthly. When a note is interest bearing but the rate is not specified on the face of the note, it is subject to the legal rate, which varies under the laws of the different states.

The days or months from the date of issue of a note to the date of its maturity (or the interest payment date) is the time for which the interest is to be computed. Thus, if a note is payable in 60 days with interest, each and every day is considered in determining the date due, and the exact number of days is used in calculating interest.

When the time in a note is specified in months, the interest should be calculated on the basis of months rather than days. For example, if a note is payable 3 months from date, the interest should be calculated on the basis of 3 months or ¼ of a year. However, when the due date is specified in a note, the time should be computed by figuring the exact number of days that will elapse from the date of the note to the date of its maturity. The interest should then be computed on the basis of this number of days. For example, if a note is dated March 1 and the due date is specified as June 1, the time should be computed in the manner shown at the right.

Days in March	31
Date of note, March	1
Days remaining in March .	30
Days in April	30
Days in May	31
Note matures on June ...	1
Total time in days	92

Notice that in this computation the date of maturity was counted but the date of the note was not counted. If the note had specified "3 months after date" instead of June 1, the interest should be computed on the basis of 90 days instead of 92 days.

In the case of long-term notes, the interest may be payable periodically, such as semiannually or annually.

In computing interest it is customary to consider 360 days as a year. Most banks and business firms follow this practice, though some banks and government agencies use 365 days as the base in computing daily interest. In any case, the formula for computing interest is:

PRINCIPAL × RATE × TIME (usually a fraction of a 360-day year) =
AMOUNT OF INTEREST

The 60-Day, 6 Percent Method. There are many short cuts that may be used in computing interest on the basis of a 360-day year. The interest on any amount for 60 days at 6 percent can be determined simply by moving the decimal point in the amount two places to the left. The reason for this is that 60 days is $\frac{1}{6}$ of a year and the interest on any amount at 6 percent for $\frac{1}{6}$ of a year is the same as the interest at 1 percent for a full year. Thus, the interest on $550 for 60 days at 6 percent is $5.50.

The 60-day, 6 percent method may be used to advantage in many cases even though the actual time may be more or less than 60 days. The following examples will serve to illustrate this fact:

FACTORS

(a) Principal of note, $1,000
(b) Time, 30 days
(c) Rate of interest, 6%

CALCULATION

When the decimal point is moved two places to the left the result is $10
30 days = $\frac{1}{2}$ of 60 days; so the interest amounts to $\frac{1}{2}$ of $10 or $5

FACTORS

(a) Principal of note, $2,000
(b) Time, 120 days
(c) Rate of interest, 6%

CALCULATION

When the decimal point is moved two places to the left the result is $20
120 days = 2 times 60 days; so the interest amounts to 2 times $20 or $40

The 60-day, 6 percent method may also be used to advantage when the actual rate is more or less than 6 percent. The following examples will serve to illustrate this fact:

FACTORS

(a) Principal of note, $1,000
(b) Time, 30 days
(c) Rate of interest, 4%

CALCULATION

Interest at 6% for 60 days = $10
Interest at 6% for 30 days = $5
Interest at 4% = $\frac{2}{3}$ of $5 or $3.33

FACTORS

(a) Principal of note, $3,000
(b) Time, 120 days
(c) Rate of interest, 8%

CALCULATION

Interest at 6% for 60 days = $30
Interest at 6% for 120 days = $60
Interest at 8% = $1\frac{1}{3}$ times $60 or $80

Sometimes it is helpful to determine the interest for 6 days at 6 percent and to use the result as the basis for calculating the actual interest. The interest on any sum for 6 days at 6 percent may be determined simply by moving the decimal point three places to the left. For example, the interest on $1,000 at 6 percent for 6 days is $1. If the actual time were 18 days instead of 6 days, the interest would be three times $1 or $3. This method differs from the 60-day, 6 percent method only in that 6 days is used in the basic computation instead of 60 days.

177

Published tables are available for reference use in determining the amount of interest on stated sums at different rates for any length of time. Such tables are widely used by financial institutions and may also be used by other firms.

Present Value. The *present value* or *present worth* of a note is its value on any day between the date of the note and its maturity. If a note is interest bearing, the present value may be determined by adding the accrued interest to the face of the note. If a note is non-interest bearing, the present value may be determined by subtracting an amount at the discount rate from the face value of the note. This amount is computed for the time that will elapse from the present date to the date of maturity.

It may be necessary to determine the present value of a note **(1)** when the note is being transferred for credit or **(2)** when it is being sold for cash. Consider the following alternative transactions involving the note illustrated on page 175:

    (a) June 16, John Thomas transferred the note to the Hayward Hardware Co. Mr. Hayward agreed to allow him credit for its present value; or

    (b) June 16, John Thomas sold the note to the First National Bank at a discount of 8 percent.

In transaction (a) the note is transferred for credit at its present value. The factors involved in computing its present value are as follows:

FACTORS
(a) Principal of note, $465.75
(b) Time interest has accrued, 42 days (May 5 to June 16)
(c) Rate of interest, 7%

CALCULATION
Interest accrued on $465.75 at 7% for 42 days = $3.80
$465.75 + $3.80 = $469.55, present value

In transaction (b) the note was sold to the First National Bank at a discount of 8 percent. Such a transaction is often referred to as *discounting a note*. It is the custom of banks to calculate the discount on the maturity value of a note. The amount of the discount is then subtracted from the maturity value to find the present value of the note.

FACTORS
(a) Principal of note, $465.75
(b) Time from date of note to date of maturity, 90 days (May 5 to August 3)
(c) Rate of interest, 7%
(d) Time from date of discount to date of maturity, 48 days (June 16 to August 3)
(e) Rate of discount, 8%

CALCULATION
Interest on $465.75 at 7% for 90 days = $8.15
$465.75 + $8.15 = $473.90, maturity value
Discount on $473.90 at 8% for 48 days = $5.05
$473.90 − $5.05 = $468.85, present value

Thus, the interest is computed on the face of the note, while the discount is computed on the maturity value of the note. Interest collected in advance by a bank is called bank discount. Bank discount should not be confused with either *trade discount* or *cash discount*. A trade discount is a discount from the list price of merchandise, while a cash discount is a discount allowed for the payment of an invoice within a specified time. Discounting a note receivable at the bank is a method of borrowing money and using the note as security. Since the party discounting the note must indorse it, he is liable for its maturity value in case the maker does not pay it at maturity. This possible future obligation is known as a *contingent liability*.

Accounting for notes receivable

The following types of transactions involve notes receivable:

(a) Note received in exchange for merchandise or other property.

(b) Note received from customer in return for an extension of time for payment of his obligation.

(c) Note received as security for cash loan.

(d) Note discounted prior to maturity.

(e) Note collected at maturity.

(f) Note renewed at maturity.

(g) Note dishonored.

Note Received in Exchange for Merchandise or Other Property. A note may be accepted in exchange for merchandise or other property. For example, on April 29, C. J. Hayward accepted a 60-day, 7 percent note for $242.50 in exchange for hardware sold to Charles Palmer. This transaction was recorded in the books of the Hayward Hardware Co. by debiting Notes Receivable and by crediting Sales for $242.50.

Note Received from Customer to Obtain an Extension of Time for Payment. When a customer wishes to obtain an extension of time for the payment of his account, he may be willing to issue a note for all or part of the amount due. A merchant may be willing to accept a note in such a case because the note will be a written acknowledgment of the debt and, if cash is needed before the note matures, it may be possible to discount the note at the bank.

Peter Jay owes the Hayward Hardware Co. $522.36 on open account. The account is past due and Mr. Hayward insists upon a settlement. Mr. Jay offers to give his 60-day, 7 percent note. Mr. Hayward accepts Mr. Jay's offer; the note is dated April 10. It was recorded in the books of the Hayward Hardware Co. as indicated by the general journal entry at the top of page 180.

```
April 10.  Notes Receivable..................................   522.36
              Accounts Receivable...........................              522.36
                 Received note from Peter Jay.
```

If, instead of giving a note for the full amount, Mr. Jay gave a check for $22.36 and a note for the balance, the transaction would have been recorded in Mr. Hayward's books as indicated by the following general journal entry:

```
April 10.  Cash..........................................    22.36
              Notes Receivable..............................   500.00
              Accounts Receivable...........................              522.36
                 Received check and note from Peter Jay.
```

(While the foregoing entry is shown in general journal form, it actually would be recorded in the combined cash journal or other appropriate book of original entry being used. This observation applies to all illustrations of entries involving the receipt and disbursement of cash.)

Note Received as Security for Cash Loan. Loans may be secured by notes receivable. For example, Mr. Hayward might lend George Tabor, an employee, $100 on his 90-day, 6 percent note. Such a transaction may be recorded in the books of the Hayward Hardware Co. as indicated by the following general journal entry:

180
```
April 1.  Notes Receivable..................................   100.00
              Cash..........................................              100.00
                 Loaned George Tabor $100.
```

If it is the practice of a firm to make frequent loans to employees, it is generally advisable to keep a separate account for such notes. An appropriate title for such an account is Notes Receivable from Employees.

Note Discounted Prior to Maturity. As previously explained, a note may be discounted at a bank prior to its maturity. It sometimes happens that a merchant is in need of money and, in order to obtain it, he may discount at a bank one or more notes that he owns. Suppose, for example, that on May 1 Mr. Hayward discounted at the First National Bank the note received from Charles Palmer on April 29 and received credit for the proceeds. The rate of discount was 8 percent. The proceeds were computed as follows:

```
Face value of note..............................................   $242.50
Interest at 7% for 60 days......................................      2.83
Maturity value of note..........................................   $245.33
```
Discount period May 1 to June 28 = 58 days
$245.33 at 8% for 58 days = $3.16
$245.33 − $3.16 = $242.17, proceeds

Since the note had been accepted originally by Mr. Hayward at its face value of $242.50 and the proceeds from discounting the note amounted to only $242.17, the difference of 33 cents represents interest expense, which should be debited to an account so titled. This transaction should be recorded in the books of the Hayward Hardware Co. as indicated by the following general journal entry:

```
May 1.  Cash..............................................  242.17
        Interest Expense..................................     .33
          Notes Receivable................................           242.50
          Discounted Charles Palmer's note at the bank.
```

If the proceeds from discounting the note had amounted to more than the face of the note, the difference would represent a gain which should be credited to a revenue account titled *Interest Earned* (or *Interest Income*).

Contingent Liability on Notes Discounted. In discounting the Palmer note at the bank it was necessary for Mr. Hayward to indorse the note. This indorsement had the effect of guaranteeing payment of the note at maturity, because Mr. Hayward would have to pay it if Mr. Palmer should fail to do so. The Hayward Hardware Co. acquired a *contingent liability* — contingent upon Mr. Palmer's failure to pay the note at maturity.

In preparing a balance sheet, it is customary to determine the total amount of any notes that have been discounted but have not yet been paid by their makers (because their maturity dates have not yet arrived) and to indicate the resulting contingent liability. This is usually accomplished by means of a footnote on the balance sheet. The usual plan is to place an asterisk (*) after the amount of the asset notes receivable and to state the amount of the contingent liability at the bottom of the report. For example, if the notes receivable amounted to $14,000 and notes discounted but not yet paid amounted to $3,000, the following statement should be added to the balance sheet in a footnote:

*Contingent liability on notes discounted, $3,000.

If a note that was discounted at a bank is not paid at maturity, the bank will immediately inform the person or firm that indorsed the note and request payment.

Note Collected at Maturity. When a note receivable matures, it may be collected by the holder or he may leave it at his bank for collection. If the maker of the note resides in another locality, the note may be forwarded to a bank in that locality for collection. It is customary for banks to charge a fee for making such collections. When the bank makes the collection, it notifies the holder on a form similar to the credit advice at the top of page 182 that the net amount has been credited to his account. Usually the maker is notified a few days before the maturity of a note so that he may know the due date and the amount that must be paid.

```
                  FIRST NATIONAL BANK
                  ELMWOOD PARK     ILLINOIS

OFFSETTING DR. ●●●●●●●●●●●●●●●●●●●●●●●●●●●●●●●●●●●●●        June 9      19 72
               ●●●●●●●●●●●●●●●●●●●●●●●●●●●●●●●●●●●●●
               ●●●●●●●●●●●●●●●●●●●●●●●●●●●●●●●●●●●●●

         WE CREDIT YOUR ACCOUNT AS FOLLOWS:
         Peter Jay's note                    $522.36
         Interest for 60 days @ 7%              6.09
                                             $528.45
         Less collection charge                10.00     $  518.45

         Hayward Hardware Co.

               1121 Deerfield Avenue      APPROVED  L. G. W.

               Elmwood Park, IL  60635
```

Credit Advice

If George Tabor pays his note in full plus the interest when both are due, the transaction should be recorded in the books of the Hayward Hardware Co. as indicated by the following general journal entry:

```
June 30.  Cash.............................................. 101.50
             Notes Receivable...............................          100.00
             Interest Earned.................................            1.50
                Received $101.50 from George Tabor in settlement of
                his note for $100 and interest $1.50.
```

182

Suppose Mr. Hayward left Peter Jay's note for $522.36 at the First National Bank for collection and on June 9 received the notice of collection reproduced above.

The transaction should be recorded as indicated by the following general journal entry:

```
June 9.  Cash............................................. 518.45
         Collection Expense................................  10.00
             Notes Receivable...............................          522.36
             Interest Earned.................................            6.09
                Received credit for the proceeds of Peter Jay's note
                collected by the bank.
```

Note Renewed at Maturity. If the maker of a note is unable to pay the amount due at maturity, he may be permitted to renew all or part of the note. If, instead of paying his note for $100 at maturity, George Tabor was permitted to pay the interest and renew the note for another 90 days at the same rate of interest, the transaction should be recorded in the books of the Hayward Hardware Co. as indicated by the following general journal entry:

```
June 30.  Notes Receivable (new note)......................... 100.00
          Cash................................................   1.50
             Notes Receivable (old note)......................          100.00
             Interest Earned.................................             1.50
                Received a new note for $100 from George Tabor in
                renewal of his note due today and $1.50 in cash in
                payment of the interest on the old note.
```

Note Dishonored. If the maker of a note refuses or is unable to pay or renew it at maturity, the note is said to be *dishonored*. It thereby loses the quality of negotiability which, in effect, means that it loses its legal status as a note receivable. Usually, the amount is transferred from the notes receivable account to the accounts receivable account pending final disposition of the obligation involved. Suppose, for example, that Mr. Hayward was unable to collect a non-interest-bearing note for $400 received a few weeks before from Paul Johnson, a customer. The following entry should be made in the books of the Hayward Hardware Co.:

```
July 17.  Accounts Receivable..............................   400.00
              Notes Receivable..................................            400.00
          Paul Johnson's note dishonored.
```

If the claim against Mr. Johnson should turn out to be completely worthless, the $400 will have to be removed from the accounts receivable account and recognized as a bad debt loss. The manner of accounting for this type of transaction will be discussed in the next chapter.

Notes receivable register

When many notes are received in the usual course of business, it may be advisable to keep an auxiliary record of such notes that will provide more detailed information than a ledger account. Such an auxiliary record is usually known as a *notes receivable register*. One form of a notes receivable register is reproduced at the bottom of pages 184 and 185. The notes recorded in the illustration were those received by the R. C. Mathews Co. during the period indicated by the record.

The information recorded in the register is obtained directly from the notes received. The notes are numbered consecutively as they are entered in the register. (This number should not be confused with the maker's number.) The due date of each note is calculated and entered in the proper When Due column. The interest to maturity is calculated and entered in the Interest Amount column. When a note is discounted, the name of the bank at which it is discounted and the date are entered in the Discounted columns. When a remittance is received in settlement of a note, the date is entered in the Date Paid column.

Notes receivable account

The information recorded in the notes receivable account should agree with that entered in the notes receivable register. The account shown on page 184 contains a record of the notes that were entered in the notes receivable register of the R. C. Mathews Co. Notice that each note is identified by the number assigned to the note. If the notes are not numbered, each note should be identified by writing the name of the maker in the Item column of the account.

NOTES RECEIVABLE

1972				1972			
Mar. 28	No. 1		250.00	May 27	No. 1		250.00
30	No. 2		300.00	29	No. 4		541.50
30	No. 3		350.00	29	No. 2		300.00
Apr. 1	No. 4		541.50	29	No. 3		350.00
May 1	No. 5		400.00	29	No. 7		450.00
3	No. 6		348.60				*1,891.50*
18	No. 7		450.00				
25	No. 8		264.20				
29	No. 9		250.00				
		1,262.80	*3,154.30*				

Proving the notes receivable account

Periodically (usually at the end of each month) the notes receivable account should be proved by comparing the balance of the account with the total of the notes owned as shown by the notes receivable register. A schedule of the notes owned on May 31 is given below.

184

Notice that the total of this schedule is the same as the balance of the notes receivable account illustrated above.

SCHEDULE OF NOTES OWNED

No. 5	$ 400.00
No. 6	348.60
No. 8	264.20
No. 9	250.00
Total	$1,262.80

PAGE *12* NOTES RECEIVABLE REGISTER

	DATE RECEIVED	No.	BY WHOM PAYABLE	WHERE PAYABLE		DATE MADE		
				BANK OR FIRM	ADDRESS	Mo.	Day	Year
1	*1972* Mar. 28	1	Bronson + Murray	Central Trust	City	Mar.	28	1972
2	30	2	Ralph Steiner	Valley Savings Bk.	Hamilton	Mar.	30	1972
3	30	3	M. R. Nelson	State Bank, Inc.	Dayton	Mar.	30	1972
4	Apr. 1	4	C. A. Arnold	West Side Savings	City	Apr.	1	1972
5	May 1	5	John Weyland	Central Trust	City	May	1	1972
6	3	6	R. S. Whitney	Third National Bk.	Middlefield	Apr.	29	1972
7	18	7	O. M. Olson	Citizens Bank	City	May	18	1972
8	25	8	Walker Brothers	State Bank, Inc.	Dayton	May	23	1972
9	29	9	M. R. Nelson	State Bank, Inc.	Dayton	May	29	1972
10								
11								

Notes Receivable Register (Left Page)

Indorsement of notes

A promissory note is usually made payable to a specified person or firm, though some notes are made payable to "Bearer." If the note is payable to the order of a specified party, he must *indorse* the note to transfer the promise to pay to another party. The two major types of indorsements are **(1)** the *blank indorsement* and (2) the *special indorsement.* When the payee signs only his name on the left end of the back of the note, he is indorsing it in blank. If, instead, he writes the words "Pay to the order of" followed by the name of a specified party and his signature, he is giving a special indorsement. The legal effect of both types of indorsement is much the same. However, a blank indorsement makes a note payable to the bearer, while a special indorsement identifies the party to whose order payment is to be made.

Under certain circumstances the maker of a note may arrange for an additional party to join in the promise to pay, either as a *cosigner* or as an indorser of the note. In the first instance, this other party signs his name below that of the maker of the note on its face. In the second case, the other party makes a blank indorsement on the back of the note, called an *accommodation indorsement.* In either event the payee of the note has two persons to look to for payment. This presumably adds security to the note.

If a partial payment is made on a note, it is common practice to record the date of the payment and the amount paid on the back of the note. This is called *indorsing the payment.*

Shown at the top of page 186 is a reproduction of the back of a promissory note originally made payable to the order of John Maynard. The

185

NOTES RECEIVABLE REGISTER   PAGE *12*

TIME	WHEN DUE				AMOUNT	INTEREST		DISCOUNTED		DATE PAID	REMARKS	
	J	M	J	J	D		RATE	AMT.	BANK	DATE			
60.ds.			27			250 00	7%	2 92			May 27		1
60.ds.			29			300 00	—				May 29	Sent for coll. 5/22	2
60.ds			29			350 00	6%	3 50			May 29	Renewal for $250	3
90.ds.				30		541 50	6%	8 12	Second National	May 29			4
60.ds.				30		400 00	6%	4 00					5
90.ds.				28		348 60	6%	5 23					6
60.ds.				17		450 00	—		Second National	May 29			7
60.ds.				22		264 20	—						8
60.ds.				28		250 00	6%	2 50				Renewal of Note No.3	9
													10
													11

Notes Receivable Register (Right Page)

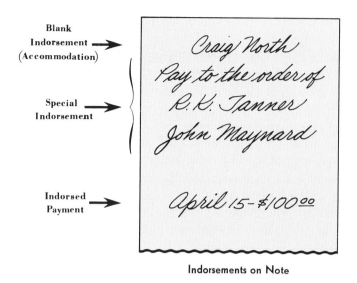

Blank Indorsement (Accommodation)

Special Indorsement

Indorsed Payment

Craig North
Pay to the order of
R. K. Tanner
John Maynard

April 15 - $100⁰⁰

Indorsements on Note

maker of the note (whoever he was) was able to get Craig North to become an accommodation indorser. Later, the payee, Maynard, transferred the note to R. K. Tanner by a special indorsement. On April 15, $100 was paid on the note.

186

Accounting for notes payable

The following types of transactions involve notes payable:

(a) Note issued in exchange for merchandise or other property purchased.

(b) Note issued to a supplier in return for an extension of time for payment of obligation.

(c) Note issued as security for cash loan.

(d) Note paid at maturity.

(e) Note renewed at maturity.

Note Issued in Exchange for Merchandise or Other Property. A note may be issued in exchange for merchandise, long-lived assets, or other property. For example, C. J. Hayward issued a 30-day, 7 percent interest-bearing note for $365 to the Carey Store Equipment Co. in exchange for store equipment purchased April 1. This transaction was recorded in the books of the Hayward Hardware Co. by debiting Store Equipment and by crediting Notes Payable for $365.

Note Issued to a Supplier in Return for Extension of Time for Payment. When a firm wishes to obtain an extension of time for the payment of an account, a note for all or part of the amount due may be acceptable to the supplier. Assume, for example, that the Hayward Hardware Co. owes

Miles & Co. $347.60 and by agreement on May 14 a check on the First National Bank for $47.60 and a 90-day, 7 percent interest-bearing note for $300 are issued. This transaction should be recorded in the books of the Hayward Hardware Co. as indicated by the following general journal entry:

May 14. Accounts Payable...............................	347.60	
Cash...		47.60
Notes Payable......................................		300.00
Issued check for $47.60 and note for $300 to Miles & Co.		

Note Issued as Security for Cash Loan. Many firms experience periods in which receipts from customers in the usual course of business are not adequate to finance their operations. During such periods, it may be necessary to borrow money from banks. Business firms commonly borrow money from banks on short-term notes to help finance their business operations. Assume, for example, that on May 15, C. J. Hayward borrows $3,000 from the First National Bank on a 60-day, 7 percent interest-bearing note. The transaction should be recorded in general journal form as follows:

May 15. Cash..	3,000.00	
Notes Payable...............................		3,000.00
Borrowed $3,000 at the bank on a 60-day, 7% note.		

Commercial banks often deduct interest in advance. If, instead of the transaction described above, Mr. Hayward had issued a $3,000, 60-day, non-interest-bearing note which the bank had discounted at 7 percent, the bank account of the Hayward Hardware Co. would have increased $2,965, and interest expense of $35 would have been recorded as follows:

May 15. Cash..	2,965.00	
Interest Expense..............................	35.00	
Notes Payable..............................		3,000.00
Discounted at 7% a $3,000, 60-day, non-interest-bearing note.		

The $35 debit to Interest Expense at this point is really prepaid interest but, since the amount will become interest expense by the end of the accounting period, it is debited immediately to Interest Expense.

Note Paid at Maturity. When a note payable matures, payment may be made directly to the holder or to a bank where the note was left for collection. The maker will know who the payee is but he may not know who the holder is at maturity because the payee may have transferred the note to another party or he may have left it with a bank for collection. When a note is left with a bank for collection, it is customary for the bank to mail the maker a notice of maturity. For example, the Carey Store Equipment Co. might forward the one-month, 7 percent note of C. J. Hayward for $365 (dated April 1) to the First National Bank for collection, and the bank might notify Mr. Hayward by sending a notice similar to the one reproduced at the top of the next page.

187

```
FIRST NATIONAL BANK
••••••••••••••••••••••
ELMWOOD PARK    ILLINOIS

YOUR NOTE DESCRIBED BELOW WILL BE DUE——▼

MAKER - CO-SIGNER - COLLATERAL   | NUMBER  | DATE DUE |        | AMOUNT
C. J. Hayward                    |         |          | Prin.  | $365.00
Hayward Hardware Co.             | 24-007  | 5-1-72   | Int.   |    2.13
                                 |         |          | Total  | $367.13

ENDORSER


        ┌                                      ┐
        C. J. Hayward
TO      Hayward Hardware Co.
        1121 Deerfield Avenue
        Elmwood Park, IL  60635

        └                                      ┘

NOTE: PLEASE BRING THIS NOTICE WITH YOU.
```

Notice of Maturity of Note

If, upon receiving this notice, Mr. Hayward issued a check to the bank for $367.13 in payment of the note and interest, the transaction should be recorded in the books of the Hayward Hardware Co. as indicated by the following general journal entry:

188

```
May  1.  Notes Payable.....................................  365.00
         Interest Expense..................................    2.13
         Cash..............................................           367.13
         Paid note issued April 1 to the Carey Store Equipment
         Co., plus interest.
```

Note Renewed at Maturity. If the maker is unable to pay a note in full at maturity, he may arrange to renew all or a part of the note. For example,

PAGE 14   NOTES PAYABLE REGISTER

DATE ISSUED		No.	TO WHOM PAYABLE	WHERE PAYABLE		DATE MADE		
				BANK OR FIRM	ADDRESS	Mo.	Day	Year
1972 Mar.	15	1	H. G. Kirk Co.	Valley Savings Bk.	Hamilton	Mar.	15	1972
May	16	2	Pinkney Equipment	Third National Bk.	Middlefield	May	16	1972
	20	3	Third National Bk.	" " "	City	May	20	1972
	22	4	Warner + Young	" " "	"	May	22	1972
	22	5	Davis Trucking	" " "	"	May	22	1972
	29	6	Third National Bk.	" " "	"	May	29	1972

Notes Payable Register (Left Page)

on August 12 Mr. Hayward might pay the $5.25 interest and $100 on the principal of the note for $300 issued to Miles & Co. on May 14 and give them a new 60-day, 7 percent note for $200. This transaction should be recorded as indicated in the following general journal entry:

Aug. 12. Notes Payable (old note)............................	300.00	
Interest Expense...................................	5.25	
Cash..		105.25
Notes Payable (new note)........................		200.00
Issued a check for $105.25 and a note for $200 to Miles & Co. in settlement of a note for $300 plus interest.		

Notes payable register

When many notes are issued in the usual course of business, it may be advisable to keep an auxiliary record of such notes that will provide more detailed information than a ledger account. Such an auxiliary record is usually known as a *notes payable register*. One form of such a register is reproduced on the previous page and below. The notes recorded in the illustration were those issued by the R. C. Mathews Co. during the period indicated by the record.

The information recorded in the register may be obtained directly from the note before it is mailed or given to the payee, or from a note stub. Blank notes are usually made up in pads with stubs attached on which spaces are provided for recording such essential information as amount, payee, where payable, date, time, rate of interest, and number. The due date of each note is calculated and entered in the proper When Due column of the register. The interest at maturity is also calculated and entered in the Interest Amount column. When a note is paid, the date is entered in the Date Paid column.

NOTES PAYABLE REGISTER — PAGE 14

	TIME	WHEN DUE												AMOUNT	INTEREST		DATE PAID	REMARKS	
		J	F	M	A	M	J	J	A	S	O	N	D		RATE	AMOUNT			
1	90 ds.						13							225 00	—		June 13	In settlement of Jan. 15 inv.	1
2	60 ds.							15						478 80	6%	4 79			2
3	90 ds.								18					2000 00	7%	35 00			3
4	3 mo.								22					400 00	6%	6 00			4
5	6 mo.											22		350 00	6%	10 50		Purchased used truck	5
6	60 ds.						28							2500 00	7%	29 17			6
7																			7
8																			8
9																			9
10																			10

Notes Payable Register (Right Page)

Notes payable account

The information recorded in the notes payable account should agree with that recorded in the notes payable register. The following account contains a record of the notes that were entered in the notes payable register of the R. C. Mathews Co.

NOTES PAYABLE

1972				1972					
June 13	No. 1		225.00	Mar. 15	No. 1			225.00	
				May 16	No. 2			478.80	
				20	No. 3			2,000.00	
				22	No. 4			400.00	
				22	No. 5			350.00	
				29	No. 6			2,500.00	
							5,728.80	5,953.80	

Proving the notes payable account

Periodically (usually at the end of each month) the notes payable account should be proved by comparing the balance of the account with the total notes outstanding as shown by the notes payable register. A schedule of the notes outstanding on June 30 is given below. Notice that the total of this schedule is the same as the balance of the notes payable account.

SCHEDULE OF NOTES OUTSTANDING

No. 2............................	$ 478.80
No. 3............................	2,000.00
No. 4............................	400.00
No. 5............................	350.00
No. 6............................	2,500.00
Total........................	$5,728.80

Accrued interest receivable

While interest on a note literally accrues day by day, it is impractical to keep a daily record of such accruals. If the life of a note receivable is entirely within the accounting period, no record need be made of interest until the amount is received.

If, however, the business owns some interest-bearing notes receivable at the end of the accounting period, neither the net income for the period nor the assets at the end of the period will be correctly stated unless the interest accrued on notes receivable is taken into consideration. It is, therefore, customary to adjust the accounts by debiting Accrued Interest Receivable and by crediting Interest Earned for the amount of interest that has accrued to the end of the period. The amount of the accrual may be computed by reference to the notes themselves or to the record provided by a notes receivable register. Suppose, for example, that at the end of a fiscal year ending June 30, a business owns four interest-bearing notes. The amount of each note, the date of issue, the rate of interest, the number of days from issue date to June 30, and the interest accrued on June 30 are shown in the following schedule:

SCHEDULE OF ACCRUED INTEREST ON NOTES RECEIVABLE

PRINCIPAL	DATE OF ISSUE	RATE OF INTEREST	DAYS FROM ISSUE DATE TO JUNE 30	ACCRUED INTEREST JUNE 30
$500.00	April 16	6%	75	$ 6.25
300.00	May 4	7%	57	3.33
348.50	May 31	6%	30	1.74
500.00	June 15	6%	15	1.25

Total accrued interest on notes receivable................$12.57

The entry, in general journal form, to record the interest accrued on June 30 is as follows:

June 30. Accrued Interest Receivable...................... 12.57
        Interest Earned................................. 12.57
        Interest accrued on notes receivable as of June 30.

In preparing the financial statements at the end of the year, the balance of the interest earned account (which will include the $12.57 interest earned but not yet received) will be reported in the income statement, while the balance of the account with Accrued Interest Receivable will be reported in the balance sheet as a current asset.

Accrued interest payable

Neither the expenses of a period nor the liabilities at the end of the period will be correctly stated unless the interest accrued on notes payable is taken into consideration. The mechanics of calculating the amount of interest accrued on notes payable are the same as in the case of notes receivable. If a notes payable register is kept, it should provide the information needed in computing the amount of interest accrued on notes payable. If the total amount of such accrued interest was calculated to be $34.87, and the fiscal period ended June 30, the proper adjusting entry may be made in general journal form as follows:

June 30. Interest Expense................................. 34.87
        Accrued Interest Payable...................... 34.87
        Interest accrued on notes payable as of June 30.

In preparing the financial statements at the end of the year, the balance of the interest expense account (which will include the $34.87 interest incurred but not yet paid) will be reported in the income statement, while the balance of the account with Accrued Interest Payable will be reported in the balance sheet as a current liability.

Drafts and trade acceptances

In addition to promissory notes, there are some other documents or instruments which are sometimes used in connection with the extension of business credit or the settlement of business obligations that have certain qualities in common with notes. Examples include drafts (some versions of which are called "bills of exchange") and trade acceptances. Essentially, a *draft* is an order by one party (the *drawer*) to another party (the *drawee*) to pay a specified amount of money to a third party (the *payee*). There are several varieties of drafts. An ordinary bank check is a draft. Commercial banks often have money on deposit in other banks. Withdrawals are made by using *bank drafts*. When a seller of goods is not well acquainted with a buyer in a different locality, he may draw a *sight draft* (one that is to be paid as soon as the drawee sees it) on the buyer and attach to the draft the *bill of lading* that relates to the property involved. (A bill of lading is prepared by the transporting company, such as a railroad, trucking company, or airline.) Usually the buyer is ordered to pay a bank. The draft and attached bill of lading are sent to this bank. An employee of the bank "presents" these documents to the buyer (the drawee of the draft). It is only by paying ("honoring") such a draft that the buyer can get the bill of lading and thereby obtain the property. The bank remits the amount collected (less a fee for the service) to the seller. The accounting for all this is usually quite simple. The seller either waits until he is paid and then records the collection as a cash sale, or he treats the sale as having been on account when the shipment was made, followed by a cash collection. On the other hand, the buyer accounts for the transaction as a cash purchase — usually a purchase of merchandise, but other property such as equipment might be involved.

Drafts of the type referred to are not essentially credit instruments; rather, they are devices used to facilitate the transfer of money from one person or firm to another under certain circumstances. The characteristic that these drafts have in common with notes is that normally they are negotiable instruments. This is because they are in writing, use the proper legal phraseology, specify the amount involved, are signed, dated, etc.

When one party orders another to make payment at some later date (for example, "60 days after sight" or "60 days after date") and the party addressed agrees to do so in writing on the face of the instrument, it becomes, in effect, a promissory note. Instruments of this type are known as *time drafts* or *trade acceptances*. They may be accounted for in the same manner as notes — notes receivable from the standpoint of the drawer of the instrument and notes payable from the standpoint of the one who accepts it. Normally, time drafts and trade acceptances do not specifically call for any interest. However, as with non-interest-bearing notes, interest will arise if discounting of drafts and trade acceptances is involved — which is often the case.

Report No. 7-1

Complete Report No. 7-1 in the workbook and submit your working papers to the instructor for approval. Then continue with the next study assignment in Chapter 8 until Report No. 8-1 is required.

193

chapter 8

accrual accounting applied to a retail business

A business enterprise that purchases and sells goods on account, maintains a stock of merchandise, and has long-lived assets must account for periodic income or loss on the accrual basis. This is a necessity both for the sake of measuring the success of the business from the standpoint of the owner and in order to comply with federal and state income tax laws. Several of the features of this type of accounting have been introduced in the preceding pages. A more detailed consideration of these procedures and the introduction of the other major practices that constitute accrual accounting will be presented in this and the two following chapters. To make the discussion realistic, it will center around the accounting records of a retail appliance business called The Adams Appliance Store, owned and operated by R. L. Adams. It should be recognized, however, that most of the principles and procedures discussed and illustrated are equally applicable to many other types of businesses.

Principles and procedures

The discussion will continue to be a blend of accounting principles and bookkeeping practices. It is important to keep in mind that the principles relate to goals and objectives while bookkeeping practices are designed to attain these goals and objectives. Such procedures as double entry and the use of business papers, journals, and ledger accounts are employed to make the record-keeping process complete, orderly, and as error-free as possible. While most accounting principles are broad enough to allow considerable flexibility, it is in the area of bookkeeping procedures that wide latitude is found. Within limits, the records for each business can be styled to meet the particular requirements of the management.

Accrual accounting

The *accrual basis of accounting* consists of recording revenue in the period in which it is earned and expenses in the period in which they are incurred. The receipt or disbursement of cash in the same period may or may not be involved. Revenue is considered to be earned when, in exchange for something of value, money is received or a legal claim to money comes into existence. To a merchant, this normally means the time at which the customer buys the goods and either pays for them or agrees to pay for them. In terms of changes in the accounting elements, revenue arises or accrues when an increase in cash or in a receivable causes an increase in owner's equity (except in cases where the increase is due to an investment of assets in the business by the owner). In comparable terms, expense accrues or is incurred when either a reduction in some asset or an increase in a liability causes the owner's equity to be reduced (except in cases where the owner's withdrawal of assets reduces the owner's equity).

195

In keeping business records the accountant must think in terms of time intervals. He must be sure that revenue and expense are accounted for in the proper accounting period. Within a period, the recognition of many types of revenue and expense at precisely the moment this revenue or expense arises is not so important nor is it usually practicable. For example, the expense of having a salaried employee literally accrues minute by minute during each working day; but if the salary will be paid by the end of the period, no record is made of the expense until it is paid. If, on the other hand, the employee was not paid by the end of the period, the accountant should record the liability and expense at that time. A lag in recording revenue and expense is not serious within the accounting period, but steps must be taken at the end of the period to be sure that all revenue earned and expenses incurred are recorded. These steps consist of making what are called *end-of-period adjustments* in the accounts.

The accrual basis of accounting is widely used because it is suited to the needs of enterprises employing it. It involves the period-by-period matching of revenue with the expenses that caused or aided in producing revenue. The revenue from sales, for example, must be matched against the cost of the goods sold and the various expenses that were incurred in conducting the business. A simple matching of cash received from customers during a period with the cash paid for goods purchased in that period would be almost meaningless in most cases. The collections might relate to sales of a prior period and the payments to purchases of the current period, or vice versa. The expense related to most long-lived assets does not arise when the property is acquired; the expense occurs as the usefulness of the property is gradually exhausted. The accrual basis recognizes changes in many types of assets and liabilities in computing net income for a specified period — not just changes in the cash account.

The chart of accounts

The importance of classifying accounts in an orderly and systematic manner, identifying each account by assigning it a number to assist in locating it in the ledger, and maintaining a list of the accounts — called a *chart of accounts* — has been discussed and illustrated in preceding chapters. The chart of accounts for the retail business that is used as a basis of the discussion and illustration in this chapter and in the two chapters that follow is shown at the top of page 197.

The pattern of numbers or code shown in the illustration is fairly typical of the arrangement used by many businesses. However, numerous variations are possible. Sometimes letters as well as numbers are made a part of the code. When numbers are used, it is not uncommon for special columns in journals to be headed by just the number, rather than the name, of the account involved. In a system of records that requires numerous accounts, the use of account numbers virtually displaces account names for all but statement purposes. This has been the case for many decades. Furthermore, in recent years account numbers have become essential to the development of a computer-based accounting system. (Note that no account number ends in zero. This is because a zero at the end of a number has no special significance in electronic data processing.)

The nature of many of the accounts included in the chart of accounts for The Adams Appliance Store should be apparent as they have been described and their use has been illustrated. However, the chart includes certain accounts that are needed in recording several types of transactions and events that have either not yet been considered, or only briefly mentioned. These accounts will be discussed prior to illustrating the accounting records of The Adams Appliance Store.

If this chart of accounts is compared with the accounts in the general ledger illustrated on pages 228–233, it will be noted that the ledger illustra-

THE ADAMS APPLIANCE STORE

CHART OF ACCOUNTS

Assets*

  Cash
    111 Columbia National Bank
    112 Petty Cash Fund

  Receivables
    121 Notes Receivable
    122 Accrued Interest Receivable
    123 Accounts Receivable
       012 Allowance for Bad Debts

  Merchandise Inventory
    131 Merchandise Inventory

  Prepaid Expenses
    141 Prepaid Insurance
    151 Stationery and Supplies

  Long-Lived Assets
    181 Store Equipment
       018 Accumulated Depreciation
          —Store Equipment
    191 Delivery Equipment
       019 Accumulated Depreciation
          —Delivery Equipment

Liabilities
    211 Notes Payable
    221 Accrued Interest Payable
    231 Accounts Payable
    241 Sales Tax Payable
    251 FICA Tax Payable
    261 Employees Income Tax Payable
    271 FUTA Tax Payable
    281 State Unemployment Tax Payable

Owner's Equity
    311 R. L. Adams, Capital
    031 R. L. Adams, Drawing
    321 Expense and Revenue Summary

Revenue from Sales
    411 Sales
       041 Sales Returns and Allowances

Cost of Goods Sold
    511 Purchases
       051 Purchases Returns and Allowances
       052 Purchases Discount

Operating Expenses
    611 Rent Expense
    612 Depreciation Expense
    613 Salaries and Commissions Expense
    614 Payroll Taxes Expense
    615 Heating and Lighting Expense
    616 Stationery and Supplies Expense
    617 Telephone and Telegraph Expense
    618 Advertising Expense
    619 Bad Debts Expense
    621 Insurance Expense
    622 Truck Expense
    623 Charitable Contributions Expense
    624 Miscellaneous Expense

Other Revenue
    711 Interest Earned

Other Expenses
    811 Interest Expense

Words in italics represent headings and not account titles.

tion does not include accounts 122, 221, 321, 612, 616, 619 and 621. This is because these accounts are not needed to record routine transactions. When the matter of adjusting entries and closing entries is discussed and illustrated in the following chapters, these accounts will be shown.

Accounting for bad debts

Businesses that sell goods or services on account realize that all of the customers may not pay all that they owe. The amounts that cannot be collected are called *bad debts*, *bad debts expense*, or *loss from bad debts*. The last designation is slightly misleading because, while the amounts that cannot be collected are certainly losses, they are losses that may reasonably be expected since they are the direct result of selling on account to encourage a larger volume of sales. The amount of such losses depends to a large degree upon the credit policy of a business. The seller should seek to avoid the two extremes of either having such a "liberal" credit policy that bad debts become excessive, or having such a "tight" credit policy that bad debt losses are minimized at the sacrifice of a larger volume of sales and greater net income.

It would be possible to wait until it was certain that the amount due from a customer would never be collected before writing off the amount by a debit to Bad Debts Expense and by a credit to Accounts Receivable. This procedure is sometimes followed. However, it is considered to be better accounting to estimate the amount of bad debt losses that will eventually result from the sales of a period and to treat the estimated amount of expected losses as an expense of that same period. The latter treatment is considered to result in better periodic matching of revenue and expense. The procedure is to use a *contra* account entitled Allowance for Bad Debts (sometimes called Allowance for Doubtful Accounts or Reserve for Bad Debts). This account is contra to the receivable accounts which means its balance will be deducted from the total of the receivable accounts. At the end of the accounting period, an estimate of the expected bad debt losses is made, and an adjusting entry is made by debiting Bad Debts Expense and by crediting Allowance for Bad Debts. To illustrate, suppose that in view of past experience, it is expected that there will be a loss of an amount equal to one half of one percent of the sales on account during the year. If such sales amounted to $100,000, the estimated bad debt losses would be $500 which should be recorded as follows:

```
Dec. 31. Bad Debts Expense.............................  500.00
            Allowance for Bad Debts.......................              500.00
            Bad debts expense provision for the year.
```

The amount of the debit balance in the bad debts expense account is reported in the income statement as an operating expense. The amount of the credit balance in the allowance for bad debts account is reported in the balance sheet as a deduction from the sum of the receivables. This arrangement serves to show the net amount of receivables that is expected to be collected.

It should be apparent that the credit part of the adjusting entry cannot be made directly to one of the receivable accounts because, at the time this entry is made, there is no way of knowing exactly which of the debtors will not pay. Experience gives virtual assurance that some of the amounts due will be uncollectible but only time will reveal which ones.

When it is determined that a certain account will not be collected, an entry should be made to write off the account and to charge the loss against the allowance. Suppose, for example, that on April 22 of the next year, it is determined that $75 owed by Stuart Palmer cannot be collected. Perhaps he died sometime before and it is found that he left no property, or perhaps he became bankrupt, or left town and cannot be traced. Whatever the circumstance, if it is fairly certain that the amount will not be collected, the following journal entry should be made:

```
April 22.  Allowance for Bad Debts......................   75.00
           Accounts Receivable..........................          75.00
               To write off account of Stuart Palmer found to
               be uncollectible.
```

Sometimes the allowance for bad debts account will show a debit balance at the end of the accounting period. This happens when the total amount of estimated uncollectible customers' accounts for the year is smaller than the total amount of such accounts actually written off during the year. When this condition is encountered, the adjusting entry for estimated bad debts must **(1)** cover this debit balance, and **(2)** provide for the expected bad debt losses of the coming year. To illustrate, assume sales on account for the year of $100,000, estimated bad debt losses of $500, and a $250 debit balance in the allowance for bad debts account. The required adjusting entry would be as follows:

```
Dec. 31.  Bad Debts Expense............................   750.00
          Allowance for Bad Debts......................          750.00
              To record deficiency in bad debts expense for
              previous year and bad debts expense provision for
              coming year.
```

The chart of accounts for The Adams Appliance Store includes Allow-   **199**
ance for Bad Debts, Account No. 012, and Bad Debts Expense, Account
No. 619, to provide for recording bad debts expense and subsequent write-
offs of the uncollectible accounts.

Accounting for prepaid expenses

The term *prepaid expense* is largely self-explanatory. It refers to something that has been bought that is properly considered an asset when acquired, but which will eventually be consumed or used up and thus become an expense. Prepaid (unexpired) insurance and supplies of various sorts are leading examples. At the end of the period, the portion of such assets that has expired or has been consumed must be determined and an entry made debiting the proper expense accounts and crediting the proper prepaid expense accounts.

The chart of accounts for The Adams Appliance Store includes two prepaid expense accounts, Prepaid Insurance, Account No. 141, and Stationery and Supplies, Account No. 151. These accounts are classified as assets in the chart of accounts. The account with Prepaid Insurance should be debited for the cost of the insurance purchased. At the end of the year the account should be credited for the portion of the cost that relates to the year then ending with an offsetting debit to Insurance Expense, Account No. 621. The account with Stationery and Supplies should be debited for the cost of stationery and supplies purchased. At the end of the year the account should be credited for the cost of stationery and supplies consumed or used during the year with an offsetting debit to Stationery and Supplies Expense, Account No. 616.

Accounting for depreciation

Depreciation accounting is the process of attempting to allocate the cost of most long-lived assets to the periods expected to benefit from the use of these assets. Most long-lived assets eventually become useless to the business either because they wear out or because they become inadequate or obsolete. Sometimes all three of these causes combine to make the assets valueless except, perhaps, for some small value as scrap or junk.

Generally, in computing depreciation, no consideration is given to what these assets might bring if they were to be sold. Assets of this type are acquired to be used and not to be sold. During their useful life their resale value is of no consequence unless the business is about to cease. For a going business, the idea is to allocate the net cost of such assets over the years they are expected to serve. By "net cost" is meant original cost less estimated scrap or salvage value. Inasmuch as the possibility of scrap or salvage value is commonly ignored, it is usually the original cost of the assets that is allocated.

It should be apparent that depreciation expense can be no more than an estimate. Usually there is no way of knowing just how long an asset will serve. However, with past experience as a guide, the estimates can be reasonably reliable.

There are several ways of calculating the periodic depreciation write-off. Traditionally, the so-called *straight-line method* has been widely used. With this method, the original cost (or cost less any expected scrap value) of an asset is divided by the number of years the asset is expected to serve to find the amount that is to be considered as depreciation expense each year. It is common practice to express depreciation as a percentage of the original cost of the asset. For example, in the case of an asset with a 10-year life, 10 percent of the original cost should be written off each year; for a 20-year asset, 5 percent should be written off.

There are some depreciation methods that permit larger write-offs in the earlier years of the life of the asset. In 1954 the Internal Revenue Code was revised to permit taxpayers to use certain of these methods in calculating net income subject to tax, though these methods primarily are useful only in the case of new assets. This change in the law has stimulated the use of

200

these "reducing-charge" methods. ("Reducing-charge" means a successively smaller write-off each year.) However, the straight-line method has been very popular in the past, and it has a number of virtues including simplicity. Straight-line depreciation is widely used. The straight-line method of accounting for depreciation is used by The Adams Appliance Store.

Depreciation expense is recorded by an end-of-period adjusting entry that involves debiting one or more depreciation expense accounts and crediting one or more accumulated depreciation (sometimes called allowance for depreciation) accounts. The latter accounts are contra accounts — contra to the accounts for the assets that are being depreciated. In theory there would be no objection to making the credits directly to the asset accounts themselves (in the same way that the asset accounts for prepaid expenses are credited to record their decreases). However, in order that the original cost of the assets will be clearly revealed, any portions of this cost written off are credited to the contra accounts. The amounts of the credit balances of the contra accounts are reported in the balance sheet as deductions from the costs of the assets to which they relate.

The credit balances in the accumulated depreciation accounts get larger year by year. When the amounts become equal to the cost of the assets, no more depreciation may be taken.

The difference between the allowance for bad debts account and the accumulated depreciation account should be recognized. Both are credited by adjusting entries at the end of the period. In both cases, the offsetting debits go to expense accounts. In both cases, the balances in the contra accounts are shown in the balance sheet as subtractions from the amounts of the assets to which they relate. However, the allowance for bad debts account is debited whenever anticipated bad debts materialize. The balance of this allowance account does not get continually larger. (If it does, this indicates that the estimate of bad debt losses has been excessive.) In contrast, the credit balances of the accumulated depreciation accounts will get larger year by year, often for many years. The credit balances remain in these accounts for as long as the assets to which they relate are kept in service.

Since The Adams Appliance Store has two classes of long-lived assets that are subject to depreciation — store equipment and delivery equipment — there are two contra accounts, Accumulated Depreciation—Store Equipment, Account No. 018, and Accumulated Depreciation—Delivery Equipment, Account No. 019. Although depreciation expense could be classified by the type of asset to which the depreciation relates, just one account, Depreciation Expense, Account No. 612, is used by The Adams Appliance Store.

Purchases discount

Purchase invoices representing purchases on account may be subject to discount if paid within a specified time. Retailers may be allowed a discount by wholesalers on invoices that are paid within a specified time, such as five days, ten days, or fifteen days, from the date of the invoice. This is known as a *cash discount* and it should not be confused with trade discounts allowed by wholesalers.

Trade discounts are the discounts allowed retailers from the list or catalog prices of wholesalers. Such trade discounts are usually shown as deductions on the invoice and only the net amount is recorded as the purchase price. If the invoice is subject to an additional discount for cash, it will be indicated on the invoice under the heading of "Terms." For example, the terms may be specified as "2/10, n/30," which means that if paid within ten days from the date of the invoice a discount of 2 percent may be deducted; otherwise the net amount of the invoice (after any trade discounts) is payable within thirty days.

To facilitate the payment of invoices in time to be entitled to any discount offered, Mr. Adams follows the policy of filing each invoice in an unpaid invoice file according to the date it should be paid. It is, therefore, only necessary to refer to the file each day to determine which invoices are due on that date and which may be subject to discount. Any amount of cash discount deducted when paying an invoice should be recorded as a credit to Purchases Discount, Account No. 052. Thus, if an invoice for $140, subject to a discount of 2 percent if paid within ten days, is paid within the specified time, the payment should be recorded by debiting Accounts Payable for $140, by crediting the bank account for $137.20, and by crediting Purchases Discount for $2.80. The purchases discount account has a credit balance and (along with Purchases Returns and Allowances) is reported as a deduction from the gross amount of purchases in the cost of goods sold section of the income statement. Some businesses report the credit balance in the purchases discount account as "other revenue." Although this latter practice is not uncommon, the trend definitely favors the practice of regarding discount earned for prompt payment of purchase invoices as a deduction from the gross amount of purchases rather than as other revenue.

Accounts with suppliers and customers

As previously explained, a record of the amounts due to suppliers for purchases on account and the amounts due from customers for sales on account may be kept without maintaining a separate ledger account for each supplier and for each customer. A file of unpaid vendors' invoices and another of sales slips for sales on account may suffice. Many merchants, however, prefer to keep a separate ledger account for each supplier and for each customer.

Subsidiary Ledgers. When the character of the enterprise and the volume of business are such that it is necessary to keep relatively few accounts, it may be satisfactory to keep all of the accounts together in a single general ledger, which may be bound, loose-leaf, or a set of cards. However, when the volume of business and the number of transactions warrant employment of more than one bookkeeper to keep the records, it may be advisable to subdivide the ledger. In some businesses it is necessary to keep separate accounts with thousands of customers and suppliers. In such cases it usually is considered advisable to segregate the accounts with customers and the accounts with suppliers from the other accounts and to keep them in separate ledgers known as *subsidiary ledgers.*

Balance-Column Account Form. A special account form known as the balance-column account form is widely used in keeping the individual accounts with customers and suppliers. While the standard account form, shown in the illustration on page 12, may be used satisfactorily for customers' and suppliers' accounts, most accountants favor the use of the *balance-column account form* shown below for such accounts. It will be noted that three parallel amount columns are provided for recording debits, credits, and balances. Following each entry the new balance may be determined and recorded in the Balance column, or if preferred, the balance may be determined and recorded at the end of each month.

NAME

ADDRESS

DATE	ITEM	POST. REF.	DEBIT	CREDIT	BALANCE

Balance-Column Account Form

Control accounts

When subsidiary ledgers are kept for suppliers and for customers, it is customary to keep *control accounts* for the subsidiary ledgers in the general ledger. Thus, if accounts with suppliers are kept in a subsidiary accounts payable ledger, a control account for accounts payable should be kept in the general ledger; if accounts with customers are kept in a subsidiary accounts receivable ledger, a control account for accounts receivable should be kept in the general ledger. The use of control accounts in the general ledger makes it possible to take a trial balance of the general ledger accounts without reference to the subsidiary ledgers.

Accounts Payable Control. The accounts payable control account provides a summary of the information recorded in the individual accounts with suppliers kept in a subsidiary accounts payable ledger. Transactions affecting suppliers' accounts are posted separately to the individual accounts in the subsidiary ledger. These transactions may also be posted separately, or may be summarized periodically and the totals posted, to the control account in the general ledger. The balance of the accounts payable control account may be proved by preparing a schedule of the individual account balances in the accounts payable ledger.

Accounts with suppliers normally have credit balances. If a supplier's account has a debit balance, the balance may be circled or be written in red ink. In preparing the schedule of accounts payable, the total of the accounts with debit balances should be deducted from the total of the accounts with credit balances, and the difference should agree with the balance of the accounts payable control account.

Accounts Receivable Control. The accounts receivable control account provides a summary of the information recorded in the individual accounts with customers kept in a subsidiary accounts receivable ledger. Transactions affecting customers' accounts are posted separately to the individual accounts in the subsidiary ledger. These transactions may also be posted separately, or may be summarized periodically and the totals posted to the control account in the general ledger. The balance of the accounts receivable control account may be proved by preparing a schedule of the individual account balances in the accounts receivable ledger.

Accounts with customers normally have debit balances. If a customer's account has a credit balance, the balance may be circled or be written in red ink. In preparing the schedule of accounts receivable, the total of the accounts with credit balances should be deducted from the total of the accounts with debit balances and the difference should agree with the balance of the accounts receivable control account.

Posting from the books of original entry

Posting to the individual accounts with suppliers and customers in the respective subsidiary ledgers may be done either from the books of original entry or directly from vouchers or other documents that represent the transactions. When the posting is done from the books of original entry, each item should, of course, be posted separately to the proper account and as the posting is completed the proper cross-reference should be made in the Posting Reference column of the book of original entry and in the Posting Reference column of the ledger account. Under this plan the voucher or other document that represents the transaction may be filed after the transaction is recorded in the appropriate book of original entry. As each transaction is recorded in a book of original entry, care must be taken to enter all of the information that will be needed when posting.

Posting from vouchers or other documents

When the posting is done directly from the vouchers or other documents that represent the transactions, the transactions usually will be recorded first in the proper books of original entry, after which the vouchers or other documents will be referred to the bookkeeper in charge of the suppliers' and customers' accounts for direct posting.

Posting to the individual accounts with suppliers

It is necessary to post all items that represent increases or decreases in the amount owed to each supplier. A list of vouchers or other documents that usually represent transactions completed with suppliers is shown below. The usual posting reference is also indicated.

VOUCHER OR DOCUMENT	TRANSACTION REPRESENTED	POSTING REFERENCE
(a) Purchase invoice No. 1	Purchase	P 1
(b) Charge-back invoice No. 1	Return or allowance	CB 1
(c) Check stub No. 1	Payment on account	Ck 1
(d) Note issued No. 1	Temporary settlement of account	N 1

The purchase invoices and charge-back invoices are usually numbered consecutively as they are received and issued. These numbers should not be confused with the numbers used by the vendor (supplier). The check stubs should be numbered consecutively to agree with the numbers of the checks issued. As the posting is completed, the proper cross-reference should be made in the Posting Reference column of the account and on the voucher or other document. If a loose-leaf ledger is used and accounts with suppliers are kept in alphabetic order, the posting may be indicated by means of a distinctive check mark on the voucher or other document.

Posting to the individual accounts with customers

It is necessary to post all items that represent increases or decreases in the amount owed by each customer. Following is a list of vouchers or other documents that usually represent transactions completed with customers. The usual posting reference is also indicated.

VOUCHER OR DOCUMENT	TRANSACTION REPRESENTED	POSTING REFERENCE
(a) Sale ticket No. 1	Sale	S 1
(b) Credit memo No. 1	Return or allowance	CM 1
(c) Remittance received	Collection on account	C
(d) Note received	Temporary settlement of account	N

The sales tickets usually are prepared in duplicate or triplicate and are numbered consecutively. Each salesperson may use a different series of numbers. One copy is retained for the use of the bookkeeper and another copy is given to the customer.

Credit memorandums issued to customers in connection with sales returns or allowances are usually prepared in duplicate and are numbered consecutively. One copy goes to the customer and the other copy is retained for the use of the bookkeeper.

Remittances received from customers may consist of cash or cash items, such as checks, bank drafts, and money orders. When the remittance is in the form of cash, it is customary to issue a receipt. The receipt may be issued in duplicate, in which case the duplicate copy will provide the information needed for the purpose of posting to the customer's account. Sometimes receipt stubs are used to record the information for posting purposes. When the remittance is in the form of a check, it is not necessary to issue a receipt as the canceled check will serve as a receipt for the customer.

Posting a credit to the customer's account may be made directly from the check or from a list of checks received. Sometimes all remittances received daily are listed in such a manner as to provide the information needed for posting purposes. When this plan is followed, the bookkeeper need not handle the remittances at all. It is a quite common practice to use a form of monthly statement of account in which the upper portion (containing the customer's name and address) is to be detached and sent in along with the remittance. The amount of the remittance is noted on this slip of paper which then contains all the information needed to post the correct credit to the proper customer's account. If the customer does not send in (or bring in) the top part of the statement, a receipt or memo is prepared to serve the same purpose. This procedure is especially suitable when it is possible to separate the functions of **(1)** handling the cash and cash items, and **(2)** recording the credits to the customers' accounts.

As the posting is completed, the proper cross-reference should be made in the Posting Reference column of the account and on the voucher or other document. If a loose-leaf ledger is used and accounts with customers are kept in alphabetic order, the posting may be indicated by means of a distinctive check mark or by initialing the voucher or other document.

Accountants generally prefer to post from the basic documents rather than from the books of original entry to the individual accounts with suppliers and customers because such procedure provides better control and promotes accuracy. When a purchase invoice is recorded in a purchases journal by one person and is posted directly from the invoice to the proper supplier's account by another person, it is unlikely that both persons will make the same mistake. Even if the posting is done by the person who also keeps the purchases journal, there is less likelihood of making a mistake than when the posting is done from the purchases journal. If a mistake were made in recording the amount of the invoice in the purchases journal, the same mistake would almost certainly be made in posting from the purchases journal to the supplier's account. The same reasoning may be applied to the recording of sales transactions and all other transactions that affect accounts with suppliers and customers.

Statement of account

When merchandise is sold on account, it is customary to render a monthly statement of account to each charge customer. Usually the statements are mailed as soon as they can be completed following the close of each month. In order that statements may be mailed on the first of each month, some firms follow the policy of including transactions completed up to the 25th of the preceding month. Such statements are an aid to collection. When a remittance is not received from the customer within the usual credit period, a copy of the statement of account may be referred to the credit department for such action as the credit manager may wish to take. A model filled-in copy of a statement of account is reproduced below. This is a statement of the account of V. T. Roberts for the month ended December 31. It shows **(1)** the balance at the beginning of the month amounting to $614.06; **(2)** a charge of $894.09 (for a sale of $859.70 plus

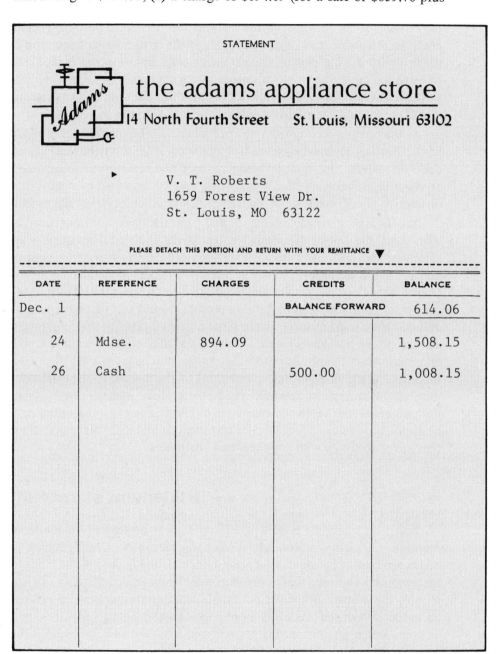

STATEMENT

the adams appliance store

14 North Fourth Street   St. Louis, Missouri 63102

▶
V. T. Roberts
1659 Forest View Dr.
St. Louis, MO 63122

PLEASE DETACH THIS PORTION AND RETURN WITH YOUR REMITTANCE ▼

DATE	REFERENCE	CHARGES	CREDITS	BALANCE
Dec. 1			BALANCE FORWARD	614.06
24	Mdse.	894.09		1,508.15
26	Cash		500.00	1,008.15

208

Statement of Account

tax of $34.39) made on December 24; **(3)** a credit of $500 for cash received on December 26; and **(4)** the balance at the close of the month amounting to $1,008.15. Note that the customer is asked to tear off the upper portion of the statement and to send it along with his remittance.

Report No. 8-1

Complete Report No. 8-1 in the workbook and submit your working papers to the instructor for approval. After completing the report, continue with the following study assignment until the next report is required.

Application of
accounting principles

The accrual basis of accounting as applied to a merchandising enterprise is illustrated on the following pages by a reproduction of the records of The Adams Appliance Store, owned and operated by R. L. Adams. The records include the following:

BOOKS OF ORIGINAL ENTRY

Combined cash journal
Purchases journal
Sales journal

BOOKS OF FINAL ENTRY

General ledger
Accounts receivable ledger
Accounts payable ledger

AUXILIARY RECORDS

Petty cash disbursements record
Checkbook
Employees' earnings records

Combined cash journal

The form of combined cash journal used is the same as the one illustrated on pages 168 and 169, except that the first two amount columns are used in recording banking transactions including deposits and checks. These columns serve the same purpose as though they were headed Cash Receipts and Disbursements. Mr. Adams follows the practice of depositing all cash receipts in a checking account at the Columbia National Bank and of making all disbursements by check (except for the payment of small items, which may be paid from a petty cash fund). For these reasons, a bank account rather than a cash account is kept in the general ledger. The posting to the bank account is from the combined cash journal, the account being debited for the total receipts (deposits) and being credited for the total disbursements (checks).

All items entered in the General Debit and Credit columns of the combined cash journal are posted individually to the proper accounts in the general ledger. No individual posting to the general ledger is required from any of the other amount columns. Instead, the totals of these columns are posted at the end of the month.

Purchases journal

The form of purchases journal used is the same as the one illustrated on page 151. It was described in detail in Chapter 6. All transactions involving the purchase of merchandise *on account* are recorded in this journal. Because the posting of the individual credits to the accounts with suppliers is done directly from the purchase invoices, the only posting required from the purchases journal is the total purchases for each month. This involves a debit to Purchases, Account No. 511, and a credit to Accounts Payable, Account No. 231.

Sales journal

The form of sales journal used is the same as the one illustrated on page 160. It was described in detail in Chapter 6. All transactions involving the sale of merchandise *on account* are recorded in this journal. Because the posting of individual charges to the accounts with customers is done directly from the sales tickets, the only posting required from the sales journal is the total sales for each month. This involves a debit to Accounts Receivable, Account No. 123, and credits to Sales, Account No. 411, and to Sales Tax Payable, Account No. 241.

General ledger

A general ledger with the accounts arranged in numerical order is used. A chart of the accounts appears on page 197. The standard account form is used in the general ledger.

Accounts receivable ledger

An accounts receivable ledger with the accounts for customers arranged in alphabetic order is used. The balance-column account form is used in this ledger. Posting to the individual accounts with customers is done directly from the sales tickets or other documents. As each item is posted, the balance is extended immediately so that reference to the account of any customer at any time will reveal without any delay the amount due from him. This is important since it is often necessary to determine the status of a particular customer's account before extending additional credit.

Accounts payable ledger

An accounts payable ledger with the accounts for suppliers arranged in alphabetic order is used. The balance-column account form is used in this ledger. Posting to the individual accounts with suppliers is done directly from the invoices or other documents. As each item is posted, the balance is extended immediately so that reference to the account of any supplier at any time will reveal the amount owed to that supplier.

Auxiliary records

As previously stated, certain auxiliary records are used, including a petty cash disbursements record and a checkbook. The form of petty cash disbursements record is similar to that illustrated on pages 56 and 57. A record of deposits made and checks issued is kept on the check stubs as well as in the combined cash journal. At the end of each month, when the summary posting from the combined cash journal has been completed, the balance of the bank checking account in the ledger should be the same as the balance recorded on the check stubs. The earnings records maintained for each of Mr. Adams' four employees are similar to the one illustrated on pages 86 and 87. (To conserve space, these records are not reproduced in this chapter.)

Accounting procedure

The books of account containing a record of the transactions completed during the month of December are reproduced on pages 221 to 238. These books include the combined cash journal, the purchases journal, the sales journal, the petty cash disbursements record, the general ledger, the accounts receivable ledger, and the accounts payable ledger. Before recording any transactions for December, the balance of the bank checking account was entered in the combined cash journal and the balance in the petty cash fund was entered in the petty cash disbursements record. The balance at the beginning of the month of December is shown in each of the accounts in the general, accounts receivable, and accounts payable ledgers. These balances along with those at the end of the month are summarized in the trial balances and schedules reproduced on pages 239 and 240.

Following is a narrative of the transactions completed during December. Transactions of a type that have not been previously introduced are analyzed to show their effect upon the accounts.

THE ADAMS APPLIANCE STORE

NARRATIVE OF TRANSACTIONS

Monday, December 2

Issued checks as follows:

No. 867, Glick Realty Co., $600, in payment of December rent.
No. 868, The Penn-Central Railroad Co., $53.18, in payment of freight on merchandise purchased.

It will be noted that both checks were recorded in the combined cash journal. Check No. 867 was recorded by debiting Rent Expense, Account No. 611, and by crediting the bank account. Check No. 868 was recorded by debiting Purchases, Account No. 511, and by crediting the bank account. Since the freight charge increases the cost of the merchandise, the purchases account should be debited.

Note that the account titles were written in the Description column. The account numbers were inserted in the Posting Reference column when the individual posting was completed at the end of the week.

Tuesday, December 3

Bought merchandise from the Ferguson Electric Co., Ferguson, Missouri, $457.30, per Invoice No. 204 of November 30. Terms, net 30 days.

It will be noted that after receiving the merchandise and checking the invoice, the transaction was recorded in the purchases journal. A check mark was placed in the Posting Reference column to indicate that individual posting is not done from the purchases journal. The invoice was then posted directly to the credit of the Ferguson Electric Co. account in the accounts payable ledger, after which the invoice was filed in an unpaid invoice file according to its due date.

Wednesday, December 4

Received check from K. G. Watson, $317.23.

Note that the credit was immediately posted to the customer's account. The remittance was then recorded in the combined cash journal by debiting the bank account and by crediting Accounts Receivable. The name of the customer was written in the Description column. Since the credit had already been posted to the customer's account, a check mark was placed in the Posting Reference column.

Thursday, December 5

Sold merchandise on account as follows:

No. 271A, K. G. Watson, 51 Webster Woods, St. Louis, Missouri, $379.50, tax $15.18.

No. 257B, R. F. Ambrose, 5245 Kingwood, St. Louis, Missouri, $458.75, tax $18.35.

No. 235C, J. C. Burns, 9440 Arban, St. Louis, Missouri, $1,694.60, tax $67.78.

Unless otherwise specified, all charge sales are payable on the 10th of the following month. No cash discount is allowed. Note that these transactions were recorded in the sales journal. A check mark was placed in the Posting Reference column to indicate that individual posting is not done from the sales journal. The sales tickets were then posted directly to the proper customers' accounts in the accounts receivable ledger, after which each ticket was filed under the name of the customer for future reference. The numbers of the sales tickets indicate that there are three salespersons identified by the letters A, B, and C. Each of these persons uses a separate pad of sales tickets numbered consecutively.

Friday, December 6

Issued checks as follows:

No. 869, Globe Publishing Co., $61.04, in payment for circulars to be used for advertising purposes.

No. 870, State Treasurer, $876.45, in payment of sales taxes for November.

Both checks were recorded in the combined cash journal by debiting the proper accounts and by crediting the bank account. Check No. 869 was charged to Advertising Expense and Check No. 870 was charged to Sales Tax Payable. The numbers of the checks were written in the Check No. column and the titles of the accounts to be charged were written in the Description column.

213

Bought merchandise from the Clayshire Electric Co., Richmond Heights, Missouri, $1,941.80, per Invoice No. 205 of December 6. Terms, net 30 days.

Sold merchandise on account as follows:

No. 259B, A. K. Young, Des Peres, Missouri, $752.75, tax $30.11.

Saturday, December 7

Cash sales for the week:

SALESPERSON	MERCHANDISE	TAX	TOTAL
A	$ 704.60	$28.18	$ 732.78
B	821.95	32.88	854.83
C	390.70	15.63	406.33
	$1,917.25	$76.69	$1,993.94

As each cash sale was completed a sales ticket was prepared. This ticket provided the information needed in recording the sale on the cash register when ringing up the amount of cash received. As each amount was thus recorded it was added to the previous total of cash sales made by each salesperson on a mechanical accumulator in the register. Usually the total cash sales are recorded daily, but to save time and to avoid unnecessary duplication of entries the total cash sales are here recorded at the end of each week and on the last day of the month. This transaction was recorded in the combined cash journal by debiting the bank account for $1,993.94 and by crediting Sales for $1,917.25 and Sales Tax Payable for $76.69.

Made petty cash disbursements as follows:

Postage stamps, $8. Petty Cash Voucher No. 73.
Collect telegram, $1.60. Petty Cash Voucher No. 74.
Messenger fee, $3. Petty Cash Voucher No. 75.

All disbursements from the petty cash fund are recorded in the petty cash disbursements record. This record is ruled so as to facilitate the classification of such expenditures. It will be noted that the cost of the postage stamps was recorded as a charge to Stationery and Supplies, Account No. 151, the cost of the telegram to Telephone and Telegraph Expense, Account No. 617, and the messenger fees to Miscellaneous Expense, Account No. 624.

END-OF-THE-WEEK WORK

(1) Proved the footings of the combined cash journal. **(2)** Deposited $2,311.17 in the Columbia National Bank and proved the bank balance ($8,061.87). **(3)** Posted each entry individually from the General Debit and Credit columns of the combined cash journal to the proper general ledger accounts. When Check No. 870, issued December 6, was posted to the account with Sales Tax Payable, the account was in balance; hence, it was ruled with a double line as illustrated on page 230. **(4)** Proved the footings of the petty cash disbursements record and proved the balance of the petty cash fund ($87.40). **(5)** Proved the footings of the sales journal.

Monday, December 9

Issued checks as follows:

No. 871, Clayshire Electric Co., $2,000, on account.
No. 872, Ferguson Electric Co., $700, on account.

Checks Nos. 871 and 872 were recorded in the combined cash journal by debiting Accounts Payable and by crediting the bank account, the names of the creditors being written in the Description column. Check marks were placed in the Posting Reference column to indicate that checks issued to creditors are not posted individually from the combined cash journal. The checks were posted directly to the proper creditors' accounts in the accounts payable ledger from the check stubs.

Tuesday, December 10

Issued Check No. 873 for $390.32 to the Columbia National Bank, a U.S. depositary, in payment of the following taxes:

Employees' income tax withheld during November............		$305.90
FICA tax imposed —		
On employees (withheld during November)................	$ 42.21	
On the employer......................................	42.21	84.42
Total...		$390.32

This transaction resulted in decreases in FICA tax payable and in employees income tax payable with a corresponding decrease in the bank account; hence, it was recorded in the combined cash journal by debiting FICA Tax Payable for $84.42 and Employees Income Tax Payable for $305.90, and by crediting the bank account for $390.32.

Sold merchandise on account as follows:

No. 275A, E. E. Wellman, 5520 Wren, St. Louis, Missouri, $646.90, tax $25.88.

Wednesday, December 11

Received the following remittances from customers:

A. D. Bowen, $500, on account.

C. M. Furr, $600, on account.

B. T. Vincent, $82.11, in full payment of account.

Thursday, December 12

Made the following disbursements from the petty cash fund:

Boy Scouts of America, $5. Petty Cash Voucher No. 76.

R. L. Adams, $10, for personal use. Petty Cash Voucher No. 77.

Friday, December 13

Received the following invoices for merchandise purchased on account:

Mack Electric Co., 4581 Gravois, St. Louis, Missouri, $1,462.50, per Invoice No. 206 of December 13. Terms 2/10, n/30.

Tipton Electric Co., Lemay, Missouri, $682.60, per Invoice No. 207 of December 12. Terms, net 30 days.

Saturday, December 14

Cash sales for the week:

SALESPERSON	MERCHANDISE	TAX	TOTAL
A	$ 840.70	$ 33.63	$ 874.33
B	1,385.60	55.42	1,441.02
C	736.90	29.48	766.38
	$2,963.20	$118.53	$3,081.73

Issued Check No. 874 payable to Payroll for $1,490.24.

Mr. Adams follows the policy of paying his employees on the 15th and last day of each month. Since December 15 fell on Sunday, the employees were paid on the 14th. The following statement was prepared from the payroll record:

PAYROLL STATEMENT FOR PERIOD ENDED DECEMBER 15

Total wages and commissions earned during period............		$1,666.73
Employees' taxes to be withheld:		
Employees' income tax....................................	$151.60	
FICA tax, 5.5% of $452.50..............................	24.89	176.49
Net amount payable to employees.........................		$1,490.24
Employer's payroll taxes:		
FICA tax, 5.5% of $452.50..............................		$24.89
Unemployment compensation taxes —		
State unemployment tax, 2.7% of $225....................		6.07
FUTA tax, 0.5% of $225................................		1.13
Total..		$32.09

The earnings of two employees had reached the $9,000 point in an earlier month. Accordingly, only $452.50 of the wages and commissions earned during the period is subject to the FICA tax. All but one employee had reached the $4,200 State Unemployment and FUTA tax limits in an earlier month. As a result, only $225 of wages and commissions earned during the period is subject to these unemployment taxes.

Two entries were required to record the payroll in the combined cash journal — one to record the total earnings of the employees, the amounts withheld for FICA tax and income tax, and the net amount paid; the other to record the social security tax imposed on the employer.

END-OF-THE-WEEK WORK

(1) Proved the footings of the combined cash journal. **(2)** Deposited $4,263.84 in the Columbia National Bank and proved the bank balance ($7,745.15). **(3)** Posted each entry individually from the General Debit and Credit columns of the combined cash journal to the proper general ledger accounts. When Check No. 873, issued December 10, was posted to the accounts with FICA Tax Payable and Employees Income Tax Payable, the accounts were found to be in balance; hence, each account was ruled with a double line as illustrated on page 230. **(4)** Proved the footings of the petty cash disbursements record and proved the balance of the petty cash fund ($72.40). **(5)** Proved the footings of the sales journal.

Monday, December 16

Issued checks as follows:

No. 875, General Appliance Co., $800, on account.
No. 876, Mack Electric Co., $673.80, on account.

Tuesday, December 17

Received the following remittances from customers:

A. K. Young, $813.52, on account.

R. M. Nelson, $769.90, in full payment of account.

P. R. Worth, $367.57 and a 30-day, 7 percent note dated December 16 payable to R. L. Adams for $2,500.

Mr. Adams agreed to accept the $2,500 note in order to extend the time of settlement of Mr. Worth's obligation. The transaction was recorded in the combined cash journal by a debit to the bank account for $367.57, a debit to Notes Receivable, Account No. 121, for $2,500, and a credit to Accounts Receivable for the total, $2,867.57. In posting to Mr. Worth's account in the accounts receivable ledger, two lines were used; one to show the amount of the cash receipt, and another to record the receipt of the note.

Wednesday, December 18

Sold merchandise on credit as follows:

No. 239C, B. T. Vincent, 1017 Veronica, Baden, Missouri, $883.10, tax $35.32.

No. 277A, D. W. Paige, Webster Groves, Missouri, $1,345.55, tax $53.82.

No. 262B, O. W. Peck, 1685 Avignon Ct., St. Louis, Missouri, $1,214.95, tax $48.60.

Issued Check No. 877 to Milner Garage, $65.40, in payment of storage, gasoline, oil, and service.

This check was recorded in the combined cash journal by crediting the bank account and by debiting Truck Expense, Account No. 622.

Thursday, December 19

Made petty cash disbursements as follows:

Advertising, $6.29. Petty Cash Voucher No. 78.
Supplies, $8.35. Petty Cash Voucher No. 79.
Miscellaneous expense, $1.75. Petty Cash Voucher No. 80.

Bought merchandise from Morganford Appliance Co., 4214 Arsenal, St. Louis, Missouri, $1,374.90, per Invoice No. 208 of December 19. Terms 2/30, n/60.

Friday, December 20

Issued charge-back Invoice No. 791 for $60 to Tipton Electric Co., for merchandise returned; to be applied on Invoice No. 207 received December 13.

This transaction was recorded in the combined cash journal by debiting Accounts Payable and by crediting Purchases Returns and Allowances. It was also posted directly to the account of the Tipton Electric Co. in the accounts payable ledger from the charge-back invoice.

Saturday, December 21

Issued Check No. 878 for $1,000 to Mr. Adams for personal use.

Cash sales for the week:

SALESPERSON	MERCHANDISE	TAX	TOTAL
A	$ 768.25	$30.73	$ 798.98
B	802.20	32.09	834.29
C	728.60	29.14	757.74
	$2,299.05	$91.96	$2,391.01

END-OF-THE-WEEK WORK

(1) Proved the footings of the combined cash journal. **(2)** Deposited $4,342 in the Columbia National Bank and proved the bank balance ($9,547.95). **(3)** Posted each entry individually from the General Debit and Credit columns of the combined cash journal to the proper general ledger accounts. **(4)** Proved the footings of the petty cash disbursements record and proved the balance of the petty cash fund ($56.01). **(5)** Proved the footings of the sales journal.

Monday, December 23

Issued Check No. 879 for $1,433.25 to Mack Electric Co. in payment of its invoice of December 13, less 2 percent discount.

The amount of the check is computed as follows:

Amount of invoice.........................	$1,462.50
Discount, 2%..............................	29.25
Balance due...............................	$1,433.25

This transaction was recorded in the combined cash journal by debiting Accounts Payable for $1,462.50 and by crediting Purchases Discount for $29.25 and crediting the bank account for $1,433.25. In posting the check directly to the account of the Mack Electric Co. in the accounts payable ledger, the amount of the check was entered on one line and the amount of the discount on another line.

Tuesday, December 24

Sold merchandise on credit as follows:

No. 269B, K. G. Watson, 51 Webster Woods, St. Louis, Missouri, $2,073.40, tax $82.94.

No. 281A, V. T. Roberts, 1659 Forest View Dr., St. Louis, Missouri, $859.70, tax $34.39.

No. 256C, C. M. Furr, 5374 Delmar, St. Louis, Missouri, $1,218.30, tax $48.73.

Thursday, December 26

Received the following remittances from customers:

O. W. Peck, $1,500, on account.
V. T. Roberts, $500, on account.

Made petty cash disbursements as follows:

Advertising, $4.80. Petty Cash Voucher No. 81.
Supplies, $9.13. Petty Cash Voucher No. 82.
Miscellaneous expense, $2.90. Petty Cash Voucher No. 83.

Friday, December 27

Issued Credit Memorandum No. 12 for $82.58 to O. W. Peck for merchandise returned. (Sales price of merchandise, $79.40, tax $3.18.)

Issued Check No. 880 for $421.30 to the Globe Publishing Co. in payment of advertising bill.

Issued Check No. 881 for $769.90 to the Columbia National Bank for R. M. Nelson's check which was returned unpaid (NSF).

R. M. Nelson's check was received on December 17, and was deposited in the bank December 21. The bank returned the check with a notice advising that the maker did not have sufficient funds on deposit to cover the check. Check No. 881 was recorded in the combined cash journal by debiting Accounts Receivable and by crediting the bank account. The amount of the check was debited immediately to Mr. Nelson's account in the accounts receivable ledger. The notation "NSF" was made in the Item column, and the number of the check (881) was shown in the Posting Reference column beside the $769.90 debit to Mr. Nelson's account.

(Since a page of the combined cash journal was filled at this point, the totals of the amount columns were recorded on the double ruled line at the bottom of the page, after which they were carried forward and entered at the top of the next page.)

Saturday, December 28

Cash sales for the week:

SALESPERSON	MERCHANDISE	TAX	TOTAL
A	$ 895.40	$ 35.82	$ 931.22
B	976.50	39.06	1,015.56
C	681.20	27.25	708.45
	$2,553.10	$102.13	$2,655.23

Issued checks as follows:

No. 882, The Bell Telephone Co., $32.15, for telephone service.
No. 883, The Union Gas & Electric Co., $73.28, for gas and electricity.

END-OF-THE-WEEK WORK

(1) Proved the footings of the combined cash journal. **(2)** Deposited $4,655.23 in the Columbia National Bank and proved the bank balance ($11,473.30). **(3)** Posted each entry individually from the General Debit and Credit columns of the combined cash journal to the proper general ledger accounts. **(4)** Proved the footings of the petty cash disbursements record and proved the balance of the petty cash fund ($39.18). **(5)** Proved the footings of the sales journal.

Monday, December 30

Received invoice from Mack Electric Co., 4581 Gravois, St. Louis, Missouri, $594.20, for merchandise purchased per Invoice No. 209 of December 27. Terms, 2/10, n/30.

Tuesday, December 31

Received the following invoices:

Cabany Electric Co., Maplewood, Missouri, $815.10, merchandise purchased per Invoice No. 210 of December 30. Terms 2/30, n/60.
Watson Safe & Lock Co., Chicago, Illinois, $562, safe purchased per invoice of December 30. Terms 2/30, n/60.

The invoice received from the Cabany Electric Co. was recorded in the purchases journal in the usual manner. The invoice received from the Watson Safe & Lock Co. was recorded in the combined cash journal by debiting Store Equipment and by crediting Accounts Payable. In this enterprise the purchases journal is used only for recording invoices covering merchandise purchased on credit.

Cash sales:

SALESPERSON	MERCHANDISE	TAX	TOTAL
A	$ 611.70	$24.47	$ 636.17
B	490.65	19.63	510.28
C	382.60	15.30	397.90
	$1,484.95	$59.40	$1,544.35

Issued Check No. 884 payable to Payroll for $1,641.21.

PAYROLL STATEMENT FOR PERIOD ENDED DECEMBER 31

Total wages and commissions earned during period........... •		$1,839.00
Employees' taxes to be withheld:		
Employees' income tax.................................	$172.90	
FICA tax, 5.5% of $452.50.............................	24.89	$ 197.79
Net amount payable to employees.........................		$1,641.21
Employer's payroll taxes:		
FICA tax, 5.5% of $452.50.............................		$ 24.89
Unemployment compensation taxes —		
State unemployment tax, 2.7% of $225...................		6.07
FUTA tax, 0.5% of $225..............................		1.13
Total...		$ 32.09

Issued Check No. 885 for $60.82 to replenish the petty cash fund.

The following statement of the petty cash disbursements for December served as a voucher authorizing the issuance of the check to replenish the petty cash fund:

STATEMENT OF PETTY CASH DISBURSEMENTS FOR DECEMBER

R. L. Adams, drawing	$10.00
Stationery and supplies..	25.48
Telephone and telegraph expense....................................	1.60
Advertising expense...	11.09
Charitable contributions expense....................................	5.00
Miscellaneous expense...	7.65
Total disbursements...	$60.82

Before the above statement was prepared the petty cash disbursements record was proved by footing the amount columns, the totals were entered in ink, and the record was ruled with single and double lines. The balance was then brought down below the double rules. The amount received to replenish the fund was added to the balance and the total, $100, was entered in the Description column.

The amount of the check issued was entered in the combined cash journal by debiting the proper accounts and by crediting the bank account. It should be remembered that no posting is done from the petty cash disbursements record; the proper accounts will be charged for the petty cash disbursements when the posting is completed from the combined cash journal.

ROUTINE END-OF-THE-MONTH WORK

(1) Proved the footings and entered the totals in the combined cash journal and the sales journal; entered the total in the purchases journal. **(2)** Deposited $1,544.35 in the Columbia National Bank and proved the bank balance ($11,315.62). **(3)** Completed the individual posting from the

General Debit and Credit columns of the combined cash journal. **(4)** Completed the summary posting of the columnar totals of the combined cash journal, the purchases journal, and the sales journal to the proper accounts in the general ledger. **(5)** Ruled the combined cash journal, the purchases journal, and the sales journal. **(6)** Prepared a trial balance and schedules of accounts receivable and accounts payable.

PURCHASES JOURNAL — PAGE 32

	DATE	INVOICE NO.	FROM WHOM PURCHASED	POST. REF.	AMOUNT	
1	19— Dec. 3	204	Ferguson Electric Co.	✓	457 30	1
2	6	205	Clayshire Electric Co.	✓	1941 80	2
3	13	206	Mack Electric Co	✓	1462 50	3
4	13	207	Tipton Electric Co.	✓	682 60	4
5	19	208	Morganford Appliance Co.	✓	1374 90	5
6	30	209	Mack Electric Co.	✓	594 20	6
7	31	210	Cabany Electric Co	✓	815 10	7
8			Purchases Dr.—Accounts Payable Cr.	511/231	7328 40	8
9						9
10						10
11						11
12						12
13						13
14						14

The Adams Appliance Store — Purchases Journal

SALES JOURNAL — PAGE 44

	DATE	SALE NO.	TO WHOM SOLD	POST REF.	ACCOUNTS RECEIVABLE DR.	SALES CR.	SALES TAX PAYABLE CR.	
1	19— Dec. 5	271a	K. G. Watson	✓	394 68	379 50	15 18	1
2	5	2578	R. F. Ambrose	✓	477 10	458 75	18 35	2
3	5	235C	J. C. Burns	✓	1762 38	1694 60	67 78	3
4	6	2598	A. K. Young	✓	782 86 3417 02	752 75 3285 60	30 11 131 42	4
5	10	275a	E. E. Wellman	✓	672 78 4089 80	646 90 3932 50	25 88 157 30	5
6	18	239C	B. J. Vincent	✓	918 42	883 10	35 32	6
7	18	277a	D. W. Paige	✓	1399 37	1345 55	53 82	7
8	18	2628	O. W. Peck	✓	1263 55 7671 14	1214 95 7376 10	48 60 295 04	8
9	24	2698	K. G. Watson	✓	2156 34	2073 40	82 94	9
10	24	281a	V. J. Roberts	✓	894 09	859 70	34 39	10
11	24	256C	C. M. Furr	✓	1267 03	1218 30	48 73	11
12					11988 60 11988 60	11527 50 11527 50	461 10 461 10	12
13					(123)	(441)	(244)	13
14								14

The Adams Appliance Store — Sales Journal

221

	COLUMBIA NATIONAL BANK		CK. NO.	DAY	DESCRIPTION	POST. REF.	
	DEPOSITS 111 DR.	CHECKS 111 CR.					
1					AMOUNTS FORWARDED *Balance* 7,341.37		1
2		600 00	867	2	Rent Expense	611	2
3		53 18	868	2	Purchases	511	3
4	317 23			4	K. G. Watson	✓	4
5		61 04	869	6	Advertising Expense	618	5
6		876 45	870	6	Sales Tax Payable	241	6
7	1993 94			7	Cash sales for week	✓	7
8	2311 17	1590 67	871	9	Clayshire Electric Co. 3,061.87	✓	8
		2000 00					
9		700 00	872	9	Ferguson Electric Co.	✓	9
10		390 32	873	10	F I C A Tax Payable	251	10
11					Employees Income Tax Payable	261	11
12	500 00			11	A. D. Bowen	✓	12
13	600 00			11	C. M. Furr	✓	13
14	82 11			11	B. T. Vincent	✓	14
15	3081 73			14	Cash sales for week	✓	15
16		1490 24	874	14	Salaries & Commissions Expense	613	16
17					F I C A Tax Payable	251	17
18					Employees Income Tax Payable	261	18
19				14	Payroll Taxes Expense	614	19
20					F I C A Tax Payable	251	20
21					F U T A Tax Payable	271	21
22					State Unemployment Tax Payable 7,745.15	281	22
23	6575 01	6171 23					23
		800 00	875	16	General Appliance Co.	✓	
24		673 80	876	16	Mack Electric Co.	✓	24
25	813 52			17	A. K. Young	✓	25
26	769 90			17	R. M. Nelson	✓	26
27	367 57			17	Notes Receivable—P. R. Worth	121	27
28		65 40	877	18	Truck Expense	622	28
29				20	Purchases R. & A.—Tipton Electric Co.	051	29
30		1000 00	878	21	R. L. Adams, Drawing	031	30
31	2394 01	7710 43		21	Cash sales for week	✓	31
	10911 01						
32		1433 25	879	23	Purchases Disc.—Mack Electric Co. 9,547.95	052	32
33	1500 00			26	O. W. Peck	✓	33
34	500 00			26	V. T. Roberts	✓	34
35				27	Sales R. & A.—O. W. Peck	041	35
36					Sales Tax Payable	241	36
37		421 30	880	27	Advertising Expense	618	37
38		769 90	881	27	Accounts Rec.—R. M. Nelson	123	38
39	12917 01	11334 88		27	Carried forward		39
	12917 01	11334 88					

222

	GENERAL DEBIT	GENERAL CREDIT	ACCOUNTS PAYABLE 231 DR.	ACCOUNTS RECEIVABLE 123 CR.	SALES 411 CR.	SALES TAX PAYABLE 241 CR.	
1							1
2	60000						2
3	5318						3
4				31723			4
5	6104						5
6	87645						6
7					191725	7669	7
8	159067		200000	31723	191725	7669	8
9			70000				9
10	8442						10
11	30590						11
12				50000			12
13				60000			13
14				8211			14
15					296320	11853	15
16	166673						16
17		2489					17
18		15160					18
19	3209						19
20		2489					20
21		113					21
22		607					22
23	367981	20858	270000	149934	488045	19522	23
			80000				
24			67380				24
25				81352			25
26				76990			26
27	250000			286757			27
28	6540						28
29		6000		6000			29
30	100000						30
31					229905	9196	31
32	724521	26858	423380	595033	717950	28718	32
		2925	146250				
33				150000			33
34				50000			34
35	7940			8258			35
36	318						36
37	42130						37
38	76990						38
39	851899	29783	569630	803291	717950	28718	39
	851899	29783	569630	803291	717950	28718	

The Adams Appliance Store — Combined Cash Journal (Right Page)

(continued on next page)

223

COLUMBIA NATIONAL BANK		CK. NO.	DAY	DESCRIPTION	POST. REF.	
DEPOSITS 111 DR.	CHECKS 111 CR.					
1291701	1133488			AMOUNTS FORWARDED		1
265523			28	Cash sales for week	✓	2
	3215	882	28	Telephone + Telegraph Expense	617	3
	7328	883	28	Heating and Lighting Expense	615	4
1557224	1144031		31	Store Equipment 11,473.30	181	5
				Accounts Pay.-Watson Safe & Lock Co.	231	6
154435			31	Cash sales, 12/29-31	✓	7
	164121	884	31	Salaries & Commissions Expense	613	8
				FICA Tax Payable	251	9
				Employees Income Tax Payable	261	10
			31	Payroll Taxes Expense	614	11
				FICA Tax Payable	251	12
				FUTA Tax Payable	271	13
				State Unemployment Tax Pay.	281	14
	6082	885	31	R. L. Adams, Drawing	031	15
				Stationery and Supplies	151	16
				Telephone + Telegraph Expense	617	17
				Advertising Expense	618	18
				Charitable Contributions Expense	623	19
				Miscellaneous Expense 11,315.62	624	20
1711659	1314234					21
1711659	1314234					21
(111)	(111)					22

224

The Adams Appliance Store — Combined Cash Journal (Left Page)

(concluded)

	GENERAL		ACCOUNTS PAYABLE 231 DR.	ACCOUNTS RECEIVABLE 123 CR.	SALES 411 CR.	SALES TAX PAYABLE 241 CR.	
	DEBIT	CREDIT					
1	851899	29783	569630	803291	717950	28718	1
2					255310	10213	2
3	3215						3
4	7328						4
5	862442	29783	569630	803291	973260	38931	5
	56200						
6		56200					6
7					148495	5940	7
8	183900						8
9		2489					9
10		17290					10
11	3209						11
12		2489					12
13		113					13
14		607					14
15	1000						15
16	2548						16
17	160						17
18	1109						18
19	500						19
20	765						20
	1111833	108971	569630	803291	1121755	44871	
21	1111833	108971	569630	803291	1121755	44871	21
22	(✓)	(✓)	(231)	(123)	(411)	(241)	22

The Adams Appliance Store — Combined Cash Journal (Right Page)
(*concluded*)

225

	DAY	DESCRIPTION	VOU. NO.	TOTAL AMOUNT	031	151	
1		AMOUNTS FORWARDED *Balance* 100.00					1
2	7	Postage, stamps	73	8 00		8 00	2
3	7	Collect telegram	74	1 60			3
4	7	Messenger fee	75	3 00			4
5	12	Boy Scouts of America 87.40	76	12 60		8 00	5
6	12	R. L. Adams, Drawing	77	5 00	10 00		6
7	19	Advertising 72.40	78	10 00	10 00	8 00	7
8	19	Supplies	79	27 60			8
9	19	Miscellaneous expense	80	6 29		8 35	9
10	26	Advertising 56.01	81	8 35			10
11	26	Supplies	82	1 75	10 00	16 35	11
12	26	Miscellaneous expense 39.18	83	43 99		9 13	12
13				4 80			13
				2 90			
				60 82	10 00	25 48	
				60 82	10 00	25 48	
14	31	Balance 39.18					14
15	31	Received in fund 60.82					15
16		Total 100.00					16

226

The Adams Appliance Store — Petty Cash Disbursements Record (Left Page)

DISTRIBUTION OF CHARGES

617	618	623	624			ACCOUNT	AMOUNT	
								1
								2
1 60								3
			3 00					4
1 60		5 00	3 00					5
								6
1 60	6 29	5 00	3 00					7
								8
			1 75					9
1 60	6 29 / 4 80	5 00	4 75					10
								11
			2 90					12
1 60 / 1 60	11 09 / 11 09	5 00 / 5 00	7 65 / 7 65					13

The Adams Appliance Store — Petty Cash Disbursements Record (Right Page)

ACCOUNT _Columbia National Bank_   ACCOUNT NO. _111_

DATE	ITEM	POST. REF.	DEBIT	DATE	ITEM	POST. REF.	CREDIT
19— Dec. 1	Balance	✓	734137	19— Dec. 31		CJ48	1314234
31		CJ48	1711659				
	11,315.62		2445796				

ACCOUNT _Petty Cash Fund_   ACCOUNT NO. _112_

DATE	ITEM	POST. REF.	DEBIT	DATE	ITEM	POST. REF.	CREDIT
19— Dec. 1	Balance	✓	100.00				

ACCOUNT _Notes Receivable_   ACCOUNT NO. _121_

DATE	ITEM	POST. REF.	DEBIT	DATE	ITEM	POST. REF.	CREDIT
19— Dec. 17		CJ47	2500.00				

ACCOUNT _Accounts Receivable_   ACCOUNT NO. _123_

DATE	ITEM	POST. REF.	DEBIT	DATE	ITEM	POST. REF.	CREDIT
19— Dec. 1	Balance	✓	856599	19— Dec. 31		CJ48	803291
27		CJ47	76990				
31		S44	1198860				
	13,291.58		2132449				

ACCOUNT _Allowance for Bad Debts_   ACCOUNT NO. _012_

DATE	ITEM	POST. REF.	DEBIT	DATE	ITEM	POST. REF.	CREDIT
				19— Dec. 1	Balance	✓	18612

ACCOUNT _Merchandise Inventory_   ACCOUNT NO. _131_

DATE	ITEM	POST. REF.	DEBIT	DATE	ITEM	POST. REF.	CREDIT
19— Dec. 1	Balance	✓	4251865				

ACCOUNT _Prepaid Insurance_   ACCOUNT NO. _141_

DATE	ITEM	POST. REF.	DEBIT	DATE	ITEM	POST. REF.	CREDIT
19— Dec. 1	Balance	✓	52616				

The Adams Appliance Store — General Ledger

228

ACCOUNT *Stationery and Supplies*   ACCOUNT NO. *151*

DATE	ITEM	POST. REF.	DEBIT	DATE	ITEM	POST. REF.	CREDIT
19— Dec. 1	Balance	✓	170 34				
31		CJ48	25 48				
			195 82				

ACCOUNT *Store Equipment*   ACCOUNT NO. *181*

DATE	ITEM	POST. REF.	DEBIT	DATE	ITEM	POST. REF.	CREDIT
19— Dec. 1	Balance	✓	2312 90				
31		CJ48	562 00				
			2874 90				

ACCOUNT *Accumulated Depreciation—Store Equipment*   ACCOUNT NO. *018*

DATE	ITEM	POST. REF.	DEBIT	DATE	ITEM	POST. REF.	CREDIT
				19— Dec. 1	Balance	✓	829 40

ACCOUNT *Delivery Equipment*   ACCOUNT NO. *191*

DATE	ITEM	POST. REF.	DEBIT	DATE	ITEM	POST. REF.	CREDIT
19— Dec. 1	Balance	✓	3426 80				

ACCOUNT *Accumulated Depreciation—Delivery Equipment*   ACCOUNT NO. *019*

DATE	ITEM	POST. REF.	DEBIT	DATE	ITEM	POST. REF.	CREDIT
				19— Dec. 1	Balance	✓	2104 10

ACCOUNT *Notes Payable*   ACCOUNT NO. *211*

DATE	ITEM	POST. REF.	DEBIT	DATE	ITEM	POST. REF.	CREDIT
				19— Dec. 1	Balance	✓	1243 70

ACCOUNT *Accounts Payable*   ACCOUNT NO. *231*

DATE	ITEM	POST. REF.	DEBIT	DATE	ITEM	POST. REF.	CREDIT
19— Dec. 31		CJ48	5696 30	19— Dec. 1	Balance	✓	3281 60
				31		CJ48	562 00
				31		P32	7328 40
			5,475.70				11172 00

The Adams Appliance Store — General Ledger (*continued*)

Chapter 8 / Accrual Accounting Applied to a Retail Business

ACCOUNT *Sales Tax Payable* ACCOUNT NO. 241

DATE	ITEM	POST. REF.	DEBIT	DATE	ITEM	POST. REF.	CREDIT
19-- Dec. 6		CJ47	876 45	19-- Dec. 1	Balance	✓	876 45
27		CJ47	3 18	31		CJ48	448 71
				31		S44	46 10
					906.63		909 81

ACCOUNT *FICA Tax Payable* ACCOUNT NO. 251

DATE	ITEM	POST. REF.	DEBIT	DATE	ITEM	POST. REF.	CREDIT
19-- Dec. 10		CJ47	84 42	19-- Dec. 1	Balance	✓	84 42
				14		CJ47	24 89
				14		CJ47	24 89
				31		CJ48	24 89
				31		CJ48	24 89
							99 56

ACCOUNT *Employees Income Tax Payable* ACCOUNT NO. 261

DATE	ITEM	POST. REF.	DEBIT	DATE	ITEM	POST. REF.	CREDIT
19-- Dec. 10		CJ47	305 90	19-- Dec. 1	Balance	✓	305 90
				4		CJ47	151 60
				31		CJ48	172 90
							324 50

ACCOUNT *FUTA Tax Payable* ACCOUNT NO. 271

DATE	ITEM	POST. REF.	DEBIT	DATE	ITEM	POST. REF.	CREDIT
				19-- Dec. 1	Balance	✓	55 94
				14		CJ47	1 13
				31		CJ48	1 13
							58 20

ACCOUNT *State Unemployment Tax Payable* ACCOUNT NO. 281

DATE	ITEM	POST. REF.	DEBIT	DATE	ITEM	POST. REF.	CREDIT
				19-- Dec. 1	Balance	✓	20 62
				14		CJ47	6 07
				31		CJ48	6 07
							32 76

The Adams Appliance Store — General Ledger (*continued*)

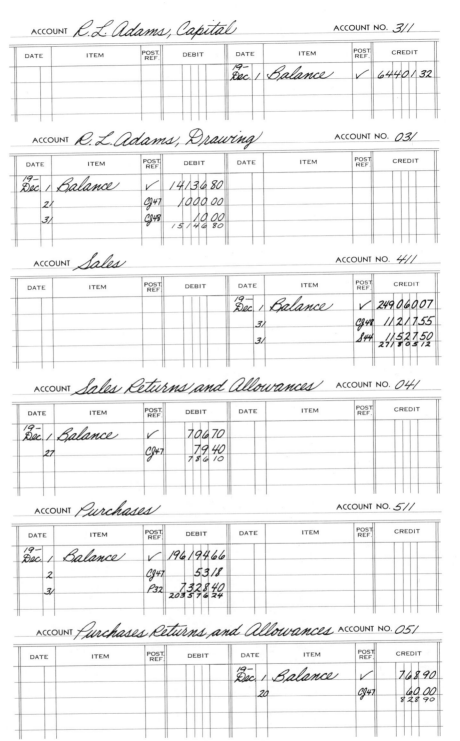

ACCOUNT R. L. Adams, Capital   ACCOUNT NO. 311

DATE	ITEM	POST. REF.	DEBIT	DATE	ITEM	POST. REF.	CREDIT
				19— Dec. 1	Balance	✓	6440132

ACCOUNT R. L. Adams, Drawing   ACCOUNT NO. 031

DATE	ITEM	POST. REF.	DEBIT	DATE	ITEM	POST. REF.	CREDIT
19— Dec. 1	Balance	✓	1413680				
21		CJ47	100000				
31		CJ48	1000				
			1514680				

ACCOUNT Sales   ACCOUNT NO. 411

DATE	ITEM	POST. REF.	DEBIT	DATE	ITEM	POST. REF.	CREDIT
				19— Dec. 1	Balance	✓	24906007
				31		CJ48	1121755
				31		S44	1152750
							27180512

ACCOUNT Sales Returns and Allowances   ACCOUNT NO. 041

DATE	ITEM	POST. REF.	DEBIT	DATE	ITEM	POST. REF.	CREDIT
19— Dec. 1	Balance	✓	70670				
27		CJ47	7940				
			78610				

ACCOUNT Purchases   ACCOUNT NO. 511

DATE	ITEM	POST. REF.	DEBIT	DATE	ITEM	POST. REF.	CREDIT
19— Dec. 1	Balance	✓	19619466				
2		CJ47	5318				
31		P32	732840				
			20357624				

ACCOUNT Purchases Returns and Allowances   ACCOUNT NO. 051

DATE	ITEM	POST. REF.	DEBIT	DATE	ITEM	POST. REF.	CREDIT
				19— Dec. 1	Balance	✓	76890
				20		CJ47	6000
							82890

The Adams Appliance Store — General Ledger (*continued*)

ACCOUNT *Purchases Discount*   ACCOUNT NO. *052*

DATE	ITEM	POST. REF.	DEBIT	DATE	ITEM	POST. REF.	CREDIT
				19— Dec. 1	Balance	✓	686 06
				23		CJ47	29 25
							715 31

ACCOUNT *Rent Expense*   ACCOUNT NO. *611*

DATE	ITEM	POST. REF.	DEBIT	DATE	ITEM	POST. REF.	CREDIT
19— Dec. 1	Balance	✓	6600 00				
2		CJ47	600 00				
			7200 00				

ACCOUNT *Salaries and Commissions Expense*   ACCOUNT NO. *613*

DATE	ITEM	POST. REF.	DEBIT	DATE	ITEM	POST. REF.	CREDIT
19— Dec. 1	Balance	✓	32742 64				
14		CJ47	1666 73				
31		CJ48	1839 00				
			36248 37				

ACCOUNT *Payroll Taxes Expense*   ACCOUNT NO. *614*

DATE	ITEM	POST. REF.	DEBIT	DATE	ITEM	POST. REF.	CREDIT
19— Dec. 1	Balance	✓	1548 63				
14		CJ47	32 09				
31		CJ48	32 09				
			1612 81				

ACCOUNT *Heating and Lighting Expense*   ACCOUNT NO. *615*

DATE	ITEM	POST. REF.	DEBIT	DATE	ITEM	POST. REF.	CREDIT
19— Dec. 1	Balance	✓	636 86				
28		CJ47	73 28				
			710 14				

ACCOUNT *Telephone and Telegraph Expense*   ACCOUNT NO. *617*

DATE	ITEM	POST. REF.	DEBIT	DATE	ITEM	POST. REF.	CREDIT
19— Dec. 1	Balance	✓	284 45				
28		CJ47	32 15				
31		CJ48	1 60				
			318 20				

The Adams Appliance Store — General Ledger (*continued*)

ACCOUNT *Advertising Expense* ACCOUNT NO. 618

DATE		ITEM	POST. REF.	DEBIT	DATE	ITEM	POST. REF.	CREDIT
19— Dec.	1	Balance	✓	4733 49				
	6		CJ47	61 04				
	27		CJ47	421 30				
	31		CJ48	11 09				
				5226 92				

ACCOUNT *Truck Expense* ACCOUNT NO. 622

DATE		ITEM	POST. REF.	DEBIT	DATE	ITEM	POST. REF.	CREDIT
19— Dec.	1	Balance	✓	570 02				
	18		CJ47	65 40				
				635 42				

ACCOUNT *Charitable Contributions Expense* ACCOUNT NO. 623

DATE		ITEM	POST. REF.	DEBIT	DATE	ITEM	POST. REF.	CREDIT
19— Dec.	1	Balance	✓	320 00				
	31		CJ48	5 00				
				325 00				

233

ACCOUNT *Miscellaneous Expense* ACCOUNT NO. 624

DATE		ITEM	POST. REF.	DEBIT	DATE	ITEM	POST. REF.	CREDIT
19— Dec.	1	Balance	✓	4555 86				
	31		CJ48	7 65				
				4563 51				

ACCOUNT *Interest Earned* ACCOUNT NO. 711

DATE	ITEM	POST. REF.	DEBIT	DATE		ITEM	POST. REF.	CREDIT
				19— Dec.	1	Balance	✓	44 90

ACCOUNT *Interest Expense* ACCOUNT NO. 811

DATE		ITEM	POST. REF.	DEBIT	DATE	ITEM	POST. REF.	CREDIT
19— Dec.	1	Balance	✓	57 18				

The Adams Appliance Store — General Ledger (*concluded*)

NAME _R. F. Ambrose_

ADDRESS _5245 Kingwood, St. Louis, MO 63123_

DATE	ITEM	POST. REF.	DEBIT	CREDIT	BALANCE
19— Dec. 5		S257B	477 10		477 10

NAME _A. D. Bowen_

ADDRESS _14811 Pont Dr., St. Louis, MO 63129_

DATE	ITEM	POST. REF.	DEBIT	CREDIT	BALANCE
19— Dec. 1	Dr. Balance	✓			1214 86
11		C		500 00	714 86

NAME _J. C. Burns_

ADDRESS _9440 Arban, St. Louis, MO 63126_

DATE	ITEM	POST. REF.	DEBIT	CREDIT	BALANCE
19— Dec. 5		S235C	1762 38		1762 38

234

NAME _C. M. Furr_

ADDRESS _5374 Delmar, St. Louis, MO 63112_

DATE	ITEM	POST. REF.	DEBIT	CREDIT	BALANCE
19— Dec. 1	Dr. Balance	✓			832 40
11		C		600 00	232 40
24		S256C	1267 03		1499 43

NAME _R. M. Nelson_

ADDRESS _875 Glenway Dr., St. Louis, MO 63122_

DATE	ITEM	POST. REF.	DEBIT	CREDIT	BALANCE
19— Dec. 1	Dr. Balance	✓			769 90
17		C		769 90	— 0 —
27	N S F	Ck881	769 90		769 90

The Adams Appliance Store — Accounts Receivable Ledger

NAME *D. W. Paige*
ADDRESS *Webster Groves, MO 63119*

DATE		ITEM	POST. REF.	DEBIT	CREDIT	BALANCE
19– Dec.	1	Dr. Balance	✓			3 1 2 15
	18		S277Q	1 39 9 37		1 7 1 1 52

NAME *O. W. Peck*
ADDRESS *1685 Avignon Ct., St. Louis, MO 63122*

DATE		ITEM	POST. REF.	DEBIT	CREDIT	BALANCE
19– Dec.	1	Dr. Balance	✓			7 42 19
	18		S262B	1 26 3 55		2 00 5 74
	26		C		1 50 0 00	5 0 5 74
	27		CM12		82 58	4 23 16

235

NAME *V. T. Roberts*
ADDRESS *1659 Forest View Dr, St. Louis, MO 63122*

DATE		ITEM	POST. REF.	DEBIT	CREDIT	BALANCE
19– Dec.	1	Dr. Balance	✓			6 14 06
	24		S281Q	8 94 09		1 5 08 15
	26		C		5 00 00	1 0 08 15

NAME *B. T. Vincent*
ADDRESS *1017 Veronica, Baden, MO 63147*

DATE		ITEM	POST. REF.	DEBIT	CREDIT	BALANCE
19– Dec.	1	Dr. Balance	✓			82 11
	11		C		82 11	– 0 –
	18		S239C	9 18 42		9 18 42

The Adams Appliance Store — Accounts Receivable Ledger (*continued*)

NAME *K. G. Watson*

ADDRESS *51 Webster Woods, St. Louis, MO 63119*

DATE	ITEM	POST. REF.	DEBIT	CREDIT	BALANCE
19— Dec. 1	Dr. Balance	✓			317 23
4		C		317 23	—0—
5		S271Q	394 68		394 68
24		S269B	2156 34		2551 02

NAME *E. E. Wellman*

ADDRESS *5520 Wren, St. Louis, MO 63120*

DATE	ITEM	POST. REF.	DEBIT	CREDIT	BALANCE
19— Dec. 10		S275Q	672 78		672 78

NAME *P. R. Worth*

ADDRESS *23 Stratford Ln., Brentwood, MO 63144*

DATE	ITEM	POST. REF.	DEBIT	CREDIT	BALANCE
19— Dec. 1	Dr. Balance	✓			2867 57
17		C		367 57	
17		N		2500 00	—0—

NAME *A. K. Young*

ADDRESS *Des Peres, MO 63131*

DATE	ITEM	POST. REF.	DEBIT	CREDIT	BALANCE
19— Dec. 1	Dr. Balance	✓			813 52
6		S259B	782 86		1596 38
17		C		813 52	782 86

The Adams Appliance Store — Accounts Receivable Ledger (*concluded*)

NAME *Cabany Electric Co.*
ADDRESS *Maplewood, MO 63143*

DATE	ITEM	POST. REF.	DEBIT	CREDIT	BALANCE
19— Dec. 31	12/30 – 2/30, n/60	P210		815 10	815 10

NAME *Clayshire Electric Co.*
ADDRESS *Richmond Heights, MO 63117*

DATE	ITEM	POST. REF.	DEBIT	CREDIT	BALANCE
19— Dec. 1	Cr. Balance	✓			411 20
6	12/6 – n/30	P205		1941 80	2353 00
9		Ck871	2000 00		353 00

NAME *Ferguson Electric Co.*
ADDRESS *Ferguson, MO 63135*

237

DATE	ITEM	POST. REF.	DEBIT	CREDIT	BALANCE
19— Dec. 1	Cr. Balance	✓			582 90
3	11/30 – n/30	P204		457 30	1040 20
9		Ck872	700 00		340 20

NAME *General Appliance Co.*
ADDRESS *Rock Hill, MO 63045*

DATE	ITEM	POST. REF.	DEBIT	CREDIT	BALANCE
19— Dec. 1	Cr. Balance	✓			1100 00
16		Ck875	800 00		300 00

The Adams Appliance Store — Accounts Payable Ledger
(*continued on next page*)

NAME *Mack Electric Co.*
ADDRESS *4581 Gravois, St. Louis, MO 63116*

DATE		ITEM	POST. REF.	DEBIT	CREDIT	BALANCE
19— Dec.	1	Cr. Balance	✓			673 80
	13	12/13 - 2/10, n/30	P206		1462 50	2136 30
	16		Ck876	673 80		1462 50
	23		Ck879	1433 25		
	23	Discount		29 25		— 0 —
	30	12/27 - 2/10, n/30	P209		594 20	594 20

NAME *Morganford Appliance Co.*
ADDRESS *4214 Arsenal, St. Louis, MO 63116*

DATE		ITEM	POST. REF.	DEBIT	CREDIT	BALANCE
19— Dec.	19	12/19 - 2/30, n/60	P208		1374 90	1374 90

238

NAME *Tipton Electric Co.*
ADDRESS *Lemay, MO 63125*

DATE		ITEM	POST. REF.	DEBIT	CREDIT	BALANCE
19— Dec.	1	Cr. Balance	✓			513 70
	13	12/12 - n/30	P207		682 60	1196 30
	20		CB791	60 00		1136 30

NAME *Watson Safe and Lock Co.*
ADDRESS *408 West Diversey, Chicago, IL 60614*

DATE		ITEM	POST. REF.	DEBIT	CREDIT	BALANCE
19— Dec.	31	12/30 - 2/30, n/60	CJ48		562 00	562 00

The Adams Appliance Store — Accounts Payable Ledger (*concluded*)

The Adams Appliance Store
Trial Balance

Account	Acct. No.	November 30, 19— Dr. Balance	Cr. Balance	December 31, 19— Dr. Balance	Cr. Balance
Columbia National Bank	111	7341 37		1131562	
Petty Cash Fund	112	10000		10000	
Notes Receivable	121			250000	
Accounts Receivable	123	856599		1329158	
Allowance for Bad Debts	012		18612		18612
Merchandise Inventory	131	4251865		4251865	
Prepaid Insurance	141	52616		52616	
Stationery + Supplies	151	17034		19582	
Store Equipment	181	231290		287490	
Accum. Depr. - Store Equip.	018		82940		82940
Delivery Equipment	191	342680		342680	
Accum. Depr. - Del. Equip.	019		210410		210410
Notes Payable	211		124370		124370
Accounts Payable	231		328160		547570
Sales Tax Payable	241		87645		90663
FICA Tax Payable	251		8442		9956
Employees' Inc. Tax Pay.	261		30590		32450
FUTA Tax Payable	271		5594		5820
State Unemp. Tax Pay.	281		2062		3276
R. L. Adams, Capital	311		6440132		6440132
R. L. Adams, Drawing	031	1413680		1514680	
Sales	411		24906007		27180512
Sales Returns + Allow.	041	70670		78610	
Purchases	511	19619466		20357624	
Purchases Returns + Allow.	051		76890		82890
Purchases Discount	052		68606		71531
Rent Expense	611	660000		720000	
Salaries + Comm. Exp.	613	3274264		3624837	
Payroll Taxes Exp.	614	154863		161281	
Heating + Lighting Exp.	615	63686		71014	
Telephone + Telegraph Exp.	617	28445		31820	
Advertising Expense	618	473349		522692	
Truck Expense	622	57002		63542	
Charitable Cont Exp.	623	32000		32500	
Miscellaneous Exp.	624	45586		46351	
Interest Earned	711		4490		4490
Interest Expense	811	5718		5718	
		32394950	32394950	34905622	34905622

The Adams Appliance Store — Trial Balance

The Adams Appliance Store
Schedule of Accounts Receivable

	Nov. 30, 19–	Dec. 31, 19–
R. F. Ambrose		477 10
A. D. Bowen	1214 86	714 86
J. C. Burns		1762 38
C. M. Furr	832 40	1499 43
R. M. Nelson	769 90	769 90
D. W. Paige	312 15	1711 52
O. W. Peck	742 19	423 16
V. T. Roberts	614 06	1008 15
B. T. Vincent	82 11	918 42
K. G. Watson	317 23	2551 02
E. E. Wellman		672 78
P. C. Worth	2867 57	
A. K. Young	813 52	782 86
	8565 99	13291 58
	8565 99	13291 58

The Adams Appliance Store — Schedule of Accounts Receivable

The Adams Appliance Store
Schedule of Accounts Payable

240

	Nov. 30, 19–	Dec. 31, 19–
Cabany Electric Co.		815 10
Clayshire Electric Co.	411 20	353 00
Ferguson Electric Co.	582 90	340 20
General Appliance Co.	1100 00	300 00
Mack Electric Co.	673 80	594 20
Morganford Appliance Co.		1374 90
Tipton Electric Co.	513 70	1136 30
Watson Safe and Lock Co.		562 00
	3281 60	5475 70
	3281 60	5475 70

The Adams Appliance Store — Schedule of Accounts Payable

Report No. 8-2

Complete Report No. 8-2 in the workbook and submit your working papers to the instructor for approval. After completing this report, continue with the textbook discussion in Chapter 9 until the next report is required.

chapter 9

the periodic summary

One of the major reasons for keeping accounting records is to accumulate information that will make it possible to prepare periodic summaries of both **(1)** the revenue and expenses of the business during a specified period and **(2)** the assets, liabilities, and owner's equity of the business at a specified date. A trial balance of the general ledger accounts will provide most of the information that is required for these summaries (the income statement and the balance sheet). However, the trial balance does not supply the data in a form that is easily interpreted, nor does it reflect changes in the accounting elements that have not been represented by ordinary business transactions. Therefore, at the end of a fiscal period it is necessary, first, to determine the kind and amounts of changes that the accounts do not reflect and to adjust the accounts accordingly and, second, to recast the information into the form of an income statement and a balance sheet. These two steps are often referred to as "the periodic summary."

End-of-period work sheet

It has already been mentioned that an end-of-period work sheet is a device that assists the accountant in three ways. It facilitates **(1)** the preparing of the financial statements, **(2)** the making of needed adjustments in the accounts, and **(3)** the closing of the temporary owner's equity accounts. In most cases the accountant is under some pressure to produce the income statement and the balance sheet as soon as possible after the period has ended. The end-of-period work sheet is of greatest assistance in helping the accountant meet this need for promptness. The help that the work sheet gives in making adjustments and in closing the accounts is secondary in importance.

Work sheets are not financial statements; they are devices used to assist the accountant in performing certain of his tasks. Ordinarily it is only the accountant who uses (or even sees) a work sheet. For this reason a work sheet (sometimes called a *working trial balance*) is usually prepared in lead pencil.

A work sheet for a retail store

While an end-of-period work sheet can be in any one of several forms, a common and widely used arrangement involves ten amount columns. The amount columns are used in pairs. The first pair of amount columns is for the trial balance. The data to be recorded consist of the name, number, and debit or credit balance of each account. Debit balances should be entered in the left-hand column and credit balances in the right-hand column. The second pair of amount columns is used to record needed end-of-period adjustments. The third pair of amount columns is used to show the account balances as adjusted. / This pair of amount columns is headed "Adjusted Trial Balance" because its purpose is to show that the debit and credit account balances as adjusted are equal in amount. The fourth pair of amount columns is for the adjusted balances of the expense and revenue accounts. This pair of columns is headed "Income Statement" since the amounts shown will be reported in that statement. The fifth, and last, pair of amount columns is headed "Balance Sheet" and shows the adjusted account balances that will be reported in that statement.

To illustrate the preparation and use of the end-of-period work sheet, the example of the accounts of The Adams Appliance Store will be continued. The journals and ledgers for this business for the month of December were reproduced in the preceding chapter. In this chapter the income statement for the year and the balance sheet at the end of the year will be reproduced, showing the use of a work sheet as a device for summarizing the data to be presented in those statements.

The work sheet for The Adams Appliance Store

The end-of-year work sheet for this business is reproduced on pages 244 and 245. Following is a description and discussion of the steps that were followed in the preparation of this work sheet. Each step should be studied carefully with frequent reference to the work sheet itself.

Trial Balance Columns. The trial balance of the general ledger accounts as of December 31 was entered in the first pair of amount columns. This trial balance is the same as the one shown on page 239 except that all of the account titles were included in the work sheet list even though certain of the accounts had no balances at this point.

The Trial Balance Debit and Credit columns were totaled. The totals should be equal. If not, the cause of any discrepancy must be found and corrected before the preparation of the work sheet can proceed.

Adjustments Columns. The second pair of amount columns on the work sheet was used to record certain entries that were necessary to reflect various changes that had occurred during the year in some of the accounting elements. In this case, adjustments were needed: **(1)** to remove the amount of the beginning-of-year merchandise inventory and to record the amount of the end-of-year inventory; **(2)** to record the amounts of interest earned but not collected, and of interest expense incurred but not paid; **(3)** to record the portions of prepaid insurance expired, and of stationery and supplies used during the year; **(4)** to record the estimated depreciation expense for the year; and **(5)** to record the estimated amount of expected bad debt losses.

243

Eight complete entries involving eight debits and nine credits were made in the Adjustments columns to reflect these changes. When an account was debited, the amount was entered on the same horizontal line as the name of the account and in the Adjustments Debit column. Amounts credited were entered, of course, in the Credit column. Each such entry made on the work sheet was identified by a small letter in parentheses to facilitate cross-reference. Following is an explanation of each of the entries:

Entry (a): In order to remove the amount of the beginning inventory of merchandise from the asset account and at the same time to include it in the determination of net income for the current year, Expense and Revenue Summary, Account No. 321, was debited, and Merchandise Inventory, Account No. 131, was credited for $42,518.65. This amount was the calculated cost of the inventory at the end of the preceding year (the beginning of the year under consideration). The amount had been in the merchandise inventory account as a debit since the accounts were adjusted as of December 31 a year ago.

Entry (b): This entry recorded the calculated cost of the merchandise on hand December 31 — often referred to as the year-end inventory. The calculation was based on a physical count of the merchandise in stock at the close of the year. The cost of the merchandise in stock was recorded

The Adams Appliance Store
Work Sheet
For the Year Ended December 31, 19—

Acct. No.	Account	Trial Balance Debit	Trial Balance Credit	Adjustments Debit	Adjustments Credit	Adj. Trial Balance Debit	Adj. Trial Balance Credit	Income Statement Debit	Income Statement Credit	Balance Sheet Debit	Balance Sheet Credit
111	Columbia National Bank	1131562				1131562				1131562	
112	Petty Cash Fund	10000				10000				10000	
121	Notes Receivable	250000				250000				250000	
122	Accrued Interest Receivable			(c) 729		729				729	
123	Accounts Receivable	1329158				1329158				1329158	
012	Allowance for Bad Debts		18612		(b) 122312		140924				140924
131	Merchandise Inventory	4251865		(d) 4712640	(a) 4251865	4712640				4712640	
141	Prepaid Insurance	52616			(e) 26308	26308				26308	
151	Stationery and Supplies	19582			(f) 16082	3500				3500	
191	Store Equipment	287490				287490				287490	
018	Accum. Depr.- Store Equip.		82940		(g) 23129		106069				106069
191	Delivery Equipment	342680				342680				342680	
019	Accum. Depr.- Delivery Equip.		210410		(g) 85670		296080				296080
211	Notes Payable		124370				124370				124370
221	Accrued Interest Payable				(d) 1161		1161				1161
231	Accounts Payable		547570				547570				547570
241	Sales Tax Payable		90663				90663				90663
251	F.I.C.A. Tax Payable		9956				9956				9956
261	Employees Income Tax Pay.		32450				32450				32450
271	F.U.T.A. Tax Payable		5820				5820				5820
281	State Unemployment Tax Pay.		3276				3276				3276
311	R.L. Adams, Capital		6440132				6440132				6440132
031	R.L. Adams, Drawing	1514680				1514680				1514680	
321	Expense + Revenue Summary			(a) 4251865	(d) 4712640	4251865	4712640	4251865	4712640		
411	Sales		27180512				27180512		27180512		
041	Sales Returns + Allowances	78610				78610		78610			
511	Purchases	20357624				20357624		20357624			
051	Purchases Returns + Allowances		82890				82890		82890		
052	Purchases Discount		71531				71531		71531		

The Adams Appliance Store — Ten-Column Work Sheet

Account	No.	Trial Balance Dr	Adjustments Dr	Adjustments Cr	Adj. Trial Balance Dr	Adj. Trial Balance Cr	Income Statement Dr	Income Statement Cr
Rent Expense	611	7200 00			7200 00		7200 00	
Depreciation Expense	612		(b) 1087 99		1087 99		1087 99	
Salaries + Commissions Exp.	613	36248 37			36248 37		36248 37	
Payroll Taxes Expense	614	1612 81			1612 81		1612 81	
Heating + Lighting Expense	615	710 14			710 14		710 14	
Stationery + Supplies Exp.	616		(f) 160 82		160 82		160 82	
Telephone + Telegraph Exp.	617	318 20			318 20		318 20	
Advertising Expense	618	5226 92			5226 92		5226 92	
Bad Debts Expense	619		(d) 1223 12		1223 12		1223 12	
Insurance Expense	620		(e) 263 08		263 08		263 08	
Truck Expense	622	635 42			635 42		635 42	
Charitable Contributions Exp.	623	325 00			325 00		325 00	
Miscellaneous Expense	624	463 51			463 51		463 51	
Interest Earned	711			(c) 7 29		52 19		52 19
Interest Expense	811	57 18	(a) 11 61		68 79		68 79	
		34905622	9239896	9239896	39851263	39851263	30242516	32052792
Net Income							1810276	
							32052792	32052792

245

by debiting Merchandise Inventory, Account No. 131, and by crediting Expense and Revenue Summary, Account No. 321, for $47,126.40.

Entry (c): This entry recorded the accrued interest that had been earned but not received by debiting Accrued Interest Receivable, Account No. 122, and by crediting Interest Earned, Account No. 711, for $7.29. The December 31 trial balance shows that Notes Receivable had a debit balance of $2,500. This was the amount of a 7 percent, 30-day note dated December 16, signed by P. R. Worth. From December 16 to December 31 was 15 days. Interest at 7 percent per year on $2,500 for 15 days is $7.29.

Entry (d): This entry recorded the accrued interest expense that had been incurred but not paid by debiting Interest Expense, Account No. 811, and by crediting Accrued Interest Payable, Account No. 221, for $11.61. The December 31 trial balance shows that Notes Payable had a credit balance of $1,243.70. This related to a 6 percent, six-month note dated November 5. From November 5 to December 31 was 56 days. Interest at the rate of 6 percent per year on $1,243.70 for 56 days is $11.61.

Entry (e): This entry recorded the insurance expense for the year by debiting Insurance Expense, Account No. 621, and by crediting Prepaid Insurance, Account No. 141, for $263.08. The December 31 trial balance shows that Prepaid Insurance had a debit balance of $526.16. This amount was the cost of a two-year policy dated January 2 of the year under consideration. By December 31 one year had elapsed and, thus, one half of the premium paid had become an expense.

Entry (f): This entry recorded the calculated cost of the stationery and supplies used during the year by debiting Stationery and Supplies Expense, Account No. 616, and by crediting Stationery and Supplies, Account No. 151, for $160.82. The December 31 trial balance shows that Stationery and Supplies had a debit balance of $195.82. This amount was the sum of the cost of any stationery and supplies on hand at the start of the year, plus the cost of stationery and supplies purchased during the year. A physical count of the stationery and supplies on hand December 31 was made and the cost determined to be $35. Thus, stationery and supplies that cost $160.82 ($195.82 − $35) had been used during the year.

Entry (g): This entry recorded the calculated depreciation expense for the year by debiting Depreciation Expense, Account No. 612, for $1,087.99 and by crediting Accumulated Depreciation — Store Equipment, Account No. 018, for $231.29 and crediting Accumulated Depreciation — Delivery Equipment, Account No. 019, for $856.70. The December 31 trial balance shows that Store Equipment had a debit balance of $2,874.90. This balance represented the $2,312.90 cost of various items of property that had been owned the entire year plus the $562 cost of the safe that was purchased on December 31. Mr. Adams follows the policy of not calculating any depreciation on assets that have been owned for less than a month. Thus, depreciation expense for the year on store equipment relates to property that had been owned for the entire year. Its cost was $2,312.90. This equipment is being depreciated at the rate of 10 percent a year. Ten percent of $2,312.90 is $231.29.

The December 31 trial balance shows that the delivery equipment account had a debit balance of $3,426.80. This was the cost of a delivery truck that had been owned the entire year. The truck is being depreciated at the rate of 25 percent per year. Twenty-five percent of $3,426.80 is $856.70.

Entry (h): This entry recorded the estimated bad debts expense for the year by debiting Bad Debts Expense, Account No. 619, and by crediting Allowance for Bad Debts, Account No. 012, for $1,223.12. Guided by past experience, Mr. Adams estimated that bad debt losses will be approximately one percent of the total sales on account for the year. Investigation of the records revealed that such sales amounted to $122,312.25. One percent of $122,312.25 is $1,223.12.

After making the required entries in the Adjustments columns of the work sheet, the columns were totaled to prove the equality of the debit and credit entries.

Adjusted Trial Balance Columns. The third pair of amount columns of the work sheet was used for the *adjusted trial balance*. To determine the balance of each account after making the required adjustments, it was necessary to take into consideration the amounts recorded in the first two pairs of amount columns. When an account balance was not affected by entries in the Adjustments columns, the amount in the Trial Balance columns was extended directly to the Adjusted Trial Balance columns.

When an account balance was affected by an entry in the Adjustments columns, the balance recorded in the Trial Balance columns was increased or decreased, as the case might be, by the amount of the adjusting entry. For example, Accumulated Depreciation — Store Equipment was listed in the Trial Balance Credit column as $829.40. Since there was an entry of $231.29 in the Adjustments Credit column, the amount extended to the Adjusted Trial Balance Credit column was found by addition to be $1,060.69 ($829.40 + $231.29). Prepaid Insurance was listed in the Trial Balance Debit column as $526.16. Since there was an entry of $263.08 in the Adjustments Credit column, the amount to be extended to the Adjusted Trial Balance Debit column was found by subtraction to be $263.08 ($526.16 − $263.08).

247

There is one exception to the procedure just described that relates to the debit and the credit on the line for Expense and Revenue Summary, Account No. 321, in the Adjustments columns. While the $4,607.75 excess of the $47,126.40 credit (the amount of the end-of-year merchandise inventory) over the $42,518.65 debit (the amount of the beginning-of-year merchandise inventory) could be extended to the Adjusted Trial Balance Credit column, it is better to extend both the debit and the credit amounts into the Adjusted Trial Balance columns. The reason is that both amounts are used in the preparation of the income statement and, accordingly, it is helpful to have both amounts appear in the Income Statement columns. Therefore, both amounts are shown in the Adjusted Trial Balance columns.

The Adjusted Trial Balance columns were totaled to prove the equality of the debits and credits.

Income Statement Columns. The fourth pair of amount columns of the work sheet was used to show the amounts that will be reported in the income statement. The manner of extending the debit and credit amounts on the line for Expense and Revenue Summary was mentioned previously. The amounts for sales, purchases returns and allowances, purchases discount, and interest earned were extended to the Income Statement Credit column. The amounts for sales returns and allowances, purchases, and all of the expenses were extended to the Income Statement Debit column.

The Income Statement columns were totaled. The difference between the totals of these columns is the amount of the increase or the decrease in owner's equity due to net income or net loss during the accounting period. If the total of the credits exceeds the total of the debits, the difference represents the increase in owner's equity due to net income; if the total of the debits exceeds the total of the credits, the difference represents the decrease in owner's equity due to net loss.

Reference to the Income Statement columns of The Adams Appliance Store work sheet will show that the total of the credits amounted to $320,527.92 and the total of the debits amounted to $302,425.16. The difference, amounting to $18,102.76, was the amount of the net income for the year.

Balance Sheet Columns. The fifth pair of amount columns of the work sheet was used to show the amounts that will be reported in the balance sheet. The Balance Sheet columns were totaled. The difference between the totals of these columns also is the amount of the net income or the net loss for the accounting period. If the total of the debits exceeds the total of the credits, the difference represents a net income for the accounting period; if the total of the credits exceeds the total of the debits, the difference represents a net loss for the period. This difference should be the same as the difference between the totals of the Income Statement columns.

Reference to the Balance Sheet columns of the work sheet will show that the total of the debits amounted to $96,087.47 and the total of the credits amounted to $77,984.71. The difference of $18,102.76 represented the amount of the net income for the year.

Completing the Work Sheet. The difference between the totals of the Income Statement columns and the totals of the Balance Sheet columns should be recorded on the next horizontal line below the totals. If the difference represents net income, it should be so designated and recorded in the Income Statement Debit and in the Balance Sheet Credit columns. If, instead, a net loss has been the result, the amount should be so designated and entered in the Income Statement Credit and in the Balance Sheet Debit columns. Finally, the totals of the Income Statement and Balance Sheet columns, after the net income (or net loss) has been recorded, are entered, and a double line is ruled immediately below the totals.

Proving the Work Sheet. The work sheet provides proof of the arithmetical accuracy of the data that it summarizes. The totals of the Trial Balance columns, the Adjustments columns, and the Adjusted Trial Balance columns must be equal in each case. The amount of the difference between the totals of the Income Statement columns must be exactly the same as the amount of the difference between the totals of the Balance Sheet columns.

249

The reason why the same amount must be inserted to cause both the Income Statement columns and the Balance Sheet columns to be in balance was mentioned in Chapter 5. Stated slightly differently, the explanation is found in the basic difference between the balance sheet accounts and the income statement accounts, and in an understanding of the real nature of net income (or net loss). The reality of net income is that the assets have increased, or that the liabilities have decreased, or that some combination of both events has taken place during a period of time. Day by day most of these changes have been recorded in the asset and liability accounts in order that they may be kept up-to-date. However, the effect of the changes on the owner's equity element is not recorded in the permanent owner's equity account. Instead, the changes are recorded in the temporary owner's equity accounts — the revenue and expense accounts.

Thus, at the end of the period after the accounts have been adjusted, each of the asset and liability accounts reflects the amount of that element *at the end of the period.* If, however, there have been no capital investments during the period and any withdrawals have been charged to a drawing account, the balance of the owner's capital account is the amount of his equity *at the beginning of the period.* (All of the changes in owner's equity are shown in the revenue and expense accounts and in the drawing account.)

As applied to the work sheet, this must mean that the Balance Sheet column totals are out of balance by the amount of the change in owner's equity that is due to net income or net loss for the period involved. If there was net income, the assets, in total, are either that much larger, or the liabilities are that much smaller, or some combination of such changes has resulted. In other words, the asset and liability accounts reflect the net income of the period, but the owner's capital account, at this point, does not. It is only after the temporary accounts are closed at the end of the period and the amount of the net income for the period has been transferred to the owner's capital account that the latter account reflects the net income of the period.

The owner's capital account lacks two things to bring its balance up-to-date (as are the balances of the asset and liability accounts): **(1)** the decrease due to any withdrawals during the period which is reflected in the debit balance of the drawing account and **(2)** the increase due to any net income for the period. On the work sheet the debit balance of the drawing account is extended to the Balance Sheet Debit column. Thus, all that is needed to cause the Balance Sheet columns to be equal is the amount of the net income for the year — the same amount that is the difference between the totals of the Income Statement columns.

250

Report No. 9-1

Complete Report No. 9-1 in the workbook and submit your working papers to the instructor for approval. After completing the report, continue with the following study assignment until the next report is required.

The financial statements

The financial statements usually consist of **(1)** an income statement and **(2)** a balance sheet. The purpose of an income statement is to summarize the results of operations during an accounting period. The income statement provides information as to the sources of revenue, types of expenses, and the amount of the net income or the net loss for the period. The purpose of a balance sheet is to provide information as to the status of a business at a specified date. The balance sheet shows the kinds and amounts of assets and liabilities and the owner's equity in the business at a specified point in time — usually at the close of business on the last day of the accounting period.

The income statement

A formal statement of the results of the operation of a business during an accounting period is called an *income statement*. Other titles commonly used for this statement include *profit and loss statement, income and expense statement, revenue and expense statement, operating statement*, and *report of earnings*. Whatever the title, the purpose of the statement or report is to show the types and amounts of revenue and expenses that the business had during the period involved, and the resulting net income or net loss for this accounting period.

Importance of the Income Statement. The income statement is now generally considered to be the most important financial statement of a business. A business cannot exist indefinitely unless it has profit or net income. The income statement is essentially a "report card" of the enterprise. The statement provides a basis for judging the overall effectiveness of the management. Decisions as to whether to continue a business, to expand it, or to contract it are often based upon the results as reported in the income statement. Actual and potential creditors are interested in income statements because one of the best reasons for extending credit or for making a loan is that the business is profitable.

Various government agencies are interested in income statements of businesses for a variety of reasons. Regulatory bodies are concerned with the earnings of the enterprises they regulate, because a part of the regulation usually relates to the prices, rates, or fares that may be charged. If the enterprise is either exceptionally profitable or unprofitable, some change in the allowed prices or rates may be needed. Income tax authorities, — federal, state and local — have an interest in business income statements. Net income determination for tax purposes differs somewhat from the calculation of net income for other purposes, but, for a variety of reasons, the tax authorities are interested in both sets of calculations.

Form of the Income Statement. The form of the income statement depends, in part, upon the type of business. For merchandising businesses, the so-called "ladder type" is commonly used. This name is applied because the final net income is calculated on a step-by-step basis. The

251

amount of gross sales is shown first with sales returns and allowances deducted. The difference is *net sales*. Cost of goods sold is next subtracted to arrive at *gross margin* (sometimes called *gross profit*). The portion of the statement down to this point is sometimes called the "trading section." Operating expenses are next listed, and the total of their amounts is subtracted to arrive at the amount of the *net operating income*. Finally, the amounts of any "other" revenue are added and any "other" expenses are subtracted to arrive at the final amount of net income (or net loss).

It is essential that the statement be properly headed. The name of the business (or of the individual if it is a professional practice or if the owner operates a business in his own name) should be shown first. The name of the statement is then shown followed by the period of time that the statement covers. It is common practice to state this as, for example, "For the Year Ended December 31, 1972" (or whatever the period and ending date happen to be).

The income statement presented to the owner (or owners) of a business, and to potential creditors or other interested parties is usually in typewritten form. Very often, however, the accountant prepares the original statement in pencil or ink on ruled paper. This is used by the typist in preparing typewritten copies. The income statement for The Adams Appliance Store for the year ended December 31, 19--, is shown on page 253. The information needed in preparing the statement was obtained from the work sheet shown on pages 244 and 245.

Income Statement Analysis. There are various procedures employed to assist in the interpretation of income statements. One device is to present income statements for two or more comparable periods in comparative form. If the figures for two periods are shown in adjacent columns, a third column showing the amount of increase or decrease in each element may be shown. This will call attention to changes which may be of major significance.

Another analytical device is to express all, or at least the major, items on the statement as a percent of net sales and then to compare these percentages for two or more periods. For example, if the net sales of $271,019.02 for The Adams Appliance Store for the year just ended are treated as 100 percent, the cost of goods sold which amounted to $197,424.28 was equal to 73 percent of net sales; the gross margin on sales which amounted to $73,594.74 was equal to 27 percent of net sales; operating expenses which amounted to $55,475.38 were equal to 20.5 percent of net sales; net operating income which amounted to $18,199.36 was equal to 6.72 percent of net sales; and net income which amounted to $18,102.76 was equal to 6.68 percent of net sales. A comparison of these percentages with the same data for one or more prior years would reveal

THE ADAMS APPLIANCE STORE
Income Statement
For the Year Ended December 31, 19--

Operating revenue:

Sales.........................			$271,805.12
Less sales returns and allowances..			786.10
Net sales.......................			$271,019.02

Cost of goods sold:

Merchandise inventory, January 1 ...		$ 42,518.65	
Purchases.....................	$203,576.24		
Less: Pur. ret. and allow. $828.90			
Purchases discount. 715.31	1,544.21		
Net purchases..................		202,032.03	
Merchandise available for sale.....		$244,550.68	
Less merchandise inv., Dec. 31 ...		47,126.40	
Cost of goods sold............			197,424.28
Gross margin on sales.............			$ 73,594.74

Operating expenses:

Rent expense...................	$ 7,200.00	
Depreciation expense...........	1,087.99	
Salaries and commissions expense...	36,248.37	
Payroll taxes expense...........	1,612.81	
Heating and lighting expense......	710.14	
Stationery and supplies expense....	160.82	
Telephone and telegraph expense..	318.20	
Advertising expense.............	5,226.92	
Bad debts expense.............	1,223.12	
Insurance expense..............	263.08	
Truck expense.................	635.42	
Charitable contributions expense....	325.00	
Miscellaneous expense...........	463.51	
Total operating expenses.......		55,475.38
Net operating income.............		$ 18,119.36

Other expenses:

Interest expense................	$ 68.79	

Other revenue:

Interest earned................	52.19	16.60
Net income......................		$ 18,102.76

The Adams Appliance Store — Income Statement

trends that would surely be of interest, and perhaps of real concern, to the management of the business.

The balance sheet

A formal statement of the assets, liabilities, and owner's equity in a business at a specified date is known as a *balance sheet*. The title of the statement had its origin in the equality of the elements, that is, in the balance between the sum of the assets and the sum of the liabilities and owner's equity. Sometimes the balance sheet is called a *statement of assets and liabilities*, a *statement of condition*, or a *statement of financial position*. Various other titles are used occasionally.

Importance of the Balance Sheet. The balance sheet of a business is of considerable interest to various parties for several reasons. The owner or owners of a business are interested in the kinds and amounts of assets and liabilities, and the amount of the owner's equity or capital element.

Creditors of the business are interested in the financial position of the enterprise, particularly as it pertains to the claims they have and the prospects for prompt payment. Potential creditors or possible lenders are concerned about the financial position of the business. Their decision as to whether to extend credit or to make loans to the business may depend, in large part, upon the condition of the enterprise as revealed by a balance sheet.

Persons considering buying an ownership interest in a business are greatly interested in the character and amount of the assets and liabilities, though this interest is probably secondary to their concern about the future earnings possibilities.

Finally, various regulatory bodies are interested in the financial position of the businesses that are under their jurisdiction. Examples of regulated businesses include banks, insurance companies, public utilities, railroads, and airlines.

Form of the Balance Sheet. Traditionally, balance sheets have been presented either in *account form* or in *report form*. When the account form is followed, the assets are listed on the left side of the page (or on the left of two facing pages) and the liabilities and owner's equity are listed on the right. This form is similar to the debit-side and credit-side arrangement of the standard ledger account. The balance sheet of The Adams Appliance Store as of December 31, 19--, in account form is reproduced on pages 256 and 257. The data for the preparation of the statement were secured from the work sheet.

When the report form of the balance sheet is followed, the assets, liabilities, and owner's equity elements are exhibited in that order on the page. The balance sheet of Howard C. Miller, Architect, was shown in report form on page 124. This arrangement is generally superior when the statement is typed on regular letter-size paper (8½″ x 11″).

Whichever form is used, it is essential that the statement have the proper heading. This means that three things must be shown: **(1)** The name of the business must be given (or the name of the individual if the business or professional practice is carried on in the name of an individual), followed by **(2)** the name of the statement — usually just "Balance Sheet," and finally **(3)** the date — month, day, and year. Sometimes the expression "As of Close of Business December 31, 1972" (or whatever date is involved) is included. It must be remembered that a balance sheet relates to a particular moment of time.

Classification of Data in the Balance Sheet. The purpose of the balance sheet and of all other financial statements and reports is to convey as much information as possible. This aim is furthered by some classification of the data being reported. As applied to balance sheets, it has become almost universal practice to classify both assets and liabilities as between those that are considered "current" and those that are considered "noncurrent" or "long-lived."

255

Current Assets. *Current assets* include cash and all other assets that may be reasonably expected to be realized in cash or sold or consumed during the normal operating cycle of the business. In a merchandising business the current assets usually will include cash, receivables, such as notes and accounts receivable, merchandise inventory, and temporary investments. Prepaid expenses, such as unexpired insurance and unused stationery and supplies, are also generally treated as current assets. This is not because such items will be realized in cash, but because they will probably be consumed in a relatively short time.

The asset cash may be represented by one or more accounts, such as bank checking accounts, bank savings accounts, or a petty cash fund. Reference to The Adams Appliance Store balance sheet will show that cash is listed at $11,415.62. Reference to the work sheet will show that this is made up of two items: the balance in the checking account at the Columbia National Bank, $11,315.62, and the amount of the petty cash fund, $100.

Temporary investments refer to those assets that have been acquired with money that would otherwise have been temporarily idle and unproductive. Such investments usually take the form of corporate stocks, bonds, or notes, or any of several types of government bonds. Quite often the policy is to invest in securities that can be liquidated in a short time with

Assets

Current assets:

Cash..........................		$11,415.62
Notes receivable................	$ 2,500.00	
Accrued interest receivable........	7.29	
Accounts receivable..............	13,291.58	
Total receivables..............	$15,798.87	
Less allowance for bad debts....	1,409.24	14,389.63
Merchandise inventory............		47,126.40
Prepaid insurance................		263.08
Stationery and supplies...........		35.00
Total current assets............		$73,229.73

Long-lived assets:

Store equipment.................	$ 2,874.90		
Less accumulated depreciation....	1,060.69	$ 1,814.21	
Delivery equipment...............	$ 3,426.80		
Less accumulated depreciation....	2,960.80	466.00	
Total long-lived assets.........			2,280.21
Total assets......................			$75,509.94

256

The Adams Appliance Store — Balance Sheet (Left Side)

little chance of loss. So-called *marketable securities* are often favored. Assets of the same type may be owned by a business for many years, and, under such circumstances, they would not be classified as temporary investments. It is the matter of intention that indicates whether the investments are to be classified as temporary and included in the current assets or considered as long-term investments and either be included in the long-lived asset classification or in a separate classification entitled *Permanent Investments.*

Reference to the balance sheet of The Adams Appliance Store above and on page 257 reveals that the current assets of this business consisted of cash, notes receivable, accrued interest receivable, accounts receivable, merchandise inventory, prepaid insurance, and stationery and supplies.

Long-Lived Assets. Property that is used in the operation of a merchandising business may include such assets as land, buildings, office equipment, store equipment, and delivery equipment. Such assets are called *long-lived*

APPLIANCE STORE
Sheet
31, 19--

Liabilities

Current liabilities:

Notes payable...................	$ 1,243.70	
Accrued interest payable..........	11.61	
Accounts payable................	5,475.70	
Sales tax payable...............	906.63	
FICA tax payable...............	99.56	
Employees income tax payable.....	324.50	
FUTA tax payable...............	58.20	
State unemployment tax payable...	32.76	
Total current liabilities..........		$ 8,152.66

Owner's Equity

R. L. Adams, capital:

Capital, January 1...............		$64,401.32	
Net income....................	$18,102.76		
Less withdrawals...............	15,146.80	2,955.96	
Capital, December 31............			67,357.28

257

Total liabilities and owner's equity....	$75,509.94

The Adams Appliance Store — Balance Sheet (Right Side)

assets. Of these assets only land is really permanent; however, all of these assets have a useful life that is comparatively long.

Reference to the balance sheet of The Adams Appliance Store will show that the long-lived assets of the business consist of store equipment and delivery equipment. In each case, the amount of the accumulated depreciation is shown as a deduction from the cost of the equipment. The difference represents the *undepreciated cost* of the equipment. This is the amount that will be written off as depreciation expense in future periods.

Current Liabilities. *Current liabilities* include those obligations that will be due in a short time and paid with monies provided by the current assets. As of December 31, the current liabilities of The Adams Appliance Store consisted of notes payable, accrued interest payable, accounts payable, sales tax payable, FICA tax payable, employees income tax payable, FUTA tax payable, and state unemployment tax payable.

Long-Term Liabilities. *Long-term liabilities* (sometimes called *fixed liabilities*) include those obligations that will not be due for a relatively long time. The most common of the long-term liabilities is mortgages payable.

A mortgage payable is a debt or an obligation that is secured by a *mortgage*, which provides for the conveyance of certain property upon failure to pay the debt at maturity. When the debt is paid, the mortgage becomes void. It will be seen, therefore, that a mortgage payable differs little from an account payable or a note payable except that the creditor holds the mortgage as security for the payment of the debt. Usually debts secured by mortgages run for a longer period of time than ordinary notes payable or accounts payable. A mortgage payable should be classified as a long-term liability if the maturity date extends beyond the normal operating cycle of the business (usually a year). The Adams Appliance Store has no long-term liabilities.

Owner's Equity. As previously explained, accounts relating to the owner's equity element may be either permanent or temporary owner's equity accounts. The permanent owner's equity accounts used in recording the operations of a particular enterprise depend upon the type of legal organization, that is, whether the enterprise is organized as a sole proprietorship, as a partnership, or as a corporation.

In the case of a sole propreitorship, one or more accounts representing the owner's interest or equity in the assets may be kept. Reference to the chart of accounts, shown on page 197, will reveal that the following accounts are classified as owner's equity accounts:

Account No. 311, R. L. Adams, Capital
Account No. 031, R. L. Adams, Drawing
Account No. 321, Expense and Revenue Summary

Account No. 311 reflects the amount of Mr. Adams' equity. It may be increased by additional investments or by the practice of not withdrawing cash or other assets in an amount as large as the net income of the enterprise; it may be decreased by withdrawals in excess of the amount of the net income or by sustaining a net loss during one or more accounting periods. Usually there will be no changes in the balance of this account during the accounting period, in which case the balance represents the owner's investment in the business as of the beginning of the accounting period and until such time as the books are closed at the end of the accounting period.

Account No. 031 is Mr. Adams' drawing account. This account is charged for any withdrawals of cash or other property for personal use. It is a temporary account in which is kept a record of the owner's personal

258

drawings during the accounting period. Ordinarily such drawings are made in anticipation of earnings rather than as withdrawals of capital. The balance of the account, as shown by the trial balance at the close of an accounting period, represents the total amount of the owner's drawings during the period.

Reference to the work sheet shown on pages 244 and 245 will reveal that the balance of Mr. Adams' drawing account is listed in the Balance Sheet Debit column. This is because there is no provision on a work sheet for making deductions from owner's equity except by listing them in the Debit column. Since the balance of the owner's capital account is listed in the Balance Sheet Credit column, the listing of the balance of the owner's drawing account in the Debit column is equivalent to deducting the amount from the balance of the owner's capital account.

Account No. 321 is used only at the close of the accounting period for the purpose of summarizing the temporary owner's equity accounts. Sometimes this account is referred to as a *clearing account*. No entries should appear in the account before the books are closed at the end of the accounting period.

The owner's equity section of the balance sheet of The Adams Appliance Store is arranged to show the major changes that took place during the year in the owner's equity element of the business. Mr. Adams' interest in the business amounted to $64,401.32 at the beginning of the period. His interest was increased $18,102.76 as the result of profitable operations, and decreased $15,146.80 as the result of withdrawals during the year. Thus, the owner's equity element of the business on December 31 amounted to $67,357.28.

Balance Sheet Analysis. The information provided by a balance sheet can be analyzed in several ways to assist in judging the financial position and soundness of the business. A few of the major analytical procedures will be briefly considered.

A balance sheet as of one date may be compared with a balance sheet as of another date to determine the amount of the increase or the decrease in any of the accounts or groups of accounts. Sometimes balance sheets as of two or more dates are prepared in comparative form by listing the amounts as of different dates in parallel columns. Thus, if balance sheets as of the close of two succeeding calendar years are compared, it is possible to determine the amount of the increase or the decrease during the intervening period in any of the accounts or groups of accounts involved. If such a comparison reveals an increase in accounts receivable, it may indicate that collections during the later period were not as favorable as they were during the preceding period. If the comparison reveals an increase in accounts payable, it may indicate an inability to pay current bills because

259

of insufficient cash. If the comparison reveals an increase in the current assets without a corresponding increase in the liabilities, it may indicate an improved financial position or status.

Too much emphasis should not be placed upon an increase or a decrease in cash. Some individuals are inclined to judge the results of operations largely by the cash balance. This practice may be misleading. The net results of operations can be properly determined only by comparison of all the assets and the liabilities. The ability of a business to meet its current obligations may be determined largely by an analysis of its current assets, particularly those assets that are sometimes referred to as the quick assets. *Quick assets* include cash and all other current assets that are readily realizable in cash, such as temporary investments in the form of marketable securities.

The relation of an account, a group of accounts, or an accounting element to another account, group of accounts, or accounting element may be referred to as the *ratio*. For example, if the total current assets amount to twice as much as the total current liabilities, the ratio is said to be 2 to 1. Ratios may be expressed in percentages or on a unit basis. Fractions of units may be expressed by means of common fractions or decimals as, for example, 7¾ to 1 or 7.75 to 1.

260

In an enterprise in which capital invested is a material revenue-producing factor, such as is the case in a merchandising enterprise, the ratio of the current assets to the current liabilities may be important. Reference to the balance sheet shown on pages 256 and 257 reveals that the total current assets amount to $73,229.73 and the total current liabilities amount to $8,152.66, a ratio of nearly 9 to 1. The total assets amount to $75,509.94 and the total liabilities amount to $8,152.66, a ratio of over 9 to 1. These ratios are sufficiently high to indicate a very favorable financial position.

Banks often consider the ratio of current assets to current liabilities when considering the advisability of making a loan. It is not expected that the long-lived assets will be sold to realize sufficient funds with which to pay a short-term loan. If the balance sheet seems to indicate that a sufficient amount of cash will not be realized from the collection of accounts receivable or from the sales of service or merchandise to repay a loan at maturity, the bank may consider the loan inadvisable. The excess of the amount of the current assets over the amount of the current liabilities is called *net current assets* or *working capital*.

It is difficult to estimate what the proper ratio of current assets to current liabilities should be, because of the variations in enterprises and industries. A 2 to 1 ratio of current assets to current liabilities may be more than sufficient in some enterprises but entirely insufficient in others.

In the milk distributing business, for example, a 1 to 1 ratio of current assets to current liabilities is considered satisfactory. The reasons are that very little capital is tied up in inventory, the amount of accounts receivable is comparatively small, and the terms on which the milk is purchased from farmers are such that settlements are slow and comparatively large amounts are due to farmers at all times. Another reason is that a large amount of capital is invested in long-lived assets, such as equipment for treating the milk and for delivering it to customers.

Generally speaking, the ratio of the current assets to the current liabilities should be maintained in a range from 2 to 1 to 5 to 1. While a standard ratio cannot be established for all enterprises, a knowledge of the working capital requirements of a particular enterprise will be helpful in determining what the ratio of current assets to current liabilities should be.

A comparison of the relationships between certain amounts in the income statement and certain amounts in the balance sheet may be informative. The leading example of this type is the ratio of net income to owner's equity in the business. The owner's equity of The Adams Appliance Store was $64,401.32 on January 1. The net income for the year of $18,102.76 was over 28 percent of this amount. A comparison of this ratio with the ratio of net income to capital invested in prior years should be of interest to the owner. It may also be of interest to compare the ratio of the net income of The Adams Appliance Store to the amount of capital invested by Mr. Adams with the same ratio for others stores of comparable nature and size. It is important to note, however, that the net income of The Adams Appliance Store was computed without regard to any salary or other compensation for the services of Mr. Adams. In comparing the results of operations of The Adams Appliance Store with those of other retail appliance businesses, some appropriate adjustment of the data might be needed to make the comparison valid.

Inventory turnover

A merchant is usually interested in knowing the rate of *inventory turnover* for each accounting period. This has reference to the number of times the merchandise available for sale is turned during the accounting period. The rate of turnover is found by dividing the cost of goods sold for the period by the average inventory. Where an inventory is taken only at the end of each accounting period, the average inventory for the period may be found by adding the beginning and ending inventories together and dividing by two. The turnover of The Adams Appliance Store for the year ended December 31 may be computed as shown at the top of the next page.

Beginning inventory.. $ 42,518.65
Ending inventory... 47,126.40
Cost of goods sold for the period............................ 197,424.28

$42,518.65 + $47,126.40 ÷ 2 = $44,822.53, average inventory
$197,424.28 ÷ $44,882.53 = 4.4, rate of turnover

This calculation indicates that, on the average, the merchandise turns over a little more often than once every three months. A careful analysis of the theory involved in computing the rate of turnover will indicate that the greater the turnover the smaller the margin need be on each dollar of sales in order to produce a satisfactory total gross margin on sales.

Report No. 9-2

Complete Report No. 9-2 in the workbook and submit your working papers to the instructor for approval. After completing the report, you may continue with the textbook discussion in Chapter 10 until the next report is required.

262

chapter 10

adjusting and closing accounts at end of accounting period

As explained in the preceding chapter, the adjustment of certain accounts at the end of the accounting period is required because of changes that have occurred during the period that are not reflected in the accounts. Since the purpose of the temporary owner's equity accounts is to assemble information relating to a specified period of time, at the end of the period the balances of these accounts must be removed to cause the accounts to be ready to perform their function in the following period. In other words, accounts of this type must be "closed."

Adjusting entries

In preparing the work sheet for The Adams Appliance Store (reproduced on pages 244 and 245), adjustments were made to accomplish the following purposes:

    (a) To transfer the amount of the merchandise inventory at the beginning of the accounting period to the expense and revenue summary.

    (b) To record the calculated cost of the merchandise inventory at the end of the accounting period.

(c) To record the amount of interest accrued on notes receivable.

(d) To record the amount of interest accrued on notes payable.

(e) To record the amount of insurance premium expired during the year.

(f) To record the cost of stationery and supplies used during the year.

(g) To record the estimated amount of depreciation of long-lived assets for the year.

(h) To record the amount of bad debt losses expected to result from the sales on account made during the year.

The effect of these adjustments was reflected in the financial statements reproduced on pages 253, 256, and 257. To bring the ledger into agreement with the financial statements, the adjustments should be recorded in the proper accounts. It is customary, therefore, at the end of each accounting period to journalize the adjustments and to post them to the accounts.

Journalizing the adjusting entries

Adjusting entries may be recorded in either a general journal or a combined cash journal. If the entries are made in a combined cash journal, the only amount columns used are the General Debit and Credit columns. A portion of a page of a combined cash journal showing the adjusting entries of The Adams Appliance Store is reproduced on page 265. It should be noted that when the adjusting entries are recorded in the combined cash journal, they are entered in exactly the same manner as they would be entered in a general journal. Since the heading "Adjusting Entries" explains the nature of the entries, a separate explanation of each adjusting entry is unnecessary. The information needed in journalizing the adjustments was obtained from the Adjustments columns of the work sheet reproduced on pages 244 and 245. The account numbers were not entered in the Posting Reference column at the time of journalizing; they were entered as the posting was completed.

Posting the adjusting entries

The adjusting entries should be posted individually to the proper general ledger accounts. The accounts of The Adams Appliance Store that were affected by the adjusting entries are reproduced in type on pages 266 and 267. The entries in the accounts for December transactions that were posted prior to posting the adjusting entries are the same as appeared in the accounts reproduced in script on pages 228–233. The number of the combined cash journal page on which the adjusting entries were recorded was entered in the Posting Reference column of the general ledger accounts affected, and the account numbers were entered in the Posting

	DAY	DESCRIPTION	POST. REF.	GENERAL DEBIT	GENERAL CREDIT	
1		AMOUNTS FORWARDED				1
2	31	*Adjusting Entries*				2
3		*Expense and Revenue Summary*	321	4251865		3
4		*Merchandise Inventory*	131		4251865	4
5		*Merchandise Inventory*	131	4712640		5
6		*Expense and Revenue Summary*	321		4712640	6
7		*Accrued Interest Receivable*	122	729		7
8		*Interest Earned*	711		729	8
9		*Interest Expense*	811	1161		9
10		*Accrued Interest Payable*	221		1161	10
11		*Insurance Expense*	621	26308		11
12		*Prepaid Insurance*	141		26308	12
13		*Stationery and Supplies Expense*	616	16082		13
14		*Stationery and Supplies*	151		16082	14
15		*Depreciation Expense*	612	108799		15
16		*Accumd. Deprec. Store Equip.*	018		23129	16
17		*Accumd. Deprec. Delivery Equip.*	019		85670	17
18		*Bad Debts Expense*	619	122312		18
19		*Allowance for Bad Debts*	012		122312	19
20				9239896	9239896	20
21						21
22						22
23						23
24						24
25						25

265

The Adams Appliance Store — Adjusting Entries

Reference column of the combined cash journal as the posting was completed. This provided a cross-reference in both books.

Ruling the merchandise inventory account

After posting the adjusting entry required to transfer the amount of the beginning inventory to the expense and revenue summary account, the merchandise inventory account was in balance. Since there was only one amount recorded on each side of the account, it was ruled by drawing a double line below the amounts across all columns except the Item columns. In posting the entry to record the inventory at the end of the period, the debit to the merchandise inventory account was recorded on the next horizontal line below the double line.

ACCRUED INTEREST RECEIVABLE   Account No. 122

19——			
Dec. 31		CJ49	7.29

ALLOWANCE FOR BAD DEBTS   Account No. 012

				19——				
				Dec. 1	Balance		√	186.12
				31		CJ49		1,223.12
								1,409.24

MERCHANDISE INVENTORY   Account No. 131

19——					19——			
Dec. 1	Balance		√	42,518.65	Dec. 31		CJ49	42,518.65
Dec. 31		CJ49	47,126.40					

PREPAID INSURANCE   Account No. 141

19——					19——			
Dec. 1	Balance		√	526.16	Dec. 31		CJ49	263.08
	263.08							

STATIONERY AND SUPPLIES   Account No. 151

19——					19——			
Dec. 1	Balance		√	170.34	Dec. 31		CJ49	160.82
31		CJ48		25.48				
	35.00			*195.82*				

ACCUMULATED DEPRECIATION — STORE EQUIPMENT   Account No. 018

				19——				
				Dec. 1	Balance		√	829.40
				31		CJ49		231.29
								1,060.69

ACCUMULATED DEPRECIATION — DELIVERY EQUIPMENT   Account No. 019

				19——				
				Dec. 1	Balance		√	2,104.10
				31		CJ49		856.70
								2,960.80

ACCRUED INTEREST PAYABLE   Account No. 221

			19——			
			Dec. 31		CJ49	11.61

EXPENSE AND REVENUE SUMMARY   Account No. 321

19——				19——			
Dec. 31	Beg. inventory	CJ49	42,518.65	Dec. 31	End. inventory	CJ49	47,126.40

DEPRECIATION EXPENSE			Account No. 612
19--			
Dec. 31	CJ49	1,087.99	

STATIONERY AND SUPPLIES EXPENSE			Account No. 616
19--			
Dec. 31	CJ49	160.82	

BAD DEBTS EXPENSE			Account No. 619
19--			
Dec. 31	CJ49	1,223.12	

INSURANCE EXPENSE			Account No. 621
19--			
Dec. 31	CJ49	263.08	

INTEREST EARNED			Account No. 711
	19—		
	Dec. 1 Balance	√	44.90
	31	CJ49	7.29
			52.19

267

INTEREST EXPENSE			Account No. 811
19--			
Dec. 1 Balance		57.18	
31	CJ49 √	11.61	
		68.79	

Report No. 10-1

Complete Report No. 10-1 in the workbook and submit your working papers to the instructor for approval. Continue with the following study assignment until Report No. 10-2 is required.

Closing procedure

After the adjusting entries have been posted, all of the temporary owner's equity accounts should be closed. This means that the accountant must remove ("close out") (1) the balance of every account that enters into the calculation of the net income (or net loss) for the accounting period and (2) the balance of the owner's drawing account. The purpose of the closing procedure is to transfer the balances of the temporary owner's equity accounts to the permanent owner's equity account. This could be accomplished simply by debiting or crediting each account involved, with an offsetting credit or debit to the permanent owner's equity account. However, it is considered better practice to transfer the balances of all accounts that enter into the net income or net loss determination to a summarizing account called Expense and Revenue Summary (sometimes called *Income Summary*, *Profit and Loss Summary*, or just *Profit and Loss*). Then, the resulting balance of the expense and revenue summary account (which will be the amount of the net income or net loss for the period) is transferred to the permanent owner's equity account.

The final step in the closing procedure is to transfer the balance of the owner's drawing account to the permanent owner's equity account. After this is done, only the asset accounts, the liability accounts, and the permanent owner's equity account have balances. If there has been no error, the sum of the balances of the asset accounts (less balances of any contra accounts) will be equal to the sum of the balances of the liability accounts plus the balance of the permanent owner's equity account. The accounts will agree exactly with what is shown by the balance sheet as of the close of the period. Reference to the balance sheet of The Adams Appliance Store reproduced on pages 256 and 257 will show that the assets, liabilities, and owner's equity as of December 31 may be expressed in equation form as follows:

$$\text{ASSETS} = \text{LIABILITIES} + \text{OWNER'S EQUITY}$$
$$\$75,509.94 \qquad \$8,152.66 \qquad \$67,357.28$$

Journalizing the closing entries

Closing entries, like adjusting entries, may be recorded in either a general journal or a combined cash journal. If the entries are made in a combined cash journal, only the General Debit and Credit columns are used. A portion of a page of a combined cash journal showing the closing entries for The Adams Appliance Store is reproduced on page 269. Since the heading "Closing Entries" explains the nature of the entries, a separate

	DAY	DESCRIPTION	POST. REF.	GENERAL DEBIT	GENERAL CREDIT	
1		AMOUNTS FORWARDED				1
2	31	*Closing Entries*				2
3		Sales	411	27180512		3
4		Purchases Returns + Allowances	051	82890		4
5		Purchases Discount	052	71531		5
6		Interest Earned	711	5219		6
7		Expense and Revenue Summary	321		27340152	7
8		Expense and Revenue Summary	321	25990651		8
9		Sales Returns + Allowances	041		78610	9
10		Purchases	511		20357624	10
11		Rent Expense	611		720000	11
12		Depreciation Expense	612		108799	12
13		Salaries and Commissions Exp.	613		3624837	13
14		Payroll Taxes Expense	614		161281	14
15		Heating and Lighting Expense	615		71014	15
16		Stationery and Supplies Expense	616		16082	16
17		Telephone and Telegraph Expense	617		31820	17
18		Advertising Expense	618		522692	18
19		Bad Debts Expense	619		122312	19
20		Insurance Expense	621		26308	20
21		Truck Expense	622		63542	21
22		Charitable Contributions Expense	623		32500	22
23		Miscellaneous Expense	624		46351	23
24		Interest Expense	811		6879	24
25		Expense and Revenue Summary	321	1810276		25
26		R. L. Adams, Capital	311		1810276	26
27		R. L. Adams, Capital	311	1514680		27
28		R. L. Adams, Drawing	031		1514680	28
29				56655759	56655759	29
30						30
31						31
32						32

The Adams Appliance Store — Closing Entries

269

explanation of each closing entry is not necessary. The information required in preparing the closing entries was obtained from the work sheet illustrated on pages 244 and 245.

The first closing entry was made to close the sales, purchases returns and allowances, purchases discount, and interest earned accounts. Since these accounts have credit balances, each account must be debited for the amount of its balance in order to close it. The debits to these four accounts are offset by a credit of $273,401.52 to Expense and Revenue Summary.

The second closing entry was made to close the sales returns and allowances, purchases, and all of the expense accounts. Since these accounts have debit balances, each account must be credited for the amount of its balance in order to close it. The credits to these accounts are offset by a debit of $259,906.51 to Expense and Revenue Summary.

Since the posting of the first two adjusting entries and the first two closing entries causes the expense and revenue summary account to have a credit balance of $18,102.76 (the net income for the year), the account has served its purpose and must be closed. The third closing entry accomplishes this by debiting the expense and revenue summary account, with an offsetting credit to R. L. Adams, Capital, for $18,102.76.

The fourth closing entry was made to close the R. L. Adams drawing account. Since this account has a debit balance, it must be credited to close it. The offsetting entry is a debit of $15,146.80 to R. L. Adams, Capital.

The account numbers shown in the Posting Reference column were not entered at the time of journalizing the closing entries — they were entered as the posting was completed.

270 Posting the closing entries

Closing entries can be posted in the usual manner — that is, exactly as each journal entry indicates. However, if it is considered desirable to have the expense and revenue summary account provide the details of the expense and revenue elements that it summarizes, posting to this account can be in detail with a notation of the nature of each amount. This "posting in detail" practice is followed in the case of The Adams Appliance Store. In any case, proper cross-references are provided by using the Posting Reference columns of the combined cash journal and the ledger accounts. After all the closing entries have been posted in the manner described, the accounts affected appear as shown on pages 271–275.

It may be observed that the first two adjusting entries described and illustrated earlier in the chapter actually qualify both as "adjusting" and as "closing" entries. They serve to adjust the merchandise inventory account by removing the amount of the beginning inventory and by recording the amount of the ending inventory. They facilitate the closing process in that they cause two amounts that enter into the calculation of net income or net loss to be entered in the Expense and Revenue Summary. It matters little which descriptive term is applied; the important thing is to be sure that needed adjustments are made and that the temporary owner's equity accounts are closed as of the end of the accounting period.

ACCOUNT R. L. Adams, Capital   ACCOUNT NO. 311

DATE	ITEM	POST. REF.	DEBIT	DATE	ITEM	POST. REF.	CREDIT
19— Dec. 31		CJ50	1514680	19— Dec. 1	Balance	✓	6440132
				31		CJ50	1810276

ACCOUNT R. L. Adams, Drawing   ACCOUNT NO. 031

DATE	ITEM	POST. REF.	DEBIT	DATE	ITEM	POST. REF.	CREDIT
19— Dec. 1	Balance	✓	1413680	19— Dec. 31		CJ50	1514680
21		CJ47	100000				
31		CJ48	1000				
			1514680				
			1514680				1514680

ACCOUNT Expense and Revenue Summary   ACCOUNT NO. 321

271

DATE	ITEM	POST. REF.	DEBIT	DATE	ITEM	POST. REF.	CREDIT
19— Dec. 31	Beg. inventory	CJ49	4251865	19— Dec. 31	End. inventory	CJ49	4712640
31	Sales R. + A.	CJ50	78610	31	Sales	CJ50	27180512
31	Purchases	CJ50	20357624	31	Pur. R. + A.	CJ50	82890
31	Rent Exp.	CJ50	720000	31	Pur. Disc.	CJ50	71531
31	Depr. Exp.	CJ50	108799	31	Int. Earned	CJ50	5219
31	Sal. + Com. Exp.	CJ50	3624837				32052792
31	Pay. Taxes Exp.	CJ50	161281				
31	Htg. + Ltg. Exp.	CJ50	71014				
31	Sta. + Sup. Exp.	CJ50	16082				
31	Tel. + Tel. Exp.	CJ50	31820				
31	Adv. Exp.	CJ50	522692				
31	Bad Debts Exp.	CJ50	122312				
31	Ins. Exp.	CJ50	26308				
31	Truck Exp.	CJ50	63542				
31	Char. Cont. Exp.	CJ50	32500				
31	Misc. Exp.	CJ50	46351				
31	Int. Exp.	CJ50	6879				
			30242516				
31	R. L. Adams, Cap.	CJ50	1810276				
			32052792				
			32052792				32052792

The Adams Appliance Store — Partial General Ledger
(*continued on next page*)

ACCOUNT _Sales_   ACCOUNT NO. 411

DATE	ITEM	POST. REF.	DEBIT	DATE	ITEM	POST. REF.	CREDIT
19— Dec. 31		CJ50	271 805 12	19— Dec. 1	Balance	✓	249 060 07
				31		CJ47	11 217 55
				31		S44	11 527 50
			271 805 12				271 805 12
							271 805 12

ACCOUNT _Sales Returns and Allowances_   ACCOUNT NO. 041

DATE	ITEM	POST. REF.	DEBIT	DATE	ITEM	POST. REF.	CREDIT
19— Dec. 1	Balance	✓	706 70	19— Dec. 31		CJ50	786 10
27		CJ47	79 40				
			786 10				
			786 10				786 10

ACCOUNT _Purchases_   ACCOUNT NO. 511

DATE	ITEM	POST. REF.	DEBIT	DATE	ITEM	POST. REF.	CREDIT
19— Dec. 1	Balance	✓	196 194 66	19— Dec. 31		CJ50	203 576 24
2		CJ47	53 18				
31		P32	7 328 40				
			203 576 24				
			203 576 24				203 576 24

ACCOUNT _Purchases Returns and Allowances_   ACCOUNT NO. 051

DATE	ITEM	POST. REF.	DEBIT	DATE	ITEM	POST. REF.	CREDIT
19— Dec. 31		CJ50	828 90	19— Dec. 1	Balance	✓	768 90
				20		CJ47	60 00
							828 90
			828 90				828 90

ACCOUNT _Purchases Discount_   ACCOUNT NO. 052

DATE	ITEM	POST. REF.	DEBIT	DATE	ITEM	POST. REF.	CREDIT
19— Dec. 31		CJ50	715 31	19— Dec. 1	Balance	✓	686 06
				23		CJ47	29 25
							715 31
			715 31				715 31

272

The Adams Appliance Store — Partial General Ledger (*continued*)

ACCOUNT *Rent Expense*   ACCOUNT NO. 611

DATE	ITEM	POST. REF.	DEBIT	DATE	ITEM	POST. REF.	CREDIT
19— Dec. 1	Balance	✓	6600 00	19— Dec. 31		CJ50	7200 00
2		CJ47	600 00				
			7200 00				
			7200 00				7200 00

ACCOUNT *Depreciation Expense*   ACCOUNT NO. 612

DATE	ITEM	POST. REF.	DEBIT	DATE	ITEM	POST. REF.	CREDIT
19— Dec. 31		CJ49	1087 99	19— Dec. 31		CJ50	1087 99

ACCOUNT *Salaries and Commissions Expense*   ACCOUNT NO. 613

DATE	ITEM	POST. REF.	DEBIT	DATE	ITEM	POST. REF.	CREDIT
19— Dec. 1	Balance	✓	32742 64	19— Dec. 31		CJ50	36248 37
14		CJ47	1666 73				
31		CJ48	1839 00				
			36248 37				
			36248 37				36248 37

273

ACCOUNT *Payroll Taxes Expense*   ACCOUNT NO. 614

DATE	ITEM	POST. REF.	DEBIT	DATE	ITEM	POST. REF.	CREDIT
19— Dec. 1	Balance	✓	1548 63	19— Dec. 31		CJ50	1612 81
14		CJ47	32 09				
31		CJ48	32 09				
			1612 81				
			1612 81				1612 81

ACCOUNT *Heating and Lighting Expense*   ACCOUNT NO. 615

DATE	ITEM	POST. REF.	DEBIT	DATE	ITEM	POST. REF.	CREDIT
19— Dec. 1	Balance	✓	636 86	19— Dec. 31		CJ50	710 14
28		CJ47	73 28				
			710 14				
			710 14				710 14

The Adams Appliance Store — Partial General Ledger (*continued*)

ACCOUNT Stationery and Supplies Expense   ACCOUNT NO. 616

DATE	ITEM	POST. REF.	DEBIT	DATE	ITEM	POST. REF.	CREDIT
19— Dec. 31		CJ49	160 82	19— Dec. 31		CJ50	160 82

ACCOUNT Telephone and Telegraph Expense   ACCOUNT NO. 617

DATE	ITEM	POST. REF.	DEBIT	DATE	ITEM	POST. REF.	CREDIT
19— Dec. 1	Balance	✓	284 45	19— Dec. 31		CJ50	318 20
28		CJ47	32 15				
31		CJ48	1 60				
			318 20				
			318 20				318 20

ACCOUNT Advertising Expense   ACCOUNT NO. 618

DATE	ITEM	POST. REF.	DEBIT	DATE	ITEM	POST. REF.	CREDIT
19— Dec. 1	Balance	✓	4733 49	19— Dec. 31		CJ50	5226 92
6		CJ47	61 04				
27		CJ47	421 30				
31		CJ48	11 09				
			5226 92				
			5226 92				5226 92

274

ACCOUNT Bad Debts Expense   ACCOUNT NO. 619

DATE	ITEM	POST. REF.	DEBIT	DATE	ITEM	POST. REF.	CREDIT
19— Dec. 31		CJ49	1223 12	19— Dec. 31		CJ50	1223 12

ACCOUNT Insurance Expense   ACCOUNT NO. 621

DATE	ITEM	POST. REF.	DEBIT	DATE	ITEM	POST. REF.	CREDIT
19— Dec. 31		CJ49	263 08	19— Dec. 31		CJ50	263 08

The Adams Appliance Store — Partial General Ledger (continued)

Truck Expense — Account No. 622

DATE	ITEM	POST. REF.	DEBIT	DATE	ITEM	POST. REF.	CREDIT
19— Dec. 1	Balance	✓	570 02	19— Dec. 31		CJ50	635 42
18		CJ47	65 40				
			635 42				
			635 42				635 42

Charitable Contributions Expense — Account No. 623

DATE	ITEM	POST. REF.	DEBIT	DATE	ITEM	POST. REF.	CREDIT
19— Dec. 1	Balance	✓	320 00	19— Dec. 31		CJ50	325 00
31		CJ48	5 00				
			325 00				
			325 00				325 00

Miscellaneous Expense — Account No. 624

DATE	ITEM	POST. REF.	DEBIT	DATE	ITEM	POST. REF.	CREDIT
19— Dec. 1	Balance	✓	455 86	19— Dec. 31		CJ50	463 51
31		CJ48	7 65				
			463 51				
			463 51				463 51

Interest Earned — Account No. 711

DATE	ITEM	POST. REF.	DEBIT	DATE	ITEM	POST. REF.	CREDIT
19— Dec. 31		CJ50	52 19	19— Dec. 1	Balance	✓	44 90
				31		CJ49	7 29
							52 19
			52 19				52 19

Interest Expense — Account No. 811

DATE	ITEM	POST. REF.	DEBIT	DATE	ITEM	POST. REF.	CREDIT
19— Dec. 1	Balance	✓	57 18	19— Dec. 31		CJ50	68 79
31		CJ49	11 61				
			68 79				
			68 79				68 79

The Adams Appliance Store — Partial General Ledger (*concluded*)

Ruling the closed accounts

After posting the closing entries, all of the temporary owner's equity accounts of The Adams Appliance Store were in balance and they were ruled in the manner illustrated on pages 271–275. Following is the recommended procedure:

(a) Where there are two or more items posted to either side of an account, foot the amounts to be sure that the total debits are equal to the total credits.

(b) Rule a single line across the debit and credit amount columns immediately below the last amount entered on the side with the most entries.

(c) Enter the totals of the debit and credit amount columns in ink on the next line.

(d) Rule a double line immediately below the totals extending through all but the Item columns.

If an account has only one item on each side, double ruling is sufficient. Note the ruling of the account with Depreciation Expense on page 273. If an account page is not filled, it may be used for recording the transactions of the following period.

276 Balancing and ruling open accounts

After the temporary owner's equity accounts have been closed, the open accounts may be balanced and ruled in order to prepare them to receive entries for the next accounting period. The open accounts include the asset accounts, the liability accounts, and the permanent owner's equity account. Prior to ruling an open account, its balance should be entered on the side which has the smaller total. The effect of this entry is to equalize the total debits and credits. The account should then be ruled with single and double lines in the manner shown on page 277. The balance should then be brought down below the ruling on the proper side of the account. However, if the page is filled, the balance may be carried forward to the top of a new page. In carrying the balance down or forward, as the case may be, care must be taken to be sure that it is entered on the side which originally had the larger total.

There is no need for balancing and ruling an open account that has entries on only one side of the account. To illustrate the procedure in balancing and ruling open accounts, the following accounts of The Adams Appliance Store are reproduced at the top of the next page.

Columbia National Bank, Account No. 111
Accounts Payable, Account No. 231
R. L. Adams, Capital, Account No. 311

ACCOUNT *Columbia National Bank*   ACCOUNT NO. *111*

DATE	ITEM	POST. REF.	DEBIT	DATE	ITEM	POST. REF.	CREDIT
19— Dec. 1	Balance	✓	7341 37	19— Dec. 31		cj48	13142 34
31	*11,315.62*	cj48	17116 59	31	Balance	✓	11315 62
			24457 96				24457 96
			24457 96				24457 96
19— Jan. 1	Balance	✓	11315 62				

ACCOUNT *Accounts Payable*   ACCOUNT NO. *231*

DATE	ITEM	POST. REF.	DEBIT	DATE	ITEM	POST. REF.	CREDIT
19— Dec. 31		cj48	5696 30	19— Dec. 1	Balance	✓	3281 60
31	Balance	✓	5475 70	31		cj48	562 00
			11172 00	31		p32	7328 40
			11172 00		*5,475.70*		11172 00
							11172 00
				19— Jan. 1	Balance	✓	5475 70

ACCOUNT *R. L. Adams, Capital*   ACCOUNT NO. *311*

DATE	ITEM	POST. REF.	DEBIT	DATE	ITEM	POST. REF.	CREDIT
19— Dec. 31		cj50	15146 80	19— Dec. 1	Balance	✓	64401 32
31	Balance	✓	67357 28	31		cj50	18102 76
			82504 08				82504 08
			82504 08				82504 08
				19— Jan. 1	Balance	✓	67357 28

The Adams Appliance Store — Balancing and Ruling Open Accounts

In the case of the account with the Columbia National Bank, the balance of the account, $11,315.62, was entered on the credit side, the totals were entered in ink, the account was ruled with single and double lines, and the balance was brought down below the ruling on the debit side. Note that in bringing the December 31 balance down below the ruling, it was entered as of January 1 to indicate that it was the balance at the beginning of a new accounting period.

In the case of Accounts Payable, the balance, $5,475.70, was entered on the debit side, the totals were entered in ink, the account was ruled with single and double lines, and the balance was brought down below the ruling on the credit side as of January 1.

In the case of R. L. Adams, Capital, the balance, $67,357.28, was entered on the debit side, the totals were entered in ink, the account was ruled with single and double lines, and the balance was brought down below the ruling on the credit side as of January 1. The balance represents the owner's equity in the business on that date.

At one time it was common practice to use *red ink* in balancing and ruling accounts. Any losses were also entered in red ink. This was the origin of the expression "in the red" to describe a loss.

Sometimes a balance-column account form is used for the general ledger accounts. In such case, the balance of each account is entered after each amount is posted. When an account is in balance, either a horizontal line or the symbol "–0–" is entered in the Balance column and no ruling of the account is required.

Trial balance after closing

A trial balance of the general ledger accounts that remain open after the temporary owner's equity accounts have been closed is usually referred to as a *post-closing trial balance*. The purpose of the post-closing trial balance is to prove that the general ledger is in balance at the beginning of a new accounting period. It is advisable to know that such is the case before any transactions for the new accounting period are recorded.

The post-closing trial balance should contain the same accounts and amounts as appear in the Balance Sheet columns of the work sheet, except that **(1)** the owner's drawing account is omitted because it has been closed, and **(2)** the owner's capital account has been adjusted for the amount of the net income (or net loss) and the amount of his drawings.

A post-closing trial balance of the general ledger of The Adams Appliance Store is shown on the next page. Some accountants advocate that the post-closing trial balance should be dated as of the close of the old accounting period, while others advocate that it should be dated as of the beginning of the new accounting period. In this illustration the trial balance is dated December 31, the end of the period.

Reversing entries for accrual adjustments

In addition to balancing and ruling the open accounts at the close of an accounting period to make ready for recording the transactions of the succeeding accounting period, many accountants reverse the adjusting entries for accruals. The purpose of such reversing entries (sometimes called "readjusting entries") is to make possible the recording of the transactions of the succeeding accounting period in a routine manner and to assure that the proper amount of revenue will be credited to the period in which earned and that the proper amount of expenses will be charged to the period in which incurred.

THE ADAMS APPLIANCE STORE
Post-Closing Trial Balance
December 31, 19—

Account	Acct. No.	Dr. Balance	Cr. Balance
Columbia National Bank...................	111	11,315.62	
Petty Cash Fund.........................	112	100.00	
Notes Receivable........................	121	2,500.00	
Accrued Interest Receivable...............	122	7.29	
Accounts Receivable.....................	123	13,291.58	
Allowance for Bad Debts.................	012		1,409.24
Merchandise Inventory...................	131	47,126.40	
Prepaid Insurance.......................	141	263.08	
Stationery and Supplies..................	151	35.00	
Store Equipment........................	181	2,874.90	
Accumulated Depr. — Store Equipment.......	018		1,060.69
Delivery Equipment......................	191	3,426.80	
Accumulated Depr. — Delivery Equipment.....	019		2,960.80
Notes Payable..........................	211		1,243.70
Accrued Interest Payable.................	221		11.61
Accounts Payable.......................	231		5,475.70
Sales Tax Payable.......................	241		906.63
FICA Tax Payable	251		99.56
Employees Income Tax Payable	261		324.50
FUTA Tax Payable	271		58.20
State Unemployment Tax Payable	281		32.76
R. L. Adams, Capital....................	311		67,357.28
		80,940.67	80,940.67

When cash is received in payment of interest, the routine manner of recording the transaction is to debit Cash (or Bank) and to credit Interest Earned. If any portion of such interest was accrued in the preceding accounting period and the adjusting entry had not been reversed at the beginning of the current accounting period, the amount credited to Interest Earned would not represent the proper amount earned in the current period. If, however, the adjusting entry at the end of the preceding period had been reversed, the interest earned account would be debited for the amount accrued and, after recording the interest collected in the current period as a credit to Interest Earned, the balance of the account would represent the correct amount of revenue applicable to the new period.

When cash is disbursed in payment of interest, the routine manner of recording the transaction is to debit Interest Expense and to credit Cash (or Bank). If any portion of such interest was accrued in the preceding accounting period and the adjusting entry had not been reversed at the beginning of the current accounting period, the amount debited to Interest Expense would not represent the proper amount of expense incurred in the current period. If, however, the adjusting entry at the end of the preceding period had been reversed, the interest expense account would be credited for the amount accrued and, after recording the interest paid in the current period as a debit to Interest Expense, the balance of the account would represent the correct amount of the interest expense for the current period.

Journalizing the reversing entries

Reversing entries, like adjusting and closing entries, may be recorded in either a general journal or a combined cash journal. If the entries are made in a combined cash journal, the only amount columns used are the General Debit and Credit columns. A portion of a page of a combined cash journal showing the reversing entries of The Adams Appliance Store is reproduced below. Usually the reversing entries are made immediately after closing the books at the end of an accounting period. However, it is customary to date the entries as of the first day of the succeeding accounting period. Thus, the reversing entries for The Adams Appliance Store are dated January 1. Since the heading "Reversing Entries" explains the nature of the entries, a separate explanation of each reversing entry is unnecessary. Following is a discussion of each of the reversing entries.

COMBINED CASH JOURNAL FOR MONTH OF *January* 19 — PAGE *51*

DAY	DESCRIPTION	POST. REF.	GENERAL DEBIT	GENERAL CREDIT	
1	AMOUNTS FORWARDED				1
2	*1*	Reversing Entries				2
3	Interest Earned	711	729		3
4	Accrued Interest Receivable	122		729	4
5	Accrued Interest Payable	221	1161		5
6	Interest Expense	811		1161	6
7			1890	1890	7
8					8

The Adams Appliance Store — Reversing Entries

Accrued Interest Receivable. Reference to the adjusting entries reproduced on page 265 will reveal that Accrued Interest Receivable, Account No. 122, was debited and Interest Earned, Account No. 711, was credited for $7.29 to record the interest accrued on the 7 percent interest-bearing note of P. R. Worth for $2,500. To reverse the adjusting entry it was necessary to debit Interest Earned, Account No. 711, and to credit Accrued

ACCOUNT *Accrued Interest Receivable*   ACCOUNT NO. *122*

DATE	ITEM	POST. REF.	DEBIT	DATE	ITEM	POST. REF.	CREDIT
19— Dec. 31		CJ49	7 29	19— Jan. 1		CJ51	7 29

ACCOUNT *Interest Earned*   ACCOUNT NO. *711*

DATE	ITEM	POST. REF.	DEBIT	DATE	ITEM	POST. REF.	CREDIT
19— Dec. 31		CJ50	52 19	19— Dec. 1	Balance	✓	44 90
				31		CJ49	7 29
			52 19				52 19
							52 19
19— Jan. 1		CJ51	7 29				

The Adams Appliance Store — Accrued Interest Receivable and Interest Earned
After Posting of Reversing Entries

Interest Receivable, Account No. 122, for $7.29. The accounts affected by this entry are reproduced above.

It will be noted that, after posting the reversing entry, the account with Accrued Interest Receivable is in balance and the account with Interest Earned has a debit balance of $7.29. If P. R. Worth pays the amount due when his note matures on January 15, his payment will be $2,514.58 (principal of note $2,500, plus interest at 7 percent for 30 days, $14.58). To record this collection it is necessary only to debit Columbia National Bank for $2,514.58 and to credit Notes Receivable, Account No. 121, for $2,500 and Interest Earned, Account No. 711, for $14.58. After posting this entry the interest earned account will have a credit balance of $7.29 ($14.58 minus $7.29). This balance represents the amount of interest earned in the year in which the note matures. If the adjusting entry had not been reversed, it would be necessary to make an analysis before recording the collection from Mr. Worth on January 15 in order to determine the amount of interest accrued in the preceding year and the amount of interest earned in the current year. This would reveal that it would be necessary to credit Accrued Interest Receivable for $7.29 and Interest Earned for $7.29, so that each year might receive credit for the correct interest earned. When the adjustment is reversed, the need for this analysis is eliminated.

The reversal procedure is particularly useful if the year-end adjustment for interest earned but not collected related to interest accrued on several notes or other interest-bearing assets. When the adjustment is reversed, all future collections of interest can be credited to the interest earned account without any concern as to when the amount was earned. The portion of any collections that was earned in the new period will automatically emerge as the balance of the interest earned account.

Accrued Interest Payable. In the adjusting entries for The Adams Appliance Store, Interest Expense, Account No. 811, was debited and Accrued Interest Payable, Account No. 221, was credited for $11.61 to record the interest accrued on a 6 percent interest-bearing note for $1,243.70 issued November 5. To reverse the adjusting entry it was necessary to debit Accrued Interest Payable, Account No. 221, and to credit Interest Expense, Account No. 811, for $11.61. The accounts affected by this entry are reproduced below.

ACCOUNT *Accrued Interest Payable*   ACCOUNT NO. 221

DATE	ITEM	POST. REF.	DEBIT	DATE	ITEM	POST. REF.	CREDIT
19— Jan. 1		CJ51	11 61	19— Dec. 31			CJ49	11 61

ACCOUNT *Interest Expense*   ACCOUNT NO. 811

DATE	ITEM	POST. REF.	DEBIT	DATE	ITEM	POST. REF.	CREDIT
19— Dec. 1	Balance	✓	57 18	19— Dec. 31		CJ50	68 79
31		CJ49	11 61				
			68 79				68 79
				19— Jan. 1		CJ51	11 61

The Adams Appliance Store — Accrued Interest Payable and Interest Expense
After Posting of Reversing Entries

It will be noted that, after posting the reversing entry, the account with Accrued Interest Payable is in balance and the account with Interest Expense has a credit balance of $11.61. If the note for $1,243.70 plus interest is paid when due on May 5, the payment will be $1,281.01 (principal of note $1,243.70, plus interest at 6 percent for six months, $37.31). To record the payment it is necessary only to debit Notes Payable, Account No. 211, for $1,243.70 and Interest Expense, Account No. 811 for $37.31 and to credit Columbia National Bank for $1,281.01. After posting this entry the interest expense account will have a debit balance of $25.70 ($37.31 minus $11.61). This balance represents the amount of interest expense incurred in the year in which the note matures. If the adjusting entry had not been reversed, it would be necessary to make an analysis before recording the payment on May 5 in order to determine the amount of interest expense incurred in the preceding year and the amount of interest expense incurred in the current year. This would reveal that it would be necessary to debit Accrued Interest Payable for $11.61 and Interest Expense for $25.70 so that each year might be charged with the correct interest expense. When the adjustment is reversed, the need for this analysis is eliminated.

The reversal procedure is particularly useful if the year-end adjustment for interest expense incurred but not paid related to interest accrued on several interest-bearing obligations. When the adjustment is reversed, all future payments of interest can be debited to the interest expense account without any concern as to when each amount paid was incurred. The portion of any payments that is an expense of the new period will automatically emerge as the balance of the interest expense account.

From the foregoing discussion it will be seen that by reversing the adjusting entries made on December 31 for accrued interest receivable and accrued interest payable, it will be possible to record the interest collected on January 15 amounting to $14.58 and the interest paid on May 5 amounting to $37.31 in an ordinary routine manner.

283

The accounting cycle

The steps involved in handling the effect of all transactions and events completed during an accounting period, beginning with entries in the books of original entry and ending with the reversing entries, collectively comprise the *accounting cycle*. In Chapter 5 (page 132) nine steps were listed. A tenth step — journalizing and posting the reversing entries — needs to be added if the accrual basis of accounting is being followed.

Income and self-employment taxes

The discussion of accounting for the revenue and expenses of a business enterprise has included frequent references to income tax considerations. It is important to note that an unincorporated business owned by one person is not taxed. The owner — not the business — is subject to income taxes. He, of course, must report the amounts of business revenue and business expenses in his personal tax return regardless of the amount of money or other property he has actually withdrawn from the business during the year. As mentioned earlier, in the case of a sole proprietorship, there is no legal distinction between the business and its owner.

In order to bring a large class of self-employed individuals into the federal social security program, the law requires all self-employed persons (except those specifically exempted) to pay a self-employment tax. The rate of tax is 2 percent more than the prevailing FICA rate. (With a combined FICA tax rate of 5.5 percent, the self-employment tax rate is 7.5 percent.) The tax is applied to "self-employment income" up to a maximum of $9,000. The rate and base of the tax may be changed by Act of Congress at any time. In general, *self-employment income* means the net income of a trade or business conducted by an individual or a partner's distributive share of the net income of a partnership whether or not any cash is distributed. Earnings of less than $400 from self-employment are ignored.

A taxable year for the purpose of the tax on self-employment income is the same as the taxpayer's taxable year for federal income tax purposes. The self-employment tax is reported along with the regular federal income tax. For calendar-year taxpayers, the tax return and full or final payment is due on April 15 following the close of the year. Like the personal income tax, the self-employment tax is treated as a personal expense of the owner. If the taxes are paid with business funds, the amount should be charged to the owner's drawing account.

284

Report No. 10-2

Complete Report No. 10-2 in the workbook and submit your working papers to the instructor for approval. You will then be given instructions as to the work to be done next.

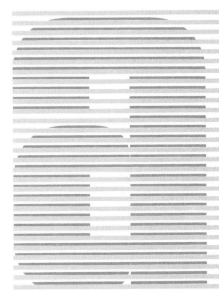

chapters 6-10

practical accounting problems

Problem 6-A

Mrs. Edythe Robinson decides to open a dress shop under the name of Edythe's Shop. The books of original entry include a purchases journal, a sales journal, and a combined cash journal. This problem involves the use of the purchases journal and the combined cash journal only. The following selected transactions were completed during the month of October:

Oct. 2. Invested $6,000 in the business.
  2. Received Invoice No. 162 dated Sept. 29 from Mini Midi Maxi, Inc., for merchandise purchased, $75.10. Terms, 30 days net.
  3. Received Invoice No. 163 dated Sept. 29 from Turner Brothers for merchandise purchased, $182.14. Terms, 10 days net.
  5. Purchased a cash register for cash, $94.31. (Debit Furniture and Fixtures.)
  6. Received Invoice No. 164 dated October 4 from Nord, Inc., for merchandise purchased, $98.60. Terms, 30 days net.
  10. Purchased merchandise for cash, $55.15.
  11. Received Invoice No. 165 dated October 9 from Mini Midi Maxi, Inc., for merchandise purchased, $131.61. Terms, 30 days net.
  12. Paid Turner Brothers $182.14 in full for Invoice No. 163, dated Sept. 29.
  13. Returned defective merchandise to Mini Midi Maxi, Inc., $26.62.
  17. Received invoice dated October 16 from the National Showcase Co. for showcases purchased, $1,432.18. Terms, 15 days net.

23. Received Invoice No. 166 dated October 18 from Turner Brothers for merchandise purchased, $246.87. Terms, 10 days net.
25. Purchased merchandise for cash, $98.16.
30. Received Invoice No. 167 dated October 26 from Merle Oberon for merchandise purchased, $45.20. Terms, 30 days net.

REQUIRED: (1) Record each transaction in the proper journal using the following accounts:

111 Cash	311 Edythe Robinson, Capital
151 Furniture and Fixtures	511 Purchases
231 Accounts Payable	051 Purchases Returns and Allowances

For the purchases journal, use a sheet of paper ruled like that shown in the illustration on page 151. For the combined cash journal, use a sheet of paper like that shown in the illustration on pages 168 and 169. (The Check No. column will not be used in this problem.) Number the pages of the journals. (2) Prove the combined cash journal by footing the amount columns; then total and rule this journal. Total the purchases journal and rule. (3) Open the necessary accounts using the standard account form of ledger paper. Post the purchases journal and combined cash journal entries for October, foot the accounts, and enter the balances. (4) Take a trial balance as of October 31, using a sheet of two-column journal paper.

Problem 6-B

286

H. C. Leffingwell decides to open a men's clothing store under the name of The Eastgate Store. The books of original entry include a sales journal, a purchases journal, and a combined cash journal. This problem involves the use of the sales journal and combined cash journal only. The following selected transactions were completed during the month of July:

July 3. Invested $9,000 in the business.
3. Sold merchandise on account to R. F. Meeks, $15.60, tax 78 cents. Sale No. 104.
5. Sold merchandise on account to K. W. Myers, $49.65, tax $2.48. Sale No. 105.
6. R. F. Meeks returned goods for credit. Sales price, $8.20, tax 41 cents.
10. Sold merchandise on account to D. W. Brady, $28.31, tax $1.42. Sale No. 106.
13. Received $7.77 from R. F. Meeks in payment of account.
14. Sold merchandise on account to W. E. Fick, $25.02, tax $1.25. Sale No. 107.
19. A customer returned some merchandise purchased earlier in the day for cash. Sales price, $9.75, tax 49 cents.
21. Received $29.73 from D. W. Brady in payment of account.
26. Sold merchandise on account to T. E. Delaney, $15.30, tax 77 cents. Sale No. 108.
28. Sold merchandise on account to R. C. Mare, $9.40, tax 47 cents. Sale No. 109.
31. Total cash sales for month, $651.80, tax, $32.59.

REQUIRED: (1) Record each transaction in the proper journal using the following accounts:

111 Cash	311 H. C. Leffingwell, Capital
123 Accounts Receivable	411 Sales
241 Sales Tax Payable	041 Sales Returns and Allowances

For the sales journal, use a sheet of paper ruled like that shown at the top of page 160. For the combined cash journal, use a sheet of paper like that shown in the illustration on pages 168 and 169. (The Check No. column will not be used in this problem.) Number the pages of the journals. (2) Prove the combined cash journal by footing the amount columns; then total and rule this journal. (3) Prove the sales journal by footing the amount columns and determining that the totals of the debit and credit columns are equal in amount. Enter the totals and rule. (4) Open the necessary accounts using the standard account form of ledger paper. Post the sales journal and combined cash journal entries for July, foot the accounts, and enter the balances. (5) Take a trial balance as of July 31, using a sheet of two-column journal paper.

Problem 6-C

Harry H. Harris is engaged in a retail merchandising business operating under the name of The HHH Store. He keeps a purchases journal, a sales journal, and a two-column general journal as books of original entry. The standard account form of general ledger is used. Individual accounts with customers and suppliers are not kept in ledger form; however, the purchase invoices and sales tickets are filed in such a manner that the amounts due to suppliers and due from customers may be determined at any time. All charge sales are payable by the tenth of the following month. The trial balance taken as of March 31, 19—, is reproduced at the top of page 288.

NARRATIVE OF TRANSACTIONS FOR APRIL

Apr. 1. (Saturday) Paid the rent for April in advance, $600.
     3. Paid the following bills:
         Gas and electric bill, $45.20.
         Telephone bill, $27.15.
     4. Received Invoice No. 61 dated April 1 from P. L. Jacoby, 412 Spring St., for merchandise purchased, $195. Terms, 30 days net.
     4. Sold merchandise on account to J. C. Sailor, 210 Main St., $26.50, tax $1.33. Sale No. 31.
     6. Sold merchandise on account to the Riverfront Inn, 20 Broadway, $82.50, tax $4.13. Sale No. 32.
     8. Sundry cash sales, $178, tax $8.90.
     10. Paid the following creditors on account:
         Campbell Bros., $153.60.
         Saxer & Co., $252.40.

THE HHH STORE
Trial Balance
March 31, 19—

Cash	111	4,296.00	
Accounts Receivable	123	7,140.00	
Merchandise Inventory	131	44,000.00	
Store Equipment	181	2,320.00	
Accounts Payable	231		7,473.24
Sales Tax Payable	241		154.14
Harry H. Harris, Capital	311		12,248.62
Harry H. Harris, Drawing	031	2,800.00	
Sales	411		97,600.00
Sales Returns and Allowances	041	850.00	
Purchases	511	53,600.00	
Purchases Returns and Allowances	051		424.00
Rent Expense	611	1,800.00	
Advertising Expense	621	480.00	
Heating and Lighting Expense	631	240.00	
Telephone and Telegraph Expense	641	144.00	
Miscellaneous Expense	651	230.00	
		117,900.00	117,900.00

11. Received the following remittances to apply on account:
    Rodeway Hotel, $76.50.
    F. D. Weber, $35.
    Mrs. B. L. Carlin, $57.40.
12. Received Invoice No. 62 dated April 10 from Rice & Simon, Cleveland, for merchandise purchased, $350. Terms, 30 days net.
13. Paid $154.14 to State Treasurer for March sales tax.
13. Made sales on account as follows:
    No. 33, Mrs. C. D. Casal, Bonne Terre, $87.45, tax $4.37.
    No. 34, Rodeway Hotel, 200 Locust, $57.25, tax $2.86.
    No. 35, Mrs. E. H. Stifel, 125 E. Fourth St., $70, tax $3.50.
14. Paid $27.50 for newspaper advertising.
15. Sundry cash sales, $142.50, tax $7.13.
17. Harry H. Harris withdrew $200 for personal use.
18. Made sales on account as follows:
    No. 36, P. L. Beffa, 406 Race St., $71.90, tax $3.60.
    No. 37, Mrs. W. J. Morris, 52 E. Fourth St., $31.90, tax $1.60.
    No. 38, Riverfront Inn, 20 Broadway, $75.16, tax $3.76.
19. Received Invoice No. 63 dated April 17 from Campbell Bros., Cincinnati, for merchandise purchased, $242.50. Terms, 30 days net.
20. Gave the Riverfront Inn credit for $12.60 on account of merchandise returned. (Sales price, $12, tax 60 cents.)
21. Received credit from Campbell Bros. for $17.80 on account of merchandise returned.
22. Sundry cash sales, $143.70, tax $7.19.
24. Received Invoice No. 64 dated April 22 from Saxer & Co., Detroit, for merchandise purchased, $92.50. Terms, 30 days net.

288

25. Made sales on account as follows:
    No. 39, F. D. Weber, 211 Elm St., $44.50, tax $2.23.
    No. 40, Rodeway Hotel, 200 Locust, $75.16, tax $3.76.
25. Allowed credit for $4.41 to P. L. Beffa for merchandise returned. (Sales price, $4.20, tax 21 cents.)
27. Paid Ebert Bros. $69.50 on account.
27. Received $122.95 from Riverfront Inn to apply on account.
28. Purchased store equipment on account from the Carter Supply Co., 61 John St., $120. Terms, 60 days net.
28. Paid freight and drayage on merchandise purchased, $25.
29. Sundry cash sales, $154.60, tax $7.73.
29. Harry H. Harris withdrew $150 for personal use.

REQUIRED: (1) Journalize the April transactions. Total the purchases journal and rule; foot the sales journal, enter the totals, and rule. Prove each page of the general journal by footing the debit and credit columns. (2) Open the necessary general ledger accounts, using the trial balance on page 288 as a guide. Record the April 1 balances as shown in the March 31 trial balance, complete the individual posting from the general journal, and complete the summary posting from the purchases and sales journals. Foot the accounts and enter the balances. (3) Take a trial balance using a sheet of two-column journal paper.

Problem 7-A

E. J. Nestor is a dealer in china and glassware. In accounting for notes, he uses a notes receivable register similar to the one reproduced on pages 184 and 185. Following is a narrative of transactions involving notes received from customers during the current year:

Mar. 6. Received from Oscar Love a 60-day, 7% note (No. 1) for $600 dated March 4 and payable at First National Bank, Willow Springs.
Apr. 26. Received from Thomas J. Nold a 90-day, 6% note (No. 2) for $500 dated April 25 and payable at Second National Bank, Lemay.
May   3. Received a check for $607 from Oscar Love in payment of his note due today plus interest.
    19. Received from William E. Forman a 60-day, 7% note (No. 3) for $525 dated May 18 and payable at Meachem Park Trust Company, Meachem Park.
July 17. Received a check for $531.13 from William E. Forman in payment of his note due today plus interest.
    24. Received a check for $507.50 from Thomas J. Nold in payment of his note due today plus interest.
Oct. 2. Received from L. R. Cole a 90-day, 6% note (No. 4) for $750 dated October 2 and payable at Kirkwood State Bank, Kirkwood.
    19. Discounted L. R. Cole's note for $750 at the Ellisville Trust Company at 7% and received credit for the proceeds.

REQUIRED: **(1)** Prepare entries in general journal form to record the foregoing transactions. Foot the amount columns as a means of proof. **(2)** Make the required entries in a notes receivable register to provide a detailed auxiliary record of the notes received by E. J. Nestor.

Problem 7-B

J. B. Hayes operates a department store. Sometimes he finds it necessary to issue notes to suppliers to obtain extensions of time for payment of their accounts. Unless otherwise stated, all such notes are made payable at the Jefferson County Bank, Jefferson. Following is a narrative of transactions involving notes issued by Mr. Hayes during the current year:

Feb. 1. Borrowed $800 from the bank on a 90-day, 6% note (No. 1).
Mar. 7. Issued a 60-day, 7% note (No. 2) for $575 to Black & Decker Co.
Apr. 20. Issued a 60-day, 6% note (No. 3) for $660 to D. R. Armstrong & Sons.
May   2. Issued a check for $812 to the bank in payment of note due today plus interest.
       6. Gave Black & Decker Co. a check for $6.71 in payment of the interest and a new note (No. 4) for $575, due in 60 days, with interest at 7%, in settlement of the note due today.
June 19. Issued a check for $666.60 to D. R. Armstrong & Sons in payment of note due today plus interest.
July 1. Borrowed $2,500 from the bank on a 90-day, 6% note (No. 5).
      5. Issued a check for $581.71 to Black & Decker Co. in payment of note due today plus interest.
Sept. 29. Gave Jefferson County Bank a check for $37.50 in payment of the interest and a new note (No. 6) for $2,500, due in 60 days, with interest at 6%, in settlement of the note due today.
Nov. 28. Issued a check for $2,525 to the bank in payment of note due today plus interest.

REQUIRED: **(1)** Prepare entries in general journal form to record the foregoing transactions. Foot the amount columns as a means of proof. **(2)** Make the required entries in a notes payable register, similar to the one reproduced on pages 188 and 189, to provide a detailed auxiliary record of the notes issued.

There are no Practical Accounting Problems for Chapter 8.

Problem 9-A

W. C. Bouchein, who is self-employed, is in the business of retail plumbing and heating. Merchandise is sold for cash and on account. On the next page is a reproduction of the Trial Balance columns of his work sheet for the current year ended December 31.

W. C. BOUCHEIN
Work Sheet
For the Year Ended December 31, 19—

Account	Acct. No.	Trial Balance Debit	Trial Balance Credit
Cash.............................	111	10,931.84	
Notes Receivable......................	131	2,800.00	
Accrued Interest Receivable.............	132		
Accounts Receivable....................	133	8,648.00	
Allowance for Bad Debts...............	013		99.44
Merchandise Inventory.................	141	21,456.00	
Prepaid Insurance.....................	151	1,120.00	
Stationery and Supplies................	152	360.00	
Store Equipment......................	161	8,800.00	
Accumulated Depreciation — Store Equipment	016		880.00
Delivery Equipment....................	171	7,200.00	
Accumulated Depreciation — Delivery Equip.	017		1,800.00
Notes Payable.......................	211		4,400.00
Accrued Interest Payable...............	221		
Accounts Payable.....................	231		13,343.40
Sales Tax Payable....................	241		160.00
FICA Tax Payable....................	261		675.00
W. C. Bouchein, Capital...............	311		50,666.00
W. C. Bouchein, Drawing..............	031	8,000.00	
Expense and Revenue Summary..........	321		
Sales...............................	411		102,870.00
Sales Returns and Allowances...........	041	358.00	
Purchases...........................	511	72,462.60	
Purchases Returns and Allowances........	051		368.60
Rent Expense........................	521	6,000.00	
Advertising Expense...................	522	780.00	
Salaries Expense.....................	523	24,000.00	
Payroll Taxes Expense.................	524	1,650.00	
Insurance Expense....................	525		
Stationery and Supplies Expense.........	526		
Depreciation Expense..................	527		
Bad Debts Expense....................	528		
Charitable Contributions Expense.........	529	500.00	
Miscellaneous Expense.................	531	210.00	
Interest Earned......................	611		70.00
Interest Expense.....................	711	56.00	
		175,332.44	175,332.44

Note: Problems 9-B and 10-A are also based on W. C. Bouchein's work sheet. If these problems are to be solved, the work sheet prepared in Problem 9-A should be retained for reference until after they are solved, when the solutions of all three problems may be submitted to the instructor.

REQUIRED: Prepare a ten-column work sheet making the necessary entries in the Adjustments columns to record the following:

(1) Merchandise inventory, end of year, $25,508.

(2) Accruals:

Interest accrued on notes receivable, $28.

Interest accrued on notes payable, $36.68.

(3) Prepaid expenses:

Prepaid insurance unexpired, $560.

Stationery and supplies on hand, $120.

(4) Depreciation:

Store equipment, 10% a year, $880.

Delivery equipment, 25% a year, $1,800.

(5) Bad debts expense:

Increase allowance for bad debts $160 to provide for estimated loss.

Problem 9-B

Refer to the work sheet for W. C. Bouchein (based on Problem 9-A) and from it prepare the following financial statements:

(1) An income statement for the year ended December 31.

(2) A balance sheet in account form as of December 31.

Problem 10-A

Refer to the work sheet for W. C. Bouchein (based on Problem 9-A) and draft the general journal entries required:

(1) To adjust the general ledger accounts so that they will be in agreement with the financial statements.

(2) To close the temporary owner's equity accounts on December 31.

(3) To reverse the accrual adjustments as of January 1.

Problem 10-B (Complete cycle problem)

H. D. Hulick is engaged in a merchandising business as a sole owner. He calls his business "Hulick's Store." He keeps a purchases journal, sales journal, combined cash journal, and general ledger. For his combined cash journal, he uses eight-column paper (8 columns divided — 2 left, 6 right) with headings arranged as follows:

Bank

    (1) Deposits Dr.

    (2) Checks Cr.

General

    (3) Debit

    (4) Credit

    (5) Accounts Payable Dr.

    (6) Accounts Receivable Cr.

    (7) Sales Cr.

    (8) Sales Tax Payable Cr.

The standard account form of ledger ruling is used. Individual accounts with customers and suppliers are not kept in ledger form; however, the purchase invoices and sales tickets are filed in such a manner that the amounts owed to suppliers and due from customers can be determined at any time. At the end of the eleventh month of this year, his trial balance appeared as shown below.

HULICK'S STORE

Trial Balance

November 30, 19—

Cash	111	20,133.84	
Notes Receivable	121	7,200.00	
Accounts Receivable	123	10,959.60	
Allowance for Bad Debts	012		278.40
Merchandise Inventory	131	83,200.00	
Prepaid Insurance	141	1,900.00	
Stationery and Supplies	151	320.00	
Store Equipment	181	7,600.00	
Accumulated Depreciation — Store Equipment	018		1,520.00
Notes Payable	211		4,800.00
Accounts Payable	231		6,439.50
Sales Tax Payable	241		608.60
Employees Income Tax Payable	251		478.40
FICA Tax Payable	261		287.04
FUTA Tax Payable	271		179.30
State Unemployment Tax Payable	281		186.00
H. D. Hulick, Capital	311		127,600.00
H. D. Hulick, Drawing	031	14,800.00	
Sales	411		334,720.00
Sales Returns and Allowances	041	505.60	
Purchases	511	252,800.00	
Purchases Returns and Allowances	051		564.40
Purchases Discount	052		440.00
Rent Expense	611	13,200.00	
Advertising Expense	612	9,600.00	
Salaries and Commissions Expense	613	51,600.00	
Payroll Taxes Expense	614	3,548.32	
Miscellaneous Expense	615	714.28	
Interest Earned	711		36.00
Interest Expense	811	56.00	
		478,137.64	478,137.64

NARRATIVE OF TRANSACTIONS FOR DECEMBER

Dec. 1. (Friday) Purchased merchandise from Bohannon Bros., Cedar Rapids, $2,600, Invoice No. 11, dated November 30. Terms, 2/10, n/30.

2. Paid the December rent, $1,200. Check No. 54.

2. Paid the telephone bill, $54. Check No. 55.

4. Paid F. J. Kern $1,865.00 in full of December 1 balance. Check No. 56.
5. Sold merchandise on account to D. L. Colby, 230 Main St., $900, tax $45.00. Sale No. 101.
6. Purchased merchandise from the Williams Supply Co., Williamstown, $2,350. Invoice No. 12, dated December 5. Terms, 30 days.
7. Received $550 from Easton Johnson in full settlement of his account.
8. Paid Bohannon Bros. $2,548 in settlement of their invoice of November 30, less 2% discount. Check No. 57.
8. Received $522.24 from Arno Becht in full settlement of his account.
9. Sold merchandise on account to A. K. Adair, Fenton, $537, tax $26.85. Sale No. 102.
11. Purchased merchandise from the Haworth Mfg. Co., St. Louis, $3,843.20. Invoice No. 13, dated December 9. Terms, 30 days.
12. Sold merchandise on account to D. C. Kutz, 102 Prince St., $750.40, tax $37.52. Sale No. 103.
13. Issued Check No. 58 to Second National Bank, a U.S. Depositary, in payment of the following taxes:

(a) Employees' income tax withheld during November............................		$478.40
(b) FICA tax:		
On employees (withheld during November).............................	$143.52	
On the employer.....................	143.52	287.04
Total.................................		$765.44

14. Sold merchandise on account to H. C. Bock, 873 Cliff St., $1,500, tax $75. Sale No. 104.
15. Issued Check No. 59 payable to State Treasurer for $608.60 for November sales tax.
18. H. D. Hulick withdrew $240 for personal use. Check No. 60.
19. Gave D. C. Kutz credit for $52.50 because a part of the merchandise sold him on the twelfth was returned. (Sales price, $50, tax $2.50.)
20. Sold merchandise on account to D. L. Colby, 230 Main St., $500, tax $25. Sale No. 105.
21. Purchased merchandise from the Brown Mfg. Co., Cincinnati, $3,748.50. Invoice No. 14, dated December 20. Terms, 30 days.
22. Received $735.42 from D. C. Kutz for balance of Sale No. 103.
23. Paid bill for advertising, $250. Check No. 61.
26. Sold merchandise on account to K. K. Kolker, 195 Johnson St., $1,570, tax $78.50. Sale No. 106.
26. Purchased merchandise from Bohannon Bros., Cedar Rapids, $1,891.40. Invoice No. 15, dated December 23. Terms, 2/10, n/30.
26. Received a check for $800 from D. L. Colby to apply on account.
27. Sold merchandise on account to D. C. Kutz, 102 Prince St., $771.90, tax $38.60. Sale No. 107.
27. Sent the Haworth Mfg. Co. a check for $1,600 to apply on account. Check No. 62.
28. Sold merchandise on account to E. O. Norman, 812 Sixth St., $1,886.30, tax $94.32. Sale No. 108.

28. Purchased store equipment from the Milton Supply Co., Milton, $480. Terms, 60 days net.
29. Received $563.85 from A. K. Adair in payment of Sale No. 102.
29. Received credit from Bohannon Bros. for $70 because a part of the merchandise purchased on the twenty-sixth was returned by agreement.
29. Sold merchandise on account to A. K. Adair, Fenton, $943.60, tax $47.18. Sale No. 109.
30. Sundry cash sales for month, $4,814.40, tax $240.72.
30. Issued Check No. 63 payable to Payroll for $2,264.90.

PAYROLL STATEMENT FOR MONTH ENDED DECEMBER 31

Total wages and commissions earned during period..........		$3,000.00
Employees' taxes to be withheld		
(a) Employees' income tax.............................	$570.10	
(b) FICA tax @ 5.5%..................................	165.00	735.10
Net amount payable to employees........................		$2,264.90
Employer's payroll taxes:		
(a) FICA tax @ 5.5%.................................		$ 165.00
(b) UC taxes —		
State @ 2.7%..................................	$ 81.00	
Federal @ 0.5%...............................	15.00	96.00
Total...		$ 261.00

(In addition to recording the amounts withheld from employees' wages for income tax purposes and for FICA tax, the social security tax imposed on the employer should also be recorded.)

295

REQUIRED: (1) Journalize the December transactions. (2) Open the necessary general ledger accounts and record the December 1 balances, using the November 30 trial balance as the source of the needed information. Complete the individual and summary posting from the books of original entry. (3) Take a trial balance of the general ledger accounts. (4) Prepare a ten-column work sheet making the required adjustments from the information given below. Number the pages of the journals as follows:

Purchases Journal....... Page 34
Sales Journal........... Page 46
Combined Cash Journal.. Pages 49–51

(a) Merchandise inventory, end of year, $117,000.

(b) Accruals:
    Interest accrued on notes receivable, $96.
    Interest accrued on notes payable, $48.

(c) Prepaid expenses:
    Prepaid insurance unexpired, $1,268.
    Stationery and supplies on hand, $100.

(d) Depreciation:
    Store equipment, 10% a year, $760.

(e) Bad debts expense:
    Increase allowance for bad debts $422.72 to provide for estimated loss.

In recording the required adjustments on the work sheet, it will be necessary to add (in numerical order) the following account titles to those already appearing in the trial balance:

Accrued Interest Receivable, Account No. 122
Accrued Interest Payable, Account No. 221
Expense and Revenue Summary, Account No. 321
Insurance Expense, Account No. 616
Stationery and Supplies Expense, Account No. 617
Depreciation Expense, Account No. 618
Bad Debts Expense, Account No. 619

(5) Prepare an income statement for the year ending December 31 and a balance sheet in report form as of December 31. **(6)** Record the adjusting entries in the combined cash journal and post. **(7)** Record the closing entries in the combined cash journal and post. **(8)** Balance and rule the accounts that are in balance after the adjusting and closing entries have been posted; also balance and rule the following accounts: Cash, H. D. Hulick, Capital, Accounts Receivable, Accounts Payable, and Sales Tax Payable, and rule the merchandise inventory account. **(9)** Take a post-closing trial balance. **(10)** Record the necessary reversing entries as of January 1 in the combined cash journal. Post and rule the accounts that are closed.

296

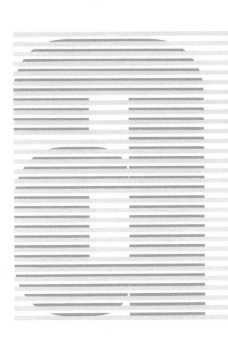

chapter 11

accounting for purchases

In Chapter 6, mention was made of the fact that the word "purchase" usually is taken to mean the purchase of merchandise. However, the word is often used in the broader sense to refer to the buying of many sorts of property. In this chapter the broader meaning applies, though much of the discussion relates to the purchase of merchandise.

Purchasing procedure

Merchandise for resale and other property for use in the operation of a business enterprise may be purchased either for cash or on account. In one enterprise the buying may be done by the owner or by an employee, and it may require only part-time attention. In a large enterprise a purchasing department may be maintained with a manager and staff who will devote their entire time to buying activities. The successful operation of such a purchasing department requires an efficient organization as well as the proper equipment.

The purchase requisition

A form used to request the purchasing department to purchase merchandise or other property is known as a *purchase requisition*. Such requests may come from any department of an enterprise. Purchase requisitions should be numbered consecutively to prevent the loss or misuse of any of the forms. Usually they are prepared in duplicate with the original going to the purchasing department and the duplicate copy being retained in the department originating the requisition.

PURCHASE REQUISITION	
HOLLING & RENZ 1111 OLIVE ST. EAST ST. LOUIS, ILLINOIS 62205	REQUISITION NO. D-129

Required for Department A	Date Issued March 27, 19--
Advise Mr. _____ Renz _____ On Delivery	Date Required April 15, 19--

QUANTITY	DESCRIPTION
40 cs. 50 20 cs.	Outside House Paint (gallons) White Primer Paint (2-gal. pail) White Primer Paint (1-gal. can)

Approved By *J. L. Holling*   Requisition Placed By *A. G. Renz*

PURCHASING AGENT'S MEMORANDUM

Purchase Order No. 211	Issued To: Celucoat Corporation
Date March 27, 19--	6161 Maple St. Louis, MO 63130

Purchase Requisition

A purchase requisition is reproduced above. The requisition specifies merchandise wanted in Department A. The merchandising business conducted by Holling & Renz is organized into two departments. Requisitions for merchandise originate with the heads of these two departments. After the purchase requisition shown in the illustration was approved by Holling, an order was placed with the Celucoat Corporation, manufacturers of paints and varnishes, as indicated by the purchasing agent's memorandum at the bottom of the form. The purchase requisition, when approved, is the purchasing department's authority to order the merchandise or other property described in the requisition.

The purchase order

A written order by the buyer for merchandise or other property specified in the buyer's purchase requisition is known as a *purchase order*. A purchase order may be prepared on a printed stock form, on a specially designed form, or on an order blank supplied by a vendor. Purchase orders should be numbered consecutively. Usually they are prepared with multiple copies. The original copy goes to the *vendor* or *supplier* — the person or firm from whom the merchandise or other property is ordered. Sometimes the duplicate copy also goes to the vendor. If this is the case, this copy — called the "acknowledgment copy" — will have a space for the vendor to sign to indicate his acceptance of the order. Such acceptance

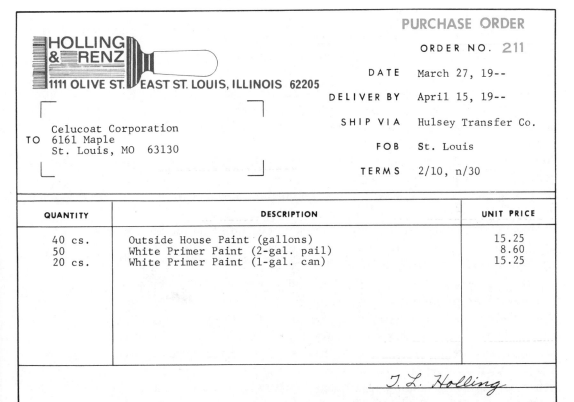

QUANTITY	DESCRIPTION	UNIT PRICE
40 cs.	Outside House Paint (gallons)	15.25
50	White Primer Paint (2-gal. pail)	8.60
20 cs.	White Primer Paint (1-gal. can)	15.25

Purchase Order

creates a formal contract. The signed acknowledgment copy is then returned to the ordering firm. Sometimes a copy of the purchase order is sent to the department that requisitioned the purchase. In many organizations a copy of the purchase order is sent to the receiving clerk. The procedure followed by some firms requires that the accounting department receive a copy of the purchase order to provide a basis for verifying the charges made by the vendor. A variety of practices are followed with respect to requisitioning purchases, placing orders, checking goods received and charges made, recording purchases, and paying vendors. Each organization adopts procedures best suited to its particular needs.

A purchase order is reproduced on page 299. The quantity and the description of the merchandise ordered are the same as were specified in the purchase requisition reproduced on page 298. The unit prices shown in the purchase order are those quoted by the vendor and it is expected that the merchandise will be billed at such prices.

The purchase invoice

A business form prepared by the seller that lists the items shipped, their cost, and the method of shipment is commonly referred to as an *invoice*. From the viewpoint of the seller, it is considered a *sales invoice;* from the viewpoint of the buyer, it is considered a *purchase invoice*.

A purchase invoice may be received by the buyer before or after delivery of the merchandise or other property ordered. As invoices are received, it is customary to number them consecutively. These numbers should not be confused with the vendors' numbers, which represent their sale numbers. After being numbered, each purchase invoice should be checked with a copy of the purchase order to determine that the quantity, the description, the prices, and the terms agree and that the method of shipment and the date of delivery conform to the instructions and specifications. A separate approval form may be used, or approval may be stamped on the invoice by means of a rubber stamp. If a separate approval form is used, it may be stapled to or be pasted on the invoice form.

An example of a purchase invoice is reproduced on page 301. A rubber stamp was used to imprint the approval form on the face of the invoice. When the merchandise is received, the contents of the shipment may be checked by the receiving clerk with a copy of the purchase order, or he may prepare a separate *receiving report*. In the latter event, the receiving report and the purchase order must be checked by a clerk in either the purchasing department or the accounting department. After the prices and extensions are verified, the purchase invoice is recorded by entering it in the *invoice register* and then posting it to the account of the proper creditor in the

300

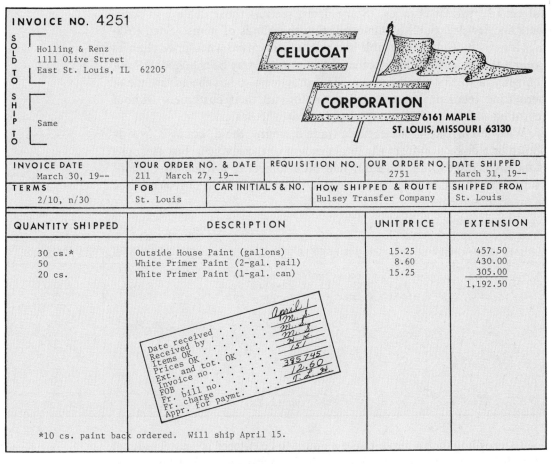

INVOICE NO. 4251

S
O
L
D
T
O

Holling & Renz
1111 Olive Street
East St. Louis, IL 62205

S
H
I
P
T
O

Same

CELUCOAT

CORPORATION 6161 MAPLE
ST. LOUIS, MISSOURI 63130

INVOICE DATE	YOUR ORDER NO. & DATE	REQUISITION NO.	OUR ORDER NO.	DATE SHIPPED
March 30, 19--	211 March 27, 19--		2751	March 31, 19--

TERMS	FOB	CAR INITIALS & NO.	HOW SHIPPED & ROUTE	SHIPPED FROM
2/10, n/30	St. Louis		Hulsey Transfer Company	St. Louis

QUANTITY SHIPPED	DESCRIPTION	UNIT PRICE	EXTENSION
30 cs.*	Outside House Paint (gallons)	15.25	457.50
50	White Primer Paint (2-gal. pail)	8.60	430.00
20 cs.	White Primer Paint (1-gal. can)	15.25	305.00
			1,192.50

Date received April 1
Received by m. f.
Items OK m. f.
Prices OK m. s.
Ext. and tot. OK 151
Invoice no. 385745
FOB bill no. 12.60
Fr. charge T. L. H.
Appr. for paymt.

*10 cs. paint back ordered. Will ship April 15.

Purchase Invoice

accounts payable ledger. The invoice is then held in an unpaid invoice file until it is paid.

Back Orders. Sometimes the vendor is unable to ship immediately a part or all of the merchandise ordered. He may, however, send an invoice immediately for the complete order and indicate on it what has been back ordered and when such items will be shipped. Reference to the purchase invoice reproduced above will indicate that while 40 cases of outside house paint were ordered, only 30 were shipped immediately by the Celucoat Corporation. Notice of this shortage was indicated on the invoice. In this instance, only the items shipped were billed.

Trade Discounts. Many manufacturers and wholesalers quote list prices (printed) which are subject to trade discounts. This makes possible the publication of catalogs with quotations of prices that will not be subject to frequent changes. Some firms, such as those dealing in hardware and jewelry, publish catalogs listing thousands of items. Such catalogs are costly, and considerable loss might be involved when price changes occur if it were not for the fact that discount rates may be changed without changing the list or catalog prices. This practice also has the advantage of permitting retail dealers to display catalogs to their customers without revealing what the items of merchandise cost the dealers.

When an invoice is subject to a trade discount, the discount is usually shown as a deduction from the total amount of the invoice. For example, if the invoice shown on page 301 had been subject to a trade discount of 10 percent, the discount might be stated in the body of the invoice in the manner shown below.

QUANTITY SHIPPED	DESCRIPTION	UNIT PRICE	EXTENSION
30 cs.*	Outside House Paint (gallons)	15.25	457.50
50	White Primer Paint (2-gal. pail)	8.60	430.00
20 cs.	White Primer Paint (1-gal. can)	15.25	305.00
			1,192.50
	Less 10% discount		119.25
			1,073.25
*10 cs. paint back ordered. Will ship April 15.			

In recording such an invoice the amount to be entered is the net amount after deducting the trade discount; trade discounts should not be entered in the accounts of either the seller or the buyer, as they represent merely a reduction in the price of the merchandise.

Sometimes a series or chain of trade discounts is allowed. For example, the list prices may be subject to discounts of 25, 10, and 5 percent. In computing the total discount where two or more trade discounts are allowed, each discount is computed separately on the successive net amounts. For example, if the gross amount of an invoice is $100 and discounts of 25, 10, and 5 percent are allowed, the net amount should be computed as follows:

Gross amount of invoice...	$100.00
Less 25%...	25.00
Balance...	$ 75.00
Less 10%...	7.50
Balance...	$ 67.50
Less 5%..	3.38
Net amount	$ 64.12

In recording this invoice only the net amount, or $64.12, should be entered.

Cash Discounts. Many firms follow the practice of allowing cash discounts as an inducement for prompt payment of invoices. The terms of payment should be clearly indicated on the invoice. It will be noted that the terms specified on the invoice reproduced on page 301 are "2/10, n/30." This means that a discount of 2 percent will be allowed if payment is made within 10 days from the date of the invoice (March 30), that is, if payment is made by April 9.

Should the invoice be paid on or before April 9, 2 percent of $1,192.50, or $23.85, may be deducted and a check for $1,168.65 may be issued in full settlement of the invoice. After April 9 no discount will be allowed, and the total amount, or $1,192.50, must be paid not later than 30 days after the date of the invoice, that is, by April 29.

Cash discounts usually are ignored at the time of recording purchase invoices, even though it may be the policy of a firm to pay all invoices in time to get the benefit of any cash discounts offered. For example, the invoice reproduced on page 301 should be recorded by debiting the proper account or accounts and by crediting Accounts Payable for $1,192.50. The discount taken at time of payment on or before April 9 will be entered at the time of recording the check issued in settlement of the invoice. At the end of the period the credit balance of the purchases discount account is shown in the income statement as a deduction from the cost of goods purchased. Sometimes purchases discount is regarded as "other revenue" but this treatment is not logical and is disappearing from practice.

A minor complication arises in treating purchases discount as a reduction in purchase cost when purchases are accounted for on a departmental basis. While it would be possible to have two or more purchases discount accounts and to analyze each discount taken to determine the department (or departments) to which it relates, such a procedure could be very time-consuming. The resulting accuracy might not be worth the trouble. An acceptable alternative is to record all purchases discount in a single account whose balance, as a part of the closing process, is allocated among the departmental cost of goods sold accounts in proportion to the net purchases of the departments. (The nature and use of cost of goods sold accounts will be explained and illustrated in Chapters 17 and 18.)

Sometimes an invoice is subject to both trade and cash discounts. In such cases the trade discount should be deducted from the gross amount of the invoice before the cash discount is computed and deducted. For example, if the invoice reproduced on page 301 were subject to a trade discount of 10 percent and the terms were 2/10, n/30, the net amount payable

303

within 10 days from the date of the invoice should be computed in the following manner:

Amount of invoice...	$1,192.50
Less trade discount, 10%.....................................	119.25
Amount subject to cash discount..............................	$1,073.25
Less cash discount, 2%.......................................	21.47
Net amount payable..	$1,051.78

Usually an entire invoice must be paid for within the time specified in order to obtain the benefit of any cash discount offered. However, in some instances, the purchaser may be allowed the usual cash discount for partial payment of an invoice within the time specified. Thus, if, instead of paying the entire invoice of the Celucoat Corporation, Holling & Renz had made a payment of $500 on the invoice by April 9, the Celucoat Corporation might agree to allow them the cash discount of 2 percent. In such case the amount of the discount should be computed in the following manner:

$100\% =$ amount for which Holling & Renz should receive credit
$100\% - 2\% = 98\%$
$98\% = \$500$
$\$500 \div 98\% = \$510.20$
$\$510.20 - \$500 = \$10.20$ discount

304

This transaction should be recorded on the books of Holling & Renz by debiting Accounts Payable for $510.20, by crediting Purchases Discount for $10.20, and by crediting the bank account for $500.

Terms. The terms commonly used in connection with purchase invoices are interpreted as follows:

30 days	The amount of the invoice must be paid within 30 days from its date.
2/10, n/30	A discount of 2% will be allowed if payment is made within 10 days from the date of the invoice; otherwise, the total amount of the invoice must be paid within 30 days from its date.
2/EOM, n/60	A discount of 2% will be allowed if payment is made before the end of the month; otherwise, the total amount of the invoice must be paid within 60 days of its date.
COD	Collect on delivery. The amount of the invoice must be paid at the time the merchandise is delivered.
FOB Shipping Point	Free on board at point of origin of the shipment. Under such terms the buyer must pay all transportation costs and assume all risks from the time the merchandise is accepted for shipment by the carrier.
FOB Destination	Free on board at destination of the shipment. The seller will pay the transportation costs and will assume all responsibility for the merchandise until it reaches the carrier's delivery point at destination.

Miscellaneous forms

In addition to the forms previously discussed, there are a number of miscellaneous forms, such as bills of lading, freight bills, drayage bills, and credit memorandums, that may be used in connection with the purchase of merchandise or other property. It is important that the function of these forms be understood in order that they may be properly processed.

Bills of Lading. The desired method of shipment is usually specified on the purchase order and the actual method of shipment is indicated on the purchase invoice. When shipment is made by railroad, highway freight, or air, the shipper is given a receipt that is known as a *bill of lading.*

A bill of lading is prepared in triplicate. The first copy is referred to as the original, the second copy as the shipping order, and the third copy as the memorandum. The freight agent signs all three copies, returning the original and the memorandum to the shipper and retaining the shipping order. The shipper in turn may send either the original or the memorandum copy to the buyer and retain the other copy for his files.

The merchandise or other property is delivered to the freight agent in cases, cartons, bundles, or packages; hence, the description in the bill of lading may differ from the description in the purchase invoice. In addition to describing the merchandise in the bill of lading, the number of packages and the weight of each are indicated. The freight rate depends upon the type of merchandise being shipped, the distance it is being

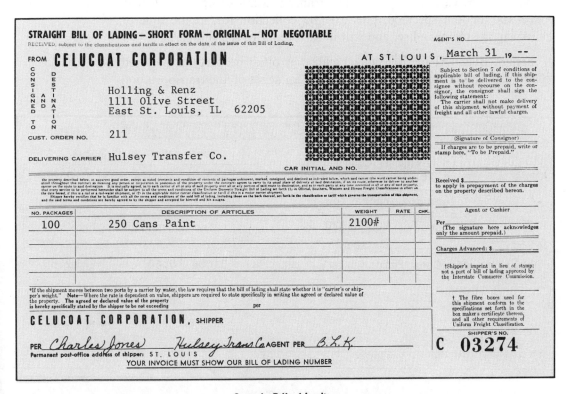

Straight Bill of Lading

shipped, and the weight of the shipment. The rate per 100 pounds on a carload (CL) is lower than the rate on less than a carload (LCL).

A model filled-in bill of lading is reproduced on page 305. This is known as a *straight bill of lading*, under the terms of which title to the merchandise passed to Holling & Renz when the merchandise was delivered to the transportation company. When Holling & Renz present a copy of this bill of lading to the local agent of the carrier, they will be entitled to receive the merchandise.

COD Purchases. Merchandise or other property may be purchased on COD terms, that is, *collect on delivery* or *cash on delivery*. COD shipments may be received by parcel post, express, or freight. When such shipments are received by parcel post or express, the recipient must pay for the property at the time of delivery. The bill may include transportation charges and COD fees. In any event, the total amount paid represents the cost of the property purchased.

When COD shipments are made by freight, the amount to be collected by the transportation company should be entered immediately below the description of the merchandise on the bill of lading. A copy of the sales invoice may be inserted in an envelope which can be pasted to the outside of the package, carton, or case. The transportation company will then collect the amount specified, plus a COD collection fee, at the time of delivering the merchandise, and will in turn remit to the shipper.

Freight Bills. At the time merchandise or other property is delivered to a transportation company for shipment, an agent of the transportation

306

Freight Bill

company prepares a *waybill* — a document which describes the shipment, shows the point of origin and destination, and indicates any special handling that may be required. The original is forwarded to the agent of the transportation company at the station to which the shipment is directed. When the shipment arrives at the destination, a bill for the transportation charges called a *freight bill* is prepared. Sometimes the recipient of the shipment is required to pay the bill before he can obtain the property.

A reproduction of a freight bill is presented on the preceding page. A comparison of this freight bill with the bill of lading reproduced on page 305 will show that it contains the same description of the shipment. In addition, however, the freight charges are shown.

Trucking companies usually make what is known as "store-to-door delivery." Freight shipments made by railroad or airline may also be delivered to the recipient's place of business at no extra charge. In case such service is not rendered by the transportation company, it may be necessary for the recipient to employ a drayage company to transport the merchandise from the freight station to his place of business. In such a case, the drayage company will submit a bill (a *drayage bill*) for its services.

Credit Memorandums. Ordinarily the buyer expects to receive the merchandise or other property ordered and to pay for it at the agreed

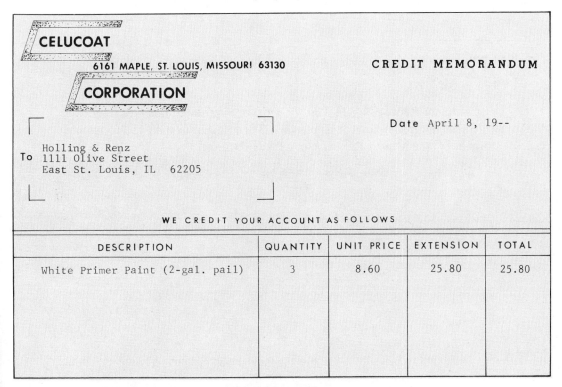

CELUCOAT				
6161 MAPLE, ST. LOUIS, MISSOURI 63130		CREDIT MEMORANDUM		
CORPORATION				

Date April 8, 19--

To Holling & Renz
    1111 Olive Street
    East St. Louis, IL 62205

WE CREDIT YOUR ACCOUNT AS FOLLOWS

DESCRIPTION	QUANTITY	UNIT PRICE	EXTENSION	TOTAL
White Primer Paint (2-gal. pail)	3	8.60	25.80	25.80

Credit Memorandum

price in accordance with the terms specified in the purchase invoice. However, part or all of the merchandise or other property may be returned to the vendor for various reasons, such as the following:

(a) It may not conform to the specifications in the purchase order.
(b) A mistake may have been made in placing the order and the vendor may give permission for it to be returned.
(c) It may have been delayed in shipment and, thus, the buyer cannot dispose of it. This sometimes happens with seasonal goods.

If the merchandise received is unsatisfactory or the prices charged are not in accord with an existing agreement or with previous quotations, an adjustment may be made that is referred to as an *allowance*.

When merchandise is to be returned to the supplier for credit, a charge-back invoice is usually issued by the buyer for the purchase price of the merchandise returned. Upon receipt of the merchandise, the supplier will usually issue a credit memorandum for the amount of the credit allowed. A model filled-in credit memorandum is reproduced on page 307. This form indicates that the Celucoat Corporation has given Holling & Renz credit for the return of three 2-gallon pails of white primer paint.

308

Report No. 11-1

Complete Report No. 11-1 in the workbook and submit your working papers to the instructor for approval. Then continue with the following study assignment until Report No. 11-2 is required.

Accounting practice

The practices followed in accounting for purchases must be tailored to conform to the nature of the business, the volume of purchases of all sorts, and the type and amount of information that is wanted. The discussion and illustration that follow explain a procedure that has wide application in accounting for purchases.

Invoice register

In many firms all incoming invoices covering purchases on account, whether they represent purchases of merchandise, supplies, or other property, are recorded in one book of original entry. Many firms also prefer to keep the merchandise accounts on a departmental basis in order that more information may be available and that better control may be exercised.

Property purchased may consist of: **(1)** merchandise bought for resale; **(2)** supplies, such as letterheads and envelopes for office use, catalogs and circulars for advertising purposes, wrapping paper and twine for use in wrapping and shipping, and cleaning supplies; or **(3)** long-lived assets, such as office equipment, store equipment, and delivery equipment, bought for use in operating the business.

The use of a properly designed columnar register facilitates the recording in one book of account of all incoming invoices covering purchases on account, regardless of whether they represent purchases of merchandise, supplies, or long-lived assets. Such a register also facilitates a proper classification of essential data and makes summary posting possible. A register of this type is often called an *invoice register.*

When all incoming invoices covering purchases on account are recorded in an invoice register, regardless of whether the invoices represent the purchase of merchandise or other property, provision should be made for a proper classification of the debits and the credits. If the merchandise accounts are kept on a departmental basis, a separate column should be provided for recording the merchandise purchased for each department. The use of special columns for this purpose will facilitate summary posting. General Ledger Debit and Credit columns should also be provided for recording items that must be posted individually to the general ledger accounts. If individual accounts with suppliers are kept in a subsidiary ledger, a summary or control account for accounts payable must be kept in the general ledger.

The procedure in recording all incoming invoices covering purchases on account in an invoice register and of keeping the merchandise accounts

INVOICE REGISTER FOR MONTH OF *April*   19 —   PAGE 34

	DEBIT					DAY	✓	DATE OF INV.	INV. NO.	NAME		CREDIT				
	PURCHASES		GENERAL LEDGER									ACCOUNTS PAYABLE	✓	GENERAL LEDGER		
	DEPT. A	DEPT. B	ACCT. NO.	AMOUNT	✓									ACCT. NO.	AMOUNT	✓
1										AMOUNTS FORWARDED						
2	1192 50					1		3/30	151	Olicent Corporation		1192 50	✓			
3		760 00				1		3/29	152	Mid-State Paint Co.		760 00	✓			
4			161	95 40	✓	1		3/31	153	Orchard Paper Co.		95 40	✓			
5			171	245 00	✓	1		4/1	154	Commercial Machine Co.				251	245 00	✓
6	12 00					5		3/29	152	Mid-State Paint Co. (Corrected Inv.)		12 00	✓			
7			541	11 78	✓	6		4/3	155	Spatz Paint Industries		954 78	✓			
8		227 60	551	2 94	✓	6		4/4	156	Paint City, Inc.		230 54	✓			
9			163	86 00	✓	6		4/5	157	L. Y. Adams Co.		86 00	✓			
10			191	396 20	✓	6		4/3	158	Business Interiors, Inc.		396 20	✓			
11			271	4 00	✓	8		4/5	157	L. Y. Adams Co. (Corrected Inv.)				163	4 00	✓
31	32 148 30	4235 11		1318 62								3745 303			249 00	
31	32 148 30	4235 11		1318 62								3745 303			249 00	
32	(511)	(521)		(✓)								(271)			(✓)	

Holling & Renz — Invoice Register

on a departmental basis will be illustrated (1) by showing the chronological recording of a group of selected transactions in an invoice register, (2) by showing the direct posting of the purchase invoices to the individual accounts of suppliers kept in a subsidiary accounts payable ledger, and (3) by showing the posting from the invoice register to the proper general ledger accounts.

Holling & Renz are engaged in the wholesale paint and varnish business. Two departments are maintained — Department A, paint, and Department B, varnish. Separate merchandise accounts are kept for each department in order that the gross margin on sales for each department may be computed separately. In addition to separate departmental purchases accounts and sales accounts, separate departmental accounts are kept for freight charges and for returns and allowances. Only one account is kept for sales discounts and one other account for purchases discounts. The balances of these two latter accounts are allocated in the adjusting and closing process at the end of the period. Following is a list of the above-mentioned accounts with appropriate account numbers:

411 Sales — Department A
   041 Sales Returns and Allowances — Department A
421 Sales — Department B
   042 Sales Returns and Allowances — Department B
   043 Sales Discount
511 Purchases — Department A
   051 Purchases Returns and Allowances — Department A
521 Purchases — Department B
   052 Purchases Returns and Allowances — Department B
   053 Purchases Discount
541 Freight In — Department A
551 Freight In — Department B

The form of the invoice register used by Holling & Renz is illustrated on page 310. A narrative of the transactions that have been entered in the invoice register follows. It will be helpful to check each transaction and to note how it was entered in the invoice register.

HOLLING & RENZ

Narrative of Transactions

Saturday, April 1

Received the following purchase invoices:

No. 151, Celucoat Corporation, St. Louis, Missouri; paint, $1,192.50; terms, March 30 — 2/10, n/30; freight collect.

No. 152, Mid-States Paint Co., Crestwood, Missouri; varnish, $760; terms, March 29 — 2/10, n/30; freight collect.

No. 153, Orchard Paper Co., St. Louis, Missouri; store supplies (Account No. 161) $95.40; terms, March 31 — 30 days.

No. 154, Commercial Machine Co., St. Louis, Missouri; store equipment (Account No. 171) $245; terms, April 1 — 30-day note with interest at 6%.

Wednesday, April 5

Received a corrected purchase invoice from Mid-States Paint Co. for $772. (See Purchase Invoice No. 152.)

Thursday, April 6

Received the following purchase invoices:

No. 155, Spatz Paint Industries, Maplewood, Missouri; paint, $943; terms, April 3 — 2/10, n/60; freight prepaid and added to invoice, $11.78.

No. 156, Paint City, Inc., St. Louis, Missouri; varnish, $227.60; terms, April 4 — 1/10, n/30; freight prepaid and added to invoice, $2.94.

No. 157, S. G. Adams Co., St. Louis, Missouri; office supplies (Account No. 163) $86; terms, April 5 — 30 days.

No. 158, Business Interiors, Inc., Kansas City, Kansas; office equipment (Account No. 191) $379.40; terms, April 3 — 2/10, n/30; freight prepaid and added to invoice, $16.80.

312

Saturday, April 8

Received a corrected purchase invoice from S. G. Adams Co. for $82. (See Purchase Invoice No. 157.)

(The transactions for April 9 through April 30 are omitted.)

Since postings to suppliers' accounts in the subsidiary accounts payable ledger will be made directly from copies of the invoices, a check mark was placed in the Check (√) column beside the Accounts Payable column as each item was entered in the invoice register.

Corrected Purchase Invoices. If a corrected purchase invoice is received before the original invoice has been entered in the invoice register, the original invoice may be discarded and the corrected invoice may be entered in the usual manner. If a corrected purchase invoice is received after the original invoice has been entered in the invoice register and has been posted to the individual account of the supplier, the corrected invoice may be entered in the invoice register if the amount of the corrected invoice is more than the amount of the original invoice. The increase should be recorded by debiting the proper account and by crediting Accounts Payable. (See Invoice No. 152.) The amount of the increase should also be posted to the credit of the proper supplier's account in the subsidiary accounts payable ledger.

If the amount of the corrected invoice is less than the amount of the original invoice, the decrease should be recorded by debiting Accounts Payable and by crediting the proper account. The entry can be recorded in the invoice register if General Ledger Debit and Credit columns are provided. (See Invoice No. 157.) If the needed columns are not provided in the invoice register, the entry must be made in the general journal. The amount of the decrease should be posted to the debit of the proper supplier's account in the subsidiary accounts payable ledger. The corrected invoice should be attached to the original invoice.

Proving the Invoice Register. The invoice register may be footed and the footings may be proved at any time by comparing the sum of the debit footings with the sum of the credit footings. The footings of Holling & Renz's invoice register were proved as of April 30 in the following manner:

COLUMN HEADINGS	DEBIT	CREDIT
Purchases, Dept. A	$32,148.30	
Purchases, Dept. B	4,235.11	
General Ledger	1,318.62	
Accounts Payable		$37,453.03
General Ledger		249.00
Totals	$37,702.03	$37,702.03

It is very common practice to make the proof simply by using an adding machine to see that the totals of the debit columns and the totals of the credit columns are the same. The adding machine tape would appear as follows:

```
                    *
        32,148.30
         4,235.11
         1,318.62

        37,702.03*

                    *
        37,453.03
           249.00

        37,702.03*
```

Ledgers

The ledgers used by Holling & Renz include a general ledger with standard ruling and a subsidiary accounts payable ledger with balance-column ruling. The accounts affected by the transactions recorded in the invoice register reproduced on page 310 are shown in skeleton form on pages 315–317.

Posting Procedure. Posting to Holling & Renz's general ledger and accounts payable ledger involves both individual posting and summary posting.

After each purchase invoice was entered in the invoice register, it was immediately posted to the proper supplier's account in the accounts payable ledger. The posting was done directly from the invoice, the invoice number being inserted in the Posting Reference column of the accounts payable ledger.

While the posting to suppliers' accounts may be done from the invoice register, there are certain advantages in posting directly from the purchase invoices. For example, the invoice provides all the information needed in posting, whereas, if the posting were done from the invoice register, it would be necessary to enter in the invoice register all the information needed in posting, regardless of whether or not it served any other purpose. Furthermore, if an error were made in entering an invoice in the invoice register, it would probably be carried over into the accounts payable ledger through the posting, whereas if the posting is done directly from the invoice, it is not likely that the same error would be made twice.

Posting directly from incoming invoices to the suppliers' accounts in the accounts payable ledger is not only efficient; it also provides a sound method of internal check and control. One bookkeeper may record the invoices in the invoice register and complete such posting as is required from the invoice register to the general ledger accounts, while another bookkeeper may post directly from the invoices to the suppliers' accounts in the accounts payable ledger. Thus the work is divided between two employees. Proof of the accuracy of their work is obtained periodically by preparing a schedule of accounts payable and comparing its total with the balance of the accounts payable control account kept in the general ledger.

Posting to the accounts of suppliers in the accounts payable ledger may be done either by hand or by machine. The use of posting machines for this purpose may be appropriate where there are a large number of accounts and a large number of transactions involved. Such machines frequently are electronic and capable of being programmed.

Individual Posting. Each invoice entered in the Accounts Payable Credit column of the invoice register was posted individually to the proper supplier's account in the accounts payable ledger shown on pages 316 and 317. In the case of invoices involving prepaid transportation charges, the amounts of the merchandise or other property purchased and the transportation charges were posted separately. In posting the invoice of April 3 received from Spatz Paint Industries, the amount of the merchandise, $943,

General Ledger (Partial)

STORE SUPPLIES   Account No. 161

19--			
April 1	Balance	√	42.11
1		IR34	95.40

OFFICE SUPPLIES   Account No. 163

19--				19--			
April 1	Balance	√	58.40	April 8		IR34	4.00
6		IR34	86.00				

STORE EQUIPMENT   Account No. 171

19--			
April 1	Balance	√	2,174.80
1		IR34	245.00

OFFICE EQUIPMENT   Account No. 191

19--			
April 1	Balance	√	4,211.70
6		IR34	396.20

315

NOTES PAYABLE   Account No. 251

				19--			
				April 1	Balance	√	4,100.00
				1		IR34	245.00

ACCOUNTS PAYABLE   Account No. 271

19--				19--			
April 8		IR34	4.00	April 1	Balance	√	6,812.64
				30		IR34	37,453.03

PURCHASES — DEPARTMENT A   Account No. 511

19--			
April 1	Balance	√	261,543.17
30		IR34	32,148.30

| | | | | PURCHASES — DEPARTMENT B | | | Account No. 521 |

19--					
April	1	Balance	√	31,212.15	
	30		IR34	4,235.11	

| | | | | FREIGHT IN — DEPARTMENT A | | | Account No. 541 |

19--					
April	1	Balance	√	2,543.59	
	6		IR34	11.78	

| | | | | FREIGHT IN — DEPARTMENT B | | | Account No. 551 |

19--					
April	1	Balance	√	604.12	
	6		IR34	2.94	

Accounts Payable Ledger (Partial)

316

S. G. ADAMS CO., ST. LOUIS, MISSOURI 63103

DATE		ITEM	POST. REF.	DEBIT	CREDIT	BALANCE
19—						
April	1	Cr. Balance	√			94.20
	6	4/5 — 30 ds.	Inv. 157		86.00	180.20
	8	Corrected invoice	Inv. 157	4.00		176.20

BUSINESS INTERIORS, INC., KANSAS CITY, KANSAS 66110

DATE		ITEM	POST. REF.	DEBIT	CREDIT	BALANCE
19—						
April	6	4/3 — 2/10, n/30	Inv. 158		379.40	
	6	Freight Prepaid	Inv. 158		16.80	396.20

CELUCOAT CORPORATION, ST. LOUIS, MISSOURI 63130

DATE		ITEM	POST. REF.	DEBIT	CREDIT	BALANCE
19—						
April	1	Cr. Balance	√			1,723.86
	1	Mdse. 3/30 — 2/10, n/30	Inv. 151		1,192.50	2,916.36

MID-STATES PAINT CO., CRESTWOOD, MISSOURI 63104

DATE		ITEM	POST. REF.	DEBIT	CREDIT	BALANCE
19—						
April	1	Cr. Balance	√			142.50
	1	Mdse. 3/29 — 2/10, n/30	Inv. 152		760.00	902.50
	5	Corrected invoice	Inv. 152		12.00	914.50

ORCHARD PAPER CO., ST. LOUIS, MISSOURI 63119

DATE		ITEM	POST. REF.	DEBIT	CREDIT	BALANCE
19—						
April	1	Cr. Balance	√			35.65
	1	3/31 — 30 ds.	Inv. 153		95.40	131.05

PAINT CITY, INC., ST. LOUIS, MISSOURI 63103

19—						
April	1	Cr. Balance	✓			871.45
	6	Mdse. 4/4 — 1/10, n/30	Inv. 156		227.60	
	6	Freight Prepaid	Inv. 156		2.94	1,101.99

SPATZ PAINT INDUSTRIES, MAPLEWOOD, MISSOURI 63102

19—						
April	1	Cr. Balance	✓			249.56
	6	Mdse. 4/3 — 2/10, n/60	Inv. 155		943.00	
	6	Freight prepaid	Inv. 155		11.78	1,204.34

and the prepaid freight charge, $11.78, were posted separately to the account of Spatz Paint Industries. The reason for doing this is that the transportation charges are never subject to discount; only the amount of the merchandise purchased may be subject to discount.

It was also necessary to post individually each item entered in the General Ledger Debit and Credit columns of the invoice register. Usually this posting is completed daily. As each item was posted, a check mark was placed in the Check (✓) column following the proper Amount column of the invoice register, and the number of the invoice was entered in the Posting Reference column of the ledger account.

Summary Posting. Summary posting is usually completed at the end of each month and involves the following procedure:

(a) The total of the column headed Purchases, Dept. A was posted to the debit of Purchases — Department A, Account No. 511, in the general ledger.

(b) The total of the column headed Purchases, Dept. B was posted to the debit of Purchases — Department B, Account No. 521, in the general ledger.

(c) The total of the column headed Accounts Payable was posted to the credit of Accounts Payable, Account No. 271, in the general ledger.

As the total of each column was posted, the account number was written in parentheses immediately below the total in the invoice register and the page number of the invoice register was written in the Posting Reference column of the general ledger as a cross-reference. A check mark was placed in parentheses below the totals of the General Ledger Debit and Credit columns in the invoice register to indicate that those totals were not posted.

Cash purchases

Holling & Renz follow the practice of entering only purchases on account in their invoice register. Cash purchases are entered in the record of checks issued, by debiting the proper departmental purchases accounts and by crediting the bank account. Usually cash purchases are not posted to the individual accounts of creditors. However, if it is desired to post cash purchases to the individual accounts of creditors, such transactions may be entered both in the invoice register and in the record of checks issued. In other words, invoices received in connection with cash purchases *may* be recorded in the same manner as invoices for purchases on account.

COD purchases

When property is purchased on COD terms, the total amount paid represents the cost of the property. Since payment must be made before possession of the property can be obtained, it is customary to treat such transactions the same as cash purchases. Thus the check issued in payment of a COD purchase is entered in the check record by debiting the proper account and by crediting the bank account. The proper account to debit depends upon the kind of property purchased. If merchandise is purchased, the proper departmental purchases account should be debited for the cost of the merchandise and the proper departmental transportation account should be debited for the amount of any transportation charges paid. If long-lived assets are purchased, the proper equipment account should be debited for the total cost, including COD fees and any transportation charges. If supplies are purchased, the proper supplies account should be debited for the total cost of the supplies, including COD fees and any transportation charges.

Transportation charges

Express and freight charges may be prepaid by the shipper or may be paid by the buyer at the time of delivery. Parcel post charges must be prepaid by the shipper. Store-to-door delivery of freight shipments may be made by the transportation companies. However, when freight shipments are not delivered to the buyer's place of business by the transportation company, the buyer must either call for the goods at a nearby freight station or must employ a trucker to deliver the goods.

Transportation Charges Prepaid. If the transportation charges are prepaid by the shipper, the amount may or may not be added to the invoice, depending upon the terms of sale. If the shipper has quoted prices FOB destination, it is understood that the prices quoted include transportation charges either to the buyer's place of business or to a nearby freight station and that no additional charge will be made for any transportation charges paid by the shipper.

If the shipper has quoted prices FOB shipping point, it is understood that the prices quoted do not include the transportation charges and that the buyer will be expected to pay the transportation costs. If shipment is made prepaid, the transportation charges will be added to the invoice, and the shipper will be reimbursed by the buyer when the invoice is paid.

Transportation Charges Collect. If prices are quoted FOB shipping point and shipment is made collect, the buyer must pay the transportation charges before obtaining possession of the shipment. Such transportation charges represent an addition to the cost of the merchandise or other property purchased. The method of recording the transportation charges in this case is the same as if the charges had been prepaid by the shipper and added to the invoice.

If prices are quoted FOB destination but for some reason shipment is made collect, the buyer must pay the transportation charges before he can obtain possession of the shipment. In such cases the transportation charges paid by the buyer should be recorded as a debit to the account of the creditor from whom the merchandise or other property was ordered. In other words, the payment of the transportation charges in such case should be treated the same as a partial payment of the amount due the shipper.

Transportation Accounts. As explained in Chapter 6, transportation charges applicable to merchandise purchased may be recorded by debiting the purchases account. However, it is common practice to record transportation charges on incoming merchandise in a separate account, which may be entitled Freight In or Transportation In. This account is treated as a subdivision of the purchases account and the balance must be taken into consideration in computing the cost of goods sold at the close of each accounting period.

The merchandise accounts of Holling & Renz are kept on a departmental basis, with separate accounts for Purchases and for Freight In being kept for Departments A and B. The only time transportation charges are entered in the invoice register is when they are prepaid by the shipper and are added to the invoice. For example, in recording Invoice No. 155, the freight prepaid amounting to $11.78 was charged to Freight In — Department A, Account No. 541. In recording Invoice No. 156, the freight prepaid amounting to $2.94 was charged to Freight In — Department B, Account No. 551. On all shipments sent freight collect, the transportation charges will be entered in the check record. For example, when the freight charges applicable to Invoice No. 151 are paid, the amount of the check issued will be entered in the check record as a debit to Freight In — Department A, Account No. 541, and as a credit to the bank account.

Transportation charges applicable to long-lived assets, such as office equipment, store equipment, or delivery equipment, should be treated as an addition to the cost of such equipment. For example, in entering the invoice of April 3 received from Business Interiors, Inc., in the invoice register of Holling & Renz, the total amount of the invoice, $396.20, including transportation charges amounting to $16.80, was charged to Office Equipment, Account No. 191. It is immaterial whether the freight charges are prepaid by the shipper and added to the invoice or whether shipment is made collect. If the freight is prepaid and added to the invoice, the total cost, including the invoice price and the transportation charges, may be recorded as a debit to the office equipment account in one amount. On the other hand, if shipment is made freight collect, the amount of the invoice and the amount of the freight charges must be posted as separate debits to the office equipment account.

Parcel Post Insurance. Merchandise or other property shipped by parcel post mail may be insured against loss or damage in transit. Such insurance may be purchased from the government through the post office, or it may be purchased from private insurance companies. If the cost of insurance is charged to the customer and is added to the invoice, it represents an addition to the cost of the merchandise or other property purchased. Thus, if an invoice is received for merchandise purchased and the merchandise is billed at a total cost of $125 plus postage of $1.50 and insurance of 40 cents, the total cost of the merchandise is $126.90.

320

The cost of insurance is seldom recorded separately on the books of the buyer, but either is charged directly to the purchases account or is included with transportation charges and is charged to Freight In.

The purchaser may indicate in placing an order that he does not want the merchandise insured. When the purchaser indicates that he does not want a parcel post shipment of merchandise insured, he implies that he is willing to assume the risk for any loss or damage sustained in transit. Title to merchandise ordinarily passes to the purchaser when it is placed in the hands of the post office for delivery.

Purchases returns and allowances

When a credit memorandum is received as a result of merchandise returned for credit or because of an allowance made by the seller, it should be recorded by debiting Accounts Payable and by crediting the proper purchases returns and allowances account. The individual account of the supplier should also be debited for the amount of the credit memorandum. For example, if a credit memorandum for $165 is received from Paint City, Inc., for varnish returned, it should be recorded as follows:

Accounts Payable	165.00	
Purchases Returns and Allowances — Department B		165.00

This amount should also be posted to the debit of the individual account of Paint City, Inc., in the subsidiary accounts payable ledger.

Computerized processing of purchasing records

If a business has a very large volume of purchases, it may be feasible to adopt some type of computerized purchasing system. It has been noted that purchasing involves several steps: requisitioning, issuing purchase orders, receiving, inspection, storing; checking vendors' invoices with respect to prices, extensions, and footings; handling returns and allowances, determining the proper amounts to be charged and credited to the proper accounts; maintaining detailed records of accounts payable, and making timely payments to suppliers. In this process, various calculations must be made and various source documents, forms, and records must be prepared. In some cases, the information on certain source documents (for example, purchase orders and vendors' invoices) can be punched into cards or written on magnetic tapes. These cards or tapes can be fed into computers that will make the necessary calculations and verifications and classify the information to provide certain needed records, such as an invoice register that gives a breakdown showing the amounts to be charged and credited to the proper accounts. Because of the relationship between purchasing and inventory and between purchasing and cash disbursements, it is likely that the system will include both inventory and cash disbursement procedures.

(For a further discussion of computer-based accounting systems, see Appendix, page A-1.)

Report No. 11-2

Complete Report No. 11-2 in the workbook and submit your working papers to the instructor for approval. Then continue with the next study assignment in Chapter 12 until Report No. 12-1 is required.

chapter 12

accounting for sales

The organization of a sales department and the procedure in handling orders received may vary widely depending upon many factors, such as the nature of the merchandise sold, the volume of sales, the methods of selling, and the terms. Each order received must be interpreted, the terms determined, the credit approved, a sales invoice prepared, goods packed and shipped or delivered, and collection made before the sales transaction is entirely completed.

Terms of sale; processing orders received

The terms on which merchandise is sold affect the procedure in handling orders and in recording the sales transactions. Goods may be sold under any of the following conditions:

(a) For cash
(b) On account
(c) COD
(d) On approval
(e) Will call sales
(f) On installment
(g) On consignment

Cash sales

Some businesses sell merchandise for cash only, while others sell merchandise either for cash or on account. A variety of practices are followed in the handling of cash sales. If such transactions are numerous, it is probable that one or more types of cash register will be used. In many cases the original record of the sale is made in the register. Often, registers that have the capability of accumulating more than one total are used. This means that by using the proper key, each amount that is "punched in" the register can be classified in the desired manner — perhaps by type of merchandise, by department, or by salesperson. Where sales taxes are involved, the amount of the tax may be separately recorded. In many retail establishments, the procedure in handling cash sales is for the salesclerks to prepare sales tickets in duplicate or in triplicate. Usually one copy is given to the customer and another copy is sent to the accounting department for analysis and recording purposes. Sometimes the preparation of the sales tickets involves the use of a type of cash register that provides means for the tickets (and any copies) to be inserted in the register in such a way that the amount being recorded is printed on the tickets. At the end of each day the cash received is checked with the record that the register provides. The receipts may also be checked with the total of the cash-sale tickets, if the system makes use of the latter.

323

Sales on account

Sales on account are often referred to as "charge sales" because the seller exchanges merchandise for the buyer's promise to pay which, in accounting terms, means that the asset accounts receivable is increased by a debit or charge. Selling goods on account is common practice at both the wholesale and retail levels of the distribution process. Firms that sell goods on account should investigate the financial reliability of those to whom they sell. A business of some size may have a separate credit department whose major function is to establish credit policies and to pass upon requests for credit from persons and firms who wish to buy goods on account. Seasoned judgment is needed to avoid a credit policy that is so stringent that profitable business may be refused, or a credit policy that is so liberal that bad debt losses may become excessive.

Generally, no goods are delivered until the salesclerk has assured himself that the buyer has established credit — that he "has an account" with the company. In the case of many retail businesses, customers with established credit are provided with *credit cards* or *charge plates*. These cards or plates not only provide evidence that the buyer has an account; they also are used in mechanical contrivances to print the customer's name and other identification on the sales tickets or sales invoices (and copies). (This type of credit card should not be confused with bank credit cards and other types of credit card plans that are in operation. These were described and discussed in Chapter 6.) In the case of *wholesale* merchants who commonly secure a large portion of their orders through the mail, by phone, or by telegraph, this confirmation of the buyer's status can be handled as a matter of routine before the goods are delivered. There is no pressing problem in this respect because the buyer is not personally waiting for the merchandise.

COD sales

Merchandise or other property may be sold on COD terms. Under this arrangement payment must be made at the time the goods are delivered by the seller or his agent. The agent may be an employee of the seller, a messenger, the post office, an express company, a railroad company, a trucking company, a steamship company, an airline, or any common carrier.

In wholesale merchandising, COD sales are usually recorded in the same manner as charge sales. When such sales are made to out-of-town customers, the merchandise is usually delivered by parcel post, express, or freight.[1] If shipment is made by parcel post or express, the post office or the express company will collect for the merchandise before giving the customer possession of it and, in turn, will remit to the seller by means of a money order or check. When this remittance is received by the seller, it is handled in the same manner as a remittance received from any other customer in full or part payment of his account.

By way of contrast, in retail merchandising, COD sales are usually recorded as cash sales. The COD sales tickets are segregated each day and a COD list is prepared for control purposes. The merchandise is then delivered to the customer and the sale price is collected upon delivery. When the money is turned in by the driver or other agent of the seller, he is given credit for the collection on the COD list and the sale is then recorded in the same manner as a cash sale. If, for any reason, the customer refuses to accept the merchandise, it is returned to stock and the sale is canceled. It should be understood that, under this plan of handling COD sales, title to the merchandise does not pass to the customer until the goods are delivered and collection has been made; therefore, the merchandise is considered to be a part of the inventory of the seller until a remittance is

___

[1]The method of making COD shipments by freight and of collecting for the merchandise before delivery was explained in the preceding chapter under the heading of COD Purchases.

received. Usually, retail merchants who sell merchandise on COD terms make their own deliveries and collections; however, delivery may be made through the post office or any common carrier.

Sales on approval

When sales are made on approval, the customer is given the right to return the goods within a specified time. Accordingly, the sale is not complete until it is known whether the customer will retain the goods or return them. Such sales may be handled as ordinary charge sales, and any returns may be handled as ordinary sales returns. On the other hand, sales on approval may be handled the same as ordinary cash sales. Under this plan a memorandum record of the sale is kept until such time as it is definitely known that the goods will be retained by the customer. The customer must either pay for the goods or return them by a specified date. If the sale is not recorded until a remittance is received, it may be treated the same as an ordinary cash sale.

Will call sales

Sales on approval should not be confused with *will call sales*. Will call sales may be made for cash or on account, but in either case the customer agrees to call for the goods. Sometimes a deposit is made by the buyer with the understanding that merchandise will be held until some future date, at which time he will call for the merchandise or at his request the merchandise will be delivered to him. Accounting for such deposits is not uniform, but the usual plan is to record the deposits in the same manner as cash sales. When this plan is used, a charge sales ticket is prepared for the balance due and is recorded by debiting a special accounts receivable control account and by crediting the proper sales account. Individual accounts with such customers may be kept in a special subsidiary ledger, sometimes referred to as a *will call ledger*.

Instead of calling for the merchandise, the customer may request delivery on a COD basis. In this case a COD slip is made for the proper amount. When the remittance is received, it is recorded in the same manner as if the customer had called for the merchandise and paid cash.

At the end of the accounting period the total amount due from customers who have made deposits on will call sales is treated in the same manner as ordinary accounts receivable. The cost of the merchandise that is being held for future delivery is not included in the inventory because it is considered to be the property of the customer.

(Installment sales and consignment sales will be discussed in Chapter 13.)

Procedure in handling incoming purchase orders

Sales by wholesale merchants usually are made in response to purchase orders received by mail, telephone, telegram, or cablegram. Purchase orders received by mail may be written on the purchase order form, letterhead, or other stationery of the buyer or on an order blank furnished by the seller. Orders received by telephone should be carefully recorded on forms provided for that purpose. The procedure in handling purchase orders varies widely with different firms; nevertheless, it is important that there be a well-organized plan for handling orders. The purpose of such a plan should be to promote efficiency and to maintain an internal check that will tend to prevent mistakes in handling orders. The following five steps constitute the heart of such a plan:

(1) **Interpretation.** Each purchase order received should be interpreted as to (a) identity of the customer and (b) quantity and description of items ordered. Orders may be received from old or new customers. Sometimes it is difficult to identify a new customer, particularly where there has been no previous correspondence with him or where he has not been contacted by the seller's representative. In some cases the identity of the items ordered involves considerable difficulty because customers frequently are careless in describing the merchandise wanted. Different items of merchandise may be specified by name, stock number, or code word. Care should be used to make sure that the stock number or the code word agrees with the description of the item. Code words are commonly used in ordering by telegram or cablegram.

(2) **Transportation.** In handling each purchase order, it is necessary to determine how shipment will be made and how the transportation charges will be handled. Shipment may be made by parcel post, express, or freight. Parcel post packages may be insured. Express shipments may be made by rail or air. Freight shipments may be made by rail, air, truck, or water.

The transportation charges must be prepaid on shipments made by parcel post. The transportation charges on express and freight shipments may be prepaid by the shipper or may be paid by the customer upon receipt of the shipment. When transportation charges are prepaid by the shipper, they may or may not be added to the invoice, depending upon whether prices have been quoted FOB shipping point or FOB destination.

If shipment is to be made by freight, it is also necessary to determine the routing of the shipment. The buyer may specify how he prefers to have shipment made. When the buyer does not indicate any preference, the shipper must determine whether to make shipment by rail, truck, air, or water, and also frequently must make a choice of transportation companies to be used. Shipment to certain points may be made via a variety of different trucking companies, airlines, or railroads.

(3) **Credit Approval.** All purchase orders received that involve credit in any form should be referred to the credit department for approval before being billed or shipped. COD orders should also be approved by the credit department, because some customers have a reputation for not accepting COD shipments, which are then returned at the seller's expense. Customers who abuse the COD privilege may be required thereafter to send cash with the order, either in full or part payment. Some firms follow a policy of requiring part payment in cash with all orders for merchandise to be shipped COD.

(4) **Check for Accuracy of Purchase Orders.** The unit prices specified on purchase orders should be checked, the proper extensions should be

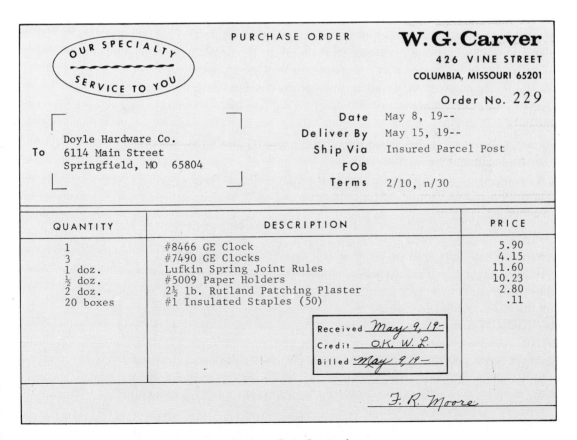

Purchase Order Received

made, and the total should be recorded. The clerks performing this function usually use calculating machines.

(5) Billing. The next step in the handling of an order is billing or preparing the sales invoice.

The purchase order reproduced on page 327 was received from W. G. Carver by the Doyle Hardware Co. The information recorded in the spaces provided by the rubber stamp impression added by Doyle Hardware Co. shows that the order was received by them on May 9, that the credit of the purchaser was approved by Doyle's credit department, and that the goods were billed by them on the same day the order was received. After the goods were billed, the purchase order was filed alphabetically by Doyle Hardware Co. under the name of the customer for future reference.

In the case of a wholesale merchant, the sales invoice is usually prepared on a typewriter or a billing machine. By using carbon paper or some other duplicating device, additional copies may be prepared. At least three copies usually are considered necessary, the original copy going to the customer as an acknowledgment of his order, a copy going to the accounting department for recording purposes, and a copy going to the shipping department as authority for packing and shipping the merchandise. The copy of the sales invoice reproduced at the top of the next page is based on the purchase order received from W. G. Carver reproduced on page 327. Sales invoices should be numbered consecutively.

Additional copies of the sales invoice may also be used for the following purposes:

(a) One copy may go to the salesman in whose territory the sale is made.

(b) One copy may go to a branch office, if the sale is made in a territory served by such an office.

(c) One copy may serve as a label to be pasted on the carton or package in which shipment is made. Usually this copy is perforated so that only that part containing the name and the address of the customer is used.

Discounts

Any trade discounts allowed on sales are usually shown as a deduction in arriving at the total of the sales invoice. Such discounts should not be entered in the accounts of the seller, as they represent merely a reduction in the selling price of the merchandise.

Any cash discounts offered should be indicated in the terms. Retail merchants seldom allow cash discounts, but wholesale merchants com-

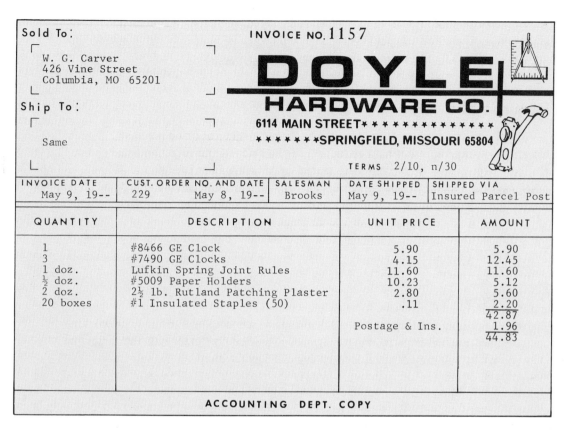

Copy of Sales Invoice for Accounting Department

monly allow cash discounts as an inducement for prompt payment of sales invoices. Cash discounts should be ignored at the time of recording sales invoices, for it cannot be known at that time that the customers will pay the invoices in time to get the discounts offered. <u>Any cash discount that is deducted from an invoice by the customer when making a remittance can be regarded by the seller either as an expense or as a reduction in gross sales (similar to sales returns and allowances).</u> Some accountants accept the view that sales discounts are expenses, but to most accountants it seems more logical to regard such discounts as a reduction of sales price. Accordingly, <u>the debit balance of the sales discount account is shown as a subtraction from sales in the income statement.</u>

A minor complication arises in treating sales discounts as a reduction of sales when the latter are accounted for on a departmental basis. While it would be possible to have two or more sales discount accounts and to analyze each discount taken to determine the department (or departments) to which it relates, such a procedure would be burdensome. In most cases the resulting accuracy would not be worth the trouble involved.

An acceptable alternative is to record all sales discounts in a single account and, in preparing the income statement, to allocate the amount of such discounts in proportion to the net sales of the departments.

Returns and allowances

Merchandise may be returned by the customer for credit or he may ask for an allowance representing a reduction in the price of the merchandise. If credit is given for merchandise returned or an allowance is made, it is customary to issue a credit memorandum for the amount involved. A model filled-in copy of a credit memorandum was reproduced on page 307.

Report No. 12-1

Complete Report No. 12-1 in the workbook and submit your working papers to the instructor for approval. Then continue with the following study assignment until Report No. 12-2 is required.

330

Accounting procedure

When the merchandise accounts are kept on a departmental basis and all sales invoices covering charge sales are recorded in a columnar sales record, often called a *sales register*, provision should be made for a proper classification of the debits and the credits. Separate columns should be provided for recording the charge sales of each department so as to facilitate periodic summary posting of the totals. General Ledger Debit and Credit columns should also be provided for recording items that must be posted individually to the general ledger accounts. If individual accounts with customers are kept in a subsidiary ledger, a summary or control account for accounts receivable must be kept in the general ledger.

The procedure of recording all charge sales invoices in a sales register and of keeping the merchandise accounts on the departmental basis will be illustrated **(1)** by showing the chronological recording of a narrative of selected transactions in the sales register, **(2)** by showing the direct posting from copies of the sales invoices to the individual accounts of customers kept in a subsidiary accounts receivable ledger, and **(3)** by showing the posting from the sales register to the proper general ledger accounts.

Holling & Renz is a partnership engaged in the wholesale paint and varnish business. Separate departments are maintained as follows:

Department A — Paint
Department B — Varnish

Separate departmental accounts are kept for sales and for sales returns and allowances as follows:

411 Sales — Department A
    041 Sales Returns and Allowances — Department A
421 Sales — Department B
    042 Sales Returns and Allowances — Department B

All charge sales are made on uniform terms of 2/10, n/30. Unless otherwise specified, freight and express shipments are made on a basis of transportation charges collect. In the case of parcel post shipments, the postage is prepaid and added to the invoice as an additional charge to the customer. As each invoice is entered in the sales register, the amount of postage prepaid is credited to Postage Stamps, Account No. 164, in the General Ledger column.

Sales register

The form of the sales register used by Holling & Renz is illustrated on page 332. All of their sales are made to dealers. The merchandise is intended for resale. Accordingly, Holling & Renz do not have to collect retail sales taxes. A narrative of the transactions that have been entered in the sales register follows. It will be helpful to check each transaction and to note how it was entered in the sales register.

HOLLING & RENZ

Narrative of Transactions

Saturday, April 1

Made charge sales as follows:

No. 418, Glaze Hardware Co., paint, $341.60; varnish, $280; freight collect.

No. 419, Morgan Paint Co., paint, $1,172.70; varnish, $52.50; express collect.

No. 420, Laclede Hardware Co., paint, $618.40; express collect.

SALES REGISTER FOR MONTH OF *April*   19 —   PAGE 65

Line	Debit ACCT. NO.	Debit GENERAL LEDGER AMOUNT	✓	ACCOUNTS RECEIVABLE	✓	DAY	NAME	SALE NO.	SALES DEPT. A	SALES DEPT. B	Credit ACCT. NO.	Credit GENERAL LEDGER AMOUNT	✓
							AMOUNTS FORWARDED						
1				621 60	✓	1	Village Hardware Co.	418	341 60	280 00			
2				1225 20	✓	1	Morgan Paint Co.	419	1172 70	52 50			
3				618 40	✓	1	Laslade Hardware Co.	420	618 40				
4				200 35	✓	1	Fischer Paints	421		172 00	164	28 35	✓
5				106 70	✓	1	Upton Paints	422		93 90	164	12 80	✓
6				6 75		5	Fischer Paints	421		6 75			
7				529 50	✓	6	Caldwell Paint Co.	423	480 00	49 50			
8				263 80	✓	6	Morgan Paint Co.	424	195 00	68 80			
9				22 40	✓	6	Upton Paints	425		41 20			
10	042	18 80	✓			7	Morgan Paint Co.	424			133	12 00	✓
11	421	12 00	✓			7	Mitchell Hardware	426		212 00			
12	131	22 00	✓										
32		242 80		36543 38					31120 60	5612 43		53 15	
32		242 80		36543 38					31120 60	5612 43		53 15	
33		(✓)		(133)					(411)	(421)		(✓)	

Holling & Renz — Sales Register

No. 421, Fischer Paints, varnish, $172; postage added to invoice, $28.35.

No. 422, Affton Paints, varnish, $93.90; insured parcel post, $12.80.

Sent Fischer Paints a corrected invoice for Sale No. 421, amounting to $207.10. (The original postage charge was correct but the varnish was underpriced $6.75.)

Made charge sales as follows:

No. 423, Caldwell Paint Co., paint, $480; varnish, $49.50; freight collect.

No. 424, Morgan Paint Co., paint, $195; varnish, $68.80; freight collect.

No. 425, Affton Paints, varnish, $41.20; less credit for varnish returned, $18.80. Note that Accounts Receivable is debited for the difference between the new amount of varnish sold and the amount of varnish returned.

333

Sent Morgan Paint Co. a corrected invoice for Sale No. 424; paint, $195; varnish, $56.80. In the sales register note that Sales, Department B — (Account No. 421) was debited for $12 and that Accounts Receivable (Account No. 133) was credited for a like amount.

Sold Mitchell Hardware varnish, $212, and received a 60-day, 6 percent interest-bearing note. (Sale No. 426.) In the sales register note that Notes Receivable (Account No. 131) was debited for $212.

(The transactions for April 8 through April 30 are omitted.)

Since postings to the customers' accounts in the subsidiary accounts receivable ledger will be made directly from copies of the sales invoices, a check mark was placed in the Check ($\sqrt{}$) column beside the Accounts Receivable column as each item was entered in the sales register.

Corrected Sales Invoices. If an error in the preparation of a sales invoice is discovered and a corrected sales invoice is prepared before the original invoice has been entered in the sales register, the original invoice may be canceled and the corrected one may be entered in the usual manner.

If a corrected sales invoice is prepared after the original sales invoice has been entered in the sales register and has been posted to the individual account of the customer, the corrected invoice may be entered in the sales register if the amount of the corrected invoice is more than the amount of the original invoice. (See Sale No. 421.) The increase should be recorded by debiting Accounts Receivable and by crediting the proper departmental sales account. The amount of the increase should also be posted to the debit of the proper customer's account in the subsidiary accounts receivable ledger.

If the amount of the corrected invoice is less than the amount of the original invoice, the decrease should be recorded by debiting the proper departmental sales account and by crediting Accounts Receivable. (The entry can be made in the sales register if General Ledger Debit and Credit columns are provided; if not, the entry must be made in the general journal.) The amount of the decrease should also be posted to the credit of the proper customer's account in the subsidiary accounts receivable ledger. (See Sale No. 424.)

A copy of the corrected invoice should be attached to the copy of the original invoice.

Proving the Sales Register. The sales register may be footed and the footings may be proved at any time by comparing the sum of the debit footings with the sum of the credit footings. The footings of Holling & Renz's sales register were proved as of April 30 by the use of an adding machine. The tape appeared as follows:

```
                          *
              242.80
           36,543.38

           36,786.18*

                          *
           31,120.60
            5,612.43
               53.15

           36,786.18*
```

Ledgers

The ledgers used by Holling & Renz include a general ledger with standard ruling and a subsidiary accounts receivable ledger with balance-column ruling. The accounts affected by the transactions entered in the sales register reproduced on page 332 are shown in skeleton form on pages 335 and 336. The March 31 balances are recorded in the accounts as of April 1. An accounts receivable control account is kept in the general ledger.

Posting Procedure. The use of a general ledger and an accounts receivable ledger involves both individual posting and summary posting. After each sales invoice was entered in the sales register, it was immediately posted to the proper customer's account in the accounts receivable ledger. The posting was done directly from the invoice, the invoice number being inserted in the Posting Reference column.

While the posting to customers' accounts might be done from the sales register, there are certain advantages in posting directly from the sales invoice. For example, the invoice provides all the information needed in posting, whereas, if the posting were done from the sales register, it would

General Ledger (Partial)

NOTES RECEIVABLE   Account No. 131

19--			
April 1 Balance	√	2,850.00	
7	SR65	212.00	

ACCOUNTS RECEIVABLE   Account No. 133

19--				19--			
April 1 Balance	√	11,218.68		April 7		SR65	12.00
30	SR65	36,543.38					

335

POSTAGE STAMPS   Account No. 164

				19--			
				April 1		SR65	28.35
				1		SR65	12.80

SALES — DEPARTMENT A   Account No. 411

				19--			
				April 1 Balance	√		457,952.30
				30	SR65		31,120.60

SALES — DEPARTMENT B   Account No. 421

19--				19--			
April 7	SR65	12.00		April 1 Balance	√		42,785.40
				30	SR65		5,612.43

SALES RETURNS AND ALLOWANCES — DEPARTMENT B   Account No. 042

19--			
April 1 Balance	√	642.30	
6 Returns	SR65	18.80	

Accounts Receivable Ledger (Partial)

AFFTON PAINTS, CENTERVILLE, MISSOURI 63633

DATE		ITEM	POST. REF.	DEBIT	CREDIT	BALANCE
19—						
April	1	Dr. Balance				321.40
	1	Mdse.	S422	93.90		
	1	Postage	S422	12.80		428.10
	6	Mdse.	S425	22.40		450.50

CALDWELL PAINT CO., ST. LOUIS, MISSOURI 63129

DATE		ITEM	POST. REF.	DEBIT	CREDIT	BALANCE
19—						
April	1	Dr. Balance				216.95
	6	Mdse.	S423	529.50		746.45

FISCHER PAINTS, LOGAN, MISSOURI 63950

DATE		ITEM	POST. REF.	DEBIT	CREDIT	BALANCE
19—						
April	1	Dr. Balance				472.30
	1	Mdse.	S421	172.00		
	1	Postage	S421	28.35		672.65
	5	Corrected invoice	S421	6.75		679.40

GLAZE HARDWARE CO., ST. LOUIS, MISSOURI 63115

DATE		ITEM	POST. REF.	DEBIT	CREDIT	BALANCE
19—						
April	1	Dr. Balance				723.90
	1	Mdse.	S418	621.60		1,345.50

LACLEDE HARDWARE CO., ST. LOUIS, MISSOURI 63114

DATE		ITEM	POST. REF.	DEBIT	CREDIT	BALANCE
19—						
April	1	Dr. Balance				84.65
	1	Mdse.	S420	618.40		703.05

MORGAN PAINT CO., ST. LOUIS, MISSOURI 63113

DATE		ITEM	POST. REF.	DEBIT	CREDIT	BALANCE
19—						
April	1	Dr. Balance				215.20
	1	Mdse.	S419	1,225.20		1,440.40
	6	Mdse.	S424	263.80		1,704.20
	7	Corrected invoice	S424		12.00	1,692.20

be necessary to enter in the sales register all the information needed in posting whether or not it served any other purpose. Furthermore, if an error had been made in entering an invoice in the sales register, it would probably be carried over into the accounts receivable ledger through the posting, whereas, if the posting were done directly from the invoice, it is not likely that the same error would be made twice.

Posting directly from the sales invoices to the customers' accounts in the accounts receivable ledger is not only efficient, but it also provides a sound method of internal check and control. One bookkeeper may enter the invoices in the sales register and may complete such posting as is required from the sales register to the general ledger accounts, while another bookkeeper may post directly from the sales invoices to the customers' accounts in the accounts receivable ledger. Thus the work is divided between two employees. Proof of the accuracy of their work is obtained periodically by preparing a schedule of accounts receivable and comparing its total with the balance of the accounts receivable control account that is kept in the general ledger.

Posting to the accounts of customers in the accounts receivable ledger may be done either manually or with a machine. A large volume of transactions makes it feasible to use posting machines or, in some cases, electronic equipment. This is discussed further on page 340.

Some firms use the *microfilm* method of accounting for charge sales. Under this method it is customary to keep a chronological record of charge sales in the same manner as in other methods of accounting. An individual account of the transactions with each customer is also kept until the end of the month, when it is photographed. The film is then filed as a permanent record of the business done with each customer, while the individual account becomes the customer's monthly statement.

Individual Posting. Each sales invoice entered in the Accounts Receivable Debit column of the sales register was posted individually to the proper customer's account in the accounts receivable ledger shown on page 336. In the case of sales invoices involving prepaid transportation charges, the amount of the merchandise sold and the amount of the prepaid transportation charges were posted separately. For example, in posting Sales Invoice No. 421, Fischer Paints was debited separately for the amount of the merchandise sold, $172, and for the amount of the postage, $28.35. The reason for posting the transportation charges as separate items is that these amounts are never subject to discount; only the amount of the merchandise sold is subject to discount.

It was also necessary to post each item in the General Ledger Debit and Credit columns of the sales register. Usually this posting is completed daily. As each such item was posted, a check mark was placed in the Check ($\sqrt{}$) column beside the proper amount, and the page number of the sales register was entered in the Posting Reference column of the affected general ledger account.

Summary Posting. The summary posting from the sales register is usually completed at the end of each month and involves the following procedure:

   (a) The total of the column headed Accounts Receivable was posted to the debit of Accounts Receivable, Account No. 133, in the general ledger.

(b) The total of the column headed Sales, Dept. A was posted to the credit of Sales — Department A, Account No. 411, in the general ledger.

(c) The total of the column headed Sales, Dept. B was posted to the credit of Sales — Department B, Account No. 421, in the general ledger.

As the total of each column was posted, the account number was written in parentheses immediately below the total in the sales register and the page of the sales register was written in the Posting Reference column of the general ledger as a cross-reference. A check mark was placed in parentheses below the totals of the General Debit and Credit columns in the sales register to indicate that those totals were not posted.

Cash sales

Holling & Renz follow the practice of entering charge sales only in their sales register. Cash sales are entered in the record of cash receipts by debiting the bank account and by crediting the proper departmental sales accounts. Cash sales are not posted to the individual accounts of customers. In a wholesale business there are relatively few cash sales, as most of the business is usually done on a charge basis.

338

COD sales

Holling & Renz follow the practice of recording COD sales in the same manner as charge sales. Since they are engaged in a wholesale business, a relatively large percentage of their sales is made to out-of-town customers; hence, several days may elapse from the date of sale until the date a remittance is received. COD sales are therefore recorded in the sales register in the same manner as ordinary sales. When the remittance is received from the post office, express company, trucking company, railroad company, or other common carrier, it is entered in the record of cash receipts in the same manner as other remittances received from customers to apply on account.

Transportation charges

In the case of parcel post shipments, the postage must be prepaid. If such packages are insured, the total amount of the postage and the insurance is added to the invoice. Holling & Renz follow the practice of making all express and freight shipments with transportation charges collect, unless the customer requests that they be prepaid and added to the invoice. Since most shipments are made collect, it is not considered necessary to provide a special column in the sales register for recording express and freight charges prepaid; instead, they are entered in the General Ledger Credit column as a credit to Freight Out, Account No. 6119.

When the express and freight charges are prepaid, the payments are entered in the record of checks issued by debiting Freight Out and by crediting the bank account. The freight out account should be in balance after all posting is completed at the end of the month, provided all prepaid express and freight charges have been charged to customers' accounts. If, however, any shipments are made FOB destination, the freight charges represent a selling expense. In this case the freight out account will have a debit balance, which represents the amount of such expense incurred.

Where numerous shipments are made by parcel post, express, and freight and the transportation charges are prepaid and charged to customers, it is advisable to provide a special credit column in the sales register for entering the transportation charges. All prepaid transportation charges on outgoing shipments that are added to the invoices and charged to customers should be entered in this column. At the end of the month when the summary posting is completed, the total of the column should be posted to the credit of Freight Out.

339

Sales returns and allowances

When a credit memorandum is issued to a customer for the price of merchandise returned for credit or because of an allowance made on merchandise sold, it should be recorded by debiting the proper sales returns and allowances account and by crediting Accounts Receivable. The individual account of the customer should also be credited for the amount of the credit memorandum. For example, if a credit memorandum for $43.40 is issued to the Harris Lumber Co. for some varnish returned for credit, it should be recorded as indicated in the following general journal entry:

```
Sales Returns and Allowances — Department B...................  43.40
    Accounts Receivable.......................................        43.40
        Issued credit memorandum to Harris Lumber Co.
```

The amount should also be posted to the credit of the individual account of the Harris Lumber Co. in the subsidiary accounts receivable ledger.

If transactions involving the issuance of credit memorandums are numerous, a special sales returns and allowances register may be used to advantage. The design of such a register would be similar to that of the sales register reproduced on page 332, except that there should be columns provided on the debit side for recording departmental sales returns and allowances and a column provided on the credit side for recording accounts receivable. The effect of an entry to record credit allowed for merchandise returned is the reverse of an entry to record merchandise sold; therefore, if a special register is used, its columnar arrangement should be the reverse of the columnar arrangement of the sales register.

Computerized processing of sales records

If a business has a very large volume of sales, it may be feasible to adopt some type of computerized sales system. It has been noted that selling involves several steps: receiving and interpreting orders, assembling the orders, shipping, billing, handling returns and allowances, determining the proper amounts to be charged and credited to the proper accounts, and maintaining a record of accounts receivable. In this process, various calculations must be made and various source documents, forms, and records must be prepared. In some cases, the information on certain source documents (incoming purchase orders, for example) can be punched into cards or written on magnetic tapes. The cards or tapes can be fed into computers that will make the necessary calculations and verifications, and classify the information to provide certain needed records such as a sales register that gives a detailed breakdown of the amounts to be charged and credited to the proper accounts. Computer equipment may be used to prepare sales invoices, to keep the accounts receivable ledger, and to facilitate the preparation of customers' monthly statements. It is probable that computer equipment also will be used to obtain detailed analyses of sales (by products or product line, by different classes of customers, by regions, etc.). Because of the relationship between sales and inventory and between sales and cash receipts, it is likely that the system will include both inventory and cash receipts records. (For a further discussion of computer-based accounting systems, see Appendix, page A-1.)

Report No. 12-2

Complete Report No. 12-2 in the workbook and submit your working papers to the instructor for approval. Then continue with the following study assignment in Chapter 13 until Report No. 13-1 is required.

chapter 13

installment sales and consignment sales

In the preceding chapter, the accounting for what are sometimes called "ordinary" sales — meaning cash sales and short-term charge sales — was considered. This chapter is concerned with the accounting for sales of two special types: *installment* sales and *consignment* sales. Since sales on the installment plan are more common, that subject is considered first.

Installment sales

Personal property, such as automobiles, household appliances, radio and television sets, phonographs, musical instruments, furniture, and many other types of durable merchandise, is commonly marketed on the *installment plan*. This is also true of many types of real property (real estate).

The installment plan refers to a sales arrangement in which the buyer secures physical possession of the property in return for his promise to pay for it in a number of fractional payments at regular intervals over a period of time. The agreement between the buyer and the seller is usually in writing and takes a legal form described as a *conditional sales contract*. Usually, a *down payment* is required at the time the buyer signs the contract and secures physical possession of the property. As a means of attempting to protect the seller against loss in the event that the buyer defaults on payments, the contract usually takes one of the following forms:

(a) Title to the property remains with the seller until the purchaser has remitted the full amount of the sales price.

(b) Title passes to the purchaser immediately, subject to a lien (claim) for the unpaid portion of the sales price.

(c) Title passes to the purchaser immediately, but at the same time the purchaser gives the seller a chattel mortgage for the unpaid portion of the sales price.

(d) Title passes to a trustee until the provisions of the contract have been completely fulfilled.

A business may be more lenient in extending credit to customers who buy on the installment plan, because the merchandise involved does not become the outright property of the buyer until the full amount of the sales price has been collected. Because of the long collection period (sometimes as much as two or three years; as contrasted with thirty to sixty days for ordinary sales on account), a higher price may be charged for goods sold on the installment plan to compensate the seller for (1) the greater risk involved, (2) the long wait to collect the money, and (3) the increased amount of record keeping.

342

Accounting for installment sales

Sales on the installment plan can be accounted for either on (1) the conventional accrual basis or (2) the installment basis. If the accrual basis

PAGE *5*   SALES REGISTER

	GENERAL LEDGER			ACCOUNTS RECEIVABLE	√	INSTALLMENT ACCOUNTS RECEIVABLE	√	DAY	NAME	
	ACCT. NO.	AMOUNT	√							
1									AMOUNTS FORWARDED	1
2						60000	√	20	*W. R. Ayers*	2
3										3
4										4
5										5
6										6
7										7
8										8

Sales Register with Installment Sales (Left Page)

is used, the profit on installment sales is accounted for in the same manner as the profit on ordinary charge sales. If the installment basis is used, the profit is accounted for in the period in which cash is received rather than in the period in which the sale is made. The installment basis is popular with firms selling on the installment plan, since it is acceptable for income tax purposes and its use results in the postponement of the income tax until the money is collected from customers. Following is a more detailed discussion of the two methods.

Accrual Basis. When installment sales are accounted for on the accrual basis, they should be recorded in the same manner as charge sales, that is, by debiting Accounts Receivable and by crediting Sales. Usually an installment sales contract will be drawn up at the time of the sale and a notation of the terms will be made in the individual account of the customer in the subsidiary accounts receivable ledger. Under this plan, any anticipated loss on deferred installments should be provided for in the same manner as on ordinary charge sales, that is, through an allowance for bad debts. Since the dealer usually retains title to the merchandise until the final installment is paid, he can recover the merchandise in case of failure to collect as agreed. (The act of recovering merchandise sold on an installment contract is known as *repossession*.) Any loss sustained will be the difference between the amount charged to the customer under the contract and the total amount collected in cash installments, plus any amount realized from the resale of the repossessed merchandise. All losses sustained on repossessions should be charged to the allowance for bad debts.

Installment Basis. When installment sales are accounted for on the installment basis, a control account with the title Installment Accounts

FOR MONTH OF *April* 19 —   PAGE 5

SALE NO.	CREDIT						
	SALES		INSTALLMENT SALES		GENERAL LEDGER		
	DEPT. A	DEPT. B	DEPT. A	DEPT. B	ACCT. NO.	AMOUNT	√
1							
2			60000				
3							
4							
5							
6							
7							
8							

Sales Register with Installment Sales (Right Page)

343

Receivable should be kept in the general ledger, and the individual accounts of installment customers should be kept in a subsidiary installment accounts receivable ledger. To simplify the recording of transactions affecting installment accounts receivable, it is advisable to provide a special debit column in the sales register for installment accounts receivable and a special credit column for installment sales. If the business is departmentalized, a separate installment sales column should be provided in the sales register for each department. Such a sales register is illustrated on pages 342 and 343. (If sales are subject to sales tax, a credit column for Sales Tax Payable will be needed.)

This form of sales register may be used in recording both installment sales and ordinary sales on account. After each installment sales invoice is recorded in the sales register, it should be posted directly to the individual account of the customer in the subsidiary installment accounts receivable ledger. (Sometimes a special account form is used for this ledger. Such an account form is reproduced below.)

Collection Day 1 2 3 4 5 6 7 8 9 10 11 12 13 14 15 16 17 18 19 (20) 21 22 23 24 25 26 27 28 29 30 31

INSTALLMENT LEDGER

Name *W. B. Ayers*   Employed by *The Wilding Company*
Address *3640 Winding Way*   Address *5421 Elm Street*
Reference *The First National Bank*   Position *Salesman*   How Long *3 yrs.*
                          Married *Yes*   Spouse's Name *Alice*
Payment $ 30   Own property
Weekly   Semimonthly   Monthly ✓ Property location

| CHARGES | | | | PAYMENTS | | | |
DATE	ITEM	POST. REF.	AMOUNT	DATE	POST. REF.	AMOUNT	BALANCE
19— Apr. 20	Furniture	SR5	60000	19— Apr. 20	CR9	3000	57000

Installment Sales Account Receivable Form

At the end of the month when the summary posting is being completed, the total of the Installment Accounts Receivable column of the sales register should be posted as a debit to the installment accounts receivable control account in the general ledger. The totals of the departmental sales columns should also be posted as a credit to the proper departmental sales accounts in the general ledger.

To facilitate the recording of amounts received to apply on installment accounts receivable, a special column headed Installment Accounts Receivable Credit should be provided in the record of cash receipts. After each receipt is recorded in this journal, it should be posted directly as a credit to the individual customer's account in the installment accounts receivable ledger. At the end of the month when the summary posting is being completed, the total of the Installment Accounts Receivable Credit column should be posted as a credit to the installment accounts receivable control account in the general ledger.

Determining Gross Profit on Total Installment Sales. At the end of the year, the percentage of gross profit to be realized on the total installment sales of that year should be determined. This rate should be applied to the sum of (a) the down payments and (b) the installment collections received during the year on that year's sales to find the gross profit realized on the installment sales for the year. The difference between the gross profit to be realized and the gross profit actually realized on the basis of installments collected should be treated as an unrealized profit applicable to installment accounts receivable. The procedure in computing the gross profit on installment sales realized during the accounting period may be summarized as follows:

(a) Determine the gross profit to be realized on installment sales by deducting the cost of the merchandise sold on installment terms from the total installment sales.

(b) Determine the percentage of gross profit to be realized on installment sales by dividing the gross profit to be realized by the total installment sales.

(c) Apply this rate of gross profit to the sum of the down payments and the installment collections received during the year to determine the amount of the gross profit actually realized.

345

To illustrate, assume that the installment sales of a furniture dealer amounted to $70,000 for his first year of operation. Cash collections (down payments and installment collections) on these sales amounted to $30,000 during the year. At the end of the year it is determined that the cost of merchandise sold on the installment plan was $40,600. The gross profit realized on installments collected during the year may be computed as follows:

First Step. Find the gross profit to be realized.

Total installment sales	$70,000.00
Less cost of goods sold	40,600.00
Gross profit to be realized	$29,400.00

Second Step. Find the percentage of gross profit to be realized.

Gross profit to be realized, $29,400 ÷ total installment sales, $70,000 = 42%

Third Step. Apply the rate of gross profit to collections during year.

Total collections during year	$30,000.00
Gross profit percentage	42%
Gross profit realized	$12,600.00

When the installment sales account in the general ledger is closed at the end of the year, the gross profit realized should be credited to Realized Gross Profit on Installment Sales and the remainder of the gross profit still to be realized should be credited to Unrealized Gross Profit on Installment Sales. An illustrative general journal entry based on the foregoing steps is presented below.

Installment Sales	70,000.00	
Cost of Goods Sold		40,600.00
Realized Gross Profit on Installment Sales		12,600.00
Unrealized Gross Profit on Installment Sales		16,800.00
Closing the installment sales account and transferring the gross profit to the proper accounts.		

In preparing the balance sheet at the end of the year, the balance of the installment accounts receivable account, amounting to $40,000 (the difference between total installment sales, $70,000, and total collections during the year, $30,000), should be classified as a current asset. The unrealized gross profit on installment sales, amounting to $16,800, should be listed as a *deferred credit* (revenue received but not yet earned) immediately following the current liabilities.

In preparing the income statement at the end of the year, the gross profit realized on installment sales, amounting to $12,600, should be included in the total gross profit on sales.

In subsequent years, the accounting for gross profit from installment selling must include both the gross profit realized from collections on the sales of the current year and the gross profit realized from collections of installment accounts receivable related to installment sales of prior years.

To illustrate, assume that in the second year of operation, the furniture dealer had installment sales of $80,000 on which he collected $50,000, and that he collected $32,000 on installment receivables that related to sales of the first year. At the end of the second year, it was determined that the cost of goods sold on the installment plan in that year was $48,000. The gross profit realized during the second year may be computed as follows at the top of the next page:

346

(a) From collection of installment accounts receivable that related to sales of the first year:

Amount collected	$32,000	
Gross profit percentage	42%	
Gross profit realized		$13,440

(b) From collections on installment sales made in the second year:

(1) Gross profit to be realized:

$80,000 − $48,000	$32,000	

(2) Percentage to be realized:

$32,000 ÷ $80,000	40%	

(3) Gross profit realized:

$50,000 × 40%		20,000
Total gross profit realized during the second year		$33,440

The general journal entries required at the end of the second year would be as follows:

Unrealized Gross Profit on Installment Sales	13,440	
Realized Gross Profit on Installment Sales		13,440

Gross profit realized on collection of installment accounts receivable related to sales of 19−−. (Prior year)

13,440 — Debit —closed out liability

13,440 ?. equity

Installment Sales	80,000	
Cost of Goods Sold		48,000
Realized Gross Profit on Installment Sales		20,000
Unrealized Gross Profit on Installment Sales		12,000

Closing the installment sales account and transferring the gross profit to the proper accounts.

347

At the end of the second year, the total of installment accounts receivable would be $38,000 ($8,000 from sales of the first year and $30,000 from sales of the second year). The total amount of unrealized gross profit on installment sales would be $15,360 (42% of $8,000 plus 40% of $30,000).

It may be necessary to keep installment accounts receivable separately by years and to have an unrealized gross profit account for each year.

Report No. 13-1

Complete Report No. 13-1 in the workbook and submit your working papers to the instructor for approval. Then continue with the following study assignment until Report No. 13-2 is required.

Consignment sales

In the marketing of certain products, a procedure known as "consignment" selling is used. In consignment selling, goods are shipped to an agent dealer with the understanding that he is not obligated to pay for them unless and until they are sold. Title to produce and merchandise so consigned is retained by the shipper until the goods are sold by the agent dealer. The owner of goods shipped on consignment is called the *consignor*. The agent dealer who receives the goods is called the *consignee*. At the time that the goods are shipped to the consignee, an *invoice of shipment* is prepared. While this invoice of shipment is similar to a sales invoice, it should be understood that a consignment shipment is not a sale. The function of the invoice of shipment is to inform the consignee of the descriptions and quantities of the items in the shipment. Unit prices may or may not be shown on the invoice of shipment depending upon whether the goods are to be sold at current market prices or at prices specified by the consignor.

Produce, such as livestock, poultry, eggs, fresh fruits, and vegetables, is widely marketed on the consignment basis. Such shipments are usually made to commission merchants on consignment to be sold at the prevailing market prices. At the time of remitting for the produce, the consignee renders a statement of consignment sales, sometimes referred to as an *account sales*. The account sales shows the amount of the sales, the amounts of the expenses charged to the consignor, and the amount of the net proceeds. Expenses charged to the consignor may include transportation charges, storage, insurance, and other similar expenses incurred in handling the consigned goods. If the consignee is allowed a commission on consignment sales or a discount from the selling price, the amount of his commission or discount will also be deducted in arriving at the amount of the net proceeds to be remitted to the consignor.

Light bulbs, radio and television tubes, electric motors, garden seeds, and many other products are also widely marketed on the consignment basis. Such goods are usually shipped to agent dealers to be sold at prices specified by the consignor. Instead of receiving a commission, the consignee may be allowed certain discounts from the consignor's list prices based upon the consignee's sales volume.

Invoice of shipment

A model filled-in copy of an invoice of shipment covering electric lamp (light) bulbs shipped by a wholesale distributor to a retail hardware store on consignment is reproduced below. The original copy of the invoice of shipment goes to the consignee and a duplicate copy is retained by the consignor as his record of the shipment. Note that the invoice of shipment provides the agent dealer with detailed information relative to the merchandise that has been charged to his account, including the quantities, the specifications of the items, the unit list prices, the extended amount of each item, and the total amount of the shipment.

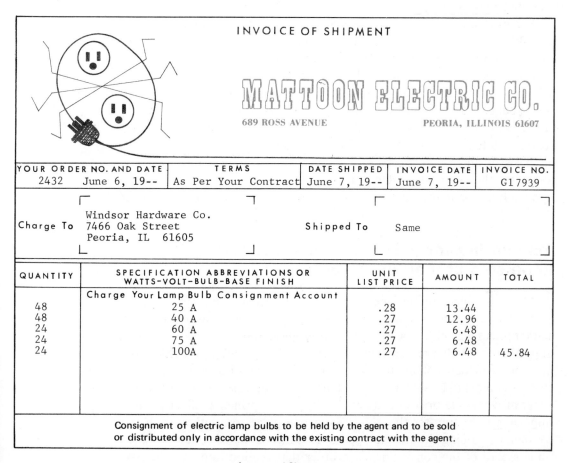

INVOICE OF SHIPMENT

MATTOON ELECTRIC CO.

689 ROSS AVENUE   PEORIA, ILLINOIS 61607

YOUR ORDER NO. AND DATE	TERMS	DATE SHIPPED	INVOICE DATE	INVOICE NO.
2432 June 6, 19--	As Per Your Contract	June 7, 19--	June 7, 19--	G17939

Charge To Windsor Hardware Co.
7466 Oak Street   Shipped To   Same
Peoria, IL 61605

QUANTITY	SPECIFICATION ABBREVIATIONS OR WATTS-VOLT-BULB-BASE FINISH	UNIT LIST PRICE	AMOUNT	TOTAL
	Charge Your Lamp Bulb Consignment Account			
48	25 A	.28	13.44	
48	40 A	.27	12.96	
24	60 A	.27	6.48	
24	75 A	.27	6.48	
24	100A	.27	6.48	45.84

Consignment of electric lamp bulbs to be held by the agent and to be sold or distributed only in accordance with the existing contract with the agent.

Invoice of Shipment

349

The duplicate copy of the invoice of shipment provides the information needed by the consignor in recording merchandise shipped on consignment. The invoice may be recorded in his general journal; or a special consignment shipments record may be kept. Accounts with consignees may be kept in his general ledger; or, if preferred, a subsidiary consignment ledger may be kept with a control account in the general ledger.

Statement of consignment sales

Periodically — usually at the end of each month — the consignor prepares and mails to the consignee a partially completed statement of merchandise shipped. The purpose of such a statement is to show **(1)** the value of the consigned merchandise in the consignee's hands at the beginning of the month, **(2)** a summary of the consignment shipments made during the month, and **(3)** the total amount of consigned merchandise for which the consignee must account.

A model filled-in statement of consignment sales is reproduced on page 351. In the statement reproduced, the balance forwarded from the previous month's statement, $418.62, represents the amount charged to the consignee at the beginning of June. The items listed in the body of the statement indicate the value of the merchandise shipped to the consignee during June. The amount listed on line 3, $595.94, is the sum of the items in the body of the statement, including the balance forwarded from the previous statement plus the sum of the shipments during the month. On the basis of an inventory taken at the end of the month, the consignee completes the statement. Thus, the consignor prepared this statement through Item 3, and the consignee prepared the remainder of the statement.

350

Accounting for consigned merchandise to be sold at market prices

Methods of accounting for consignment sales are not uniform. Produce or merchandise that is shipped on consignment to be sold at prevailing market prices may either be charged to the consignee at wholesale prices or shipped without charge. In the latter case a memorandum record of the shipment will be kept by the consignor. Merchandise that is shipped on consignment to be sold at specified prices may be billed to the consignee either at wholesale prices or at retail prices. The principal effect of such shipments is to transfer the goods from one place to another, with the consignor retaining title to the goods. It is advisable, of course, to keep some record of the consignments in order that the location and the cost of the goods may be determined at any time. The cost of the goods out on consignment must be included in the consignor's inventory, although it is customary to list the inventory of consigned goods separately in the balance sheet, using the same method of costing that is used for the inventory of merchandise in stock.

When a statement of consignment sales is received from a commission merchant, the sales should be recorded on the books of the consignor. The proper entries will vary depending upon the method of accounting for

2062
(1-55)   ⊕ PAT'D

FROM: . Mattoon Electric Co.
          . 689 Ross Avenue
          . Peoria, IL 61607
          .
                    LARGE LAMP DEPARTMENT

SERVING AGENT FOR **GENERAL ⑰ ELECTRIC,** CONSIGNOR
                              C O M P A N Y
          TO: . Windsor Hardware Co.
                  . 7466 Oak Street
                  . Peoria, IL 61605
                  .
                  .

REPORT FOR MONTH ENDED	FORM AND BASIS	APPOINTMENT EXPIRES	TOTAL LIST SALES		
			INCL. LAST REPORT	REQ'D THIS BASIS	QUALIFY NEXT BASIS
6/30/19--	A-300	9/1/19--	840.99		

MONTHLY STATEMENT OF GENERAL ELECTRIC LARGE LAMP SALES

DATE OR OTHER REFERENCE	DEBIT	CREDIT	BALANCE
1. BALANCE FORWARDED FROM PREVIOUS STATEMENT			418.62
2. CHARGES (CREDITS)			
6/7 G1 7939	45.84		
6/19 G1 7579	42.26		
6/21 G1 7795	33.16		
6/27 G1 8311	31.46		
6/30 G1 7691	24.60		

351

3	TOTAL ACCOUNTABILITY (LINE 1 + 2)		595.94
4	LESS WORKING STOCK (OR ATTACHED INVENTORY)	(−)	394.31
5	LIST SALES FOR MONTH		201.63
6	LESS 30 % BASIC COMPENSATION	(−)	60.49
7	NET		141.14
8	LESS 2% SPECIAL COMPENSATION, IF EARNED (SEE NOTE BELOW)	(−)	2.82
9	NET AMOUNT (AFTER DEDUCTING 2% SPECIAL COMPENSATION, IF EARNED) →		138.32
10	OTHER CHARGES AND/OR CREDITS		
11			
12	REMITTANCE DUE →		138.32

Sales

AGENT PLEASE NOTE: TO EARN YOUR **2%** SPECIAL COMPENSATION DEDUCTED ON LINE 8,
YOU MUST MAIL ONE COPY OF THIS REPORT WITH YOUR CHECK TO YOUR
SERVING AGENT ON OR BEFORE **7**TH OF THE MONTH.

Statement of Consignment Sales

consignment shipments. Usually a separate account will be kept for consignment sales so that such sales may be recorded separately from ordinary sales. If it is desired to record consignment sales in the sales register along with ordinary charge sales, it may be advisable to provide a special credit column to simplify the summary posting of the total consignment sales at the end of each month. If it is customary for the consignee to remit the proceeds at the time of rendering a statement of consignment sales, the entire transaction may be entered in the consignor's record of cash receipts in much the same manner as ordinary cash sales. It may be advisable, however, to provide a special credit column in the cash receipts record so as to simplify summary posting of the total consignment sales at the end of each month.

To illustrate, it will be assumed that a statement of consignment sales has been received from a commission merchant covering the sale of a shipment of poultry. The consignor had made no entry on his books for the shipment; he simply kept a copy of the invoice of shipment as a memorandum record. The statement of consignment sales showed that the total sales amounted to $1,500 and that the following expenses were incurred by the consignee and charged to the consignor:

Freight charges..	$165.00
Commission...	150.00

A remittance for the proceeds, amounting to $1,185, accompanied the statement. The effect of this transaction on the accounts of the consignor is indicated by the following general journal entry:

Freight Out...	165.00	
Commission Expense.....................................	150.00	
Bank..	1,185.00	
Consignment Sales.....................................		1,500.00
Received statement of consignment sales.		

Since a remittance for the amount of the proceeds was received with the statement, the transaction may be recorded completely in the consignor's record of cash receipts.

Accounting for consigned merchandise to be sold at specified prices

When merchandise is shipped on consignment to an agent dealer under contract to be sold at prices specified by the consignor, an entirely different accounting procedure may be advisable.

Consignor's Books. An invoice of shipment of electric lamp bulbs to the Windsor Hardware Co. by the Mattoon Electric Co. is reproduced on page 349. This invoice was recorded on the books of the Mattoon Electric Co. as shown by the following general journal entry:

Windsor Hardware Co., Consignee......................	45.84	
Consignment Shipments.............................		45.84
Invoice of shipment No. Gl 7939.		

The Mattoon Electric Co. follows the practice of charging the consigned merchandise to the consignee and of crediting Consignment Shipments at list or retail prices. A separate account may be kept in the general ledger for each consignee, or these accounts may be kept in a subsidiary ledger with a control account in the general ledger. An account is also kept in the general ledger for consignment shipments. The accounts with the consignees are not ordinary accounts receivable because the consignees are not obligated to pay for the merchandise unless it is sold. The Mattoon Electric Co., therefore, follows the practice of treating the accounts with the consignees and with consignment shipments as memorandum or offsetting accounts that are never shown in the balance sheet. On the other hand, some firms follow the practice of treating the consignees' accounts as assets and the account with consignment shipments as *deferred revenue* to be shown as offsetting or contra items in the balance sheet.

A statement of consignment sales received from the Windsor Hardware Co. by the Mattoon Electric Co. is reproduced on page 351. It shows that **353** in addition to the shipment of June 7, which amounted to $45.84, four other shipments from the Mattoon Electric Co. were received during the month. When this statement was received by the Mattoon Electric Co., the following entries were made to record consigned merchandise sold by the Windsor Hardware Co. and the remittance received:

Consignment Shipments....................................	201.63	
Consignment Sales..		201.63
Consigned merchandise sold by Windsor Hardware Co. during June.		
Bank...	138.32	
Consignment Sales Commission Expense......................	63.31	
Windsor Hardware Co., Consignee.........................		201.63
Statement of consignment sales received from Windsor Hardware Co. with remittance of $138.32.		

The first entry was made to record the June sales of merchandise consigned to the Windsor Hardware Co. The second entry was made to record the remittance received and the commission expense involved.

Assuming that the Windsor Hardware Co. was the only consignee to whom merchandise was shipped on consignment, the consignment accounts would appear in the general ledger of the Mattoon Electric Co., after the June transactions were posted, as illustrated on the following page.

19--			19--		
June 1 Balance		418.62	June 30		201.63
7		45.84			
19		42.26			
21		33.16			
27		31.46			
30		24.60			
	394.31	*595.94*			

CONSIGNMENT SHIPMENTS

19--			19--		
June 30		201.63	June 1 Balance		418.62
			7		45.84
			19		42.26
			21		33.16
			27		31.46
			30		24.60
				394.31	*595.94*

It should be noted that the debit balance of the Windsor Hardware Co. consignee account is the same as the credit balance of the consignment shipments account. This balance represents the June 30 inventory of merchandise out on consignment to the Windsor Hardware Co.

354

Consignee's Books. At the time of receiving the invoice of shipment reproduced on page 349, the Windsor Hardware Co. recorded the transaction on its books as indicated by the following general journal entry:

Consigned Merchandise................................	45.84	
Mattoon Electric Co., Consignor.......................		45.84
Invoice of shipment No. Gl 7939.		

Other invoices of shipment received from the same consignor during the month were recorded in a like manner. The account with the Mattoon Electric Co. is not an ordinary account payable, as there is no obligation to pay for the consigned merchandise unless and until it is sold. The Windsor Hardware Co. follows the practice of treating the accounts with consignors and with consigned merchandise as memorandum offsetting accounts that need not appear in the balance sheet.

As the consigned merchandise was sold by the Windsor Hardware Co., the sales were recorded by debiting the bank account or Accounts Receivable, depending upon whether the sales were for cash or on account, and by crediting Sales for the selling price. At the end of the month an inventory of the consigned merchandise was taken, and the statement of consignment sales, reproduced on page 351, was completed by filling in the agent's monthly report at the bottom of the form. This statement, together with a remittance of $138.32, was then mailed to the Mattoon Electric Co. prior to July 7 in order to get the benefit of the special 2 percent compensation allowance. This transaction was recorded on the books of the Windsor Hardware Co. as indicated by the following general journal entries:

Sales...	201.63	
Consigned Merchandise.............................		201.63
Consigned merchandise sold during June.		
Mattoon Electric Co., Consignor......................	201.63	
Commissions on Consignment Sales....................		63.31
Bank..		138.32
Statement of consignment sales rendered to the Mattoon Electric Co. with remittance of $138.32 in payment of amount due.		

Since, at the time of each consignment sale, the Windsor Hardware Co. follows the practice of crediting Sales for the selling price of consigned merchandise, the first entry was made to record the total June sales of merchandise consigned by the Mattoon Electric Co. After this entry was posted, the balance of the sales account represented the amount of the regular merchandise sales during the month. The second entry was made **355** to record the commissions earned on sales of the consigned merchandise and the check issued in payment of the net proceeds. The difference ($63.31) between the amount of such sales ($201.63) and the payment ($138.32) is regarded as the total amount of commission, even though $2.82 is considered by the consignor to be "special compensation" for prompt payment.

Assuming that the Mattoon Electric Co. is the only consignor from whom merchandise is received on consignment, the consignment accounts after the June transactions were posted would appear in the general ledger of the Windsor Hardware Co. as illustrated below and at the top of the following page.

MATTOON ELECTRIC CO., CONSIGNOR

19--		19--		
June 30	201.63	June 1 Balance		418.62
		7		45.84
		19		42.26
		21		33.16
		27		31.46
		30		24.60
			394.31	*595.94*

19--			19--	
June 1 Balance		418.62	June 30	201.63
7		45.84		
19		42.26		
21		33.16		
27		31.46		
30		24.60		
	394.31	*595.94*		

It should be noted that the credit balance of the account for the Mattoon Electric Co., Consignor, is the same as the debit balance of the consigned merchandise account.

Report No. 13-2

Complete Report No. 13-2 in the workbook and submit your working papers to the instructor for approval. Then continue with the next study assignment in Chapter 14 until Report No. 14-1 is required.

chapter 14

accounting for inventory and prepaid expenses

357

Merchandise inventory and prepaid expenses have an important characteristic in common: both represent costs incurred in one accounting period that are expected in part to benefit the following period. Because the benefit is expected to be realized within a relatively short time, these assets are considered to be current rather than long-lived. In most cases, the dollar amount of merchandise inventory is much larger than that for prepaid expenses. For this reason, accounting for merchandise inventory poses a much greater problem and receives much more care and attention.

Merchandise inventory

One of the major reasons for keeping accounting records is to make it possible to determine the net income (or net loss) of a business on a periodic basis. If the business is engaged in the purchase and sale of merchandise, it is essential that the cost of all merchandise available for sale during the accounting period (goods on hand at the start of the period plus net purchases) be apportioned in a reasonable manner between the expense called cost of goods sold and the asset commonly called merchandise inventory.

The routine bookkeeping procedure involved in accounting for merchandise, using accounts for purchases, purchases returns and allowances, purchases discount, and merchandise inventory, has been discussed and illustrated in preceding chapters. The problem of determining the quantity of goods on hand at the end of the period and of assigning cost to these goods remains to be considered.

Taking a physical inventory

In many cases there is no record that shows the quantity and the cost of the merchandise on hand. Lacking such a record, the first step in attempting to apportion merchandise costs between sold and unsold goods consists of counting the goods that are on hand (or otherwise measuring their quantity) at the end of the period. This process is called *taking an inventory* or *taking a physical inventory*.

Taking a physical inventory of a stock of merchandise can be a sizable task. Frequently it must be done after regular business hours. Some firms cease operations for a few days to take inventory. The ideal time to count the goods is when the quantity on hand is at its lowest level. A fiscal year may be selected so as to start and end at the time that the stock of goods is normally at its lowest level. This is known as a *natural business year*. Such a year is used by many businesses for accounting purposes.

It would be desirable if all goods on hand could be inventoried within a few hours. Sometimes extra help is employed so as to take the inventory in as short a time as possible. Even if this is done, however, the taking of an inventory may require several days. If regular business is carried on during this time, special records must be kept of additions to and subtractions from the stock during the inventory-taking period. In this way the quantities of goods that were on hand at the end of the last day of the fiscal period can be determined.

Various procedures are followed in taking an inventory so as to be sure that no items are missed and that no items are included more than once. It is customary for persons taking inventory to work in pairs; one counts the items and "calls out" the information to the other who records it. Usually such information is recorded on a form commonly known as an *inventory sheet.* The sheet is arranged with space to show the description of each type of item, the quantity on hand, the cost per unit, and the extension — the amount that results from multiplying the quantity by the unit cost. (The cost per unit can be determined and the extensions completed after the count is finished.) Inventory sheets commonly provide spaces **(1)** to note the date of the inventory count, **(2)** to record the location of the items listed, and **(3)** to record the names or initials of the person who did the calling, the person who recorded the quantities, the person who entered the unit costs, the person who made the extensions, and the person who checked the information. A reproduction of part of an inventory sheet of a furniture store is shown below. Two extension columns are provided so that subtotals may be separated from item extensions.

INVENTORY May 31, 19 72 Page 1				
Sheet No. 1			Costed by R. M.	
Called by T. G. P.	Department A		Extended by R. M.	
Entered by W. S. E.	Location Storeroom		Examined by W. G. R.	

Description	Quantity	Unit	Unit Cost	Extensions	
Table Lamp	20	ea.	10 40	208 00	
Wall Rack	18	ea.	2 80	50 40	
Bookcase	7	ea.	29 40	205 80	
End Table	13	ea.	7 90	102 70	
Desk	6	ea.	35 90	215 40	
Total					1,261 92

Inventory Sheet

In taking a physical inventory, care must be exercised to be sure that only the goods that are the property of the firm are included. Goods that have been sold and are awaiting delivery and goods held on consignment must not be included in the count. It is also important to be sure to include goods that are owned on the date of the inventory but which may not be in the store or warehouse. Examples are goods out on consignment and goods which may have been recorded as purchases but which have not been received. Such goods are said to be *in transit* (on their way in a freight car, truck, ship, or airplane). Goods which have arrived but have not yet been unloaded must also be included.

359

Assigning cost to the inventory

After the quantities of goods that are owned at the end of the accounting period have been determined, the next step is to decide how much cost should be assigned to each unit. At first thought, this might seem to be an easy, though perhaps a time-consuming job. If all purchases of the same article had been made at the same price per unit, reference to any purchase invoice covering such items would show the unit cost. The unit cost times the number of units in the inventory would give the total cost to be assigned to those units. However, it is frequently the case that identical articles have been purchased at different times at different costs per unit. The question then arises as to which unit cost should be assigned to the goods in the inventory. Often there is no way of knowing exactly which price was paid for the specific goods that are on hand. As a workable solution to this problem, one of several different bases of inventory costing must be adopted. The most common bases are **(1)** first-in, first-out costing, **(2)** weighted average costing, and **(3)** last-in, first-out costing.

First-In, First-Out Costing. A widely used method of allocating cost between goods sold during an accounting period and goods on hand at the end of that period has been to assume that the first goods bought were the first goods sold. Accordingly, the items on hand at the end of the period are considered to be those most recently purchased. This is known as the *first-in, first-out* method, frequently referred to as the "fifo" method. To illustrate how this method works, assume the following circumstances with respect to a particular article of merchandise:

On hand at start of period, 100 units assigned a cost of $1.56 each......	$ 156.00
Purchased during period:	
First purchase, 500 units @ $1.60 each...........................	800.00
Second purchase, 400 units @ $1.75 each........................	700.00
Last purchase, 600 units @ $1.80 each..........................	1,080.00
Total cost of 1,600 units available for sale...........................	$2,736.00
On hand, end of period, 400 units	

If it is assumed that the first units purchased were the first ones sold, then the 400 units left at the end of the period were among those purchased last at a cost of $1.80 each. Accordingly, the total cost to be assigned to these units would be $720 (400 units × $1.80). The cost assigned to the units sold would be $2,016 ($2,736 − $720).

First-in, first-out costing became popular because of two features: **(1)** Whenever a merchant is able to control the flow of merchandise, he will see to it that the older goods are moved out first. Thus, fifo costing is often in harmony with what actually happened. **(2)** Fifo costing assigns the most current costs to the ending inventory. The amount of that inventory is shown on the balance sheet among the current assets.

Another reason for the continuing widespread use of fifo costing is the reluctance of accountants to change a long followed method of accounting, if such a change would destroy the comparability of their calculations over a period of years. Consistency is important in accounting. Firms that have used the fifo method for a long time are reluctant to abandon it.

Weighted Average Costing. Another method of allocating merchandise cost between goods sold and those in the inventory is on the basis of the average cost of identical units. In the example above, the total cost of the 1,600 units that were available for sale during the period was $2,736. Dividing $2,736 by 1,600 units results in a weighted average cost of $1.71 per unit. This is described as a *weighted average* because both the quantities involved and the unit costs are taken into consideration. On a weighted average cost basis, the 400 units in the ending inventory would be assigned a total cost of $684 (400 × $1.71). The cost assigned to the units sold would be $2,052 ($2,736 − $684).

There is a logical appeal to the use of the weighted average basis to allocate cost between goods sold and goods on hand. In this example, one fourth (400) of the total units available (1,600) were unsold. The weighted average cost basis assigns one fourth ($684) of the total cost ($2,736) to these goods.

Last-In, First-Out Costing. A third method of allocating cost between goods sold and goods on hand is to assume that all of the sales in the period were of the goods most recently purchased. This is called the *last-in, first-out* or "lifo" method. As applied to the data shown on page 360, this would mean that the 400 units on hand at the end of the period would be assumed to include the 100 units that were on hand at the start of the period with an assigned cost of $1.56 per unit plus 300 of the units from the first purchase at a cost of $1.60 each. Therefore, the cost assigned to the inventory would be calculated as follows:

361

100 units @ $1.56	$156.00
300 units @ $1.60	480.00
Total	$636.00

The cost assigned to the units sold would be $2,100 ($2,736 − $636).

Sometimes the lifo method has been justified on the grounds that the physical movement of goods in some businesses is actually last-in, first-out. This is rarely the case, but the method has become popular for other reasons. One persuasive argument for the use of lifo is that the method attempts to match the cost of the items purchased most recently against the current sales revenue. In many cases in which the lifo method is used, the calculated amount called "cost of goods sold" is really the *cost to replace the goods sold*. When this amount is subtracted from sales revenue, the resulting gross margin figure is not inflated or deflated by gain or loss due merely to price changes. In the opinion of many accountants, this is proper and desirable.

Another argument in favor of the lifo method is that a going business must keep a minimum or base quantity of inventory on hand at all times. While this portion of the inventory is considered to be a current asset, it is, in reality, more like a long-lived asset. Because long-lived assets are carried at original cost, it is logical to assign original cost to the base amount of inventory. Lifo accomplishes this result for the most part.

Probably the major reason for the growing popularity of the lifo method is the fact that when prices are rising, net income calculated by using the lifo method is smaller than the amount that would result from using either the fifo or the weighted average method. As a result, the related income tax is smaller. The reverse would be true if prices were falling. That has not been the trend for many years, however.

The lifo method is used by firms in many industries. Procedures have been developed to apply the "lifo principle" to situations in which the goods sold are not literally replaced. (High-fashion merchandise is an example.) Index numbers are used to convert costs to a lifo basis.

Opponents of the lifo method contend that its use causes old, out-of-date inventory costs to be shown in the balance sheet. The theoretical and practical merits of fifo and lifo are the subject of much debate.

Comparison of Methods. To compare the results obtained by the use of the three inventory-costing methods discussed, assume that the 1,200 units that were sold brought $3,300 and that operating expenses for the period were $1,000. (The amount of the revenue from sales and the amount of operating expenses will not be affected by the method used to apportion cost between goods sold and goods on hand.) The tabulation below contrasts calculated net income and the cost assigned to the ending inventory under each of the three cost allocation methods. It must be remembered, however, that the example relates to a period in which costs were rising.

	FIFO COSTING	WEIGHTED AVERAGE COSTING	LIFO COSTING
Sales.....................................	$3,300	$3,300	$3,300
Cost of goods sold....................	2,016	2,052	2,100
Gross profit......................	$1,284	$1,248	$1,200
Operating expenses..................	1,000	1,000	1,000
Net income......................	$ 284	$ 248	$ 200
Cost assigned to ending inventory......	$ 720	$ 684	$ 636

Note that, in all cases, the total cost of goods available for sale ($2,736) was apportioned between goods sold and goods on hand at the end of the period. For example, under fifo costing, $2,016 is apportioned to cost of goods sold and $720 to ending inventory. It is common practice to describe the methods that have been discussed as methods of inventory valuation. It should be apparent, however, that a process of valuing the cost of goods sold also is involved. The term valuation is somewhat misleading, since what is involved is really *cost apportionment*.

Cost or market, whichever is lower

There is a well-established tradition in accounting that unrealized profits should not be recorded except in very unusual cases. If the value of an asset increases, no formal record of the fact is entered on the books because the gain has not been actually realized. Nevertheless, in many cases, if the value or usefulness of an asset declines, it is generally considered proper to recognize that an expense or a loss has been incurred and to record the fact even though the loss has not been realized. These practices have given rise to the so-called *rule of conservatism* (sometimes designated as the *principle of conservatism*). This rule or principle says: "Provide for all losses, but anticipate no gains." This practice is criticized as being inconsistent and often overdone. Some think that the force of the conservative tradition in accounting is lessening; however it continues to exert considerable influence.

The practice of assigning "cost or market, whichever is lower" to the items that comprise the inventory of merchandise at the end of an accounting period is an important application of the rule of conservatism. In this connection, "cost" means the amount calculated on either the fifo or the weighted average basis. "Market" means cost to replace. It is the prevailing price in the market in which the goods are purchased — not the prevailing price in the market in which they are sold — that is involved. An improved statement of the practice is *cost or cost to replace, whichever is lower*.

The lower of cost or market rule is not applied if inventory cost is calculated on a lifo basis. The reason is that the lifo method is usually adopted because of its possible income tax advantage. The tax law does not permit the use of the lower of "lifo cost" or market for tax purposes. Lifo users must follow the tax rule for all business income calculations.

To illustrate the application of the lower of cost or market rule to the previous example, suppose that the replacement cost or market price of the items in question was $1.70 on the last day of the period. This is less than the fifo cost per unit ($1.80) or the weighted average cost per unit ($1.71). Accordingly, the 400 units in the ending inventory would be assigned a total cost of $680 (400 × $1.70) and the cost of goods sold would be $2,056 ($2,736 − $680). Gross margin and net income would be reduced accordingly. Actually the cost of goods sold figure would then include an amount that can be described as a loss due to a decline in the replacement cost of unsold goods.

Since the merchandise will probably be sold for considerably more than either market or cost (however calculated), the reason for following such a conservative practice may be questioned. (Not all businesses do follow

363

the lower of cost or market rule. Some firms assign cost — fifo or weighted average — to the ending inventory even if market is less.) The purpose in using the "cost or market, whichever is lower" rule is to carry the goods into the next period with an assigned cost that will result in no less than an average or normal percentage of margin when the units are sold in the new period. If replacement cost has fallen, competition may cause some reduction in selling price.

To adhere strictly to the rule, the lower of cost or market should be used for each item in the inventory; it is not simply a matter of using the lower of total cost or total replacement cost of the entire inventory. Special applications of the rule have been developed to take care of nonreplaceable, damaged, or shopworn goods.

In determining the cost to be assigned to goods in an inventory, it is proper to assign to the goods on hand a fair share of any transportation costs that have been incurred on goods purchased. In other words, cost means cost at the buyer's place of business, not cost at the supplier's shipping point. In some cases, transportation charges are an important part of the total cost of merchandise acquired.

In calculating the cost to be assigned to goods on hand, the matter of purchases discounts should not be overlooked. It may be that the unit costs entered on the inventory sheets exclude cash discounts. If purchases discounts are regarded as a reduction of cost (and this practice is recommended), the amount of cost assigned to the ending inventory should reflect purchases discounts taken. It is not necessary to adjust every unit cost figure for discounts. The total cost before cash discounts can be calculated and this amount can then be reduced by a percentage determined by the relationship of purchases discounts to purchases for the year. For example, if purchases (less purchases returns and allowances) for the year amounted to $100,000 and purchases discounts taken were $1,500, the latter would be equal to 1½ percent of purchases. If the calculated fifo or weighted average cost (exclusive of discounts) of the ending inventory was $20,000, the corrected cost amount would be $19,700 ($20,000 less 1½% of $20,000). This $19,700 amount would be assigned to the ending inventory unless the lower of cost or market basis was being followed and the replacement cost of the goods was less than $19,700.

Estimated allocation of merchandise cost

The taking of a physical inventory may be such a sizable task that it is not attempted more than once a year. If so-called *interim* income statements and balance sheets are to be prepared, the portions of the cost of goods available for sale during the interim period to be allocated to goods sold during the period and to goods on hand at the end of the period must be estimated. One way of doing this uses a gross margin approach. The amount of sales during the period is reduced by what is considered to be the normal percentage of gross margin (gross profit) to determine the estimated cost of goods sold. Deducting this amount from the total cost of goods available for sale gives the estimated amount of the ending inventory.

To illustrate, assume that a firm normally has a gross margin of 40 percent on sales. At the start of its fiscal year, the balance in the merchandise inventory account was $45,000. Net purchases for the first month of the year amounted to $35,000. Net sales for the month amounted to $78,000. **(1)** What was the estimated cost of the goods that were sold during the month? **(2)** What was the estimated amount of the merchandise inventory at the end of the month?

> **(a)** Since gross margin is assumed to have been 40% of sales, cost of goods sold is assumed to have been 60% of sales (100% − 40%).
> Therefore, the estimated cost of goods sold = 60% of $78,000 (net sales for the month), or $46,800.
>
> **(b)** Cost of goods available for sale was $80,000 (opening inventory of $45,000 plus net purchases of $35,000).
> The estimated inventory at the end of the month would be equal to goods available for sale, $80,000, less estimated cost of goods sold, $46,800, or $33,200.

365

Such computed amounts are only reasonable if the normal gross margin on sales has prevailed during the period and is expected to prevail during the following periods when the goods in the inventory will be sold. This type of calculation can be used to check the general reasonableness of the amount of an inventory that has been computed on the basis of a physical count. Any sizable difference in the two calculations might serve to call attention to a possible mistake in the count, in costing the items, or a marked change in the realized rate of gross margin. The gross margin procedure can also be used to estimate the cost of an inventory that may have been destroyed by fire or other casualty. Such a calculation might be useful in negotiating an insurance settlement.

The retail method of inventory

Many retail merchants use a variation of the gross margin method to calculate cost of goods sold and ending inventory for interim-statement purposes. The procedure employed is called the *retail method of inventory.* Its use requires keeping records of the prices at which purchased goods are marked to sell. This information, together with the record of the cost of goods purchased, will make it possible to compute the ratio between cost and retail prices. When the amount of retail sales is subtracted from the retail value of all goods available for sale, the result is the estimated retail value of the ending inventory. Multiplying this amount by the ratio of cost to selling price gives the estimated cost of the ending inventory.

Following is an example of the calculation of the estimated cost of an ending inventory of merchandise by the retail method:

	Cost	Retail
Inventory, start of period...............................	$38,160	$54,000
Net purchases during period...........................	24,840	36,000
Merchandise available for sale...........................	$63,000	$90,000
Less sales for period....................................		60,000
Inventory, end of period, at retail........................		$30,000
Ratio of cost to retail prices of merchandise available for sale ($63,000 ÷ $90,000)...................................		70%
Estimated inventory, end of period, at cost (70% of $30,000).	$21,000	

366

The foregoing example was simplified by assuming that there were no changes in the prices at which the goods were marked to sell. In practice, such changes are commonplace and the calculation must take such adjustments into consideration.

In addition to using the retail method in estimating the cost of inventory for interim-statement purposes, the cost-retail ratio that is developed can be used to convert the amount of a physical inventory which originally has been priced at retail to its approximate cost.

Perpetual inventories

Firms that deal in certain types of merchandise sometimes find it feasible to keep up-to-date records of the quantities and costs of goods on hand at all times. Such records are known as *perpetual inventories*. The general ledger account for Merchandise Inventory under such a system is somewhat like the account for Cash or Bank; chronological records of additions (purchases) and subtractions (sales) are maintained. The balance of the account at any time shows the cost of goods that should be on hand.

When a perpetual inventory is kept, the merchandise inventory account in the general ledger is usually a control account. A subsidiary ledger with an account for each type of goods is maintained. These accounts are often in the form of cards which provide spaces to show additions, subtractions, and the balance after each change. Goods sold can be assigned cost on either a fifo, a weighted average, or a lifo basis. The day-to-day costing of sales on either the weighted average or lifo basis will give results that differ somewhat from those obtained when lifo or weighted average costing is applied at the end of the period. (The results will be the same if the fifo basis is used.) Perpetual inventories do not eliminate the need for taking periodic physical inventories. The records must be checked from time to time to discover and correct any errors. However, it is not always necessary to count everything at almost the same time. The stock can be counted and the records verified by groups of items, by departments, or by sections.

A business that sells a wide variety of comparatively low-cost goods (such as a 5 and 10 cent store) will not find it practical to keep a perpetual inventory. In contrast, a business that sells relatively few high-cost items (an automobile dealer, for example) can maintain such a record without incurring excessive clerical cost.

Many types of businesses often keep supplementary or auxiliary records of goods in terms of quantities only. These are called stock records. Stock records serve as a guide in purchasing operations, help to reveal any shortages, and provide information as to the goods on hand as a basis for assigning merchandise cost for interim-statement purposes.

Perpetual inventory records in computer-based accounting systems

Some businesses with very large volumes of transactions and inventories composed of substantial numbers of different items have found it advantageous to use electronic computers in keeping their perpetual inventory records. Some of these computers have very large data storage capacities and the capability of retrieving any item of stored information in fractions of a second. Each item in the inventory is given a code number. By means of punched cards or magnetic tapes, data relating to the amounts of additions to and subtractions from each inventory item are fed into the computer. It makes the necessary addition or subtraction and computes the new balance in each case. In response to coded instructions, the status of any particular inventory item can be determined at will. Whenever desired, the machine will provide a listing of the status of all of the items in the inventory. Computer capacity can be purchased or leased sufficient to maintain records for inventories of many thousands of different items. (For a further discussion of computer-based accounting systems, see Appendix, page A-1.)

Prepaid expenses

Office supplies, store supplies, advertising supplies, fuel, and other supplies purchased may not be wholly consumed in the period in which they are acquired. The premiums on insurance policies covering merchandise, equipment, and buildings may be prepaid, but the terms of the policies may extend beyond the current accounting period. Rent and interest may be paid in advance, but the expenses may not be wholly incurred in the same accounting period. The cost of unused supplies on hand at the close of an accounting period and the portion of such prepayments that will benefit future periods should be treated as current assets because the benefits will be realized within a comparatively short time. Current assets of this type are known as *prepaid expenses*.

When accounts are kept on the accrual basis, it is necessary to adjust certain of them at the close of each accounting period for the following:

(a) The amounts of any supplies or services purchased during the period that were recorded as assets at time of purchase and that were consumed or used during the period.

(b) The amounts of any supplies or services purchased during the period that were recorded as expenses at time of purchase and that were not consumed or used during the period.

Asset method of accounting for supplies and prepayments

Supplies, such as office supplies, store supplies, advertising supplies, fuel, and postage, which may not be wholly consumed in the accounting period in which they are acquired, are usually recorded as assets at the time of purchase.

Office Supplies. Office supplies include letterheads and envelopes, pencils, carbon paper, ink, notebooks, typewriter ribbons, rubber bands, paper clips, and other miscellaneous supplies that are normally consumed in the operation of an office. Transactions arising from the purchase of such supplies on account should be entered in the invoice register. When such supplies are purchased for cash, the transactions should be entered in the record of checks issued. In either case, the purchases are posted to the account for office supplies in the general ledger.

At the end of each accounting period, an inventory of the office supplies on hand is taken and an adjusting entry is made to record the amount of the office supplies consumed during the period. For example, if on December 31 the office supplies account has a debit balance of $400 and an inventory reveals that the cost of the supplies on hand amounts to $150, it must be that the supplies expense during the period was $250. The following adjusting entry would be made:

```
Office Supplies Expense....................................  250.00
    Office Supplies.........................................         250.00
        Office supplies consumed during period.
```

After this entry is posted, the office supplies account will have a debit balance of $150, which should be reported in the balance sheet as a current asset. The account for office supplies expense will have a debit balance of $250, which should be reported in the income statement as an operating expense.

369

Store Supplies. Store supplies include wrapping paper and twine, corrugated board, paper bags and other containers, cleaning supplies, and other miscellaneous supplies that are normally consumed in the operation of a store. Transactions arising from the purchase of such supplies should be recorded in the same manner as transactions arising from the purchase of office supplies; that is, purchases should be recorded by debiting Store Supplies and by crediting either Accounts Payable or the bank account, depending upon whether the purchases are made on account or for cash.

At the end of each accounting period, an inventory of the store supplies on hand is taken and an adjusting entry is made to record the amount of the store supplies consumed during the period. For example, if on December 31 the store supplies account has a debit balance of $260 and an inventory reveals that the cost of the supplies on hand amounts to $75, it must be that the supplies expense during the period was $185. The following adjusting entry would be made:

```
Store Supplies Expense.....................................  185.00
    Store Supplies..........................................         185.00
        Store supplies consumed during period.
```

After this entry is posted, the store supplies account will have a debit balance of $75, which should be reported in the balance sheet as a current asset. Store Supplies Expense will have a debit balance of $185, which should be reported in the income statement as an operating expense.

Advertising Supplies. Advertising supplies include catalogs, circulars, price lists, order blanks, and other miscellaneous supplies that are normally consumed in an advertising program. Transactions arising from the purchase of such supplies should be recorded in the same manner as transactions arising from the purchase of other types of supplies; that is, purchases should be recorded by debiting Advertising Supplies and by crediting either Accounts Payable or the bank account, depending upon whether the purchases are made on account or for cash.

At the end of each accounting period, an inventory of the advertising supplies on hand is taken and an adjusting entry is made to record the amount of the advertising supplies consumed during the period. For example, if on December 31 the advertising supplies account has a debit balance of $275 and an inventory reveals that the cost of the supplies on hand amounts to $145, it must be that the supplies expense during the period was $130. The following adjusting entry would be made:

Advertising Supplies Expense.	130.00	
Advertising Supplies.		130.00
Advertising supplies consumed during period.		

After this entry is posted, the advertising supplies account will have a debit balance of $145, which should be reported in the balance sheet as a current asset. The account for advertising supplies expense will have a debit balance of $130, which should be reported in the income statement as an operating expense.

Postage Stamps. The cost of postage stamps purchased is usually recorded by debiting Postage Stamps and by crediting the bank account. Usually a check is made payable to Postage and, after it is cashed, the money is used to purchase stamps in the desired denominations. Some of the stamps may be used on parcel post packages and others on ordinary mail. If stamps used on parcel post packages are billed to the customer, the entry to record the sale will include a credit to the postage stamps account. Usually no record is kept of the stamps used on ordinary mail each day, but periodically the stamps on hand are counted and their value is determined. The difference between the amount of the unused stamps on hand and the debit balance of the postage stamps account represents the amount of the stamps used and not billed to customers.

If the account for postage stamps is debited **(1)** for the amount of the stamps on hand at the beginning of the month, $17, and **(2)** for the amount of stamps purchased during the month, $95, and is credited for the amount of the stamps used on parcel post packages during the month, $60, the account will have a debit balance of $52 at the end of the month. If, at that time, the amount of the stamps on hand is found to be $14, the difference, or $38, represents the amount of the stamps that must have been used and not billed to customers during the month. The following adjusting entry would be made:

Postage Expense..	38.00	
Postage Stamps..		38.00
Amount of stamps used on ordinary mail.		

After this is posted, the account for postage stamps will have a debit balance of $14, which should be reported in the balance sheet as a current asset. The postage expense account will have a debit balance of $38, which should be reported as an operating expense in the income statement.

A business may meet its postage requirements by **(1)** buying postage stamps, **(2)** making a deposit under the postal permit system for a certain amount of postage, or **(3)** using a postage meter. In the latter case, a certain amount of postage is paid for and the meter is set so that the postage may be used as needed. Regardless of whether postage stamps are purchased, whether a deposit is made under the permit system, or whether metered postage is purchased, the accounting procedure can be the same. The prepaid postage can be charged to an account with postage stamps, and when the stamps are used or the postage is consumed, the amount should be charged to the proper expense account.

Insurance. Insurance against loss from fire, water, windstorm, burglary, or other casualties is a form of protection provided by insurance companies. A contract under which an insurance company (the insurer) agrees to protect the owner of property (the insured) from loss on such property is known as an *insurance policy*. The amount that the insured is required to pay for such protection is known as the *premium*. The premium is usually stated as a specified rate per $1,000 of insurance for one or more years. If the rate is quoted on a one-year basis, it is known as an *annual rate*. If it is quoted for a longer period than one year, it is known as a *term rate*. Since insurance is usually purchased for a period of one or more years and the premium must be paid in advance by the insured, the amount paid is usually charged to an account for prepaid insurance. This account is classified as a current asset.

Expired Insurance. The portion of an insurance premium that is prepaid decreases day by day, but it is not customary to keep a daily record of expired insurance. Instead the usual plan is to record, at the close of each accounting period (usually a year but, sometimes, a month), the total

371

amount of the prepayment that has expired during the period just ended. The expired amount is recorded as an expense.

Many businesses keep an auxiliary record of insurance policies similar to the one reproduced below and on the opposite page. The left page is used to record the essential information with respect to each policy. (No figure is shown in the Amount column for the delivery truck policy because the amounts of coverage with respect to various risks are different.) The left page also provides the information needed to distribute the insurance premium on each policy in the columns provided on the right page. To determine the amount of the expired premium to be entered in the column provided for each month, it is necessary to divide the total premium by the number of months in the term of the policy. Thus, if the total premium amounts to $30 and the term of the policy is one year, the amount of monthly insurance expense will be $2.50 ($30 ÷ 12 months). In the case of Policy No. 86743 issued on August 5, 1971, the prepaid premium amounted to $292.32. This amount, divided by 36, the term of the policy in months, establishes that the insurance expiring monthly is $8.12. Since five months of insurance expired in 1971, the amount of unexpired insurance at the beginning of 1972 was $251.72, as indicated. The total of each monthly column is the amount of insurance expired during that month. Before this amount can be recorded, it is necessary to make a proper distribution of the insurance expense. The insurance expired during January (amounting to $42.18) was distributed as follows:

Expired insurance on merchandise...................................... $ 6.92
Expired insurance on office equipment................................   8.12
Expired insurance on store equipment................................   4.00
Expired insurance on delivery equipment.............................   23.14
                                                                      _____
    Total... $42.18

INSURANCE POLICY

Date of Policy	Policy No.	Insurer	Property Insured	Amount	Term	Expiration Date	Unexpired Premium	
7–1–69	35420	Standard Insurance Co.	Merchandise	15,000	3	7–1–72	41	52
8–5–71	86743	U.S. Fire Ins. Co.	Office Equip.	5,000	3	8–5–74	251	72
1–1–72	74882	U.S. Fire Ins. Co.	Store Equip.	4,000	3	1–1–75	144	00
1–3–72	61141	World Auto Ins. Co.	Del. Truck		1	1–3–73	277	68
7–1–72	98165	Standard Insurance Co.	Merchandise	15,000	3	7–1–75	264	96
9–1–72	42381	National Insurance Co.	Store Equip.	3,000	3	9–1–75	109	44
							1089	**32**

(Left Page)

The amount of the expired insurance was recorded by the following general journal entry:

Merchandise Insurance Expense...............................	6.92	
Office Equipment Insurance Expense..........................	8.12	
Store Equipment Insurance Expense...........................	4.00	
Delivery Equipment Insurance Expense.........................	23.14	
Prepaid Insurance...		42.18
Insurance expired during January.		

After the insurance expense is recorded for each month during the year, the balance of the prepaid insurance account at the end of the year should be the same as the total of the unexpired premium column in the insurance policy register.

At the beginning of each year, it is necessary to forward the data in the insurance policy register to a new page as shown in the illustration at the top of page 374. Only the left page of the register is reproduced in this illustration. In bringing forward the data, information about each policy still in effect and the unexpired premium are recorded. Thus, it is possible to calculate the amount of premium to be charged off each month. For example, the unexpired premium on Policy No. 86743 amounted to $154.28 and the policy had nineteen months to run. Therefore, 1/19 of the unexpired premium, or $8.12, should be charged off each month during the coming year. The unexpired premium on Policy No. 98165 amounted to $220.80 and the policy had thirty months to run. Therefore, 1/30 of the unexpired premium, or $7.36, should be charged off each month. The unexpired premium on Policy No. 42381 amounted to $97.28 and the policy had thirty-two months to run. Therefore, 1/32 of the unexpired premium, or $3.04, should be charged off each month. At the time of forwarding the

REGISTER — 1972

	EXPIRED PREMIUM													UNEXPIRED PREMIUM
JAN.	FEB.	MAR.	APR.	MAY	JUNE	JULY	AUG.	SEPT.	OCT.	NOV.	DEC.	TOTAL	
6 92	6 92	6 92	6 92	6 92	6 92							41 52	
8 12	8 12	8 12	8 12	8 12	8 12	8 12	8 12	8 12	8 12	8 12	8 12	97 44	154 28
4 00	4 00	4 00	4 00	4 00	4 00	4 00	4 00	8 20*				40 20	
23 14 42 18	23 14 42 18	23 14 42 18	23 14 42 18	23 14 42 18	23 14 42 18	23 14	23 14	23 14	23 14	23 14	23 14	277 68	
						7 36 42 62	7 36 42 62	7 36	7 36	7 36	7 36	44 16	220 80
								3 04 49 86	3 04 41 66	3 04 41 66	3 04 41 66	12 16 513 16	97 28 472 36

*Policy #74882 canceled August 31.

(Right Page)

Chapter 14 / Accounting for Inventory and Prepaid Expenses

amount of unexpired insurance to a new page, the total of the Unexpired Premium column should be in agreement with the debit balance of the prepaid insurance column.

DATE OF POLICY	POLICY NO.	INSURER	PROPERTY INSURED	AMOUNT	TERM	EXPIRATION DATE	UNEXPIRED PREMIUM
8–5–71	86743	U.S. Fire Ins. Co.	Office Equip.	5,000	3	8–5–74	154 28
7–1–72	98165	Standard Insurance Co.	Merchandise	15,000	3	7–1–75	220 80
9–1–72	42381	National Insurance Co.	Store Equip.	3,000	3	9–1–75	97 28

(Left Page)

Canceled Insurance. Either the insurance company or the insured may cancel an insurance policy at any time before expiration of the policy. If a policy is canceled, the insured is entitled to receive a refund of that part of the premium applicable to the unexpired period. The amount of the refund will depend upon whether the policy is canceled by direct action of the insurance company or at the request of the insured. When the policy is canceled directly by the insurance company, the premium for the expired period is computed on a pro rata basis. When the policy is canceled at the request of the insured, the premium for the expired period is usually computed on a *short-term rate* basis. To record the amount refunded, it is only necessary to debit the bank account and to credit the prepaid insurance account. At the same time an entry should be made in the insurance policy register to indicate that the policy has been canceled and to record the additional cost of insurance due to the short-term rate computation. This increased cost should be recorded in the column for the month in which the refund was received.

Policy No. 74882, purchased on January 1, was canceled on August 31. At that time the policy had twenty-eight months to run. At $4 a month this would amount to $112. The insurance company refunded $103.80 in September, and the loss of $8.20, representing the difference between the short-term rate and the annual rate, was recorded in the September column, as illustrated on page 373. It could not be recorded in the August column because the amount of the loss was not known until the refund was received in September. When the $103.80 was received, it was recorded by a debit to the bank account and by a credit to Prepaid Insurance.

Prepaid Interest. Sometimes interest is prepaid on a note payable. When this is done and the note does not mature in the same accounting period, the amount of interest paid may be recorded as a charge to a prepaid interest account, which should be classified as a current asset.

At the end of the accounting period the amount of the interest expense actually incurred during the period should be calculated and an adjusting entry should be made to transfer that portion of the interest from the prepaid interest account to an interest expense account. For example, on December 1 a note for $1,000 due in three months with interest at 7 percent was issued to a bank, and the interest amounting to $17.50 was paid in advance. On December 31 it was determined that one third of the interest expense was incurred during the current accounting period; therefore, the following adjusting entry was made:

Interest Expense...	5.83	
Prepaid Interest..		5.83
Prepaid interest transferred to Interest Expense.		

After this entry is posted, the prepaid interest account will have a debit balance of $11.67, which should be reported in the balance sheet as a current asset. The debit balance of the interest expense account should be reported in the income statement under the heading of "Other Expenses."

One advantage of using the asset method of accounting for prepaid expenses is that the adjusting entries that are required at the end of the period are of the write-off type. Such adjustments do not need to be reversed at the start of the new period.

Expense method of accounting for prepaid expenses

Supplies and services that may not be wholly consumed in the period in which they are purchased may be recorded as expenses at the time of purchase. Under this method of accounting, it is necessary to adjust the accounts at the end of each accounting period in order that the unused portions may be recorded as assets. For example, if office supplies purchased during an accounting period are charged to the account for office supplies expense, it will be necessary to adjust the account at the end of the period for the cost of the supplies on hand. If Office Supplies Expense had been charged for a total of $250 during the period and an inventory taken at the end of the period showed that the supplies on hand amounted to $95, it would be necessary to make the following adjusting entry:

Office Supplies...	95.00	
Office Supplies Expense.....................................		95.00
Office supplies on hand.		

After this entry is posted, the account for office supplies expense will have a debit balance of $155, which should be reported in the income statement as an operating expense. The account for office supplies will have a debit balance of $95, which should be reported in the balance sheet as a current asset.

When the expense method of accounting is followed, the adjustments made at the end of the period may be called *deferral adjustments* — they defer expenses to the next period. Adjustments of this type should be reversed at the start of the new period. In such case, the effect of the adjusting, closing, and reversing procedure is to remove the unused or unexpired amount from an expense account at the end of the period, to transfer the remaining amount to the expense and revenue summary account, and, at the start of the new period, to transfer back to the expense account the amount of expense that had been deferred.

A detailed comparison of the asset method and the expense method of accounting for supplies and other prepaid expenses is shown in parallel columns below and on the next page.

The final results are the same under both methods of accounting, but the adjusting entries required at the close of each accounting period differ. Reversing or readjusting entries are needed if the expense method is used.

Accounting for Prepaid Expenses

Asset Method	Expense Method

TRANSACTION. March 1. Purchased office supplies, $250. Terms, 30 days.

JOURNAL ENTRY	JOURNAL ENTRY
Mar. 1. Office Supplies....... 250	Mar. 1. Office Supplies Expense 250
Accounts Payable.. 250	Accounts Payable.. 250
Purchased office supplies on account.	Purchased office supplies on account.

ADJUSTMENT DATA. December 31. Inventory of office supplies on hand, $95.

JOURNAL ENTRY	JOURNAL ENTRY
Dec. 31. Office Supplies Expense.............. 155	Dec. 31. Office Supplies.......... 95
Office Supplies.... 155	Office Supplies Expense. 95
Office supplies consumed during period.	Office supplies on hand.

Asset Method

LEDGER ACCOUNTS

OFFICE SUPPLIES (An asset account)

Mar. 1	250 *95*	Dec. 31	155

OFFICE SUPPLIES EXPENSE

Dec. 31	155		

ACCOUNTS PAYABLE

		Mar. 1	250

The balance of the account for office supplies, amounting to $95, should be reported as a current asset in the balance sheet, while the balance of the account for office supplies expense, amounting to $155, should be reported as an operating expense in the income statement.

Expense Method

LEDGER ACCOUNTS

OFFICE SUPPLIES EXPENSE

Mar. 1	250 *155*	Dec. 31	95

OFFICE SUPPLIES
(An asset account)

Dec. 31	95		

ACCOUNTS PAYABLE

		Mar. 1	250

The balance of the account for office supplies expense, amounting to $155, should be reported as an operating expense in the income statement, while the balance of the account for office supplies, amounting to $95, should be reported as a current asset in the balance sheet. As of the start of the new period, the adjusting entry for $95 should be reversed so as to transfer the deferred amount back to the expense account.

Report No. 14-2

Complete Report No. 14-2 in the workbook and submit your working papers to the instructor for approval. Then continue with the next study assignment in Chapter 15 until Report No. 15-1 is required.

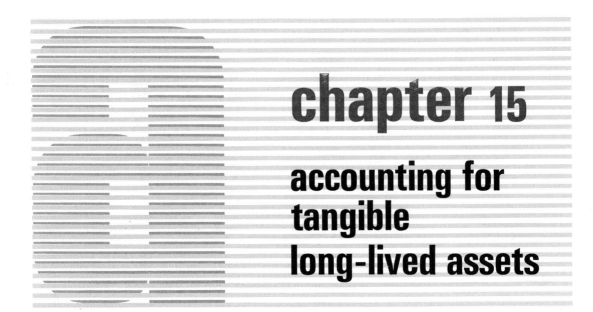

chapter 15

accounting for tangible long-lived assets

Many types of business assets are acquired with the expectation that they will remain in service for a number of accounting periods. Assets of this type are called *long-lived assets* or *fixed assets.* (The descriptions *plant assets* and *capital assets* are used sometimes.) Such assets can be classified in various ways. From a legal standpoint all property is either *real property* or *personal property.* Real property (realty or real estate) includes land and anything attached to the land; personal property includes everything else that can be owned other than real property. In nearly all cases, any real property owned by a business is considered to be a long-lived asset. (Real estate acquired as a short-term investment is an exception.) Many kinds of personal property are classified as long-lived assets. Furniture, equipment, motor vehicles, machinery, patents, and copyrights are common examples of personal property that is owned and used by a business for a number of accounting periods.

Another way of classifying long-lived assets is on the basis of tangibility. All real property is tangible (has physical substance). The same is true of such personal property as furniture, equipment, and machinery. Major examples of *intangible* long-lived assets are patents, copyrights, leases, franchises, trademarks, and goodwill. While these latter assets do not have physical substance, they do have existence in either an economic or a legal sense.

Sometimes businesses own interests in other incorporated businesses in the form of capital stock, bonds, or long-term notes. Not infrequently, government bonds or notes are also owned. It is logical to classify such assets as intangibles; however, because of their special nature, they are usually classified as investments. If it is expected that such assets will be owned for a long time, they will be considered long-term investments and will be shown in the balance sheet under some such heading. If investments are temporary in nature, they should be classified as current assets.

For accounting purposes, a common classification of long-lived assets is on the basis of how the original cost of the property is handled in the process of determining net income period by period. The cost of land used only as a site for a store, a factory, a warehouse, or a parking lot is normally left undisturbed in the accounts as long as the land is owned. Because land does not lose its capability to serve for these purposes, it does not depreciate. Assets such as buildings, furniture, and equipment are usually called *depreciable assets,* because their value or usefulness is diminished as time passes. In determining net income period by period, a portion of the cost of such assets is charged off as depreciation expense. In a similar fashion, the cost of such intangible properties as patents, copyrights, and leaseholds is gradually charged off as expense to the periods benefited by the ownership of the assets. As applied to these assets, however, the periodic write-off is termed *amortization* (in contrast to *depreciation* of certain tangible assets). Actually, the meaning of the word amortization is broad enough to include depreciation, but customarily the write-off of the cost of most tangible long-lived assets is called depreciation, while the write-off of the cost of intangibles is called amortization.

Finally, certain long-lived assets whose physical substance is consumed in the operation of a business are called *wasting assets.* Common examples include mines, stands of timber, and oil and gas wells. As might be expected, an effort is made to allocate the cost of such property to the periods in which its removal or exhaustion occurs. In this case, the periodic write-off is called *depletion.*

The subject of wasting assets and their depletion will be considered briefly at the end of the chapter. Because land, buildings, and various types of equipment are more common, the major features of accounting for these latter types of property will be considered first. For the sake of brevity, such items will be referred to simply as "long-lived assets," though it will be understood that those discussed in this chapter are all in the "tangible" category.

379

Land, buildings, and equipment

Long-lived assets may be purchased for cash or on account. The amount at which long-lived assets should be recorded initially is the total of all outlays needed to put them in place ready for use. This total may include the purchase price, transportation charges, installation costs, and any other costs that are incurred up to the point of placing the assets in service. In some cases interest may be included in the cost. For example, if money is borrowed for the purpose of constructing a building or other facilities, it is considered sound accounting to add the interest incurred during the period of construction to the cost of such building or facilities. It is important that the cost of depreciable assets be properly accounted for, because the total cost becomes the basis for the periodic depreciation write-off.

Transactions involving the purchase of long-lived assets may be recorded in the appropriate book of original entry by debiting the proper asset accounts and by crediting the bank account for the amount paid, or by crediting the proper liability account, such as Accounts Payable, Notes Payable, or Mortgages Payable, for the obligations incurred.

Additions or improvements representing an increase in the value of long-lived assets should be recorded by debiting the proper asset accounts and by crediting the bank account or the proper liability account. For example, if an addition to a building is constructed, the total cost incurred should be debited to the building account. In the same manner, such improvements as the installation of partitions, shelving, hardwood floors, a sprinkler system, an air conditioning system, or any other improvements that increase the usefulness of the property, should be recorded by debiting the proper asset accounts for the cost of the improvements. The cost of landscaping grounds surrounding an office or factory building, constructing new driveways, or planting trees and shrubbery represent improvements in the land which enhance its value. Assessments for street improvements, sidewalks, sewers, flood prevention or parks also represent improvements in, or enhancement of the value of, the land. Such costs and assessments should be recorded by debiting the land account.

Depreciation

The central task in attempting to determine net income or loss on a periodic basis is to allocate revenue to the period in which it is earned and to assign expenses to the periods that are benefited. Long-lived assets frequently last for many years and, accordingly, benefit a number of periods. The process of determining and recording the depreciation of most long-lived assets is carried on in an effort to assign their cost to the periods that they benefit or serve.

Causes of Depreciation. Depreciation is the loss of usefulness of an asset. There are two major types of depreciation:

Physical Depreciation. This term refers to the loss of usefulness because of deterioration from age and from wear. This type of depreciation is generally continuous, though not necessarily uniform from period to period. Assets exposed to the elements may wear out at a fairly regular rate. Assets not exposed to the elements may slowly deteriorate whether in use or not, but the speed at which they deteriorate often is related to the extent to which they are used.

Functional Depreciation. This term refers to loss of usefulness because of inadequacy or obsolescence. The growth of a business may result in some of its long-lived assets becoming inadequate. The assets remain capable of doing the job for which they were acquired, but the job has become too big for them. Assets may become obsolete because of a change in the demand for products or services, or because of the development of new methods, equipment, or processes which either reduce costs, or increase quality, or both.

Calculating the Amount of Depreciation for a Period. The net cost of an asset should be apportioned over the periods the asset is expected to serve. Net cost means original cost less scrap or salvage value. Scrap or salvage value is difficult to predict in most cases. Quite often, the assumption is made that the scrap value will be zero. The major problem connected with depreciation accounting, however, is to attempt to foretell either how many periods the asset will serve or how many units of service the asset will provide. If it were possible to know that a machine would operate for 100,000 hours, it would be easy to decide that 5 percent of its net cost should be charged to the first year in which it was used 5,000 hours. Likewise, a certain knowledge that an asset would last 10 years and equally serve each of those years would solve the problem of how to apportion its cost. Unfortunately, there is no way of knowing exactly how long an asset will last or exactly what its output will be. All that can be done is to make estimates based upon past experience. In attempting to make such estimates, the accountant may be assisted by information relating to assets previously owned by the business or he may be guided by the experience of others. Statistics supplied by trade associations and government agencies (such as the Internal Revenue Service) may help. Opinions of engineers or appraisal companies may be sought. Past experience with respect to

381

physical depreciation may be a very good guide for the future. Past events, however, are not much help in attempting to predict depreciation caused by inadequacy or obsolescence. Uncertainty surrounds all depreciation calculations.

Methods of Calculating Depreciation. There are several different ways of calculating the amount of depreciation to be recorded each period. The most commonly used methods are the following:

(a) Straight-line method.

(b) Declining-balance method.

(c) Sum-of-the-years-digits method.

A fourth method, based on the estimated productive capacity of the asset, will be described, though it is not used as frequently as the other three methods mentioned.

Depreciation may be taken into consideration in calculating income subject to federal and state income taxes. A business is not required to calculate depreciation in the same way both for income tax and for business accounting purposes. However, because depreciation can be only an estimate, many firms adopt depreciation practices that are acceptable for income tax determination purposes. This does not impose severe limitations since the tax laws generally allow any method that is reasonable and consistently followed.

382

Straight-Line Method. When the *straight-line* method is used, the net cost of an asset is apportioned equally over its estimated useful life in terms of months or years. For example, assume that a frame building cost $30,000 and is expected to last 20 years. The estimated salvage or scrap value at the end of 20 years is $2,000. The amount of depreciation each year, then, would be $1,400. This is computed as follows:

$$\frac{\$30,000 - \$2,000}{20} = \$1,400$$

The annual rate of depreciation would be 4.67 percent ($1,400 ÷ $30,000).

A month is usually the shortest period that is considered in depreciation accounting. An asset purchased before the fifteenth of the month is considered to have been owned for the full month. An asset purchased after the middle of the month is not considered to have been acquired until the first of the next month.

The difference between the cost of an asset and the total amount of such cost that has been charged off as depreciation as of a certain date is its *undepreciated cost* (sometimes called *book value*) at that time. When the straight-line method is used, the undepreciated cost of the asset decreases uniformly period by period. Shown on a graph, the undepreciated cost over a number of periods is a downward-sloping, but perfectly straight line. That is how the method got its name.

The straight-line method of calculating depreciation closely reflects the facts in many cases. The method's outstanding advantage is its simplicity. Since depreciation is based upon estimates in any case, many businessmen and accountants believe that the use of more complicated procedures is not warranted. The calculation of depreciation on a straight-line basis is still the most widely followed practice.

Depreciation can be calculated on each individual asset or on each group of substantially identical assets. It is possible to calculate a *group* or *composite rate* to be applied to a number of assets that may include various related types of property. For example, suppose that the general ledger account Office Furniture included the following:

ITEM	QUANTITY	ESTIMATED LIFE, YEARS	TOTAL COST
Desks	12	20	$3,000
Chairs...........	20	15	1,200
Tables...........	5	12	400
Filing Cabinets ...	20	15	960
			$5,560

Further suppose that it is estimated that the salvage values of the four groups of items will be, respectively, $300, $150, $40 and $60. The composite or group rate of depreciation would be 5.306 percent computed as follows:

ITEM	COST	SALVAGE VALUE	DEPRECIABLE COST	ESTIMATED LIFE	ANNUAL DEPRECIATION
Desks...........	$3,000	$300	$2,700	20	$135
Chairs...........	1,200	150	1,050	15	70
Tables..........	400	40	360	12	30
Filing Cabinets...	960	60	900	15	60
	$5,560	$550	$5,010		$295

$$\$295 \div \$5,560 = 5.306\%$$

The rate probably would be rounded to 5.3 percent. As long as the relative proportions of the items in the groups stay about the same, and no reason arises to alter the estimated life of any of the items, the composite rate of 5.3 percent can be applied to the group total to determine the annual depreciation write-off.

When depreciation is calculated on the basis of a group or composite rate, no attempt is made to relate the depreciation to specific units. No depreciation is recorded in the subsidiary record (if any) for each individual unit. Therefore, when disposition is made of a unit, its original cost, less any salvage or trade-in value, is charged to the accumulated depreciation account for the appropriate group. No gain or loss is recognized upon the disposition of a unit. (The group method is an averaging device. It is expected that some units will have lives shorter than the average, and some will serve longer.)

Declining-Balance Method. Many long-lived assets require repairs and parts replacements to keep them in service. Such expenses usually increase as the assets grow older. Some accountants believe that depreciation expense should be higher in early years to offset the higher repair and maintenance expenses of the later years. Another reason advanced in support of a depreciation method that gives a greater write-off at first is the contention that many, if not most, assets contribute proportionately more to the business during the years that the assets are comparatively new. For these reasons, it may be desirable to calculate depreciation in a way that will give larger write-offs in the early years of the life of the unit. One way to accomplish this result is to apply a fixed or uniform rate to the undepreciated cost of the property each year. As the undepreciated cost diminishes year by year, the depreciation charges are successively smaller. This method is called the *declining-balance* or the *fixed percentage of diminishing value* method.

There is a formula which can be used to calculate a rate which will leave a predetermined amount at the end of a predetermined number of years.[1] This rate must be applied each year to the difference between original cost and amounts already written off. (There must always be some salvage or scrap value involved; any rate less than 100 percent will never reduce the original amount to zero.)

In practice, however, the rate used is rarely calculated by a formula. Instead, a rate equal to twice the straight-line rate is employed because this is the maximum allowed for federal income tax purposes. (The law was changed in 1954 to permit this rate of depreciation on any *new* assets acquired after December 31, 1953. Prior to that time, the law did not allow a rate greater than 1.5 times the straight-line rate. One and one-half times the straight-line rate is still the limit in connection with assets that were *used* when acquired.)

Suppose, for example, that an asset with a cost of $1,000 and an expected life of 5 years is to be depreciated on the declining-balance basis. It was new when acquired. Assume that the company wishes to handle depreciation in the same way for both income tax and business accounting purposes. Accordingly, since the straight-line rate would be 20 percent ($100\% \div 5$ years), the company would use a declining-balance rate of 40 percent ($2 \times 20\%$). The annual depreciation, the balance in the accumulated depreciation account, and the undepreciated cost at the end of each year would be as shown at the top of the next page.

---

[1]The formula is:
$$\text{Rate} = 1 - \sqrt[n]{s \div c}$$
when n = number of years of estimated life, s = estimated salvage value, and c = original cost.

YEAR	ANNUAL DEPRECIATION	ACCUMULATED DEPRECIATION END OF YEAR	UNDEPRECIATED COST END OF YEAR
0......			$1,000.00
1......	$400.00	$400.00	600.00
2......	240.00	640.00	360.00
3......	144.00	784.00	216.00
4......	86.40	870.40	129.60
5......	51.84	922.24	77.76

For income tax purposes, the declining-balance rate can be abandoned at any time without permission, and the undepreciated cost at that date, less any estimated salvage value, can be written off in equal installments over the estimated remaining life. Suppose, for example, that the estimated salvage value of the asset in the foregoing illustration was $50. At the end of 3 years, the undepreciated cost of the asset was $216. In each of the fourth and fifth years, $83 might be taken as depreciation. ($216 − $50 = $166. $166 ÷ 2 = $83.) If the expected salvage value was approximately $75 or $80, however, there would be no reason to depart from the declining-balance procedure.

Sum-of-the-Years-Digits Method. Another method of writing off smaller amounts of depreciation year by year is known as the *sum-of-the-years-digits* method. This method is similar in effect to the declining-balance method. However, with the "years-digits" method, a write-down to the exact amount of estimated salvage value (which might be, and often is, zero) is possible. The write-off each year is based on a schedule of fractions obtained by listing the digits that represent the years of the estimated life of the asset and adding these digits to get a denominator for all of the fractions. The largest digit is used as the numerator for the first year, the next largest digit as the numerator for the second year, etc. For example, suppose that the estimated life of the asset is 5 years. $5 + 4 + 3 + 2 + 1 = 15$. Therefore, write off $5/15$ of the net cost (original cost less estimated salvage value) the first year, $4/15$ the second year, $3/15$ the third year, etc. As applied to an asset costing $1,000, with an estimated salvage value of $100, the results would be as follows:

385

YEAR	ANNUAL DEPRECIATION	ACCUMULATED DEPRECIATION END OF YEAR	UNDEPRECIATED COST END OF YEAR
0......			$1,000.00
1......	$300.00	$300.00	700.00
2......	240.00	540.00	460.00
3......	180.00	720.00	280.00
4......	120.00	840.00	160.00
5......	60.00	900.00	100.00

(This method became popular when the Internal Revenue Act passed in 1954 specifically allowed its use in depreciating new assets acquired after December 31, 1953.)

Comparison of Methods. The following tabulation contrasts the results of using straight-line, declining-balance, and sum-of-the-years-digits depreciation methods for an asset costing $1,000 with a ten-year estimated life and an estimated salvage value of $100:

| YEAR | STRAIGHT-LINE METHOD | | DECLINING-BALANCE METHOD | | SUM-OF-THE-YEARS-DIGITS METHOD | |
	DEPRECIATION CHARGE	UNDEPRECIATED COST END OF YEAR	DEPRECIATION CHARGE	UNDEPRECIATED COST END OF YEAR	DEPRECIATION CHARGE	UNDEPRECIATED COST END OF YEAR
0...		$1,000.00		$1,000.00		$1,000.00
1...	$90.00	910.00	$200.00	800.00	$163.64	836.36
2...	90.00	820.00	160.00	640.00	147.27	689.09
3...	90.00	730.00	128.00	512.00	130.91	558.18
4...	90.00	640.00	102.40	409.60	114.55	443.63
5...	90.00	550.00	81.92	327.68	98.18	345.45
6...	90.00	460.00	65.54	262.14	81.82	263.63
7...	90.00	370.00	52.43	209.71	65.45	198.18
8...	90.00	280.00	41.94	167.77	49.09	149.09
9...	90.00	190.00	33.55	134.22	32.73	116.36
10...	90.00	100.00	26.84	107.38	16.36	100.00

The annual depreciation charge under the straight-line method was determined by dividing the net cost of $900 ($1,000 − $100) by 10.

In using the declining-balance method in the preceding comparison, salvage value was ignored (since it was a "built-in" factor) and twice the straight-line rate was applied to the undepreciated cost at the start of each year. With a ten-year life, the straight-line rate was 10 percent, so twice this, or 20 percent, was used. In this case, the undepreciated cost at the end of ten years ($107.38) was very close to the estimated salvage value stated at the outset of the comparison. If this were not the case, the declining-balance procedure could have been dropped at some point and in the years remaining, equal charges could have been made to write off all but the estimated salvage value.

In using the sum-of-the-years-digits method in the preceding comparison, salvage value was taken into consideration. The sum of the digits one through ten is 55. Therefore, under the years-digits method, the charge for the first year was 10/55 of the net cost, 9/55 in the second year, and so on.

Effect of Different Depreciation Methods on Net Income Calculation. Over a number of years, the *total* of the amounts of the calculated annual net incomes (deducting, perhaps, net losses in some years) will be about the same regardless of the method of depreciation used. For any one year, however, the method of depreciation used may make a significant difference in the amount of the calculated net income. For example, consider the case of a new business with a number of new depreciable assets which have just been acquired at a cost of $50,000, with an estimated life of 10 years

386

and an estimated scrap value of $5,000. Suppose that, for the first year, revenue was $125,000 and all costs and expenses except depreciation amounted to $100,000. Following is a comparison of three very condensed income statements of the new business showing the net income for the first year after applying each of the depreciation methods so far discussed. (To check the depreciation calculation, refer to Year 1 of the previous comparison and multiply by 50 since that example was based on a $1,000 asset and this illustration assumes that the depreciable assets cost $50,000.)

	STRAIGHT-LINE DEPRECIATION METHOD USED		DECLINING-BALANCE DEPRECIATION METHOD USED		SUM-OF-THE-YEARS-DIGITS DEPRECIATION METHOD USED	
Revenue..........		$125,000		$125,000		$125,000
Costs and expenses except depreciation....	$100,000		$100,000		$100,000	
Depreciation.....	4,500	104,500	10,000	110,000	8,182	108,182
Net income....		$ 20,500		$ 15,000		$ 16,818

Note that the calculated amount of net income in the first case is over one-third greater than the amount in the second case. When such differences may result from the choice of depreciation methods, and it is recalled that the choice of method of allocating cost between goods sold and inventory on hand may make an important difference, it is apparent that periodic business income calculation is not an exact science, but rather an art involving careful judgement.

387

Units-of-Output Method. Another method of calculating the amount of depreciation for each period is the *units-of-output* or *units-of-production* method. If it is possible to estimate the number of units of service or output that can be secured from an asset, then it is logical to allocate the net cost of the asset to the periods it serves on the basis of the use or output during each period. Obviously such a measure of service does not exist in the case of many assets. In the case of certain types of machinery, equipment, and vehicles, however, the units-of-output method may be used.

For example, a company may have found from experience that it usually can obtain 70,000 miles of service from certain types of trucks before they become so worn out that the need for extensive repairs and replacements makes it advisable for the company to dispose of them. Suppose a new truck of this type is purchased. The cost of the truck (apart from tires, which are separately depreciated on the basis of shorter lives) is $4,000. The company expects that the truck can be traded in for $1,200 after 70,000 miles. The estimated net cost to be charged to operations during the life of the truck is, therefore, $2,800. The estimated depreciation per mile is 4 cents ($2,800 ÷ 70,000 miles). If the truck were driven 22,000 miles the first year, the depreciation charge for that year with respect to that truck would be $880 (22,000 × .04).

Accounting procedure

The number of accounts for tangible long-lived assets that will be kept in the general ledger will depend upon the number of such assets, the type of information required by the management, and, in the case of all but land, the sort of depreciation procedure that is to be followed. If there are very few long-lived assets, a separate account for each one with a related depreciation account (except for land, which is not subject to depreciation) can be kept in the general ledger. In such a case, the periodic depreciation for each one would be calculated and recorded separately.

If the business has a considerable number of depreciable long-lived assets, it is likely that there will be relatively few accounts for them in the general ledger. Summary accounts will be kept for each major class of assets, such as one account for buildings, one for machinery and equipment, one for office furniture and equipment, and one for delivery trucks. Each of these summary accounts will have a related accumulated depreciation account. It is highly desirable that such summary accounts be supported by some sort of supplementary or subsidiary records of the items that comprise the general ledger account totals. If depreciation is calculated on a *unit basis* (meaning a separate calculation and record of depreciation for each unit), it is common practice to maintain a subsidiary record of each unit. Such records are commonly in the form of cards. Space is provided on each card to show the details about the asset, including the cost of the unit (which supports the debit in the general ledger asset account), and the amount of depreciation taken each period. (These entries support the credits in the general ledger accumulated depreciation accounts.) Space is also provided to record matters relating to the disposition of the asset. A typical long-lived asset record card of this type is shown below. Following is a narrative of the transactions that were recorded on the card:

January 7, 1970. Purchased Olivetti Underwood Typewriter, No. 6200625, from the Office Supply Co., City, for $240.

December 31, 1970. Depreciation of typewriter at annual rate of 20 percent of net cost, $40. (A salvage value of $40 and a five-year life are estimated.)

December 31, 1971. Depreciation of typewriter at annual rate of 20 percent of net cost, $40.

July 1, 1972. Sold typewriter for $145 cash.

Before the sale of the typewriter on July 1, 1972, was recorded, depreciation for the half year, amounting to $20, was recorded by debiting Depreciation of Office Equipment and by crediting Accumulated Depreciation — Office Equipment. The amount of this depreciation was also entered on the record card. The sale was then recorded as indicated by the following general journal entry:

Bank...	145.00	
Accumulated Depreciation — Office Equipment................	100.00	
Office Equipment......................................		240.00
Gain on Sale of Office Equipment.........................		5.00
Sold Olivetti Underwood typewriter #6200625.		

LONG-LIVED ASSET RECORD

Description   Typewriter   Account   Office Equipment

Age when acquired   New   Estimated salvage value $40

Estimated life   5 years   Rate of annual depreciation 20%

COST				DEPRECIATION RECORD			
Date Purchased	Description	Amount		Year	Rate	Amount	Total To Date
1970				1970	20%	40 00	40 00
Jan. 7	Olivetti Underwood Typewriter	240 00		1971	20%	40 00	80 00
	#6200625			1972	20%	20 00	100 00
	Office Supply Co.			19			
	City			19			
				19			
				19			
				19			
				19			

SOLD, EXCHANGED, OR DISCARDED							
Date	Explanation	Amount Realized	More than ✓ / less than	Undepr. Cost	Accum. Depr.		
1972						19	
July 1	Sold	145 00		5 00	100 00	19	
						19	

Long-Lived Asset Record

The sale was also entered on the record card, after which the card was transferred from a file of assets owned to a file of assets sold, exchanged, or discarded. Such an asset record, when properly kept, will provide all the information needed in claiming the proper amount of depreciation of long-lived assets as a deduction from gross income in the annual income tax returns. The gain resulting from the sale of the typewriter for $5 more than its undepreciated cost represents taxable income, which must be reported in the income tax return for the year in which the sale was made.

In some accounting systems, no effort is made to calculate separately the periodic depreciation on each unit. Instead, depreciation is calculated for groups of assets. The grouping is usually by similar types of assets and similarity of average length of life. If this procedure is followed, there will be relatively few summary asset and related accumulated depreciation accounts in the general ledger, and there are not likely to be very extensive subsidiary records. No record is kept of the periodic depreciation on each unit; depreciation is calculated for each group as a whole, using an average or composite rate. Even if the group procedure is followed, however, it is desirable to have some sort of an individual record for each asset that will show its acquisition date, cost, location, and date and nature of disposition.

390 Recording depreciation

It has been seen that depreciation usually is recorded at the end of the period, along with other necessary adjusting entries. One or more depreciation expense accounts may be debited, and one or more accumulated depreciation accounts may be credited. The number of each of these accounts that will be used will depend upon the degree of detail that is desired in the general ledger accounts and for the periodic statements. Usually there is one depreciation expense account for each major type of asset, such as Depreciation of Buildings, Depreciation of Furniture and Fixtures, and Depreciation of Delivery Equipment. A business that classifies expenses on a departmental basis may use a considerable number of depreciation expense accounts.

In the normal course of events, the only entries in the accumulated depreciation accounts are those made at the end of each period to record the depreciation for the period then ended. When some disposition is made of a depreciable asset (such as its sale, exchange, retirement, or destruction by fire), depreciation should be recorded for the interval between the date of the last regular adjustment of the accounts and the date of the disposition of the asset. (Usually the depreciation is calculated to the nearest full month.)

Disposition of long-lived assets

A long-lived asset may be disposed of in any one of the following ways:

(a) It may be discarded or retired.

(b) It may be sold.

(c) It may be exchanged or traded in for property of like kind or for other property.

If the record of the cost of, and any depreciation on, the asset being removed is a part of some long-lived asset group records, no gain or loss will be recognized when the asset is removed. The cost of the item must be credited to the proper (group) asset account. The cost less any amount received for the item is charged to the proper (group) accumulated depreciation account. The discussion in the paragraphs that follow relates to assets that have been depreciated on a unit basis.

Discarding or Retiring Long-Lived Assets. A long-lived asset may be discarded or retired whether or not it has been fully depreciated. If it has been fully depreciated, no gain or loss will be realized. If it has not been fully depreciated, the undepreciated cost of the discarded asset will represent a loss. Such a loss may be the result of underestimating the depreciation of the asset for the period of time that it has been in use, or it may be the result of obsolescence. Often it is better to scrap an obsolete machine and to buy a new one even though a loss is realized on the old machine.

On July 16, Holling & Renz discarded parcel post scales that had no exchange or sale value. The long-lived asset record indicated that the scales originally had cost $80 and that depreciation amounting to a total of $60 had been recorded as a credit to the accumulated depreciation — store equipment account.

This transaction involved a loss of $20 resulting from the discard of the asset, which had an undepreciated cost of $20. The transaction should be recorded as indicated by the following general journal entry:

```
Loss on Discarded Store Equipment...........................   20.00
Accumulated Depreciation — Store Equipment...................   60.00
   Store Equipment..........................................           80.00
      Discarded parcel post scales.
```

When this entry is posted, the debit of $60 to the accumulated depreciation account and the credit of $80 to the store equipment account will have the effect of eliminating the parcel post scales from the balances of these accounts. The debit of $20 to Loss on Discarded Store Equipment records the realized loss.

391

When a long-lived asset is discarded after it has been fully depreciated, no gain or loss will result from the transaction, but the discarded asset should be eliminated from the account balances by debiting the accumulated depreciation account and by crediting the asset account for the original cost of the asset.

Selling Long-Lived Assets. If a long-lived asset is sold, it is necessary to know its undepreciated cost before the proper amount of any gain or loss resulting from the transaction can be determined. The undepreciated cost of an asset is the difference between its cost and the amount of depreciation recorded. Thus, if an adding machine that cost $200 depreciates at the rate of 10 percent a year and the annual depreciation is recorded by debiting Depreciation of Office Equipment and by crediting Accumulated Depreciation — Office Equipment, the undepreciated cost of the adding machine at the end of three years will be $140, the difference between the cost price of the adding machine and the credit balance of the accumulated depreciation account. When a long-lived asset is sold at its undepreciated cost, no gain or loss results from the transaction; when it is sold for more than its undepreciated cost, the difference represents a gain; when it is sold for less than its undepreciated cost, the difference represents a loss.

Assuming that the adding machine was sold at the end of three years for $150 cash, the transaction should be recorded as indicated by the following general journal entry:

Bank..	150.00	
Accumulated Depreciation — Office Equipment.................	60.00	
Office Equipment..		200.00
Gain on Sale of Office Equipment..........................		10.00
Sold adding machine.		

When this entry is posted, the debit of $60 to the accumulated depreciation account will offset the amount recorded previously as a credit to the accumulated depreciation account because of the estimated depreciation of the adding machine over a period of three years. The amount credited to Office Equipment will offset the purchase price previously recorded as a debit to Office Equipment. These entries have the effect of completely eliminating the old adding machine from the office equipment and accumulated depreciation accounts. The gain realized from the sale of the adding machine for $10 more than its undepreciated cost is reported as a "Gain on Sale of Office Equipment." This gain should be listed under the heading of "Other Revenue" in the income statement.

If the adding machine referred to was sold at the end of three years for $110 instead of $150, there would be a loss of $30 instead of a gain of $10. The transaction should be recorded as indicated by the following general journal entry:

392

```
Bank...................................................................  110.00
Accumulated Depreciation — Office Equipment..................   60.00
Loss on Sale of Office Equipment.............................   30.00
   Office Equipment..........................................                200.00
      Sold adding machine.
```

When this entry is posted, the debit of $60 to the accumulated depreciation account and the credit of $200 to the office equipment account will eliminate the old adding machine from these accounts. The loss resulting from the sale of the old adding machine for $30 less than its undepreciated cost will be reported as a "Loss on Sale of Office Equipment." This loss should be listed under the heading of "Other Expenses" in the income statement.

Exchange of Long-Lived Assets. A long-lived asset may be exchanged or traded in for other property. While in a simple trade each party must expect to benefit, it is not likely that either would record any gain. In most cases, the asset acquired would be assigned a cost equal to the undepreciated cost of the asset given.

If one asset is traded in on the purchase of another, the *trade-in allowance* may be equal to, greater than, or less than the undepreciated cost of the asset turned in. If the allowance is greater, a gain results; if less, a loss is sustained. However, gains or losses of this sort are not always "recognized." To simplify the preparation of income tax returns, it is common practice to record trade-ins in a way that conforms to the tax regulations. These regulations state that no gain or loss is recognized if property held for productive use is exchanged for property *of like kind* acquired for similar use. The cost (the tax laws call it the "basis") of the new property acquired is the undepreciated cost of the old property exchanged for it, plus the additional cash paid.

For example, suppose that a delivery truck that cost $3,200 has been owned for three years. Depreciation in the amount of $960 has been taken each year — a total of $2,880. Thus, the undepreciated cost of the truck is $320 ($3,200 − $2,880). If this truck is traded in on a new one to be used for a similar purpose and $3,500 is paid in cash, the cost of the new truck is $3,820 ($3,500 + $320). The transaction should be recorded as indicated in the following general journal entry:

```
Delivery Equipment (new truck)..........................  3,820.00
Accumulated Depreciation — Delivery Equipment............  2,880.00
   Delivery Equipment (old truck).........................              3,200.00
   Bank...................................................              3,500.00
      Purchased a new truck.
```

When this journal entry is posted, the cost of the old truck will be eliminated from the delivery equipment account and that account will be charged for the cost of the new truck, a figure which constitutes the basis for future depreciation charges. The amount of the depreciation of the old truck will also be eliminated from the accumulated depreciation account. No gain or loss is recognized in recording the transaction. This method of accounting conforms to the income tax regulations.

Some accountants prefer to take into consideration the amount of the exchange allowance rather than the undepreciated cost of an asset given in exchange in determining the cost of the new asset acquired. However, if this practice is followed, it will be necessary to make special calculations when preparing the annual income tax return. These calculations can become quite complicated where there are frequent transactions involving the exchange of long-lived assets. It is, therefore, generally preferable from a practical standpoint to follow the income tax regulations in recording such transactions.

In any transaction involving an exchange in which property is exchanged for property *not of like kind,* any gain or loss resulting from the transaction should be recorded, since it must be taken into consideration in preparing the income tax return.

For example, suppose that the $175 cost of a typewriter was charged to the office equipment account and depreciation on the typewriter amounting to $35 had been credited to the accumulated depreciation account each year for two years. At the end of two years the typewriter was traded in on a new cash register costing $450. The trade-in allowance amounted to $130, the balance, $320, being paid in cash. Since this transaction did not involve an exchange of property for other property of like kind, any gain realized or loss involved would be recognized for income tax purposes. Because $130 was allowed for an asset that had an undepreciated cost of $105 ($175 − $70), the transaction involved a gain of $25. The transaction should be recorded as indicated in the following general journal entry:

Store Equipment...	450.00	
Accumulated Depreciation — Office Equipment.................	70.00	
Office Equipment...		175.00
Bank..		320.00
Gain on Sale of Office Equipment...........................		25.00
Purchased a new cash register.		

When this entry is posted, the debit of $70 to the accumulated depreciation account will offset the amount recorded previously as a credit to that account because of the estimated depreciation of the typewriter over a period of two years. The amount credited to Office Equipment will offset the purchase price of the typewriter previously recorded as a debit to that account. These entries have the effect of completely eliminating the old typewriter from the office equipment account and the related accumulated depreciation account. The gain realized on the old typewriter is recorded as a credit to Gain on Sale of Office Equipment. Had the trade-in allowance been less than the undepreciated cost of the typewriter, the difference would have represented a loss to be charged to Loss on Sale of Office Equipment.

Fully depreciated long-lived assets

A long-lived asset is said to be fully depreciated when the recorded depreciation is equal to the cost of the asset. When an asset is fully depreciated, no further depreciation should be recorded. Since the rate of depreciation is based on its estimated useful life, an asset may be continued in use after it is fully depreciated. In this case, the cost of the asset and an equal amount of accumulated depreciation are usually retained in the accounts. When a fully depreciated asset is scrapped, the cost of the asset and the total amount of depreciation should be removed from the accounts. Such an adjustment involves a debit to the proper accumulated depreciation account and a credit to the proper long-lived asset account for the cost of the asset.

In some states a taxable value is placed on a fully depreciated long-lived asset if the asset is continued in use. Under such circumstances, the taxable value of the fully depreciated asset should be stated in the long-lived asset record as a guide in preparing the property tax schedule. The taxable values of fully depreciated long-lived assets and the undepreciated costs of other long-lived assets should be listed so that the total taxable value of the long-lived assets may be determined.

Depreciation in the statements

Most accountants and businessmen consider depreciation to be an operating expense and so classify it in the income statement. There may be as much subclassification as the management desires. Depreciation of delivery equipment, for example, may be classed as a selling expense, while depreciation of office furniture and equipment may be classed as an office or general administrative expense.

In view of the close relationship between long-lived asset accounts and their accumulated depreciation accounts, the preferred practice in the preparation of balance sheets is to show the amount of the accumulated depreciation as a deduction from the cost of the asset. The difference, representing undepreciated cost, is extended to be included in the asset total.

Accumulated depreciation accounts, like allowances for bad debts, are sometimes called asset valuation accounts. An accumulated depreciation account, however, only values the asset in a very limited and remote sense.

The difference between the cost of the asset and the balance of the accumulated depreciation account is not expected to have any relation to the market value of the asset. Such assets are not intended for sale. What they might bring, if sold, is usually of small consequence. Those who understand accounting interpret the difference between the gross amount of the long-lived assets and the related accumulated depreciation accounts as being simply costs not yet charged to operations. Some companies so describe this difference in their balance sheets.

Wasting assets

The term *wasting asset* is applied to real property which is acquired for the purpose of removing or extracting the valuable natural resource on or in the property. Stands of timber, mines, oil wells, gas wells, or land acquired in the belief that the property contains minerals, oil, or gas that can be extracted, are examples of this type of asset. The adjective "wasting" is applied because, in most cases, it is expected that the valuable product eventually will be removed or exhausted so as to leave the property relatively valueless. In the case of many types of mines and wells, only the valuable material below the surface is owned. The land, as such, may not be owned by the mining, oil, or gas company.

Depletion. The consumption or exhaustion of wasting assets is called *depletion*. Apart from income tax considerations, the accounting problem is to apportion the cost of such assets to the periods in which they are consumed. The procedure is very similar to that involved in computing depreciation on a units-of-output basis. The cost of the property is reduced by estimated salvage or residual value, if any, and the difference is divided by the estimated number of units that the property contains. The result is the depletion expense per unit. This amount times the number of units removed and sold during the period will give the depletion expense for the period.

The following example is used to illustrate both the method of computing depletion and the proper accounting procedure:

A coal mine is acquired at a cost of $300,000. No salvage value is expected. The estimated number of units available for production is 1,000,000 tons. During the current year 145,000 tons of coal are mined and sold.

COMPUTATION OF AMOUNT OF DEPLETION EXPENSE

$300,000 ÷ 1,000,000 tons = 30¢ per ton
145,000 tons × 30¢ per ton = $43,500, amount of depletion expense

The depletion may be recorded by means of the following general journal entry:

```
Depletion Expense.......................................  43,500
    Accumulated Depletion — Coal Mine......................         43,500
    Depletion based on 145,000 tons of coal at a unit rate of 30¢ a
    ton.
```

The difference between the cost of the mine and the amount of the accumulated depletion is the undepleted cost of the property.

```
Cost of coal mine............................................  $300.000
    Less accumulated depletion...............................    43,500
Undepleted cost of mine......................................  $256,500
```

It is customary to show the accumulated depletion as a deduction from the property account in the balance sheet to indicate the undepleted cost of the property. Depletion Expense is a temporary account that is closed into Expense and Revenue Summary at the end of the accounting period. It should be reported as an operating expense in the income statement.

From time to time the estimate of the quantity of the resource that remains in the property has to be changed. The usual practice is to make a new calculation of the depletion per unit, starting with the most recently determined undepleted cost of the property and dividing that amount (less estimated salvage value, if any) by the number of units extracted during the current year plus the current estimate of the number of units remaining. For example, the mine mentioned in the previous illustration had an undepleted cost of $256,500 at the start of the second year. During that year 200,000 tons were extracted and at the end of the year the engineers estimate that 700,000 tons remain. The calculation of the revised depletion expense per unit would be as follows:

$$\frac{\$256,500}{200,000 \text{ tons} + 700,000 \text{ tons}} = 28\tfrac{1}{2}¢ \text{ per ton}$$

200,000 tons × 28½¢ = $57,000, depletion expense for the second year

Depletion Expense for Federal Income Tax Purposes. Special rules govern the amount of the deduction for depletion expense that can be taken for federal income tax purposes. The taxpayer may compute the amount in the manner explained in the preceding paragraphs. However, taxpayers who own and operate oil and gas wells and certain types of mines may take deductions equal to certain specified percentages (which vary from 5 percent to 22 percent) of the amount of the sales of the period subject to stated maximum and minimum limits. This procedure is commonly known as *percentage depletion.*

Report No. 15-2

Complete Report No. 15-2 in the workbook and submit your working papers for approval. Then continue with the next study assignment in Chapter 16 until Report No. 16-1 is required.

398

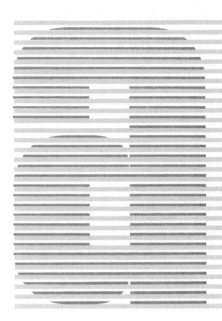

chapters 11-15

practical
accounting
problems

Problem 11-A

Miller Upton, is a wholesale distributor of office furniture and supplies. The merchandise accounts are kept on the departmental basis, Dept. A comprising furniture and Dept. B all other merchandise. The following general ledger accounts are affected by this problem:

171 Store Equipment	531 Purchases — Dept. A
181 Office Equipment	541 Purchases — Dept. B
251 Notes Payable	551 Freight In — Dept. A
261 Accounts Payable	561 Freight In — Dept. B

Following is a narrative of purchases made during February:

Feb. 1. (Tuesday) No. 206, The Shaw-Walker Co., Philadelphia; desks, $361.40; terms, January 27 — 2/10, n/30; Penn-Central freight collect.

    1. No. 207, Utility Supply Co., Detroit; memo books, $47.95; terms, January 28 — 2/10, n/30.

    1. No. 208, Midwest Office Supply Co., Chicago; ledger outfits, $162.80; terms, January 28 — 2/10, n/60; postage prepaid and added to invoice, $7.60.

    1. No. 209, Mohawk Chair, Inc., Oneida; chairs, $93.50; terms January 28 — 3/10, n/30; Penn-Central freight collect.

    1. No. 210, Wakefield Furniture Co., Grand Rapids; Tables, $175.95; terms, January 27 — 30 days; Michigan Central freight collect.

14. No. 211, The Wormwood Bros. Co., Columbia; tables, $120; terms, February 11 — 30 days; Missouri Pacific freight prepaid and added to invoice, $9.80.

14. No. 212, Waterman's, New York City; desk sets, $282.40; terms, February 10 — 30 days; express prepaid and added to invoice, $17.75.

21. No. 213, The Shaw-Walker Co., Philadelphia; filing cabinets (for their own store use), $284; terms, February 18 — 2/10, n/30; Penn-Central freight collect.

21. Received a corrected purchase invoice, dated January 27, from Wakefield Furniture Co., Grand Rapids, $185.95. (See Purchase Invoice No. 210.)

21. No. 214, Rocky Mount Furniture Co., Rocky Mount; desks, $525; terms, February 19 — 30-day note with interest at 6%.

28. No. 215, Olivetti Underwood Corporation, Detroit; typewriter (for their own office use), $175; terms, February 26 — 30 days.

REQUIRED: As the accountant for the business, (1) enter each invoice in an invoice register similar to the one reproduced on page 310 and post directly to the proper supplier's account in a subsidiary accounts payable ledger. (Invoice No. 214 is not to be so posted.) (2) Complete the individual posting from the invoice register to the general ledger. (3) Foot, prove the footings, enter the totals, and rule the invoice register. (4) Complete the summary posting. (5) Prove the balance of the accounts payable account by preparing a schedule of accounts payable as of February 28. Use standard ledger paper for the general ledger and balance-column ledger paper for the accounts payable ledger.

Problem 12-A

Wenzil Dolva is a wholesale distributor of musical instruments. The merchandise accounts are kept on the departmental basis. Following is a list of the general ledger accounts that are affected by this problem, with the September 1 balances indicated:

131 Notes Receivable, $1,600.00
133 Accounts Receivable, $3,050.80
411 Sales — Dept. A, $15,926.42
    041 Sales Returns and Allowances — Dept. A, $695.00
421 Sales — Dept. B, $13,842.44
    042 Sales Returns and Allowances — Dept. B, $282.70
619 Freight Out, $582.80

As of September 1, the accounts receivable had debit balances as follows:

Cornell & Stanford, 211 Main Street, Janesville; $600.
Hanley Bros., 462 Spruce Street, Quincy; $556.80.
Howe's Department Store, 1241 Main Street, Springfield; $591.80.
Mallory & Son, 1622 Division Street, Rockford; $584.64.
Thorp's Department Store, 2531 Virginia Avenue, Bloomington; $717.56.

All charge sales are subject to a discount of 2% if paid within ten days from date of invoice, net 30 days.

The narrative of the September charge sales is given below:

Sept.
1. (Friday) Sale No. 262, Thorp's Department Store; Dept. A, $106.40.
2. Sale No. 263, Mallory & Son; Dept. B, $126.80; express prepaid and added to invoice, $5.75.
5. Sale No. 264, Cornell & Stanford; Dept. A, $65.60, Dept. B, $48.30.
8. Sale No. 265, J. T. Carter, 2518 Blair, Bowling Green; Dept. A, $126.20.
11. Sale No. 266, Hanley Bros.; Dept. A, $96.40; Dept. B, $16.60; freight prepaid and added to invoice, $8.50.
13. Sale No. 267, Thorp's Department Store; Dept. A, $125; Dept. B, $165.30.
15. Sale No. 268, Ladd & Doody Furniture Store, 221 Green Street, Fond du Lac; Dept. B, $64.20; express prepaid and added to invoice, $3.62.
16. Sale No. 269, Howe's Department Store; Dept. A, $59.40; Dept. B, $62.80.
16. Sent J. T. Carter a corrected invoice for Sale No. 265 amounting to $149.60.
20. Sale No. 270, Calhoun's Hi-Fi Shop, 422 Bloomfield Street, Paducah; Dept. A, $175. Received 60-day, 6% interest-bearing note.
22. Sent Ladd & Doody Furniture Store a corrected invoice for Sale No. 268 amounting to $69.52.
27. Sale No. 271, Thorp's Department Store; Dept. A, $42.80; parcel post charges added to invoice, $3.22.
28. Sale No. 272, Mallory & Son; Dept. A, $55; Dept. B, $56.40. Less credit for merchandise returned, Dept. A, $8.60.
30. Sale No. 273, Cornell & Stanford; Dept. B, $134.50; freight prepaid and added to invoice, $5.32.

401

REQUIRED: (1) Using standard ledger paper, open the necessary general ledger accounts and enter the September 1 balances. (2) Using balance-column ledger paper, open the necessary accounts receivable ledger accounts and enter the September 1 balances. (3) Using a sales register similar to the one reproduced on page 332, enter the charge sales for September and post (except for Sale No. 270) directly to the proper customers' accounts. (4) Complete the individual posting from the sales register to the general ledger accounts. (5) Foot, prove the footings, enter the totals, and rule the sales register; complete the summary posting. (6) Foot the general ledger accounts and prove the balance of the accounts receivable account by preparing a schedule of the accounts receivable as of September 30.

Problem 13-A

Warren's Washing Machine Shop uses the installment plan of accounting for sales of washing machines on an installment collection basis. The information at the top of the next page was obtained from the general ledger accounts at the end of the first year of operations.

Installment sales...		$20,250
Cost of goods sold..		$16,200
Total down payments and collections from installment customers.........		$17,500

REQUIRED: **(1)** Determine the amount of the gross profit to be realized on the installment sales. **(2)** Determine the percentage of the gross profit to be realized on the installment sales. **(3)** Determine the amount of the gross profit actually realized during the year. **(4)** Prepare an entry in general journal form to close the installment sales account at the end of the year.

Problem 13-B

The Sangamon Electric Co. distributes electric motors to local dealers on the consignment basis. Shipments to agent dealers on consignment are charged to the consignees at list prices. The dealer's basic compensation is a commission of 30% of the list prices. The dealer is also allowed an additional commission of 2% of list price less basic commission for settlement in full on or before the 5th of the month for merchandise sold during the preceding month.

On October 2, The Sangamon Electric Co. made a shipment of electric motors to Good & Son on consignment. The invoice of shipment amounted to a total of $1,050, computed at list (retail) prices. During October, Good & Son sold all of the electric motors that were consigned to them on the October 2 shipment. On November 5, Good & Son rendered a statement of consignment sales to The Sangamon Electric Co., at the same time remitting the net proceeds which were computed as follows:

Sales..			$1,050.00
Less: Commission, 30%..............................		$315.00	
Additional commission, 2%.......................		14.70	329.70
Net proceeds remitted...			$ 720.30

REQUIRED: **(1)** As the accountant for The Sangamon Electric Co., prepare the entries in general journal form necessary to record (a) the invoice of shipment to Good & Son on October 2 and (b) the sale of consigned merchandise by Good & Son during October, per statement received November 5 with a remittance for $720.30 in the amount of the net proceeds. **(2)** Assuming that you are one of the employees of Good & Son and keep the books, prepare the entries in general journal form necessary to record (a) the invoice of shipment to Good & Son on October 2 and (b) the sale of consigned merchandise by Good & Son during October, per statement rendered November 5 with a check for $720.30, the net proceeds.

Problem 14-A

Neely Brothers Company is in the wholesale hardware business. Stock records are kept of all merchandise handled. The data with respect to Article Z were assembled from their stock records and appeared as shown below:

On hand at beginning of period, 600 units.
First purchase during period, 700 units @ $25.00.
Second purchase during period, 560 units @ $22.00.
Last purchase during period, 580 units @ $26.00.
In stock at end of period, 550 units.

REQUIRED: Assuming that the units in stock at the beginning of the period were assigned a cost of $24 each under the fifo method, or $24.50 each under the lifo method, compute (1) the total cost of the units in stock at the end of the period and (2) the total cost of the units sold during the period under (a) the fifo method and (b) the lifo method of cost assignment.

Problem 14-B

Bessler & Herbst operate a mail-order house as partners. Metered postage is used on parcel post packages. As required, deposits are made for postage under the postal permit system. Postage stamps are purchased for other purposes. All prepaid postage is charged to Postage Stamps, Account No. 164, and periodically the postage used is charged to the following expense accounts:

619 Freight Out (Parcel Post)
624 Advertising Postage Expense
639 General Postage Expense

403

Before adjusting entries had been made on April 30, the postage stamps account had a debit balance of $1,960.

REQUIRED: (1) Open the necessary accounts and enter the balance of the postage stamps account before adjustment. (2) Assuming that (a) during the month of April the postage used on parcel post packages amounted to $654 and on advertising matter, $608, and (b) that on April 30 the unused stamps on hand amounted to $190 and the unused metered postage amounted to $320, make the required adjusting entry in general journal form to record all postage expense for the month. (3) Post. (4) Balance and rule the postage stamps account and bring down the balance as of May 1.

Problem 14-C

Beginning on January 3 of the current year, Edward Crane goes into the distribution of soft drinks. In accounting for insurance, the following accounts are used:

165 Prepaid Insurance
621 Merchandise Insurance Expense
631 Store Equipment Insurance Expense
641 Office Equipment Insurance Expense

The premiums paid for insurance policies are charged to the prepaid insurance account. At the end of each month the expired insurance is charged to the proper expense accounts and credited to Prepaid Insurance. The firm keeps an auxiliary record of insurance in the form of a policy register similar to the one on pages 372 and 373.

Following is a record of the insurance transactions completed during the current year:

Jan. 3. Paid the premiums on the following insurance policies:
No. 42270 dated January 1, Guardian Accident, Fire & Life Insurance Co.; merchandise, $40,000; term, one year; premium, $537.60.
No. 62142 dated January 1, Travelers' Mutual Insurance Company of Iowa; merchandise, $6,000; term, three years; premium, $240.
No. 738240 dated January 1, Bankers' Mutual Insurance Co.; office equipment, $2,000; term, one year; premium, $24.
No. 21464 dated January 1, Baker's Mutual Fire Insurance Co.; store equipment, $2,000; term, one year; premium, $21.60.

Feb. 2. Paid $150 premium on Policy No. 149120 dated February 1, Brokers' Fire Insurance Co.; merchandise, $10,000; term, one year.

Mar. 6. Paid $54 premium on Policy No. 42360 dated March 1, Monroe Mutual Fire Insurance Co.; merchandise, $2,000; term, three years.

Sept. 12. Received a check for $44 from the Brokers' Fire Insurance Co. representing a refund on Policy No. 149120 canceled as of September 1.

Nov. 10. Paid $48 premium on Policy No. 21360 dated November 1, Alton Mutual Fire Insurance Co.; store equipment, $3,000; term, one year.

404

REQUIRED: (1) Journalize the transactions involving the premiums paid on insurance policies purchased during January. Enter these policies on the left page of an insurance policy register form, and extend the portion of the premium on each policy in effect during January to the January column on the right page of the register. Then foot the column in small figures. (2) Prepare a journal entry to record the amount of the insurance expired during January. (3) Continue the work required each month to record any new insurance policies purchased during the month and to record the total insurance expired during the month. In recording the transactions for September, it will also be necessary to prepare a journal entry to record the amount refunded on September 12 on Policy No. 149120. (4) As of December 31, enter the total expired premium and unexpired premium on each policy in the last two columns on the right page of the insurance policy register and foot the columns in small figures. (5) Open an account for Prepaid Insurance, Account No. 165. Post the debit and credit entries affecting the prepaid insurance account from the general journal. After completing the posting to the prepaid insurance account, foot the amount columns, determine the balance, and enter it on the proper side of the account in small figures. Prove your work by comparing the balance of the account with the footing of the unexpired premium column on the right page of the insurance policy register.

Problem 15-A

On February 1 of the current year, Trump & Whitaker begin the wholesale distribution of air-conditioning equipment as partners. In accounting for their long-lived assets, the following accounts are used:

171 Store Equipment
    017 Accumulated Depreciation — Store Equipment
181 Delivery Equipment
    018 Accumulated Depreciation — Delivery Equipment
191 Office Equipment
    019 Accumulated Depreciation — Office Equipment
271 Accounts Payable
625 Depreciation of Store Equipment
626 Depreciation of Delivery Equipment
641 Depreciation of Office Equipment

Transactions involving the purchase of long-lived assets on account are recorded in an invoice register from which they are posted to the proper general ledger accounts. Accounts with suppliers are kept in a subsidiary accounts payable ledger and the posting to these accounts is done directly from the invoices and other documents representing transactions completed with suppliers. The following is a narrative of transactions involving the purchase of long-lived assets during the year ended December 31:

Feb. 2. Invoice No. 248; purchased cabinet file for office use from The Gray & Pease Co.; $200; terms, February 1 — 30 days. Estimated useful life, 10 years. Estimated trade-in value at end of 10 years, $50.

Mar. 6. Invoice No. 262; purchased a small truck for delivery purposes from Monarch Motors, Inc.; $3,200; terms, March 4 — 30 days. Estimated useful life, 4 years. Estimated trade-in value at end of 4 years, $400.

April 8. Invoice No. 279; purchased an office table from The American Furniture Co.; $100; terms, April 7 — 30 days. Estimated useful life, 20 years. No salvage value.

July 12. Invoice No. 304; purchased showcases from A. G. Smith Co.; $450; terms, July, 11 — 2/10, n/30. Estimated useful life, 15 years. No salvage value.

Aug. 18. Invoice No. 321; purchased used double-pedestal desk for use in storeroom from Superior Store Equipment Co.; $140; terms, August 16 — 2/10, n/30. Estimated useful life, 20 years. No salvage value.

Sept. 19. Invoice No. 342; purchased used Olivetti Underwood typewriter, No. S5738582-11, from Olivetti Underwood Corporation; $125; terms, September 18 — 30 days. Estimated useful life, 5 years. Estimated trade-in value at end of 5 years, $25.

REQUIRED: (1) Using an invoice register similar to the one reproduced on page 310, record the foregoing transactions. (2) Foot the amount columns, prove the footings, enter the totals, and rule the invoice register. (3) Determine the annual rate of depreciation (straight-line method) applicable to each of the long-lived assets purchased, compute the amount of the depreciation accumulated during the current year ended December 31, and prepare an entry in general journal form to record the depreciation.

405

(4) Assume that on January 5, after recording twenty-two months' depreciation, the delivery truck purchased on March 6 was traded in for a new truck, with $1,600 in cash being paid. Prepare a general journal entry to record the transaction. (No gain or loss to be recognized.)

Problem 15-B

Stonebraker Enterprises, Inc., owns a gravel pit that had been purchased a few years before for $40,000. The accountant has been calculating depletion on the basis of 8 cents for every cubic yard of gravel excavated. At the beginning of the current year the balance of the accumulated depletion account was $3,680. During the first four months of this year 30,000 cubic yards of gravel were excavated, and on May 2 the pit was sold for $38,600 cash.

REQUIRED: Prepare entries in general journal form, to record **(1)** the depletion accumulated for the first four months of the year, and **(2)** the sale of the gravel pit, recognizing any gain or loss on the sale.

406

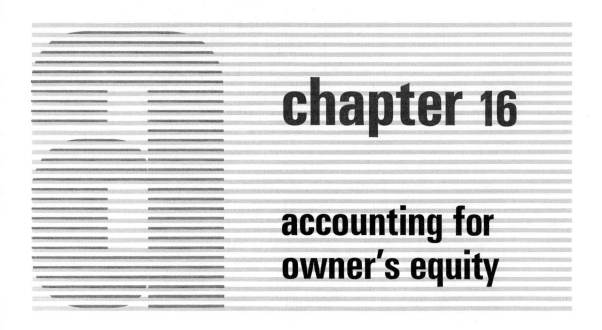

chapter 16

accounting for owner's equity

The assets of a business are subject to the claims of its creditors and of its owners. The claims of the creditors are known as the liabilities of a business. The dollar amount of the difference between the assets and the liabilities of a business is the amount of the equity of the owner or owners.

The single proprietorship

When there is only one owner, the amount of his interest in the business is called owner's equity. At one time, the term *proprietorship* was widely used to indicate owner's equity. Sometimes the designations *net worth* or *capital* are used. The word "Capital" commonly follows the name of the owner as a part of the title of the account that shows the amount of the owner's equity element of the business.

In small merchandising enterprises and in personal service enterprises the single proprietorship form of organization predominates. The medical and dental professions, for example, are composed largely of individuals who are engaged in practice as sole owners. One reason for the popularity of the single proprietorship form of operation is that it is easily organized, involving no formal or legal agreement with others as to owner-ship or conduct. Anyone may engage in a lawful enterprise merely by complying with state and local laws.

Organization of a single proprietorship

When engaging in an enterprise as a sole owner, an individual decides the amount that he will invest and the nature of the property that he will invest. The original investment may consist of cash only, or of cash and any other property that he owns, such as merchandise, office equipment, store equipment, or delivery equipment. The property invested usually is segregated from any other property that may be owned by the proprietor. An individual may engage in more than one enterprise and may operate each enterprise separately as a single proprietorship. In such cases, it may be desirable to keep separate records of the activities of each enterprise.

In comparison with other forms of business organization, the single proprietorship offers certain advantages, such as:

    (a) Simplicity of organization.
    (b) Freedom of initiative and industry.
    (c) Fewer government reports required.
    (d) Strong incentive to individual enterprise.

The single proprietorship form of organization has some disadvantages, of which the following are the most significant:

    (a) The amount of available capital may be limited.
    (b) The amount of available credit may be restricted.
    (c) The proprietor is solely responsible for all debts incurred.

Accounting procedure

In general, the accounting procedure in recording the ordinary oper-ating transactions of an enterprise is not affected by the type of ownership. Whether an enterprise is operated as a single proprietorship by an indi-vidual, as a partnership by two or more partners, or as a corporation by stockholders through directors and officers has little bearing on the ac-counting procedure in recording the routine transactions in connection with the ordinary operations of the business. However, the owner's equity accounts required depend largely upon the type of ownership.

Owner's Equity Accounts. There are two types of owner's equity ac-counts: **(1)** permanent owner's equity accounts and **(2)** temporary owner's equity accounts.

In a single proprietorship, the owner's capital account is the only permanent owner's equity account. The account is usually given the name of the owner of the enterprise followed by "Capital" or "Proprietor."

The temporary owner's equity accounts are those in which increases and decreases in owner's equity arising from the transactions completed during an accounting period are recorded. The owner's drawing or personal account and all of the revenue and expense accounts are temporary owner's equity accounts. At the end of each year, it is customary to close the temporary revenue and expense accounts by transferring their balances to one or more summary accounts. In a service type of enterprise, the only summary account kept may be Expense and Revenue Summary. In a merchandising type of enterprise, there also may be a Cost of Goods Sold account. In the closing process, this latter account is debited for (1) the amount of the merchandise inventory at beginning of the year and (2) the amount of the purchases for the year; it is credited for (1) the amount of purchases returns and allowances for the year, (2) the amount of purchase discounts for the year, and (3) the amount of the merchandise inventory at end of the year. The balance of the account, representing the cost of goods sold during the year, is in turn transferred to the debit of Expense and Revenue Summary. The balances of all expense and revenue accounts are also transferred to Expense and Revenue Summary whose balance then represents the net income or net loss for the year. The cost of goods **409** sold account and the expense and revenue summary account are the most temporary of all accounts; they are used only at the end of the year in summarizing the revenue and expense accounts.

Opening Entries. An individual may invest cash and other property in a single proprietorship enterprise. Certain liabilities may attach to the property invested. If the investment consists solely of cash, the opening entry will involve a debit to Cash or the bank account and a credit to the owner's capital account for the amount invested.

If cash and other property, such as office equipment, store equipment, or other equipment, are invested, the opening entry will involve a debit to Cash or the bank account for the amount of cash invested, debits to appropriate equipment accounts for the amounts of the other property items invested, and a credit to the owner's capital account for the total amount of the investment.

If, at the time of organizing an enterprise, there are any liabilities, such as accounts payable, notes payable, or mortgages payable applicable to the property invested, appropriate accounts representing the liabilities should be credited and the owner's capital account should be credited only for the excess of the amount of the assets invested over the total amount of the liabilities.

EXAMPLE: J. D. McDonough decides to engage in a merchandising business and invests cash amounting to $2,500, office equipment amounting to $900, store equipment amounting to $800, and delivery equipment amounting to $1,500. He owes $300 on the office equipment, and there is a mortgage amounting to $600 on the delivery equipment. The opening entry in general journal form to record McDonough's investment is as follows:

Bank[1]...	2,500.00	
Office Equipment..	900.00	
Store Equipment..	800.00	
Delivery Equipment.....................................	1,500.00	
Accounts Payable....................................		300.00
Mortgages Payable...................................		600.00
J. D. McDonough, Capital............................		4,800.00
Investment in business.		

Some small business enterprises are started and operated for a time with very scanty records. No journals or ledgers are used. The record of cash receipts and disbursements is kept on check stubs. The amounts of accounts receivable and payable can be found only by consulting files of uncollected charge-sale slips and unpaid bills. At the end of a period, various calculations relating to inventory, bad debts, expired insurance, depreciation, and accruals are made in informal fashion and the several bits of information are pieced together to prepare an income statement and a balance sheet. These statements are often incorrect. Conditions and facts may have been overlooked. Business papers may have been lost. The absence of double-entry records means that one method of checking the mathematical accuracy of the figures assembled is not available.

While such informal accounting practices may barely suffice when the enterprise is small and transactions are few, the time will come when a formal accounting system is needed. To get this started, it is necessary to prepare a balance sheet from the information at hand and to use this as the basis for an opening journal entry to record the assets, liabilities, and owner's equity of the enterprise.

For example, assume that P. R. Munn has been operating a business without any formal, double-entry accounting records. After several months he decides that proper records are necessary. With the help of an accountant, he constructs the balance sheet reproduced on page 411 for his business. The information supplied by the balance sheet is used in preparing the general journal entry shown below the statement.

---

[1]The bank account is debited for the amount of cash invested for the reason that it is the usual custom of business firms to deposit all cash receipts in the bank and to make all disbursements by check. Under this plan a cash account need not be kept in the general ledger. Instead, all receipts may be debited to the bank account and all disbursements may be credited to the bank account. It should be understood, however, that a cash account and one or more bank accounts may be kept in the general ledger, if desired.

P. R. MUNN
Balance Sheet
December 31, 1972

Assets			Liabilities		
Cash..............		$ 1,750.00	Notes payable........	$1,500.00	
Accounts receivable....	$2,800.00		Accounts payable......	2,200.00	
Less allow. for bad			Total liabilities........		$ 3,700.00
debts...........	300.00	2,500.00			
Mdse. inventory.......		6,670.00	Owner's Equity		
Store equipment.......	$4,000.00				
Less accumulated de-			P. R. Munn, capital.....		10,820.00
preciation........	400.00	3,600.00	Total liabilities and		
Total assets..........		$14,520.00	owner's equity.......		$14,520.00

Jan 1. Bank..	1,750.00	
Accounts Receivable.............................	2,800.00	
Merchandise Inventory...........................	6,670.00	
Store Equipment................................	4,000.00	
Notes Payable...............................		1,500.00
Accounts Payable.............................		2,200.00
Allowance for Bad Debts.......................		300.00
Accumulated Depreciation — Store Equipment......		400.00
P. R. Munn, Capital...........................		10,820.00
Opening a set of books.		

After the necessary accounts in the general ledger have been opened,
the debits and the credits of the opening journal entry should be posted in
the usual manner. As a result of such posting each asset account is debited
and each liability account is credited for the respective amounts shown in
the balance sheet. These amounts represent the balances of the accounts.
The accounts for allowances for bad debts and accumulated depreciation
are credited for their balances. Mr. Munn's capital account is credited
for his equity in the business. The balances of the accounts with
customers in the accounts receivable ledger may be entered directly from
a schedule of accounts receivable. The balances of the accounts with
creditors in the accounts payable ledger may be entered directly from a
schedule of accounts payable.

Proprietary Transactions Completed During the Accounting Period.
Certain types of transactions may be referred to as proprietary transactions because they affect either the owner's drawing account or his
capital account. The following are typical proprietary transactions:

(a) Periodic withdrawals of cash for personal use of owner.
(b) Payment of owner's personal or family bills with business cash.
(c) Withdrawal of cash or other assets by the owner intended as a partial
liquidation of the business.
(d) Investment of cash or other assets by owner intended as a permanent increase in assets and owner's equity.

411

Cash withdrawn periodically by the owner for personal use is usually charged to his drawing or personal account on the assumption that such amounts represent withdrawals in anticipation of income. Such withdrawals are sometimes regarded as salary or compensation for personal services rendered; however, they represent charges to the owner's drawing or personal account and should not be treated as an operating expense of the enterprise.

The payment of personal or family bills or accounts with business funds should be recorded as a withdrawal of cash by the owner. It is quite common for an individual engaged in a business or professional enterprise as a sole owner to pay all personal and family or household bills by issuing checks against the same bank account as that used for business expenditures of the enterprise. However, care should be used in recording all checks issued, and those representing personal or family expenditures should be charged to the owner's drawing or personal account. Those representing business expenditures should be charged to the proper expense, asset, or liability accounts.

An owner may, at any time, withdraw a portion of the cash or other assets invested in his business, or he may make additional investments in the business in the form of cash or other property. Withdrawals that are considered to be decreases in the permanent invested capital should be charged to his capital account; his investments in the business should be credited to his capital account.

Disposition of the Balance of the Expense and Revenue Summary Account at End of Accounting Period. It is customary to close the temporary owner's equity accounts at the end of each year. As the temporary accounts are closed, their balances usually are transferred to an account entitled Expense and Revenue Summary. The difference between the footings of this summary account represents the amount of the net income or the net loss for the year. If the summary account has a credit balance, it represents net income; if the account has a debit balance, it represents net loss. The simplest way to dispose of the balance of the expense and revenue summary account at the end of the accounting period is to transfer its balance to the owner's capital account by means of a journal entry. If the expense and revenue summary account has a credit balance, the journal entry will involve a debit to Expense and Revenue Summary and a credit to the owner's capital account for the amount of the net income. If the summary account has a debit balance, the journal entry will involve a debit to the owner's capital account and a credit to Expense and Revenue Summary for the amount of the net loss.

Closing the Owner's Drawing Account. The owner's drawing account usually is closed at the end of each year by transferring its balance to the owner's capital account. The drawing account usually has a debit balance, and it may be closed by means of a journal entry debiting the owner's capital account and crediting the drawing account for the amount of its balance.

After transferring the balances of the expense and revenue summary account and the owner's drawing account to the owner's capital account, the balance of the owner's capital account represents the owner's equity in the enterprise at the end of the year.

Owner's Equity Section of the Balance Sheet. The method of exhibiting the equity of the owner of the business in the balance sheet is shown on pages 43, 124, and 257. There may be some variation in the account titles used by different enterprises. However, the final results should be the same since the balance sheet is an exhibit of the accounting elements: **(1)** the assets, **(2)** the liabilities, and **(3)** the owner's equity. The owner's equity section of the balance sheet should be arranged to show the owner's equity in the business at the beginning of the accounting period, the net increase or the net decrease in his equity during the period, and his equity in the business at the end of the period.

413

Report No. 16-1

Complete Report No. 16-1 in the workbook and submit your working papers to the instructor for approval. Then continue with the following study assignment until Report No. 16-2 is required.

The partnership

When two or more individuals engage in an enterprise as co-owners, the organization is known as a partnership. This form of organization is prevalent in practically all types of enterprises. However, it is more popular among personal service enterprises than among merchandising enterprises. For example, the partnership form of organization is quite common in the legal and public accounting professions.

Organization of a partnership

The Uniform Partnership Act states that "a partnership is an association of two or more persons who carry on, as co-owners, a business for profit." The partners may, by agreement, unite their capital, labor, skill, or experience in the conduct of a business for their mutual benefit. While under certain circumstances a partnership may be formed by means of an oral or an implied agreement, it is desirable that a partnership agreement be evidenced by a written contract. A written agreement containing the various provisions under which a partnership is to operate is known as a *partnership agreement.* There is no standard form of partnership agreement, but there are certain provisions that are uniformly desirable, such as the following:

414

(a) Date of agreement.
(b) Names of the partners.
(c) Kind of business to be conducted.
(d) Length of time the partnership is to run.
(e) Name and location of the business.
(f) Investment of each partner.
(g) Basis on which profits or losses are to be shared by the partners.
(h) Limitation of partners' rights and activities.
(i) Salary allowances to partners.
(j) Division of assets upon dissolution of the partnership.
(k) Signatures of the partners.

The conventional form of partnership agreement is reproduced on page 415.

In comparison with the single proprietorship form of organization, the partnership form offers certain advantages, such as:

(a) The ability and the experience of the partners are combined in one enterprise.
(b) More capital may be raised because the resources of the partners are combined.
(c) Credit may be improved because each general partner is personally liable for partnership debts.

PARTNERSHIP AGREEMENT

THIS CONTRACT, made and entered into on the first day of July, 19--, by and between T. L. Holling of East St. Louis, Illinois, and A. G. Renz of the same city and state.

WITNESSETH: That the said parties have this day formed a partnership for the purpose of engaging in and conducting a wholesale paint and varnish business in the city of East St. Louis under the following stipulations, which are a part of this contract:

FIRST: The said partnership is to continue for a term of twenty-five years from July 1, 19--.

SECOND: The business is to be conducted under the firm name of Holling & Renz, at 1111 Olive St., East St. Louis, Illinois.

THIRD: The investments are as follows: T. L. Holling, cash, $35,000; A. G. Renz, cash, $35,000. These invested assets are partnership property in which the equity of each partner is the same.

FOURTH: Each partner is to devote his entire time and attention to the business and to engage in no other business enterprise without the written consent of the other partner.

FIFTH: During the operation of this partnership, neither partner is to become surety or bondsman for anyone without the written consent of the other partner.

SIXTH: Each partner is to receive a salary of $12,000 a year, payable $500 in cash on the fifteenth day and last business day of each month. At the end of each annual fiscal period, the net income or the net loss shown by the income statement, after the salaries of the two partners have been allowed, is to be shared as follows: T. L. Holling, 50 percent; A. G. Renz, 50 percent.

SEVENTH: Neither partner is to withdraw assets in excess of his salary, any part of the assets invested, or assets in anticipation of net income to be earned, without the written consent of the other partner.

EIGHTH: In the case of the death or the legal disability of either partner, the other partner is to continue the operations of the business until the close of the annual fiscal period on the following June 30. At that time the continuing partner is to be given an option to buy the interest of the deceased or incapacitated partner at not more than 10 percent above the value of the deceased or incapacitated partner's proprietary interest as shown by the balance of his capital account after the books are closed on June 30. It is agreed that this purchase price is to be paid one half in cash and the balance in four equal installments payable quarterly.

NINTH: At the conclusion of this contract, unless it is mutually agreed to continue the operation of the business under a new contract, the assets of the partnership, after the liabilities are paid, are to be divided in proportion to the net credit to each partner's capital account on that date.

IN WITNESS WHEREOF, the parties aforesaid have hereunto set their hands and affixed their seals on the day and year above written.

T. L. Holling   (Seal)

A. G. Renz   (Seal)

Partnership Agreement

There are some disadvantages that are peculiar to the partnership form of organization, including the following:

(a) Each partner is individually liable for all of the debts of the partnership. The liability of each partner is not limited to a pro rata share of the partnership debts; he is personally liable for all of the debts of the business to the same extent as if he were the sole owner. Under the laws of some states, certain partners may limit their liability. At least one partner, however, must be a general partner who is responsible for all of the debts of the partnership.

(b) A partner cannot transfer his interest in the partnership without the consent of the other partners.

(c) Termination of the partnership agreement, bankruptcy of the firm, or death of one of the partners dissolves the partnership.

Accounting procedure

In accounting for the operations of a partnership, it is necessary to keep a separate capital account for each partner. It is also customary to keep a separate drawing or personal account for each partner. While no new principles are involved in keeping these accounts, care should be used in preparing the opening entry and in recording any transactions thereafter that affect the respective interests of the partners.

Opening Entries. When two or more individuals engage in an enterprise as partners, each may invest cash and other property. Certain liabilities may be assumed by the partnership, such as accounts payable, notes payable, and mortgages payable. In opening the books for a partnership, it is customary to prepare a separate journal entry to record the investment of each partner. The proper asset accounts should be debited for the amounts invested, the proper liability accounts should be credited for the amounts of obligations assumed, and each partner's capital account should be credited for his equity in the assets. The opening entries for Holling & Renz based on the partnership agreement reproduced on page 415 may be made in general journal form as follows:

Bank..	35,000.00	
T. L. Holling, Capital............................		35,000.00
T. L. Holling invested $35,000 in cash.		
Bank..	35,000.00	
A. G. Renz, Capital............................		35,000.00
A. G. Renz invested $35,000 in cash.		

If, instead of investing $35,000 in cash only, Holling were to invest office equipment valued at $600 on which he owes $200, delivery equipment valued at $1,900 on which he owes $400 represented by a mortgage, and $33,100 in cash, the proper opening entry in general journal form to record his investment should be as follows:

Bank...	33,100.00	
Office Equipment..	600.00	
Delivery Equipment.......................................	1,900.00	
Accounts Payable......................................		200.00
Mortage Payable.......................................		400.00
T. L. Holling, Capital.................................		35,000.00
T. L. Holling's investment in partnership.		

Sometimes two or more individuals who have been engaged in business as sole owners form a partnership for the purpose of combining their businesses. Their respective balance sheets may be the basis for the opening entries to record the investments of such partners. For example, on April 1, A. G. Dale and J. P. Jones form a partnership under the firm name of Dale and Jones to continue the conduct of the businesses which they have been operating as sole owners. They agree to invest the assets shown in their respective balance sheets. It is also agreed that the partnership shall assume the liabilities shown in their respective balance sheets. Each partner is to receive credit for his equity in the assets invested by him, and the profits and losses are to be shared on the basis of Dale, two fifths, and Jones, three fifths. In case of dissolution, the assets are to be distributed between the partners in the ratio of their capital interests at the time of dissolution. The balance sheets reproduced on page 418 were made a part of the partnership agreement.

Since the partnership is taking over the long-lived assets at their undepreciated cost, the cost of such property should be adjusted for prior accumulated depreciation up to the date of the transfer. Thus, the cost of the store equipment contributed by Dale should be adjusted for the depreciation accumulated prior to the organization of the partnership. The adjusted value is the difference between the cost of $1,200 and the accumulated depreciation of $319, or $881. Likewise, the cost of the office equipment and the store equipment contributed by Jones should be adjusted for the depreciation accumulated prior to the organization of the partnership. The adjusted value of the office equipment is $1,050 and of the store equipment is $1,100.

Since it cannot be determined now which of the accounts receivable may later prove to be uncollectible in whole or in part, the amount of the accounts receivable cannot be adjusted for the accumulated allowance for bad debts. It is, therefore, necessary to record the full amount of the accounts receivable as a debit and the amount of the allowance for bad debts as a credit in journalizing each partner's investment in the books of the partnership.

The proper entries in general journal form to record the partners' investments are shown under the statements on the next page.

A. G. DALE
Balance Sheet
March 31, 1972

Assets			Liabilities		
Cash..............		$ 2,033.00	Notes payable........	$1,000.00	
Accounts receivable....	$1,771.32		Accounts payable......	3,231.60	
Less allow. for bad			Total liabilities........		$ 4,231.60
debts...........	137.52	1,633.80			
Mdse. inventory.......		7,875.86	**Owner's Equity**		
Store equipment.......	$1,200.00				
Less accumulated de-			A. G. Dale, capital.....		8,192.06
preciation........	319.00	881.00			
			Total liabilities and		
Total assets..........		$12,423.66	owner's equity.......		$12,423.66

J. P. JONES
Balance Sheet
March 31, 1972

Assets			Liabilities		
Cash..............		$ 1,136.30	Notes payable........	$2,000.00	
Accounts receivable....	$1,700.00		Accounts payable......	4,243.00	
Less allow. for bad			Total liabilities........		$ 6,243.00
debts...........	200.00	1,500.00			
Mdse. inventory.......		9,517.22	**Owner's Equity**		
Supplies..............		91.90	J. P. Jones, capital.....		8,152.42
Office equipment......	$1,400.00				
Less accumulated de-					
preciation	350.00	1,050.00			
Store equipment.......	$1,500.00				
Less accumulated de-					
preciation........	400.00	1,100.00			
			Total liabilities and		
Total assets..........		$14,395.42	owner's equity.......		$14,395.42

418

April 1.	Bank..	2,033.00	
	Accounts Receivable..............................	1,771.32	
	Merchandise Inventory............................	7,875.86	
	Store Equipment.................................	881.00	
	Notes Payable.................................		1,000.00
	Accounts Payable..............................		3,231.60
	Allowance for Bad Debts		137.52
	A. G. Dale, Capital............................		8,192.06
	A. G. Dale's investment in partnership.		
1.	Bank..	1,136.30	
	Accounts Receivable..............................	1,700.00	
	Merchandise Inventory............................	9,517.22	
	Supplies...	91.90	
	Office Equipment.................................	1,050.00	
	Store Equipment.................................	1,100.00	
	Notes Payable.................................		2,000.00
	Accounts Payable..............................		4,243.00
	Allowance for Bad Debts........................		200.00
	J. P. Jones, Capital............................		8,152.42
	J. P. Jones' investment in partnership.		

Had the long-lived assets of Dale and Jones been taken over by the partnership at other than their undepreciated cost, the assets should be recorded in the books of the partnership at the value agreed upon. For example, if it had been agreed that the store equipment invested by Dale was to be valued at $1,000 instead of its undepreciated cost, Store Equipment should be debited for $1,000 instead of $881, and Dale's capital account should be credited for $8,311.06 instead of $8,192.06. Thus, the undepreciated cost of the store equipment as shown in Dale's balance sheet of March 31 would be ignored and the store equipment would be recorded on the books of the partnership at the value agreed upon by the partners. Such agreed value represents the cost of the store equipment to the partnership.

It will be observed that the ratio of the partners' investments in the partnership ($8,192.06 to $8,152.42) is not exactly the same as their profit-and-loss-sharing ratio (two fifths to three fifths). The basis on which profits and losses are to be shared is a matter of agreement between the partners, and it is not necessarily the same as their investment ratio. It should be recognized that there are factors other than the assets invested that may enter into a profit-and-loss-sharing agreement. For example, one partner may contribute most of the assets but may render no services, while the other partner may contribute less in assets but may devote his full time to the activities of the partnership.

419

Admitting a New Partner. A new partner may be admitted to a partnership by agreement among the existing partners. For example, Dale and Jones may admit W. E. Carey as a partner and agree to share profits and losses on the basis of their capital interests. If his investment consisted of cash only, the proper entry to admit him to the partnership would involve a debit to the bank account and a credit to his capital account for the amount invested. If Carey has been operating a business of his own as a sole owner and his business is taken over by the partnership, his balance sheet will serve as a basis for preparing the opening entry. Assume that, as of July 1, Carey was admitted to the partnership. The assets listed in his balance sheet are taken over, his liabilities are assumed, and he is given credit for his equity in the assets of his business. His balance sheet is shown at the top of page 420.

The proper entry in general journal form to admit Carey as a partner is shown beneath the balance sheet on page 420.

The admission of a new partner calls for the dissolution of the old partnership and the creation of a new partnership. A new partnership agreement that includes all of the necessary provisions should be drawn.

W. E. CAREY
Balance Sheet
June 30, 1972

Assets			Liabilities		
Cash.................		$ 1,917.82	Notes payable........	$2,900.00	
Accounts receivable....	$4,580.00		Accounts payable......	2,419.65	
Less allow. for bad			Total liabilities........		$ 5,319.65
debts...........	345.43	4,234.57			
Mdse. inventory.......		8,747.25	Owner's Equity		
			W. E. Carey, capital...		9,579.99
			Total liabilities and		
Total assets..........		$14,899.64	owner's equity.......		$14,899.64

July 1. Bank...		1,917.82	
Accounts Receivable.............................		4,580.00	
Merchandise Inventory...........................		8,747.25	
Notes Payable.................................			2,900.00
Accounts Payable..............................			2,419.65
Allowance for Bad Debts.......................			345.43
W. E. Carey, Capital...........................			9,579.99
W. E. Carey admitted to partnership.			

420   Goodwill. Some business organizations consistently are able to earn profits that are very large in relation to the amount of the recorded assets. This unique earning power may be due to exceptional management, good location, or one or more of several other factors. When such a condition exists, the business is said to possess *goodwill.* Because of the fact that goodwill is difficult to measure and may not prove to be permanent, accountants do not favor its formal recognition as an asset unless it has been purchased.

For example, suppose that Dale and Jones purchased the business of W. E. Carey for $13,082.18 cash, acquiring all of his business assets except cash and assuming his business liabilities. If the undepreciated cost ($12,981.82; that is, $4,234.57 plus $8,747.25) of the assets purchased from Carey was considered to be their fair value, Dale and Jones paid $5,420.01 more for the business than the net value of the assets acquired. This amount may be considered to be the price paid for the goodwill of Carey's business. The transaction may be recorded as follows:

July 1. Accounts Receivable............................		4,580.00	
Merchandise Inventory...........................		8,747.25	
Goodwill..		5,420.01	
Notes Payable.................................			2,900.00
Accounts Payable..............................			2,419.65
Allowance for Bad Debts.......................			345.43
Bank...			13,082.18
Purchased W. E. Carey's business.			

It is permissible to record goodwill if a new partner is taken into a firm and is allowed a capital interest in excess of the net assets he invests. For example, suppose that, instead of purchasing Carey's business, Dale and Jones had agreed to take him into the firm as a partner and to give him a capital interest of $15,000 for his business (including his business cash). Carey's investment may be recorded as follows:

July 1. Bank...	1,917.82	
Accounts Receivable.............................	4,580.00	
Merchandise Inventory...........................	8,747.25	
Goodwill..	5,420.01	
Notes Payable................................		2,900.00
Accounts Payable.............................		2,419.65
Allowance for Bad Debts......................		345.43
W. E. Carey, Capital.........................		15,000.00
W. E. Carey admitted to partnership.		

Goodwill is considered to be an *intangible asset*. When goodwill is recorded in the accounts, it is usually reported in the balance sheet as the last item in the asset section.

Compensation of Partners. The compensation of partners (other than their shares of profits) may be in the nature of salaries, royalties, commissions, bonuses, or other compensation. The amount of each partner's compensation and the method of accounting for it should be stated in the partnership agreement. For example, in the partnership agreement shown on page 415, it is stated that each partner is to receive a salary of $1,000 a month. When all partners receive the same salaries and when profits and losses are shared equally, it is immaterial whether the salaries are treated as an expense of the partnership or as withdrawals of anticipated profits. Under the federal income tax law, salaries or other compensation paid to partners for services rendered may not be claimed as a deduction from gross income in the income tax information return of the partnership unless such salaries are guaranteed. In this latter event, the amounts may be treated as deductions. (The partners, of course, must report such income in their individual returns.) However, apart from income tax considerations, the partnership agreement may provide that partners' salaries are to be treated as operating expenses in computing the net income or the net loss to be shared by the partners.

If partners' salaries are not treated as an expense of the partnership, it is not necessary to keep a salary account for each partner. Thus, amounts withdrawn by the partners as compensation for services may simply be charged to their respective drawing accounts. If partners' salaries are treated as operating expenses, it is usually advisable to keep a separate salary account for each partner. For example, the salaries specified in the partnership agreement between T. L. Holling and A. G. Renz are to be treated as

421

operating expenses. If the salaries are paid regularly, such as monthly or semimonthly, it will be necessary only to debit each partner's salary account and to credit the bank account. Instead of paying partners' salaries regularly in cash, they may be credited to the partners' drawing accounts. The partners may then draw against such salaries at will. Under this plan the proper entry to record each partner's salary on each payday is to debit his salary account and to credit his drawing account for the proper amount.

Allocation of Partnership Profits and Losses. The partnership agreement should specify the basis on which profits and losses are to be shared by the partners. In the absence of any agreement between the partners, profits and losses must be shared equally regardless of the ratio of the partners' investments. If the partnership agreement specifies how profits are to be shared, but does not specify how losses are to be shared, the losses must be shared on the same basis as that indicated for the profits.

After closing the temporary accounts into Expense and Revenue Summary at the end of the accounting period, the balance of the summary account represents either net income or net loss. If the account has a credit balance, it represents net income; if the account has a debit balance, it represents net loss.

The balance of the expense and revenue summary account should be allocated in accordance with the partnership agreement. If the account has a credit balance, the entry to close the account requires a debit to Expense and Revenue Summary and credits to either the partners' drawing or capital accounts for the proper share of the net income in each case. Because the partners may formally or informally agree that they will not withdraw any of their permanent investments without mutual consent, it may be preferable to credit their drawing accounts with their respective shares of net income. Any credit balances in partners' drawing or personal accounts can then be reduced by withdrawals without restriction.

Dissolution of a Partnership. Dissolution of a partnership may be brought about through bankruptcy or the death of one of the partners. No partner can retire from the partnership before its termination without the consent of the remaining partners. To do so would constitute a violation of the partnership agreement and would make the retiring partner liable to the remaining partners for any loss resulting from his retirement.

By agreement, a partner may retire and be permitted to withdraw assets equal to, greater than, or less than the amount of his capital interest in the partnership. The book value of a partner's interest is shown by the credit balance of his capital account after all profits or losses have been allocated in accordance with the agreement and the books are closed. Should the retiring partner withdraw cash or other assets equal to the credit balance of his capital account, the transaction will have no effect upon the capital of the remaining partners.

Suppose, for example, that sometime after W. E. Carey had been taken into the partnership of Dale and Jones, he expressed a desire to retire and his partners agreed to his withdrawal of cash equal to the amount of his equity in the assets of the partnership. After closing the temporary owner's equity accounts into Expense and Revenue Summary, and after allocating the net income and closing the partners' drawing accounts, assume that the partners' capital accounts had credit balances as follows:

A. G. Dale	$ 7,000.00
J. P. Jones	9,000.00
W. E. Carey	12,000.00

This indicates that the book value of Carey's interest in the partnership amounts to $12,000. If this amount is withdrawn in cash, the entry in general journal form to record the transaction on the books of the partnership is as follows:

W. E. Carey, Capital	12,000.00	
Bank		12,000.00
W. E. Carey retired, withdrawing $12,000 in settlement of his equity.		

While the transaction involves a decrease in the asset Cash with a corresponding decrease in the total capital of the partnership, it does not affect the equity of the remaining partners. Dale still has an equity of $7,000 and Jones an equity of $9,000 in the partnership assets.

If a retiring partner agrees to withdraw less than the book value of his interest in the partnership, the effect of the transaction will be to increase the capital accounts of the remaining partners. To record such a transaction it is necessary to debit the retiring partner's account for the amount of its credit balance, to credit the assets withdrawn, and to credit the difference to the capital accounts of the remaining partners.

Thus, if Carey had agreed to withdraw only $10,000 in settlement of his interest in the partnership, the transaction should be recorded in the books of the partnership as follows:

W. E. Carey, Capital	12,000.00	
Bank		10,000.00
A. G. Dale, Capital		875.00
J. P. Jones, Capital		1,125.00
W. E. Carey retired, withdrawing $10,000 in settlement of his equity.		

The difference between Carey's equity in the assets of the partnership and the amount of cash withdrawn is $2,000. This difference is divided between the remaining partners on the basis stipulated in the partnership agreement, the ratio of their capital interests after allocating net income and closing their drawing accounts. Thus, Dale is credited for 7/16 of $2,000, or $875, while Jones is credited for 9/16 of $2,000, or $1,125.

If a partner is permitted to withdraw more than the book value of his interest in the partnership, the effect of the transaction will be to decrease the capital accounts of the remaining partners. Thus, if Dale and Jones had agreed to Carey's withdrawal of $14,000 in settlement of his interest in the partnership, the transaction should be recorded in the books of the partnership as follows:

W. E. Carey, Capital	12,000.00	
A. G. Dale, Capital	875.00	
J. P. Jones, Capital	1,125.00	
Bank		14,000.00
W. E. Carey retired, withdrawing $14,000 in settlement of his equity.		

The excess of the amount of cash withdrawn over Carey's equity in the partnership is divided between the remaining partners on the basis stipulated in the partnership agreement. Thus, Dale is debited for 7/16 of $2,000, or $875, while Jones is debited for 9/16 of $2,000, or $1,125.

When a partner retires from the business his interest may be purchased by one or more of the remaining partners or by an outside party. If he sells his interest to one of the remaining partners, his equity is merely transferred to the other partner. Thus, if instead of withdrawing cash in settlement of his equity in the partnership, Carey sells his interest to Dale, the entry to record the transaction on the books of the partnership is as follows:

W. E. Carey, Capital	12,000.00	
A. G. Dale, Capital		12,000.00
A. G. Dale purchased W. E. Carey's interest in the partnership.		

The amount paid to Carey by Dale is a personal transaction not recorded on the books of the partnership and is immaterial to the firm. Any gain or loss resulting from the transaction is a personal gain or loss of the withdrawing partner and not of the firm. Thus, a general journal entry should be made debiting Carey's capital account and crediting Dale's capital account for $12,000.

Owners' Equity Section of a Partnership Balance Sheet. The method of showing the equity of the partners in the balance sheet of a partnership is similar to that of a single proprietorship, except that the equity of each partner should be shown separately. Following is an illustration of the owners' equity section of a balance sheet for a partnership whose accounts are kept on a calendar year basis.

Owners' Equity

P. W. Weston
Capital, January 1, 1972............ $46,790.15
Net income
(½ of $26,543.80)..... $13,271.90
Less withdrawals....... 10,426.20   2,845.70

Capital, December 31, 1972.......... $49,635.85

A. D. Smithfield
Capital, January 1, 1972............ $39,671.60
Net income
(½ of $26,543.80)..... $13,271.90
Less withdrawals....... 12,134.80   1,137.10

Capital, December 31, 1972..........   40,808.70

Total owners' equity.................. $90,444.55

Report No. 16-2

Complete Report No. 16-2 in the workbook and submit your working papers to the instructor for approval. Then continue with the following study assignment until Report No. 16-3 is required.

The corporation

A private corporation is an artificial person created by law for a specific purpose. A corporation differs from a single proprietorship or a partnership with respect to organization, ownership, and distribution of net income or net loss.

In contrast to a partnership, the corporate form of organization has several advantages. The most important of these are that:

(a) Except in very unusual cases, the owners (stockholders) have no personal liability for the debts of the corporation.

(b) The shares of ownership are easily transferred from one person to another.

(c) The corporation has a perpetual life that is independent of the lives of its owners.

The outstanding disadvantage of the corporate form of organization is that the net income of a corporation is taxed and any cash dividends resulting from that income are also taxable to the stockholders.

Organization of a corporation

426

In order to incorporate an enterprise, a charter must be obtained from the state in which the corporation is to be formed. The persons who file articles of incorporation are known as the *incorporators.* Such persons must be competent to contract, some or all of them must be citizens of the state in which the articles are filed, and usually each incorporator is required to be a subscriber for one or more shares of the capital stock. All of the incorporators must sign the articles.

The procedure in incorporating an enterprise must conform to the laws of the state in which it is desired to incorporate. The laws of the different states vary considerably in their provisions relating to the organization of corporations. Persons desiring to incorporate a business should acquaint themselves with the laws of the particular state in which they wish to incorporate, as it will be necessary to comply with the laws of that state. The following excerpts from the laws of one of the states will illustrate a typical procedure to be observed in forming a corporation:

"Private corporations may be created by the voluntary association of three or more persons for the purposes authorized by law and in the manner hereinafter mentioned.

"A charter must be prepared, setting forth:

1. The name of the corporation;
2. The purpose for which it is formed;

3. The place or places where the business is to be transacted;
4. The term for which it is to exist;
5. The number of directors or trustees, and the names and residences of those who are appointees for the first year; and
6. The amount of the capital stock, if any, and the number of shares into which it is divided.

"It must be subscribed by three or more persons, two of whom must be citizens of this State, and must be acknowledged by them, before an officer duly authorized to take acknowledgments of deeds.

"The articles of incorporation shall also set forth the minimum amount of capital with which the corporation will commence business, which shall not be less than $1,000. The articles of incorporation may also contain any provision which the incorporators may choose to insert for the management of the business and for the conduct of the affairs of the corporation, and any provisions creating, defining, limiting, and regulating the powers of the corporation, the directors and the stockholders, or any class of the stockholders.

"The affidavit of those who executed the charter shall be furnished to the Secretary of State, showing:

1. The name, residence, and post office address of each subscriber to the capital stock of such company;
2. The amount subscribed by each, and the amount paid by each;
3. The cash value of any property received, with its description, location, and from whom and the price at which it was received; and
4. The amount, character, and value of labor done, and from whom and the price at which it was received."

The Charter. After the articles of incorporation have been filed, and other conditions, such as the payment of incorporation fees, have been fulfilled, the document is examined by a court or an administrative officer. If the instrument is satisfactory and the other requirements have been met, a license, a certificate of incorporation, or a charter is issued and recorded or filed as required by the particular statute of the state concerned. While, as previously stated, the provisions of law governing corporate organization vary in different states, in general they include such matters as the name, purpose, duration, location, and capitalization.

Ownership of a Corporation. Ownership in a corporation is represented by _capital stock._ To make it possible to have many owners — often with different ownership interests — the capital stock is divided into _shares._ The persons forming a corporation (the incorporators) and others who wish to become owners _subscribe_ for shares. Each agrees to buy a certain number of shares for a certain amount per share. Often payment is to be made in cash. Sometimes the subscription is paid for by transferring assets other than cash to the corporation.

Subscriptions to the capital stock of a corporation may be made before or after incorporation. A subscription made before incorporation is an agreement to subscribe for stock. It is a contract entered into between the subscriber and the incorporator or promoter and not between the subscriber and the corporation. The corporation, as such, does not exist until after the articles of incorporation have been filed with the proper state official and approved. A subscription for capital stock after incorporation is a contract between the subscriber and the corporation.

Stockholders. All parties owning shares of stock in a corporation are known as *stockholders* (sometimes called *shareholders*). In order to possess all of the rights of a stockholder of record, the party owning stock must have his ownership properly recorded on the books of the corporation. If stock is acquired from a previous stockholder, the transfer is not complete until it is recorded on the appropriate record of the corporation. Until this takes place, the new shareholder cannot have a *certificate of stock* issued in his name, he cannot vote at a stockholder's meeting, nor can he share in any dividends declared by the board of directors.

Directors. The stockholders elect a *board of directors* that is charged with the management and direction of corporate affairs. It would be impractical for all of the stockholders of a large corporation to meet periodically or at special times to decide upon questions in connection with the direction and management of company affairs. For this reason the stockholders elect a board of directors that is responsible to the stockholders for the proper management of corporate affairs. The directors are the legal agents of the corporation.

A board of directors usually consists of three or more stockholders. Where the board is unusually large in number, it is customary to appoint an *executive committee* of from three to five members of the board, which is given authority to administer the affairs of the corporation.

Officers. The board of directors elects the officers. Usually a president, vice-president, secretary, and treasurer are elected as executive officers. One person may hold two positions; for instance, the same person may serve both as secretary and treasurer. All of the officers are responsible to the board of directors and receive their instructions from the board. The officers have no authority other than to perform the duties required by the by-laws of the corporation and the statutes of the state. Generally they are liable for fraud or misrepresentation, or for exceeding the rights and powers conferred upon them by the by-laws of the company or the statutes of the state.

428

Capital Stock. The charter obtained by a business corporation specifies the amount of capital stock that it is authorized to issue. The state of incorporation authorizes a corporation to issue a certain number of shares of stock, and it is illegal for a company to issue a greater number of shares than is authorized in its charter. A certificate of stock issued to M. N. Dolan by The Wesley Company, Inc., with the stub completed, is reproduced below. It will be noted that the stub of the stock certificate book provides information as to the number of shares issued, the date of issue, and the name of the previous owner of the shares (if any). In this illustration, no previous owner is shown. This indicates that Mr. Dolan is the original purchaser of these shares.

Capital stock may or may not have *par value.* Par value is a technical legal matter. Its practical significance is not very great in most cases. In general, par represents the smallest amount that the corporation can accept in exchange for a share of stock at the time it is originally issued without the buyer of the stock incurring some liability to the corporation. In many states par-value stock cannot be sold originally by the corporation for less than par value. In most states it is possible for corporations to issue stock that has no par value.

If the corporation issues only one type of capital stock, it is called *common stock.* The stockholders own the corporation "in common." Among other things, the stockholders have the right to vote for directors

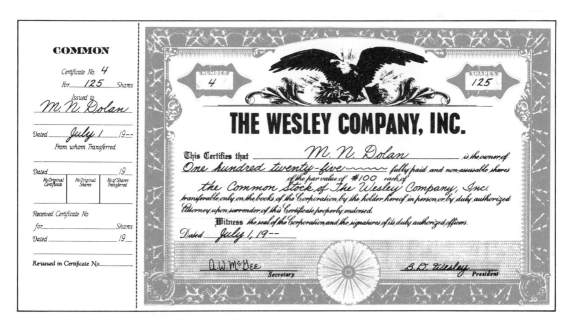

Certificate of Stock with Stub Attached

and upon certain other matters, including the right to share in any distributions (called *dividends*) resulting either from profitable operations, or from the fact that the corporation is being dissolved. In all cases these rights are in direct proportion to the number of shares of stock owned.

Some corporations have more than one class or type of stock. The classes differ with respect to the rights which go with the ownership of the stock. In addition to common stock, a corporation may have one or more types of *preferred stock*. Stock of this type may entitle the owner to receive a limited share of the earnings before the common stockholders receive any dividends and may involve a first or "prior" claim upon assets in the event that the corporation is dissolved. Sometimes preferred stock has a "preference" as to both dividends and assets. Frequently, preferred stockholders do not have voting rights.

If a corporation has only one class of common stock outstanding, the *book value* per share of such stock is equal to the total owners' equity of the corporation (assets less liabilities) divided by the number of shares outstanding. If the corporation also has preferred stock outstanding, the book value per share of common stock will be the total owners' equity less the portion that is allocated to the preferred stock, divided by the number of shares of common stock outstanding.

It is not to be expected that the book value per share and the *market value* per share will be the same. The latter is influenced by a number of factors, particularly the corporation's chances for success in the future. Market value is easy to determine if the corporation's stock is listed and actively traded on an organized stock exchange. If not, market value can only be estimated. In most cases the par value (if any), the book value, and the market value of the stock of a corporation are three different amounts.

Transactions peculiar to a corporation

The day-to-day operating transactions of a corporation are similar to those of a single proprietorship or of a partnership business of a like nature. Certain transactions involving the owners' equity of a business are unique if the enterprise is incorporated. Examples of such transactions include:

(a) Capital stock subscriptions.
(b) Amounts received to apply on capital stock subscriptions.
(c) Issuance of capital stock to subscribers.
(d) Transfer of capital stock from one stockholder to another stockholder.
(e) Declaration and payment of dividends.

Accounts peculiar to a corporation

A list of the major accounts that are peculiar to the corporate form of organization is shown below.

ACCOUNT	CLASSIFICATION
Capital Stock	Owners' equity
Subscriptions Receivable	Asset
Capital Stock Subscribed	Owners' equity
Retained Earnings (sometimes called *Earnings Retained in the Business*; at one time known as *Earned Surplus*)	Owners' equity
Dividends Payable	Liability

One of the features of accounting for corporate owners' equity is the distinction that usually is maintained in the records between owners' equity that results from investments by stockholders and that which results from retention of earnings (profitable operations coupled with a moderate dividend policy). In the case of certain types of corporate transactions, this distinction as to the source of the owners' equity is not evident, but in most cases the difference is reflected in the accounts. When the corporation exchanges its stock for cash or other property equal in amount to the par value of the shares issued, the transaction should be recorded by debiting the proper asset account and by crediting Capital Stock. If there is more than one type of capital stock, there should be an account for each type.

Sometimes a corporation obtains *subscriptions* to its stock in which each subscriber agrees to buy a certain number of shares at an agreed price (possibly par, if the stock has par value) and to pay for the shares at or within a specified time, either in full at one time or in installments over a period of time. If, for example, a subscription were received for 100 shares at a price of $50 each (assumed to be the par value of the shares in this case), the transaction should be recorded by debiting Subscriptions Receivable and by crediting Capital Stock Subscribed for $5,000. Collections on the subscription should be debited to Cash (or whatever is accepted in lieu of cash) and credited to Subscriptions Receivable. When the subscription is paid in full, the stock will be issued and an entry should be made debiting Capital Stock Subscribed and crediting Capital Stock for $5,000. As long as Subscriptions Receivable has a balance representing an amount that is expected to be collected, the account is treated as an asset and should be so shown on the balance sheet. Capital Stock Subscribed is an owners' equity account, the balance of which indicates the amount that eventually will be added to Capital Stock.

431

At the end of each accounting period, the balance of the expense and revenue summary account is transferred to the retained earnings account. If a corporation is operated at a loss, the amount of the net loss which is transferred from the expense and revenue summary account to the retained earnings account might result in the retained earnings account having a debit balance. In such event, this balance is termed a *deficit* and it will appear as a deduction in the owners' equity section of the corporation's balance sheet.

A decision on the part of the directors of a corporation to pay a dividend is commonly referred to as a *declaration of dividends*. When dividends are declared and such dividends are payable in cash at a later date, it is customary to record the declaration by debiting Retained Earnings and by crediting Dividends Payable. The dividends payable account will have a credit balance until all dividends declared have been paid in full. When dividends are paid immediately upon being declared, there is no need for setting up an account with Dividends Payable. Usually the dividends are not paid until some time after being declared by the directors. In the meantime, the dividends declared represent a liability of the corporation.

Accounting procedure

432

Following is a narrative of corporate transactions with illustrative general journal entries:

(a) The Wesley Company, Inc., was incorporated with an authorized issue of 500 shares of common capital stock, par value $100 per share. At the time of incorporation, subscriptions had been received as follows:

B. D. Wesley	250 shares
M. N. Dolan	125 shares
A. W. McGee	125 shares

The stock was subscribed for at par value and one half of the subscription price was paid in cash, the balance to be paid on demand.

To record this transaction it is necessary **(1)** to record the stock subscriptions received, and **(2)** to record the cash received to apply on the subscription price. These entries may be made in general journal form as illustrated below and at the top of the next page.

(1)

Subscriptions Receivable	50,000.00.	
Capital Stock Subscribed		50,000.00
Received subscriptions to capital stock at par as follows:		
B. D. Wesley, 250 shares		
M. N. Dolan, 125 shares		
A. W. McGee, 125 shares		

```
Bank............................................  25,000.00
    Subscriptions Receivable.............................        25,000.00
        Received cash on account of subscriptions to capital
    stock as follows:
                B. D. Wesley, $12,500
                M. N. Dolan, $6,250
                A. W. McGee, $6,250
```

(b) Received cash from subscribers to capital stock in settlement of balances due as follows:

```
        B. D. Wesley.................................  $12,500.00
        M. N. Dolan..................................    6,250.00
        A. W. McGee..................................    6,250.00
```

This transaction involves an increase in the asset cash and a decrease in the asset subscriptions receivable. The transaction may be recorded in general journal form as illustrated as follows:

```
Bank............................................  25,000.00
    Subscriptions Receivable.............................        25,000.00
        Received cash in settlement of the balance due from
    subscribers to capital stock as follows:
                B. D. Wesley, $12,500
                M. N. Dolan, $6,250
                A. W. McGee, $6,250
```

(c) Issued certificates of stock to the following subscribers who had remitted their subscriptions in full:

433

```
        B. D. Wesley.................................  250 shares
        M. N. Dolan..................................  125 shares
        A. W. McGee..................................  125 shares
```

Usually certificates of stock are not issued until subscriptions are remitted in full. In this case the subscribers have remitted their subscriptions in full and the stock certificates have been issued. The transactions may be recorded in general journal form as follows:

```
Capital Stock Subscribed.............................  50,000.00
    Capital Stock² .....................................        50,000.00
        Capital stock issued to subscribers as follows:
                B. D. Wesley, 250 shares
                M. N. Dolan, 125 shares
                A. W. McGee, 125 shares
```

After posting the above entry, the capital stock account will have a credit balance of $50,000, the par value of the capital stock outstanding.

(d) B. D. Wesley returned his stock certificate for 250 shares and requested that 50 shares be transferred to T. F. Parker and that a new certificate for 200 shares be issued to himself.

---

²When both common stock and preferred stock are authorized in the charter of a corporation, separate accounts should be kept for each class of stock. A memorandum entry of the number of shares authorized should be entered in the Item column of each capital stock account.

This transaction indicates that Wesley has sold 50 shares of his stock to Parker. Transferring capital stock from one stockholder to another involves the cancellation of an old certificate and the issuance of new certificates for the proper numbers of shares. In this case, it is necessary to cancel the original certificate for 250 shares issued to Wesley and to issue two new certificates, one to Parker for 50 shares and one to Wesley for 200 shares. This transaction has no effect upon the assets, liabilities, or capital of the corporation. It is merely a transfer of stock between stockholders and the only entry required is a transfer entry in the capital stock records kept by the corporation.

(e) The board of directors at its annual meeting held on June 15 voted to pay a cash dividend of $6 per share, the dividend to be paid on July 1 to stockholders of record June 15.

The board of directors has the right to decide when dividends shall be paid to stockholders. After dividends have been declared, they constitute a liability of the corporation, and this liability should be recorded at the time that the dividend is declared. The transaction may be recorded in general journal form as follows:

```
June 15.  Retained Earnings...............................  3,000.00
             Dividends Payable............................            3,000.00
                Dividend declared by the directors.
```

Dividends may be paid immediately upon being declared or at some later date. Large corporations usually do not pay dividends until sometime after the date of declaration. The directors usually specify that the dividends shall be paid to the stockholders of record as of a certain date. This means that only stockholders whose stock is recorded in their names on that date are entitled to receive dividends. Any stockholder who acquires stock after that date is not entitled to share in the dividend previously declared. To record the payment of the dividend declared in transaction (e), it is necessary to debit Dividends Payable and to credit the bank account as in the following general journal entry:

```
July  1.  Dividends Payable...............................  3,000.00
             Bank.........................................            3,000.00
                Paid dividend declared June 15.
```

This transaction has the effect of decreasing the liability dividends payable $3,000 with a similar decrease in the asset cash. After the transaction is posted, the dividends payable account will be in balance (that is, the account will have a zero balance).

Incorporating a Single Proprietorship. The legal steps involved in incorporating a single proprietorship are the same as in organizing a new corporation. Usually the sole proprietor becomes the principal stockholder in the corporation and transfers the assets of his business to the corporation in exchange for capital stock. The business liabilities may also be assumed by the corporation. The same books of account may be continued or an entirely new set of records may be installed. Suppose, for example, that The Gibbs Company, Inc., was organized to take over the business formerly conducted by J. J. Gibbs as a single proprietorship. Gibbs subscribes for 200 shares of the capital stock at $100 per share and transfers his equity in his business ($15,300) to apply on his subscription. Just before the transfer at the end of the year, the balance sheet of the business appeared as reproduced below:

J. J. GIBBS
Balance Sheet
December 31, 1972

Assets			Liabilities		
Cash...............		$ 4,750.00	Notes payable........	$1,000.00	
Accounts receivable....	$3,800.00		Accounts payable......	3,200.00	
Less allow. for bad debts...........	400.00	3,400.00	Total liabilities........		$ 4,200.00
Mdse. inventory.......		7,950.00			
Office equipment	$1,600.00			**Owner's Equity**	
Less accumulated depreciation........	400.00	1,200.00	J. J. Gibbs, capital....		15,300.00
Store equipment.......	$1,200.00				
Less accumulated depreciation........	300.00	900.00			
Delivery equipment.....	$2,900.00				
Less accumulated depreciation........	1,600.00	1,300.00			
			Total liabilities and		
Total assets..........		$19,500.00	owner's equity		$19,500.00

If Gibbs plans to continue to use the same set of books with only those modifications needed because of the change to the corporate form of enterprise, the entries to record his subscription and its partial payment by the transfer of his business assets and liabilities to the corporation should be as follows:

Subscriptions Receivable..............................	20,000.00	
Capital Stock Subscribed............................		20,000.00
J. J. Gibbs subscribed for 200 shares of stock at par.		
J. J. Gibbs, Capital....................................	15,300.00	
Subscriptions Receivable............................		15,300.00
Assets and liabilities of J. J. Gibbs transferred to corporation at book value.		

When the foregoing entries are posted, Gibbs' capital account will be in balance. The corporate accounts listed at the top of page 436 will take the place of Gibbs' capital account in the general ledger.

Capital Stock
Subscriptions Receivable
Capital Stock Subscribed

If, instead of using the same books of account that were used by Gibbs, a new set of books is installed by the corporation, a general journal entry should be made to record the transfer of the accounts of the single proprietorship to the corporation. If the long-lived assets are being taken over at their undepreciated cost, it is customary to record them in the books of the corporation at their net value after making adjustment for prior accumulated depreciation. If the long-lived assets are being taken over at any value other than their undepreciated cost, they should be recorded on the books of the corporation at the value agreed upon. Such value represents the cost of the assets to the corporation. The accounts of Gibbs may be transferred to The Gibbs Company, Inc., by means of a general journal entry entered on the books of the corporation as follows:

Bank...	4,750.00	
Accounts Receivable.................................	3,800.00	
Merchandise Inventory...............................	7,950.00	
Office Equipment....................................	1,200.00	
Store Equipment....................................	900.00	
Delivery Equipment.................................	1,300.00	
Notes Payable....................................		1,000.00
Accounts Payable....................................		3,200.00
Allowance for Bad Debts.............................		400.00
Subscriptions Receivable.............................		15,300.00
Assets and liabilities of J. J. Gibbs transferred to corporation at book value.		

Assuming that Gibbs paid the balance due on his subscription and that a stock certificate for 200 shares was issued to him, the transactions should be recorded on the books of the corporation as follows:

Bank...	4,700.00	
Subscriptions Receivable.............................		4,700.00
Cash received from J. J. Gibbs in settlement of balance due on subscription to capital stock.		
Capital Stock Subscribed.............................	20,000.00	
Capital Stock.......................................		20,000.00
Issued 200 shares of common capital stock to J. J. Gibbs.		

Incorporating a Partnership. A partnership may be terminated by incorporation, and the partners may become stockholders of the corporation. The same books of account may be continued or a new set of books may be installed by the corporation. Suppose, for example, that The Benson Company, Inc., is organized with an authorized capital of $50,000 to take over the business formerly conducted by Benson and Estes, partners. The partners subscribe for capital stock of the corporation as follows:

A. Y. Benson, 300 shares @ $50 a share.........................	$15,000.00
Carl O. Estes, 200 shares at @ $50 a share.......................	10,000.00

Benson and Estes, as individuals, are to receive credit toward their subscriptions for their respective equities in the assets of the partnership.

The following balance sheet for the partnership was prepared just prior to the time of incorporating the business (April 1, 1972):

BENSON AND ESTES
Balance Sheet
March 31, 1972

Assets			Liabilities		
Cash................		$ 6,600.00	Notes payable........	$2,000.00	
Notes receivable.......	$ 750.00		Accounts payable......	3,738.75	
Accounts receivable....	3,800.00		Total liabilities........		$ 5,738.75
	$4,550.00				
Less allow. for bad debts...........	300.00	4,250.00	**Owners' Equity**		
Mdse. inventory.......		9,800.00	A. Y. Benson, capital...	$ 8,246.50	
Office equipment	$1,600.00		Carl O. Estes, capital...	8,364.75	
Less accumulated depreciation........	500.00	1,100.00	Total owners' equity....		16,611.25
Delivery equipment.....	$1,200.00				
Less accumulated depreciation........	600.00	600.00			
			Total liabilities and		
Total assets..........		$22,350.00	owners' equity.......		$22,350.00

The subscriptions to the capital stock should be recorded as indicated in the following general journal entry:

Subscriptions Receivable............................	25,000.00	
Capital Stock Subscribed...........................		25,000.00
Received subscriptions to capital stock as follows:		
A. Y. Benson, 300 shares		
Carl O. Estes, 200 shares		

If the books of the partnership are to be continued in use by the corporation, the transfer of the partners' equities to the corporation may be made by means of the following general journal entry:

A. Y. Benson, Capital..................................	8,246.50	
Carl O. Estes, Capital..................................	8,364.75	
Subscriptions Receivable.............................		16,611.25
Assets and liabilities of Benson and Estes transferred to corporation at book value.		

When this entry is posted, the partners' accounts will be in balance. If, instead of using the same books of account as were used by Benson and Estes, a new set of books is installed by the corporation, a general journal entry on the books of the corporation is required to transfer the accounts of the partnership to the corporation. This journal entry is shown at the top of the next page.

Bank...	6,600.00	
Notes Receivable....................................	750.00	
Accounts Receivable.................................	3,800.00	
Merchandise Inventory..............................	9,800.00	
Office Equipment....................................	1,100.00	
Delivery Equipment.................................	600.00	
Notes Payable....................................		2,000.00
Accounts Payable.................................		3,738.75
Allowance for Bad Debts..........................		300.00
Subscriptions Receivable..........................		16,611.25
Assets and liabilities of Benson and Estes transferred to corporation at book value.		

It will be noted that the long-lived assets of Benson and Estes are recorded on the books of the corporation at their undepreciated cost after making adjustments for prior accumulated depreciation. Had the long-lived assets been taken over at any value other than their undepreciated cost, they should be recorded on the books of the corporation at the value agreed upon.

Assuming that Benson and Estes paid the balance due on their subscriptions and that stock certificates were issued to them, the transactions should be recorded on the books of the corporation as follows:

Bank...	8,388.75	
Subscriptions Receivable...........................		8,388.75
Received cash from subscribers as follows: A. Y. Benson, $6,753.50 Carl O. Estes, $1,635.25		
Capital Stock Subscribed............................	25,000.00	
Capital Stock.....................................		25,000.00
Issued common capital stock to subscribers.		

Owners' Equity Section of a Corporation Balance Sheet. The difference between the amounts of the assets and of the liabilities of a corporation is called either "capital" or "stockholders' equity" and is so described in the balance sheet of the corporation. Generally, the amount resulting from the issuance of capital stock and the amount resulting from undistributed earnings are shown. At the end of the first year of operations, the owners' equity section of the balance sheet of The Benson Company, Inc., appeared as follows:

Stockholders' Equity

Capital stock (1,000 shares authorized; 500 shares issued).....................	$25,000.00
Retained earnings.....................................	8,000.00
Total stockholders' equity..........................	$33,000.00

It should be understood that, because of differences in capital structure, there may be considerable variation in the capital section of balance sheets prepared for different corporations. If more than one kind of capital stock is issued, each kind should be listed separately. There may be retained earnings (accumulated income) or a deficit (accumulated losses) at the end of the year. A deficit should be shown as a deduction from the amount resulting from the issuance of the capital stock in arriving at the net stockholders' equity of a corporation.

Report No. 16-3

Complete Report No. 16-3 in the workbook and submit your working papers to the instructor for approval. Then continue with the following study assignment in Chapter 17 until Report No. 17-1 is required.

chapter 17

accrual accounting applied to a wholesale business

440

In a wholesale merchandising enterprise, the merchandise handled is usually purchased directly from manufacturers, importers, or producers and is sold to retailers and distributors, who in turn sell to consumers at retail prices. The wholesaler usually buys in sizable quantities and has storage facilities to enable him to carry a large stock of merchandise. He may purchase the goods for cash or on account and, likewise, may sell the goods for cash or on account. A large percentage of the wholesale business involves the use of credit.

Factors affecting accounting records used

The books of account and the auxiliary records of a wholesale business will vary depending upon a number of factors, such as the following:

    (a) Type of business organization.
    (b) Volume of business.
    (c) Office equipment used.
    (d) Information desired on the part of the management and others concerned
        with the operation of the business.

Type of Business Organization. A wholesale merchandising enterprise may be conducted as a single proprietorship, a partnership, or a corporation. So far as the single proprietorship and the partnership forms of organization are concerned, there are no distinctive records to be kept. With the corporate form of organization, however, certain corporate records, such as a minute book, a stock certificate record, and a stockholders ledger, may be kept. The type of organization will also affect the accounts that are kept. In the case of a single proprietorship, it may be necessary to keep two accounts for the proprietor — one for recording his capital and the other for recording his personal transactions. In the case of a partnership, it is necessary to keep separate accounts for each partner. In the case of a corporation, it is necessary to keep separate accounts for capital stock, retained earnings, and dividends payable.

Volume of Business. The volume of business is an important factor in determining the types of records and the number of accounts to be maintained. Obviously, the records and the accounts of a firm with annual sales of a million dollars will differ considerably from one with annual sales of only $50,000 a year. In a big business with numerous departments, there will be a demand for more financial and statistical information for management and a greater need for adequate control.

When manual methods are used, there is a fairly direct relationship between the size of a business and the number of persons engaged in keeping its accounting records. When several persons are required, the work must be divided in some logical fashion. Generally, this means that a separate record or book of original entry will be kept for each major type of business transaction, and that the books of final entry (the ledgers) will be subdivided. For example, one journal may be provided to record purchases, another journal to record sales, another to record cash receipts, another to record checks drawn, and a general journal to record transactions that cannot be recorded in the special journals. It is likely that there will be one or more subsidiary ledgers to record the details about some of the elements that are shown in summary in certain of the general ledger accounts. Each employee engaged in accounting activity will specialize in keeping one of these records.

A functional division of the accounting activity has, among others, the following advantages:

    (a) Provides for better internal check and control.

    (b) Makes possible an equitable distribution of work among several employees.

    (c) Provides for a more detailed classification of transactions in the books of original entry.

    (d) Makes possible periodic summary posting to the general ledger.

Office Equipment. The accounting system is certain to be affected by the use of various types of office equipment. In recent years there has been a great expansion in the use of accounting, calculating, and other office machines. In the modern office of a big business enterprise, it is not uncommon to find a large share of the bookkeeping work being done with the aid of mechanical and electronic devices, including posting machines, accounting machines, and photographic equipment. Many large companies are using computers and other data processing equipment.

Regardless of the extent to which equipment is used in the accounting department, the fundamental principles involved in keeping the accounts continue to apply. A knowledge of accounting theory on the part of those employed in the accounting department is just as essential as if no machines were used.

Information Desired. The accounting system must be designed to provide management and others concerned with the operation of a business with the desired information. The management will wish to know where the business stands financially from time to time, as well as the results of operations for given periods of time. The accounting department may be required to supply much information of a statistical nature as well as the usual accounting reports. For example, the manager of the purchasing department may expect the accounting department to keep detailed stock records of all merchandise handled. The accounts must be kept so as to provide all the information needed for all the various tax reports required by the federal, state, and local governments. In recent years there has been a tremendous increase in the number of tax reports and in the amount of tax information that must be furnished. Many large firms have found it necessary to organize a tax accounting department separate from the general accounting department.

Accounting procedure

Holling and Renz are partners who conduct a wholesale paint and varnish business. Paint is handled in Department A, varnish in Department B. Such merchandise is purchased on account from various manufacturers. The terms of purchase may vary considerably. Most of the firms from whom Holling & Renz buy allow discounts ranging from 1 to 3 percent for cash in from 10 to 30 days. Holling & Renz sell the merchandise to local dealers and distributors both on account and for cash. On charge sales their terms usually are 2 percent discount for cash in

10 days, net 30 days, frequently expressed as 2 percent, 10 days, net 30; or in an abbreviated form as 2/10, n/30.

The records maintained by Holling & Renz consist of the following:

(a) Books of original entry

    (1) Invoice register
    (2) Sales register
    (3) Record of cash receipts
    (4) Record of checks drawn
    (5) General journal

(b) Books of final entry

    (1) General ledger
    (2) Subsidiary ledgers

        a. Accounts receivable ledger
        b. Accounts payable ledger
        c. Operating expense ledger

(c) Auxiliary records

    (1) Notes receivable register
    (2) Petty cash disbursements record
    (3) Insurance policy register
    (4) Check stubs
    (5) Stock record
    (6) Long-lived asset record

Invoice register

A comparison of Holling & Renz's invoice register reproduced on page 310 with the invoice register reproduced on page 464 will reveal that they are identical. This form of invoice register was described in detail in Chapter 11.

Sales register

A comparison of Holling & Renz's sales register reproduced on page 332 with the sales register reproduced on page 465 will reveal that they are identical. This form of sales register was described in detail in Chapter 12.

Record of cash receipts

Holling & Renz keep a multicolumn record of cash receipts. Reference to their record of cash receipts reproduced on page 466 will reveal that

General Ledger Debit and Credit columns are provided. In addition, special debit amount columns are provided for (1) Sales Discount and (2) Bank. Special credit amount columns are provided for (1) Accounts Receivable, (2) Sales, Department A, and (3) Sales, Department B. All cash and cash items are recorded by debiting the bank account immediately. This practice usually is followed where it is the custom to deposit all cash receipts in a bank and to make all disbursements (other than petty cash) by check.

Proving the Record of Cash Receipts. The record of cash receipts may be footed and the footings may be proved daily or periodically by comparing the sum of the debit footings with the sum of the credit footings. When a page is filled, the amount columns should be footed, the footings should be proved, and the totals should be carried forward to the top of the next page. It is customary to start a month at the top of a new page.

Posting from the Record of Cash Receipts. Completing the posting from the record of cash receipts involves both individual posting and summary posting. Individual posting is required from the General Ledger Debit and Credit columns. This posting usually is done daily. As each such item is posted, a check mark should be entered in the Check (√) column following the Amount column of the record of cash receipts. The initials "CR" and the page number of the record of cash receipts then should be entered in the Posting Reference column of the proper general ledger account preceding the amount posted.

The summary posting usually is completed at the end of each month and involves the following procedure:

(a) The total of the column headed Sales Discount should be posted as a debit to Sales Discount, Account No. 043, in the general ledger.

(b) The total of the column headed Bank should be posted as a debit to American National Bank, Account No. 111, in the general ledger.

(c) The total of the column headed Accounts Receivable should be posted as a credit to Accounts Receivable, Account No. 133, in the general ledger.

(d) The total of the column headed Cash Sales, Dept. A, should be posted as a credit to Sales — Department A, Account No. 411, in the general ledger.

(e) The total of the column headed Cash Sales, Dept. B, should be posted as a credit to Sales — Department B, Account No. 421, in the general ledger.

As the total of each column is posted, the account number should be written in parentheses immediately below the total in the record of cash receipts. The page number of the record of cash receipts then should be entered in the Posting Reference column of the proper general ledger account as a cross-reference. A check mark should be placed in parentheses below the totals of the General Ledger Debit and Credit columns to indicate that these totals are not posted.

Record of checks drawn

Holling & Renz keep a multicolumn record of checks drawn. Reference to the record of checks drawn reproduced on pages 467 and 468 will reveal that General Ledger Debit and Credit columns are provided. In addition, special debit amount columns are provided for (1) Operating Expenses and (2) Accounts Payable. Special credit amount columns are provided for (1) Purchases Discount and (2) Bank.

Proving the Record of Checks Drawn. The record of checks drawn may be footed and the footings may be proved daily or periodically by comparing the sum of the debit footings with the sum of the credit footings. When a page is filled, the amount columns should be footed, the footings should be proved, and the totals should be carried forward to the top of the next page. It is customary to start a month at the top of a new page.

445

Posting from the Record of Checks Drawn. Completing the posting from the record of checks drawn involves both individual posting and summary posting. Individual posting is required from the General Ledger Debit and Credit columns. This posting usually is done daily. As each item is posted, a check mark should be entered in the Check ($\sqrt{}$) column following the Amount column of the record of checks drawn. The initials "CD" and the page number of the record of checks drawn then should be entered in the Posting Reference column of the ledger account to the left of the amount posted.

Individual posting is also required from the Operating Expenses Debit column. This posting usually is done daily. As each item is posted, a check mark should be entered in the Check ($\sqrt{}$) column following the Amount column of the record of checks drawn. The initials "CD" and the page number of the record of checks drawn then should be entered in the Posting Reference column of the proper operating expense ledger account to the left of the amount posted.

The summary posting usually is completed at the end of each month and involves the following procedure:

    (a) The total of the column headed Operating Expenses should be posted as a debit to Operating Expenses, Account No. 611, in the general ledger.

(b) The total of the column headed Accounts Payable should be posted as a debit to Accounts Payable, Account No. 271, in the general ledger.

(c) The total of the column headed Purchases Discount should be posted as a credit to Purchases Discount, Account No. 053, in the general ledger.

(d) The total of the column headed Bank should be posted as a credit to American National Bank, Account No. 111, in the general ledger.

As the total of each column is posted, the account number should be written in parentheses immediately below the total in the record of checks drawn. The page number of the record of checks drawn then should be entered in the Posting Reference column of the proper general ledger account as a cross-reference. A check mark should be placed in parentheses below the totals of the General Ledger Debit and Credit columns to indicate that these totals are not posted.

General journal

Holling & Renz use a multicolumn general journal. Reference to the general journal reproduced on page 469 will reveal that General Ledger Debit and Credit columns are provided. In addition, special debit amount columns are provided for **(1)** Operating Expenses and **(2)** Accounts Payable. Special credit amount columns are provided for **(1)** Accounts Payable and **(2)** Accounts Receivable. The general journal is used for recording all transactions that cannot be recorded in the special journals. Adjusting, closing, and reversing entries also are recorded in the general journal.

Proving the General Journal. The general journal may be footed and the footings may be proved daily or periodically by comparing the sum of the debit footings with the sum of the credit footings. When a page is filled, the amount columns should be footed, the footings should be proved, and the totals should be carried forward to the top of the next page. It is customary to start a month at the top of a new page.

Posting from the General Journal. Completing the posting from the general journal involves both individual posting and summary posting. Individual posting is required from the General Ledger Debit and Credit columns. This posting usually is done daily. As each item is posted, a check mark should be entered in the Check ($\sqrt{}$) column following the Amount column of the general journal. The initial "G" and the page number of the general journal then should be entered in the Posting Reference column of the proper general ledger account to the left of the amount posted.

Individual posting is also required from the Operating Expenses Debit column. As each item is posted, a check mark should be entered in the Check (√) column following the Amount column of the general journal. The initial "G" and the page number of the general journal then should be entered in the Posting Reference column of the proper operating expense ledger account to the left of the amount posted.

The summary posting usually is completed at the end of each month and involves the following procedure:

(a) The total of the debit column headed Operating Expenses should be posted as a debit to Operating Expenses, Account No. 611, in the general ledger.

(b) The total of the debit column headed Accounts Payable should be posted as a debit to Accounts Payable, Account No. 271, in the general ledger.

(c) The total of the credit column headed Accounts Payable should be posted as a credit to Accounts Payable, Account No. 271, in the general ledger.

(d) The total of the credit column headed Accounts Receivable should be posted as a credit to Accounts Receivable, Account No. 133, in the general ledger.

As the total of each column is posted, the account number should be written in parentheses immediately below the total in the general journal. The page number of the general journal then should be entered in the Posting Reference column of the proper general ledger account as a cross-reference. A check mark should be placed in parentheses below the totals of the General Ledger Debit and Credit columns to indicate that these totals are not posted.

General ledger

Holling & Renz use a general ledger with standard ledger account ruling. The accounts are arranged in this ledger in numerical order. A chart of accounts is reproduced on the next page. It will be noted that the chart includes several accounts of a type not previously used in this presentation. A brief discussion of each of these accounts follows.

Government Bonds, Account No. 121. This account is used to record the cost of the United States government bonds owned by Holling & Renz. From time to time, the partners find that the firm's bank balance is larger than necessary. In order to supplement earnings from regular operations, the excess cash is temporarily invested in certain types of government bonds which have a high degree of safety even though the rate of return is low. Whenever the money is needed, the bonds can be sold or redeemed with little risk of loss. Because there is no present intention to hold the

CHART OF GENERAL LEDGER ACCOUNTS

*Assets**

Cash
111 American National Bank
112 Petty Cash Fund

Temporary Investments
121 Government Bonds

Receivables
131 Notes Receivable
132 Accrued Interest Receivable
133 Accounts Receivable
   013 Allowance for Bad Debts

Merchandise Inventory
141 Merchandise Inventory
     — Department A
151 Merchandise Inventory
     — Department B

Supplies and Prepayments
161 Store Supplies
162 Advertising Supplies
163 Office Supplies
164 Postage Stamps
165 Prepaid Insurance

Long-Lived Assets
171 Store Equipment
   017 Accumulated Depreciation —
      Store Equipment
181 Delivery Equipment
   018 Accumulated Depreciation —
      Delivery Equipment
191 Office Equipment
   019 Accumulated Depreciation —
      Office Equipment

Liabilities
211 FICA Tax Payable
221 FUTA Tax Payable
231 State Unemployment Tax Payable
241 Employees Income Tax Payable
251 Notes Payable
261 Accrued Interest Payable
271 Accounts Payable

Owners' Equity
311 T. L. Holling, Capital
  031 T. L. Holling, Drawing
321 A. G. Renz, Capital
  032 A. G. Renz, Drawing
331 Expense and Revenue Summary

Revenue from Sales
411 Sales — Department A
  041 Sales Returns and Allowances
     — Department A
421 Sales — Department B
  042 Sales Returns and Allowances
     — Department B
  043 Sales Discount

Cost of Goods Sold
511 Purchases — Department A
  051 Purchases Returns and Allow-
     ances — Department A
521 Purchases — Department B
  052 Purchases Returns and Allow-
     ances — Department B
  053 Purchases Discount
541 Freight In — Department A
551 Freight In — Department B
561 Cost of Goods Sold
     — Department A
571 Cost of Goods Sold
     — Department B

Operating Expenses
611 Operating Expenses

Other Revenue
711 Interest Earned

Other Expenses
811 Interest Expense
821 Charitable Contributions Expense
831 Collection Expense

Words in italics represent headings and not account titles.

448

same bonds for a long period of time, they are regarded as a temporary investment and classified as a current asset of the firm.

Sales Discount, Account No. 043. It is the practice of most wholesale businesses to offer their customers cash discounts for prompt payment of purchases on account. As previously mentioned, Holling & Renz allow a discount of 2 percent if an amount due is paid within ten days from date of purchase. When a sale on account is made, the customer is billed for the gross amount due. If a remittance is received within the discount period, the entry to record it involves debits to American National Bank and Sales

Discount with a credit to Accounts Receivable. In preparing the income statement at the end of the fiscal year, the amount of sales discount is prorated on the basis of the amount of sales, less sales returns and allowances, of each department. While sales discount could be treated as an expense, a preferred treatment is to consider it (like sales returns and allowances) as a reduction of sales revenue in calculating the amount of net sales.

Freight In — Department A and Freight In — Department B, Accounts Nos. 541 and 551. These accounts are charged with the amount of freight paid by Holling & Renz on incoming shipments of merchandise. The balances of these accounts are treated as additions to the cost of merchandise purchased and are so reported in the income statement.

Cost of Goods Sold — Department A and Cost of Goods Sold — Department B, Accounts Nos. 561 and 571. These two accounts are similar to Expense and Revenue Summary in that they are used at the end of the accounting period in the closing process. Such accounts are used to summarize the elements that enter into the calculation of the cost of goods sold by each department. The debit balances of the merchandise inventory accounts (representing the beginning inventories), the purchases accounts, and the freight in accounts, together with the credit balances of the purchases returns and allowances accounts and the purchases discount account, are closed to the respective cost of goods sold accounts. When the amounts of the ending inventories are recorded, the respective cost of goods sold accounts are credited. The balance of each of these accounts then represents the cost of goods sold for the indicated department. These balances then are closed to the expense and revenue summary account.

449

Charitable Contributions Expense, Account No. 821. This account is not new, but classifying it as an "other expense" differs from the treatment in the case of The Adams Appliance Store. In the Adams chart of accounts (see page 197) this expense was classified as an "operating expense." There is a difference of opinion among accountants as to which is the preferred classification of charitable contributions expense.

Accounts receivable ledger

Holling & Renz use an accounts receivable ledger with balance-column account ruling. The accounts are arranged in this ledger in alphabetic order. A control account for accounts receivable (Account No. 133) is kept in the general ledger. At the end of each month it is customary to prepare a schedule of the accounts receivable, the total of which should be the same as the balance of the accounts receivable control account.

Posting to the customers' accounts in the accounts receivable ledger may be done either from the books of original entry or directly from vouchers or other documents that represent the transactions. The accountant for Holling & Renz follows the latter practice.

Accounts payable ledger

Holling & Renz use an accounts payable ledger with balance-column account ruling. The accounts are arranged in this ledger in alphabetic order. A control account for accounts payable (Account No. 271) is kept in the general ledger. At the end of each month it is customary to prepare a schedule of the accounts payable, the total of which should be the same as the balance of the accounts payable control account.

Posting to creditors' accounts in the accounts payable ledger may be done either from the books of original entry or directly from vouchers or other documents that represent the transactions. The accountant for Holling & Renz follows the latter practice.

450

Operating expense ledger

Holling & Renz use an operating expense ledger with balance-column account ruling. The accounts are arranged in this ledger in numerical order. A chart of the accounts appears below. A control account for operating

HOLLING & RENZ

CHART OF OPERATING EXPENSE LEDGER ACCOUNTS

Selling Expenses

6111 Advertising Expense
6112 Store Clerks Salary Expense
6113 Truck Drivers Wage Expense
6114 A. G. Renz, Salary Expense
6115 A. G. Renz, Traveling Expense
6116 Truck Gas and Oil Expense
6117 Truck Repairs Expense
6118 Garage Rent Expense
6119 Freight Out
6121 Merchandise Insurance Expense
6122 Delivery Equipment Insurance Expense
6123 Store Equipment Insurance Expense
6124 Store Supplies Expense
6125 Postage Expense (Selling)
6126 Depreciation of Store Equipment
6127 Depreciation of Delivery Equipment
6128 Miscellaneous Selling Expense

Administrative Expenses

6131 Rent Expense
6132 T. L. Holling, Salary Expense
6133 Office Salaries Expense
6134 Light and Water Expense
6135 Telephone and Telegraph Expense
6136 Bad Debts Expense
6137 Property Tax Expense
6138 Office Supplies Expense
6139 Postage Expense (Administration)
6141 Office Equipment Insurance Expense
6142 Depreciation of Office Equipment
6143 Payroll Taxes Expense
6144 Miscellaneous General Expense

expenses (Account No. 611) is kept in the general ledger. At the end of each month it is customary to prepare a schedule of the operating expenses, the total of which should be the same as the balance of the operating expenses control account.

All posting to the operating expense accounts is done from the books of original entry. As each item is posted, the page of the journal from which it is posted is entered in the Posting Reference column of the account.

Auxiliary records

Holling & Renz keep certain auxiliary records. These are as follows: a petty cash disbursements record, a notes receivable register, an insurance policy register, a long-lived asset record, check stubs, and a stock record. Their record of petty cash disbursements for June is reproduced on pages 470 and 471. The form of the notes receivable register is similar to that shown on pages 184 and 185. The form of the insurance policy register is similar to that shown on pages 372 and 373. The form of the long-lived asset record is not shown. (Since Holling & Renz use the group method of depreciation accounting, the long-lived asset record does not show the periodic depreciation of each unit.) A discussion of check stubs and the stock record follows.

451

Check Stubs. Holling & Renz use a checkbook bound with two checks to a page with stubs attached. The purpose of the stubs is **(1)** to provide spaces for recording the current bank balance, deposits, and the information needed to keep the records of checks drawn, and **(2)** to post to the accounts with creditors in the accounts payable ledger. Space is also provided on the stubs of the checks to record the account number of the account to be debited.

Stock Record. Holling & Renz keep a stock record as a means of control and as an aid to good business management. Such a record may serve several purposes. It indicates when the supply of any item is low and its replenishment is needed. A physical count should be made at least once a year even if the stock record is maintained, because the record shows the quantity that should be on hand and indicates the need for closer control if a substantial discrepancy is discovered. With a stock record, it is not essential that a physical count of the entire inventory be made at the same time. Businesses that want *interim* financial statements (monthly or quarterly) can base their calculation of cost of goods sold and of inventory at the statement date upon information provided by a stock record. (A complete physical count at the end of each month or each quarter may not be practical, and calculations based upon estimates may not be sufficiently reliable.)

One form of stock record is shown below. The information needed in keeping such a record is obtained from the purchase invoices, sales invoices, charge-back invoices, and credit memorandums. In recording receipts, sales, returns, and balances, only quantities are entered. Minimum quantities are indicated and, whenever the quantity in stock reaches the minimum, more of the item is ordered.

STOCK RECORD

DATE	INV. NO.	RECEIVED	ISSUED	BALANCE	DATE	INV. NO.	RECEIVED	ISSUED	BALANCE
May 1				1062					
5	104		30	1032					
9	108		40	992					
10	821	100		1092					
16	CM 881	4		1096					
18	111		60	1036					
20	114		40	996					
25	CB 14		5	991					
27	839	80		1071					

ARTICLE	DESCRIPTION		MINIMUM	DEPARTMENT
Oil-Base Paint	White Primer 2-gal. pail	1 ea.	1000	A

Stock Record

Accounting procedure illustrated

The accounts of Holling & Renz are being kept on the basis of a fiscal year ending June 30. Their books of original entry (invoice register, sales register, record of cash receipts, record of checks drawn, and general journal) are reproduced on pages 464 to 469, inclusive. The only auxiliary record reproduced is the petty cash disbursements record, pages 470 and 471. The general and subsidiary ledgers are not reproduced in this illustration. Following is a narrative of the June transactions that are shown recorded in the illustrations.

HOLLING & RENZ

WHOLESALE DEALERS IN PAINT AND VARNISH

NARRATIVE OF TRANSACTIONS

Wednesday, June 1

Issued Check No. 830 for $450 to T. R. Walsh in payment of the June rent.

Received a check for $573.30 from Don V. Davis for our invoice of May 23 for $585, less 2 percent discount.

Before the check received from Don V. Davis was recorded, it was reconciled by referring to his account in the accounts receivable ledger. The account showed that on May 23 he had been charged for merchandise amounting to $585. A discount of 2 percent is allowed for cash in ten days. The amount of his remittance was therefore verified in the following manner:

Merchandise sold	$585.00
Less 2% discount	11.70
Net amount due	$573.30

When the check was found to be for the proper amount, it was posted immediately to the credit of the account with Don V. Davis in the accounts receivable ledger. The amount of the check, $573.30, was entered on one line and the amount of the discount, $11.70, on the next line. The check was then entered in the record of cash receipts by debiting the bank account for the amount of the check, $573.30, by debiting Sales Discount for the amount of the discount, $11.70, and by crediting Accounts Receivable for the total of the invoice, $585. A check mark was placed in the Check ($\checkmark$) column following the amount entered in the Accounts Receivable column to indicate that the posting to Don V. Davis' account had been completed.

Made charge sale as follows:

No. 104, Don V. Davis, St. Louis, Missouri; paint, $268.90; varnish, $151.50; terms, 2/10, n/30.

The information needed by the bookkeeper in recording each sale is obtained from a carbon copy of the sales invoice prepared by the billing clerk. As this invoice was entered in the sales register, a check mark was placed in the Check ($\checkmark$) column following the Accounts Receivable Debit column to indicate that the invoice would be posted directly to the account of Don V. Davis. The invoice was then posted to Mr. Davis' account in the accounts receivable ledger. A copy of the sales invoice was used to make appropriate entries on the affected stock record cards — the date, invoice number, quantity issued, and balance remaining. (Refer to Stock Record form illustrated on page 452.)

Holling & Renz follow the practice of depositing at the end of each day all checks and other cash items received during the day.

Thursday, June 2

Issued checks as follows:

No. 831, U.S. Paint Company, $826.73, in payment of its invoice of May 24 for $852.30, less 3 percent discount.

No. 832, M.F.A. Insurance Co., $170, in payment of bill for one-year policy on delivery truck.

As these checks were entered in the record of checks drawn, check marks were placed in the Check (√) column following the amounts entered in the Accounts Payable and General Ledger Debit columns to indicate that the checks would be posted directly from the check stubs to the proper accounts in the subsidiary ledgers. In posting to the account of U.S. Paint Company, the amount of the check, $826.73, was entered on one line and the amount of the discount, $25.57, was entered on the next line.

Friday, June 3

Received the following invoices:

Celucoat Corporation, St. Louis, Missouri; paint, $576; terms, June 2 — 2/10, n/30.

Phelan-Faust Paint Manufacturing Co., St. Louis, Missouri; varnish, $394.20; terms, June 2 — 3/10, n/30.

Sunbrite Supply Co., St. Louis, Missouri; office supplies, $38.90; terms, June 3 — n/30.

As these invoices were received they were numbered consecutively, beginning with No. 741, and were entered in the invoice register. Check marks were placed in the Check (√) column following the Accounts Payable Credit column to indicate that the invoices would be posted directly to the proper creditors' accounts in the accounts payable ledger. These invoices were used to make appropriate entries on the affected stock record cards — the date, invoice number, quantity received, and new balance.

Saturday, June 4

454 Issued Check No. 833 for $1,166.69 to Celucoat Corporation in payment of its invoice of May 25 for $1,190.50, less 2 percent discount.

Received the following invoices:

Celucoat Corporation, St. Louis, Missouri; paint, $375.40; terms, June 4 — 2/10, n/30; shipped directly to Kaplan Lumber Co., St. Charles, Missouri, freight collect.

Holling & Renz are agents for Celucoat Corporation. However, they do not necessarily carry in stock the entire line of that corporation's paint. When an order is received for items that are not carried in stock, an order is placed with the supplier with instructions to ship directly to the customer, transportation charges collect. After the invoice was recorded in the invoice register and was posted to the account of Celucoat Corporation in the accounts payable ledger, the invoice was referred to the billing clerk with instructions to bill the Kaplan Lumber Co. (See related charge sale No. 107 of June 6.)

U.S. Paint Company, St. Louis, Missouri; varnish, $570; terms, June 3 — 3/10, n/30.

Steelcote Paper Products, St. Louis, Missouri; office supplies, $42; terms, June 4 — n/30.

END-OF-THE-WEEK WORK

(1) Footed the amount columns in the invoice register and record of checks drawn and proved the footings. **(2)** Proved the bank balance in the following manner:

```
Balance, June 1 ...................................................    $2,616.27*
Total receipts June 1–4 per record of cash receipts..................        573.30
Total ...........................................................    $3,189.57
    Less total checks issued June 1–4 per record of checks drawn .......    2,613.42
Balance, June 4 ...................................................    $  576.15
```

*Indicated by General Ledger Account No. 111 not reproduced in this illustration.

(3) Completed the individual posting from the books of original entry to the general ledger and to the operating expense ledger accounts.

Monday, June 6

Received a check for $767.34 from Famous-Barr Co. for merchandise sold on May 27 amounting to $783, less 2 percent discount.

Made charge sales as follows:

No. 105, St. John Hardware, St. John, Missouri; paint, $307.50; terms, 2/10, n/30.

No. 106, Morris Hardware, St. Louis, Missouri; paint, $143.60; postage, $1.65; terms, 2/10, n/30.

In entering Sales Invoice No. 106 in the sales register, the postage was charged to the customer's account and was credited to Postage Stamps, Account No. 164. In posting this invoice to the account of Morris Hardware Co. in the accounts receivable ledger, the amount of the merchandise sold, $143.60, was entered on one line, and the amount of the postage prepaid, $1.65, was entered on the next line.

No. 107, Kaplan Lumber Co., St. Charles, Missouri; paint, $500.50; terms, 2/10, n/30; shipped directly from factory, freight collect.

The paint billed to the Kaplan Lumber Co. on Sales Invoice No. 107 was shipped directly by Celucoat Corporation on June 3, and an invoice was received by Holling & Renz on June 4.

Issued Check No. 834 for $820.81 to Phelan-Faust Paint Manufacturing Co. in payment of its invoice of May 27 for $846.20, less 3 percent discount.

Tuesday, June 7

Issued Credit Memorandum No. 892 to Don V. Davis, $17.80, for paint returned.

The paint returned had been billed on Sales Invoice No. 104. The return transaction was recorded in the general journal, after which the credit memorandum was posted directly to the account of Don V. Davis in the accounts receivable ledger. The stock record was adjusted accordingly.

Made the following cash sales:

No. 151, Badger Paint Stores; paint, $454.50.
No. 152, M. J. Rosen; paint, $286.80.

At the end of each day the carbon copies of the cash sales tickets are analyzed to determine the total sales by departments, after which an entry is made in the record of cash receipts debiting the Bank for the total amount of cash received and crediting Cash Sales by departments for the total sales made in each department.

Issued the following checks:

No. 835, $40, payable to Postage. (Cashed the check at the bank and purchased $40 worth of stamps.)

No. 836, Banner Paint Co., $272.74, in payment of its invoice of May 30 for $275.50, less 1 percent discount.

No. 837, Celucoat Corporation, $349.66, in payment of merchandise purchased May 30 amounting to $356.80, less 2 percent discount.

Wednesday, June 8

Issued Credit Memorandum No. 893 to Atlas Hardware, $8.60, for varnish returned.

Received the following checks:

Wittenberg Lumber Co., $895.72, in payment of merchandise sold May 30 amounting to $914, less 2 percent discount.

Atlas Hardware, $589.50, in payment of merchandise sold May 10.

Made the following cash sales:

No. 153, W. E. Brubaker; paint $370; varnish, $195.80.
No. 154, C. R. Wannen; paint $177.20.

Made petty cash disbursements as follows:

Typewriter repairs, $4.50. Voucher No. 56.
500 circular letters, $8.25. Voucher No. 57.

Issued charge-back Invoice No. 15 to Celucoat Corporation, $52.80, for paint returned; paint purchased May 30.

> This transaction was recorded in the general journal, after which the charge-back invoice was posted directly to the account of Celucoat Corporation in the accounts payable ledger.

Issued the following checks:

No. 838, Celucoat Corporation, $583.88, in payment of balance due on merchandise purchased May 30 for $595.80, less 2 percent discount.

> In computing the amount of the check to be issued it was necessary to refer to the account of Celucoat Corporation and to make the following calculations:
>
> | | |
> |---|---:|
> | Merchandise purchased May 30 | $648.60 |
> | Less merchandise returned for credit June 8 | 52.80 |
> | Amount subject to discount | $595.80 |
> | Less 2% discount | 11.92 |
> | | $583.88 |

456

No. 839, Phelan-Faust Paint Manufacturing Co., $500.42, in payment of its invoice of May 30, $515.90, less 3 percent discount.

Thursday, June 9

Received the following invoices:

Vane-Calvert Paint Co., St. Louis, Missouri; varnish, $47.30; terms, June 8 — 1/10, n/30; delivered to United Lumber Co., City.

Celucoat Corporation, St. Louis, Missouri; paint, $964.20; terms, June 8 — 2/10, n/30.

Office Equipment Co., St. Louis, Missouri; calculator, $502.85; terms, June 9 — n/30.

Friday, June 10

Made charge sales as follows:

No. 108, Warson Village Hardware, Warson Village, Missouri; paint, $455.80; terms, 2/10, n/30; express collect.

No. 109, County Lumber Co., Jennings, Missouri; paint, $396.60; varnish, $593.10; terms, 2/10, n/30; express collect.

No. 110, Famous-Barr Co., St. Louis, Missouri; paint, $2,761.50; varnish, $94.80; terms, 2/10, n/30.

No. 111, United Lumber Co., St. Louis, Missouri; varnish, $63.40; terms, 2/10, n/30.

The varnish billed to the United Lumber Co. on Sales Invoice No. 111 was delivered directly by the Vane-Calvert Paint Co. on June 9 and an invoice was received on June 9.

Received a 30-day, 6 percent interest-bearing note (No. 104), dated June 9, for $750 from the United Lumber Co. in temporary settlement of the balance due on its account June 1.

The note was recorded in the general journal and in the notes receivable register.

Issued Credit Memorandum No. 894 to St. John Hardware, $54.20, for paint returned. Since the paint was defective, it was returned immediately to Celucoat Corporation for credit at cost, $40.40. Issued charge-back Invoice No. 16.

Both of these transactions were recorded in the general journal. It will be noted that St. John Hardware was given credit for the wholesale price of the paint, while Celucoat Corporation was charged for the manufacturer's price.

Issued Check No. 840 to The Daily Post for $15.90 in payment of an advertisement in the Sunday edition of June 5.

Received the following check:

Zephyr Hardware, $651.90, in full settlement of our invoice of May 31, $665.20, less 2 percent discount.

Saturday, June 11

Issued Check No. 841 for $148.47 to the American National Bank in payment of a dishonored check of the Forest Park Lumber Co. Its check was returned unpaid by the bank on which it was drawn with a notice stating the reason as "not sufficient funds."

The dishonored check was originally received for a sales invoice issued May 19 for $151.50, less 2 percent discount. Holling & Renz have arranged with the bank for all dishonored checks to be presented to them for reimbursement. When the dishonored check of the Forest Park Lumber Co. was presented, Mr. Holling issued Check No. 841 in settlement and wrote A. L. Jinks, President of the Forest Park Lumber Co., advising him that his check of May 31 had been returned unpaid and had been charged back to his account.

Received the following invoices:

Sunbrite Supply Co., St. Louis, Missouri; advertising supplies, $57.50; terms, June 11 — n/30.

458

Celucoat Corporation, St. Louis, Missouri; paint, $1,015.50; terms, June 10 — 2/10, n/30.

Glidden Co., St. Louis, Missouri; paint, $345.70; terms, June 10 — 3/10, n/30; delivered directly to Famous-Barr Co., City.

Morris Paper Co., St. Louis, Missouri; store supplies, $35.45; terms, June 10 — n/30.

Vane-Calvert Paint Co., St. Louis, Missouri; varnish, $45.20; terms, June 10 — 1/10, n/30; shipped by the supplier to Beyers Lumber Co., Olivette, Missouri; express collect.

Issued the following checks:

No. 842, Celucoat Corporation, $564.48, in payment of its invoice of June 2 for $576, less 2 percent discount.

No. 843, Phelan-Faust Paint Manufacturing Co., $382.37, in payment of its invoice of June 2 for $394.20, less 3 percent discount.

Received a check for $394.55 from Don V. Davis, in settlement of the balance of our invoice of June 1; merchandise, $402.60, less 2 percent discount.

END-OF-THE-WEEK WORK

(1) Footed the amount columns in all the books of original entry and the petty cash disbursements record and proved the footings. **(2)** Proved the bank balance as follows:

Balance, June 1..	$2,616.27
Total receipts for the period June 1–11 per record of cash receipts......	5,356.61
Total..	$7,972.88
Less total checks issued during period June 1–11 per record of checks drawn..	6,292.15
Balance, June 11...	$1,680.73

(3) Completed the individual posting from the books of original entry to the general ledger and the operating expense ledger accounts.

Monday, June 13

Discounted the United Lumber Co. note (No. 104) for $750 (received June 10) at the American National Bank at 6 percent and deposited the proceeds amounting to $750.48.

> Two lines were required to record the transaction in the record of cash receipts. A notation was also made in the Discounted column of the notes receivable register.

Made charge sales as follows:

No. 112, Beyers Lumber Co., Olivette, Missouri; paint, $135; varnish, $60.70; postage, $2.38; terms, 2/10, n/30. (The varnish was shipped directly from the factory, express collect. See the related transaction of June 11.)

No. 113, Hoffman Paint Co., Rock Hill, Missouri; paint, $98.10; varnish, $155.40; terms, 2/10, n/30.

No. 114, Famous-Barr Co., St. Louis, Missouri; paint, $484; terms, 2/10, n/30; delivered directly from factory on June 11, freight collect.

No. 115, Brod-Dugan Co., Clayton, Missouri; paint, $3,174.30; terms, 2/10, n/30.

Received the following check:

E. E. Wilson, $685.50, in full settlement of account.

Made the following cash sale:

No. 155, R. J. Powell; paint, $462.70; varnish, $62.40.

Issued the following checks:

No. 844, Celucoat Corporation, $367.89, in payment of merchandise purchased June 4 for $375.40, less 2 percent discount.

459

No. 845, U.S. Paint Company, $552.90, in payment of its invoice of June 3, $570, less 3 percent discount.

Tuesday, June 14

Issued Check No. 846 for $138.48 to the Lion Oil Co. in payment of gasoline and oil supplied during May.

Paid $4.80 out of the petty cash fund for repairs on truck. Voucher No. 58.

Sent a corrected invoice to the Warson Village Hardware, Warson Village, Missouri; for $83.10.

> On Sales Invoice No. 94 dated May 25 the paint, through an error, was billed at $81.30.
> In recording this transaction in the sales register, it was necessary only to debit Accounts Receivable and to credit Sales — Department A for $1.80, which represented the increased amount of the corrected invoice. Since the transaction related to Sale No. 94, that number was entered in the Sale No. column of the sales register.

Wednesday, June 15

Made petty cash disbursements as follows:

460

> Water bill, $7.95. Voucher No. 59.
> 1M shipping tags, $5.70. Voucher No. 60.
> 100 sheets carbon paper, $1.80. Voucher No. 61.
> Painting window sign, $6. Voucher No. 62.

Made the following cash sales:

> No. 156, Affton Hardware; paint, $116.40.
> No. 157, Badger Paint Stores; varnish, $226.50.

Received the following checks:

St. John Hardware, $301.35, in settlement of balance due on merchandise sold June 6; merchandise, $307.50, less 2 percent discount.

Morris Hardware, $142.38, for merchandise sold June 6, $143.60, less 2 percent discount, plus postage $1.65.

Kaplan Lumber Co., $490.49, in payment of merchandise sold June 6 for $500.50, less 2 percent discount.

Central Hardware, $390.20, to apply on account and a 60-day, 6 percent note (No. 105) for $800 dated June 15, in temporary settlement of the balance due.

> After entering both the check and the note in the cash receipts record, they were posted immediately as a credit to the account of Central Hardware in the accounts receivable ledger. The amount of the check was entered on one line and the amount of the note on the next line. The note was also recorded in the notes receivable register.

Mr. Holling reported that he had clipped interest coupons, amounting to $75, from government bonds owned and had deposited them in the American National Bank.

This transaction was recorded in the record of cash receipts.

Issued Check No. 847 for $611.40 to the American National Bank, a United States depositary, in payment of the following taxes:

Employees' income tax (withheld during May)		$323.20
FICA tax imposed —		
On employees (withheld during May)	$144.10	
On employer	144.10	288.20
Total		$611.40

Issued Check No. 848 payable to Payroll for $2,076.35.

Holling & Renz follow the policy of paying their employees on the 15th and the last day of each month. They are subject to the taxes imposed under the Federal Insurance Contributions Act for old-age benefits and hospital insurance, and under the Federal Unemployment Tax Act for unemployment insurance purposes. They are also required to make contributions to the state unemployment compensation fund. They are required to withhold a percentage of their employees' wages both for old-age and hospital insurance benefits and for income tax purposes. In addition to the wages paid to employees, the Holling & Renz partnership agreement provides that each partner is to receive a salary of $1,000 a month, payable semimonthly. While the salaries of the partners constitute an operating expense of the business, they do not represent "wages" as defined in the social security and income tax laws; hence, such salaries are not subject to the FICA tax imposed upon employers and employees. Neither are such salaries subject to withholding for employees' income tax.

461

Each payday the bookkeeper is supplied with a report prepared by the payroll clerk showing the total amount of wages and salaries earned during the pay period, the amount of the payroll deductions, and the net amount of cash needed for payroll purposes. The report for June 15 appears as follows:

PAYROLL STATEMENT FOR PERIOD BEGINNING JUNE 1 AND ENDING JUNE 15

			DEDUCTIONS	
CLASSIFICATION	TOTAL EARNINGS	FICA TAX	EMPLOYEES' INCOME TAX	NET AMOUNT PAYABLE
Salaries of store clerks	$ 650.00	$35.75	$ 89.40	$ 524.85
Wages of truck driver	275.00	15.13	26.90	232.97
Office salaries	385.00	21.17	45.30	318.53
Partners' salaries:				
T. L. Holling	500.00	None	None	500.00
A. G. Renz	500.00	None	None	500.00
	$2,310.00	$72.05	$161.60	$2,076.35

Employer's payroll taxes:		
FICA tax, 5.5% of $1,310		$ 72.05
Unemployment compensation tax —		
State unemployment tax, 2.7% of $1,265	$34.16	
FUTA tax, 0.5% of $1,265	6.33	40.49
Total		$112.54

A check made payable to Payroll was issued for the net amount payable. This check was then cashed at the American National Bank and currency and coins in the right denominations needed to pay each employee were obtained. The bookkeeper was instructed by Messrs. Holling and Renz to deposit their salaries in their individual bank accounts and to furnish them with duplicate copies of the deposit tickets.

The payroll check is entered in the record of checks drawn by debiting the proper salary accounts for the earnings, by crediting the proper liability accounts for the taxes withheld, and by crediting the bank account for the amount of the check issued. The payroll taxes imposed on the employer are recorded in the general journal by debiting Payroll Taxes Expense and by crediting the proper liability accounts for the taxes imposed.

The double waved lines appearing at this point in the records illustrated indicate omission of the transactions completed on the days between June 15 and 30.

Thursday, June 30

Received the following invoices (numbered consecutively beginning with 768):

Vane-Calvert Paint Co., St. Louis, Missouri; varnish, $126.70; terms, June 30 — 1/10, n/30.

Celucoat Corporation, St. Louis, Missouri; paint, $2,370.50; terms, June 29 — 2/10, n/30.

U.S. Paint Company, St. Louis, Missouri; varnish, $951.10; terms, June 28 — 3/10, n/30.

462

Office Equipment Co., St. Louis, Missouri; one checkwriter, $75, less credit for exchange allowance on old checkwriter, $5; terms, June 29 — n/30.

The original cost of the old checkwriter was $45. Since the group method of accounting for depreciation is used, the accumulated depreciation account must be charged with the cost of the old checkwriter less the $5 trade-in allowance. This transaction was recorded in the invoice register by debiting Office Equipment, Account No. 191, for $75, the cost of the new checkwriter; by debiting Accumulated Depreciation — Office Equipment, Account No. 019, for $40, the difference between the cost and the trade-in allowance on the old checkwriter; by crediting Office Equipment, Account No. 191, for $45, the original cost of the old checkwriter; and by crediting Accounts Payable, Account No. 271, for $70, the balance due the Office Equipment Co.

Received cashier's check for $300.75 from the Wellston Bank, Wellston, Missouri, in payment of Pearl Paint Store note (No. 101) for $300 plus interest $1.50, less collection charges, 75 cents.

John J. Baker, attorney at law, advises that he is unable to collect the $45 owed by Raymond Hall, and Mr. Holling has instructed that the account be charged off.

This transaction is recorded in the general journal by debiting Allowance for Bad Debts, Account No. 013, and by crediting Accounts Receivable for $45. It is then posted immediately as a credit to the account of Raymond Hall in the accounts receivable ledger.

Made charge sales as follows:

No. 139, Joe Miller Lumber Co., Centerville, Missouri; varnish, $87; terms, 2/10, n/30.

No. 140, Branneky and Sons, St. Ann, Missouri; paint, $1,438.25; varnish, $996.10; terms, 2/10, n/30; freight collect.

No. 141, County Lumber Co., Jennings, Missouri; paint, $610.40; varnish, $371.05; terms, 2/10, n/30; shipped by prepaid express, $6.15.

It will be noted from the entry in the sales register that the express prepaid on the merchandise sold to the County Lumber Co. at Jennings, Missouri, was credited to Freight Out, Account No. 6119. Since this account is kept in the subsidiary operating expense ledger, it is also necessary to credit the freight to the general ledger control account for Operating Expenses, Account No. 611. The double posting is provided for by drawing a diagonal line in the Account No. column.

As a part of the foregoing transaction, paid $6.15 out of the petty cash fund for express charges on merchandise shipped to the County Lumber Co., Jennings, Missouri. Voucher No. 67.

Beyers Lumber Co. has advised that the paint and varnish shipped directly from the factory on June 24 arrived by express collect, $3.75, even though a delivered price had been quoted them. Mr. Holling, therefore, directed that a credit memorandum (No. 897) be issued to Beyers Lumber Co. for the amount of the express charges.

This transaction was recorded in the general journal by debiting Freight Out, Account No. 6119, in the Operating Expenses column, and by crediting Accounts Receivable for $3.75. The credit memorandum was also posted directly to the account of Beyers Lumber Co. in the accounts receivable ledger.

Made petty cash disbursement of $1.30, for collect telegram. Voucher No. 68.

Issued the following checks:

No. 868, Pine Street Garage, $25, in payment of May storage.

No. 869, Vane-Calvert Paint Co., $20.79, in payment of its invoice of June 22, $21, less 1 percent discount.

No. 870, Hulsey Transfer Co., $96.10, in payment of freight and drayage on incoming merchandise received during June.

According to Mr. Holling's instructions, freight and drayage on incoming merchandise should be distributed on a basis of the cost of the merchandise purchased for each department during the month. On this basis, Freight In — Department A should be charged for $86.30 and Freight In — Department B should be charged for $9.80.

Issued Check No. 871 payable to Payroll for $2,076.35.

The payroll for the second half of June was the same as that for the first half of the month. Refer to payroll statement, page 461.

Issued Check No. 872 for $94.55 payable to Petty Cash to replenish the petty cash fund. The petty cash disbursements for June are shown at the top of page 472.

INVOICE REGISTER FOR MONTH OF June 19 —

PAGE 38

PURCHASES DEBIT		GENERAL LEDGER DEBIT			DAY	DATE OF INV.	INV. NO.	NAME	ACCOUNTS PAYABLE CREDIT	✓	GENERAL LEDGER CREDIT		✓
DEPT. A	DEPT. B	AMOUNT	ACCT. NO.	✓							ACCT. NO.	AMOUNT	
								AMOUNTS FORWARDED					
576 00					3	6/2	741	Celucoat Corporation	576 00	✓			
	394 20				3	6/2	742	Phelan-Faust Paint Mfg. Co.	394 20	✓			
		38 90	163	✓	3	6/3	743	Sunbrite Supply Co.	38 90	✓			
375 40					4	6/4	744	Celucoat Corporation	375 40	✓			
	570 00				4	6/3	745	R.L. Paint Company	570 00	✓			
		42 00	163	✓	4	6/4	746	Stalcoat Paper Products	42 00	✓			
		99 60							99 60	✓			
	96 420				9	6/8	747	Vane-Calvert Paint Co.	47 30	✓			
	47 730				9	6/8	748	Celucoat Corporation	964 20	✓			
95 140		502 85	191	✓	9	6/9	749	Office Equipment Co.	502 85	✓			
96 420		57 50	162	✓	11	6/11	750	Sunbrite Supply Co.	57 50	✓			
101 550					11	6/10	751	Celucoat Corporation	1015 50	✓			
34 570					11	6/10	752	Glidden Co.	345 70	✓			
		35 45	161	✓	11	6/10	753	Morris Paper Co.	35 45	✓			
	45 20				11	6/10	754	Vane-Calvert Paint Co.	45 20	✓			
327 680	105 270	67 670							5070 20				
237 050	126 70				30	6/30	768	Vane-Calvert Paint Co.	126 70	✓			
					30	6/29	769	Celucoat Corporation	237 050	✓			
	95 110	75 00	191	✓	30	6/23	770	R.L. Paint Company	951 10	✓			
		40 00	019	✓	30	6/29	771	Office Equipment Co.	70 00	✓	191	45 00	✓
2080 490	534 280	90 320							2700 590			45 00	
2080 490	534 280	90 320							2700 590			45 00	
(511)	(521)	(✓)							(271)			(✓)	

Holling & Renz — Invoice Register

ACCT. NO.	AMOUNT	✓	ACCOUNTS RECEIVABLE	✓	DAY	NAME	SALE NO.	DEPT. A	DEPT. B	ACCT. NO.	AMOUNT	✓
						AMOUNTS FORWARDED						
			42040	✓	1	Don V. Davis	104	26890	15150			
			30750	✓	6	St. John Hardware	105	30750				
			14525	✓	6	Morris Hardware	106	14360		164	165	✓
			50050	✓	6	Kaplan Lumber Co.	107	50050				
			45580	✓	10	Watson Village Hardware	108	45580				
			98970	✓	10	County Lumber Co.	109	39660	59310			
			285630	✓	10	Famous-Barr Co.	110	276150	9480			
			56340	✓	10	United Lumber Co.	111	45 34440	6340		166	
			573 85 / 19808	✓	13	Beyers Lumber Co.	112	13500	7020 / 6070	164	238	
			25350	✓	13	Hoffman Paint Co.	113	9810	15540			
			48400	✓	13	Famous-Barr Co.	114	48400				
			317430	✓	13	Brod-Dugan Co.	115	317430				
			180	✓	14	Watson Village Hardware	94	180				
			8700	✓	30	Joe Miller Lumber Co.	139		8700			
			243435	✓	30	Branneby and Sons	140	143825	99610	611		
			98760	✓	30	County Lumber Co.	141	61040 / 5010420	37105 / 5693760	619	615	✓
			3593235 / 3593235					5010420	5693760		13055 / 13055	
			(133)					(411)	(421)		(✓)	

Holling & Renz — Sales Register

465

466

	DEBIT							CREDIT					
GENERAL LEDGER			SALES DISCOUNT	BANK NET AMOUNT	DAY	RECEIVED FROM — DESCRIPTION	ACCOUNTS RECEIVABLE	✓	CASH SALES		GENERAL LEDGER		
ACCT. NO.	AMOUNT	✓							DEPT. A	DEPT. B	ACCT. NO.	AMOUNT	✓
						AMOUNTS FORWARDED							
			1170	57330	1	Don V. Davis	58500	✓					
			1566	76734	6	Famous-Bass Co.	78300	✓					
				74130	7	Cash Sales			74130				
			1828	89572	8	Wittenberg Lumber Co.	91400	✓					
				58950	8	Atlas Hardware	58950	✓					
				74300	8	Cash Sales			54720	19580			
			1330	65190	10	Zephyr Hardware	66520	✓					
			805	39455	11	Don V. Davis	40760	✓					
			6299	535650			333930		129850	19570			
				75048	13	Bank Note No. 104 disc.					131	75000	✓
					13	Interest Earned					711	48	✓
				68550	13	E.E. Wilson	68550	✓					
				52510	13	Cash Sales			46270	6240			
				34290	15	Cash Sales			11640	22650			
			615	30135	15	St. John Hardware	30750	✓					
			287	14238	15	Morris Hardware	14525	✓					
			1001	49049	15	Kaplan Lumber Co.	50050	✓					
131	80000	✓		39020	15	Central Hardware-Note No.105	119020	✓					
				7500	15	Interest on government bonds					711	7500	✓
831	30075	✓		30075	30	Wellston Bank-Note No.101					131	30000	✓
					30	Interest Earned					711	150	✓
	80075		52190	3816235			3407742		298830	101740		113138	
	80075		52190	3416235			3417742		291870	101740		113138	
	(✓)		(043)	(111)			(133)		(411)	(421)		(✓)	

Holling & Renz — Record of Cash Receipts

GENERAL LEDGER (DEBIT) ACCT. NO.	v	AMOUNT	OPERATING EXPENSES ACCT. NO.	v	AMOUNT	ACCOUNTS PAYABLE	v	DAY	v	DRAWN TO THE ORDER OF	GENERAL LEDGER (CREDIT) ACCT. NO.	v	AMOUNT	PUR- CHASES DISC.	v	CK. NO.	BANK NET AMOUNT	
										AMOUNTS FORWARDED								
			6131	v	45000			1		J. C. Walsh						830	45000	1
						85230	v	2		U.S. Paint Company				2557		831	82673	2
165		17000						2		Mr. F.O. Insurance Co.						832	17000	3
					45000	119050		4		Celucoat Corporation				2381 / 4935		833	116669 / 26342	4
						84620	v	6		Phelan-Faust Paint Mfg. Co.				2539		834	872081	5,6
144	v	4000						7		Postage						835	4000	7
						27550	v	7		Benner Paint Co.				276		836	27274	8
						35680	v	7		Celucoat Corporation				714		837	34966	9
						59580	v	8		Celucoat Corporation				1192		838	58388	10
						51590	v	8		Phelan-Faust Paint Mfg. Co.				1548		839	50042	11
			6111	v	1590			10		The Daily Post						840	1590	12
133	v	15150						11		American National Bank	043		303 v			841	148847	13
						57600	v	11		Celucoat Corporation				1152		842	56448	14
					36590	39420	v	11		Phelan-Faust Paint Mfg. Co.				1183		843	38237	15
						37540	v	13		Celucoat Corporation	303			751		844	36789	16
						57000	v	13		U.S. Paint Company				1710		845	55290	17
			6116	v	13848			14		Lion Oil Co.						846	13848	18
244	v	32320						15		American National Bank						847	61140	19
2/1	v	28820																20
			6112	v	65000			15		Payroll	2/1		7205 v			848	207635	21
			6113	v	27500						241		16160 v					22
			6114	v	50000													23
			6132	v	50000													24
			6133	v	38500													25
			6118	v	2500			30		Pine Street Garage						868	2500	38
						2100 / 2/1430	v	30		Vance-Calvert Paint Co.				21 / 49127		869	2079 / 32/3/08	39
		14861			350995	2814430				Carried forward			17751	49127			32/3/08	40

RECORD OF CHECKS DRAWN FOR MONTH OF *June* 19 ___   PAGE 78

DEBIT GENERAL LEDGER ACCT. NO.	AMOUNT	√	OPERATING EXPENSES ACCT. NO.	AMOUNT	√	ACCOUNTS PAYABLE	DAY	DRAWN TO THE ORDER OF	√	CREDIT GENERAL LEDGER ACCT. NO.	AMOUNT	√	PUR-CHASES DISC.	CK. NO.	BANK NET AMOUNT	
	1 148 61			3 509 95		28 141 30	30	AMOUNTS FORWARDED			177 51		491 27		32 131 08	1
544	86 30	√					30	*Hulsey Transfer Co.*						870	96 10	2
551	9 80	√														3
			6112	650 00	√		30	*Payroll*		211	72 05	√		871	2076 35	4
			6113	275 00	√					244	16 60	√				5
			6114	500 00	√											6
			6132	500 00	√											7
			6133	385 00	√											8
163	1 80	√	6111	8 25	√		30	*Petty Cash*						872	94 55	9
			6117	4 80	√											10
			6119	8 60	√											11
			6123	7 65	√											12
			6134	7 95	√											13
			6135	3 60	√											14
	1 244 51		6144	51 90	√	28 141 30					411 16		491 27		34 398 08	15
	1 244 51			5 912 70		28 141 30					411 16		491 27		34 398 08	16
	(√)			(611)		(271)					(√)		(053)		(111)	17
																18
																19
																20
																21
																22
																23

Holling & Renz — Record of Checks Drawn *(concluded)*

Line	DAY	DESCRIPTION	GL Debit Acct. No.	GL Debit Amount	Accounts Payable (Dr.)	Op. Exp. Acct. No.	Op. Exp. Amount	GL Credit Acct. No.	GL Credit Amount	Accounts Payable (Cr.)	Accounts Receivable (Cr.)
		AMOUNTS FORWARDED									
1	7	Don V. Davis, CM 892	044	1780							1780 ✓
2	8	Atlas Hardware, CM 893	042	860							860 ✓
3	8	Celucoat Corporation, C-B15			5280 ✓			051	5280 ✓		
4–5	10	United Lumber Co., N 104	131	75000							75000 ✓
6	10	St. John Hardware, CM 894	044	5420							5420 ✓
7	10	Celucoat Corporation, C-B16			4040 ✓			051	4040 ✓		
				83060	9320				9320 ✓		$3060 (83060) ✓
8	15	Payroll Taxes				6443	11254 ✓	211	7205 ✓		
9								221	633 ✓		
10								231	3416 ✓		
≈≈≈											
27	30	Raymond Hall	013	4500							4500 ✓
28	30	Byers Lumber Co., CM 897				6419	375 ✓				375 ✓
29						6443	11254 ✓	211	7205 ✓		
30	30	Payroll Taxes						221	633 ✓		
31								231	3416 ✓		
32				195412 / 195412	21460 / 21460			22883 / 22883		45075 / 45075		194650 / 194680
33				(✓)	(271)		(611)		(✓)		(133)

	DAY	DESCRIPTION	VOU. NO.	TOTAL AMOUNT		6111		6117		
1		AMOUNTS FORWARDED *Balance 100.00*								1
2	8	Typewriter repairs	56	4 50						2
3	8	Circular letters	57	8 25 *12 75*		8 25				3
4	14	Repairs on truck	58	4 80		*8 25*		4 80		4
5	15	Water bill	59	7 95						5
6	15	Shipping tags	60	5 70						6
7	15	Carbon paper	61	1 80						7
8	15	Painting window signs	62	6 00						8
13	30	Express charges	67	6 15						13
14	30	Collect telegram	68	1 30 *94 55*		8 25		4 80		14
15				94 55		8 25		4 80		15
16	30	Balance 5.45								16
17		Received in fund 94.55								17
18		100.00								18

DISTRIBUTION OF CHARGES

	6119	6128	6134	6135	6144	ACCOUNT	AMOUNT	
1								1
2					4 50			2
3								3
4					4 50			4
5			7 95					5
6		5 70						6
7						163	1 80	7
8					6 00			8
≈≈≈								
13	6 15							13
14				1 30				14
15	8 60	7 65	7 95	3 60	5 90		1 80	14
15	8 60	7 65	7 95	3 60	51 90		1 80	15

Holling & Renz — Petty Cash Disbursements (Right Page)

STATEMENT OF PETTY CASH DISBURSEMENTS FOR JUNE

Acct. No.	Account	Amount
163	Office Supplies	$ 1.80
6111	Advertising Expense	8.25
6117	Truck Repairs Expense	4.80
6119	Freight Out	8.60
6128	Miscellaneous Selling Expense	7.65
6134	Light and Water Expense	7.95
6135	Telephone and Telegraph Expense	3.60
6144	Miscellaneous General Expense	51.90
	Total disbursements	$94.55

END-OF-THE-MONTH WORK

(1) Footed the amount columns, proved the footings, entered the totals, and ruled each of the books of original entry and the petty cash disbursements record. (2) Proved the bank balance as illustrated below:

Balance, June 1	$ 2,616.27
Total receipts for June per record of cash receipts	38,162.35
Total	$40,778.62
Less total checks issued during June per record of checks drawn	34,398.08
Balance, June 30	$ 6,380.54

(3) Completed the individual posting from the books of original entry to the general ledger and to the operating expense ledger accounts. (4) Completed the summary posting of the totals of the special columns of each of the books of original entry to the general ledger accounts. (5) Prepared a trial balance and schedules of accounts receivable, accounts payable, and operating expenses.

Step (5) would be completed as a part of the normal routine at the end of each month. However, since the end of June is also the end of the fiscal year for Holling & Renz, the procedure is varied slightly. The preparation of the general ledger trial balance and the schedule of operating expenses is combined with the preparation of the end-of-year work sheets used to assist in producing the income statement for the year and the balance sheet as of June 30. This process is described and illustrated in the following chapter. (The schedules of accounts receivable and accounts payable are shown on page 504.)

Report No. 17-1

The workbook contains an analysis test that should be completed at this time. Before beginning work on the test, this chapter should be reviewed thoroughly. The narrative of transactions for June should be checked with the illustrations to see how each transaction is recorded and to note the effect of each transaction on the accounts involved. Special attention should be given to the analyses following certain transactions. Unless the procedure involved in recording the transactions completed by Holling & Renz during the month of June is thoroughly understood, you cannot hope to make a satisfactory grade on the test.

473

chapter 18

accounting procedure at end of year

474

One of the several reasons for maintaining a set of accounting records is to make it possible to prepare periodic financial reports. At the very least, an income statement for the fiscal year and a balance sheet as of the close of that year are needed. Long experience has shown that one of the fastest ways to produce these statements is **(1)** to use the information provided by the accounts — as reflected by the year-end trial balance taken after the regular posting has been completed, **(2)** to determine the needed adjustments, and **(3)** to bring these amounts together in a manner that facilitates statement preparation. The device most commonly used is the work sheet (or, sometimes, work *sheets*). A work sheet can be described in modern terminology as one means of processing data.

Summary and supplementary year-end work sheets

A simple eight-column work sheet for a personal service enterprise was discussed and illustrated in Chapter 5. A ten-column work sheet for a retail merchandising business was introduced in Chapter 9. Following is a discussion and illustration of a ten-column summary work sheet supplemented by a three-column operating expenses work sheet. The illustrations relate to the firm of Holling & Renz, wholesale distributors of paint and varnish. In the preceding chapter, a partial narrative of transactions for this firm for the month of June, 19--- (the last month of the fiscal year) was given. These transactions were shown as recorded in the books of original entry and in certain of the auxiliary records. The books of original entry were reproduced as they would appear after both the individual and the summary posting had been completed. Neither the general ledger accounts nor the accounts in each of the three subsidiary ledgers (accounts receivable, accounts payable, and operating expenses) were reproduced. However, it may be assumed that trial balances of all ledgers were taken, and that everything was found to be in order. That is, the general ledger was found to be in balance, and the total of the account balances in each subsidiary ledger was found to agree with the balance of the related control account in the general ledger.

Summary end-of-year work sheet

This work sheet is reproduced on pages 476 and 477. It is identical in form to that used for The Adams Appliance Store reproduced on pages 244–245. The first step in its preparation was to write the proper heading at the top, to insert the proper headings in the space provided at the top of each of the five pairs of amount columns, and to list the general ledger account titles and numbers in the spaces provided at the left. Note that, with one exception, the title and number of every general ledger account was listed even though certain of the accounts had no balances at the time the trial balance was taken. (Refer to the Chart of Accounts given on page 448 for the complete list.) The one exception was Expense and Revenue Summary, Account No. 331. That account is used in the formal process of adjusting and closing the books, but it is not needed on the work sheet. Note also that in the cases of Cost of Goods Sold — Department A, Account No. 561, and Cost of Goods Sold — Department B, Account No. 571, three lines were allowed in each case to accommodate the several debits and credits that will be involved. (The purpose of each cost of goods sold account is to provide a means of bringing together all the elements that are involved in calculating the amount of this cost: (1) beginning inventory, (2) purchases, (3) purchases returns and allowances, (4) purchases discount, (5) freight in, and (6) ending inventory.)

The account balances were entered in the first pair of columns and these columns were totaled to prove their equality.

Holling & Berg
Work Sheet
For the Year Ended June 30, 19—

Account	Acct. No.	Trial Balance Debit	Trial Balance Credit	Adjustments Debit	Adjustments Credit	Adj. Trial Balance Debit	Adj. Trial Balance Credit	Income Statement Debit	Income Statement Credit	Balance Sheet Debit	Balance Sheet Credit
American National Bank	111	638054				638054				638054	
Petty Cash Fund	112	1000				1000				1000	
Government Bonds	121	500000				500000				500000	
Notes Receivable	131	430326				430326				430326	
Accrued Interest Receivable	132			(l) 2566		2566				2566	
Accounts Receivable	133	1615905				1615905				1615905	
Allowance for Bad Debts	013		51480		(a) 192654		244134				244134
Merchandise Inventory-Dept. 2	141	12947210		(b) 13665915	(a) 12947210	13665915				13665915	
Merchandise Inventory-Dept. B	151	982152		(b) 1060715	(b) 982152	1060715				1060715	
Store Supplies	161	141562			(c) 127544	14018				14018	
Advertising Supplies	162	37319			(d) 24979	12340				12340	
Office Supplies	163	139210			(e) 117246	21964				21964	
Postage Stamps	164	104860			(f) 77970	26890				26890	
Prepaid Insurance	165	100248			(g) 61634	38614				38614	
Store Equipment	171	258360				258360				258360	
Accum. Depr.-Store Equip.	017		64604		(h) 25836		90440				90440
Delivery Equipment	181	457832				457832				457832	
Accum. Depr.-Delivery Equip.	018		286146		(i) 114458		400604				400604
Office Equipment	191	439940				439940				439940	
Accum. Depr.-Office Equip.	019		71384		(j) 38666		110050				110050
F.I.C.A. Tax Payable	211		28820				28820				28820
F.U.T.A. Tax Payable	221		7596				7596				7596
State Unemployment Tax Pay.	231		20496				20496				20496
Employees Income Tax Pay.	241		30796				30796				30796
Notes Payable	251		450000				450000				450000
Accrued Interest Payable	261				(m) 4425		4425				4425
Accounts Payable	271		712050				712050				712050
J. L. Holling, Capital	311		7573212				7573212				7573212
J. L. Holling, Drawing	031	2017615				2017615				2017615	

Holling & Renz — Ten-Column Work Sheet

Account	No.	Trial Balance Dr	Trial Balance Cr	Adjustments Dr	Adjustments Cr	Adjusted Trial Balance Dr	Adjusted Trial Balance Cr	Income Statement Dr	Income Statement Cr	Balance Sheet Dr	Balance Sheet Cr
O. L. Renz, Capital	321		1894730				1894730				1894730
O. L. Renz, Drawing	032	7541951				7541951				7541951	
Sales - Department A	411		5424246				5424246		5424246		
Sales Ret. and Allow.-Dept. A	041	728510				728510		728510			
Sales - Department B	421		5835568				5835568		5835568		
Sales Ret. and Allow.-Dept. B	042	91060				91060		91060			
Sales Discount	043	579526				579526		579526			
Purchases - Department A	511	4898260			(a) 4898260						
Purchases Ret.+Allow.-Dept. A	051		213452	(c) 213452							
Purchases - Department B	521	4533720			(b) 4533720						
Purchases Ret.+Allow.-Dept. B	052		13916	(d) 13916							
Purchases Discount	053		871412	(e) 871412							
Freight In - Department A	541	367243			(f) 367243						
Freight In - Department B	551	62190			(g) 62190						
Cost of Goods Sold - Dept. A	561			(adjustments)		40547332		40547332			
Cost of Goods Sold - Dept. B	571			(adjustments)		4418033		4418033			
Operating Expenses	611	6972868		180987		7153855		7153855			
Interest Earned	711		18032		2566		20598		20598		
Interest Expense	811	21471		4425		25896		25896			
Charitable Contributions Exp.	821	58500				58500		58500			
Collection Expense	831	3490				3490		3490			
		78032161	78032161	77404163	77404163	77311984	77311984	54206202	60097412	23105784	17214574
Net Income								5891210			5891210
								60097412	60097412	23105784	23105784

Adjustment of the Merchandise Accounts. Eleven entries were made in the adjustments columns on the work sheet to show the calculation of the cost of goods sold for each department and to adjust the merchandise inventory accounts:

Entry (a): The amount of the beginning inventory for Department A, $129,472.10, was transferred to Cost of Goods Sold — Department A by a debit to that account (No. 561) and by a credit to Merchandise Inventory — Department A, Account No. 141.

Entry (b): The amount of the beginning inventory for Department B, $9,821.52, was transferred to Cost of Goods Sold — Department B by a debit to that account (No. 571) and by a credit to Merchandise Inventory — Department B, Account No. 151.

Entry (c): The amount of the purchases for the year for Department A, $418,982.60, was transferred to Cost of Goods Sold — Department A by a debit to that account (No. 561) and by a credit to Purchases — Department A, Account No. 511.

Entry (d): The amount of the purchases for the year for Department B, $45,337.20, was transferred to Cost of Goods Sold — Department B by a debit to that account (No. 571) and by a credit to Purchases — Department B, Account No. 521.

Entry (e): The amount of the purchases returns and allowances for the year for Department A, $2,134.52, was transferred to the proper cost of goods sold account by a debit to Purchases Returns and Allowances — Department A, Account No. 051, and by a credit to Cost of Goods Sold — Department A, Account No. 561.

Entry (f): The amount of the purchases returns and allowances for the year for Department B, $139.16, was transferred to the proper cost of goods sold account by a debit to Purchases Returns and Allowances — Department B, Account No. 052, and by a credit to Cost of Goods Sold — Department B, Account No. 571.

Entry (g): The amount of the purchases discount taken during the year, $8,714.12, was prorated between the cost of goods sold accounts in proportion to the amount of the purchases (less returns and allowances) of the two departments. Purchases (less returns and allowances) of Department A were $416,848.08 ($418,982.60 − $2,134.52). Purchases (less returns and allowances) of Department B were $45,198.04 ($45,337.20 − $139.16). Thus the total purchases (less returns and allowances) amounted to

$462,046.12. Of this total, 90.2 percent were those of Department A, and 9.8 percent were those of Department B. Therefore, $7,860.14 was credited to Cost of Goods Sold — Department A, Account No. 561, and $853.98 to Cost of Goods Sold — Department B, Account No. 571, with a debit of $8,714.12 to Purchases Discount, Account No. 053.

Entry (h): The amount of the freight in on Department A purchases for the year, $3,672.43, was transferred to Cost of Goods Sold — Department A by a debit to that account (No. 561) and by a credit to Freight In — Department A, Account No. 541.

Entry (i): The amount of the freight in on Department B purchases for the year, $621.90, was transferred to Cost of Goods Sold — Department B by a debit to that account (No. 571) and by a credit to Freight In — Department B, Account No. 551.

Entry (j): The cost assigned to the June 30 merchandise inventory of Department A, $136,659.15, was debited to that account (No. 141) with an offsetting credit to Cost of Goods Sold — Department A, Account No. 561. Holling & Renz use the first-in, first-out method of accounting for inventory. A physical count of the goods on hand at the year's end had been made. Reference to recent purchase invoices provided unit costs for the various items. (While it would be quite reasonable to slightly reduce the inventory cost because of purchase discounts taken and to slightly increase the amount because of freight in, the amounts of both of these are small in relation to the cost of the goods, and they partially offset each other. For these reasons, they are ignored in calculating the cost to be assigned to the inventory.) Each time a physical inventory is taken, the quantities found to be on hand are compared with the stock records. The latter are corrected if any discrepancy is discovered.

Entry (k): The cost assigned to the June 30 merchandise inventory of Department B, $10,607.15, was debited to that account (No. 151) with an offsetting credit to Cost of Goods Sold — Department B, Account No. 571. (The description of the procedure followed in connection with the inventory cost assignment in Department A likewise applies to Department B.)

At this point the amount of the cost of goods sold for each department was determined by subtracting the sum of the three credits from the sum of the three debits to each of the cost of goods sold accounts. The amounts, $405,473.32 for Department A and $44,180.33 for Department B, were extended to the Adjusted Trial Balance Debit column.

Adjustment of the Interest Accounts. In order to have the calculation of the net income for the year reflect the correct amounts of both interest earned and interest expense, accruals of both types had to be taken into consideration. The notes receivable register was the source of the information required to make the following calculation relative to accrued interest on notes receivable.

SCHEDULE OF ACCRUED INTEREST ON NOTES RECEIVABLE

No.	PRINCIPAL AMOUNT	RATE OF INTEREST	DATE OF NOTE	DAYS ACCRUED	ACCRUED INTEREST
97	$1,250.00	6%	May 4	57	$11.87
98	500.00	—	May 7	—	—
100	750.00	6	May 21	40	5.00
105	800.00	6	June 15	15	2.00
106	601.76	—	June 20	—	—
107	401.50	6	June 22	8	.54
	Total interest accrued on notes receivable......................				$19.41

In addition to the notes owned on June 30, Holling & Renz owned five $1,000, 3 percent United States treasury bonds. Semiannual interest totaling $75 had been collected on June 15. Since that date, interest for 15 days amounting to $6.25 had accrued. Thus total interest accrued June 30 was $25.66 ($19.41 + $6.25).

Entry (l): On the work sheet the accrued interest receivable on June 30, $25.66, was debited to that account (No. 132) and credited to Interest Earned, Account No. 711.

Holling & Renz had only one note payable outstanding on June 30. It was a $4,500, 90-day, 6 percent note, dated May 2. On June 30, 59 days' interest amounting to $44.25 had accrued.

Entry (m): The accrued interest payable was recorded on the work sheet by debiting Interest Expense, Account No. 811, and by crediting Accrued Interest Payable, Account No. 261, for $44.25. At this point, work on the summary end-of-year work sheet was suspended temporarily.

Supplementary work sheet for operating expenses

To provide the desired information, the income statement that was to be prepared had to be supplemented by a schedule of operating expenses. The accounting records of Holling & Renz include a subsidiary operating expenses ledger which is controlled by the account, Operating Expenses (No. 611), in the general ledger. A considerable number of the operating expenses accounts required end-of-year debit adjustments (with, of course, a summary debit to the general ledger control account). These adjustments involved offsetting credits to various general ledger accounts.

In order to assemble all of the information needed both for the income statement and for the supporting schedule of operating expenses, as well as to facilitate the recording of adjustments in the general ledger and subsidiary ledger accounts (which must be done later), an operating expenses work sheet was used. As will be seen, it is very closely tied in with the summary work sheet. This operating expenses work sheet is reproduced on page 482. Note that it was given an appropriate heading that included the period involved. This work sheet needed only three amount columns: **(1)** to show the account balances when the trial balance was taken, **(2)** to provide space for certain adjustments, and **(3)** to show the adjusted amounts. In every case only debits were involved. The titles and numbers of all of the accounts in the subsidiary operating expenses ledger were placed in the columns provided. (Refer to the Chart of Accounts given on page 450 for the complete list.) It will be observed that a considerable number of the accounts had no balance when the trial balance was taken. The balance of each account (that had a balance) was entered in the Trial Balance Debit column. That column was totaled. If its total, $69,728.68, had not agreed with the balance shown for Operating Expenses, Account No. 611 (the control account), on the summary work sheet, it would have been necessary to discover and correct the discrepancy before the preparation of either work sheet could proceed.

All of the adjustments that follow (for depreciation, supplies used, insurance expired, and the bad debts provision) involved both the summary and the supplementary work sheet. One or more operating expense accounts were debited on the operating expenses work sheet, and one or more general ledger accounts were credited on the summary work sheet.

Depreciation Expense. Holling & Renz use the group method of accounting for long-lived assets and their depreciation. In the general ledger, three long-lived asset accounts (with related accumulated depreciation accounts) are kept: store equipment, delivery equipment, and office equipment. In the operating expenses ledger, three depreciation expense accounts (that correspond to the asset classifications) are kept. Depreciation is not considered on assets owned for less than one month. The schedule reproduced at the top of page 483 was prepared to determine the estimated depreciation expense for the year.

Based upon the calculations shown on the schedule, the following adjustments were made on the work sheets — the debits on the operating expenses work sheet and the credits on the summary work sheet:

Entry (n): Depreciation of Store Equipment, Account No. 6126, was debited, and Accumulated Depreciation — Store Equipment, Account No. 017, was credited for $258.36.

Holling & Renz
Operating Expenses Work Sheet
For the Year Ended June 30, 19—

Account	Acct. No.	Trial Bal. Debit	Adjustments Debit	Adj. Trial Bal. Debit
Advertising Expense	6111	269945	(n) 24979	294924
Store Clerks Salary Expense	6112	1560000		1560000
Truck Drivers Wage Expense	6113	660000		660000
A. G. Renz, Salary Expense	6114	1200000		1200000
A. G. Renz, Traveling Expense	6115	117685		117685
Truck Gas and Oil Expense	6116	131921		131921
Truck Repairs Expense	6117	21460		21460
Garage Rent Expense	6118	30000		30000
Freight Out	6119	1840		1840
Merchandise Insurance Expense	6121		(u) 29210	29210
Delivery Equipment Insurance Exp.	6122		(u) 24016	24016
Store Equipment Insurance Expense	6123		(u) 3240	3240
Store Supplies Expense	6124		(q) 127544	127544
Postage Expense (Selling)	6125		(t) 38760	38760
Depreciation of Store Equipment	6126		(m) 25836	25836
Depreciation of Delivery Equipment	6127		(o) 114458	114458
Miscellaneous Selling Expense	6128	23835		23835
Rent Expense	6131	540000		540000
J. L. Holling, Salary Expense	6132	1200000		1200000
Office Salaries Expense	6133	924000		924000
Light and Water Expense	6134	11965		11965
Telephone and Telegraph Expense	6135	20940		20940
Bad Debts Expense	6136		(u) 192654	192654
Property Tax Expense	6137	41635		41635
Office Supplies Expense	6138		(a) 117246	117246
Postage Expense (Administration)	6139		(t) 39210	39210
Office Equipment Insurance Expense	6141		(u) 5168	5168
Depreciation of Office Equipment	6142		(p) 38666	38666
Payroll Taxes Expense	6143	190514		190514
Miscellaneous General Expense	6144	27128		27128
		6972868	780987	7753855

Holling & Renz — Operating Expenses Work Sheet

SCHEDULE OF DEPRECIATION EXPENSE

FOR THE YEAR ENDED JUNE 30, 19--

ASSET	COST	ANNUAL (STRAIGHT-LINE) RATE OF DEPRECIATION	DEPRECIATION FOR THE YEAR
Store Equipment	$2,583.60	10%	$ 258.36
Delivery Equipment	4,578.32	25	1,144.58
Office Equipment	3,866.55*	10	386.66

*It may be noted that the balance of the office equipment account shown on the work sheet on page 476 is $4,399.40. That is because the costs of a desk calculator purchased on June 9 and of a checkwriter purchased on June 30 are included. However, since those assets have been owned for less than one month, no depreciation is taken on them.

Entry (o): Depreciation of Delivery Equipment, Account No. 6127, was debited, and Accumulated Depreciation — Delivery Equipment, Account No. 018, was credited for $1,144.58.

Entry (p): Depreciation of Office Equipment, Account No. 6142, was debited, and Accumulated Depreciation — Office Equipment, Account No. 019, was credited for $386.66.

Supplies Expense. The general ledger of Holling & Renz includes four asset accounts for supplies — store supplies, advertising supplies, office supplies, and postage stamps. When purchased, the supplies are recorded as assets. An inventory of unused supplies (and postage stamps) is taken **483** at the end of the year so that the cost of the supplies used can be calculated and charged to the proper operating expense accounts. The following schedule was prepared to determine the needed adjustments:

SCHEDULE OF SUPPLIES USED

FOR THE YEAR ENDED JUNE 30, 19--

ASSET	ACCOUNT BALANCE JUNE 30, 19--	AMOUNT ON HAND JUNE 30, 19--	EXPENSE FOR YEAR
Store Supplies	$1,415.62	$140.18	$1,275.44
Advertising Supplies	373.19	123.40	249.79
Office Supplies	1,392.10	219.64	1,172.46
Postage Stamps	1,048.60	268.90	779.70*

*Memorandum records kept by the shipping clerk indicate that $387.60 should be treated as a selling expense and the remainder, $392.10, as an administrative expense.

Based upon the foregoing calculations, the following adjustments were made on the work sheets:

Entry (q): Store Supplies Expense, Account No. 6124, was debited, and Store Supplies, Account No. 161, was credited for $1,275.44.

Entry (r): Advertising Expense, Account No. 6111, was debited, and Advertising Supplies, Account No. 162, was credited for $249.79.

Entry (s): Office Supplies Expense, Account No. 6138, was debited, and Office Supplies, Account No. 163, was credited for $1,172.46.

Entry (t): Postage Expense (Selling), Account No. 6125, was debited for $387.60; Postage Expense (Administration), Account No. 6139, was debited for $392.10; and Postage Stamps, Account No. 164, was credited for $779.70.

Insurance Expense. Prepaid insurance premiums are recorded by Holling & Renz in the same manner as supplies. At the time of payment of a premium, the amount paid is recorded as an asset. The prepaid insurance account (No. 165) in the general ledger is debited. At the end of the fiscal year, June 30, calculations are made to determine the fraction of the total term of each policy that has elapsed during the year. That fraction of the original premium is an expense of the year. Each such amount is classified according to the type of asset insured to determine the proper total amount to be charged to each insurance expense account. The operating expenses ledger of Holling & Renz includes insurance expense accounts for the insurance on merchandise, the delivery truck, store equipment, and office equipment.

Since the accounting records of Holling & Renz include an insurance policy register, this record was used to provide the information needed for the calculations. The following summary was based upon information supplied by the insurance policy register:

SCHEDULE OF INSURANCE EXPENSE

FOR THE YEAR ENDED JUNE 30, 19--

Type of Property Insured	Expense for Year
Merchandise	$292.10
Delivery Truck	240.16
Store Equipment	32.40
Office Equipment	51.68
Total	$616.34

Based upon this summary, the following adjustment was made on the work sheets:

Entry (u): Merchandise Insurance Expense, Account No. 6121, was debited for $292.10; Delivery Equipment Insurance Expense, Account No. 6122, was debited for $240.16; Store Equipment Insurance Expense, Account No. 6123, was debited for $32.40; Office Equipment Insurance Expense, Account No. 6141, was debited for $51.68; and Prepaid Insurance, Account No. 165, was credited for $616.34.

Bad Debts. Holling & Renz use the allowance method of accounting for bad debts. Past experience indicates that accounts that have turned out to be uncollectible have averaged ½ of 1 percent of sales on account. For the year ended June 30, 19—, sales on account totaled $385,308.20. One half of one percent of this amount is $1,926.54. The following entry was made on the work sheets:

Entry (v): Bad Debts Expense, Account No. 6136, was debited, and Allowance for Bad Debts, Account No. 013, was credited for $1,926.54.

Completing the operating expenses work sheet

It will be noted that only one of the thirteen debits in the Adjustments column of this work sheet had to be added to a previous debit balance in the account — the $249.79 debit to Advertising Expense, Account No. 6111. This was added to the $2,699.45 shown in the Trial Balance column, and their sum, $2,949.24, was extended into the Adjusted Trial Balance column. In every other case, either the unadjusted amount or the amount of the adjustment was extended into the last column.

The Adjustments and Adjusted Trial Balance columns were totaled. Since only debits were involved in this work sheet, the total of the Adjusted Trial Balance column, $77,538.55, had to be equal to the totals of the first two columns ($69,728.68 and $7,809.87).

A double rule was made below the three totals.

Completing the summary work sheet

To complete the adjustments on the summary work sheet, the balance of the control account for operating expenses had to be increased to reflect the total of all of the debits to the operating expenses that had been made on the supplementary work sheet. Accordingly, that total, $7,809.87, was entered on the line for Operating Expenses, Account No. 611, in the Adjustments Debit Column. Note that the debit was identified as "(n–v)," since it was offset by credits to nine general ledger accounts made when adjustments (n) through (v) were entered on the work sheets to adjust the operating expense accounts.

The Adjustments columns were totaled to prove their equality. The amounts in the Trial Balance columns, altered where indicated by amounts in the Adjustments columns, were extended to the Adjusted Trial Balance columns. The latter were totaled to prove their equality. Each amount in the Adjusted Trial Balance columns was extended to the proper Income Statement or Balance Sheet column. The last four columns were totaled.

485

It was found that the Income Statement Credit column exceeded the Debit column by $58,912.10, and that the Balance Sheet Debit column exceeded the Credit column by the same amount. "Net Income" was written on the next line at the left, and the amount was placed in the two proper places. The Income Statement and Balance Sheet columns were totaled to prove that each pair was in balance. Double rules were made below the final totals in all ten columns.

The summary work sheet then could be used to prepare the income statement for the fiscal year (shown on page 498) and the balance sheet as of the last day of that year (shown on pages 502 and 503). The supplementary work sheet provided the information for the schedule of operating expenses (shown on page 499).

Report No. 18-1

Complete Report No. 18-1 in the workbook. Do not submit the report at this time. Since Reports Nos. 18-1 and 18-2 are related, you should retain the working papers until you have completed both reports. Continue with the next study assignment until Report No. 18-2 is required.

Adjusting, closing, and reversing entries

The most important function of the end-of-year work sheet (or work sheets) is to facilitate the preparation of the income statement and the balance sheet as soon as possible after the end of the accounting period. Having completed the work sheets illustrated and discussed in the preceding pages, the accountant for Holling & Renz would next prepare the financial statements. A secondary function of the work sheets is to aid in the process of formally recording the adjusting and closing entries in the books. However, for the purpose of organization of subject matter in this textbook, adjusting, closing, and reversing entries will be considered next. The financial statements will be illustrated and discussed in Chapter 19.

Journalizing the adjusting entries

The adjusting entries had to be recorded in the general journal. The page of the general journal containing the adjusting entries as of June 30, 19--, is reproduced on page 488. In the form of general journal used by Holling & Renz, a special Debit column is provided for charges to the accounts in the operating expenses subsidiary ledger. Journalizing the adjusting entries involved the use of this column as well as the General Ledger Debit and Credit columns. Several features of these entries should be noted: **(1)** The titles of the accounts involved appear only as a part of the explanation of the entries. The identification of the accounts was accomplished by entering the account numbers in the space provided for this purpose when the journalizing was done, *not* as a step in the posting. **(2)** The entries are made in the same order as shown alphabetically, (a) through (v), on the work sheets (pages 476, 477, and 482). While this order was not essential, the danger of omitting an entry was slightly reduced by using the work sheets as a guide in journalizing the entries. **(3)** In order to be sure that the total of the debits equaled the total of the credits, and because the total of the Operating Expenses Debit column had to be posted, the three columns were footed, the totals were entered, and the usual rulings were made.

Posting the adjusting entries

As the individual amounts in the General Ledger Debit and Credit columns were posted to the accounts (indicated by the account numbers), a check mark (√) was made to the right of each amount in the column provided. A check mark was made in parentheses below the total of each of those two columns to indicate that, in this case, the amount was *not* posted anywhere. In the case of the entries in the Operating Expenses Debit column, a check mark was placed to the right of each amount as it was posted. The number "611" was placed in parentheses below the total of that column to indicate that the amount, $7,809.87, was posted as a debit to Operating Expenses, Account No. 611, in the general ledger. In both the general ledger and the operating expenses ledger, the page of the general journal (G 44) was placed in the Posting Reference column as each posting was made.

Journalizing the closing entries

The page of the general journal showing the closing entries as of June 30, 19--, is reproduced on page 489. Certain features of these entries

488

DAY	GL DR ACCT NO.	GL DR AMOUNT	OP EXP ACCT NO.	OP EXP AMOUNT	DESCRIPTION	GL CR ACCT NO.	GL CR AMOUNT
30					Adjusting Entries		
	561	12947210 ✓			To transfer beg. inv. to Cost of Goods Sold - Depts. A and B	141	12947210 ✓
	571	98252 ✓				151	98252 ✓
	561	4898260 ✓			To transfer purchases to Cost of Goods Sold - Depts. A and B	511	4898260 ✓
	571	4533720 ✓				521	4533720 ✓
	051	213452 ✓			To transfer pur. ret. & allow. to Cost of Goods Sold - Depts. A and B	561	213452 ✓
	052	13916 ✓				571	13916 ✓
	053	871412 ✓			Cost of Goods Sold - Depts. A and B To allocate pur. disc. to Cost of Goods Sold - Depts. A and B	561	786044 ✓
						571	85398 ✓
	561	367243 ✓			To transfer freight in to Cost of Goods Sold - Depts. A and B	541	367243 ✓
	571	6290 ✓				551	6290 ✓
	141	13665915 ✓			To record ending inventories of Depts. A and B	561	13665915 ✓
	151	1060715 ✓				571	1060715 ✓
	132	2566 ✓			Accrued interest receivable	711	2566 ✓
	811	4425 ✓			Accrued interest payable	261	4425 ✓
			6426	25836 ✓	Deprec. of store equipment	017	25836 ✓
			6427	114458 ✓	Deprec. of delivery equipment	018	114458 ✓
			6442	38066 ✓	Deprec. of office equipment	019	38066 ✓
			6424	1275544 ✓	Store supplies used	161	1275544 ✓
			6411	24979 ✓	Advertising supplies used	162	24979 ✓
			6438	117246 ✓	Office supplies used	163	117246 ✓
			6425	38760 ✓	Postage stamps used	164	77970 ✓
			6439	39210 ✓			
			6421	2920 ✓			
			6420	24016 ✓	Insurance expired	165	61634 ✓
			6423	3240 ✓			
			6441	5168 ✓			
			6436	1926454 ✓	Provision for bad debts	013	1926454 ✓
	76623176			7809877			77404163
	76623176			7809877			77404163
	(✓)			(611)			(✓)

Holling & Renz — Adjusting Entries

Op. Exp. Acct. No.	Op. Exp. Amount	A/P Debit	G/L Acct. No.	G/L Amount (Debit)	Day	Description	G/L Acct. No.	G/L Amount (Credit)	A/P Credit	A/R Credit
						AMOUNTS FORWARDED				
					30	Closing Entries				
			411	5424124 ✓		Sales—Department A				
			421	5835568 ✓		Sales—Department B				
			711	20598 ✓		Interest Earned				
						Expense & Revenue Summary	331	6009741 2 ✓		
			331	5420620 2 ✓		Expense & Revenue Summary				
						Sales R. and A. – Dept. A	041	728510 ✓		
						Sales R. and A. – Dept. B	042	91060 ✓		
						Sales Discount	043	579626 ✓		
						Cost of Goods Sold – Dept. A	561	40547332 ✓		
						Cost of Goods Sold – Dept. B	571	4418033 ✓		
						Operating Expenses	611	7753855 ✓		
						Interest Expense	811	25896 ✓		
						Charitable Cont. Expense	821	58500 ✓		
						Collection Expense	831	3490 ✓		
			331	5891210 ✓		Expense & Revenue Summary				
						J. L. Holling, Capital	311	2945605 ✓		
						A. H. Renz, Capital	321	2945605 ✓		
			311	2017615 ✓		J. L. Holling, Capital				
						J. L. Holling, Drawing	031	2017615 ✓		
			321	1894730 ✓		A. H. Renz, Capital				
						A. H. Renz, Drawing	032	1894730 ✓		
				12410769				12410769		
				12410769				12410769		
				(✓)				(✓)		

Holling & Renz — Closing Entries

Chapter 18 / Accounting Procedure at End of Year

should be noted: **(1)** Each closing entry was made in conventional form — the names of the accounts both to be debited and to be credited were given. The names of the accounts to be credited were slightly indented. As in the case of the adjusting entries, however, the numbers of the accounts were entered at the time of journalizing. The check marks were made later as the posting was completed. **(2)** The order of the closing entries follows a logical sequence. The revenue accounts are closed first, followed by the expense accounts. The third entry closes the expense and revenue summary account by dividing the income ($58,912.10) equally between T. L. Holling and A. G. Renz (as their partnership agreement specifies). The last two closing entries transfer the amount of each partner's withdrawals to his capital account. The amount columns were footed to prove the equality of the debits and credits.

It should be noted that, while there was a credit of $77, 538.55 to close Operating Expenses, Account No. 611, the individual credits to close the thirty accounts in the operating expenses subsidiary ledger were not shown. One reason is that the form of the journal page does not accommodate credits to the operating expenses accounts, because these accounts rarely are credited (except when they are closed). The occasional transaction that requires a credit to an operating expense account can be handled by noting *both* the number of the control account (611) and the number of the subsidiary ledger account in the account number column provided just to the left of the General Ledger Credit column. The amount of the credit will then be posted as a credit to both accounts. It must be understood, however, that the operating expenses accounts in the subsidiary ledger *must be closed.* The manner of doing so is illustrated by the reproduction of the account for Advertising Expense, Account No. 6111, shown on page 491. The accountant knows that when a general ledger control account is closed, all accounts in a ledger that is subsidiary to that control account also must be closed. Knowing this, the space and time required to list all of the subsidiary ledger accounts, numbers, and balances (thirty in the case at hand) is not warranted.

Posting the closing entries

The postings were made to the general ledger accounts indicated. A check mark was placed in the column provided in the general journal as each posting was made. The page of the general journal (G 45) was noted in the Posting Reference column of the account involved. As mentioned in the preceding paragraph, the balance of each account in the subsidiary operating expenses ledger was closed in the manner indicated by the entry

490

on the last line of the illustration of the account for Advertising Expense shown below. (Note that "G 45" was entered in the Posting Reference column, since that is the page of the general journal that called for the closing entry in the operating expenses control account.) The other twenty-nine operating expenses accounts were closed in a similar fashion.

ACCOUNT *Advertising Expense*					ACCOUNT NO. *6111*
DATE	ITEM	POST. REF.	DEBIT	CREDIT	BALANCE
19— June 1	Dr. Balance	✓			2675 30
10		CD77	15 90		2691 20
30		CD77	8 25		2699 45
30		G44	249 79		2949 24
30		G45		2949 24	—0—

Closed Subsidiary Operating Expense Ledger Account

491

The expense and revenue summary account and the two cost of goods sold accounts after the adjusting and closing entries had been posted are reproduced on page 492. Note that the former account was posted in detail. Remember that all three of these accounts are summarizing accounts that are used only at the end of the accounting period. (In some accounting systems, cost of goods sold accounts are used throughout the year, if such cost is known at the time of sale. This is possible if so-called *perpetual inventories* are maintained. While Holling & Renz keep stock records, these records show physical quantities only. In the accounting system of Holling & Renz, the cost of goods sold accounts are used only at the end of the fiscal year.)

Post-closing trial balance

After the closing entries were posted, a trial balance of the general ledger accounts that remained open was taken to prove the equality of the

ACCOUNT Expense and Revenue Summary   ACCOUNT NO. 331

DATE	ITEM	POST. REF.	DEBIT	DATE	ITEM	POST. REF.	CREDIT
19— June 30	S.R.+A.-Dept.A	J45	7 285 10	19— June 30	Sales-Dept.A	J45	542 412 46
30	S.R.+A.-Dept.B	J45	910 60	30	Sales-Dept.B	J45	58 355 68
30	Sales Disc.	J45	5 795 26	30	Int. Earned	J45	205 98
30	C.of G.S.-Dept.A	J45	405 473 32				600 974 12
30	C.of G.S.-Dept.B	J45	44 180 33				
30	Oper. Exp.	J45	77 538 55				
30	Int. Exp.	J45	258 96				
30	Char. Cont. Exp.	J45	585 00				
30	Collection Exp.	J45	34 90				
30	J.L. Holling, Cap.	J45	29 456 05				
30	A.G. Renz, Cap.	J45	29 456 05				
			600 974 12				600 974 12
			600 974 12				600 974 12

ACCOUNT Cost of Goods Sold - Department A   ACCOUNT NO. 561

492

DATE	ITEM	POST. REF.	DEBIT	DATE	ITEM	POST. REF.	CREDIT
19— June 30	Beg. inventory	J44	129 472 10	19— June 30	Pur. R.+A.	J44	2 134 52
30	Purchases	J44	418 982 60	30	Pur. Disc.	J44	7 860 14
30	Freight In	J44	3 672 43	30	End. inventory	J44	136 659 15
			552 127 13	30	Exp.+Rev. Sum.	J45	405 473 32
							552 127 13
			552 127 13				552 127 13

ACCOUNT Cost of Goods Sold - Department B   ACCOUNT NO. 571

DATE	ITEM	POST. REF.	DEBIT	DATE	ITEM	POST. REF.	CREDIT
19— June 30	Beg. inventory	J44	9 821 52	19— June 30	Pur. R.+A.	J44	139 16
30	Purchases	J44	45 337 20	30	Pur. Disc.	J44	853 98
30	Freight In	J44	621 90	30	End. inventory	J44	10 607 15
			55 780 62	30	Exp.+Rev. Sum.	J45	44 180 33
							55 780 62
			55 780 62				55 780 62

Closed General Ledger Summary Accounts

debit and credit balances. This post-closing trial balance of the general ledger of Holling & Renz is reproduced below.

HOLLING & RENZ

Post-Closing Trial Balance

June 30, 19--

Account	Acct. No.	Dr. Balance	Cr. Balance
American National Bank................	111	6,380.54	
Petty Cash Fund.....................	112	100.00	
Government Bonds...................	121	5,000.00	
Notes Receivable....................	131	4,303.26	
Accrued Interest Receivable...........	132	25.66	
Accounts Receivable.................	133	16,159.05	
Allowance for Bad Debts..............	013		2,441.34
Merchandise Inventory — Department A...	141	136,659.15	
Merchandise Inventory — Department B...	151	10,607.15	
Store Supplies......................	161	140.18	
Advertising Supplies..................	162	123.40	
Office Supplies.....................	163	219.64	
Postage Stamps.....................	164	268.90	
Prepaid Insurance...................	165	386.14	
Store Equipment....................	171	2,583.60	
Accumulated Depreciation — Store Equip..	017		904.40
Delivery Equipment..................	181	4,578.32	
Accumulated Depreciation — Del. Equip...	018		4,006.04
Office Equipment....................	191	4,399.40	
Accumulated Depreciation — Office Equip.	019		1,100.50
FICA Tax Payable...................	211		288.20
FUTA Tax Payable..................	221		75.96
State Unemployment Tax Payable.......	231		204.96
Employees Income Tax Payable	241		307.96
Notes Payable......................	251		4,500.00
Accrued Interest Payable..............	261		44.25
Accounts Payable	271		7,120.50
T. L. Holling, Capital.................	311		85,012.02
A. G. Renz, Capital..................	321		85,928.26
		191,934.39	191,934.39

Not all accountants feel that it is necessary to prepare a post-closing trial balance in the form illustrated. Some think that it is sufficient merely to use an adding machine tape to list and total (1) the amounts of the debit balances and (2) the amounts of the credit balances to be sure that the totals are the same. If this proves to be the case, the tapes usually are thrown away. (The cause of any discrepancy would have to be located and remedied if the ledger was found not to be in balance.) However, many accountants feel that it is desirable to prepare the post-closing trial balance in a formal fashion and file it with various other records.

Reversing entries

Two adjusting entries of the "accrual type" had been made as of June 30, 19—. One was for accrued interest receivable ($25.66), and the other for accrued interest payable ($44.25). In order that interest collections and payments may be handled in routine fashion in the new period, the accountant for Holling & Renz follows the practice of reversing accrual adjustments. A reproduction of part of the first page of the general journal for the next month (July, 19—, the first month of the next fiscal year) is given below. The first entries for the new period are the reversals of the previous accrual adjustments.

√	GENERAL LEDGER ACCT. NO.	AMOUNT	√	DAY	DESCRIPTION	GENERAL LEDGER ACCT. NO.	AMOUNT	√
					AMOUNTS FORWARDED			
	711	25 66	√	1	To reverse adjusting entries	132	25 66	√
	261	44 25	√		for accrued interest	811	44 25	√

GENERAL JOURNAL FOR MONTH OF *July* 19 —   PAGE 46

Holling & Renz — Reversing Entries

Report No. 18-2

Complete Report No. 18-2 in the workbook and submit Reports Nos. 18-1 and 18-2 for approval. Continue with the next study assignment in Chapter 19 until Report No. 19-1 is required.

chapter 19

the annual report

496   The term *annual report* as applied to a business usually refers to the financial statements and schedules relating to the accounting (fiscal) year of the enterprise. At the very least, the report includes an income statement and a balance sheet. The practice of including a statement of changes in financial position is growing. The nature and preparation of this statement is discussed and illustrated later in this chapter. In the case of business corporations with many stockholders (thousands, even hundreds of thousands, in some cases), the annual report may be a thirty- to forty-page printed publication — sometimes in full color with numerous pictures of the company's products, plants, officers, and sundry graphs and statistics in addition to the financial statements. In reports of this type, it is customary to include a letter addressed to the stockholders signed by the president of the corporation and, sometimes, by the chairman of the board of directors also. The letter is printed in the report booklet and constitutes a verbal report — often described as "highlights" of the year. Such annual reports invariably include a reproduction of the *opinion* (sometimes referred to as the *Auditor's Report*) of the CPA firm that performed the audit.

Annual reports of the elaborate type just mentioned are not used if the business has few owners. In the case of a partnership, it is probable that no one other than the partners and, possibly, one or two of the officials at their bank will ever see their reports. The annual report of Holling & Renz consists of the following statements and schedules:

The income statement

The income statement for the year ended June 30, 19--, is reproduced on page 498. It was prepared from information provided by the Income Statement columns of the work sheet reproduced on pages 476 and 477. The statement was arranged to show the sales, the detailed calculations of cost of goods sold, and the gross margin on sales for each department as well as in total. The manner of handling sales discounts should be noted: The amount of sales discounts taken by customers during the year, $5,795.26, had been recorded in one account (Sales Discount, No. 043). In preparing the income statement, the amount was allocated to the two departments in proportion to the sales less sales returns of each department. In the case of Department A, the amount is $535,127.36 ($542,412.46 − $7,285.10). For Department B, it is $57,445.08 ($58,355.68 − $910.60). The total is, accordingly, $592,572.44. Sales of Department A were 90.31 percent of the total and those of Department B, 9.69 percent. The amount of the sales discount was allocated in this proportion, that is, $5,233.70 to Department A and $561.56 to Department B.

The schedule of operating expenses reproduced on page 499 was prepared from information provided by the operating expenses work sheet shown on page 482. It should be evident that the purpose of the schedule is to provide the detail of what makes up the total amount of operating expenses ($77,538.55) shown on the income statement. If there had been only ten or twelve accounts for operating expenses it is probable that (1) there would have been no subsidiary ledger for them and (2) the comparatively few items would have been included in the income statement — no schedule would have been needed. It must be understood that there is wide variation in the form and content of financial statements. Some accountants, for example, have thought that it would have been better to use only one line in the income statement to show the amounts of cost of goods sold with a "supporting" schedule to show how the amounts were calculated. The form illustrated on page 498 was used since there was sufficient space on a regular letter-size page (8½″ x 11″) to include the details relating to cost of goods sold.

497

HOLLING & RENZ

Income Statement

For the Year Ended June 30, 19—

	Department A	Department B	Total
Sales	$542,412.46	$ 58,355.68	$600,768.14
Less: Sales returns and allowances	(7,285.10)	(910.60)	(8,195.70)
Sales discounts	(5,233.70)	(561.56)	(5,795.26)
Net sales	$529,893.66	$ 56,883.52	$586,777.18
Cost of goods sold:			
Merchandise inventory, July 1	$129,472.10	$ 9,821.52	$139,293.62
Purchases	$418,982.60	$ 45,337.20	$464,319.80
Less: Purchases returns and allowances	(2,134.52)	(139.16)	(2,273.68)
Purchases discounts	(7,860.14)	(853.98)	(8,714.12)
Net purchases	$408,987.94	$ 44,344.06	$453,332.00
Freight in	3,672.43	621.90	4,294.33
Delivered cost of purchases	$412,660.37	$ 44,965.96	$457,626.33
Merchandise available for sale	$542,132.47	$ 54,787.48	$596,919.95
Less merchandise inventory, June 30	136,659.15	10,607.15	147,266.30
Cost of goods sold	405,473.32	44,180.33	449,653.65
Gross margin on sales	$124,420.34	$ 12,703.19	$137,123.53
Operating expenses			77,538.55
Net operating income			$ 59,584.98
Other revenue:			
Interest earned			205.98
			$ 59,790.96
Other expenses:			
Interest expense			$258.96
Charitable contributions expense			585.00
Collection expense			34.90
Total other expenses			878.86
Net income			$ 58,912.10

Holling & Renz — Income Statement

HOLLING & RENZ

Schedule of Operating Expenses

For the Year Ended June 30, 19—

Selling expenses:

Advertising expense..	$ 2,949.24
Store clerks salary expense..................................	15,600.00
Truck drivers wage expense.................................	6,600.00
A. G. Renz, salary expense..................................	12,000.00
A. G. Renz, traveling expense..............................	1,176.85
Truck, gas, and oil expense.................................	1,319.21
Truck repairs expense..	214.60
Garage rent expense...	300.00
Freight out...	18.40
Merchandise insurance expense............................	292.10
Delivery equipment insurance expense....................	240.16
Store equipment insurance expense.......................	32.40
Store supplies expense.......................................	1,275.44
Postage expense (selling)....................................	387.60
Depreciation of store equipment...........................	258.36
Depreciation of delivery equipment.......................	1,144.58
Miscellaneous selling expense..............................	238.35
Total selling expenses..................................	$44,047.29

Administrative expenses:

Rent expense..	$ 5,400.00
T. L. Holling, salary expense...............................	12,000.00
Office salaries expense......................................	9,240.00
Light and water expense....................................	119.65
Telephone and telegraph expense.........................	209.40
Bad debts expense...	1,926.54
Property tax expense..	416.35
Office supplies expense.....................................	1,172.46
Postage expense (administration)..........................	392.10
Office equipment insurance expense......................	51.68
Depreciation of office equipment.........................	386.66
Payroll taxes expense	1,905.14
Miscellaneous general expense............................	271.28
Total administrative expenses.........................	$33,491.26
Total operating expenses..............................	$77,538.55

Holling & Renz — Schedule of Operating Expenses

Interpreting the income statement: percentage analysis

In order of importance, the most significant items shown by the annual income statement are the total amounts of **(1)** net income, **(2)** sales, **(3)** cost of goods sold and gross margin (taken together because of their interrelationship), and **(4)** operating expenses. The dollar amounts take on added meaning if their proportionate relationship to each other is computed. The customary way of expressing this is to consider net sales ($586,777.18) to be the base, 100 percent. Cost of goods sold ($449,653.65) is, then, 76.6 percent of net sales and gross margin, 23.4 percent. Operating expenses equal 13.2 percent of net sales and net operating income equals 10.2 percent of net sales. When the relatively minor amounts of other revenue and other expenses are considered, net income is just slightly more than 10 percent of net sales. Each dollar of net sales resulted in ten cents of net profit.

The same type of analysis can be applied to the data for the net sales, cost of goods sold, and gross margin of each department. For example, considering net sales for each department as the base (100 percent), gross margin was 23.5 percent of the net sales of Department A and 22.3 percent in the case of Department B.

Merchandise turnover; comparative analysis

The data reported in the income statement make it possible to compute the *turnover* of merchandise during the year. For the business as a whole, the average inventory was $143,279.96 (beginning inventory, $139,293.62, plus ending inventory, $147,266.30, divided by two). Since the total cost of goods sold was $449,653.65, the turnover was slightly more than 3 times ($449,653.65 ÷ $143,279.96). This means that, on the average, goods remained in stock for almost four months. Making the same type of calculation for each department reveals that the turnover in Department A was 3.047, and in Department B, 4.325.

Added meaning is given to the information supplied by an income statement if it is compared with statements for past periods. In this way answers will be provided to such vital questions as: Are sales growing or shrinking? How much has net income increased or decreased (both absolutely and relatively)? Has the gross margin percentage become larger or smaller? It may be assumed that the first thing that each partner did after looking at the income statement for the year just ended was to compare it with the statement for the preceding year — probably for several preceding years. Often, income statements (and other financial statements) are prepared in comparative form to aid in their interpretation.

The balance sheet

The balance sheet of Holling & Renz as of June 30, 19--, is reproduced on pages 502 and 503. It was prepared from information provided by the Balance Sheet columns of the work sheet reproduced on pages 476 and 477. The statement was arranged in "account form" since the data could be arranged better in that fashion on the pages. On the asset side, the conventional practice of placing the current assets at the top was followed. The current assets were arrayed in their probable order of liquidity. Government bonds were shown just below cash since these bonds are regarded as temporary investments which can be liquidated readily if a shortage of cash should occur. Receivables — notes, interest, and accounts (less the allowance for bad debt losses likely to arise) — logically followed. The inventories of merchandise (in terms of dollar amount, the most important assets of the firm) were shown last, except for a rather minor amount of supplies and prepayments. These latter items are included as current assets because the fact that they are now owned means that less money will have to be spent for such purposes in the near future. It is not expected that these items will be directly converted into cash. The long-lived assets of Holling & Renz are shown last.

The liabilities of the firm are all of the current variety. The owners' equity section is arranged to show the nature and amount of the change in each partner's equity during the year.

Assets

Current assets:

Cash....................		$ 6,480.54	
Government bonds............		5,000.00	
Notes receivable.............	$ 4,303.26		
Accrued interest receivable.....	25.66		
Accounts receivable..........	16,159.05		
	$ 20,487.97		
Less allowance for bad debts.	2,441.34	18,046.63	

Merchandise inventories:

Department A..............	$136,659.15		
Department B..............	10,607.15	147,266.30	

Supplies and prepayments:

Store supplies.............	$ 140.18		
Advertising supplies........	123.40		
Office supplies............	219.64		
Postage stamps............	268.90		
Prepaid insurance..........	386.14	1,138.26	
Total current assets.......			$177,931.73

Long-lived assets:

Store equipment.............	$ 2,583.60		
Less accumulated depreciation	904.40	$ 1,679.20	
Delivery equipment..........	$ 4,578.32		
Less accumulated depreciation	4,006.04	572.28	
Office equipment............	$ 4,399.40		
Less accumulated depreciation	1,100.50	3,298.90	
Total long-lived assets.....			5,550.38
Total assets...................			$183,482.11

502

Holling & Renz — Balance Sheet (Left Page)

& RENZ

Sheet

19—

Liabilities

Current liabilities:

FICA tax payable.............	$ 288.20	
FUTA tax payable.............	75.96	
State unemployment tax payable..	204.96	
Employees income tax payable ...	307.96	
Notes payable................	4,500.00	
Accrued interest payable........	44.25	
Accounts payable.............	7,120.50	
Total current liabilities........		$ 12,541.83

Owners' Equity

T. L. Holling, capital:

Capital, July 1, beginning of year.		$75,732.12	
Net income (½ of $58,912.10).....	$29,456.05		
Less withdrawals..	20,176.15	9,279.90	
Capital, June 30...............		$85,012.02	

A. G. Renz, capital:

Capital, July 1, beginning of year.		$75,419.51	
Net income (½ of $58,912.10).....	$29,456.05		
Less withdrawals..	18,947.30	10,508.75	
Capital, June 30...............		85,928.26	
Total owners' equity..........			170,940.28
Total liabilities and owners' equity ...			$183,482.11

503

Holling & Renz — Balance Sheet (Right Page)

The balance sheet is supported by schedules of accounts receivable and of accounts payable as of June 30, 19--. These schedules, reproduced below, are really just trial balances of the subsidiary accounts receivable and accounts payable ledgers as of the close of the year.

HOLLING & RENZ

Schedule of Accounts Receivable

June 30, 19—

Atlas Hardware	$ 452.90
Baden Paint Co.	391.85
Beyers Lumber Co.	815.20
Branneky & Sons	2,432.35
Brod-Dugan Co.	4,127.10
County Lumber Co.	987.60
Don V. Davis	520.20
Famous-Barr Company	2,182.40
Hoffman Paint Co.	215.05
Kaplan Lumber Co.	1,236.75
Joe Miller Lumber Co.	87.00
Morris Hardware	105.95
St. John Hardware	1,032.60
United Lumber Co.	51.90
Warson Village Hardware	889.20
Wittenberg Lumber Co.	631.00
	$16,159.05

504

Holling & Renz — Schedule of Accounts Receivable

HOLLING & RENZ

Schedule of Accounts Payable

June 30, 19—

Celucoat Corporation	$4,257.50
Glidden Company	602.90
Morris Paper Co.	35.45
Office Equipment Co.	572.85
Phelan-Faust Paint Manufacturing Co.	516.50
Sunbrite Supply Co.	57.50
U.S. Paint Co.	951.10
Vane-Calvert Paint Co.	126.70
	$7,120.50

Holling & Renz — Schedule of Accounts Payable

Interpreting the balance sheet

One use of the balance sheet is to aid in judging the *current position* of a business — that is, the ability of the enterprise to pay its debts promptly. Not only the relative amounts of current assets and current liabilities, but the composition of these resources and obligations must be considered. The ratio of the current assets ($177,931.73) to current liabilities ($12,541.83) is over 14 to 1. This is very good, but of equal or greater significance is the fact that the "quick" assets (cash, temporary investments, and current receivables) total $29,527.17 — more than twice the current liabilities. This indicates that the firm more than passes the *acid test* (a ratio of quick current assets to total current liabilities of at least 1 to 1).

It must be remembered that the *undepreciated cost* of the long-lived assets (the difference between the cost of these assets and the depreciation so far charged off as an expense), does not indicate what those assets would bring if they were sold. They are not expected to be sold. The difference ($5,550.38, in total) represents the amount, less any expected scrap or salvage value, that is to be charged against future revenues.

As in the case of income statements, a comparison of current and past balance sheets may be informative. Comparative balance sheets are often presented. In some cases, an analysis that involves expressing one amount as a percent of another may be helpful. For example, it is interesting to note that on June 30, 19--, the current assets of Holling & Renz amounted to 97 percent of the total assets. The liabilities (all current) were equal to only 6.8 percent of the total of both liabilities and owners' equity.

505

Analysis of profitability

The amount of annual net income does not mean too much by itself. When this amount is contrasted with the volume of sales, the total amount of the assets, or the total of the owners' equity element of the business, a better indication of profitability is provided. It has been noted (see page 500) that Holling & Renz had net income equal to 10 percent of net sales. The net income of $58,912.10 was equal to over 32 percent of total assets. The total owners' equity was $151,151.63 ($75,732.12 + $75,419.51) at the start of the fiscal year. The net income for the year was equal to nearly 39 percent of that amount. In judging these relationships, however, it must be remembered that no income tax is taken into consideration, since partnerships, as such, do not pay income taxes. In his individual income tax return, each partner must include his share of the partnership net income along with any "salary" payment or allowance. (The amount of any cash or other assets received from the firm is not relevant to the calculation of his taxable income.) The amount of income tax that each partner must pay depends upon the total amount of his income from various sources, the amount of various deductions that he may take, and the number of exemptions to which he is entitled.

Report No. 19-2

Complete Report No. 19-2 in the workbook. Do not submit the report at this time. Since Reports Nos. 19-1, 19-2, and 19-3 are related, you should retain the working papers until you have completed all three reports. Continue with the next study assignment until Report No. 19-3 is required.

The statement of changes in financial position

The annual report of Holling & Renz includes a *statement of changes in financial position* for the year. Since this type of statement has not been discussed or illustrated in earlier chapters, its nature and purpose will be explained before the one for Holling & Renz is considered.

Nature and purpose of the statement

The managers of a business have the dual objective of generating net income and of keeping the enterprise solvent. It would seem that success in the matter of profitability would automatically assure solvency. Net income brings in cash — either at once, or as soon as receivables are collected. To assure solvency is not that simple, however. The cash inflow resulting from profitable operations may be used to acquire more long-lived assets, to discharge long-term indebtedness, or it may be withdrawn by the owners. Many profitable and growing businesses suffer from a continual shortage of *working capital* (current assets minus current liabilities). Sometimes the reverse is the case. There may be little or no net income, and yet by occasional sales of long-lived assets, by borrowing on a long-term basis, or by additional investments by the owners, the business maintains ample working capital. The increase or decrease in working capital is the result of the interplay of various circumstances, management decisions, and actions.

In analyzing the affairs of a business, it is helpful to know the reasons for an increase or a decrease in working capital during the period under review (often a year). To provide this information, a special type of financial statement that explains the change in working capital has been developed. It is called the *statement of changes in financial position*, the *statement of source and application of funds*, the *statement of application of funds*, the *fund-change statement*, or the *statement of changes in working capital*.

In this connection, the word "funds" means working capital. The word has other meanings. In a semislang sense, "funds" is sometimes used as a synonym for cash. The term "fund" (singular) is used to describe cash or other assets set aside for a specified purpose such as a *petty cash fund*. In government finance and accounting, a fund is a segregated collection of cash and other assets (and, sometimes, related liabilities) held or used for a certain purpose, such as a *highway construction fund*. A statement of changes in financial position, however, usually is a statement explaining the increase or decrease in the working capital of a business during a specified period of time. (It may be noted that the term "financial position" can be used to encompass more and, sometimes, less than working capital, but the prevailing practice is to limit the statement to an explanation of working capital, i.e., "funds," changes.)

The question may arise as to why a statement of source and application of cash would not better serve to explain what has been happening to the business. For certain purposes, periodic statements of cash receipts and disbursements are needed. However, in judging the current position and the changes in it that have occurred, it can be very misleading to look only at what has happened to cash. To illustrate, consider the following comparative statement of the current assets and current liabilities of a business at the start and close of a year:

Current Assets	BEGINNING OF YEAR	END OF YEAR
Cash...	$ 10,000	$ 60,000
Temporary investments.............................	20,000	5,000
Receivables (net).................................	40,000	20,000
Inventories and prepayments........................	30,000	35,000
Total...	$100,000	$120,000
Current Liabilities		
Notes, accounts, and taxes payable....................	25,000	80,000
Working capital.................................	$ 75,000	$ 40,000

507

Cash increased 500 percent but the current position of the company deteriorated seriously. The current ratio changed from 4 to 1 to only 1.5 to 1, and the acid-test ratio from 2.8 to 1 to 1.06 to 1. In analyzing what has been happening in the business, the reasons for the $35,000 decrease in working capital are of far more concern than the explanation of why cash is $50,000 greater. Thus, a statement of changes in financial position is much more informative than a summary of cash receipts and disbursements.

Sources of funds

Funds may be secured or obtained in four ways:

Investments by Owners. If the owners invest cash or other current assets in the business, working capital is increased.

Profitable Operations. If there has been net income for an accounting period, the increase in cash and receivables due to sales (and, sometimes, due to other revenue) must have been more than the total of the decrease in inventory (because of goods sold) and either the decrease in cash or the increase in current payables that took place when most expenses were incurred. (The special problem of depreciation and a few other expenses that do not reduce working capital when incurred will be discussed at a later point.)

Long-Term Borrowing. When money is borrowed and the promised date of repayment is many years in the future, working capital is increased. (Short-term borrowing does not affect working capital because the increase in cash is exactly offset by the increase in a current liability — usually notes payable.)

Sale of Long-Lived Assets. Selling long-lived assets, such as land, buildings, equipment, or trucks, usually increases either cash or current receivables.

Applications of funds

Funds may be applied or used in four ways:

Withdrawals by Owners. When the owners of a business take money out (either because there has been a profit or as a withdrawal of their capital investment) working capital is reduced. In the case of corporations, the payment of cash dividends is the usual example of this type of application of funds.

Unprofitable Operations. Working capital is reduced if the decrease in inventory (because of goods sold) and either the decrease in cash or the increase in current payables that takes place when most expenses are incurred are, in total, larger than the addition to cash and receivables due to sales (and, sometimes, due to other revenue).

Repayment of Long-Term Borrowing. When long-term liabilities, such as mortgages payable, are paid, cash (and, thus working capital) is reduced. (The discharge of short-term obligations does not affect working capital because the decrease in cash is offset by an equal decrease in a current liability.)

Purchase of Long-Lived Assets. When a long-lived asset (land, building, equipment, etc.) is purchased, usually either cash is reduced or accounts payable is increased. In either case, working capital is diminished.

Example of statement of changes in financial position

The statement of changes in financial position is prepared from information supplied by the balance sheets at the beginning and end of the accounting period involved, plus certain other data found in the income statement. To illustrate, assume that the balance sheets of Cooper & Mann at the beginning and end of the year 19-- were as shown below:

	BEGINNING OF YEAR	END OF YEAR
Assets		
Cash...	$ 30,000	$ 40,000
Receivables.......................................	90,000	80,000
Inventory..	100,000	80,000
Total current assets.............................	$220,000	$200,000
Building and equipment...........................		100,000
Land..	20,000	20,000
	$240,000	$320,000
Liabilities and Owners' Equity		
Notes payable....................................	$ 20,000	$ 30,000
Accounts payable.................................	90,000	50,000
Total current liabilities..........................	$110,000	$ 80,000
Mortgage payable.................................		70,000
Cooper, capital..................................	70,000	90,000
Mann, capital...................................	60,000	80,000
	$240,000	$320,000

During the year Cooper and Mann each invested an additional $5,000. Neither partner withdrew anything. The net income for the year was $30,000.

The amount of working capital at the start of the year was $110,000 ($220,000 — $110,000). At the end of the year the amount was $120,000 ($200,000 — $80,000). The change, then, was an increase of $10,000. The statement of changes in financial position must explain how this happened.

Comparison of the two balance sheets reveals that building and equipment increased from nothing to $100,000. (A building was constructed during the year. It was completed just before the year ended. At that time the equipment was purchased.) This was a $100,000 application of funds. Mortgage payable increased from nothing to $70,000 — a source of funds. (The money was borrowed on a long-term basis by giving a note secured by a mortgage on the land and building.) The owners' equity in the business increased from $130,000 ($70,000 + $60,000) to $170,000 ($90,000 + $80,000). This $40,000 increase in funds was from two sources: (1) the net income for the year, $30,000, and (2) the partners' additional investment of $10,000. These findings can be classified to produce the following statement:

COOPER & MANN

Statement of Changes in Financial Position

For the Year Ended December 31, 19—

Sources of funds:

Net income for the year.....................	$ 30,000	
Investments by partners.....................	10,000	
Long-term borrowing.......................	70,000	$110,000

Applications of funds:

Purchase of building and equipment..........		100,000
Increase in working capital..................		$ 10,000

Cooper & Mann — Statement of Changes in Financial Position

Assembling the data for the Holling & Renz statement of changes in financial position

There are various techniques for assembling and organizing data to produce a statement of changes in financial position. If the calculations are likely to be complicated, it may be advisable to use a special form of work sheet. If no special problems are involved, the use of a work sheet is not warranted. The first step is to summarize, in comparative form, the balance sheets at the beginning and end of the period. The accountant for Holling & Renz used the balance sheet at the close of the preceding year (not reproduced in this textbook) and the balance sheet at the close of the year just ended (reproduced on pages 502 and 503). He summarized the statements and noted the changes in each element, as follows:

	BEGINNING OF YEAR	END OF YEAR	INCREASE (DECREASE)
Cash..	$ 9,216.11	$ 6,480.54	$ (2,735.57)
Government bonds..........................		5,000.00	5,000.00
Receivable (net)............................	15,871.40	18,046.63	2,175.23
Merchandise inventories.....................	139,293.62	147,266.30	7,972.68
Supplies and prepayments....................	987.14	1,138.26	151.12
Total current assets........................	$165,368.27	$177,931.73	$ 12,563.46
Long-lived assets (less accumulated depreciation)..	6,767.13	5,550.38	(1,216.75)
Total assets..............................	$172,135.40	$183,482.11	$ 11,346.71
Payroll taxes payable........................	$ 726.14	$ 877.08	$ 150.94
Notes and interest payable...................	8,963.76	4,544.25	(4,419.51)
Accounts payable...........................	11,293.87	7,120.50	(4,173.37)
Total current liabilities.....................	$ 20,983.77	$ 12,541.83	$ (8,441.94)
Owners' equity.............................	151,151.63	170,940.28	19,788.65
Total liabilities and owners' equity............	$172,135.40	$183,482.11	$ 11,346.71

The first fact to be noted from the foregoing summary is that working capital increased $21,005.40 (the current assets increased $12,563.46 and **511** the current liabilities decreased $8,441.94). The purpose of the statement of changes in financial position will be to explain this $21,005.40 increase. (It should be observed that cash decreased $2,735.57, but this was overshadowed by the increase in temporary investments, the increase in inventories, and the substantial reduction in the amount of the current liabilities. It was mentioned earlier that the change in the amount of cash is not nearly so significant as the change in working capital.)

In order to be sure that nothing was missed, the accountant mentally went over the list of sources and applications of funds to see which ones applied to this case. As enumerated on page 508, the possible sources are (1) investments by owners, (2) profitable operations, (3) long-term borrowing, and (4) sale of long-lived assets. Items (1), (3) and (4) could be ignored: the partners had made no investments during the year, there had been no long-term borrowing, and no sales of long-lived assets. The only source of funds for the year under review was No. (2), profitable operations. This source of funds will be examined in the following section. As enumerated on pages 508 and 509, the possible applications of funds are: (1) withdrawals by owners, (2) unprofitable operations, (3) repayment of long-term borrowing, and (4) purchase of long-lived assets. Item (2) did not apply since the year had been very profitable, and item (3) was eliminated since Holling & Renz had not started the year with any long-term debt that could have been repaid. Item **(1)** certainly applied since both partners had made substantial withdrawals, and item **(4)** was relevant because two pieces of office equipment had been purchased. These applications of funds will be considered shortly.

Funds provided by operations

The income statement of Holling & Renz for the year ended June 30, 19--, revealed a net income of $58,912.10. Did this mean that the working capital of the business had been increased by that amount during the year? The answer is: "Yes — and then some." There were two types of revenue: sales and interest earned. In both cases, either cash was collected or a current receivable (accounts receivable, notes receivable, or accrued interest receivable) was increased. In any event, the current assets (and, accordingly, working capital) were increased by the amount of both types of revenue.

Almost every type of expense that was incurred caused working capital to be reduced. Cost of goods sold reduced the merchandise inventory — an important current asset. Prepaid Insurance — a current asset — was reduced by an amount equal to the cost of the insurance that expired during the period. The provision for bad debt losses was, in effect, a reduction of current receivables. Nearly every one of the many sorts of expenses caused an immediate reduction in cash or an increase in a current payable of some sort. Whether the current assets were reduced or the current liabilities were increased, working capital was reduced.

The single exception (in this case) to the foregoing analysis of the effect of expenses upon working capital is the matter of *depreciation expense.* When the depreciation of the three types of long-lived assets was recorded (refer to adjustments (n), (o), and (p) in the work sheets on pages 476 and 477) the offset to the depreciation expense debit was a credit to the proper accumulated depreciation account. Accumulated depreciation represents the amount of asset cost so far charged to operations. An addition to accumulated depreciation is a reduction in the undepreciated cost of the long-lived asset — *not a reduction in a current asset.*

The total amount of Holling & Renz's depreciation expense for the year was $1,789.60 ($258.36 + $1,144.58 + $386.66). Since this expense did not reduce working capital (funds), for statement of changes in financial position purposes the amount of the net income for the year, $58,912.10, was modified by the amount of the depreciation expense for the year and reported as follows:

Funds provided by operations:

Net income (per income statement)	$58,912.10
Add expenses not requiring funds:	
Depreciation	1,789.60
Total funds provided by operations	$60,701.70

512

It is unfortunate that a great deal of misunderstanding has arisen about depreciation in the statement of changes in financial position. The idea that "depreciation is a source of funds" is widely accepted. This notion is entirely incorrect. Depreciation, while difficult to measure on a periodic basis, is a very real expense. It differs from most other expenses only in that most others reduce working capital, while depreciation expense is a reduction in certain long-lived assets. In the long run, depreciation *is* just like other expenses. When the assets that are being depreciated were bought, cash was disbursed. In point of time, the disbursement may have been years before. In the case of most other expenses, the disbursement of cash is closely related. In most instances, the money is spent in the same period that the expenses arise; in a few cases the money was spent in the preceding period (such as payments for inventory and supplies that are not sold or used until the next period); and in some cases the money will not be disbursed until the next period (for example, employer's payroll taxes that relate to one year but are not paid until the next). Depreciation is too often misunderstood because the time that the money was spent for the depreciable asset and the time to which the depreciation expense relates may be far apart.

Another method of showing "funds provided by operations" that could be used would be to show total revenue (sales and interest earned) and deduct therefrom "expenses that reduced working capital." In the present case the difference would be $60,701.70 — just as shown at the bottom of page 512. Nothing would need to be said about depreciation if this method were used. The reason that this treatment is not followed is that it is considered desirable to have the statement of changes in financial position start with the amount shown as the net income in the income statement. It is felt that this treatment serves to tie the financial statements together in a more desirable manner.

Another argument that may be used to show that depreciation is *not* a source of funds is as follows: Suppose that depreciation expense had been overlooked in calculating the net income for a period. Would the funds provided by operations be any less? The answer, clearly, is "no." If the accountant for Holling & Renz had failed to record the depreciation expense totalling $1,789.60, the net income for the year would have been (incorrectly) calculated to be $60,701.70. In the statement of changes in financial position, that amount would be shown as funds provided by operations — just as it is when the net income calculation includes the depreciation expense.

It should be mentioned that there are a few other expenses that have the same characteristics as depreciation. They, too, arise when something that was purchased is gradually written off as an expense over a number of succeeding years. A good example is the case of a patent. Patents have a legal life of 17 years. A company may have purchased a patent soon after it was issued. The management of the acquiring company may not think that the patent will be valuable for 16 to 17 years, but it may believe that ownership of the patent will be of benefit, perhaps, for 10 years. Accordingly, one tenth of the cost may be charged to an expense for each of the ten years. This is described as *amortizing* the cost. The portion written off each year is described as *amortization expense*. The asset, patent, is classed as long-lived. As portions of its cost are taken into expense, no decrease in working capital is involved. Accordingly, amortization expense, like depreciation expense, must be "added back" to determine the amount of funds provided by operations.

Occasions may arise when the net income figure must be further modified to arrive at funds provided by operations. If, for example, a piece of land that cost $10,000 some years before was sold for $12,000 and the $2,000 profit was reported in the income statement, that amount ($2,000) would have to be shown as a reduction of funds provided by operations. (Unless the business was engaged in buying and selling land, such a transaction would not be considered a part of regular operations.) The $12,000 received from the sale of the land would be reported separately as a source of funds in the statement of changes in financial position.

Regular operations were the only source of funds for Holling & Renz during the year ended June 30, 19--. The two types of funds applications during that year will be considered next.

Applications of funds: owners' withdrawals

Reference to the owners' equity section of the balance sheet for the year ended June 30, 19-- (reproduced on pages 502 and 503) shows that during the year, T. L. Holling withdrew $20,176.15 and A. G. Renz, $18,947.30. These amounts are shown in the *applications* section of the statement of changes in financial position.

Applications of funds: purchase of long-lived assets

In the analysis of the changes in the balance sheets of Holling & Renz shown on page 511, it will be noted that there was a decrease in the total undepreciated cost (cost less accumulated depreciation) of the long-lived assets in the amount of $1,216.75. A decrease in the total undepreciated cost amounting to $1,789.60 was due to the amounts of cost written off as depreciation expense for the year. This amount of depreciation has already been taken into consideration in preparing the statement. If the decrease in undepreciated cost due to depreciation for the year was $1,789.60, but the total decrease was only $1,216.75, it must be that there was an application of funds in the amount of $572.85 to purchase some new long-lived assets. An examination of the long-lived asset accounts revealed that on June 9, a desk calculator was purchased at a cost of $502.85, and that on June 30, a new checkwriter was purchased at a net cost of $70. (The list price of the checkwriter was $75 but a $5 trade-in allowance was given for the old one.) As it happens, both of these items had been purchased from the Office Equipment Co., and since neither had yet been paid for, the amount of accounts payable on June 30, 19--, included $572.85 due to that company. (See the schedule of accounts payable on page 504.) Since an increase in a current liability is just as effective as a decrease in cash in reducing working capital, the purchases of office equipment certainly were applications of funds for the year. These acquisitions were so reported in the statement of changes in financial position.

The Holling & Renz statement of changes in financial position with supporting schedule of changes in working capital

The annual report of Holling & Renz includes a statement of changes in financial position with a supporting schedule of changes in working capital. These are reproduced on page 516. The statement of changes in financial position explains the net change in working capital that occurred between the start and the close of the fiscal year. The supporting schedule shows the amounts of the changes in the elements that comprise working capital (current assets and current liabilities). The balance sheets as of the beginning and end of the year provided the data for the schedule.

Statements of changes in financial position are not always presented in the form illustrated. Various other arrangements of the data are possible. One form sometimes used begins with the amount of working capital at the beginning of the period (usually a year). To this is added the amount of funds secured, appropriately classified. The applications of funds are then shown and their total is subtracted to show the amount of working capital at the end of the period. It was mentioned that titles other than "statement of changes in financial position" sometimes are used. By whatever name it may be called, the inclusion of the statement in the annual report is becoming widespread practice.

HOLLING & RENZ

Statement of Changes in Financial Position

For the Year Ended June 30, 19—

Sources of funds:

Funds provided by operations:
Net income (per income statement)..........................	$58,912.10
Add expenses not requiring funds:	
Depreciation.......................................	1,789.60
Total funds provided by operations......................	$60,701.70

Application of funds:

Partners' withdrawals:
T. L. Holling...............................	$20,176.15
A. G. Renz..............................	18,947.30
Purchase of office equipment..................	572.85
Total funds applied........................	39,696.30
Increase in working capital.....................	$21,005.40

Holling & Renz — Statement of Changes in Financial Position

516

HOLLING & RENZ

Schedule of Changes in Working Capital

For the Year Ended June 30, 19—

	Beginning of Year	End of Year	Working Capital Increase	Working Capital Decrease
Cash......................	$ 9,216.11	$ 6,480.54		$ 2,735.57
Government bonds.........		5,000.00	$ 5,000.00	
Receivables (net)...........	15,871.40	18,046.63	2,175.23	
Merchandise inventories.....	139,293.62	147,266.30	7,972.68	
Supplies and prepayments...	987.14	1,138.26	151.12	
Payroll taxes payable......	726.14	877.08		150.94
Notes and interest payable..	8,963.76	4,544.25	4,419.51	
Accounts payable..........	11,293.87	7,120.50	4,173.37	
			$23,891.91	$ 2,886.51
Increase in working capital...				21,005.40
			$23,891.91	$23,891.91

Holling & Renz — Schedule of Changes in Working Capital

Report No. 19-3

Complete Report No. 19-3 in the workbook and submit your working papers for Reports Nos. 19-1, 19-2, and 19-3 for approval. Continue with the next study assignment in Chapter 20 until Report No. 20-1 is required.

chapter 20

interim financial statements

In accounting for business operations, it has become a nearly universal practice to determine income or loss on an annual basis and to prepare balance sheets at annual intervals. While the calendar year is widely used as the fiscal year, the practice of adopting a so-called *natural business year* (meaning a year that starts and ends at the time when business activity is the lowest) is increasing. In any case, a year is the basic time interval. It is easy to understand, however, that interested parties — notably owners and managers — may have reason to wish for more frequent reports of the affairs of a business. For this reason, it is more and more becoming the practice to prepare *interim financial statements*. Interim means "between." An income statement shorter than, and within the limits of, the fiscal year is an interim income statement. A balance sheet as of a date other than the close of the fiscal year is an interim balance sheet. (It would be possible to have interim statements of changes in financial position, but this is not customary.)

Interim periods

It would be possible to prepare interim statements for any segment of a year. Two circumstances, however, make it impractical to use a very short period (such as a day or a week): **(1)** the considerable amount of work involved in producing the statements, and **(2)** the fact that the shorter the period, the more unreliable the determination of income. Many of the problems of accounting (in contrast to pure data gathering, recording, and storing) arise because numerous items of value are acquired in one period, but are not sold or used entirely within that period. Two important examples are **(1)** the problem of allocating cost between goods sold (or used) and goods unsold (or unused) at the end of the period, and **(2)** the problem of cost allocation in the case of most long-lived assets — the matter of depreciation. The shorter the period, the greater the problem.

The constraints just mentioned combine to cause the month to be the smallest time segment generally used for interim-statement purposes. Monthly time segments have the advantage of being universally understood. A disadvantage of using monthly segments is the fact that they are uneven in length. February has only 28 days (29 once every four years), four months have 30 days, and seven months have 31 days. This unevenness may be further accentuated by the dates on which weekends and holidays happen to fall. These circumstances should be kept in mind when comparing the results of successive months and the results of a certain month compared with the same month of the preceding year (or years).

Interim statements often are prepared on a quarterly (three months) basis. In contrast to monthly statements, much less effort is required, the longer time interval gives somewhat more reliability, and quarters are more comparable in length. Quarterly statements in very condensed form commonly are furnished to the stockholders of large business corporations. Usually it is noted that the statements were "prepared without audit."

In the majority of cases, interim statements must be regarded as very provisional or tentative in nature. At the end of the fiscal year physical inventories may be taken to determine (or, in some cases, to verify) the quantities of merchandise inventory and various supplies on hand. The procedure is likely to be time consuming and, thus, expensive. It cannot be done every month — or even every three months. Estimates may have to be used for interim-statement purposes. However, even with their imperfections, interim financial statements can be useful.

Producing interim financial statements with the aid of work sheets

It has been shown that the end-of-year work sheet (or work sheets, if circumstances require) is a useful device to **(1)** assist in the production of the annual income statement and the year-end balance sheet, and (2) aid in the year-end process of formally adjusting and closing the accounts. For interim-statement purposes the same type of work sheet can materially assist in the statement-production function. (No aid is needed in formally adjusting and closing the accounts because this is not done at the close of interim periods.)

To illustrate the use of interim period work sheets, an example is presented. The example relates to the Wilson & Son Wholesale Drug Company owned and operated as a partnership by John H. Wilson and his son, Robert S. Wilson. They share profits and losses in a 60%–40% ratio. (The determination of net income takes partners' "salaries" into account.) The firm uses the calendar year as its fiscal year. The accountant for the company prepares monthly income statements and what are called "year-to-date" income statements, as well as balance sheets, as of the last day of each month. (The income statement for January is, actually, a year-to-date statement in which the "date" is January 31. The income statement for January and February together is a year-to-date statement in which the date is February 28, and so on.) For purposes of this illustration, the business is not departmentalized, and the general ledger contains comparatively few accounts. There is no subsidiary operating expenses ledger. It may be assumed that appropriate books of original entry and auxiliary records are used.

Work sheet for month ended January 31, 19—

This work sheet is reproduced on pages 522 and 523. Actually, a ten-column work sheet was used, but to conserve space the Adjusted Trial Balance columns are not shown. The amounts in the Trial Balance columns were taken from the general ledger after the posting for the month of January had been completed. The reasons why certain of the accounts had no balance will become apparent in the discussion that follows.

The adjustments enumerated starting below were made in the second pair of amount columns.

Entry (a): The amount of the beginning inventory of merchandise, $1,883,246.41, was transferred by a debit to Cost of Goods Sold, Account No. 531, and by a credit to Merchandise Inventory, Account No. 141.

Entry (b): The amount of the purchases for the month, $868,439.20, was transferred by a debit to Cost of Goods Sold, Account No. 531, and by a credit to Purchases, Account No. 511.

Entry (c): The amount of the purchases returns and allowances for the month, $10,421.15, was transferred by a debit to Purchases Returns and Allowances, Account No. 051, and by a credit to Cost of Goods Sold, Account No. 531.

Entry (d): The amount of the purchases discount for the month, $17,329.06, was transferred by a debit to Purchases Discount, Account No. 052, and by a credit to Cost of Goods Sold, Account No. 531.

Entry (e): The amount assigned to the merchandise inventory at January 31, $1,742,500, was taken into account by a debit to Merchandise Inventory, Account No. 141, and by a credit to Cost of Goods Sold, Account No. 531. Note that a "round" amount (rounded to the nearest hundred dollars) was used. This is because the figure was, in part, an estimate. The firm of Wilson & Son maintains a stock record of certain "high value" items. That record provided the quantities of those items that were presumed to be on hand at January 31. (No physical count was made. The record was considered reliable, since careful physical control of these items is enforced. Very little discrepancy had been found when a physical count was made at the end of the last year.) The quantities were costed by reference to recent purchase invoices. The amount of various low value items was estimated. Accordingly, the cost assigned to the entire inventory was considered to be a reliable estimate. Nevertheless, to avoid the appearance of great precision and accuracy, a round-amount figure was used. For interim-statement purposes, this is considered to be satisfactory.

521

Entry (f): The interest accrued since January 1, $9,000, on the mortgage payable was debited to Interest Expense, Account No. 811, and was credited to Accrued Interest Payable, Account No. 251. It will be noted that Wilson & Son has a $1,800,000 mortgage payable. (Actually it is a note payable that is secured by a mortgage on the real estate — land and building — of the firm. Custom sanctions referring to such a liability as a *mortgage payable*.) This long-term liability is of the type that is to be paid off in full at a distant maturity date — not in monthly installments. Interest at 6 percent per annum is payable semiannually each January 1 and July 1. Interest for the six months ended last December 31 ($54,000) was paid on January 2 (since January 1 was a holiday). The determination of net income (or loss) for January must take into account the interest that has accrued during that month.

Entry (g): The amount of the insurance expense for January, $3,212.49, was debited to Insurance Expense, Account No. 615, and was credited to Prepaid Insurance, Account No. 152. The insurance policy register used by Wilson & Son provided the information needed to calculate the amount.

522

Account	Acct. No.	Trial Balance Debit	Trial Balance Credit
First National Bank	111	46 052 32	
Accounts Receivable	131	240 541 64	
Allowance for Bad Debts	013		3 681 07
Merchandise Inventory	141	1 883 246 41	
Store Supplies	151	9 134 87	
Prepaid Insurance	152	14 256 63	
Furniture and Equipment	161	328 357 70	
Accumulated Depreciation — Furniture and Equipment	016		112 054 78
Delivery Equipment	171	115 796 64	
Accumulated Depreciation — Delivery Equipment	017		59 342 15
Building	181	2 714 433 60	
Accumulated Depreciation — Building	018		1 392 431 21
Land	191	650 000 00	
FICA Tax Payable	211		7 139 66
FUTA Tax Payable	221		317 24
State Unemployment Tax Payable	231		2 142 59
Employees Income Tax Payable	241		11 897 60
Accrued Interest Payable	251		
Accounts Payable	261		298 613 70
Mortgage Payable	271		1 800 000 00
John H. Wilson, Capital	311		1 279 215 40
John H. Wilson, Drawing	031	10 278 90	
Robert S. Wilson, Capital	321		852 529 20
Robert S. Wilson, Drawing	032	6 847 35	
Sales	411		1 183 768 05
Sales Returns and Allowances	041	11 654 23	
Sales Discount	042	22 878 16	
Purchases	511	868 439 20	
Purchases Returns and Allowances	051		10 421 15
Purchases Discount	052		17 329 06
Cost of Goods Sold	531		
Salaries and Commissions Expense	611	79 315 80	
Payroll Taxes Expense	612	6 814 32	
Partners' Salaries Expense	613	4 000 00	
Depreciation Expense	614		
Insurance Expense	615		
Property Tax Expense	616		
Utilities Expense	617	2 374 72	
Telephone and Telegraph Expense	618	769 15	
Delivery Expense	619	3 145 96	
Supplies Expense	621		
Bad Debts Expense	622		
Miscellaneous Expense	623	5 183 12	
Interest Expense	811		
Accrued Property Tax Payable		7 027 201 79	7 027 201 79
Net Income			

WHOLESALE DRUG COMPANY

Sheet

January 31, 19--

Adjustments Debit	Adjustments Credit	Income Statement Debit	Income Statement Credit	Balance Sheet Debit	Balance Sheet Credit
				46 052 32	
				240 541 64	
					2 065 11
(e) 1 742 500 00	(j) 5 746 18				
	(a) 1 883 246 41			1 742 500 00	
	(h) 2 334 87			6 800 00	
	(g) 3 212 49			11 044 14	
				328 357 70	
	(i) 1 710 20				113 764 98
	(i) 2 412 43			115 796 64	
					61 754 58
	(i) 5 655 07			2 714 433 60	
					1 398 086 28
				650 000 00	
					7 139 66
					317 24
					2 142 59
					11 897 60
	(f) 9 000 00				9 000 00
					298 613 70
					1 800 000 00
					1 279 215 40
				10 278 90	
					852 529 20
				6 847 35	
			1 183 768 05		
		11 654 23			
		22 878 16			
(c) 10 421 15	(b) 868 439 20				
(d) 17 329 06					
(a) 1 883 246 41	(c) 10 421 15	981 435 40			
(b) 868 439 20	(d) 17 329 06				
	(e) 1 742 500 00				
		79 315 80			
		6 814 32			
		4 000 00			
(i) 9 777 70		9 777 70			
(g) 3 212 49		3 212 49			
(k) 6 872 13		6 872 13			
		2 374 72			
		769 15			
		3 145 96			
(h) 2 334 87		2 334 87			
(j) 5 746 18		5 746 18			
		5 183 12			
(f) 9 000 00		9 000 00			
	(k) 6 872 13				6 872 13
4 558 879 19	4 558 879 19	1 154 514 23	1 183 768 05	5 872 652 29	5 843 398 47
		29 253 82			29 253 82
		1 183 768 05	1 183 768 05	5 872 652 29	5 872 652 29

Work-Sheet for One-Month Period

Entry (h): The estimated cost of store supplies used during the month, $2,334.87, was debited to Supplies Expense, Account No. 621, and was credited to Store Supplies, Account No. 151. The amount was determined by subtracting the estimated cost of the store supplies on hand January 31, $6,800.00, from the balance of the store supplies account, $9,134.87. It will be noted that the firm uses the asset method of accounting for supplies.

Entry (i): The calculated amount of depreciation for the month, $9,777.70, was debited to Depreciation Expense, Account No. 614, with credits to Accumulated Depreciation — Furniture and Equipment, Account No. 016, $1,710.20, Accumulated Depreciation — Delivery Equipment, Account No. 017, $2,412.43, and Accumulated Depreciation — Building, Account No. 018, $5,655.07. The firm uses straight line depreciation calculated at the following *annual* rates: furniture and equipment, 6 1/4 percent; delivery equipment, 25 percent; and building, 2 1/2 percent. Since no long-lived assets had been purchased during January, these rates were applied to the cost of the assets as shown in the trial balance, and 1/12 was taken as the amount for January.

Entry (j): The amount of the bad debts provision for the month, $5,746.18, was debited to Bad Debts Expense, Account No. 622, and was credited to Allowance for Bad Debts, Account No. 013. Experience has indicated that bad debt losses average 1/2 of 1 percent of net sales. Net sales for January amounted to $1,149,235.66 ($1,183,768.05 − $11,654.23 − $22,878.16). One half of one percent of $1,149,235.66 is $5,746.18. While it may be assumed that the allowance account had a credit balance on January 1, it should be noted that the January 31 trial balance shows that the account had a debit balance of $3,681.07. Evidently the write-offs of uncollectible accounts receivable used up the January 1 balance and related to some of the charge sales made in January. It is possible that the January 1 balance of the allowance for bad debts account was insufficient, but if the sum of the January 1 balance and the $5,746.18 provision prove to be adequate to take care of losses relating to sales on account to January 31, no error in prior provisions will be indicated.

Entry (k): The property tax assignable to January, $6,872.13, was debited to Property Tax Expense, Account No. 616, and was credited to Accrued Property Tax Payable. It will be noted that the latter title had to be added to the list and that no account number is shown. The reason is that there is no need for such an account in the general ledger of Wilson & Son Wholesale Drug Company. Property taxes pose a special accounting problem. Such taxes do not accrue in the conventional sense. The tax relates to certain property that is owned *on a specific date* — usually on a specified day in the spring of the year. (It does not matter whether the property has just been purchased or has been owned for many years.) Usually the amount of the tax is not known until the tax bill is received several months after the assessment date. Frequently the tax may be paid in two installments: one half by a specified day late in the year (a day in November or December), and the other half by a specified day in the following spring. (If not paid by the due date, penalties and interest are assessed.)

Property tax expense commonly is accounted for on a cash basis; that is, no record is made until a payment occurs. By the end of the year, the property tax expense account shows the amount of tax actually paid during the year. Wilson & Son follows this practice: In the year just ended they paid $40,659.42 in April, and $41,232.78 in December. Another $41,232.78 must be paid in April of the current year. Since it seems reasonable to allocate the total expense for the year over twelve months and it may be reasoned that the April payment relates to the first half of the year, one sixth of the amount is assigned to each of the first six months. Entry (k) accomplishes this by a debit to the expense account and a credit to the liability. The real purpose of the entry is to cause January to bear a reasonable share of the year's property tax expense. The credit to the liability is incidental. (During the second half of the year, the amount must be estimated until the tax bill arrives in late October or early November and the exact amount is shown. Usually, however, the estimate can be fairly accurate.) It should be mentioned that not all accountants would treat property tax expense in precisely this manner, but some procedure would be followed to cause a reasonable amount to be included in the income determination for each interim period.

The work sheet was completed by (1) totaling the adjustments columns to prove their equality, (2) extending the amounts (as adjusted, in many cases) into the Adjusted Trial Balance columns (not shown) and totaling those columns to prove their equality, (3) showing each amount in the proper Income Statement or Balance Sheet columns, (4) footing the last four columns to determine the net income for the month and entering this amount, $29,253.82, in the Income Statement Debit and the Balance Sheet Credit columns, and (5) entering the totals and making the rulings.

The interim statements for January

The income statement for the month of January, 19--, for Wilson & Son Wholesale Drug Company is reproduced on page 526. The balance sheet as of January 31, 19--, is shown on pages 527 and 528. It will be observed that, in the owners' equity section, the net income for the month was apportioned between the partners in the agreed ratio: 60% - 40%.

The procedure followed in the production of these interim financial statements was almost identical to the steps that normally are followed at the end of the year. At year-end, however, the end-of-period work of the accountant would not have ceased with statement preparation. The adjusting entries would have been journalized and posted, followed by the journalizing and posting of the needed closing entries. It is likely that a post-closing trial balance would have been taken. In many cases, certain

WILSON & SON WHOLESALE DRUG COMPANY

Income Statement

For the Month of January, 19—

Sales.....................................			$1,183,768.05
Less: Returns and allowances.............			(11,654.23)
Sales discounts....................			(22,878.16)
Net sales.............................			$1,149,235.66
Cost of goods sold:			
Merchandise inventory, January 1.........		$1,883,246.41	
Purchases............................		868,439.20	
Less: Returns and allowances...........		(10,421.15)	
Purchases discounts..............		(17,329.06)	
Cost of merchandise available for sale......		$2,723,935.40	
Less merchandise inventory, January 31		1,742,500.00	981,435.40
Gross margin on sales.....................			$ 167,800.26
Operating expenses:			
Salaries and commissions expense.........	$	79,315.80	
Payroll taxes expense..................		6,814.32	
Partners' salaries expense..............		4,000.00	
Depreciation expense...................		9,777.70	
Insurance expense.....................		3,212.49	
Property tax expense..................		6,872.13	
Utilities expense......................		2,374.72	
Telephone and telegraph expense........		769.15	
Delivery expense......................		3,145.96	
Supplies expense......................		2,334.87	
Bad debts expense....................		5,746.18	
Miscellaneous expense.................		5,183.12	
Total operating expenses.............			129,546.44
Net operating income...................		$	38,253.82
Interest expense......................			9,000.00
Net income...........................		$	29,253.82

Wilson & Son Wholesale Drug Company — Income Statement

reversing entries would have been journalized and posted. At the end of each interim period, none of these bookkeeping steps is involved.

WILSON & SON WHOLESALE DRUG COMPANY

Balance Sheet

January 31, 19—

Assets

Current assets:

Cash..................................		$ 46,052.32	
Accounts receivable.........	$ 240,541.64		
Less allowance for bad debts	2,065.11	238,476.53	
Merchandise inventory.....................		1,742,500.00	
Store supplies...........................		6,800.00	
Prepaid insurance.......................		11,044.14	
Total current assets....................			$2,044,872.99

Long-lived assets:

Furniture and equipment......	$ 328,357.70		
Less accumd. depreciation..	113,764.98	$ 214,592.72	
Delivery equipment..........	$ 115,796.64		
Less accumd. depreciation..	61,754.58	54,042.06	
Building..................	$2,714,433.60		
Less accumd. depreciation..	1,398,086.28	1,316,347.32	
Land.....................................		650,000.00	
Total long-lived assets..................			2,234,982.10
Total assets.............................			$4,279,855.09

Liabilities

Current liabilities:

FICA tax payable........................	$ 7,139.66	
FUTA tax payable.......................	317.24	
State unemployment tax payable............	2,142.59	
Employees income tax payable	11,897.60	
Accrued interest payable.................	9,000.00	
Accrued property tax payable..............	6,872.13	
Accounts payable.......................	298,613.70	
Total current liabilities...................		$ 335,982.92

Long-term liability:

Mortgage payable......................		1,800,000.00
Total liabilities.............................		$2,135,982.92

Wilson & Son Wholesale Drug Company — Balance Sheet
(*continued on next page*)

Owners' Equity

John H. Wilson, capital:

Capital, January 1.......... $1,279,215.40		
Add: Net income (60% of		
$29,253.82)	17,552.29	
Less withdrawals.........	(10,278.90)	
Capital, January 31.....................		$1,286,488.79

Robert S. Wilson, capital:

Capital, January 1.......... $ 852,529.20		
Add: Net income (40% of		
$29,253.82)	11,701.53	
Less withdrawals..........	(6,847.35)	
Capital, January 31.....................	857,383.38	
Total owners' equity...................		2,143,872.17
Total liabilities and owners' equity............		$4,279,855.09

Wilson & Son Wholesale Drug Company — Balance Sheet (*concluded*)

Work sheet for two months ended February 28, 19—

528

This work sheet is reproduced on pages 530 and 531. The amounts in the Trial Balance columns were the balances of all of the general ledger accounts after the posting for the month of February had been completed. A comparison of the January 31 trial balance on page 522 with the trial balance for February 28 on page 530 reveals that there were no changes in the balances of several accounts. The balance of the merchandise inventory account (No. 141) will remain unchanged until the accounts are adjusted at the end of the year. There were no changes in the balances of the delivery equipment and land accounts (Nos. 171 and 191) because none of these types of assets had been acquired, nor disposed of during February. None of the accumulated depreciation accounts (Nos. 016, 017 and 018) received any debits, since none of the related assets were retired or sold during February, and the accumulated depreciation accounts will receive no credits until the year-end adjustments are recorded.

Accrued Interest Payable, Account No. 251, had no balance at the end of either month since the accrual is not recorded on a monthly basis. There was no transaction during February that affected the balance of Mortgage Payable, Account No. 271. The partners' capital accounts (Nos. 311 and 321) were unchanged, since neither partner made any additional investment in February, and the accounts will be unaffected by withdrawals and net income (or loss) until the annual closing entries are posted at the end of the year. The accounts for Depreciation Expense (No. 614), Insurance Expense (No. 615), Supplies Expense (No. 621), and Bad Debts Expense (No. 622) had no balances at the end of either month, since they normally are not debited until the year-end adjustments are recorded: Property Tax Expense, Account No. 616, and Interest Expense, No. 811, had no balances at the end of either month, since no payments of property taxes had been made during either month, and the payment of mortgage interest on January 2 had discharged the liability recorded at the end of the previous year. Cost of Goods Sold, Account No. 531, and Expense and Revenue Summary, Account No. 331 (not shown), had no balances at either date, since these accounts are used solely in the end-of-year process of formally adjusting and closing the accounts.

The entries in the Adjustments columns of the work sheet for the two months ended February 28 involved exactly the same accounts as the entries on the work sheet for the month ended January 31:

Entry (a): Cost of Goods Sold, Account No. 531, was debited and Merchandise Inventory, Account No. 141, was credited for exactly the same amount, $1,883,246.41, as on the earlier work sheet, since the January 1 inventory was involved in the calculations of cost of goods sold both for January alone and for the two-month period ended February 28.

Entries (b), (c), and (d): The balances of Purchases, Account No. 511 ($1,650,034.86), Purchases Returns and Allowances, Account No. 051 ($19,797.87), and Purchases Discount, Account No. 052 ($32,925.68) were transferred to Cost of Goods Sold, Account No. 531. In every case, the balance represented the amount for the two months.

Entry (e): Merchandise Inventory, Account No. 141, was debited and Cost of Goods Sold, Account No. 531, was credited for $1,621,000, the estimated amount of the inventory on February 28.

Entry (f): Interest Expense, Account No. 811, was debited and Accrued Interest Payable, Account No. 251, was credited for $18,000, the mortgage interest accrued for the two months.

Entry (g): Insurance Expense, Account No. 615, was debited and Prepaid Insurance, Account No. 152, was credited for $6,370.31, the share of insurance premiums applicable to the two months. (The amount was not exactly twice the amount for January alone because one policy expired early in February and was renewed at a slightly lower rate.)

Entry (h): Supplies Expense, Account No. 621, was debited and Store Supplies, Account No. 151, was credited for $4,510.98, the calculated cost

529

530

Account	Acct. No.	Trial Balance Debit	Trial Balance Credit
First National Bank	111	60 552 69	
Accounts Receivable	131	247 582 15	
Allowance for Bad Debts	013	8 740 16	
Merchandise Inventory	141	1 883 246 41	
Store Supplies	151	11 010 98	
Prepaid Insurance	152	15 902 78	
Furniture and Equipment	161	367 926 00	
Accumulated Depreciation — Furniture and Equipment	016		112 054 78
Delivery Equipment	171	115 796 64	
Accumulated Depreciation — Delivery Equipment	017		59 342 15
Building	181	2 715 234 60	
Accumulated Depreciation — Building	018		1 392 431 21
Land	191	650 000 00	
FICA Tax Payable	211		6 879 48
FUTA Tax Payable	221		623 10
State Unemployment Tax Payable	231		4 206 09
Employees Income Tax Payable	241		11 025 80
Accrued Interest Payable	251		
Accounts Payable	261		212 547 76
Mortgage Payable	271		1 800 000 00
John H. Wilson, Capital	311		1 279 215 40
John H. Wilson, Drawing	031	25 115 70	
Robert S. Wilson, Capital	321		852 529 20
Robert S. Wilson, Drawing	032	16 391 55	
Sales	411		2 249 115 76
Sales Returns and Allowances	041	22 144 39	
Sales Discount	042	43 459 58	
Purchases	511	1 650 034 86	
Purchases Returns and Allowances	051		19 797 87
Purchases Discount	052		32 925 68
Cost of Goods Sold	531		
Salaries and Commissions Expense	611	155 780 90	
Payroll Taxes Expense	612	13 388 78	
Partners' Salaries Expense	613	8 000 00	
Depreciation Expense	614		
Insurance Expense	615		
Property Tax Expense	616		
Utilities Expense	617	4 544 22	
Telephone and Telegraph Expense	618	1 481 63	
Delivery Expense	619	6 152 61	
Supplies Expense	621		
Bad Debts Expense	622		
Miscellaneous Expense	623	10 207 65	
Interest Expense	811		
		8 032 694 28	8 032 694 28
Accrued Property Tax Payable			
Net Income			

WHOLESALE DRUG COMPANY

Sheet

Period Ended February 28, 19--

	Adjustments		Income Statement		Balance Sheet	
	Debit	**Credit**	**Debit**	**Credit**	**Debit**	**Credit**
					60 552 69	
					247 582 15	
		(j) 10 917 56				2 177 40
	(e) 1 621 000 00	(a) 1 883 246 41			1 621 000 00	
		(h) 4 510 98			6 500 00	
		(g) 6 370 31			9 532 47	
					367 926 00	
		(i) 3 420 40				115 475 18
					115 796 64	
		(i) 4 824 86				64 167 01
					2 715 234 60	
		(i) 11 310 14				1 403 741 35
					650 000 00	
						6 879 48
						623 10
						4 206 09
						11 025 80
		(f) 18 000 00				18 000 00
						212 547 76
						1 800 000 00
						1 279 215 40
					25 115 70	
						852 529 20
					16 391 55	
				2 249 115 76		
			22 144 39			
			43 459 58			
		(b) 1 650 034 86				
	(c) 19 797 87					
	(d) 32 925 68					
	(a) 1 883 246 41	(c) 19 797 87	1 859 557 72			
	(b) 1 650 034 86	(d) 32 925 68				
		(e) 1 621 000 00				
			155 780 90			
			13 388 78			
			8 000 00			
	(i) 19 555 40		19 555 40			
	(g) 6 370 31		6 370 31			
	(k) 13 744 26		13 744 26			
			4 544 22			
			1 481 63			
			6 152 61			
	(h) 4 510 98		4 510 98			
	(j) 10 917 56		10 917 56			
			10 207 65			
	(f) 18 000 00		18 000 00			
		(k) 13 744 26				13 744 26
	5 280 103 33	5 280 103 33	2 197 815 99	2 249 115 76	5 835 631 80	5 784 332 03
			51 299 77			51 299 77
			2 249 115 76	2 249 115 76	5 835 631 80	5 835 631 80

531

Work-Sheet for Two-Month Period

of supplies used during the two months. That amount was determined by subtracting the estimated cost of supplies on hand February 28, $6,500, from the amount of the balance of the store supplies account on February 28, $11,010.98.

Entry (i): Depreciation Expense, Account No. 614, was debited for $19,555.40, and Accumulated Depreciation — Furniture and Equipment, Account No. 016, was credited for $3,420.40, Accumulated Depreciation — Delivery Equipment, Account No. 017, was credited for $4,824.86, and Accumulated Depreciation — Building, Account No. 018, was credited for $11,310.14. In every case the amount was exactly twice that for January alone. During February, $39,568.30 had been added to the furniture and equipment account and $801.00 to the building account, but depreciation was not considered on assets owned for less than one month. There had been no change in the amount of delivery equipment.

Entry (j): Bad Debts Expense, Account No. 622, was debited and Allowance for Bad Debts, Account No. 031, was credited for $10,917.56. This amount was determined by taking 1/2 of 1 percent of the net sales for the two months, $2,183,511.79 ($2,249,115.76 — $22,144.39 — $43,459.58).

Entry (k): Property Tax Expense, Account No. 616, was debited and Accrued Property Tax Payable was credited for $13,744.26. This amount represented the share of property tax expense for two months. It was exactly twice the amount of the adjustment for January.

It should be noted that in calculating the amounts of insurance expense, depreciation expense, interest expense, and property tax expense, the fact that January had more days than February was ignored. The month — not the number of days — was the unit of time used.

The work sheet was completed in the usual manner. Net income for the two-month period ended February 28, 19--, in the amount of $51,299.77 was disclosed.

Interim statements — successive periods

The work sheet reproduced on pages 530 and 531 assembled the data needed for an income statement covering the two-month period ended February 28, 19--, and a balance sheet as of the same date. The accountant for Wilson & Son Wholesale Drug Company uses the same procedure to develop a succession of year-to-date income statements and month-end balance sheets. Income statements of this type are valuable for comparative purposes. Owners and managers are interested in learning how the progress in the current year compares with that of preceding years.

WILSON & SON WHOLESALE DRUG COMPANY

Income Statements

	For Two Months Ended February 28, 19—	For January, 19—	For February, 19—
Sales	$2,249,115.76	$1,183,768.05	$1,065,347.71
Less: Returns and allowances	(22,144.39)	(11,654.23)	(10,490.16)
Sales discounts	(43,459.58)	(22,878.16)	(20,581.42)
Net sales	$2,183,511.79	$1,149,235.66	$1,034,276.13
Cost of goods sold:			
Merchandise inventory, beginning of period	$1,883,246.41	$1,883,246.41	$1,742,500.00
Purchases	1,650,034.86	868,439.20	781,595.66
Less: Returns and allowances	(19,797.87)	(10,421.15)	(9,376.72)
Purchases discounts	(32,925.68)	(17,329.06)	(15,596.62)
Cost of merchandise available for sale	$3,480,557.72	$2,723,935.40	$2,499,122.32
Less merchandise inventory, end of period	1,621,000.00	1,742,500.00	1,621,000.00
	1,859,557.72	981,435.40	878,122.32
Gross margin on sales	$ 323,954.07	$ 167,800.26	$ 156,153.81
Operating expenses:			
Salaries and commissions expense	$ 155,780.90	$ 79,315.80	$ 76,465.10
Payroll taxes expense	13,388.78	6,814.32	6,574.46
Partners' salaries expense	8,000.00	4,000.00	4,000.00
Depreciation expense	19,555.40	9,777.70	9,777.70
Insurance expense	6,370.31	3,212.49	3,157.82
Property tax expense	13,744.26	6,872.13	6,872.13
Utilities expense	4,544.22	2,374.72	2,169.50
Telephone and telegraph expense	1,481.63	769.15	712.48
Delivery expense	6,152.61	3,145.96	3,006.65
Supplies expense	4,510.98	2,334.87	2,176.11
Bad debts expense	10,917.56	5,746.18	5,171.38
Miscellaneous expense	10,207.65	5,183.12	5,024.53
Total operating expenses	254,654.30	129,546.44	125,107.86
Net operating income	$ 69,299.77	$ 38,253.82	$ 31,045.95
Interest expense	18,000.00	9,000.00	9,000.00
Net income	$ 51,299.77	$ 29,253.82	$ 22,045.95

Wilson & Son Wholesale Drug Company — Income Statements

WILSON & SON WHOLESALE DRUG COMPANY

Balance Sheet

February 28, 19—

Assets

Current assets:

Cash....................................		$ 60,552.69
Accounts receivable.........	$ 247,582.15	
Less allowance for bad debts	2,177.40	245,404.75
Merchandise inventory.....................		1,621,000.00
Store supplies..........................		6,500.00
Prepaid insurance.......................		9,532.47
Total current assets....................		$1,942,989.91

Long-lived assets:

Furniture and equipment......	$ 367,926.00		
Less accumd. depreciation..	115,475.18	$ 252,450.82	
Delivery equipment..........	$ 115,796.64		
Less accumd. depreciation..	64,167.01	51,629.63	
Building..................	$2,715,234.60		
Less accumd. depreciation..	1,403,741.35	1,311,493.25	
Land..................................		650,000.00	
Total long-lived assets.................			2,265,573.70
Total assets..............................			$4,208,563.61

534

Liabilities

Current liabilities:

FICA tax payable........................	$ 6,879.48	
FUTA tax payable.......................	623.10	
State unemployment tax payable...........	4,206.09	
Employees income tax payable	11,025.80	
Accrued interest payable.................	18,000.00	
Accrued property tax payable.............	13,744.26	
Accounts payable.......................	212,547.76	
Total current liabilities...................		$ 267,026.49

Long-term liability:

Mortgage payable.......................		1,800,000.00
Total liabilities.............................		$2,067,026.49

Wilson & Son Wholesale Drug Company — Balance Sheet
(continued on next page)

Owners' Equity

John H. Wilson, capital:

Capital, January 1..........	$1,279,215.40	
Add: Net income (60% of $51,299.77)	30,779.86	
Less withdrawals...........	(25,115.70)	
Capital, February 28....................		$1,284,879.56

Robert S. Wilson, capital:

Capital, January 1..........	$ 852,529.20	
Add: Net income (40% of $51,299.77)	20,519.91	
Less withdrawals...........	(16,391.55)	
Capital, February 28....................	856,657.56	
Total owners' equity....................		2,141,537.12
Total liabilities and owners' equity.............		$4,208,563.61

Wilson & Son Wholesale Drug Company — Balance Sheet (*concluded*)

In addition to the cumulative, year-to-date income statement, an interim income statement is needed for each period by itself. Little effort is required to produce such statements using the year-to-date information. The technique is illustrated on page 533. At the left is the income statement of the company for the two-month period ended February 28, 19––. (This was prepared from the Income Statement columns of the work sheet reproduced on pages 530 and 531.) Next shown is the income statement for January, 19––. This statement is exactly the same as the one shown on page 526 (developed from the Income Statement columns of the January work sheet on pages 522 and 523). At the right is the income statement for February, 19––, that was derived by subtracting the amounts in the January statement from those in the January-February statement (with the two exceptions noted in the following paragraph).

Since the income statements show the manner in which cost of goods sold was calculated, the amounts of the beginning and ending merchandise inventories shown in the February statement were not derived by subtraction. The beginning inventory for February, $1,742,500, was the ending inventory for January. The ending inventory for February, $1,621,000, was also the ending inventory for the two-month period.

The balance sheet as of February 28, 19––, is reproduced above and on the preceding page. This was prepared from the Balance Sheet columns of the work sheet on pages 530 and 531. It should be noted that the owners' equity section shows each partner's equity as of January 1, plus his share of the net income for the two-month period, less his withdrawals during the two-month period, to arrive at the amount of his equity on February 28. If desired, each calculation could have started with his equity on January 31 (as shown in the balance sheet on pages 527 and 528), with his net income share for February added and his February withdrawals deducted. The result would have been the same.

It should be evident that a similar procedure would have been employed if quarterly, rather than monthly, interim statements had been prepared.

Report No. 20-1

Complete Report No. 20-1 in the workbook and submit your working papers to the instructor for approval. The instructor will then give directions as to the work to be done next.

536

chapters 16-20

practical accounting problems

Problem 16-A

On May 1, H. A. Weitman organized a photographic equipment and supplies enterprise and opened a new set of books. Following is a list of the assets that he invested in the business:

Cash	$10,438.50
Office equipment	5,120.00
Store equipment	6,839.00
Delivery truck	5,680.00
Total	$28,077.50

He owed $1,680 on the delivery truck that had been purchased on account.

REQUIRED: Prepare the opening entry in general journal form.

Problem 16-B

HIRAM GRANT
Balance Sheet
December 31, 19 — —

Assets			Liabilities		
Cash..............		$ 4,544.30	Accounts payable......	$5,945.00	
Accounts receivable....	$8,643.20		Social security tax pay-		
Less allow. for bad			able	104.62	
debts...........	682.56	7,960.64	Employees income tax		
Mdse. inventory.......		17,238.90	payable...........	79.10	
Prepaid insurance......		312.46	Total liabilities........		$ 6,128.72
Store equipment.......	$7,000.00		Owner's Equity		
Less accumd. depr....	640.00	6,360.00	Hiram Grant, capital...		30,287.58
			Total liabilities and		
Total assets..........		$36,416.30	owner's equity.......		$36,416.30

Hiram Grant, who has been conducting a wholesale wallpaper and paint enterprise, decides to install a formal set of books as of January 2.

REQUIRED: Prepare the opening entry in general journal form.

538 Problem 16-C

D. L. Davis is engaged in the wholesale leather goods business. After closing his revenue and expense accounts for the calendar year ended December 31, his expense and revenue summary account, No. 321, had a credit balance of $19,080.50. At the same time his capital account, No. 311 had a credit balance of $54,990 and his drawing account, No. 031, had a debit balance of $16,000.

REQUIRED: (1) Using the standard account form of ledger paper, open Mr. Davis's capital account and drawing account, and an expense and revenue summary account, and enter the December 31 balances. (2) Assuming that Mr. Davis wishes to have the balances of both the expense and revenue summary and drawing accounts transferred to his capital account, journalize and post the required entries. After completing the posting, total and rule the accounts and bring down Mr. Davis's present equity below the ruling.

Problem 16-D

Ernest B. Williams has been operating a wholesale hardware business as a single proprietor. His balance sheet prepared as of September 30 is shown below. On October 1 of the current year he admits James R. Cooper as a partner with a one-half interest in the business to be conducted under the firm name of Williams & Cooper. Under the partnership agreement, Mr. Cooper invests $23,563.24 in cash. The assets of Mr. Williams become the property of the partnership and his liabilities are assumed by the partnership.

ERNEST B. WILLIAMS
Balance Sheet
September 30, 19 — —

Assets			Liabilities		
Cash.................		$ 7,240.44	Notes payable........	$6,000.00	
			Accounts payable......	5,000.20	
Accounts receivable....	$9,600.60		Social security tax payable	120.00	
Less allow. for bad debts...........	980.00	8,620.60	Employees income tax payable...........	90.00	
Mdse. inventory.......		15,392.40	Total liabilities........		$11,210.20
Store equipment.......	$4,800.00			Owner's Equity	
Less accumd. depr....	1,280.00	3,520.00	Ernest B. Williams, capital.............		23,563.24
			Total liabilities and		
Total assets..........		$34,773.44	owner's equity.......		$34,773.44

REQUIRED: Assuming that a new set of books is installed by the partnership, prepare the necessary opening entries in general journal form to record the investments of the partners.

Problem 16-E

George E. Bohl and Donald E. Wilson have been competitors in the wholesale drug business. On July 1 of the current year they form a partnership, to be operated under the firm name of Bohl & Wilson. Their balance sheets as of June 30 are reproduced on page 540. The partnership agreement provides that the assets are to be taken over at their book value and that the liabilities are to be assumed by the partnership. The agreement also provides that Mr. Wilson is to contribute a sufficient amount of additional cash to make his investment equal to Mr. Bohl's investment. It is also agreed that the partners will share profits and losses equally and that the assets will be distributed equally between them in case of dissolution of the partnership.

REQUIRED: Assuming that a new set of books is installed by the partnership, prepare the necessary opening entries in general journal form to record the investments of the partners.

GEORGE E. BOHL
Balance Sheet
June 30, 19 — —

Assets			Liabilities		
Cash...............		$ 7,000.38	Notes payable........	$2,400.00	
Accounts receivable....	$5,921.00		Accounts payable......	4,824.20	
Less allow. for bad			Social security tax pay-		
debts...........	137.40	5,783.60	able	116.00	
Mdse. Inventory.......		9,781.34	Employees income tax		
Delivery equipment.....	$6,600.00		payable...........	90.00	
Less accumd. depr....	1,750.00	4,850.00	Total liabilities........		$ 7,430.20
Office equipment......	$2,800.00				
Less accumd. depr....	1,200.00	1,600.00	Owner's Equity		
			George E. Bohl, capital.		21,585.12
			Total liabilities and		
Total assets..........		$29,015.32	owner's equity.......		$29,015.32

DONALD E. WILSON
Balance Sheet
June 30, 19 — —

Assets			Liabilities		
Cash...............		$ 9,000.40	Accounts payable......	$5,818.32	
Accounts receivable....	$4,598.20		Social security tax pay-		
Less allow. for bad			able	104.00	
debts...........	106.40	4,491.80	Employees income tax		
Mdse. inventory.......		7,081.24	payable...........	88.00	
Delivery equipment.....	$6,000.00		Total liabilities........		$ 6,010.32
Less accumd. depr....	1,600.00	4,400.00			
Office equipment......	$2,400.00		Owner's Equity		
Less accumd. depr....	800.00	1,600.00	Donald E. Wilson,		
			capital............		20,563.12
			Total liabilities and		
Total assets..........		$26,573.44	owner's equity.......		$26,573.44

Problem 16-F

The Woodward Upholstering Co., a partnership, is engaged in the wholesale upholstering business. Ownership of the firm is vested in Charles L. Woodward, D. R. Conroy, H. E. Cusick, and W. E. Thomas. Profits and losses are shared equally.

Mr. Cusick died on July 5. His widow is entitled to receive his share in the distribution of the partnership assets. The remaining partners agreed to buy his widow's interest at 95% of its book value. When the books were closed as of the date of Mr. Cusick's death, his capital account had a credit balance of $17,304.20. On August 15, a partnership check was issued to Mrs. Cusick in final settlement.

REQUIRED: Compute the amount to be paid Mrs. Cusick under the agreement and prepare the general journal entry required to record the check on the books of the partnership.

Problem 16-G

January 1. The Lincoln Carpet Co. was incorporated with an authorized issue of 1,000 shares of common capital stock, par value $100 per share. Subscriptions were received from the following:

G. W. Ober, 300 shares, $30,000
H. L. Ober, 300 shares, $30,000
R. P. Holt, 200 shares, $20,000
D. L. Colby, 200 shares, $20,000

On January 6, all subscribers paid the amounts due. The stock certificates were issued on January 10.

Following is a list of the corporate accounts to be kept:

Capital Stock
Subscriptions Receivable
Capital Stock Subscribed

REQUIRED: Prepare the general journal entries required to record **(1)** the stock subscriptions received, **(2)** cash received to apply on subscriptions, and **(3)** the capital stock issued to subscribers on January 10.

Problem 16-H

August 28. The board of directors of The Southland Rolling Mill Co. declared a cash dividend of $3 per share on its 6% cumulative preferred stock, payable October 16 to holders of record September 15. There were 34,350 shares of this stock outstanding.

October 16. The company mailed dividend checks amounting to a total of $103,050 to stockholders.

REQUIRED: Using standard two-column journal paper, record **(1)** the dividend declaration on August 28 and **(2)** the dividend payment on October 16.

Problem 16-I

Fred Freeman, Walter Mitty, and Roy Ryder were in business as a partnership under the firm name of Freeman, Mitty, & Ryder. On January 2, The Gateway City Distributing Co., with an authorized capital of $100,000, consisting of 5,000 shares of common capital stock, par value $20 per share, was organized to take over the business formerly conducted by the partnership. The following balance sheet of the partnership was prepared at the time of incorporating the business:

FREEMAN, MITTY, & RYDER

Balance Sheet

December 31, 19 — —

Assets			Liabilities		
Cash...............		$13,900.48	Accounts payable.....	$ 7,813.00	
Accounts receivable...	$15,901.36		Social security tax pay-		
Less allow. for bad			able	133.20	
debts...........	1,964.00	13,937.36	Employees income tax		
Mdse. inventory......		25,226.20	payable..........	112.44	
Office equipment.....	$ 4,800.00		Total liabilities.......		$ 8,058.64
Less accumd. depr...	1,600.00	3,200.00			
Delivery equipment...	$ 6,600.00		Owners' Equity		
Less accumd. depr...	3,600.00	3,000.00	Fred Freeman, capital.	$18,888.44	
			Walter Mitty, capital..	16,612.64	
			Roy Ryder, capital....	15,704.32	51,205.40
			Total liabilities and		
Total assets.........		$59,264.04	owners' equity.....		$59,264.04

The partners subscribed for capital stock of the corporation as follows:

Fred Freeman, 2,000 shares at $20 a share...........................	$40,000
Walter Mitty, 2,000 shares at $20 a share...........................	40,000
Roy Ryder, 1,000 shares at $20 a share.............................	20,000

The partners, as individuals, received credit toward their subscriptions for their respective equities in the assets of the partnership and gave their personal checks for the balance of their respective subscriptions. A new set of books is to be installed by the corporation.

REQUIRED: Prepare entries in general journal form to record the following: **(1)** The partners' subscriptions to the capital stock of the corporation, **(2)** the transfer of the assets and liabilities of the partnership to the corporation, **(3)** the receipt of cash from the partners collectively in settlement of the balances due on their respective subscriptions, and **(4)** the issuance of stock certificates to the partners.

Problem 16-J

Stanley M. Jones has been operating a wholesale grocery business as a single proprietor. His balance sheet prepared as of April 30 is shown below. On May 1 of the current year he admits John M. Good as a partner with a one-half interest in the business to be conducted under the firm name of Jones & Good. Under the partnership agreement, Mr. Good invests merchandise inventory valued at $21,874.84, store equipment valued at $6,000, and $19,251.64 in cash. The assets of Mr. Jones become the property of the partnership and his liabilities are assumed by the partnership.

STANLEY M. JONES

Balance Sheet

April 30, 19 — —

Assets			Liabilities		
Cash..............		$14,480.88	Notes payable.......	$12,000.00	
Accounts receivable...	$19,201.20		Accounts payable.....	10,000.40	
Less allow. for bad			Social security tax		
debts..........	1,960.00	17,241.20	payable	240.00	
			Employees income tax		
Mdse. inventory......		30,784.80	payable..........	180.00	
			Total liabilities.......		$22,420.40
Store equipment......	$ 9,600.00				
Less accumd. depr...	2,560.00	7,040.00	Owner's Equity		
			Stanley M. Jones,		
			capital...........		47,126.48
			Total liabilities and		
Total assets.........		$69,546.88	owner's equity.....		$69,546.88

543

REQUIRED: Assuming that a new set of books is installed by the partnership, prepare the necessary opening entries in general journal form to record the investments of the partners.

There are no Practical Accounting Problems for Chapter 17.

Problem 18-A

Lewis & Bartell are partners in a wholesale mercantile business. Their accounts are kept on a fiscal year basis, with the year ending on June 30. The accounts with customers, suppliers, and operating expenses are kept in

LEWIS & BARTELL
Trial Balance
June 30, 19—

Drovers Bank	111	10,843.00	
Petty Cash Fund	112	60.00	
Notes Receivable	131	7,116.96	
Accrued Interest Receivable	132		
Accounts Receivable	133	14,475.70	
Allowance for Bad Debts	013		1,372.80
Merchandise Inventory	151	144,593.28	
Store Supplies	161	1,350.00	
Office Supplies	163	1,323.24	
Fuel	164	567.00	
Postage Stamps	165	910.76	
Prepaid Insurance	166	1,184.36	
Store Equipment	171	2,880.00	
Accumd. Depreciation — Store Equip.	017		739.44
Delivery Equipment	181	5,760.00	
Accumd. Depreciation — Delivery Equip.	018		1,440.00
Office Equipment	191	4,800.00	
Accumd. Depreciation — Office Equip.	019		858.26
Social Security Tax Payable	211		479.28
Employees Income Tax Payable	221		288.00
Notes Payable	231		5,684.16
Accrued Interest Payable	241		
Accounts Payable	251		7,111.80
C. S. Lewis, Capital	311		74,888.10
C. S. Lewis, Drawing	031	11,100.00	
H. R. Bartell, Capital	321		74,888.10
H. R. Bartell, Drawing	032	10,980.00	
Sales	411		1,084,234.56
Sales Returns and Allowances	041	7,780.32	
Sales Discount	042	6,744.00	
Purchases	511	854,731.62	
Purchases Returns and Allowances	051		5,281.44
Purchases Discount	052		4,680.00
Freight In	531	8,972.18	
Cost of Goods Sold	551		
Operating Expenses	611	165,788.00	
Interest Earned	711		298.32
Interest Expense	811	283.84	
		1,262,244.26	1,262,244.26

544

subsidiary ledgers with control accounts in the general ledger. Any necessary adjustments in the operating expense accounts are made at the end of each year after a trial balance is taken. Since the accountant is required to prepare annual financial statements, he follows the practice of preparing a ten-column summary work sheet and a three-column supplementary operating expenses work sheet at the end of each year as a means of compiling and classifying the information needed in financial statement preparation.

The following accounts in the operating expense ledger require adjustment as of June 30:

Insurance Expense	6121	
Store Supplies Expense	6123	
Postage Expense	6124	
Depreciation of Store Equipment	6125	
Depreciation of Delivery Equipment	6126	
Fuel Expense	6134	$ 701.52
Bad Debts Expense	6136	
Office Supplies Expense	6138	
Depreciation of Office Equipment	6141	
All others (to balance)		165,086.48
		$165,788.00

The trial balance of the general ledger taken as of June 30 is shown on page 544.

REQUIRED: Assuming that you are employed as the accountant for Lewis & Bartell, you are required to prepare a ten-column summary work sheet for the year ended June 30, 19—, and a supplementary work sheet for operating expenses. Use as your guide the model work sheets reproduced on pages 476, 477, and 482. Allow 3 lines for Cost of Goods Sold on the summary work sheet. The following data provide the information needed in adjusting the general ledger accounts and the operating expenses ledger accounts.

Merchandise inventory, June 30	$148,302.52
Allowance for bad debts for year should total	1,807.06
Store supplies used	1,170.00
Office supplies used	1,154.82
Fuel inventory, June 30	135.00
Postage expense	868.10
Insurance expense	772.58
Depreciation of store equipment	10% of cost
Depreciation of delivery equipment	25% of cost
Depreciation of office equipment	10% of cost
Interest accrued on notes receivable, June 30	$50.86
Interest accrued on notes payable, June 30	43.04

Retain the solution to this problem for use in Problem 18-B.

Problem 18-B

The work sheets for Lewis & Bartell for the year ended June 30, 19--, completed in Problem 18-A, will be used to solve this problem.

REQUIRED:

(1) Prepare the entries necessary to adjust the general ledger accounts and the operating expense ledger accounts as of June 30, 19--. Use as your guide the model general journal illustration reproduced on page 488.

(2) After making the required entries, foot the amount columns of each general journal page to prove the footings.

(3) Prepare the entries required to close the following types of accounts in the general ledger: revenue accounts, expense accounts, the expense and revenue summary account, No. 331, and the partners' drawing accounts. Distribute the balance of the expense and revenue summary account equally between the two partners. Use as your guide the model general journal illustration reproduced on page 489.

(4) Prepare the necessary entries to reverse the accrual adjustments as of January 1, 19--. Use as your guide the model general journal illustration reproduced on page 494.

(5) After making the required entries, foot the amount columns of each general journal page to prove the footings.

(6) Assuming that the individual posting to the general ledger accounts and the operating expense ledger accounts has been completed, insert the necessary check marks in the general journal. Enter the totals of the amount columns on each page and rule each page of the general journal. Assuming that the summary posting has been completed, make the necessary notations in the general journal.

Problem 19-A

King & Lazares conduct a wholesale merchandising business as partners. They keep their accounts on a fiscal year basis, with their year ending June 30. Accounts with customers, suppliers, and operating expenses are kept in subsidiary ledgers with control accounts in the general ledger. Adjustments to the operating expense accounts are made at the end of each fiscal year by means of a supplementary work sheet before completing a ten-column summary work sheet. The accountant is required to prepare annual financial statements with appropriate supporting schedules.

The completed ten-column summary work sheet and supplementary operating expenses work sheet of King & Lazares as of June 30 of the current year are given on the following three pages. Their subsidiary accounts receivable and accounts payable ledgers in T-account form, containing final June 30 balances, are given below.

KING & LAZARES

Accounts Receivable Ledger

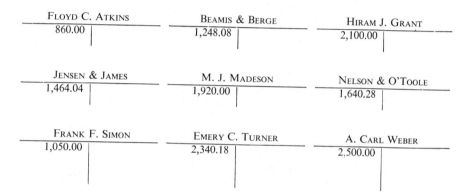

Floyd C. Atkins	Beamis & Berge	Hiram J. Grant
860.00	1,248.08	2,100.00

Jensen & James	M. J. Madeson	Nelson & O'Toole
1,464.04	1,920.00	1,640.28

Frank F. Simon	Emery C. Turner	A. Carl Weber
1,050.00	2,340.18	2,500.00

KING & LAZARES

Accounts Payable Ledger

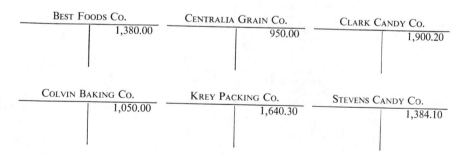

Best Foods Co.	Centralia Grain Co.	Clark Candy Co.
1,380.00	950.00	1,900.20

Colvin Baking Co.	Krey Packing Co.	Stevens Candy Co.
1,050.00	1,640.30	1,384.10

REQUIRED: **(1)** Prepare an income statement for the year ended June 30, similar in form to the one illustrated on page 498. **(2)** Prepare a schedule of operating expenses for the year ended June 30, similar in form to the one illustrated on page 499.

Account	Acct. No.	Trial Balance Debit	Trial Balance Credit	Adjustments Debit	Adjustments Credit
Merchants National Bank......	111	5,245.50			
Petty Cash Fund.............	112	90.00			
Government Bonds...........	121	4,800.00			
Notes Receivable............	131	3,844.04			
Accrued Interest Receivable....	132			(l) 20.06	
Accounts Receivable.........	133	15,122.58			
Allowance for Bad Debts......	013	713.04			(v) 1,539.50
Mdse. Inventory — Dept. A....	141	123,434.64		(j) 127,804.26	(a)123,434.64
Mdse. Inventory — Dept. B....	151	12,905.88		(k) 13,350.42	(b) 12,905.88
Store Supplies..............	161	1,478.74			(q) 1,436.56
Advertising Supplies..........	162	317.04			(r) 283.68
Office Supplies..............	163	1,353.72			(s) 1,237.92
Postage Stamps.............	164	1,060.20			(t) 1,026.24
Prepaid Insurance............	165	949.92			(u) 663.04
Store Equipment.............	171	2,620.32			
Accumd. Depr. — Store Equip..	017		754.78		(n) 262.04
Delivery Equipment..........	181	4,293.98			
Accumd. Depr. — Deliv. Equip..	018		202.94		(o) 1,073.50
Office Equipment............	191	4,379.28			
Accumd. Depr. — Office Equip..	019		971.38		(p) 392.00
FICA Tax Payable...........	211		223.58		
FUTA Tax Payable...........	221		112.53		
State Unemp. Tax Payable....	231		147.64		
Employees Inc. Tax Payable ...	241		225.17		
Notes Payable..............	251		4,200.00		
Accrued Interest Payable......	261				(m) 41.30
Accounts Payable............	271		8,304.60		
P. J. King, Capital...........	311		74,421.98		
P. J. King, Drawing..........	031	19,968.30			
D. E. Lazares, Capital........	321		73,716.92		
D. E. Lazares, Drawing.......	032	18,687.06			
Sales — Dept. A............	411		506,466.06		
Sales R. & A. — Dept. A......	041	6,931.08			
Sales — Dept. B.............	421		53,346.12		
Sales R. & A. — Dept. B......	042	730.32			
Sales Discount..............	043	4,925.00			
Purchases — Dept. A........	511	389,046.72			(c)389,046.72
Purchases R. & A. — Dept. A ..	051		1,945.62	(e) 1,945.62	
Purchases — Dept. B........	521	40,347.66			(d) 40,347.66
Purchases R. & A. — Dept. B ..	052		120.96	(f) 120.96	
Purchases Discount...........	053		8,504.06	(g) 8,504.06	
Freight In — Dept. A........	541	3,758.62			(h) 3,758.62
Freight In — Dept. B........	551	656.08			(i) 656.08
Cost of Goods Sold — Dept. A.	561			(a)123,434.64 (c)389,046.72 (h) 3,758.62	(e) 1,945.62 (g) 7,703.52 (j) 127,804.26
Cost of Goods Sold — Dept. B.	571			(b) 12,905.88 (d) 40,347.66 (i) 656.08	(f) 120.96 (g) 800.54 (k) 13,350.42
Operating Expenses..........	611	65,433.98		(n–v) 7,914.48	
Interest Earned..............	711		216.40		(l) 20.06
Interest Expense.............	811	202.94		(m) 41.30	
Charitable Cont. Expense	821	548.40			
Collection Expense...........	822	35.70			
		733,880.74	733,880.74	729,850.76	729,850.76
Net Income................					

548

LAZARES
Sheet
ed June 30, 19—

Adj. Trial Balance		Income Statement		Balance Sheet	
Debit	Credit	Debit	Credit	Debit	Credit
5,245.50				5,245.50	
90.00				90.00	
4,800.00				4,800.00	
3,844.04				3,844.04	
20.06				20.06	
15,122.58				15,122.58	
	826.46				826.46
127,804.26				127,804.26	
13,350.42				13,350.42	
42.18				42.18	
33.36				33.36	
115.80				115.80	
33.96				33.96	
286.88				286.88	
2,620.32				2,620.32	
	1,016.82				1,016.82
4,293.98				4,293.98	
	1,276.44				1,276.44
4,379.28				4,379.28	
	1,363.38				1,363.38
	223.58				223.58
	112.53				112.53
	147.64				147.64
	225.17				225.17
	4,200.00				4,200.00
	41.30				41.30
	8,304.60				8,304.60
	74,421.98				74,421.98
19,968.30				19,968.30	
	73,716.92				73,716.92
18,687.06				18,687.06	
	506,466.06		506,466.06		
6,931.08		6,931.08			
	53,346.12		53,346.12		
730.32		730.32			
4,925.00		4,925.00			
378,786.58		378,786.58			
39,637.70		39,637.70			
73,348.46		73,348.46			
	236.46		236.46		
244.24		244.24			
548.40		548.40			
35.70		35.70			
725,925.46	725,925.46	505,187.48	560,048.64	220,737.98	165,876.82
		54,861.16			54,861.16
		560,048.64	560,048.64	220,737.98	220,737.98

549

KING & LAZARES

Operating Expenses Work Sheet

For the Year Ended June 30, 19 — —

Account	Acct. No.	Trial Balance Debit	Adjustments Debit	Adj. Tr. Bal. Debit
Advertising Expense........	6111	2,339.66	(r) 283.68	2,623.34
Store Clerks' Salary Expense.	6112	13,800.00		13,800.00
Truck Drivers' Wage Expense.	6113	6,480.00		6,480.00
D. E. Lazares, Salary Exp....	6114	11,520.00		11,520.00
D. E. Lazares, Travel Exp....	6115	1,010.58		1,010.58
Truck Gas and Oil Expense..	6116	1,220.90		1,220.90
Truck Repairs Expense......	6117	222.20		222.20
Garage Rent Expense......	6118	360.00		360.00
Freight Out..............	6119	22.44		22.44
Mdse. Insurance Expense....	6121		(u) 315.00	315.00
Delivery Equip. Insur. Expense	6122		(u) 267.30	267.30
Store Equip. Insur. Expense..	6123		(u) 27.00	27.00
Store Supplies Expense.....	6124		(q) 1,436.56	1,436.56
Postage Expense (Selling)...	6125		(t) 555.72	555.72
Depreciation of Store Equip..	6126		(n) 262.04	262.04
Depr. of Delivery Equipment.	6127		(o) 1,073.50	1,073.50
Miscellaneous Selling Expense	6128	229.40		229.40
Rent Expense.............	6131	5,040.00		5,040.00
P. J. King, Salary Expense...	6132	11,520.00		11,520.00
Office Salaries Expense.....	6133	8,928.00		8,928.00
Light and Water Expense...	6134	118.02		118.02
Tel. and Tel. Expense.......	6135	196.96		196.96
Bad Debts Expense........	6136		(v) 1,539.50	1,539.50
Property Tax Expense......	6137	459.36		459.36
Office Supplies Expense....	6138		(s) 1,237.92	1,237.92
Postage Expense (Admin.)...	6139		(t) 470.52	470.52
Office Equip. Insur. Expense.	6141		(u) 53.74	53.74
Depreciation of Office Equip.	6142		(p) 392.00	392.00
Payroll Taxes Expense......	6143	1,779.08		1,779.08
Misc. General Expense......	6144	187.38		187.38
		65,433.98	7,914.48	73,348.46

550

Problem 19-B

REQUIRED: Using the work sheets and subsidiary accounts receivable and accounts payable ledgers of King & Lazares from Problem 19-A: **(1)** Prepare a balance sheet as of June 30. **(2)** Prepare supporting schedules of accounts receivable and accounts payable as of June 30.

Problem 19-C

REQUIRED: Using the work sheets of King & Lazares from Problem 19-A, and the balance sheet information from the beginning of the year given below: **(1)** Prepare a statement of changes in financial position for the year ended June 30. **(2)** Prepare a schedule of changes in working capital for the year ended June 30.

BEGINNING OF YEAR BALANCE SHEET INFORMATION

Cash...	$ 11,449.90
Government bonds...	—
Receivables (net)..	17,401.52
Merchandise inventories.....................................	136,340.52
Supplies and prepayments....................................	470.56
Total current assets.....................................	$165,662.50
Long-lived assets (less accumulated depreciation).................	9,364.48
Total assets..	$175,026.98
Payroll taxes payable.......................................	$ 561.74
Notes and interest payable..................................	9,656.64
Accounts payable...	16,669.70
Total current liabilities................................	$ 26,888.08
Owners' equity...	148,138.90
Total liabilities and owners' equity.........................	$175,026.98

Problem 20-A

The Broad Brothers are partners in the wholesale grocery business. They share profits and losses in the following ratio: R. L. Broad, senior partner, 65%; S. S. Broad, junior partner, 35%. "Salaries" are included in the profit shares. The calendar year is used as a fiscal year.

Broad Brothers' accountant prepares quarterly and "year-to-date" income statements, as well as balance sheets as of the last day of each quarter. The completed trial balance for Broad Brothers for the quarter ended March 31, 19-- is shown on the next page.

BROAD BROTHERS

Trial Balance

For the Quarter Ended March 31, 19 ——

First Community Bank	111	24,942.67	
Accounts Receivable	131	65,602.23	
Allowance for Bad Debts	013	1,125.90	
Merchandise Inventory	161	513,493.84	
Store Supplies	181	3,678.48	
Prepaid Insurance	183	5,775.59	
Furniture and Equipment	211	89,551.98	
Accumd. Depreciation — Furn. & Equip.	021		32,719.44
Delivery Equipment	221	31,738.99	
Accumd. Depreciation — Delivery Equip.	022		13,952.80
Building	231	783,729.84	
Accumulated Depreciation — Building	023		382,527.62
Land	251	180,000.00	
FICA Tax Payable	311		1,947.14
FUTA Tax Payable	312		86.53
State Unemployment Tax Payable	313		584.15
Employees Income Tax Payable	314		3,244.92
Accrued Interest Payable	315		—
Accounts Payable	316		81,439.85
Mortgage Payable	411		600,000.00
R. L. Broad, Capital	511		336,184.17
R. L. Broad, Drawing	051	2,554.86	
S. S. Broad, Capital	521		233,965.83
S. S. Broad, Drawing	052	1,934.26	
Sales	611		309,382.47
Sales Returns and Allowances	061	2,960.52	
Sales Discount	062	6,040.55	
Purchases	711	255,960.81	
Purchases Returns and Allowances	071		2,522.14
Purchases Discount	072		5,091.63
Cost of Goods Sold (allow 3 lines)	721		
Salaries and Commissions Expense	811	21,634.77	
Payroll Taxes Expense	812	1,644.24	
Partners' Salaries Expense	813	8,100.00	
Depreciation Expense	814	—	
Insurance Expense	815	—	
Property Tax Expense	816	—	
Utilities Expense	817	652.24	
Telephone and Telegraph Expense	818	268.85	
Delivery Expense	819	844.39	
Supplies Expense	821	—	
Bad Debts Expense	822	—	
Miscellaneous Expense	823	1,413.68	
Interest Expense	911	—	
		2,003,648.69	2,003,648.69
Accrued Property Tax Payable			—

REQUIRED: **(1)** Using the trial balance on page 552 and the data and information given below, prepare a work sheet for Broad Brothers for the quarter ended March 31, 19--. Use as your guide the model work sheet reproduced on pages 530 and 531 (which is complete except for the Adjusted Trial Balance columns). Enter the trial balance in the trial balance columns of a ten-column work sheet. Then, enter the necessary adjustments in the adjustments columns of the ten-column work sheet as follows:

(a) Transfer the beginning merchandise inventory to Cost of Goods Sold.

(b) Transfer the purchases for the quarter to Cost of Goods Sold.

(c) Transfer the purchases returns and allowances for the quarter to Cost of Goods Sold.

(d) Transfer the purchases discounts for the quarter to Cost of Goods Sold.

(e) Amount of ending merchandise inventory, $507,450.

(f) Interest accrued on mortgage since January 1, $2,500.

(g) Insurance expense for quarter, $876.18.

(h) Store supplies used during quarter, $1,143.48.

(i) Depreciation of furniture and equipment, $497.50.
Depreciation of delivery equipment, $661.23.
Depreciation of building, $1,632.76.

(j) Bad debts provision for quarter, $1,501.90.

(k) Property tax assignable to quarter, $1,995.84.

553

(2) Extend the adjusted amounts to the adjusted trial balance columns and foot the columns as a means of proof. **(3)** Complete the work sheet, determine the amount of net income or net loss, and foot the income statement and balance sheet columns as a means of proof.

The solution to this problem will be needed in solving Problem 20-C.

Problem 20-B

This is a continuation of Problem 20-A. The completed trial balance for Broad Brothers for the six-month period ended June 30, 19--, is shown on the next page.

REQUIRED: **(1)** Using the trial balance on page 554 and the data and information given at the top of page 555, prepare a work sheet for Broad Brothers for the six-month period ended June 30, 19--. Use as your guide the model work sheet reproduced on pages 530 and 531 (which is complete except for the Adjusted Trial Balance columns). Enter the trial balance in the trial balance columns of a ten-column work sheet. Then,

BROAD BROTHERS

Trial Balance

For the Six-Month Period Ended June 30, 19 ——

First Community Bank................	111	27,793.72	
Accounts Receivable.................	131	74,132.58	
Allowance for Bad Debts.............	013	2,514.98	
Merchandise Inventory...............	161	513,493.84	
Store Supplies.....................	181	4,548.62	
Prepaid Insurance..................	183	6,287.00	
Furniture and Equipment.............	211	101,422.47	
Accumd. Depreciation — Furn. & Equip..	021		32,719.44
Delivery Equipment.................	221	31,738.99	
Accumd. Depreciation — Delivery Equip.	022		13,952.80
Building.........................	231	783,729.74	
Accumulated Depreciation — Building...	023		382,527.62
Land............................	251	180,000.00	
FICA Tax Payable..................	311		1,915.23
FUTA Tax Payable.................	312		171.66
State Unemployment Tax Payable......	313		1,158.70
Employees Income Tax Payable	314		3,192.09
Accrued Interest Payable.............	315		—
Accounts Payable..................	316		86,526.21
Mortgage Payable..................	411		600,000.00
R. L. Broad, Capital................	511		336,184.17
R. L. Broad, Drawing................	051	5,444.20	
S. S. Broad, Capital................	521		233,965.83
S. S. Broad, Drawing...............	052	4,146.42	
Sales...........................	611		600,457.96
Sales Returns and Allowances.........	061	5,631.78	
Sales Discount.....................	062	11,576.76	
Purchases........................	711	486,325.55	
Purchases Returns and Allowances......	071		4,819.01
Purchases Discount.................	072		9,704.10
Cost of Goods Sold (allow 3 lines).....	721		
Salaries and Commissions Expense......	811	42,915.12	
Payroll Taxes Expense..............	812	3,261.54	
Partners' Salaries Expense...........	813	16,200.00	
Depreciation Expense...............	814	—	
Insurance Expense..................	815	—	
Property Tax Expense...............	816	—	
Utilities Expense...................	817	1,397.67	
Telephone and Telegraph Expense.....	818	506.56	
Delivery Expense...................	819	1,574.06	
Supplies Expense...................	821	—	
Bad Debts Expense.................	822	—	
Miscellaneous Expense..............	823	2,653.22	
Interest Expense...................	911	—	
		2,307,294.82	2,307,294.82

Accrued Property Tax Payable........   —

enter the necessary adjustments in the adjustments columns of the ten-column work sheet as follows:

(a) Transfer the beginning merchandise inventory to Cost of Goods Sold.

(b) Transfer the purchases for the six-month period to Cost of Goods Sold.

(c) Transfer the purchases returns and allowances for the six-month period to Cost of Goods Sold.

(d) Transfer the purchases discounts for the six-month period to Cost of Goods Sold.

(e) Amount of ending merchandise inventory, $503,400.

(f) Interest accrued on mortgage since January 1, $5,000.

(g) Insurance expense for six-month period, $1,745.56.

(h) Store supplies used during period, $2,112.61.

(i) Depreciation of furniture and equipment, $995.
Depreciation of delivery equipment, $1,322.46.
Depreciation of building, $3,265.52.

(j) Bad debts provision for period, $2,916.25.

(k) Property tax assignable to period, $3,991.68.

(2) Extend the adjusted amounts to the adjusted trial balance columns and foot the columns as a means of proof. (3) Complete the work sheet, determine the amount of net income or net loss, and foot the income statement and balance sheet columns as a means of proof.

555

The solution to this problem will be needed in solving Problem 20-C.

Problem 20-C

This is a continuation of Problems 20-A and 20-B. The ten-column work sheets completed in these two previous problems will be used here.

REQUIRED: (1) Using the income statement columns of the work sheets completed in Problems 20-A and 20-B, prepare a year-to-date income statement for the six-month period ended June 30, 19--, an income statement for the quarter ended March 31, 19--, and an income statement for the quarter ended June 30, 19--. Use as your guide the model comparative income statement reproduced on page 533. (2) Using the balance sheet columns of the work sheet completed in Problem 20-B, prepare a balance sheet in report form as of June 30, 19--. Use as your guide the model balance sheet reproduced on pages 534 and 535.

HILGERT & NORD

Trial Balance

For the Quarter Ended September 30, 19—

Lemay State Bank	111	16,628.45	
Accounts Receivable	131	43,734.82	
Allowance for Bad Debts	013	750.60	
Merchandise Inventory	161	342,329.23	
Store Supplies	181	2,452.32	
Prepaid Insurance	183	3,850.38	
Furniture and Equipment	211	59,701.32	
Accumd. Depreciation — Furn. & Equip.	021		21,812.96
Delivery Equipment	221	21,159.33	
Accumd. Depreciation — Delivery Equip.	022		9,301.87
Building	231	522,486.56	
Accumulated Depreciation — Building	023		255,018.41
Land	251	120,000.00	
FICA Tax Payable	311		1,298.09
FUTA Tax Payable	312		57.69
State Unemployment Tax Payable	313		389.43
Employees Income Tax Payable	314		2,163.28
Accrued Interest Payable	315		—
Accounts Payable	316		54,293.23
Mortgage Payable	411		400,000.00
Raymond L. Hilgert, Capital	511		224,122.78
Raymond L. Hilgert, Drawing	051	1,703.24	
Walter R. Nord, Capital	521		155,977.22
Walter R. Nord, Drawing	052	1,289.51	
Sales	611		206,254.98
Sales Returns and Allowances	061	1,973.68	
Sales Discount	062	4,027.03	
Purchases	711	170,640.54	
Purchases Returns and Allowances	071		1,681.43
Purchases Discount	072		3,394.42
Cost of Goods Sold (allow 3 lines)	721		
Salaries and Commissions Expense	811	14,423.18	
Payroll Taxes Expense	812	1,096.16	
Partners' Salaries Expense	813	5,400.00	
Depreciation Expense	814	—	
Insurance Expense	815	—	
Property Tax Expense	816	—	
Utilities Expense	817	434.83	
Telephone and Telegraph Expense	818	179.23	
Delivery Expense	819	562.93	
Supplies Expense	821	—	
Bad Debts Expense	822	—	
Miscellaneous Expense	823	942.45	
Interest Expense	911	—	
		1,335,765.79	1,335,765.79
Accrued Property Tax Payable			—

Problem 20-D

Hilgert and Nord are partners in the wholesale hardware business. They share profits and losses in the following ratio: Raymond L. Hilgert, senior partner, 60%; Walter R. Nord, junior partner, 40%. "Salaries" are included in the profit shares. The fiscal year of this business runs from July 1 to the following June 30.

Hilgert & Nord's accountant prepares quarterly and "year-to-date" income statements, as well as balance sheets as of the last day of each quarter. The completed trial balance for Hilgert & Nord for the quarter ended September 30, 19––, is shown on page 556.

REQUIRED: (1) Using the trial balance on page 556 and the data and information given below, prepare a work sheet for Hilgert & Nord for the quarter ended September 30, 19––. Use as your guide the model work sheet reproduced on pages 530 and 531 (which is complete except for the Adjusted Trial Balance columns). Enter the trial balance in the trial balance columns of a ten-column work sheet. Then, enter the necessary adjustments in the adjustments columns of the ten-column work sheet as follows:

557

    (a) Transfer the beginning merchandise inventory to Cost of Goods Sold.
    (b) Transfer the purchases for the quarter to Cost of Goods Sold.
    (c) Transfer the purchases returns and allowances for the quarter to Cost of Goods Sold.
    (d) Transfer the purchases discounts for the quarter to Cost of Goods Sold.
    (e) Amount of ending merchandise inventory, $338,300.
    (f) Interest accrued on mortgage since July 1, $1,666.67.
    (g) Insurance expense for quarter, $584.12.
    (h) Store supplies used during quarter, $762.32.
    (i) Depreciation of furniture and equipment, $331.67.
        Depreciation of delivery equipment, $440.82.
        Depreciation of building, $1,088.51.
    (j) Bad debts provision for quarter, $1,001.27.
    (k) Property tax assignable to quarter, $1,330.56.

(2) Extend the adjusted amounts to the adjusted trial balance columns and foot the columns as a means of proof. (3) Complete the work sheet, determine the amount of net income or net loss, and foot the income statement and balance sheet columns as a means of proof. Rule all of the amount columns.

The solution to this problem will be needed in solving Problem 20-F.

HILGERT & NORD

Trial Balance

For the Six-Month Period Ended December 31, 19——

Lemay State Bank....................	111	18,529.15	
Accounts Receivable.................	131	49,421.72	
Allowance for Bad Debts.............	031	1,676.65	
Merchandise Inventory...............	161	342,329.23	
Store Supplies......................	181	3,032.41	
Prepaid Insurance...................	183	4,191.33	
Furniture and Equipment.............	211	67,614.98	
Accumd. Depreciation — Furn. & Equip..	021		21,812.96
Delivery Equipment..................	221	21,159.33	
Accumd. Depreciation — Delivery Equip..	022		9,301.87
Building............................	231	522,486.56	
Accumulated Depreciation — Building...	023		255,018.41
Land................................	251	120,000.00	
FICA Tax Payable....................	311		1,276.82
FUTA Tax Payable...................	312		114.44
State Unemployment Tax Payable......	313		772.47
Employees Income Tax Payable	314		2,128.06
Accrued Interest Payable.............	315		—
Accounts Payable....................	316		57,684.14
Mortgage Payable...................	411		400,000.00
Raymond L. Hilgert, Capital..........	511		224,122.78
Raymond L. Hilgert, Drawing.........	051	3,629.47	
Walter R. Nord, Capital..............	521		155,977.22
Walter R. Nord, Drawing.............	052	2,764.28	
Sales...............................	611		400,305.31
Sales Returns and Allowances........	061	3,754.52	
Sales Discount......................	062	7,717.84	
Purchases..........................	711	324,217.03	
Purchases Returns and Allowances......	071		3,212.67
Purchases Discount..................	072		6,469.40
Cost of Goods Sold (allow 3 lines).....	721		
Salaries and Commissions Expense......	811	28,610.08	
Payroll Taxes Expense...............	812	2,174.36	
Partners' Salaries Expense............	813	10,800.00	
Depreciation Expense................	814	—	
Insurance Expense...................	815	—	
Property Tax Expense................	816	—	
Utilities Expense....................	817	931.78	
Telephone and Telegraph Expense.....	818	337.71	
Delivery Expense....................	819	1,049.37	
Supplies Expense....................	821	—	
Bad Debts Expense..................	822	—	
Miscellaneous Expense...............	823	1,768.75	
Interest Expense....................	911	—	
		1,538,196.55	1,538,196.55
Accrued Property Tax Payable........			—

Problem 20-E

This is a continuation of Problem 20-D. The completed trial balance for Hilgert & Nord for the six-month period ended December 31, 19--, is shown on page 558.

REQUIRED: (1) Using that trial balance and the data and information given below, prepare a work sheet for Hilgert & Nord for the six-month period ended December 31, 19--. Use as your guide the model work sheet reproduced on pages 530 and 531 (which is complete except for the Adjusted Trial Balance columns). Enter the trial balance in the trial balance columns of a ten-column work sheet. Then, enter the necessary adjustments in the adjustments columns of the ten-column work sheet as follows:

(a) Transfer the beginning merchandise inventory to Cost of Goods Sold.
(b) Transfer the purchases for the six-month period to Cost of Goods Sold.
(c) Transfer the purchases returns and allowances for the six-month period to Cost of Goods Sold.
(d) Transfer the purchases discounts for the six-month period to Cost of Goods Sold.
(e) Amount of ending merchandise inventory, $335,600.
(f) Interest accrued on mortgage since July 1, $3,333.33.
(g) Insurance expense for the six-month period, $1,163.71.
(h) Store supplies used during period, $1,408.41.
(i) Depreciation of furniture and equipment, $663.33.
    Depreciation of delivery equipment, $881.64.
    Depreciation of building, $2,177.02.
(j) Bad debts provision for period, $1,944.17.
(k) Property tax assignable to period, $2,661.12.

559

(2) Extend the adjusted amounts to the adjusted trial balance columns and foot the columns as a means of proof. (3) Complete the work sheet, determine the amount of net income or net loss, and foot the income statement and balance sheet columns as a means of proof. Rule all of the amount columns.

The solution to this problem will be needed in solving Problem 20-F.

Problem 20-F

This is a continuation of Problems 20-D and 20-E. The ten-column work sheets completed in these two previous problems will be used here.

REQUIRED: **(1)** Using the income statement columns of the work sheets completed in Problems 20-D and 20-E, prepare a year-to-date income statement for the six-month period ended December 31, 19--, an income statement for the quarter ended September 30, 19--, and an income statement for the quarter ended December 31, 19--. Use as your guide the model comparative income statement reproduced on page 533. **(2)** Using the balance sheet columns of the work sheet completed in Problem 20-E, prepare a balance sheet in report form as of December 31, 19--. Use as your guide the model balance sheet reproduced on pages 534 and 535.

560

chapter 21

the corporate organization

561

A century and a half ago, John Marshall, then Chief Justice of the United States Supreme Court, described a corporation as follows:

> "A corporation is an artificial being, invisible, intangible, and existing only in contemplation of law."

The definition draws attention to the fact that corporations possess *legal entity*. Entity means oneness — something set apart, separate and distinct — a unit. Legally a corporation is separate and distinct from its owners. A corporation can own property, enter into contracts, and incur debt in its own name. A corporation can sue and be sued.

The characteristic of legal entity does not exist for businesses organized as sole proprietorships. Partnerships have only partial legal entity. The assets of businesses organized as sole proprietorships or partnerships legally belong to the proprietors or to the partners, and the debts of such businesses are legally the personal debts of the owners. However, the assets and the liabilities of a corporation are those of the business.

In accounting, every business is considered to be a separate entity regardless of whether the enterprise is a sole proprietorship, a partnership, or a corporation. In each case, the assets and the liabilities are considered to be those of the business itself.

Organization and management

More businesses are organized as sole proprietorships and partnerships than as corporations in the United States. However, although corporations are fewer in number, they do considerably more business, in the aggregate, than the other two types of business organizations combined.

Characteristics of the corporation

Some of the characteristics of the corporate form of organization are the following:

Limited Liability of Owners. Ownership in a corporation is divided into shares of capital stock. The owners of a corporation cannot be compelled to contribute additional capital to the company if their stock is fully paid for at the time of issuance. (This is usually the case and often is required by law.) These stockholders have no personal liability for the debts of the corporation. Contrast this with the legal status of sole proprietors and general partners who have unlimited personal liability for the debts of their businesses. The limited-liability feature is a major reason for the popularity of the corporate form of organization.

Transferable Ownership Units. Usually, any stockholder can transfer his stock to another person without the knowledge or the consent of the other stockholders and without disturbing the normal activities of the corporation. Contrast this with the status of a partner who cannot transfer his interest without the consent of the other partner or partners, and who automatically dissolves the partnership if he withdraws.

Unlimited Life. A sole proprietorship ends with the death of the proprietor. A partnership ends with the death or withdrawal of any partner. Corporations, however, are chartered either with perpetual life or with provision for renewal if the charter specifies a limit.

Suitability for Large-Scale Operations. While there are many small corporations, certain types of businesses must be operated on a relatively large scale. The corporate form of organization makes it possible to secure large amounts of capital. Furthermore, various economies are possible with large-scale operations. If large amounts of capital are to be obtained, there usually must be a considerable number of investors. The corporate form of enterprise is the most suitable for a business that must obtain capital from many people.

Investment Opportunity. Capital stock may be purchased as an investment for revenue purposes by those who do not care to participate in the management of a business. Investors in the stocks of corporations provide most of the capital required for their operation. At the same time, few of the stockholders in the larger companies actually participate in the management of those companies.

Taxation of Corporate Earnings. A major disadvantage of the corporate form of organization is the fact that corporations must pay income taxes. Sole proprietorships and partnerships, as such, do not have to pay income taxes. A sole proprietor reports the net income or the net loss from his business in his personal income tax return. Partnerships file information tax returns but they are not required as such to pay income taxes. Each partner reports his distributive share of the firm's net income or net loss in his personal income tax return. These amounts are taken into account in calculating the tax liabilities of the sole proprietors or partners.

Corporations are subject to a special corporation income tax, and the individual stockholders of corporations are subject to personal income tax on the dividends that they receive from their companies. A distribution of cash or other property by a corporation to its stockholders is called a *dividend*. Unless specifically labeled otherwise, dividends represent taxable income. In the usual case, the corporation is "dividing up" its earnings.

The process of taxing corporate income both to the company that earns it and to the stockholders of the company who receive it is considered by many to be unfair. Such "double taxation" has hindered more widespread adoption of the corporate form of organization by smaller businesses.

563

Domestic corporations and foreign corporations

All states have general laws, known as *statutes*, authorizing the creation of corporations by specified numbers of persons who comply with the statutory requirements. It is not necessary that a company be incorporated in the state in which it expects to do all or some portion of its business. A company may be incorporated under the laws of one state and operate exclusively in another state. Corporations are classified as **(1)** domestic corporations or **(2)** foreign corporations. A company incorporated under the laws of the state in which its business is conducted is called a *domestic corporation*. A company incorporated under the laws of any state other than the one in which it is doing business is considered by the latter state to be a *foreign corporation*. It usually is necessary for a corporation to maintain an office in the state from which its certificate of incorporation was obtained. It is not necessary, however, to conduct the regular business operations of the company from that office. The maintenance of an office with an authorized agent in charge usually is sufficient. It also may be necessary to keep certain corporate records in that office.

A corporation must obtain a license from a state other than the one in which it is incorporated before it can do business in that other state. A company may incorporate under the laws of any state and may obtain separate licenses as a foreign corporation entitling it to do business in all of the other states.

A corporation organized under the laws of one state takes a serious risk when it transacts business within the borders of another state without first obtaining a license to do business in that state. A corporation that does not have a license to do business in a state may not have the right to take action in the courts of that state to enforce its contracts or to collect its receivables. In some states specific penalties are provided, imposing fines or imprisonment (or both) on the agents of corporations doing business without such a license.

State incorporation laws

Before incorporating a company, the organizers should be familiar with the general corporation laws of the state in which they desire to incorporate. Variations in the corporation laws of the different states make some states more attractive than others for the purpose of incorporation. Delaware is noted for the great number of companies incorporated under its laws. Following are some of the reasons often given for the popularity of Delaware's corporation laws:

(a) Capital stock may be issued for cash, for services performed, for personal property (such as patents or contracts) or for real estate or real estate leases. In the absence of actual fraud, the judgment of the directors of the corporation as to the value of the property for which the stock was issued is conclusive, and stock so issued is considered fully paid.

(b) Voting power may be vested in one or more classes of stock, to the exclusion of other classes. This makes it possible for an individual or a group of individuals with an idea for a patent, or possessing a going business, to obtain capital through the sale of stock without losing control of the corporation.

(c) The directors need not be stockholders. Less than a majority of the whole board of directors may constitute a quorum. When vacancies occur in the board of directors, they may be filled by a vote of a majority of the remaining directors. The right to elect all or a majority of the directors may be confined to one class of stock. The board of directors may appoint an executive committee consisting of two or more of its members who may exercise the powers of the board of directors in the management of the business.

(d) Shares of capital stock owned by persons or by corporations outside of the state are not subject to taxation. Cash and securities of the corporation may be kept on deposit in the state without the payment of any personal property taxes.

(e) The stock and transfer books are open for inspection only to stockholders and there is no state tax on the issue or transfer of stock.

Many of the provisions just stated and others that are considered attractive will be found in the corporation laws of other states. In view of the many variations of the corporations laws of the several states, it is advisable for organizers to consult a competent attorney before taking steps to obtain a certificate of incorporation from any state.

The formation of a private corporation for the purpose of conducting a business enterprise is not as simple as the formation of a sole proprietorship or a partnership for business purposes. A corporation may be formed only with the expressed or the implied permission of a government body. In the United States, the power to create corporations rests largely with the various state legislatures. All of the states have general laws authorizing the creation of corporations. Persons desiring to incorporate must comply with the laws of the state in which incorporation is desired. These provisions vary in the different states. Under the Model Business Corporation Act, in effect in several states, the incorporators may consist of "three or more natural persons of full age."

Incorporators

Individuals who unite in filing an application for articles of incorporation are known as *incorporators*. The incorporators must be legally competent to contract, and usually each incorporator is required to be a subscriber for one or more shares of the capital stock of the corporation. Incorporators must file articles of incorporation or articles of association that comply with the requirements of the state statutes.

Before the election of directors, the incorporators have the direction of the affairs and the organization of a corporation and may take such steps as are proper to perfect the organization of the corporation. After the articles of incorporation have been filed and recorded, the incorporators may hold the so-called "first meeting of incorporators" for the purpose of adopting bylaws, electing directors, and transacting any other business that may properly be brought before the meeting.

Articles of incorporation

When the incorporators have complied with the legal requirements, including the payment of required fees, *articles of incorporation* (sometimes known as a *certificate of incorporation*) are approved by the Secretary of

State or other official whose duty it is to approve articles of incorporation that meet the requirements of the state law. The articles of incorporation are frequently referred to as a *charter*. Usually the incorporators must sign the articles of incorporation and acknowledge the document before a notary public or other officer authorized by law. When the articles of incorporation have been signed and acknowledged by the incorporators, the original must be filed in the proper state office and a copy thereof, certified by the proper state official, should be filed with the recorder of the county in which the principal office of the corporation is to be located. A third copy of the articles should be retained by the corporation. The procedure for incorporation of a company under the laws of the different states varies as to details, but in most states it follows substantially the procedure described heretofore. An illustration of articles of incorporation is shown on page 567.

Articles of incorporation confer certain special powers on a corporation in addition to common-law powers. The special powers conferred are those expressed in the articles of incorporation. In addition to the powers expressed in the articles, such powers as are reasonably necessary to the corporation in carrying out its expressed powers are implied. For instance, unless it is prevented by the provisions of the articles of incorporation or by the adopted bylaws, a corporation has the implied power to borrow money for use in carrying on its authorized business, to sign or endorse negotiable instruments, to issue bonds, and to mortgage or pledge its real or personal property as security for its debts.

A corporation has only such powers as are expressly conferred or implied by the articles of incorporation. For instance, a corporation has the power to do only such business as is authorized by its articles of incorporation. A natural person operating as a sole proprietor, or an ordinary partnership, may engage in any legal undertaking, but a corporation cannot engage in business foreign to the objects for which it was incorporated and which are stated in the articles of incorporation.

Corporation bylaws

The rules and regulations adopted by the stockholders of a corporation are known as *bylaws*. The bylaws are for the government and regulation of persons connected with the corporation and usually are not binding upon other persons. Reasonable bylaws, legally adopted, that are neither contrary to public policy nor inconsistent with the general law of the land, are binding upon all stockholders regardless of their knowledge or consent. Any bylaws that are not contrary to the laws of the state under which the

Articles of Incorporation

— OF —

APPROVED
FOR FILING

By ....

Date ....

Amount ....

THE PERKINS MANUFACTURING CO.
(Name of Corporation)

The undersigned, a majority of whom are citizens of the United States, desiring to form a corporation, for profit, under Sections 1701.01 et seq. of the Revised Code of Ohio, do hereby certify:

FIRST. The name of said corporation shall be ....

The Perkins Manufacturing Co. .

SECOND. The place in Ohio where its principal office is to be located is ....

Cincinnati , Hamilton County.
(City, Village or Township)

THIRD. The purposes for which it is formed are:

To manufacture, purchase or otherwise acquire, own, mortgage, pledge, sell, assign, and transfer, or otherwise dispose of, to invest, trade, deal in and deal with goods, wares, and merchandise and real and personal property of every class and description.

FOURTH. The number of shares which the corporation is authorized to have outstanding is one thousand (1,000) and the par value of each such share is One Hundred Dollars ($100), amounting in the aggregate to One Hundred Thousand Dollars ($100,000).

567

FIFTH. The amount of stated capital with which the corporation shall begin business is

.... Fifty Thousand .... Dollars ($ 50,000.00).

IN WITNESS WHEREOF, We have hereunto subscribed our names, this .... 1st .... day

of .... September ...., 19 72.

THE PERKINS MANUFACTURING CO.
(Name of Corporation)

Morton R. Perkins
Morton R. Perkins

Ralph W. Case
Ralph W. Case

A. Y. King
A. Y. King

(INCORPORATORS' NAMES SHOULD BE TYPED OR PRINTED BENEATH SIGNATURES)

N. B. Articles will be returned unless accompanied by form designating statutory agent. See Section 1701.07, Revised Code of Ohio.

Form C-101

Articles of Incorporation

BYLAWS
OF
THE PERKINS MANUFACTURING CO.

ARTICLE I — OFFICES

1. The principal office of the company shall be in the City of Cincinnati, County of Hamilton, Ohio.

2. The corporation may also have offices at such other places as the board of directors may from time to time see fit to establish in accord with the requirements of the business of the corporation.

ARTICLE II — SEAL

1. The corporate seal shall have inscribed thereon the name of the corporation, the year of its organization, and the words "Corporate Seal, Ohio." Said seal may be used by causing it or a facsimile thereof to be impressed or affixed or reproduced or otherwise.

ARTICLE III — STOCK

1. Certificates of stock shall be issued in numerical order, be signed by the president and secretary, and be sealed with the corporation seal.

2. Transfers of stock shall be made in the books of the corporation only by the person named in the certificate, or his duly authorized attorney, and upon surrender of the certificate therefor.

ARTICLE IV — STOCKHOLDERS

1. The annual meeting of the stockholders shall be held in the principal office of the company in Cincinnati, Ohio, sometime during the second week of January.

2. Special meetings of the stockholders may be called at the principal office of the company at any time, by resolution of the board of directors, or upon written request of the stockholders holding one fourth of the outstanding stock.

3. Notice of regular and special meetings of the stockholders shall be prepared by the secretary and mailed to the last known post-office address of each stockholder not less than ten days before such meeting and in the case of a special meeting, such notice shall state the object or objects thereof.

4. A quorum at any meeting of the stockholders shall consist of a majority of the stock of the company represented in person or by proxy.

5. The election of directors shall take place at the time of the annual meeting of the stockholders. The election shall be by ballot and each stockholder of record shall be entitled to cast one vote for each share of stock held by him.

ARTICLE V — DIRECTORS

1. A board of five directors shall be elected annually by the stockholders for a term of one year and they shall serve until the election and acceptance of duly qualified successors. Vacancies may be filled by the board for the unexpired term.

2. Regular meetings of the board of directors shall be held in the principal office of the company in Cincinnati, Ohio, on the last Saturday of each month at 9 a.m., if not a legal holiday; but if a legal holiday then on the following Monday.

3. Special meetings of the board of directors to be held in the principal office of the company in Cincinnati, Ohio, may be called at any time by the president or by request of a majority of the directors.

4. Notice of regular and special meetings of the board of directors shall be prepared by the secretary and mailed to each member of the board not less than five days before such meeting. Notices of special meetings shall state the purposes thereof.

5. A quorum at any meeting of the board of directors shall consist of a majority of the entire membership of the board.

6. At the first regular meeting of the board of directors after the election of directors each year, the officers of the company shall be elected for a period of one year. The board shall fix the compensation of the officers.

Corporation Bylaws

ARTICLE VI — OFFICERS

1. The officers of the company shall consist of a president, a vice-president, a secretary, and a treasurer, who shall be elected for a term of one year and shall hold office until their successors are duly elected and qualified.

2. The president shall preside at all meetings and have general supervision of the affairs of the company; shall sign all certificates, contracts, and other instruments of the company as authorized by the board of directors; shall make reports to the directors and stockholders; and shall perform all such duties as are incident to his office and are properly required of him by the board of directors. In the absence or disability of the president, the vice-president shall exercise all his functions.

3. The secretary shall issue notices for all meetings of the board of directors and stockholders; shall keep minutes of such meetings; shall have charge of the seal and the corporate records; shall sign, with the president, such instruments as will require such signature; and shall make such reports and perform such other duties as are incident to his office, or are properly required of him by the board of directors.

4. The treasurer shall have the custody of all moneys and securities of the company, and shall keep regular books of account. He shall sign such instruments as require his signature, and shall perform all duties incident to his office or that are properly required of him by the board of directors. He shall give bond for the faithful performance of his duties in such sum and with such sureties as are required by the board of directors.

ARTICLE VII — AMENDMENTS

These bylaws may be amended, repealed, or altered, in whole or in part, by a three-fourths vote of the entire outstanding stock of the company, at any regular meeting of the stockholders or at any special meeting duly called for such purpose.

CERTIFICATION OF BYLAWS

We, the undersigned, Morton R. Perkins and Ralph W. Case, respectively, the duly elected president and secretary of The Perkins Manufacturing Co., do hereby certify that the foregoing bylaws were duly adopted by the stockholders of said corporation at the first meeting held on the 11th day of September, 1972, in the principal office of the said corporation at 534 Broadway, Cincinnati, Ohio.

In Testimony Whereof, we have hereunto signed our signatures and affixed the seal of said corporation this 11th day of September, 1972.

MORTON R. PERKINS, President
RALPH W. CASE, Secretary

CORPORATE SEAL

Corporation Bylaws

company is incorporated may be adopted for the purpose of controlling the operations of a corporation. The bylaws usually provide for the time and place of holding stockholders' and directors' meetings, the number of days' notice for meetings, requirements for a quorum, the number of directors, names of committees, titles of officers, transfers of stock, signing of checks, fiscal year, annual statements; and such other matters covering the duties and the removal of officers, agents, and employees as may be decided upon from time to time.

The bylaws of a corporation usually are adopted at the first meeting of the incorporators after the filing and recording of the articles of incorporation. After that, the power to make, alter, or repeal bylaws rests with the stockholders, unless in the articles of incorporation that power is conferred upon the directors. Typical bylaws of a corporation are illustrated on pages 568 and 569.

Stockholders

The owner of the stock of a corporation is called a *stockholder* or *shareholder*. The form issued by a corporation to show the name of the stockholder and the number of shares he owns is called a *stock certificate*. (An illustration of a stock certificate appears on page 429.) Stockholders have certain rights and certain restrictions. Unless they own shares of a class of stock that carries no voting rights, they have a right to attend stockholders' meetings, to vote in the election of *directors*, and to vote upon any other matters that properly may come before the stockholders' meetings. Each share of stock usually carries one vote. If a stockholder cannot be present at a stockholders' meeting, and he authorizes another stockholder to vote his shares, this is known as *voting by proxy*. A typical proxy is shown below.

570

PROXY
THE PERKINS MANUFACTURING CO.

The undersigned hereby appoints Morton R. Perkins and Ralph W. Case, and each of them, attorneys and proxies, with power of substitution, to vote at the annual meeting of stockholders of The Perkins Manufacturing Co. to be held at Cincinnati, Ohio, on January 10, 19--, or at any adjournment thereof, according to the number of votes that the undersigned would be entitled to vote if personally present. Such proxies, and each of them, may vote for the directors named in the Proxy Statement received by the undersigned and on all other matters that may legally come before the meeting.

Date............19..   ....
                                          Signature of Stockholder

                                                                    152

Proxy

Each share of stock of a class on which a dividend may be declared entitles its owner to receive a proportionate amount of any dividends distributed by the corporation. Certain classes of stock usually give the holder the right (known as the *preemptive right*) to purchase a proportionate number of any new shares that the corporation might issue. The preemptive right gives each stockholder a chance to maintain his proportionate equity in the corporation. The stockholder is not obliged to take advantage of this right.

In the event that the corporation *liquidates* (goes out of business), each stockholder has the right to share in the distribution of the assets. The distribution is on a proportional, share-for-share basis, although there may be a rank or order of claims if the corporation has more than one class of stock outstanding.

While stockholders are actually the owners of the corporation, they do not have the right to bind the company by a contract. This right usually belongs to the officers of the corporation. The officers may be, and often are, stockholders; but it is in their capacity as officers, not as stockholders, that they can contract in the name of the corporation.

In order to enjoy any of the rights that have been mentioned, a stockholder must have his stock properly recorded on the books of the corporation. When the stockholder acquires his shares directly from the corporation as part of an original issue, the capital stock certificate will be recorded on the books of the corporation. When shares of capital stock are acquired by purchase from other stockholders rather than directly from the corporation, it is necessary to have the stock transferred on the books of the corporation before the new stockholders will be entitled to vote or to share in any dividends declared.

571

A certificate of stock may indicate ownership of any number of shares of stock. It is not necessary for a corporation to issue a separate certificate for each share of capital stock sold; instead, one certificate may be issued to each purchaser for the total number of shares purchased.

The Model Business Corporation Act requires that capital stock certificates state the following:

(a) The state of incorporation.

(b) The name of the person to whom issued.

(c) The number and the class of shares represented and the designation of the series, if any.

(d) The par value of each share or a statement that there is no par value.

(e) If there is more than one class of shares, a summary of the rights or restrictions of each class.

Directors

A group of persons elected by the stockholders to manage a corporation is known as the *board of directors*. The number of directors to be elected and eligibility for membership on a board of directors are determined by state statute, by the articles of incorporation, or by the bylaws of the corporation. In the election of directors, as in other matters, each stockholder usually is entitled to one vote for each share of stock owned.

Directors are not allowed to vote by proxy and must personally attend meetings of the board in order to be entitled to vote. The board of directors possesses the power of general management of the corporation. Usually it may appoint an executive committee to act for it between regular board meetings. The active management of a corporation usually is entrusted to the corporate officers who are elected by the board and are responsible to the board. Unless otherwise provided in the bylaws of the corporation, the board of directors has sole authority to declare dividends. As long as the directors act in good faith, they are not liable for losses resulting from their management.

Officers

The officers usually are selected from the board of directors. Unless restricted by the bylaws, however, the officers need not be members of the board of directors nor even stockholders. The officers usually consist of a president, one or more vice-presidents, a secretary, and a treasurer. One person may hold more than one office. For example, the same person may be elected secretary-treasurer. When two or more vice-presidents are elected, each may be assigned special duties. One vice-president may be put in charge of production, one in charge of sales, and a third in charge of public relations. The officers of a corporation are merely agents who are responsible to the board of directors. The duties of the officers may be prescribed by the board of directors subject to the provisions of the certificate of incorporation and the bylaws.

572

Report No. 21-1

Complete Report No. 21-1 in the workbook and submit your working papers for approval. Continue with the following study assignment until Report No. 21-2 is required.

Corporate records

In recording the usual operating transactions of a corporation, records or books of account similar to those used by sole proprietorships and by partnerships may be used. The only records peculiar to the corporate form of organization are those required for recording:

    (a) Minutes of the meetings of —
        (1) The incorporators
        (2) The stockholders
        (3) The board of directors
    (b) Subscriptions to capital stock
    (c) Issuance, ownership, and transfer of capital stock

State laws vary with respect to what corporate records must be kept. Usually a corporation is required by law to keep a minute book and a stockholders ledger. Other corporate records may be prescribed by the bylaws. Under the laws of most states stockholders have the right to examine the corporate records, but usually such inspection is limited to the original or duplicate stock records containing the names and the addresses of the stockholders and the number of shares held by each.

573

Corporation minute book

A corporation minute book is used to record the minutes of the meetings of the stockholders and of the directors. Sometimes the minutes of the stockholders' meetings are kept in one book and the minutes of the directors' meetings are kept in another book. Either a bound book or a loose-leaf book may be used. In most cases a loose-leaf type of book which makes it possible to type the minutes is desirable. Following are some of the plans used to prevent extraction or substitutions of sheets:

    (a) The pages may be numbered consecutively and the secretary may sign each page.
    (b) Watermarked paper may be used, coding each sheet with symbols consisting of letters and figures, such as "XY5AB."
    (c) Keylock binders may be used, making it impossible to extract sheets when the book is locked.

If all minutes are recorded in a single book, it is customary to allot a portion of the book to the stockholders' meetings and another portion to the directors' meetings so that the minutes of each may be recorded consecutively. While the stockholders usually meet but once a year, the directors may meet much more often. Sometimes the provisions of the articles of incorporation are copied into the minute book or a copy of the articles may be bound in the minute book. Following the articles of incorporation, it is customary to keep a record of the bylaws adopted by the incorporators at their first meeting after the articles are approved or adopted by the stockholders in subsequent meetings. In recording the minutes of a meeting of the stockholders or of the directors, it is important that the following information be recorded:

(a) The character of the meeting, that is, whether it is a stockholders' meeting or a directors' meeting.

(b) The date and the place of the meeting and whether it is a regular or a special meeting.

(c) If it is a board of directors' meeting, the names of those present, indicating whether or not a quorum was present. If it is a stockholders' meeting, the name of the presiding officer, names of other officers, and either the names of the stockholders present or the number of shares represented at the meeting.

(d) A complete record of the proceedings of the meeting, which may include decisions to purchase or sell property, declare dividends, issue bonds, or adopt or amend bylaws. Should any act of the board of directors or of the stockholders affect the accounting records, information concerning the action taken must be communicated to the accountant. For instance, the declaration of a dividend must be reported to the accountant in order that he may make the required entry in the books of account.

574

MINUTES OF FIRST MEETING OF STOCKHOLDERS
THE PERKINS MANUFACTURING CO.

Held September 11, 1972

Pursuant to written call and waiver of notice signed by all the incorporators, the first meeting of The Perkins Manufacturing Co. was held in its principal office at 534 Broadway, Cincinnati, Ohio, at 1 p.m., September 11, 1972.

Mr. Morton R. Perkins called the meeting to order and was elected chairman by motion unanimously carried. Mr. Ralph W. Case was elected secretary. There were present in person: Morton R. Perkins, Ralph W. Case, T. F. Rice, J. J. Stern, and Samuel Bay.

The chairman reported that the articles of incorporation had been filed with the Secretary of State on September 7, 1972, and that a certified copy had been filed with the County Recorder on September 8, 1972. Upon motion duly made and carried, said articles of incorporation were accepted, the directors named therein approved, and the secretary instructed to cause a copy of such articles to be inserted in the minute book of the company.

The secretary presented bylaws prepared by counsel, which were read, article by article. Upon motion, duly made, seconded and carried, it was resolved that the bylaws submitted be, and the same hereby are, adopted as the bylaws of this corporation, and that the secretary be, and he hereby is, instructed to cause the same to be inserted in the minute book immediately following the copy of the articles of incorporation.

There being no further business, the meeting was declared adjourned.

> *MORTON R. PERKINS, Chairman*
> *RALPH W. CASE, Secretary*

Corporation Minutes

The minute book is one of the most important of the corporate records and it should be kept with the utmost care. It should be considered a permanent record of the corporation. Usually it is the duty of the secretary of a corporation to keep the minutes of all regular and special meetings of both the board of directors and the stockholders. Typical minutes of a meeting of stockholders are illustrated on the preceding page.

Subscriptions records

One who agrees to purchase capital stock of a corporation is known as a *subscriber*. A list of subscribers is known as a *subscription list*. A subscription list usually consists of one or more sheets of paper with suitable headings on which subscribers may acknowledge their subscriptions for a specified number of shares of capital stock. One or more subscription lists may be circulated simultaneously. An example of a subscription list is illustrated below. Subscriptions to capital stock may be made before or after incorporation. Since a corporation does not exist until after the articles of incorporation have been approved, any subscription to capital stock made before incorporation is merely an agreement to subscribe for stock. Such an agreement is a contract between the subscriber and the promoter of the corporation or its incorporators. A subscription to capital stock made after incorporation is a contract between the subscriber and the corporation. The amount due a corporation from subscribers to its capital stock represents an asset that is usually recorded in the books of account

---

SUBSCRIPTION LIST
THE PERKINS MANUFACTURING CO.

To Be Incorporated Under the Laws of Ohio

Capital Stock $100,000   Par Value $100 a share

We, the undersigned, hereby severally subscribe for and agree to take at par value, the number of shares of the capital stock of The Perkins Manufacturing Co. set opposite our respective signatures, said subscriptions to become due upon completion of the organization of said company, and to be then payable in cash on demand of the treasurer of the company.

Cincinnati, Ohio
August 1, 1972

NAME ADDRESSES	SHARES	AMOUNT
Morton R. Perkins, 5535 Hamilton Ave., Cincinnati, Ohio 45224	300	$30,000
Ralph W. Case, 2087 Springdale Rd., Cincinnati, Ohio 45231	100	10,000
T. F. Rice, 35 W. Daniels St., Cincinnati, Ohio 45219	75	7,500
J. J. Stern, 609 Crown St., Cincinnati, Ohio 45206	15	1,500
Samuel Bay, 6332 Montgomery Rd., Cincinnati, Ohio 45213	10	1,000

Subscription List

as "subscriptions receivable." A subscriber may pay for capital stock with cash or other property.

At the time of accepting subscriptions, a record should be made in the books of the corporation. When there are many subscribers, a subscription register may serve a useful purpose. If there are only a few subscribers, their subscriptions may be recorded in an ordinary journal.

A subscription register may be either a bound book or a loose-leaf book. Usually it is ruled to provide approximately the same information as the subscription list, that is, the names and the addresses of the subscribers, the number of shares subscribed, and the amount of the subscriptions. Even when a subscription register is used, subscriptions should be recorded in summary form in the regular books of the corporation. The subscription list or any complete record of subscriptions accepted will provide the information needed in making the proper entry in the regular books of account.

The accounts with subscribers may be kept in the general ledger or in a subsidiary ledger known as a *subscription ledger* or a *stock payment record*. A subscription ledger usually is used when the stock is to be paid for in installments. A standard form of account ruling for a subscription ledger or stock payment record is illustrated below.

A narrative of the transactions recorded in the account reproduced in the illustration is given at the top of the next page.

576

STOCK PAYMENT RECORD SHEET NO. 1

NAME Paul M. Cox
ADDRESS P.O. Box 32, Cleveland, Ohio 44101

DATE	NO. SHARES PUR-CHASED	AMOUNT PER SHARE	SUB-SCRIPT. NO.	TOTAL DEBIT	DATE OF CREDIT	PAYMENTS WEEKLY—SEMIMONTHLY (MONTHLY)	AMOUNTS OF CREDIT
1972 Sept. 1	20	100 00	1	2000 00	1972 Sept. 1	Down Payment	200 00
					Oct. 1	First Installment	200 00
					Nov. 1	Second Installment	200 00
					Dec. 1	Third Installment	200 00
						TOTAL $	

NAME OF SALESMAN	COMMISSION	% PAID	19
PAID $	IN FULL AND CERTIFICATE NO.	ISSUED	19
		SIGNATURE	AUDITOR

Subscription Ledger Account

Sept. 1. Paul M. Cox subscribed for 20 shares of common stock at par value, making a down payment of $200 and agreeing to make additional payments of $200 a month until the stock is paid for in full, at which time a certificate is to be issued to him.

Oct. 1. Received $200 from Paul M. Cox to apply on stock subscription.

Nov. 1. Received $200 from Paul M. Cox to apply on stock subscription.

Dec. 1. Received $200 from Paul M. Cox to apply on stock subscription.

If a subsidiary subscription ledger is kept, a control account must be kept in the general ledger. The title of such a control account usually is Subscriptions Receivable. The function of the subscriptions receivable control account and of the subscription ledger is practically the same as the function of an accounts receivable control account and an accounts receivable ledger. The balance of the subscriptions receivable control account may be proved at any time by preparing a list of the balances of the subscribers' accounts kept in the subsidiary subscription ledger. The total amount due from subscribers as shown by this list should be the same as the balance of the control account.

Stock certificate book

When a subscriber has paid his subscription in full, the corporation issues a certificate to him for the number of shares subscribed for and fully paid. The blank certificates sometimes are bound in a book known as a *stock certificate book*. A stock certificate and its stub, representing one page of a stock certificate book, is illustrated on page 429.

In that illustration both the certificate and the stub are filled in as they should be when the certificate is ready for delivery to the subscriber. Both the certificates and the stubs should be numbered consecutively. The certificate should show the name of the stockholder, the number of shares represented, and the date of issue. It should also be signed by the president and the secretary of the corporation. The stub, when properly filled in, should show the number of shares issued, the name of the stockholder, and the date of issue. Sometimes, in the case of relatively small corporations, the stockholder is required to sign the stub as a receipt for the certificate. In the case of large corporations this procedure is impractical. Sometimes when a stock certificate is canceled it is pasted to the stub to which it was originally attached.

Stockholders ledger

The general ledger of a sole proprietorship contains the capital account of the proprietor. There is a capital account for each partner in the general ledger of a partnership. In the case of a corporation, however, there is no general ledger account for each stockholder. The general ledger of a corporation contains accounts that relate to the stockholders' equity in the company, but these accounts show the total amounts of each of the various types of owners' equity, not the name and the share of each owner. Since it is essential to have a record of the number of shares owned by each stockholder, it is common practice to maintain a ledger which contains an account for each stockholder known as a *stockholders ledger*. This is not a subsidiary ledger in the usual sense because its accounts contain information relating only to number of shares; dollar amounts usually are not shown. Since the general ledger capital stock accounts show number of shares as well as dollar amounts, however, there is a special sort of control account-subsidiary ledger relationship.

The information recorded in each stockholder's account should include the following:

(a) The date, the certificate number, and the number of shares issued to the stockholder by the corporation.
(b) The date, the certificate number, and the number of shares transferred to the stockholder from other stockholders.
(c) The date, the certificate number, and the number of shares transferred from the stockholder to other stockholders.
(d) The balance, representing the number of shares held by the stockholder.

578

The stockholders ledger is an important corporate record. This ledger and the corporation minute book are two records that most corporations are required by law to keep.

A standard form of account ruling for a stockholders ledger is illustrated below.

STOCKHOLDER *W. C. May*
ADDRESS *114 Cambridge Drive, Wilmington, Delaware 19803*

DATE	CERTIFICATE NOS.		RECEIVED FROM	TRANSFERRED TO	NO. OF SHARES	BALANCE
	OLD	NEW				
1973 July 2		23	Original Issue		50	50
Aug. 25	23	36		A. D. Short	10	40
Sept. 1	18	46	J. G. Grayson		12	52

Stockholders Ledger Account

Following is a narrative of transactions recorded in the account reproduced in the illustration:

> July 2. Issued Certificate No. 23 for 50 shares of common stock to W. C. May who has paid his subscription in full.
>
> Aug. 25. W. C. May surrendered Certificate No. 23 for 50 shares and requested that 10 shares be transferred to A. D. Short. Issued a new certificate, No. 36, for 40 shares to Mr. May.
>
> Sept. 1. T. G. Grayson surrendered Certificate No. 18 for 12 shares with a request that the stock be transferred to W. C. May. Issued Certificate No. 46 for 12 shares to Mr. May.

Stock transfer record

Since a stockholder has the right to transfer his stock in a corporation and the corporation is required to keep a record of its outstanding stock, it is advisable for the corporation to keep some sort of a stock transfer record. A standard form of transfer record is illustrated below.

STOCK TRANSFER RECORD

DATE OF TRANSFER ON BOOKS	SURRENDERED		NAMES OF STOCKHOLDERS INVOLVED IN THE TRANSFER AND SIGNATURES OF ATTORNEYS MAKING THE TRANSFERS	REISSUED	
	CERT. NOS.	NO. OF SHARES		CERT. NOS.	NO. OF SHARES
1972 Aug. 25	23	50	BY *W. C. May*	36	40
			TO *A. D. Short*	37	10
			SIGNED *A. L. Burns* (ATTORNEY)		

Stock Transfer Record

The purpose of a stock transfer record is to record transfers of capital stock from one stockholder to another and to provide the information needed in keeping the stockholders ledger. The following transaction is recorded in the illustration:

> Aug. 25. W. C. May surrendered Certificate No. 23 for 50 shares and requested that 10 shares be transferred to A. D. Short. Issued Certificate No. 36 for 40 shares to Mr. May and Certificate No. 37 for 10 shares to Mr. Short.

When stock is transferred, the transferrer must endorse the certificate and his signature must be witnessed.

Someone to whom the corporate records are properly accessible should be designated to record the transfer of the stock. This may be the corporation secretary or a transfer agent. The person who is authorized to transfer the stock is known as the attorney, but he is not necessarily a lawyer.

It is customary for corporations to close the transfer record a specified number of days before the annual meeting or before the payment of dividends. Stockholders must have their stock transferred and duly registered in the books of the corporation prior to the closing of the transfer records to be eligible to vote or to receive dividends, as the case may be. For instance, a corporation in notifying stockholders of the annual meeting to be held on June 21, 1972, advised that —

> "In accordance with Section 40 of the corporation's bylaws, the board of directors has fixed May 31, 1972, as the record date of the stockholders entitled to notice of and to vote at said meeting and only stockholders of record at the close of business on May 31, 1972, be entitled to vote thereat."

In declaring a dividend, it is customary for the board of directors to specify not only the date of payment but also the date of record in the following manner:

> "A dividend of one dollar a share is declared, payable July 1 to stockholders of record June 25."

A stockholder who acquired his stock too late to have it recorded by June 25 would not be entitled to share in this dividend.

580

Report No. 21-2

Complete Report No. 21-2 in the workbook and submit your working papers for approval. Continue with the textbook discussion in Chapter 22 until the next report is required.

chapter 22

accounting for capital stock

It has been noted that, unless specifically denied, each share of capital stock of a business corporation gives its owner certain rights: **(1)** the right to vote upon various corporate matters, **(2)** the right to share in any distribution of earnings, **(3)** the right to subscribe for any additional shares that may be later authorized, and **(4)** the right to share in the distribution of the assets if the corporation is liquidated. For a variety of reasons, some of these rights are modified or denied in connection with certain types of capital stock. The purpose of the first part of this chapter is to consider the nature and purpose of these modifications, and the several ways in which the term "value" is used in connection with capital stock.

Types and values of capital stock

The types of stock and the number of shares that a corporation may issue are specified in its articles of incorporation. The laws of the state of incorporation usually specify the minimum amount of capital that must be paid in before the corporation can begin business. This does not necessarily mean that all of the authorized stock must be issued immediately. It is necessary only to issue the number of shares needed to provide the minimum amount of paid-in capital specified by law. Additional authorized shares may be issued from time to time if the corporation finds it desirable to increase its capital. After all of the authorized shares have been issued and are outstanding, no more shares may be issued without securing an amendment to the articles of incorporation.

Par-value stock

The *par value* (sometimes called the *face value*) of a share of stock represents the minimum amount of cash or other property that the corporation may accept in exchange for the share when it is issued originally, if the share is to be fully paid. Capital stock usually is not issued until it is paid for in full. Ordinarily, stock may be paid for with cash or with other property, and sometimes with labor performed or with services rendered. When stock has been fully paid for, neither the corporation nor its creditors have any further financial claim on the stockholders.

582

If stock is issued without having been fully paid for and the corporation later becomes insolvent, its creditors may force the original purchasers (if the shares are still in their hands) to pay the difference between the purchase price and the par value of the stock. Owners of capital stock — other than the original purchasers — may also be liable for the difference between the amount originally paid in and the par value of the shares. However, it must be established that these subsequent holders acquired the stock knowing that the original purchaser had not paid for it in full.

If the shares of capital stock have a par value, its amount is always shown on the stock certificates. The incorporators may designate any amount as the par value of shares of a class of capital stock. It is unusual to have shares with a par value of less than 10 cents or more than $100. Par values of $1, $10, $25, $50, and $100 are frequently used. The number of shares authorized and the par value per share, if any, are stated in the articles of incorporation and appear on each stock certificate. The par value of each share times the number of shares authorized is known as the *authorized capital* of the corporation. The articles of incorporation of The Perkins Manufacturing Co., reproduced on page 567, specify an authorized capital of $100,000 divided into 1,000 shares with a par value of $100 each.

There was a time when all stock issued by a corporation was required to have a par value. This requirement was intended to serve as a means of protecting the interests of corporate creditors. Since the owners of a corporation ordinarily have no personal liability for its debts, it was intended that each share of stock issued by the corporation should represent a capital investment of an amount equal to at least the par value of the share. The laws either forbade the issuance of stock at a discount or, if this was permitted, provided that the purchaser of the stock would be liable for the amount of any such discount.

Generally, the various state laws make it illegal for a corporation to pay any dividends that would result in its total assets being less than the sum of all of its liabilities plus the par value of all shares outstanding. Thus, any losses up to the amount of the total par value of outstanding shares will reduce the equity or interest of the stockholders but will not impair the claims of the creditors.

It should be clear that par value is strictly a legal matter. Par value does not have any direct relationship to the market value of the shares (though, unfortunately, uninformed investors sometimes have been misled into thinking that par value represents what the stock is worth). As between the shareholders themselves, par value has little significance. Each share of stock, with or without par value, represents a proportionate interest in the owners' equity element of a corporation. If there are 10,000 shares of only one class of stock outstanding, the holder of 100 shares has a 1 percent ownership interest. His votes count 1 percent, he gets 1 percent of any earnings that are distributed as dividends, and if the corporation were to liquidate, he would get 1 percent of anything remaining after all creditors were paid in full.

No-par-value stock

Capital stock that does not designate any amount to represent the par value for each share is called *no-par-value* stock (or, simply, *no-par* stock). Most states allow corporations to issue such stock. Shares of this type can be sold for whatever they will bring and there will be no discount liability. The articles of incorporation will specify the number of such shares that may be issued.

Laws permitting the use of no-par shares came to pass because of certain abuses that arose in connection with par-value stock. Unscrupulous promoters and stock salesmen took advantage of the fact that some people did not understand the meaning of par value. Property accepted in exchange for stock sometimes was overvalued so that the shares issued would be fully paid. This overvaluation could occur because directors of a corporation have the power to place a value upon property accepted in exchange for stock. Oftentimes the directors were acting for the corporation in purchasing property from themselves as individuals. Sometimes they exchanged their property at a greatly exaggerated value for shares of stock that, technically, were issued as being fully paid.

When no-par shares are used, there is less temptation to overvalue property received in exchange for shares. Actual and potential stockholders are less likely to be misled if the shares do not have par value. There is no problem of discount liability in the case of no-par shares.

Long-established customs and legal precedents die hard, however. The laws permitting no-par stock frequently provide that each share of such stock shall be assigned a *stated value*. The corporate directors determine what this stated value shall be. Usually it is a nominal amount. A stated value of $1 may be established for shares that actually are sold for $10 or more. In such cases, the legal capital of the corporation is equal to the number of shares outstanding times the stated value per share. Stated value and par value are essentially the same thing.

In accounting for the sale of no-par shares with a stated value, some accountants credit an amount equal to the stated value to the capital stock account and the amount of any excess to an account entitled Paid-In Capital in Excess of Stated Value. The recommended procedure, however, is to credit the entire amount received to the capital stock account. The stated value of the shares can be noted parenthetically in the balance sheet.

584

Many of the older corporations have par-value stock outstanding. Corporations formed in recent years have shown some tendency to favor no-par stock, although the use of par-value shares still is popular.

Book value

The *book value* of a share of capital stock is the dollar amount of stockholder equity represented by each share. If there is only one class of capital stock, the book value per share is calculated by dividing the total stockholders' equity by the number of shares outstanding. Calculations of book value per share are made for purposes of analysis and comparison. The subject is considered further in Chapter 29.

Market value

The price at which a share of capital stock might be purchased or sold at a given time is described as its *market value*. In the case of stocks which are *listed* for trading on a stock exchange, the most recent price at which the shares were traded is regarded as the market value. (Most big cities have such exchanges — the New York Stock Exchange being the best known.) However, there is no assurance that future trades will be at the same price. *Bid* and *offered* prices for shares listed on certain exchanges are tabulated and reported in many newspapers. These listings are considered to be an indication of market value.

In the case of stocks not listed on any exchange, it may be more difficult to estimate their market value. If there has been a recent sale of an unlisted stock, its selling price may be considered the present market value. Certain brokers make a specialty of dealing in unlisted stocks. (They operate a so-called "over the counter" market.) Through such brokers, information may usually be obtained as to the bid and offered prices of unlisted stocks. Any information that will aid in forecasting the price at which stock may be bought or sold will be helpful in estimating the market value of such stock.

Many factors affect the market value of capital stock. Some of these factors are as follows: (1) the effectiveness of the company management, (2) the business outlook for the company, (3) the current rate of dividends and the past dividend record of the company, (4) the financial position of the company as indicated by its balance sheet, (5) the earnings of the most recent period as indicated by its income statement, (6) the stability of the earnings of the company over a period of years, and (7) general economic conditions.

Classes of capital stock

Basically, all capital stock represents an ownership equity or interest in a corporation. Unless specifically restricted by the articles of incorporation, each share carries the same rights with respect to voting privileges, dividends, and participation in the division of assets in the event of dissolution. If there is only one class of stock outstanding, all shares will have all of these rights. Such an issue of stock would be classed as *common stock*.

If there are classes of stock that carry certain specified preferences, or first claims, they are called *preferred stock*. Usually these preferences relate to either or both of the following:

    (a) *Preference as to Dividends.* Shares with a dividend preference entitle their owners to receive dividends of a certain amount (often expressed as a percent of the par value of the shares) before shares of an issue with secondary preferences or without preferences receive anything.

    (b) *Preference as to Assets.* Shares with a *liquidating preference* entitle the holders to receive, in the event the corporation liquidates, a certain amount before shares with secondary preference or no preference receive anything. If there is a liquidation preference, it is never less than the par value of the shares and is often a few dollars more. If the shares are *redeemable* or *callable* at the option of the corporation, there is usually a *call premium* involved. For example, an issue of $100 par-value preferred stock might have a preference in total liquidation of $103 per share and be callable at the option of the corporation on and after a specified date at $105 per share plus any unpaid dividends.

There is no promise or guarantee either that there will be any dividends or anything to distribute if the corporation liquidates, but preferred stockholders have a prior or first claim (up to a specified limit) upon whatever is available. Preferred stock usually does not have voting rights.

Corporations sometimes have more than one class of preferred stock outstanding. The issues are usually differentiated with such names as "First Preferred," or "Second Preferred." If the first preferred had a specified dividend rate of 4 percent and the second preferred 6 percent, it would mean that dividends of 4 percent per share would have to be paid on the first preferred shares before the holders of the second preferred shares could receive any dividends. Then a dividend of 6 percent per share would have to be paid on the second preferred shares before the common stockholders could receive any dividends.

Some corporations have more than one class of common stock outstanding. The different issues often are designated as "Class A Common" or "Class B Common." The differences usually relate either to dividend preferences (even though the several issues are called common stock) or voting rights. Certain classes of stock may entitle the holder to vote for only a limited number of directors. Such a device is used to enable the holders of one class of stock to maintain control of the corporation.

Participating and nonparticipating preferred stock

Preferred stock that is given a right to share with the common stock in dividends in excess of a stated dividend rate is said to be *participating*. Stock of this sort is not very prevalent; however, there is a considerable variety of participation arrangements. In all cases, the preferred stock receives its regular dividend first if there are any dividends paid during the year. Usually the participation does not begin until the holders of the common stock have received a specified amount. Beyond that amount, the preferred stock and the common stock may share according to some specified plan or ratio in any further dividends that are to be paid.

If there is an equal division of any excess dividends between the preferred shares and the common shares, without any limit as to the amount the preferred shares may receive, the preferred stock is said to be *fully participating*. Often the extent of participation is limited. The preferred stock might have a 6 percent stated dividend rate with participation up to

8 percent. In that case the owners of the preferred shares would never receive dividends in any year in excess of 8 percent of the par value of the stock held. If preferred dividends are limited to the stated dividend rate, the stock is said to be *nonparticipating*.

Cumulative and noncumulative preferred stock

Preferred stock on which the claims for dividends may be accumulated from year to year is called *cumulative preferred stock*. The holder of such stock is entitled to a specified rate of dividend and, if the directors do not declare the dividend in any year (whether because of insufficient earnings or otherwise), the unpaid amount will accumulate until it is paid out of the earnings of subsequent years. The accumulating amounts are not a liability of the corporation, except that they must be paid before the common stockholders can receive any dividends.

Preferred stock on which the claims for dividends do not accumulate from year to year is called *noncumulative preferred stock*. If the earnings of a particular year do not warrant the declaration of dividends, there is no carry-over of dividends to succeeding years. The holder of noncumulative preferred stock is only entitled to receive dividends in any year in which the earnings are sufficient to pay such dividends and if and when the board of directors declares them.

587

Convertible stock

Sometimes a class of stock is issued that is *convertible* into some other class of stock. Thus, a corporation may issue a class of preferred stock that may be converted into common stock at a specified time and in a specified ratio as to the number of common shares (or a fraction thereof) that may be obtained in exchange for each preferred share. This offers the stockholder the advantage of being able to convert his preferred stock into common stock should he so desire. Such action might become desirable on his part if the market value of the common stock became greater than the market value of the preferred stock.

Issued and unissued stock

Authorized capital stock that has not been issued is known as *unissued stock*. It has no asset value and should not be listed in the balance sheet of the company as an asset. Such stock may be considered to have potential value in that it may be issued at any time for the purpose of acquiring additional assets. When a corporation sells its capital stock, certificates are issued to the stockholders and the stock is said to be outstanding. The total amount relating to each class of stock which has been issued should be shown separately in the balance sheet. If the stock has a par value, it is shown at par. If it is no-par stock with a stated value, it is often shown at the amount of the stated value. However, the recommended practice is to show the total amount received upon the issuance of the shares. The stated value may be shown parenthetically. If there is no stated value, the total amount received upon issuance of the shares is shown and the number of shares issued is noted parenthetically.

Treasury stock

Corporations may reacquire their own shares of capital stock either by purchase or by donation. If such shares are canceled and retired, they revert to the status of unissued stock. If such shares are not retired, they are considered to be *treasury stock*. Treasury stock may not be voted at stockholders' meetings and does not share in dividends declared. The total number of shares of capital stock outstanding at any time is the total number of shares issued less the total number of any treasury shares.

When a corporation reacquires its own stock by purchase, it is usually recorded at cost and is reported in the balance sheet as a deduction from the total capital of the corporation. When a corporation reacquires its own stock by donation, or at no cost, all that is needed is a notation in the Item column on the debit side of the capital stock account to show the number of shares reacquired. In preparing a balance sheet the number of donated shares held in the treasury should be noted. Since a corporation cannot own itself in whole or in part, treasury stock should not be listed in the balance sheet as an asset.

Report No. 22-1

Complete Report No. 22-1 in the workbook and submit your working papers for approval. Continue with the following study assignment until the next report is required.

Recording capital
stock transactions

The practices followed in accounting for assets, liabilities, revenue, and expenses of corporations are generally the same as those in the cases of single proprietorships and partnerships. The peculiarities of corporate accounting relate to owners' equity. Accounting for capital stock transactions will be considered in this chapter. Accounting for corporate earnings and distributions to stockholders will be explained in the following chapter.

Corporate accounts — par-value stock

In recording corporate transactions relating to capital stock with par value, accounts of the following types may be needed. (If a corporation has more than one class of par-value stock, the number of accounts needed will be greater in order to provide for proper identification of the results of transactions involving each class.)

Capital Stock
Subscriptions Receivable
Capital Stock Subscribed
Premium on Capital Stock
Paid-In Capital in Excess of
    Stated Value

Discount on Capital Stock
Treasury Stock
Donated Capital
Paid-In Capital from Sale of Treasury Stock
Organization Costs

Accounting for authorization and
issuance of capital stock

The articles of incorporation specify the amount of the authorized capital stock of a corporation. The dollar amount of the stock and the number of shares authorized may be recorded by means of a memorandum entry in the corporation journal. Usually a memorandum entry is also made in the capital stock account to show the dollar amount and the number of shares authorized. When more than one class of stock is authorized, there should be a separate account kept for each class. For example, suppose the MNO Corporation is formed with the authority to issue 2,000 shares of 6 percent preferred stock, par value $100 per share, and 4,000 shares of common stock, par value $25 per share. Separate accounts should be kept for Preferred Stock and for Common Stock, and a notation of the number of shares of each class of stock authorized should be made in the Item column on the credit side of the accounts. If 1,200 shares of the preferred stock are sold at par for cash and 1,000 shares of the common stock are issued in exchange for land valued at $25,000, the transactions are recorded as follows:

```
Bank..................................................  120,000
    Preferred Stock....................................           120,000
        Sold 1,200 shares of preferred stock at par for cash.
Land..................................................   25,000
    Common Stock......................................            25,000
        Issued 1,000 shares of common stock at par in exchange for
        land valued at $25,000.
```

The stockholders' equity section of the balance sheet of the MNO Corporation prepared just after the preceding transactions had been recorded should appear as follows:

Paid-in capital:
Preferred stock, 6%, par $100
   (2,000 shares authorized; 1,200 shares issued) $120,000

Common stock, par $25
   (4,000 shares authorized; 1,000 shares issued)   25,000
Total paid-in capital...................... $145,000

If at some later date the charter is amended to permit the issuance of additional shares or to reduce the number of shares authorized, it is only necessary to make a memorandum entry in the corporation journal of the action taken and to make a similar entry in the capital stock accounts.

590

Accounting for capital stock subscriptions

Corporations sometimes accept subscriptions for their capital stock. The conditions of the subscription contract may call for the subscribers to make payment of the agreed amount in full at a later date or in several installments over a period of time. Subscriptions for capital stock are usually recorded by debiting Subscriptions Receivable and by crediting Capital Stock Subscribed. For example, suppose the MNO Corporation (mentioned previously) obtained subscriptions for 1,000 shares of its common stock at par value. The journal entry to record these subscriptions is as follows:

```
Common Stock Subscriptions Receivable.....................  25,000
    Common Stock Subscribed.................................          25,000
        Received subscriptions for 1,000 shares of common stock at par.
```

It should be noted that the word "Common" appears in each of the account titles. Since the corporation has two classes of stock, separate accounts for each class are kept.

If there are a number of subscribers and the conditions of the subscription contract involve installment payments of the purchase price, it is probable that a subsidiary subscription ledger will be used. See page 576 for a standard form of account for such a ledger. This ledger is controlled by the subscriptions receivable account in the general ledger.

Assume that subscribers for 500 shares pay their subscriptions in full ($12,500), while subscribers for the other 500 shares pay 20 percent, or $2,500, on their subscriptions. The journal entry to record these payments is as follows:

```
Bank...................................................  15,000
    Common Stock Subscriptions Receivable....................          15,000
        Received cash in full payment of subscription for 500 shares
        of common stock and $5 per share to apply on subscriptions
        for 500 shares of common stock.
```

The amounts received would be credited to the proper accounts in the subscription ledger. At this point the subscriptions receivable account has a debit balance of $10,000. The sum of all of the balances in the subsidiary ledger should equal this amount. If the amounts due from subscribers for capital stock represent bona fide, collectible claims, it is acceptable accounting practice to show the debit balance of the subscriptions receivable account as an asset in the balance sheet. If it is likely that the amount will be collected soon, the account may be classified as a current asset.

Because the subscriptions for 500 shares have been paid in full, the certificates will be issued. The issuance would be recorded as follows:

```
Common Stock Subscribed .................................  12,500
    Common Stock..........................................          12,500
        Capital stock certificates for 500 shares of common stock issued
        to subscribers who have paid in full.
```

591

At this point the common stock subscribed account has a credit balance of $12,500, which represents the par value of the 500 shares for which the full price has not yet been received. This account will be closed upon the issuance of the shares after the full subscription price has been received.

The balance sheet of the MNO Corporation, after all of the foregoing transactions have been recorded, should appear as follows:

MNO CORPORATION

Balance Sheet

Assets			Stockholders' Equity		
Current assets:			Paid-in capital:		
Cash..............	$135,000		Preferred stock, 6%, par $100 (2,000 shares authorized;		
Common stock subscriptions receivable......	10,000				
Total current assets.....		$145,000	1,200 shares issued) .		$ 120,000
			Common stock, par $25 (4,000 shares authorized; 1,500 shares		
Long-lived assets:					
Land...............		25,000	issued).............	$ 37,500	
			Common stock subscribed (500 shares)........	12,500	50,000
Total assets...........		$170,000	Total stockholders' equity..		$170,000

The common stock subscriptions receivable, instead of being shown as an asset, may be shown in the stockholders' equity section of the balance sheet as a deduction from common stock subscribed. The resulting difference represents the amount actually paid in by the subscribers to common stock to the date of the balance sheet. If there is any question of the collectibility of subscriptions receivable, this procedure must be followed. Some accountants prefer this treatment in any event.

It is not necessary to use subscriptions receivable and capital stock subscribed accounts when shares are sold outright for cash or are issued in exchange for other property. In such cases the proper asset accounts may be debited and the capital stock account may be credited directly. The subscription accounts are used in connection with subscription contracts that call either for a lump-sum payment at a later date or a series of payments over a period of time.

Discount or premium on capital stock

Original issues of par-value capital stock often are sold at par. However, the shares are sometimes sold for more than par. If the state law permits, they also may be sold for less than par. When shares of stock are sold or exchanged for more than par value, the excess is termed a *premium* and it should be credited to Premium on Capital Stock. If shares are sold for less than their par value, the difference is termed a *discount* and it should be debited to Discount on Capital Stock.

To illustrate, suppose that, at a date subsequent to the transactions already considered, the MNO Corporation sells 100 shares of preferred stock at $104 per share and 200 shares of common stock at $24 per share. The journal entries to record these sales are as follows:

Bank..	10,400	
Preferred Stock...		10,000
Premium on Preferred Stock		400
Sold 100 shares of preferred stock at $104 per share.		
Bank..	4,800	
Discount on Common Stock...............................	200	
Common Stock...		5,000
Sold 200 shares of common stock at $24 per share.		

Premium on capital stock is an addition to stockholders' equity and the credit balance should be so reported in the stockholders' equity section of the balance sheet. Discount on capital stock is a deduction from stockholders' equity and the debit balance should be so reported in the balance sheet. If desired, the discount account debit balance may be written off against an accumulated credit balance in the premium account. In a state where the law permits, discount on capital stock may be written off against an accumulated credit balance in the retained earnings account.

It has been mentioned that the laws pertaining to par value and stock discount have invited such subterfuges as overvaluing assets accepted in exchange for shares so that the existence of a discount is hidden. When assets are overvalued for this or any other reason, the capital stock is said to be *watered*.

Under the federal income tax law, no gain or loss arises from the original sale of capital stock by a corporation. It is immaterial whether the stock is sold at a premium or at a discount. The sale of an original issue of stock represents a capital transaction from which neither taxable gain nor deductible loss results, regardless of the selling price.

Accounting for treasury stock

Treasury stock refers to the shares of stock that have been reacquired by the issuing corporation and that have not been formally canceled. Treasury stock may be acquired either by donation or by purchase. (On rare occasions, stockholders may agree to donate some of their shares on a pro rata basis. These shares then can be sold to provide cash.) Accountants are not in universal agreement as to how treasury stock transactions should be recorded. The recommended procedure is to record treasury stock at its cost irrespective of any par value. If this practice is followed, only a memorandum entry is needed if the treasury stock is acquired by donation. When the donated shares are sold, an account entitled Donated Capital may be credited. For example, suppose that 200 shares of treasury stock that had been donated by the stockholders are sold for $40 per share. The journal entry to record this transaction is as follows:

Bank..	8,000	
Donated Capital..		8,000
Sold 200 shares of donated treasury stock at $40 per share.		

A corporation sometimes purchases its own capital stock for one of the following reasons:

(a) The corporation may wish to reduce the amount of capital stock outstanding, thereby reducing the capitalization of the corporation. This may be desirable at a time when the stock can be purchased at a discount. When the shares are formally canceled, the stock ceases to be treasury stock and reverts to the status of unissued stock.

(b) A corporation may have sold capital stock to its employees under an agreement to repurchase the shares if the workers leave the employment of the company. The price at which the shares will be repurchased usually is covered by the agreement.

(c) A corporation may purchase some of its shares to stabilize the market price of the stock.

(d) A corporation may want to obtain some of its shares to give to officers or employees as a bonus or to sell to officers or employees under a stock option agreement.

When a corporation purchases its own stock, Treasury Stock should be debited for the cost. When treasury stock is sold for more than its cost, Treasury Stock should be credited for the original cost of the stock and Paid-In Capital from Sale of Treasury Stock should be credited for the amount of the excess over cost. When treasury stock is sold for less than its cost, Treasury Stock should be credited for the original cost of the shares and Paid-In Capital from Sale of Treasury Stock should be debited for the amount of the excess of cost over selling price. For example, suppose that 3,000 shares of common stock are purchased for $8 per share. The journal entry to record the transaction would be as follows:

Common Treasury Stock	24,000	
Bank		24,000
Purchased 3,000 shares of common stock at $8 per share.		

If 1,000 of the treasury shares later were sold for $11 per share, the journal entry to record the transaction would be as follows:

Bank	11,000	
Common Treasury Stock		8,000
Paid-In Capital from Sale of Treasury Stock		3,000
Sold 1,000 treasury shares at $11 per share.		

If the other 2,000 treasury shares were sold for $7 per share, the journal entry to record the transaction would be as follows:

Bank	14,000	
Paid-In Capital from Sale of Treasury Stock	2,000	
Common Treasury Stock		16,000
Sold 2,000 treasury shares at $7 per share.		

There should be a separate treasury stock account for each class of treasury stock in the possession of the corporation. The balance of each of these accounts, representing the cost of the treasury shares on hand, is shown in the balance sheet as a deduction from the total amount of stockholders' equity of all types. This treatment is illustrated in the stockholders' equity section of a balance sheet shown on page 598.

Accountants do not accept the notion that a corporation can realize a gain or sustain a loss by dealing in its own shares. Paid-In Capital from Sale of Treasury Stock is, as its name indicates, a paid-in capital account. The amount of the balance of the account is shown in the balance sheet in the paid-in capital portion of the stockholders' equity section.

Organization costs account

In the organization of a corporation, certain costs are incurred, such as incorporation fees, attorneys' fees, and promotion expense. Such expenditures are known as *organization costs* (sometimes called *organization expenses*). Organization costs differ from operating expenses in that they apply to the entire life of a corporation rather than to one accounting period. It is, therefore, customary to treat organization costs as an intangible asset. In the interest of conservatism, it is common practice to amortize (write off) the cost over a period of years. If it is decided to amortize organization costs over a period of five years, one fifth of the original amount should be written off each year by an end-of-period adjusting entry debiting Amortization of Organization Costs and crediting Organization Costs. The amount of the Amortization of Organization Costs is treated as a nonoperating expense in the income statement. For federal income tax purposes, organization costs may be amortized over any period of time except that the period may not be less than sixty months.

Accounting for no-par-value stock

Accounting for transactions involving capital stock without par value may be somewhat simpler than is the case with par-value stock. It will not be simpler if the shares have a stated value and this value is treated in the accounts as though it were par. If, however, the stated value is ignored except for a balance sheet notation of its amount, or if there is no stated value, the accounting is simplified. When shares are issued, the capital stock account is credited for the amount of money or the value of property received. The number of shares issued should be noted in the account. There is no premium or discount.

Subscriptions for no-par stock are recorded in a manner similar to that followed in the case of par-value stock. The subscriptions receivable account is debited and the capital stock subscribed account is credited for the full amount of the subscriptions. If there are numerous subscribers, a subsidiary subscription ledger should be used. When the stock certificates are issued after the full price has been received, the capital stock subscribed account should be debited and the capital stock account should be credited for the full amount received for the stock.

The accounting for no-par treasury stock transactions does not differ from the accounting for par-value treasury stock transactions if the cost basis is used.

Capital stock transactions

To illustrate the application of some of the principles of accounting for capital stock that have been discussed to this point, the entries needed to record a narrative of corporate transactions are presented. Only the events and transactions pertaining to capital stock are included.

It is assumed that a subsidiary subscription ledger and a subsidiary stockholders ledger are maintained. A stock transfer record, similar to the one illustrated on page 579, is used to record such transactions as those occurring on August 8, October 3 and 19, and December 6.

TRANSACTIONS

July 1. The Morgan Manufacturing Company was incorporated with the authority to issue 1,000 shares of 7 percent preferred capital stock, par value $100, and 3,000 shares of common stock without par value.

1. At the first meeting of the incorporators, the following subscriptions for the capital stock were accepted:

A — 600 shares of preferred stock at $105 per share
B — 200 shares of preferred stock at $105 per share
C — 800 shares of common stock at $45 per share
D — 500 shares of common stock at $45 per share
E — 200 shares of common stock at $45 per share

17. The following was received from subscribers to apply on their subscriptions for capital stock:

A — Cash, $63,000
B — Cash, $10,500
C — Cash, $4,000; land, $32,000
D — Machinery and equipment, $22,500
E — Cash, $3,000

17. Issued stock certificates to the following subscribers, who had paid their subscriptions in full:

A — 600 shares of preferred stock
C — 800 shares of common stock
D — 500 shares of common stock

Aug. 8. Stockholder A returned his certificate for 600 shares of preferred stock and requested that 150 shares of his stock be transferred to F. (He had sold these shares to F.) Issued a new certificate to A for 450 shares and a certificate to F for 150 shares.

23. Sold 200 shares of preferred stock to G at a price of $104 per share. Received cash in full settlement and issued the certificate.

26. Sold 10 shares of common stock to H at a price of $42 per share. Received cash in full settlement and issued the certificate.

Oct. 3. Purchased 100 shares of the preferred stock owned by A for a total of $9,900. A returned his certificate for 450 shares and was issued a new certificate for 350 shares. The shares purchased are to be held as treasury stock; accordingly, a certificate for 100 shares was made out in the name of the company.

19. Purchased 10 shares of common stock owned by H for a total of $400. The stock is to be held in the treasury.

Dec. 6. Sold the 10 shares of common treasury stock to J for $410.

July 1. Incorporated The Morgan Manufacturing Company with an authorized issue of 1,000 shares of 7% preferred stock, par value $100, and 3,000 shares of common stock without par value.

1. Preferred Stock Subscriptions Receivable......................	84,000	
Common Stock Subscriptions Receivable......................	67,500	
Preferred Stock Subscribed................................		80,000
Common Stock Subscribed.................................		67,500
Premium on Preferred Stock..............................		4,000

       Received subscriptions for capital stock as follows:
       Preferred stock subscribed at $105 per share —
         A — 600 shares, B — 200 shares
       Common stock subscribed at $45 per share —
         C — 800 shares, D — 500 shares, E — 200 shares

17. Bank..	80,500	
Land..	32,000	
Machinery and Equipment.................................	22,500	
Preferred Stock Subscriptions Receivable...................		73,500
Common Stock Subscriptions Receivable...................		61,500

       Received cash and other property in settlement of subscriptions
       for capital stock as follows:
       To apply on preferred stock subscriptions:
         A — Cash, $63,000 (in full)
         B — Cash, $10,500
       To apply on common stock subscriptions:
         C — Cash, $4,000; land, $32,000 (in full)
         D — Machinery and equipment, $22,500 (in full)
         E — Cash, $3,000

17. Preferred Stock Subscribed.................................	60,000	
Common Stock Subscribed...............................	58,500	
Preferred Stock..		60,000
Common Stock..		58,500

       Stock certificates issued to subscribers as follows:
         A — 600 shares preferred stock
         C — 800 shares common stock
         D — 500 shares common stock

597

Aug. 8. (No general journal entry required.)

23. Bank..	20,800	
Preferred Stock..		20,000
Premium on Preferred Stock..............................		800

       Sold 200 shares of preferred stock to G at $104 per share.

26. Bank..	420	
Common Stock...		420

       Sold 10 shares of common stock to H at $42 per share.

Oct. 3. Preferred Treasury Stock.................................	9,900	
Bank...		9,900

       Purchased 100 shares of preferred stock from A at $99 per share.

19. Common Treasury Stock..................................	400	
Bank...		400

       Purchased 10 shares of common stock from H at $40 per share.

Dec. 6. Bank..	410	
Common Treasury Stock.................................		400
Paid-In Capital from Sale of Treasury Stock................		10

       Sold 10 shares of common treasury stock to J at $41 per share.

Assume that the records (not shown) of The Morgan Manufacturing Company disclose a net income of $8,000 for the six months ended December 31. Further assume that no dividends have been declared to that date.

Accordingly, the capital section of the balance sheet of the company as of December 31 should appear as reproduced below.

THE MORGAN MANUFACTURING COMPANY
Balance Sheet
December 31, 19--

Stockholders' Equity

Paid-in capital:

Preferred stock, 7%, par $100		
(1,000 shares authorized; 800 shares issued)	$80,000	
Preferred stock subscribed (200 shares)	20,000	$100,000
Common stock, no-par		
(3,000 shares authorized; 1,310 shares issued)	$58,920	
Common stock subscribed (200 shares)	9,000	67,920
Premium on preferred stock	$ 4,800	
Paid-in capital from sale of treasury stock	10	4,810
Total paid-in capital		$172,730
Retained earnings		8,000
		$180,730
Less preferred treasury stock (100 shares, at cost)		9,900
Total stockholders' equity		$170,830

598

After completing the posting from the journal of The Morgan Manufacturing Company, Preferred Stock Subscriptions Receivable will have a debit balance of $10,500 and Common Stock Subscriptions Receivable will have a debit balance of $6,000. The sum of these balances may be listed among the assets in the balance sheet. If it is expected that the amounts due on subscriptions will be collected in the near future, they may be listed as a current asset. Otherwise, most accountants would probably prefer to treat Preferred Stock Subscriptions Receivable as a deduction from Preferred Stock Subscribed, and Common Stock Subscriptions Receivable as a deduction from Common Stock Subscribed in the stockholders' equity section of the balance sheet.

Report No. 22-2

Complete Report No. 22-2 in the workbook and submit your working papers for approval. Continue with the textbook discussion in Chapter 23 until the next report is required.

chapter 23

accounting for corporate earnings

599

In accounting for all types of businesses it is common practice to use the term *capital* to describe the excess of the dollar amount of the assets over the dollar amount of the liabilities. The designation *owners' equity* is growing in use and is superior because the word "capital" has a variety of meanings in economics, law, and business. However, long-standing custom sanctions the use of the word capital as a synonym for owners' equity. This is particularly true in corporation accounting. In all of the discussion that follows, the terms capital and stockholders' equity are used interchangeably.

Long usage has given the term *earnings* two different, though not unrelated, meanings. The word is a synonym for *net income* — the excess of revenue over expenses. Revenue and expense are defined as *reasons* for increases and decreases in owners' equity (capital). (See page 16.) Accordingly, "earnings" is a reason for an increase in capital. The term is often used in this sense. Equally often, the word earnings is used to describe the *net assets* that resulted from having had net income — often cash and short-term receivables. The expression "earnings retained in the business" means net assets that resulted from having had profitable operations in excess of the amount of assets that have been distributed as dividends.

The way in which the term earnings is used causes it to mean either **(1)** a reason why one or more assets were obtained, or **(2)** the asset or assets that were obtained.

Earnings retained
in the business

There are two major sources of capital for every type of business: **(1)** capital that results from the investment of cash or other property by the owner or owners, and **(2)** capital that results from earnings retained in the business. In the case of single proprietorships and partnerships, little or no effort is made to distinguish between these two types of capital. In the accounts of a single proprietorship, all of the owner's equity usually is recorded in the capital account of the proprietor. The balance in the capital account of each member of a partnership usually represents his share of the owners' equity in the partnership. In corporation accounting, more attention is paid to the source of the capital, that is, to the distinction between paid-in or invested capital and capital resulting from retained earnings.

600

Paid-in capital

The original capital of a corporation is usually derived from the sale of capital stock. The amount received from the sale of capital stock represents the paid-in or invested capital of the stockholders. Subsequently, the capital of a corporation may be increased by additional contributions by stockholders or by the retention of earnings for use in the business.

Paid-in capital, sometimes referred to as invested capital, should be recorded in the proper capital stock accounts to the extent of the par value or stated value of the stock. This amount usually constitutes the legal capital of a corporation. Amounts invested in excess of the par or stated value of the capital stock should be recorded in appropriate capital accounts that indicate the source of the capital. For example, if common stock is sold for more than its par value, the excess should be credited to Premium on Capital Stock. If stock is sold for less than its par value, the difference should be debited to Discount on Capital Stock. Assuming that only common stock has been issued and that there have been no stock dividends, the amount of the paid-in or contributed capital may be determined by finding the sum of the amounts credited to the capital stock and premium on capital stock accounts or by finding the difference between the amount credited to the capital stock account and the amount debited to the discount on capital stock account.

Retention of earnings

Capital resulting from the retention of earnings should be recorded in an account with an appropriate title, such as Retained Earnings or Earnings Retained in the Business. (At one time it was common practice to use an account titled "Earned Surplus," but this designation has lost favor.) Seldom does a corporation distribute all of its net earnings to stockholders. Usually only a portion of the earnings is distributed, and the balance is retained as additional capital to help finance the growth of the business. It is not uncommon to find that a major portion of the capital of a corporation has resulted from earnings retained in the business. Many of today's large corporations started originally as small companies, and their growth was financed primarily from retained earnings. This was particularly true prior to the time of high corporate income taxes. As income tax rates have increased, it has become more difficult for corporations to finance their growth or expansion with capital derived from earnings retained in the business. The result is that under current conditions an increasing amount of the financial need of corporations must be met by the sale of additional stock or by issuing bonds or other evidences of indebtedness.

The retained earnings account

The net income of corporations is calculated in much the same manner as that of sole proprietorships and partnerships. At the end of the accounting period, the accounts are adjusted and the revenue and expense accounts are closed into the expense and revenue summary account. A credit balance in this account represents net income; a debit balance signifies a net loss. Beyond this point the accounting procedures for corporations differ from those of sole proprietorships and partnerships. The balance of the expense and revenue summary account of a corporation is transferred to the retained earnings account.

Typical debits and credits to the retained earnings account include the following:

Debits

    (a) Net loss for the period (after including any extraordinary, nonrecurring gains or losses).

    (b) Appropriations of retained earnings by the board of directors.

(c) Dividends declared by the board of directors.

(d) Adjustments relating to prior periods (if significant in amount).

Credits

(a) Net income for the period (after including any extraordinary, nonrecurring gains or losses).

(b) Adjustments relating to prior periods (if significant in amount).

It should be noted that the calculation of net income or net loss for a period should include any extraordinary, nonrecurring gains or losses. This practice was not always followed. For many years it was common practice to close only regular operating revenues and expenses into the expense and revenue summary account. Such a procedure is no longer considered to be proper, however, as it may cover up the fact that an operating profit or loss reported in the income statement was partly or wholly offset by nonoperating or extraordinary gains or losses recorded directly in the retained earnings account.

Stockholders tend to attach great importance to the net income or net loss figure that is shown in the income statement. They may overlook, or not bother to study, a statement of changes in retained earnings. For this reason, it is important that both operating and nonoperating revenues and expenses, as well as extraordinary gains and losses, be reported in the income statement. The statement can be arranged to clearly distinguish between the various types of revenues, expenses, gains, and losses. When this procedure is followed, the final net income or net loss figure gives a better indication of the total result of the activities of the period.

The list of typical debits and credits to the retained earnings account includes entries that arise from prior period adjustments (if significant in amount). Not all such adjustments involve retained earnings; but the correction of errors that had an effect on the income calculation of the immediately preceding period usually requires an adjustment in Retained Earnings. For example, suppose that after the books were closed it was discovered that the amount recorded for merchandise inventory at the end of the preceding period (the beginning of the current period) was overstated in the amount of $4,000. The journal entry to correct this overstatement would be as follows:

Retained Earnings...................................... 4,000
Merchandise Inventory................................. 4,000
    Correction of overstatement of merchandise inventory as of December 31.

This entry not only corrects the amount shown in the ledger as the amount of the opening merchandise inventory of the present period, but it also corrects whatever amount was closed to the retained earnings account at the end of the previous period purporting to be the net income or net loss for that period.

Appropriations of retained earnings

Sometimes a portion of the earnings is appropriated for special purposes, such as inventory losses, a patent infringement, or an antitrust suit. Sometimes a general appropriation is made for contingencies or contingent liabilities. The action of the directors in making such appropriations should be recorded in such a manner as to indicate the portion of retained earnings that is not available for dividends. For example, if the directors should adopt a resolution appropriating $20,000 of retained earnings for contingencies, such action may be recorded by debiting Retained Earnings and by crediting Appropriation for Contingencies. The amount of this contingency appropriation is shown in the capital section of the balance sheet.

The directors of a corporation have wide discretion in the matter of declaring cash dividends. In most cases, however, the amount of dividends that the directors will declare and pay is determined by the amount of cash available and other considerations of policy. For example, even if the corporation has ample cash, the directors may not consider it wise to pay large dividends. They may want to use some of the money to expand the business or to reduce liabilities. They may want to invest the money in marketable securities that could be converted into cash very quickly in case of an emergency. Most corporations do not regularly distribute all of their earnings as dividends.

Successful operations for a period of years coupled with a moderate dividend policy usually result in an increasing balance in the retained earnings account. It is extremely unlikely that there will be a parallel increase in the size of the bank balance. The money probably will have been used to purchase various assets or to reduce liabilities.

When the directors have no intention of paying dividends to the full extent of the balance of Retained Earnings, they may reduce the balance of the account by declaring and distributing a stock dividend or they may appropriate a portion of the retained earnings account balance. The latter amounts to nothing more than formally passing a resolution at a directors' meeting instructing the accountant to transfer a certain amount of the credit balance of the retained earnings account to a designated appropriation account, such as Appropriation for Contingencies, Appropriation for New Construction, or Appropriation for Expansion. (At one time it was common practice to title such accounts "Reserve for Contingencies," "Reserve for New Construction," etc. The use of the term *reserve*, however, is rapidly declining.)

603

Such appropriations have no effect on the assets, the liabilities, or the total stockholders' equity of a corporation. The appropriations result in nothing more than renaming a portion of retained earnings. This procedure is sometimes described as earmarking part of the retained earnings. Reporting such appropriations in the suggested manner serves to advise the readers of a balance sheet that the directors have no present intention of distributing as dividends more than an amount equal to the unappropriated retained earnings.

Statement of retained earnings

In order to explain the change in the amount of retained earnings between two successive balance sheet dates, it is customary to prepare a *statement of retained earnings*. To illustrate the relationship between such a statement and the balance sheet of a corporation, a condensed balance sheet followed by a statement of retained earnings of The Sutton Machinery Company are reproduced below and at the top of the next page.

The balance sheet shows that the capital paid in by the stockholders amounts to $18,433,278 ($17,067,850 + $1,365,428), while the capital resulting from retained earnings amounts to $16,514,623 ($800,000 +

604

THE SUTTON MACHINERY COMPANY
Balance Sheet
December 31, 1972

Total assets........	$42,194,794	Total liabilities.....		$ 7,246,893
		Stockholders' Equity		
		Common stock, $25 par value, (authorized 1,000,000 shares; outstanding 682,714 shares).........	$17,067,850	
		Premium on capital stock.........	1,365,428	
		Earnings retained for use in the business:		
		Appropriated for contingencies.....	800,000	
		Unappropriated, per statement...	15,714,623	34,947,901
		Total liabilities and stockholders' equity.........		
Total assets........	$42,194,794			$42,194,794

THE SUTTON MACHINERY COMPANY
Statement of Retained Earnings
For the Year Ended December 31, 1972

Balance, January 1	$14,531,424
Net income for year	2,548,627
	$17,080,051
Cash dividends — $2.00 per share........................	1,365,428
Balance, December 31	$15,714,623

$15,714,623). The statement of retained earnings provides an explanation of the changes in the (unappropriated) retained earnings account during the year. The balance of the account was increased by the amount of net income for the year, $2,548,627, and was reduced by the payment of cash dividends in the amount of $1,365,428. It is evident that the $800,000 shown as "Appropriated for Contingencies" had been charged to the retained earnings account in some prior year. The action taken by the directors in making this appropriation indicates that the amount appropriated is not available for dividends. While the amount of the unappropriated retained earnings is technically available for dividends, it is not to be taken for granted that the entire amount will be distributed to the stockholders.

605

It will be noted that nearly half of the capital of the business has been provided by retained earnings. As a result, the stockholders' equity has grown until their stock has a book value of $51.19 a share ($34,947,901 ÷ 682,714) though its average issue price was only $27 a share ($18,433,278 ÷ 682,714).

Combined income and retained earnings statement

Instead of presenting a separate statement of retained earnings, that statement can be combined with the income statement. Such a combined *income and retained earnings statement* for The Sutton Machinery Company (with the detail of the income statement omitted) is shown at the top of page 606. Note that this combined statement serves to account for the change in the balance of the retained earnings account during the year.

Opinion is divided as to whether such a combined statement (with either of the arrangements illustrated) is superior to presenting the income statement separate from the statement of retained earnings.

THE SUTTON MACHINERY COMPANY
Income and Retained Earnings Statement
For the Year Ended December 31, 1972

Net income..	$ 2,548,627
Retained earnings, January 1........................	14,531,424
	$17,080,051
Less cash dividends — $2.00 per share...............	1,365,428
Retained earnings, December 31......................	$15,714,623

An alternative arrangement that is often used is shown below:

Net income..	$ 2,548,627
Less cash dividends — $2.00 per share...............	1,365,428
Net increase in retained earnings...................	$ 1,183,199
Retained earnings, January 1........................	14,531,424
Retained earnings, December 31......................	$15,714,623

Recapitalization

606

With the knowledge and consent of its stockholders, a corporation may secure an amendment to its articles of incorporation to permit it to change the legal value of its stock. Usually the change is to a lower par value or to no-par value. Generally this involves calling in the old stock certificates and issuing new certificates. A major reason for reducing either the par value or the stated value of capital stock without increasing the number of shares outstanding is to eliminate an accumulated deficit. If a corporation operates at a loss for a prolonged period of time, the sum of the assets will become less than the total liabilities plus the par or stated value of the capital stock outstanding. Such a result is called a *deficit*. Officers, directors, and stockholders of a corporation dislike having to show a deficit. One way to eliminate it is to recapitalize the corporation and reduce the par or stated value of the capital stock.

Assume that The Cole Corporation had a deficit of $300,000 as shown by the condensed balance sheet at the top of the next page.

There were 20,000 shares of capital stock outstanding with a par value of $100 per share. In order to eliminate the deficit of $300,000, it was decided to obtain an amendment to the articles of incorporation to permit an exchange of the old shares of capital stock for an equal number of new shares with a par value of $50 per share. The exchange of stock certificates was recorded in the journal entry following the balance sheet on page 607.

THE COLE CORPORATION

Balance Sheet

Total assets.........	$2,600,000	Total liabilities.......		$ 900,000
		Stockholders' Equity		
		Capital stock.........	$2,000,000	
		Less deficit........	300,000	1,700,000
		Total liabilities and		
Total assets.........	$2,600,000	stockholders' equity..		$2,600,000

Capital Stock (Old)..................................	2,000,000	
Capital Stock (New)................................		1,000,000
Deficit..		300,000
Premium on Capital Stock...........................		700,000

Premium on capital stock was credited with $700,000 because the new stock was, in effect, issued at a premium. The par value of the old stock was $2,000,000, whereas the par value of the new stock was only $1,000,000. After the deficit of $300,000 was written off, the balance represented the premium on the new stock.

After the exchange of shares was recorded in the manner suggested, the capital section of the balance sheet of the company would appear as follows:

Stockholders' Equity

Capital stock.........................	$1,000,000	
Premium on capital stock.................	700,000	$1,700,000

The exchange of shares had no effect upon the assets or the liabilities. It should also be noted that the total capital after exchanging the stock and writing off the deficit is the same as before. The book value per share of stock was not affected. There are still 20,000 shares of stock outstanding and the total capital of the company is still $1,700,000; hence, the book value of each share of stock is $85 a share. A reduction of the legal capital and the elimination of the deficit in the accounts were the only results of these events.

It should be understood that corporate recapitalizations have various purposes and take a variety of forms. Sometimes a recapitalization amounts to a reorganization of the company. Recapitalizations may involve the elimination of one or more classes of stock and, sometimes, bonds. Sometimes an exchange of one share of an old issue of stock for more than one share of a new issue of essentially the same class of stock takes place. Such an exchange is known as a *stock split*. The usual purpose of a stock split is to improve the marketability of the shares by reducing the market price per share. Having a greater number of shares outstanding also makes it possible to have a wider ownership of the stock.

Earnings distributed to stockholders

A pro rata distribution of cash or other assets by a corporation to its stockholders is known as a *dividend*. When the dividend represents a distribution of earnings, it is usually paid in cash, though it may involve the distribution of other assets. Sometimes corporations issue additional shares of their own stock to the stockholders on a pro rata basis. Such a distribution is termed a *stock dividend*. When a corporation is being dissolved and any assets are distributed to the stockholders, the distribution is known as a *liquidating dividend*.

Cash dividends

Most corporation dividends are paid in cash and represent the distribution of corporate earnings. Some corporations are able to pay dividends regularly; that is, annually, semiannually, or quarterly. Other corporations pay dividends irregularly. It has been noted that the size and the frequency of dividend distributions depend upon earnings, the amount of cash available, and the plans and policies of the directors.

Three dates are involved in the declaration and the payment of dividends: **(1)** the date of declaration, **(2)** the record date, and **(3)** the date of payment. The *record date* is the day on which the names of stockholders entitled to receive the dividend will be determined. For example, a board of directors might meet on January 25 and declare a dividend of $2.50 a share on common stock, payable on February 15 to stockholders of record on February 5.

The result of such a declaration is to make the corporation liable for the dividend at the time of declaration on January 25. However, the dividend will not be paid until February 15. To be eligible to receive the dividend, a stockholder must have his stock recorded in his name in the books of the corporation not later than February 5. Thereafter any stock of the corporation that may be transferred is said to be transferred *ex-dividend*. This means that anyone acquiring the stock after February 5 will not be entitled to share in the dividend declared on January 25, even though the dividend is paid after the stock is acquired.

Sometimes each dividend declared is given a number to distinguish it from those that have been declared in the past. Dividends on different classes of capital stock should be accounted for separately. To illustrate, assume that the board of directors declares a semiannual dividend of $3 per share on 4,000 shares of preferred stock outstanding and a semi-annual dividend of $2 per share on 10,000 shares of common stock outstanding. Assume that this is the 37th dividend on the preferred stock and the 28th on the common stock. These declarations should be recorded, in general journal form, as follows:

Retained Earnings..	12,000	
Preferred Dividends Payable, No. 37........................		12,000
Declared a dividend of $3 per share on 4,000 shares of preferred stock outstanding.		
Retained Earnings..	20,000	
Common Dividends Payable, No. 28........................		20,000
Declared a dividend of $2 per share on 10,000 shares of common stock outstanding.		

When the dividends are paid, the dividends payable accounts should be debited and Bank should be credited. If a balance sheet were prepared on some date between the time the dividends were declared and the time they were paid, the balances of the two dividends payable accounts should be included among the current liabilities.

Sometimes large corporations with many stockholders draw a single check to cover a particular dividend and deposit the check in a special bank account. Such a transaction should be recorded by a debit to the special dividend checking account and a credit to the general checking account. Special check forms probably will be used in paying such a dividend. The individual dividend checks may be recorded in a special dividend check register or in a dividend record similar to the one shown on page 610. No other record need be made until the canceled checks are received from the bank together with a statement covering the special dividend deposit account. At that time the sum of the checks paid and canceled by the bank may be recorded by debiting Dividends Payable and by crediting the special dividend checking account. After all the dividend checks have been paid by the bank and the proper entries have been made in the books of the corporation, the dividends payable account and the special dividend checking account will be in balance.

DIVIDEND NO.	DATE DECLARED	RATE	NO. OF SHARES	AMOUNT	NAME OF STOCKHOLDER	HOW PAID	DATE PAID
1	1972 Jan. 15	$1.25	300	375 00	Morton R. Perkins	Check	1972 Jan. 31
1	15	$1.25	100	125 00	Ralph W. Case	"	31
1	15	$1.25	75	93 75	J. F. Rice	"	31
1	15	$1.25	15	18 75	J. J. Stern	"	31
1	15	$1.25	10	12 50	Samuel Bay	"	31

Dividend Record

In some instances dividend checks may be returned unclaimed or they may never be presented for payment to the bank on which they are drawn. Any checks that are unclaimed may be canceled when they are returned. Payment may be stopped on any checks not returned and not presented to the bank for payment within a reasonable length of time. The total of such unclaimed and uncashed checks may be recorded by debiting Dividends Payable and by crediting Unclaimed Dividends. At the same time the unused portion of the dividend checking account should be transferred back to the general checking account. The account with Unclaimed Dividends will have a credit balance as long as any dividend checks remain unpaid. This balance should be reported in the balance sheet as a current liability.

Stock dividends

A pro rata distribution of shares of a corporation's own stock to its stockholders is termed a *stock dividend*. Corporations may distribute this type of dividend for one or more of several reasons. The company may be short of cash and may be unable or unwilling to borrow to pay a cash dividend. It may be in the stockholders' interest to have more shares with a lower market price, as low-priced shares usually are more readily marketable. A greater number of shares outstanding makes wider ownership possible, and wide ownership may be desired in some cases. The corporation may have a large credit balance in Retained Earnings and the directors may deem it advisable to transfer a portion of this balance to a restricted capital category for purposes of subsequent balance sheet presentation.

When a stock dividend is declared, an amount equal to the market value of the shares to be distributed should be charged to the retained earnings account. If the stock has a par or stated value, Stock Dividend

Distributable should be credited for the par or stated value of the shares, and the excess of market value over par or stated value should be credited to Premium on Capital Stock. If the stock in question has neither par nor stated value, the market value of the dividend shares should be debited to Retained Earnings and credited to Stock Dividend Distributable. (Stock Dividend Distributable is not a liability since no money is owed. If a balance sheet were prepared as of a date between the declaration and distribution of the stock dividend, the balance of the account should be reported in the stockholders' equity section of the statement.) When the dividend shares are distributed, an entry should be made debiting Stock Dividend Distributable and crediting Capital Stock.

A stock dividend does not affect the assets, the liabilities, or the total capital of the corporation. The transaction merely transfers part of the balance of the retained earnings account to one or more paid-in capital accounts. Such a transfer serves to destroy the distinction between invested capital and earned capital, but that is not considered to be a serious matter in view of the purpose to be served.

The proportionate amount of a common stockholder's interest in a corporation is not affected by a stock dividend of the same class of shares. He will have more shares, but the book value of each one will be proportionately reduced. The owner of 100 shares of common stock of a corporation with 1,000 shares of common stock has a 10 percent interest in the total equity that belongs to the common shareholders. If a 25 percent common stock dividend is distributed, he would own 125 of 1,250 shares. He would still have a 10 percent interest in the equity — neither more nor less than he had before the dividend.

Generally, stock dividends are not regarded as income to the recipient and are not subject to income tax.

Liquidating dividends

A liquidating dividend is very different from an ordinary cash dividend. An ordinary cash dividend is a distribution of earnings — a return *on* the stockholders' investment. A liquidating dividend represents a return *of* the stockholders' investment. The liquidation of the firm need not be completed before liquidating dividends are paid. As assets are converted into cash, the money may be distributed to the stockholders. Mining companies sometimes pay partial liquidating dividends as their ore reserves are depleted. They may pay dividends that represent partly earnings and partly a return of capital.

When a corporation is being completely dissolved or liquidated, the liabilities first must be paid in full. If there are outstanding preferred shares that have a preference as to assets, the holders of such shares must receive the full amount to which they are entitled (including unpaid dividends if the stock is cumulative) before the common stockholders receive anything. Whatever is left is distributed on a pro rata basis to the common stockholders. Usually all such distributions are in cash. Sometimes, however, property other than cash is distributed to the stockholders. Upon receiving the final distribution, the stockholders will return their stock certificates. When articles of dissolution are filed with the proper state official, the corporation ceases to exist.

Application of principles

As a means of illustrating the principles involved in recording dividends declared and paid, the following selected transactions completed by The Lawson Manufacturing Company are shown recorded in the general journal on the following page.

NARRATIVE OF TRANSACTIONS

Jan. 10. The board of directors declared dividends as follows:
    On preferred stock: quarterly dividend (No. 21) of $1.50 a share on 3,000 shares.
    On common stock: dividend (No. 11) of 25 cents a share on 30,000 shares. Both dividends are payable in cash on February 1 to stockholders of record on January 20.

29. The shares of preferred stock are held by a very few people. Checks in payment of such dividends are drawn on the regular checking account. The shares of common stock are held by a large number of people. Special checks drawn on a dividend checking account are used to pay common stock dividends. Accordingly, the treasurer drew a check for $7,500 on the regular bank account and deposited it in the dividend checking account for the common stock dividend.

30. Checks drawn on the regular bank account in payment of the preferred dividend were prepared and mailed. Special checks drawn on the dividend checking account in payment of the common dividend were prepared and mailed.

Feb. 28. A statement covering the dividend checking account was received from the bank together with the canceled checks. It was noted that all checks issued had been paid.

Mar. 15. The board of directors declared a stock dividend of one share of common stock for every ten shares of common held. The market value of the common shares is $14 each. (The par value of each share is $10.) The stock will be distributed on April 5 to stockholders of record on March 25.

Apr. 5. Certificates for the 3,000 shares of dividend stock were issued to the common stockholders.

Jan.	10.	Retained Earnings...	4,500	
		Preferred Dividends Payable, No. 21........................		4,500
		Declared $1.50 per share dividend on 3,000 shares of preferred stock outstanding.		
	10.	Retained Earnings...	7,500	
		Common Dividends Payable, No. 11.........................		7,500
		Declared a dividend of 25 cents a share on 30,000 shares of common stock outstanding.		
	29.	First National Bank, Dividend Account......................	7,500	
		First National Bank, General Account......................		7,500
		Transferred $7,500 to special dividend account.		
	30.	Preferred Dividends Payable, No. 21.........................	4,500	
		First National Bank, General Account......................		4,500
		Paid preferred dividend, No. 21.		
Feb.	28.	Common Dividends Payable, No. 11..........................	7,500	
		First National Bank, Dividend Account....................		7,500
		Dividend checks issued January 30, in payment of common dividend No. 11, paid by bank per statement of this date.		
Mar.	15.	Retained Earnings...	42,000	
		Common Stock Dividend Distributable.....................		30,000
		Premium on Common Stock...............................		12,000
		Declared a dividend to common stockholders distributable in common stock on the basis of one share for every ten held.		
Apr.	5.	Common Stock Dividend Distributable......................	30,000	
		Common Stock..		30,000
		Issued 3,000 shares of common stock in satisfaction of stock dividend declared March 15.		

613

Report No. 23-2

Complete Report No. 23-2 in the workbook and submit your working papers for approval. Continue with the following study assignment in Chapter 24 until Report No. 24-1 is required.

chapter 24

accounting for corporate bonds

To supplement the funds provided by the stockholders of a corporation, additional funds may be obtained by issuing bonds. A *bond* is similar to a long-term note in that it is an interest-bearing, negotiable instrument in which the maker promises to pay a certain amount of money at a definite or determinable future date. Bonds usually are secured with respect to either principal or interest, or both, by a pledge of certain corporate assets.

Accounting for bonds sold

The right to borrow money is implied in the charter of a corporation. The board of directors usually decides when and how much to borrow. If only a small amount of money is needed or if the money will be repaid in a short time, notes usually will be issued. The notes may be secured or unsecured. If the corporation has a good credit standing, it may be able to borrow on its unsecured notes. If this is the case, the liability that arises is recorded as Notes Payable. If the notes are secured by a mortgage, the liability is recorded as Mortgage Payable.

When a corporation borrows a large sum of money for a long period of time, say from five to fifty years or more, it is customary to issue bonds instead of notes. A bond issue usually consists of a number of bonds. All of the bonds comprising the issue need not have the same denomination. Some may be for $1,000 or less, while others may have face values of $5,000 or $10,000, and sometimes more.

If bonds are secured, all of the bonds in a particular issue usually will be secured under one deed of trust. A *deed of trust* is a mortgage on certain specified properties. The deed is placed in the hands of a trustee who represents the bondholders. The deed of trust states the terms and the conditions under which the bonds are issued and under which the property is held for their security. Reference is made in the bonds to the deed of trust by which they are secured. It will be seen, therefore, that both the deed of trust and the bonds issued refer to each other in such a manner that all the terms and conditions are clearly stated in both. The trustee has the right to act in behalf of the bondholders and may begin foreclosure proceedings if it becomes necessary to do so in order to safeguard their interests.

Classification of bonds

Bonds may be classified as to **(1)** purpose of the issue, **(2)** security of the bonds, **(3)** payment of the interest, or **(4)** payment of the principal.

As to Purpose of Issue. When bonds are issued to acquire funds for a specific purpose, the bonds may be classified as:

    (a) Improvement bonds.
    (b) Purchase-money bonds.
    (c) Refunding bonds.
    (d) Adjustment bonds.

When the purpose of issuing bonds is to acquire funds for the construction of new buildings, such as an office building, a warehouse, a power plant, or some other type of permanent structure, the bonds may be classified as *improvement bonds.*

When bonds are issued in exchange for assets or as part payment of the purchase price of an asset that has already been constructed, the bonds may be designated as *purchase-money bonds.*

When a new series of bonds is issued for the purpose of raising funds to be used in paying off an old series of bonds that is soon to mature, or is issued to retire outstanding bonds prior to maturity, the bonds may be classified as *refunding bonds.*

When companies that are in financial difficulties are being reorganized, new types of securities may be issued to the holders of securities already

615

outstanding. For instance, bondholders may be given new bonds bearing a lower rate of interest in exchange for their old bonds. If a corporation is unable to pay the interest on its outstanding bonds because of reduced earnings, the bondholders may agree to take a new issue of bonds bearing a lower rate of interest in exchange for the old bonds. Such an issue of bonds may be designated as *adjustment bonds*.

As to Security. Bonds are often classified on the basis of the security offered. Such bonds may be classified as follows:

(a) Mortgage bonds.
(b) Collateral-trust bonds.
(c) Guaranteed bonds.
(d) Debenture bonds.

When bonds are secured by a mortgage on corporate assets, such as real estate, equipment, or leaseholds, they may be designated as *mortgage bonds*. Such bonds are sometimes designated as first mortgage bonds, second mortgage bonds, etc., according to the lien or claim by which they are secured. Thus, a first mortgage bond is a first lien or claim on the property covered by the mortgage. For example, the Ohio Power Company issued $25,000,000 of first mortgage bonds on April 1, 1959. These are 4⅝ percent bonds due to mature in 1989.

When bonds are secured by a deposit of stocks, bonds, mortgages, or other collateral with a trustee under a trust agreement, they may be classified as *collateral-trust bonds*.

When bonds of subsidiary or affiliated corporations are guaranteed as to the payment of principal or interest, or both, by the parent company or another affiliated company, they may be known as *guaranteed bonds*. To be effective, the guarantee must be in writing and must either be stated on the bond itself or be attached to it.

When no security is offered other than the general credit of the corporation issuing the bonds, the issue may be classified as *debenture bonds*.

As to Payment of Interest. Bonds may be classified according to how the interest is to be paid. In this respect they are classified as follows:

(a) Registered bonds.
(b) Coupon bonds.

If the bonds are *registered*, it means that the issuing corporation keeps a record of the names and the addresses of the bondholders. Sometimes the corporation keeps the record; sometimes the record is kept by the trustee of the bond issue. Some form of bond register is used. This will show the number and the denomination of each bond, to whom it was issued, and to whom it was transferred. Checks for the amount of interest due to each registered bondholder are mailed to the bondholders in accordance with the terms of the contract — often called the *bond indenture.*

Very often bonds are issued with a number of interest coupons attached. These are called *coupon bonds.* Each coupon is a promise to pay a specified amount of money on the date stated on the coupon. Because the corporation will pay the face amount of coupon bonds to whomever presents them at their maturity date, they are also known as *bearer bonds.* Likewise the corporation will pay the interest to whomever presents the interest coupons on or after the maturity date of each one. Bond interest may be paid quarterly, semiannually, or annually. Most coupon bonds pay interest semiannually on specified dates, such as January 1 and July 1, or March 15 and September 15. A 20-year, 5 percent, $10,000 coupon bond with interest payable semiannually would be issued with 40 coupons for $250 each attached to it. Each coupon would have its own maturity date. As each interest date arrives, the owner of the bond detaches the coupon and presents it for payment. Many bondholders have their banks act as their agents in collecting their bond coupons. Coupons should not be detached until they become due because they might be lost or because the owner of the bond might want to sell it to someone else.

As to Payment of Principal. Bonds are sometimes classified in accordance with the provisions made as to the payment of the principal. In this respect, bonds may be classified as follows:

    (a) Term bonds.
    (b) Serial bonds.
    (c) Convertible bonds.
    (d) Callable bonds.

The designation *term bonds* applies when all bonds of the issue have the same maturity date. There may be a provision for a sinking fund whose operation will cause a portion of the bonds to be retired before they become due, but the legal date of maturity is the same for the entire issue.

When bonds are issued so that a specified amount of the principal matures each year, the bonds may be classified as *serial bonds.* This is a means of providing for paying off a bond issue on the installment basis. Serial bonds may be secured or unsecured. If unsecured, they are similar to debenture bonds. If secured by a mortgage on certain assets covering the entire issue, provision may be made for the relinquishment of portions of the security after the redemption of each series. Otherwise, all of the mortgaged property may be tied up until the last series of bonds is redeemed.

When bonds are issued so that the holder has the option of exchanging his bonds for other securities of the corporation, the bonds may be classified as *convertible bonds.* Such a privilege may become a valuable one should the market value of these other securities of the corporation increase substantially. The basis upon which the conversion may be made is usually specified and the time within which the conversion must be made is often limited.

When bonds are issued with a provision that they may be called for redemption before the date of maturity, they may be classified as *callable bonds*. In the case of many bond issues, such a provision is made. Thus, twenty-year bonds may be issued with a provision that they are subject to call for payoff at any time after ten years from date of issue.

On page 619 is a reproduction of a first mortgage, 5½ percent, $1,000 bond of The Wilmington Transit Company. The issue date of the bond was April 15, 1952; the maturity date, April 15, 1977. It is a coupon bond. When it was issued, it had fifty coupons attached. Coupon No. 40 is reproduced below. The other coupons were identical except for their number and date.

No. 40 $27.50

   Coupon for $27.50, lawful money of the United States of America, payable to bearer on the fifteenth day of April, 1972, at the principal office of the Guaranty Trust Company of New York in the Borough of Manhattan, City and State of New York, or at the option of the holder at the office of the Central Trust Company in the City of Cincinnati, State of Ohio, without deduction for taxes, for six months' interest due on that day on the $1,000 First Mortgage, 5½% Bond, Series A, of The Wilmington Transit Company, No. M68148, subject to the terms of said bond, and of the indenture dated April 15, 1952.

                              HERMAN B. TAYLOR
                                   Treasurer

Bond Interest Coupon

Bonds and stock often are mentioned in the same breath, but basically they are very different. A bond is an obligation of the issuing corporation — a promise to pay a certain amount of money on a certain date. Stock represents corporate ownership or equity; there is no promise to pay any definite amount at any stated time. Bondholders are creditors of a corporation; stockholders are owners.

Accounting for bonds issued

The decision of the board of directors to borrow money by the use of bonds would be recorded in detail in the official minutes of their meeting. When the bonds are issued, the resulting liability is recorded in a bonds payable account. The account title may be more descriptive if desired.

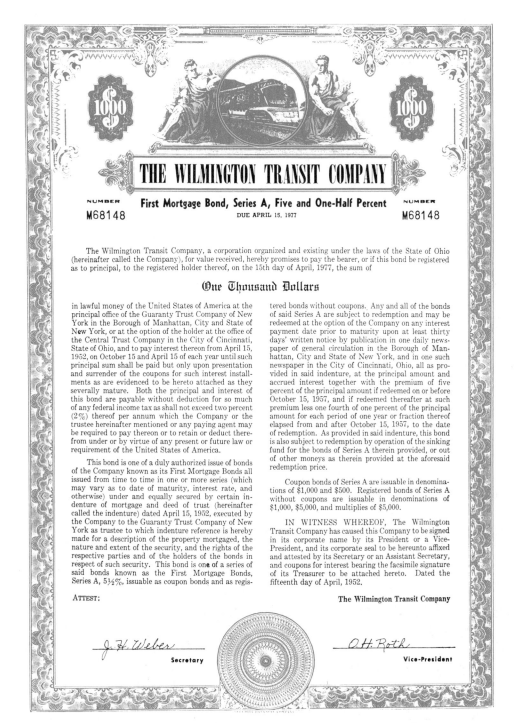

THE WILMINGTON TRANSIT COMPANY

First Mortgage Bond, Series A, Five and One-Half Percent
DUE APRIL 15, 1977

NUMBER
M68148

NUMBER
M68148

The Wilmington Transit Company, a corporation organized and existing under the laws of the State of Ohio (hereinafter called the Company), for value received, hereby promises to pay the bearer, or if this bond be registered as to principal, to the registered holder thereof, on the 15th day of April, 1977, the sum of

One Thousand Dollars

in lawful money of the United States of America at the principal office of the Guaranty Trust Company of New York in the Borough of Manhattan, City and State of New York, or at the option of the holder at the office of the Central Trust Company in the City of Cincinnati, State of Ohio, and to pay interest thereon from April 15, 1952, on October 15 and April 15 of each year until such principal sum shall be paid but only upon presentation and surrender of the coupons for such interest installments as are evidenced to be hereto attached as they severally mature. Both the principal and interest of this bond are payable without deduction for so much of any federal income tax as shall not exceed two percent (2%) thereof per annum which the Company or the trustee hereinafter mentioned or any paying agent may be required to pay thereon or to retain or deduct therefrom under or by virtue of any present or future law or requirement of the United States of America.

This bond is one of a duly authorized issue of bonds of the Company known as its First Mortgage Bonds all issued from time to time in one or more series (which may vary as to date of maturity, interest rate, and otherwise) under and equally secured by certain indenture of mortgage and deed of trust (hereinafter called the indenture) dated April 15, 1952, executed by the Company to the Guaranty Trust Company of New York as trustee to which indenture reference is hereby made for a description of the property mortgaged, the nature and extent of the security, and the rights of the respective parties and of the holders of the bonds in respect of such security. This bond is one of a series of said bonds known as the First Mortgage Bonds, Series A, 5½%, issuable as coupon bonds and as regis-

tered bonds without coupons. Any and all of the bonds of said Series A are subject to redemption and may be redeemed at the option of the Company on any interest payment date prior to maturity upon at least thirty days' written notice by publication in one daily newspaper of general circulation in the Borough of Manhattan, City and State of New York, and in one such newspaper in the City of Cincinnati, Ohio, all as provided in said indenture, at the principal amount and accrued interest together with the premium of five percent of the principal amount if redeemed on or before October 15, 1957, and if redeemed thereafter at such premium less one fourth of one percent of the principal amount for each period of one year or fraction thereof elapsed from and after October 15, 1957, to the date of redemption. As provided in said indenture, this bond is also subject to redemption by operation of the sinking fund for the bonds of Series A therein provided, or out of other moneys as therein provided at the aforesaid redemption price.

Coupon bonds of Series A are issuable in denominations of $1,000 and $500. Registered bonds of Series A without coupons are issuable in denominations of $1,000, $5,000, and multiplies of $5,000.

IN WITNESS WHEREOF, The Wilmington Transit Company has caused this Company to be signed in its corporate name by its President or a Vice-President, and its corporate seal to be hereunto affixed and attested by its Secretary or an Assistant Secretary, and coupons for interest bearing the facsimile signature of its Treasurer to be attached hereto. Dated the fifteenth day of April, 1952.

ATTEST:

The Wilmington Transit Company

J. H. Weber
Secretary

O. H. Roth
Vice-President

Corporation Mortgage Bond

A more descriptive account title would be necessary if the corporation had more than one issue outstanding. There would be a separate account, properly identified, for each issue. Bonds Payable is credited with the face or maturity value of the bonds issued, regardless of the amount that is received for them upon their issuance. In the balance sheet, bonds payable usually are classified as long-term liabilities because the principal may not be due for many years.

It is a universal custom to speak of the sale of bonds. The expression is not incorrect, but it must be understood that the issuing corporation is actually borrowing money when it "sells" its own bonds. It is selling documents containing its promise to pay specified amounts of money on specified dates to the holders of the bonds. When the owner (holder) of a bond sells it to someone else, the transaction is a sale in the usual sense of the word.

Bonds sometimes sell for exactly the amount of their face or maturity value. More often they sell for more or less than their face value. If the bonds sell for more than their face value, the excess is termed *premium*. If the bonds sell for less than their face value, the difference between the face value and the amount received is termed *discount*. A premium or a discount usually represents an adjustment of the contractual rate of interest. If the rate promised by the bonds is higher than the going or market rate for bonds of a similar quality, investors will be willing to pay a premium. If the contractual rate is below the going rate, the bonds can be sold only at a discount. For this reason, the issuing corporation considers a premium to be a partial offset to the amount of interest that must be paid at intervals in the future, while a discount represents bond interest expense in addition to the contractual amount that must be paid in the future.

Sale of Bonds for Face Amount. Most corporations sell bond issues to bankers or underwriters who, in turn, sell them to investors. If a $200,000 issue of first mortgage bonds is sold for exactly this amount, the journal entry to record the transaction would be as follows:

```
Bank.................................................  200,000
    First Mortgage Bonds Payable..........................          200,000
        Sold mortgage bonds at face value.
```

If the above bonds were sold directly to the investing public on a subscription basis, a bond subscription record similar to a stock subscription record might be maintained. In such case, accounts should be kept with Bond Subscriptions Receivable, Bonds Subscribed, and Bonds Payable to record the transactions arising from subscriptions, amounts received to apply on subscriptions, and issuance of the bonds. The transactions arising from the sale of the bonds on a subscription basis may be recorded in the general journal as illustrated at the top of the next page.

```
Bond Subscriptions Receivable..........................    200,000
    First Mortgage Bonds Subscribed.......................              200,000
        Received subscriptions to mortgage bonds at face value.
Bank........................................................    200,000
    Bond Subscriptions Receivable.........................              200,000
        Received remittances on bond subscription contracts.
First Mortgage Bonds Subscribed..........................    200,000
    First Mortgage Bonds Payable..........................              200,000
        Mortgage bonds issued to subscribers.
```

Bond subscription accounts are needed only when subscriptions are taken in advance of collections. When remittances are received at the time that the bonds are sold, there is no need for keeping subscription accounts.

Sale of Bonds at a Premium. When bonds are sold for an amount greater than their face value, the excess is credited to Premium on Bonds Payable. If the bonds referred to above were sold at 102,[1] the transaction would be recorded in the manner illustrated below.

```
Bank........................................................    204,000
    First Mortgage Bonds Payable..........................              200,000
    Premium on Bonds Payable..............................                4,000
        Sold mortgage bonds at 102.
```

Sale of Bonds at a Discount. When bonds are sold for an amount less than their face value, the difference between the face value and the amount received is debited to Discount on Bonds Payable. If the bonds in question were sold at 97, the transaction would be recorded as follows:

```
Bank........................................................    194,000
Discount on Bonds Payable...............................      6,000
    First Mortgage Bonds Payable..........................              200,000
        Sold mortgage bonds at 97.
```

It will be noted that the bonds payable account is credited for the face or maturity value of the bonds, regardless of the amount actually received upon their issuance.

Sale of Bonds Between Interest Dates. All of the preceding examples involved the sale of bonds on the very day interest began. The entries shown would have been equally correct if the bonds had been sold on any interest date. When bonds are sold between interest dates, the buyer must pay for the amount of interest that has accrued since the last interest date. Bond prices are quoted at certain amounts plus accrued interest. On the first regular interest date following his purchase, the interest that the buyer has purchased will be returned to him.

For example, suppose a corporation has a $100,000 issue of 6 percent bonds printed. The bonds are dated April 1, with interest coupons maturing semiannually. The first coupons mature October 1. Further suppose

---

[1]Bond prices are quoted on the basis of $100 per bond even though most bonds have larger denominations. A $1,000 bond selling at 102 would bring $1,020; if the price were 99½, it would bring $995.

that delays arise so that the bonds are not sold until May 1 following the issue date. Since five months later the purchasers will be able to cash their first coupons for six months' interest, they will have to pay the corporation for one month's interest accrued when the bonds are purchased. If the issue sold at 100 plus accrued interest, the total amount received would be $100,500. The sale would be recorded as follows:

May 1. Bank...	100,500	
First Mortgage Bonds Payable..........................		100,000
Bond Interest Expense...................................		500
Sold first mortgage bonds at 100 plus accrued interest, April 1–May 1.		

The additional amount received on May 1 because of the interest accrued since April 1 is recorded as a credit to Bond Interest Expense. By crediting this accrued interest to Bond Interest Expense, that account will show the amount of interest expense actually incurred, $2,500, when it is debited for the interest paid on the bonds on October 1 amounting to $3,000 ($3,000 − $500 = $2,500).

If coupon bonds were originally sold a considerable time after the issue was dated, all of the coupons that matured before the bonds were sold would be detached. Therefore, the purchasers of such bonds would be required to pay for the interest accrued since the last interest date only. Thus, if a $1,000 coupon bond dated July 1 were not sold until April 1 of the following year, the buyer would have to pay for interest accrued only from January 1 of the second year. The first interest coupon had matured on January 1 and would have been detached prior to the sale of the bond on April 1.

622

Report No. 24-1

Complete Report No. 24-1 in the workbook and submit your working papers for approval. Continue with the textbook discussion until Report No. 24-2 is required.

Accounting for bond interest expense

The interest on bonds may be payable at annual, semiannual, or quarterly intervals. Interest payment on a semiannual basis is the most common. The method used in recording bond interest expense is not necessarily affected by the kind of bonds issued; that is, the interest on registered bonds may be recorded in the same manner as the interest on coupon bonds. It is desirable to record bond interest expense separately from the interest on other obligations. The first semiannual interest payment on October 1 on the issue of 6 percent, first mortgage bonds, principal amount $100,000, dated April 1 (referred to on page 621), may be recorded in the general journal as follows:

```
Oct.  1. Bond Interest Expense....................................   3,000
             Bank..............................................           3,000
             Made semiannual payment of interest on 6% bonds out-
             standing.
```

At the close of each accounting period an adjusting entry should be made to record any interest accrued on bonds payable since the last interest payment date. For example, in the case of the bonds referred to above, as of December 31, three months' interest has accrued (October 1 to December 31). This amounts to $1,500.

It is therefore necessary to adjust the accounts as follows:

```
Dec. 31. Bond Interest Expense....................................   1,500
             Accrued Bond Interest Payable.........................           1,500
             Accrued bond interest.
```

After the posting is completed the bond interest expense account will have a debit balance of $4,000 and the account with Accrued Bond Interest Payable will have a credit balance of $1,500. The two accounts will appear as follows:

BOND INTEREST EXPENSE				ACCRUED BOND INTEREST PAYABLE		
Oct. 1	3,000	May 1	500		Dec. 31	1,500
Dec. 31	1,500					
	4,000	*4,500*				

The explanation of the May 1 credit of $500 in the bond interest expense account is that the issue was sold at 100 plus accrued interest (referred to on page 622). The balance of the account represents the total interest expense incurred from May 1 to December 31. The balance of the account with Accrued Bond Interest Payable represents the amount of the accrued liability on December 31.

623

Amortization of bond premium or discount

If bonds are sold either at a premium or at a discount, the amount of interest that actually is paid each year is not the correct interest expense for the year. The bond interest expense account must be adjusted for a pro rata share of the original premium or discount. This process is called *amortization* of the premium or discount. (Technically, premium is amortized, while discount is accumulated; but the term "amortization" often is used to describe the procedure in both cases.) Premium or discount can be amortized on a compound-interest basis. This method is the most accurate from a theoretical standpoint, but in most cases a simple straight-line method is satisfactory. Under the straight-line method, the total original discount or premium is divided by the number of months or years between the date on which the bonds were issued and the date on which they are to mature. The quotient is the amount of premium or discount to be written off each month or year.

For example, suppose that an issue of 7 percent, 10-year bonds with a value of $500,000 is sold at 104 on January 1 (the day interest begins). The entry recording this sale would include a credit to Premium on Bonds Payable in the amount of $20,000. Since the bonds mature in 10 years, one tenth of this premium would be written off each year by means of the following journal entry:

624

Dec. 31. Premium on Bonds Payable............................... 2,000
           Bond Interest Expense.................................. 2,000
           Amortization of premium on bonds for one year.

After recording the amount of the bond interest paid during the year and the amount accrued at the end of the year, the bond interest expense account will have a debit balance of $35,000, which is the contractual interest for the year. After posting the entry made to amortize one tenth of the premium on the bonds, the bond interest expense account will have a debit balance of $33,000 and the premium on bonds payable account will have a credit balance of $18,000, as follows:

BOND INTEREST EXPENSE				PREMIUM ON BONDS PAYABLE			
June 30	17,500	Dec. 31	2,000	Dec. 31	2,000	Jan. 1	20,000
Dec. 31	17,500					*18,000*	
	33,000 *35,000*						

The correct bond interest expense for the year is $33,000. That amount will be closed into the expense and revenue summary account and will be reported in the income statement for the year.

The justification for considering $33,000 to be the proper bond interest expense for each year is provided by the analysis shown at the top of the next page.

Face value of the bonds that the corporation must pay at maturity	$500,000
Total interest that must be paid ($35,000 a year for 10 years)	350,000
Total expenditures to be made with respect to both bonds and interest	$850,000
Less amount realized upon sale of bonds	520,000
Excess of total expenditures over total receipts	$330,000

$330,000 ÷ 10 years = $33,000.

To illustrate the amortization of discount on bonds, the following case is presented: 4½ percent, 20-year bonds with a face value of $200,000 are sold at 97 on October 1 (the day interest begins). The journal entry recording their sale would include a debit of $6,000 to Discount on Bonds Payable, as follows:

Oct. 1. Bank	194,000	
Discount on Bonds Payable	6,000	
Bonds Payable		200,000

Sold 4½%, 20-year bonds with face value of $200,000 at 97.

At the end of the first year, no interest would have been paid (since the bonds would have been outstanding for only three months), but an adjusting entry would be made debiting Bond Interest Expense and crediting Accrued Bond Interest Payable for $2,250 ($200,000 at 4½ percent for one-fourth year). The discount of $6,000 must be charged off to the bond interest expense account on a pro rata basis over the 20-year life of the bonds. This would amount to $300 a year. At the end of the first year, however, the bonds would have been outstanding for only three months, so that the amortization at the end of that year would be only $75. The journal entry to record this would be as follows:

625

Dec. 31. Bond Interest Expense	75	
Discount on Bonds Payable		75

Amortization of discount on bonds for three months.

After posting this entry, the bond interest expense account will have a debit balance of $2,325, representing the correct bond interest expense for the three months from October 1 to December 31; and the discount on bonds payable account will have a debit balance of $5,925, as illustrated.

BOND INTEREST EXPENSE				DISCOUNT ON BONDS PAYABLE			
Dec. 31	2,250			Oct. 1	6,000	Dec. 31	75
31	75			*5,925*			
	2,325						

The amount of the bond interest expense, $2,325, should be closed into the expense and revenue summary account and should be reported in the income statement for the year. For each of the remaining full years that the bonds are outstanding, the total bond interest expense will be $9,300. This can be calculated as follows:

Face value of the bonds that the corporation must pay at maturity	$200,000
Total interest that must be paid ($9,000 a year for 20 years)	180,000
Total expenditures to be made with respect to both bonds and interest	$380,000
Less amount realized upon sale of bonds	194,000
Excess of total expenditures over receipts	$186,000

$186,000 ÷ 20 years = $9,300.

Simple straight-line amortization of premium or discount is suitable only in cases where all of the bonds comprising the issue are issued on the same date and all mature on the same date. If all of the bonds of an issue are not outstanding for the same length of time, the amortization of any premium or discount must be in proportion to the total amount of bonds outstanding each year or fraction of a year.

The credit balance in the premium account or the debit balance in the discount account will be reduced year by year, until no balance is left on the date the bonds mature. Balance sheets prepared during the time the bonds are outstanding usually show unamortized bond discount as a deferred charge or unamortized bond premium as a deferred credit. Some accountants think that the amount of discount on bonds payable should be shown as a deduction from the face amount of bonds payable, or that the amount of premium on bonds payable should be shown as an addition to the face amount of bonds payable. Considerable logic supports this manner of handling, but it has not yet become widely accepted.

Deferred charges

There are certain expenditures that are expected to benefit a number of accounting periods. Supplies and certain prepaid items, such as prepaid insurance and prepaid interest, which will ordinarily be used up within the current operating cycle of a business, are generally treated as current assets. On the other hand, expenditures for services or benefits that are properly chargeable to a number of accounting periods should be capitalized (recorded in asset accounts) and the cost distributed over the periods benefited. The cost of issuing bonds, including any commissions paid to brokers, underwriting fees, or discounts, represents such an expenditure. Accounts of this type are usually classified as *deferred charges* and grouped together or itemized under the heading of deferred charges in the balance sheet. It is customary to list deferred charges last among the assets.

Deferred credits

Sometimes revenue is received or collected in advance of the period in which it is earned. Goods may be sold on installment terms and it may be considered desirable to distribute the profit over the periods in which the installment collections are received. When an issue of bonds is sold at a price greater than its maturity value, the premium should be distributed over the life of the bonds. Accounts of this type are usually classified as *deferred credits* and grouped together or itemized under the heading of deferred credits in the balance sheet. It is customary to list deferred credits last among the liabilities.

Report No. 24-2

Complete Report No. 24-2 in the workbook and submit your working papers for approval. Continue with the textbook discussion until Report No. 24-3 is required.

Accounting for bonds retired

Usually bonds issued by a corporation are redeemed at face value at their maturity. By that date the entire amount of any issuance premium or discount should have been written off. To record the redemption, Bonds Payable is debited and Bank is credited. The retired bonds usually are marked "Canceled" and are stored away until they are checked over by the company auditors; after that the bonds are destroyed.

Corporations may redeem part or all of a bond issue before maturity. In some cases a corporation may compel the bondholders to surrender their bonds by taking advantage of an option to call the bonds before they mature. Unless the terms of the issue include such an option, however, this procedure is not possible. Without such an option, a corporation can purchase its bonds only if it has the money and if the holders of the bonds are willing to sell.

Redemption of bonds originally sold at face value

Usually there is either a gain or a loss involved in the redemption of bonds before their maturity date. If the bonds were originally sold at face value and the corporation pays more than this when the bonds are redeemed, there is a loss. For example, suppose a corporation sells a $100,000 issue of bonds at face value. Some years later, but prior to the date of

627

maturity, $10,000 of the issue is redeemed on an interest date at 103. The bonds were sold originally for $10,000 and were redeemed for $10,300; therefore, the corporation sustained a loss of $300. The journal entry to record this transaction would be as follows:

```
Bonds Payable.........................................    10,000
Loss on Bonds Redeemed...............................       300
    Bank.............................................            10,300
        Redeemed bonds with face value of $10,000 at 103.
```

If bonds that originally were sold at face value are redeemed for a lesser amount, a gain results. If, in the preceding case, the price paid had been 97 instead of 103, there would have been a gain of $300. In this case the journal entry to record the transaction would be as follows:

```
Bonds Payable.........................................    10,000
    Bank.............................................             9,700
    Gain on Bonds Redeemed...........................              300
        Redeemed bonds with face value of $10,000 at 97.
```

Redemption of bonds
originally sold at a premium

628

If a corporation redeems part or all of its bonds that originally were sold at a premium, the calculation of the gain or the loss involved must take into account the premium amortization from the date of issue to the date of redemption. For example, suppose that an issue of 20-year bonds with a face value of $100,000 had been sold at 104. Eight years later the corporation redeems $10,000 of the issue at a price of 103. If this redemption were made at the end of the accounting period, the amortization of the premium on the bonds would be up-to-date. If the redemption were made at some other time, it would be necessary to record the amortization of the premium on the bonds for the time elapsed since the last regular premium write-off entry had been made. The proper amount should be debited to the premium account and credited to the bond interest expense account — the same accounts that are involved in the regular periodic premium-amortization entry.

After any needed entry is made to bring the amortization of the premium on the bonds redeemed up-to-date, the *unamortized premium* pertaining to these bonds would be $240. (These bonds were sold for $10,400 eight years before. Eight twentieths, or $160, of the $400 premium would have been written off, leaving $240 unamortized.) The adjusted issue price of these bonds is, thus, $10,240. Their redemption for $10,300 is a loss of $60. The journal entry to record this transaction would be:

```
Bonds Payable.........................................    10,000
Premium on Bonds Payable.............................       240
Loss on Bonds Redeemed...............................        60
    Bank.............................................            10,300
        Redeemed bonds with face value of $10,000 at 103.
```

Note that this entry writes off the portion of the balance in the premium account that relates to the bonds that are being retired. When the bonds themselves are taken out of the accounts, any unamortized premium that relates to such bonds must also be removed. The remaining balance of the premium account represents the unamortized premium on the bonds still outstanding.

The treatment of the premium would be the same no matter what price was paid when the bonds were redeemed. If these bonds had been redeemed at a price of 102 instead of 103, a gain of $40 would have resulted. The journal entry in this case would be as follows:

Bonds Payable...	10,000	
Premium on Bonds Payable...............................	240	
Bank...		10,200
Gain on Bonds Redeemed...............................		40
Redeemed bonds with face value of $10,000 at 102.		

Redemption of bonds originally sold at a discount

If a corporation redeems part or all of its bonds that originally were sold at a discount, the calculation of the gain or the loss involved must take into account the discount amortization from the date of issue to the date of redemption. For example, suppose that an issue of 20-year bonds with a face value of $100,000 had been sold at 97. Fifteen years later the corporation redeems $10,000 of the issue at a price of 99. Before recording the redemption, the amortization of the discount on the bonds must be brought up to the date of redemption. If the date of redemption was at the end of the accounting period, the amortization would be up-to-date. If this was not the case, the amount of discount amortization since the last regular discount write-off would have to be calculated and recorded. This amount would be debited to the bond interest expense account and credited to the discount account — the same accounts that are involved in the regular periodic discount-amortization entry.

After any needed entry is made to bring the amortization of the discount on the bonds being redeemed up-to-date, the *unamortized discount* pertaining to these bonds would be $75. (These bonds were sold for $9,700 fifteen years before. Fifteen twentieths, or $225, of the $300 discount would have been written off, leaving $75 unamortized.) The adjusted issue price of these bonds is, thus, $9,925. Their redemption for $9,900 results in a gain of $25. The journal entry to record this transaction is as follows:

Bonds Payable...	10,000	
Bank...		9,900
Discount on Bonds Payable...............................		75
Gain on Bonds Redeemed...............................		25
Redeemed bonds with a face value of $10,000 at 99.		

Note that this entry writes off the portion of the balance in the discount account that relates to the bonds that are being retired. When the bonds themselves are taken out of the accounts, any unamortized discount that relates to such bonds must also be removed. The remaining balance of the discount account represents the unamortized discount on the bonds still outstanding.

If these bonds had been redeemed at a price of 101 instead of 99, a loss of $175 would have resulted. The journal entry in this case would be as follows:

Bonds Payable..	10,000	
Loss on Bonds Redeemed.................................	175	
Bank...		10,100
Discount on Bonds Payable..............................		75
Redeemed bonds with a face value of $10,000 at 101.		

In all of the preceding discussion, it was assumed that the bonds were redeemed on an interest date. Presumably the interest on all of the bonds being redeemed had been paid in the usual manner. If the bonds had been redeemed between interest dates, the price in each case would have included accrued interest. The entry in each case would have included a debit to the bond interest expense account for the amount of the interest accrued, and the credit to Bank would have been correspondingly larger. As previously stated, with respect to the bonds being redeemed, a special adjustment is needed to record the amortization of premium or discount for the time elapsed since the date of the last regular write-off entry. Thus, the correct interest expense on these bonds for whatever portion of the year they were outstanding would be included in the bond interest expense account.

Bond sinking funds

In years past a variety of practices have been followed in connection with the redemption of (or the accumulation of money to redeem) corporation term bonds. In some instances, money has been set aside and invested over a period of years to provide the amount needed to redeem an issue of bonds at its maturity. These accumulations have been described as *sinking funds* or *bond retirement funds*. Sometimes the funds have been established voluntarily; more often they have been the result of requirements in bond agreements (indentures). Such requirements usually have provided that the trustee for a bond issue shall receive the money and administer the fund. In some instances, the corporation has been required to make appropriations of retained earnings equal to the specified additions to the fund.

Present practices in regard to bond sinking funds tend to differ in purpose and operation from those described in the preceding paragraph.

630

At the present time, the usual purpose of sinking funds is to provide what is termed "price support" for the bond issue. The bond indenture may require that the corporation must pay to the trustee each year a stated percentage (often 1–2 percent) of the largest amount of bonds of the issue ever outstanding. The trustee, in turn, must use the money either to purchase some of the bonds in the market or, if necessary, to acquire them by the exercise of a special "sinking fund call" provision of the indenture. In some cases, the corporation can meet the requirements by purchasing the necessary amounts of bonds and delivering them (rather than the money) to the trustee. The fact that either the trustee or the corporation periodically is buying a few bonds will both "support the market" and give greater security to the bonds that remain outstanding. These results are advantageous to the holders of the outstanding bonds.

The entries to record sinking fund transactions of this type can be very simple. If cash is paid to the trustee, all that is required is a debit to Sinking Fund and a credit to Bank. When the trustee subsequently reports the amount of bonds redeemed and the price paid, an entry to record the redemption is made. This entry will be the same as one of those described on pages 627–630 except that the credit for the amount spent is to Sinking Fund rather than to Bank. If the corporation itself redeems the bonds, the entry needed will be identical with one of those already described.

Where cash is paid to the trustee, it is probable that the amount remitted to him by the corporation and the amount he subsequently expends may not be exactly the same. (The corporation might be obligated to pay $20,000 a year, but the trustee may be able to purchase bonds with a face value of $20,000 at a price less than 100.) Any balance in the sinking fund account represents an asset and should be reported in the corporation's balance sheet.

By the date of maturity of the issue, some of the bonds already will have been redeemed. Little or no money may be in the sinking fund at this time, but probably no accumulation was intended in connection with this feature of the bond issue. The money to redeem the remaining bonds will have to be provided by other means — possibly by the sale of a new issue of bonds, by the sale of stock, or by using cash accumulated for this purpose.

Application of principles

To illustrate further the accounting for bonds issued, bond interest expense (including premium amortization), and the redemption of bonds at maturity, as well as the operation of a sinking fund of the type described, the following example is presented: The Wilcox Manufacturing Corporation issued first mortgage, 10-year, 6 percent bonds, principal amount

$500,000. Interest was payable January 1 and July 1. The bond indenture provided that the Corporation was to pay to the trustee (a bank) $10,000 by December 15 of each (except the tenth) year, the money to constitute a sinking fund to be used to purchase bonds which subsequently would be canceled.

Narrative of Transactions and Events

First Year

Jan. 2. The entire issue of bonds, principal amount $500,000, was sold at a price of 101.

July 1. Semiannual interest of $15,000 was paid.

Dec. 14. Payment to trustee, $10,000.
     31. Accrued interest on bonds, $15,000.
         Premium to be amortized, $500.

Second Year

Jan. 2. Semiannual interest of $15,000 was paid.
     23. Trustee reported that on January 16 he purchased bonds with a face value of $10,000 for $9,900 plus $25 accrued interest for fifteen days (to January 16).

July 1. Semiannual interest of $14,700 was paid.

Dec. 13. Payment to trustee, $10,000.
     31. Accrued interest on bonds, $14,700.
         Premium to be amortized, $490.

Tenth Year

> (Note: No bonds were retired during the first year; bonds in the principal amount of $10,000 were retired each year for the next eight years. As of January 1 of this (tenth) year, the balance of the bonds payable account was $420,000; of the premium on bonds payable account, $420; of the accrued bond interest payable account, $12,600; and of the sinking fund account, $10,391.40.)

Jan. 2. Semiannual interest of $12,600 was paid.
      8. Trustee reported that on January 6 he purchased bonds with a face value of $10,000 for $10,025 plus $8.33 interest for five days (to January 6).

July 1. Semiannual interest of $12,300 was paid.

Dec. 28. A check for $409,641.93 was given to the trustee. (This, together with the $358.07 left in the sinking fund — January 1 balance, $10,391.40 less January 8 credit of $10,033.33 — provides the amount needed to redeem the bonds at maturity a few days later.)
     31. Accrued interest on bonds, $12,300.
         Premium to be amortized, $410.

Eleventh Year

Jan. 2. Semiannual interest of $12,300 was paid.
     20. Trustee reported that all bonds had been redeemed.

The entries to record these transactions and events are recorded in the general journal entries on pages 633 and 634.

First Year

Jan. 2. Bank.. 505,000.00
   First Mortgage Bonds Payable.......................   500,000.00
   Premium on Bonds Payable..........................   5,000.00
   Sold ten-year, 6% bonds with face value of $500,000
   at 101.

July 1. Bond Interest Expense............................... 15,000.00
   Bank..   15,000.00
   Paid semiannual interest on bonds.

Dec. 14. Bond Sinking Fund................................. 10,000.00
   Bank..   10,000.00
   Payment to trustee for sinking fund.

  31. Bond Interest Expense............................... 15,000.00
   Accrued Bond Interest Payable.....................   15,000.00
   Six months' interest accrued on bonds payable.

  31. Premium on Bonds Payable.......................... 500.00
   Bond Interest Expense.............................   500.00
   Amortization of premium on bonds.

Second Year

Jan. 1. Accrued Bond Interest Payable...................... 15,000.00
   Bond Interest Expense.............................   15,000.00
   Reversing entry for accrued bond interest.

   2. Bond Interest Expense............................... 15,000.00
   Bank..   15,000.00
   Paid semiannual interest on bonds.

  23. First Mortgage Bonds Payable....................... 10,000.00
   Premium on Bonds Payable.......................... 90.00
   Bond Interest Expense............................. 25.00
   Bond Sinking Fund.................................   9,925.00
   Gain on Bonds Redeemed...........................   190.00
   Bonds redeemed by sinking fund trustee.

   (Note: As of January 1 of the second year, the bonds
   redeemed had an adjusted issue price of $10,090 [$10,000 +
   90% of the original premium of $100]. The amortization
   of the premium on these bonds for the few days to January 16 was ignored since the amount was so small. Accordingly, the gain on the redemption was $190 [$10,090 −
   $9,900].)

July 1. Bond Interest Expense............................... 14,700.00
   Bank..   14,700.00
   Paid semiannual interest on bonds.

   (Note: The interest for this six months' period relates
   to bonds with a face value of $490,000.)

Dec. 13. Bond Sinking Fund................................. 10,000.00
   Bank..   10,000.00
   Payment to trustee for sinking fund.

  31. Bond Interest Expense............................... 14,700.00
   Accrued Bond Interest Payable.....................   14,700.00
   Six months' interest accrued on bonds payable.

  31. Premium on Bonds Payable.......................... 490.00
   Bond Interest Expense.............................   490.00
   Amortization of premium on bonds.

   (Note: The amortization for the current year of 10% of
   the $4,900 premium that originally related to the $490,000
   of bonds outstanding for this year.)

Tenth Year

Jan. 1. Accrued Bond Interest Payable...................... 12,600.00
   Bond Interest Expense.............................   12,600.00
   Reversing entry for accrued bond interest.

633

2. Bond Interest Expense.............................	12,600.00	
Bank...		12,600.00
Paid semiannual interest on bonds.		
8. First Mortgage Bonds Payable........................	10,000.00	
Premium on Bonds Payable..........................	10.00	
Bond Interest Expense.............................	8.33	
Loss on Bonds Redeemed...........................	15.00	
Bond Sinking Fund...............................		10,033.33
Bonds redeemed by sinking fund trustee.		

        (Note: The bonds redeemed had an adjusted issue price of $10,010 as of January 1 of the tenth year [$10,000 plus 10% of the original premium of $100]. The amortization of premium on these bonds for the few days to January 6 was ignored since the amount was so small. Accordingly, the loss on redemption was $15 [$10,025 − $10,010].)

July 1. Bond Interest Expense.............................	12,300.00	
Bank...		12,300.00
Paid semiannual interest on bonds.		

        (Note: The interest for this six months' period relates to bonds with a face value of $410,000.)

Dec. 28. Bond Sinking Fund................................	409,641.93	
Bank...		409,641.93
Payment to trustee for bond redemption.		
31. Bond Interest Expense.............................	12,300.00	
Accrued Bond Interest Payable.....................		12,300.00
Six months' interest accrued on bonds payable.		
31. Premium on Bonds Payable..........................	410.00	
Bond Interest Expense.............................		410.00
Amortization of premium on bonds.		

        (Note: The amortization for the tenth year is 10% of the $4,100 premium that originally related to the $410,000 of bonds that have been outstanding for the full year.)

Eleventh Year

Jan. 1. Accrued Bond Interest Payable......................	12,300.00	
Bond Interest Expense.............................		12,300.00
Reversing entry for accrued bond interest.		
2. Bond Interest Expense.............................	12,300.00	
Bank...		12,300.00
Paid semiannual interest on bonds.		
20. First Mortgage Bonds Payable........................	410,000.00	
Bond Sinking Fund...............................		410,000.00
Payment of first mortgage bonds at maturity by trustee.		

634

Report No. 24-3

    Complete Report No. 24-3 in the workbook and submit your working papers for approval. Continue with the following study assignment in Chapter 25 until Report No. 25-1 is required.

chapter 25

accounting for investments and intangible long-lived assets

The term "investment" can be used in a very broad sense to include any expenditure made in the expectation or hope of gain. In a narrower sense, investment relates to an expenditure made in the expectation of gain in which the risk of loss is not extreme. If there is a great risk, the term "speculation" is applied. However, the distinction between investment and speculation is not sharp.

In a general sense, every asset acquired and every expense incurred by a business is an investment, since the business is being operated for gain or profit. However, when the term investment is used to refer to the asset acquired (rather than to the act of acquiring it), the word frequently is taken to mean a revenue-producing asset of a type unrelated to the major activity of the business. Just as an individual may own stocks, bonds, and savings accounts which are unrelated to his occupation or profession, so business partnerships and corporations may own such properties. While under certain circumstances a wide variety of assets would be entitled to be considered as investments, corporation stocks and bonds of numerous types are major examples. The following discussion is limited to the accounting for these latter types of investments.

Corporation stock investments

If a corporation purchases shares of capital stock in another corporation, the transaction may be recorded by debiting an investment account entitled Corporation Stocks and by crediting Bank for the amount paid for the stock. If desired, a separate account may be kept for each company's stock purchased. For example, if the corporation should purchase common stock of the General Motors Corporation, the accountant might open a separate account for the stock under the title of General Motors Corporation Common Stock. If money also was invested in the common stock of the U.S. Steel Corporation, there could be an additional account for that stock under the title of U.S. Steel Corporation Common Stock. The usual plan, however, is to keep only a summary account entitled Corporation Stocks for all capital stock purchased for investment purposes. Such a summary account should be debited at the time of purchase for the cost price of capital stock bought, and should be credited at the time of sale for the cost price of capital stock sold. If the stock is sold at a gain, the gain may be recorded by crediting a separate account entitled Gain on Corporation Stocks. If the stock is sold at a loss, the loss may be recorded by debiting an account entitled Loss on Corporation Stocks.

If The Munson Company, Inc., purchased 100 shares of the common stock of the Alba Chemical Co. through a broker at a total cost of $9,420 and paid cash for it, the transaction would have been recorded as indicated by the following journal entry:

Corporation Stocks......................................	9,420.00	
Bank..		9,420.00
Purchased 100 shares of Alba Chemical Co. common stock.		

If a dividend amounting to $1.50 per share was received while the stock was owned, the transaction would have been recorded as indicated by the following journal entry:

Bank..	150.00	
Dividends Received....................................		150.00
Dividend received on 100 shares of Alba Chemical Co. common stock.		

If the stock was subsequently sold and the net proceeds of the sale amounted to $9,650, the transaction would have been recorded as indicated by the following journal entry:

Bank..	9,650.00	
Corporation Stocks....................................		9,420.00
Gain on Corporation Stocks............................		230.00
Sold 100 shares of Alba Chemical Co. common stock.		

The receipt of a stock dividend is ordinarily not considered to be revenue and no entry other than a notation in the stock investment account is required. For example, suppose that The Munson Company, Inc., owned

100 shares of the common stock of the Lawton Manufacturing Corporation that had cost a total of $4,800 ($48 per share). Some months after the stock was purchased, the Lawton Manufacturing Corporation distributed a 20 percent common stock dividend. When the certificate for 20 additional shares was received, a notation of the receipt was made in the record of the Lawton Manufacturing Corporation investment. The acquisition of the additional shares did affect the cost basis of each share of stock. After this acquisition, the $4,800 that had applied to the original 100 shares then related to the 120 shares. Each share was assigned $40 ($4,800 ÷ 120 shares). In the event that some of the 120 shares are sold, any gain or loss will be determined by comparing the amount received with the cost basis of $40 per share times the number of shares sold.

Bond investments

The borrowing of money by means of the issuance of bonds by governments of all types (federal, state, and local) and by business corporations is a widespread practice. Bonds are popular forms of investment because (1) nearly all bonds promise to pay interest periodically as well as the principal amount at maturity, (2) many bonds are secured by the mortgage of certain property or, in the case of government bonds, by taxing power, and (3) a bondholder is a creditor, not an owner. When a bond is purchased (either upon original issuance or subsequently from another bondholder) the nature of the entry made to record the purchase depends upon whether the price paid includes any payment for accrued interest. For example, assume that a particular bond has a maturity value of $1,000, promises interest at 6 percent payable semiannually on January 1 and July 1, and matures on January 1, 1985. If this bond were purchased on January 1 or July 1, the previous owner would have collected interest to that date. If the price paid (including any broker's commission) was $1,015, the purchase would be recorded as indicated by the following journal entry:

Bond Investments......................................	1,015.00	
Bank...		1,015.00
Purchased a $1,000 bond.		

Suppose, instead, that the same bond had been purchased on either April 1 or October 1. In such event, interest amounting to $15 would have accrued since the last interest date (January 1 or July 1). The cost of the bond would be $15 larger to include accrued interest. If the total amount paid (including any broker's commission) was $1,030, the purchase would be recorded as indicated by the following journal entry:

Bond Investments......................................	1,015.00	
Interest Earned..	15.00	
Bank		1,030.00
Purchased a $1,000 bond.		

637

The $15 was charged to Interest Earned to facilitate the recording of the regular interest collection three months later. At that time $30 will be collected (6 months' interest on $1,000 at 6 percent per year). This collection of interest will be recorded by a debit to Bank and a credit to Interest Earned. The difference between the $15 debit to Interest Earned when the bond was purchased and the $30 credit to the account when six months' interest was collected is the amount ($15) of interest earned for the three months that the bond has been owned.

Bond Interest Earned. Nearly all bonds promise to pay interest at a specified rate. The interest is usually paid semiannually, generally on either the first or fifteenth day of each of two months that are six months apart (January and July, March and September, etc.).

As mentioned in Chapter 24, sometimes bonds are issued with coupons attached. A twenty-year, $5,000, 6 percent bond that pays interest semi-annually would be issued with 40 coupons, each promising to pay the bearer $150. Each coupon would show the date due: the first would be due six months from the date of the bond; the second, six months later. As each coupon becomes due, the owner of the bond detaches the coupon and sends it to the designated fiscal agent (often a bank) for collection. Frequently, the bondholder's own bank will "cash" the coupon. Bonds that do not carry coupons have to be "registered" with the government agency or with the corporation that issued the bond, and checks for interest are mailed to the registered owners as the amounts become due.

Whatever the mechanics of payment, the receipt of bond interest should be recorded by a debit to Bank and a credit to Interest Earned.

If the bondholder's records are being kept on a full accrual basis (and such is not always the case), an adjusting entry should be made at the end of the fiscal period to record any accrued bond interest earned. Assume, for example, that a $10,000, 5½ percent bond that pays interest on April 15 and October 15 is owned. From October 15 to December 31 is 2½ months. Interest at the rate of 5½ percent for 2½ months on $10,000 amounts to $114.58. The following journal entry should be made as of December 31:

Accrued Interest Receivable................................	114.58	
Interest Earned...		114.58
Bond interest accrued to December 31.		

This entry should be reversed as of January 1 of the next year.

Premium and Discount on Bond Investments. If a bond paying a contractual rate of interest of 5 percent is available for purchase, but a potential buyer can get other bonds of comparable quality that pay 6 percent, the 5 percent bond will not be purchased unless it can be acquired at a price that will give the buyer the equivalent of a 6 percent return when the bond is held to maturity. In other words, the 5 percent bond would sell at a *discount* — something less than the face or maturity value of the bond. (The exact amount of the discount would depend upon the number of years until the bond matures.) The situation might be just the reverse: the "going market rate" for a certain class of bonds might be 5½ percent and a particular bond might have a contractual rate of interest of 5¾ percent. In this case the bond would sell at a *premium* — something more than the bond's face or maturity value.

When a bond is purchased, its cost — whether more or less than face value — should be debited to the bond investment account. If the purchaser of the bond does not expect to keep it until maturity (which might be many years distant), nothing is done about any premium or discount that was involved when the bond was acquired. Stated differently, bonds held as *temporary investments* usually are carried in the accounts at original cost. If, however, the purchaser of a bond regards it as a *long-term investment* and expects to hold it to maturity, it is good accounting practice to periodically write off or *amortize* any premium or discount over the life of the bond investment.

The periodic amortization of any premium is treated as a reduction of bond interest earned; the periodic amortization of any discount is regarded as additional bond interest earned.

For example, suppose that a $1,000, 7 percent bond is purchased on January 1, 1972, for $1,096. The bond matures exactly eight years later. **639** The purchase was recorded by debiting Bond Investments and by crediting Bank for $1,096. On July 1, the collection of $35 interest was recorded by a debit to Cash and a credit to Interest Earned for $35. On December 31, an entry was made to record the $35 interest that had accrued since July 1. At this point, Interest Earned had a credit balance of $70 ($35 + $35).

Since the owner of the bond expects to hold it until maturity when he will get $96 less than the bond cost, it is proper to amortize (write off) the $96 over the eight years. This can be done on a compound-interest basis, but the simpler, straight-line method is satisfactory in many cases. $96 divided by 8 is $12 per year. Accordingly, the following adjusting entry should be made as of the end of each of the eight years:

Interest Earned..	12.00	
Bond Investments.....................................		12.00
Amortization of bond premium.		

When this entry is posted, the balance of the interest earned account is reduced to $58 ($70 − $12). The "book value" of the bond is reduced $12 each year. By the end of the eighth year, the book value will be $1,000, which is the amount that will be received when the bond is redeemed.

The logic of considering that the actual interest earned each year is $58, rather than $70, is explained by the calculation illustrated at the top of the next page.

Total amount to be received from ownership of bond:
Interest ($70 a year for 8 years)..................................... $ 560
Upon redemption.. 1,000

Total.. $1,560
Cost of bonds... 1,096

Excess of receipts over cost..................................... $ 464

$464 divided by 8 = $58 per year.

For federal income tax purposes, a taxpayer may amortize premiums on bonds owned. If interest on the bonds is tax exempt, any premium must be amortized.

Assume that the bond in the foregoing example ($1,000, 7 percent, due 8 years from purchase date on January 1, 1972) had been bought for $932. Thus, the discount was $68 ($1,000 − $932). $68 divided by 8 is $8.50 per year. The journal entry to record the amortization of the discount at the end of each year should be as follows:

Bond Investments....................................... 8.50
Interest Earned..   8.50
Amortization of bond discount.

This entry adds $8.50 to the $70 already in the interest earned account after the $35 interest receipt on July 1 and the $35 accrual as of December 31 are recorded. If $8.50 is added each year to the bond investments account, the book value of the bond will be $1,000 on the day before it is redeemable for that amount.

640

The logic of considering that the actual interest earned each year is $78.50, rather than $70, is explained by the following calculation:

Total amount to be received from ownership of bond:
Interest ($70 a year for 8 years)..................................... $ 560
Upon redemption.. 1,000

Total.. $1,560
Cost of bond.. 932

Excess of receipts over cost..................................... $ 628

$628 divided by 8 = $78.50 per year.

For federal income tax purposes, discount need not be amortized. Upon redemption, the difference between cost and maturity value is treated either as a capital gain or as ordinary income, depending on how long the bonds have been held.

Sale or Redemption of Bonds. When a bond is sold before maturity, it is probable that gain or loss will be realized. Suppose that a bond purchased a few months before at a cost of $5,265.50 is sold on an interest date for $5,337 (net after broker's commission). The journal entry to record the sale should be as follows:

Bank.. 5,337.00
Bond Investments....................................... 5,265.50
Gain on Sale of Bonds................................... 71.50
Sold bond.

If the bond had been sold sometime later and the amount received was $42.87 greater because of interest accrued, the journal entry to record the sale should be as follows:

Bank	5,379.87	
Bond Investments.....................................		5,265.50
Interest Earned..		42.87
Gain on Sale of Bonds.................................		71.50
Sold bond.		

When a bond is sold, its book value must be removed from the bond investments account. Book value may be original cost (as in the foregoing illustration), or it may be either original cost plus amortization of part of any discount, or minus amortization of part of any premium. For example, suppose that a $20,000 bond had been purchased three years ago for $20,220.34. At the date of purchase, the bond had 11½ years to go until maturity. Since the buyer originally intended to hold the bond until maturity, the accountant had been amortizing the premium at the rate of $19.16 for each full year ($20,220.34 − $20,000.00 = $220.34. $220.34 ÷ 11½ = $19.16). After three years, a total of $57.48 (3 × $19.16) would have been subtracted from the bond investment account making the book value of the bond $20,162.86 ($20,220.34 − $57.48). If the bond was sold for a net of $19,825.23, including $13.48 interest accrued, the loss on the sale of the bond would be $351.11. The journal entry to record the sale should be as follows:

Bank...	19,825.23	
Loss on Sale of Bonds..................................	351.11	
Bond Investments.....................................		20,162.86
Interest Earned..		13.48
Sold bond.		

If a bond is held to maturity and any premium or discount has been amortized, the entry to record the bond redemption is a debit to Bank and a credit to Bond Investments for the maturity value (which will be the book value). No gain or loss will be involved.

If a bond was purchased at a premium and the premium has *not* been amortized, the redemption at maturity will involve a loss equal to the amount of the premium. If a bond was purchased at a discount and the discount has *not* been amortized, the redemption at maturity will involve a gain equal to the amount of the discount.

Record of stocks and bonds

When investments in securities, such as bonds and capital stock, are sufficiently numerous to justify keeping a detailed record of them, special forms similar to the one reproduced on page 642 may be used for this purpose. Such record forms are produced by the leading manufacturers of

RECORD OF STOCKS AND BONDS

NAME U. S. Treasury Bond

DESCRIPTION #40019K

DATE OF ISSUE June 15, 1969 DATE OF MATURITY June 15, 1989 INTEREST OR DIVIDEND 4½ % PAYABLE J & D SEMI-ANNUALLY ✓

DENOMINATION $5,000.00

DATE	OF WHOM PURCHASED	DATE	SOLD TO	CERT. NO. OR BOND NO.	MATURITY	PAR VALUE	PRICE PAID	TOTAL COST	SOLD FOR	INTEREST OR DIVS. EARNED	LOSS OR GAIN
1969 June 15	Subscription			40019K	6/15/89	5,000	5,000	5,000.00			

Record of Stocks and Bonds

business forms. The forms are so designed that all necessary information may be recorded on them conveniently. A separate sheet should be used for keeping a record of each bond and of each stock certificate owned. A description of the bond or stock certificate, together with information regarding its purchase and sale, may be recorded on the front of the form as shown in the illustration. The back of the form is ruled to provide for recording interest or dividends received during the period of ownership.

This type of record is usually regarded as an auxiliary or memorandum record, and the information recorded on it is supplementary to the information recorded in the regular books of account.

Temporary investments v. long-term investments

It is not unusual for businesses to find that they have accumulated more cash than is needed for the financing of current operations. Often this surplus of cash is a temporary matter. In a few weeks or months, the money will be needed again for regular operations. Rather than merely maintaining a large bank balance, it is desirable to use the money to produce some revenue — even if a comparatively small amount. The otherwise-idle money may be invested in something likely to yield a return and also likely to be salable with little risk of loss whenever the money is needed. Investments in the form of "high grade" stocks or bonds (including *notes* or *bills* of the federal government) often are favored. Generally, securities that are actively traded on an organized exchange are preferred. If it is intended that the investment will be held for only a short time, it is called a "temporary" investment. Temporary investments are regarded as current assets and are so reported in the balance sheet — usually immediately following cash.

If there is no immediate prospect of liquidating investments, they are considered to be "long term." It was mentioned earlier that if long-term investments include bonds, it is customary to amortize any premium or discount that was involved when the bonds were purchased. Long-term investments are reported in the balance sheet following the current assets — often under the caption "Investments." Corporations sometimes maintain special funds such as bond sinking funds (for the retirement of their own bonds) and pension funds. The amounts in these funds usually are included in the investments category.

Investment earnings in the income statement

Investment (temporary or long-term) *earnings* should be reported near the bottom of the income statement following net income (or loss) from operations. Such nonoperating earnings are usually captioned "Other Revenue." Gains arising from the *disposition* of investments are similarly captioned; losses are shown as "Other Expenses."

Accounting for intangible long-lived assets

In an accounting sense, the term *intangible* has come to have a very restricted meaning. The word itself is broad enough to include all types of assets that lack physical substance. Amounts on deposit in a bank, receivables of all types, prepaid insurance, and securities are all assets that have no physical substance. The fact that some of these assets are evidenced by documents or certificates of various types does not make the properties tangible. However, none of these assets is included in the category of intangibles as the term is used in accounting. Instead, the term is used to refer to a limited group of certain valuable legal or economic rights that a firm may acquire. All of the items classified as intangibles have the common characteristic of being of comparatively long duration; they usually are considered to be long-lived assets. Major examples of intangibles include patents, copyrights, leases, leasehold improvements, franchises, trademarks, and goodwill.

Patents. A *patent* is a grant by the federal government to an inventor giving him the exclusive right to produce and sell his invention for a period of seventeen years. A firm may acquire a patent by original grant or by purchase from a prior patent owner. If a patentable invention is developed in the operation of a business, the cost associated with the patent may be either very nominal or a considerable amount depending upon various circumstances. A manufacturing company that carries on regular research activities may treat the costs of such activities as current expenses. If patents are secured on any resulting inventions, the cost of the patents is considered to include only the fees paid to the government and probably also certain fees paid to patent attorneys whose services were used. In many cases these fees are considered to be ordinary expenses of the period in which they were incurred. The patents may become very valuable, but under these circumstances they are not treated as assets in the records.

In other cases a record may be kept of all of the costs and expenses connected with a certain research project. These costs, together with any legal fees, are treated as costs of the patent that is obtained. An asset account, Patents, is charged with the total of these costs.

In many cases patents are acquired by purchase and their cost is debited to Patents. If numerous patents are owned, a subsidiary or supplementary record showing the nature, life, and cost of each one may be maintained.

Since the life of a patent is specifically limited, any cost assigned to it should be allocated over no more than the number of years that the patent right will exist. The greatest number of years would be seventeen if the firm acquired the patent at the time of its original issuance. If a patent that has already run five years has been acquired, its cost should be apportioned over a period of twelve years. In many cases, however, it is expected that the effective or economic life of a patent may be something less than its legal life. In this event, the cost should be allocated over the expected useful or economic life.

If the cost of a patent is to be written off on a straight-line basis, the charge-off each year is determined by dividing the cost of the patent right by its expected life. Suppose, for example, that a patent with thirteen years to run is purchased at a cost of $6,000. Further suppose that the buyer expects that the effective life of the patent will be only ten years. In that event, $600 ($6,000 ÷ 10) would be charged as expense for each of the ten years. The $600 is called the periodic amortization of the cost. The adjusting journal entry to record the amortization for a year would be as follows:

Patent Amortization...	600.00	
Patents...		600.00
Amortization of patent.		

Sometimes an account entitled Patent Expense is debited for the amount written off. On rare occasions the credit is to an account entitled Accumulated Amortization — Patents. The latter account is identical in nature to an accumulated depreciation account. In most cases, however, the credit is made directly to the asset account rather than to a contra account. This is not consistent with the accounting for depreciation of most tangible long-lived assets. Depreciation write-offs are almost always credited to an accumulated depreciation account.

Patent amortization is usually treated as a manufacturing expense. Since patents are assets, their unamortized cost should be reported in the balance sheet as an intangible long-lived asset.

Copyrights. A *copyright* is similar in many respects to a patent. It consists of a federal grant of the exclusive right to the reproduction and sale of a literary, artistic, or musical composition. A copyright is granted for 28 years with the privilege to renew it for another 28 years. The cost of obtaining a copyright in the first place is very nominal and would be treated as an ordinary and incidental expense by the one who secures it. However, if an existing copyright is purchased, the cost might be large enough and the expected future value sufficient to warrant charging the cost to an asset account titled Copyrights. If a number of copyrights are owned, a suitable subsidiary or supplementary record may be maintained.

It would be a rare case in which it was expected that a copyright would have an economic life as long as its legal life (56 years at the most). In most cases the cost of a copyright is written off in a very few years. The write-off can be on a straight-line basis or in the proportion of the actual sales of the copyrighted article during the period to the total expected sales of the article. The amount of the write-off for each period, however calculated, is debited to Copyright Amortization (or Copyright Expense) and credited to Copyrights. The expense should be reported in the income statement and any unamortized portion of the cost of copyrights should be reported in the balance sheet as an intangible long-lived asset.

Leases. A *lease* is a contract in which the owner of certain property (commonly real estate) agrees to let another party use it for a certain length of time in return for specified regular payments, usually monthly rental payments. In most cases the original lessee (the party who will use the property) acquires a lease at no cost apart from the monthly rental payments that must be made as the property is used. Such payments are treated as ordinary expenses when paid.

Most leases are transferable. Any one of several circumstances may cause a long-term lease to become valuable. Thus, it may happen that the original lessee can sell his rights under a lease to another party. The buyer acquires an asset with a life that can be measured exactly. For example,

645

suppose that a business buys what is left of a twenty-year lease on a certain store ten years after the lease has started. The lease may call for monthly rental payments of $300. However, the buyer considers the location to be so desirable that he is willing to pay more than that. Assume that he buys the lease (which has 10 years to run) for $18,000. He may record the purchase by a debit of $18,000 to the account Leasehold and a credit to Bank.

If the lease had exactly 10 years, or 120 months, to run, the cost would be allocated over this length of time. The cost, $18,000, divided by 10 years is $1,800 a year, or $150 a month. An adjustment would be made either monthly or annually to amortize the proper amount. If the adjustment were made at the end of each month, the entry in the general journal would be as follows:

Rent Expense...	150.00	
Leasehold...		150.00
Amortization of leasehold.		

The debit was made to the rent expense account since the recorded cost of the lease was really the same thing as prepaid rent. The rent expense account would already have been debited for the $300 cash rent paid to the owner of the property at the start of the month. However, the real rent expense to the tenant is $450 each month — $300 cash rent plus 1/120 of the $18,000 cost of the 120-month lease. Some accountants might prefer to debit the $150 to an account titled Amortization of Leasehold rather than Rent Expense but, in most cases, this serves no useful purpose.

The unamortized portion of the cost of the lease should be reported in the balance sheet as an intangible long-lived asset.

Leasehold Improvements. The party using property under a long-term lease may decide that it is to his interest to incur costs to improve the property. In most cases whatever is left of any improvements or additions will belong to the owner of the property at the termination of the lease. In the records of the lessee, the cost of any long-lived improvements is charged to an account titled Leasehold Improvements. This cost will be written off as expense over the number of years that it is expected to benefit the lessee. If the benefit from the improvements is expected to be exhausted before the lease expires, the cost is amortized over the expected economic life of the improvements. If, however, it is expected that the benefit from the improvements will extend beyond the life of the lease, then the cost of the improvements is written off over the remaining period of the lease.

Suppose, for example, that three years after taking over the lease on the store mentioned previously, the lessee spends $2,800 restyling the front of the store and installing various modern features. Let it be assumed that these improvements are expected to benefit the property for fifteen to twenty years. However, they will become a permanent part of the store and the lessee's right to use the property will end in ten years. Thus, the cost of the improvements would be amortized over a ten-year period. The adjusting journal entry, in general journal form, at the end of each year would be as follows:

```
Amortization of Leasehold Improvements ......................  280.00
  Leasehold Improvements .................................           280.00
      Annual amortization of leasehold improvements.
```

Amortization of Leasehold Improvements is an expense similar to depreciation and should be so reported in the operating section of the income statement. The unamortized portion of the cost of leasehold improvements should be reported in the balance sheet as an intangible long-lived asset. It may be noted that leasehold improvements usually have physical substance but, since they become a part of property owned by someone else, they are not considered to be a tangible asset of the lessee.

The original lessee of property might have leasehold-improvement cost to account for, even though he had incurred no cost for the lease itself other than the regular monthly rental payments.

Franchises. A *franchise* is a grant of certain rights or privileges for a specified time, an indefinite time, or forever. In many cases franchises are granted to businesses by governments. Examples of governmental franchises include the right to operate buses or other public vehicles on city streets and the monopoly right to operate a power company or a telephone company. Business organizations sometimes enter into contracts that are called franchises. A manufacturer, for example, may give a franchise to a certain dealer that gives the latter the exclusive right to sell the manufacturer's product in a specified geographic area. A franchise of this type is often called a *dealership*.

Quite often there is no cost to the party who originally secures a franchise right. However, if the right becomes valuable and its terms allow it to be transferred, a subsequent buyer of the franchise will have some cost to account for. The cost of a purchased franchise should be debited to a franchise account. Whether this cost should be written off and, if so, how fast, depends upon various circumstances. If the franchise has a specified term with no renewal option, the cost should be written off over a period no longer than the specified term. The period of the write-off might be less than the legal life if there were reason to think that the economic value would disappear before the right legally ended. Even if there is no reason to think that the value of an indefinite or perpetual franchise is diminishing, many accountants on grounds of conservatism favor amortizing the cost.

The amortization adjustment at the end of each period would be similar to that made for other intangibles. In this case the debit might be to an expense account titled Amortization of Franchise and the credit should be to the franchise account. The amount of the expense should be reported in

647

the income statement and the unamortized portion of the franchise cost should be reported in the balance sheet as an intangible long-lived asset.

Trademarks. The manufacturer or seller of a product frequently wishes to identify his merchandise in some unique fashion. The practice of using *trademarks* or trade names is widespread. The federal government offers legal protection to such designations by permitting them to be registered with the United States Patent Office. As long as the trademark or trade name is continuously used, the courts will protect the owner of a registered trademark by preventing others from using it, or by assessing damages against those who infringe upon such rights.

The person or firm who originally registers a trademark may have incurred little or no cost in its creation or, by contrast, may have incurred sizable cost in its development. Since trademarks and trade names can be sold, a buyer will have some cost to account for. Inasmuch as a trademark or trade name does not expire as long as it is used, the question arises as to whether any of the cost of such an asset should be amortized and, if so, over what period of time. The future value of a trademark or trade name is highly uncertain. Conservatism suggests that any cost incurred should be written off within a few years of its incurrence.

The periodic adjusting entry to record the amortization involves a debit to Amortization of Trademarks (or Trade Names) and a credit to Trademarks (or Trade Names). The amount written off should be reported as a nonoperating expense in the income statement. The federal income tax law does not permit a deduction of the amortization of trademarks and trade names. Any unamortized portion of the cost of trademarks or trade names should be reported in the balance sheet as an intangible long-lived asset.

Goodwill. Goodwill is usually defined as the value of excess earning capacity. Just exactly what is meant by "excess" and how to calculate such value is difficult. Usually, goodwill is not recorded as an asset unless it has been purchased. In that case its amount is known or can be determined.

Goodwill cannot be purchased by itself. It may arise in connection with such transactions as the admission of a new partner into a partnership (see Chapter 16) and the purchase of all of the assets of one business by another. If the price paid for the assets of the business that is "selling out" is larger than the reasonable value of the identifiable assets being purchased, the excess is regarded as the amount paid for the goodwill of the acquired business.

For example, suppose that James Goodsell, who owns and has been successfully operating the Goodsell Supply Company, decides to sell his business. The officers of the Olson Corporation want to buy Goodsell's business and merge it with their own business. The corporation's officers

648

inspect the assets of the Goodsell Supply Company and decide that the property has the following values:

Accounts receivable	$ 27,500
Merchandise inventory	18,600
Furniture and fixtures	15,900
Land	10,000
Building	55,000
Total	$127,000

Mr. Goodsell will pay all of the liabilities of the business and withdraw any cash that is left. He agrees that the values placed on the assets are fair, but refuses to sell unless he receives $150,000. If the Olson Corporation decides to buy at this price, it will be paying $23,000 ($150,000 − $127,000) for the goodwill that relates to Mr. Goodsell's business. Obviously the buyer would not pay the price asked unless he thought he was getting something of value. In this example, the directors of the Olson Corporation may feel that $23,000 is not too much to pay for the business contacts, patronage, and prestige that Mr. Goodsell has built up. If the offer is accepted and the price of $150,000 is paid in cash, the entry to record the transaction in the general journal would be as follows:

Accounts Receivable	27,500.00	
Merchandise Inventory	18,600.00	
Furniture and Fixtures	15,900.00	
Land	10,000.00	
Building	55,000.00	
Goodwill	23,000.00	
Bank		150,000.00
Purchased the assets of the Goodsell Supply Co.		

649

If goodwill has been purchased and charged to an asset account, the question arises as to whether it should be written off and, if so, how fast. Goodwill has no legal life; its economic life is uncertain. Since a logical basis for amortizing the cost of goodwill is lacking, conservatism dictates that it should be written off in a very few years. If it were decided that the goodwill purchased by the Olson Corporation was to be written off over five years, the adjusting journal entry at the end of each of these years would be as follows:

Amortization of Goodwill	4,600.00	
Goodwill		4,600.00
Amortization of goodwill.		

If the write-off were made in this form, the amortized portion should be reported in the income statement as a nonoperating expense. Amortization of goodwill is not deductible for federal income tax purposes. The unamortized portion of goodwill should be reported in the balance sheet as an intangible long-lived asset.

Other Intangibles. The intangible assets that have been discussed are the major examples of this type of property. Other examples include organization costs (necessary costs incurred in launching an enterprise), secret processes, and subscription lists. The usual practice is to amortize the costs of such property within a few years after its acquisition.

Under the federal income tax law, organization cost is allowed as a deduction provided it is charged off over a period of not less than sixty months, beginning with the month in which the corporation begins business. The amount written off each year is usually recorded by debiting Amortization of Organization Cost and by crediting Organization Cost.

A common practice in regard to many intangibles is to write off all of their cost except for $1 as soon as possible. The $1 is carried in the accounts and reported in the balance sheet indefinitely. This serves to call the attention of the readers of the balance sheet to the existence of such assets and the fact that the company has followed the conservative practice of amortizing their cost. To find "Patents, Trademarks, and Goodwill . . . $1" listed among the assets in the balance sheet of a hundred-million dollar corporation is not unusual.

Report No. 25-1

Complete Report No. 25-1 in the workbook and submit your working papers to the instructor for approval. Then continue with the following study assignment in Chapter 26 until Report No. 26-1 is required.

chapters 21-25

practical accounting problems

The following problems supplement those in Reports 21-1 through 25-1 in the Part 3 Workbook. Each problem is numbered to indicate the chapter of the textbook with which it correlates. Loose-leaf stationery should be used in solving these problems.

Problem 21-A

Diversified Industries is a corporation, organized under the laws of Missouri, with an authorized capital of $500,000 divided into 5,000 shares of common stock, par value $100 a share. The company uses a standard form of stockholders ledger. Following is a list of selected stock transactions:

Mar. 1. Issued Stock Certificate No. 34 for 120 shares of common stock to Wallace J. Dunham, 2000 S. 20th St., Kansas City, Missouri. This stock is fully paid and nonassessable.

April 3. Issued Stock Certificate No. 38 for 80 shares of common stock to Mrs. Donald Barnes, Route 3, Chesterfield, Missouri.

June 15. Mrs. Barnes surrendered Certificate No. 38 for 80 shares of common stock and requested that 50 shares be transferred to Mr. Dunham. Issued Certificate No. 41 for 50 shares to Mr. Dunham and Certificate No. 42 for 30 shares to Mrs. Barnes.

Chapters 21-25 / Practical Accounting Problems

Sept. 1. Mr. Dunham surrendered Certificate No. 34 for 120 shares and Certificate No. 41 for 50 shares and requested that 150 shares be transferred to Albert Tecklin, 1206 West 20th Street, Joplin, Missouri. Issued Certificate No. 43 for 150 shares to Mr. Tecklin and Certificate No. 44 for 20 shares to Mr. Dunham.

REQUIRED: Open accounts in the stockholders ledger for Mr. Dunham, Mrs. Barnes, and Mr. Tecklin, and record the foregoing transactions directly in the accounts.

Problem 21-B

Diversified Industries, referred to in the preceding problem, uses a standard stock transfer record to enter all transfers of its capital stock. This record is kept by the secretary of the company. Following is a narrative of stock transfers for the month of December:

Dec. 2. Robert J. Messey, 2315 Florida Street, Ocala, Florida, surrendered Certificate No. 31 for 60 shares of common stock and requested that it be transferred to George Marifian, 8446 Bayside, St. Petersburg, Florida. Issued Certificate No. 51 for 60 shares to Mr. Marifian.

5. Leonard R. Hayes, 1835 Speedway Avenue, Indianapolis, Indiana, surrendered Certificate No. 36 for 44 shares and requested that 22 shares of the stock be transferred to H. L. Williamson, 811 Indiana Avenue, Muncie, Indiana. Issued Certificate No. 52 for 22 shares to Mr. Williamson and Certificate No. 53 for 22 shares to Mr. Hayes.

15. Mr. Marifian surrendered Certificate No. 51 for 60 shares and requested that it be transferred to his daughter, Miss Jo Ann Marifian, 8446 Bayside, St. Petersburg, Florida. Issued Certificate No. 54 for 60 shares to Miss Marifian.

21. L. Vinson Freeman, 2214 Center Street, Golden, Colorado, surrendered Certificate No. 37 for 160 shares and requested that 60 shares be transferred to the First National Bank, Golden, Colorado. Issued Certificate No. 55 for 60 shares to the First National Bank and Certificate No. 56 for 100 shares to Mr. Freeman.

REQUIRED: (1) Record the foregoing transactions in the stock transfer record of Diversified Industries. (2) Open the necessary accounts in the stockholders ledger and post the entries from the transfer record to the stockholders ledger. In opening the stockholders accounts, record the following balances as of December 1:

First National Bank..................................... 0 shares
L. Vinson Freeman.....................................160 shares
Leonard R. Hayes....................................... 44 shares
George Marifian..120 shares
Jo Ann Marifian....................................... 0 shares
Robert J. Messey...................................... 60 shares
H. L. Williamson...................................... 28 shares

(3) After posting the stock transfers for December, prepare a list of the stockholders showing the number of shares held by each as of December 31.

Problem 22-A

R. E. Burlew and J. G. Hoffman were partners. They decided to incorporate their business. On January 2, the company was incorporated under the name of The Burhoff Company. The authorized capital was $2,000,000, divided into 200,000 shares of common stock, par value $10 each.

Burlew and Hoffman decided to transfer all of the assets except cash and all of the liabilities of the partnership to the corporation in exchange for 164,000 shares of stock at par. The corporation was to accept the assets and the liabilities at their net book value in each case. Burlew and Hoffman divided the cash of the partnership and the stock of the corporation in the ratio of their capital interests in the partnership.

The balance sheet of the partnership on December 31 appeared as follows:

BURLEW AND HOFFMAN
Balance Sheet
December 31, 19 --

Assets			Liabilities		
Cash.................	$	40,000	Notes payable.................	$	400,000
Accounts receivable....		600,000	Accounts payable.............		160,000
Materials inventory....		400,000	Total liabilities.................	$	560,000
Machinery & equip.....	$480,000				
Less accumd. deprec..	80,000	400,000	Owners' Equity		
Buildings.............	$800,000				
Less accumd. deprec..	160,000	640,000	R. E. Burlew, capital.............		1,008,000
Land.................		160,000	J. G. Hoffman, capital		672,000
Total assets..........		$2,240,000	Total liabilities and owners' equity.		$2,240,000

653

REQUIRED: **(1)** Prepare an entry in general journal form to record the acquisition of the partnership assets and liabilities in exchange for stock. **(2)** Calculate the number of shares of stock each partner received.

Problem 22-B

The Apex Manufacturing Co. was organized under the laws of Illinois with authority to issue 8,000 shares of preferred stock, par value $100 a share, and 20,000 shares of common stock with no par value.

Feb. 1. Subscriptions for capital stock, collectible on demand, were accepted as follows:
4,000 shares of preferred stock at par
7,000 shares of common stock at $50 a share

Mar. 1. Cash was received from subscribers in full for their subscriptions accepted February 1 and stock certificates were issued to all subscribers.

July 3. Issued Certificate No. 31 for 400 shares of common stock to Donald C. Kutz in payment for land valued at $20,000 to be used as a site for a new factory.

Oct. 2. Donald C. Kutz sold 200 shares of the common stock owned by him to C. W. Mattox and requested that the transfer be made on the records of the company. Certificate No. 31 for 400 shares was canceled and Certificates Nos. 32 and 33 were issued to Mr. Kutz and Mr. Mattox respectively for 200 shares each.

REQUIRED: Record the foregoing corporate transactions in the general journal of The Apex Manufacturing Co.

Problem 22-C

The Queen City Manufacturing Co. was incorporated on January 3 with the authority to issue 2,000 shares of preferred stock with a par value of $100 per share and 40,000 shares of common stock with a par value of $10 per share.

Jan. 4. All of the common stock was issued to the founders of the corporation in exchange for patents valued at $400,000.

5. The common stockholders donated 8,000 shares to the corporation to be sold to raise working capital.

26. All of the donated shares were sold for cash at $12 per share.

Feb. 8. Eight hundred shares of the preferred stock were exchanged for machinery and equipment valued at $88,000.

Dec. 31. The expense and revenue summary account will have a credit balance of $75,000 after the revenue and expense accounts are closed into it.

REQUIRED: Prepare the entries in general journal form to record the foregoing transactions and to close the expense and revenue summary account to Retained Earnings.

Problem 23-A

The following information was taken from an annual report, dated June 30, 19B, of Inter-Action, Inc., a corporation engaged in business as a magazine publisher:

Balance of retained earnings at beginning of period, July 1, 19A, $18,312,731.
Net income for the year ended June 30, 19B, $6,740,441.
Appropriation for contingencies, $650,000.
Cash dividends paid during the year on common stock, $2,535,000.

REQUIRED: From the foregoing information, prepare a statement of retained earnings showing the balance of retained earnings at the end of the period.

Problem 23-B

The Cherokee Oil Co. was incorporated with an authorized issue of 2,000 shares of 6% preferred stock, par value $100 a share, and 4,000 shares of common stock without par value. At the time of the annual meeting of the board of directors on July 1, all of the preferred stock had been issued and was outstanding, and 2,000 shares of the common stock had been issued at a price of $10 a share, the entire selling price having been credited to the common stock account. The balance sheet of the company showed that it had retained earnings amounting to $64,000.

After declaring a cash dividend (No. 31) of 6% on the preferred stock outstanding, the board declared a dividend (No. 27) on the common stock, payable in cash at the rate of $1 a share and in unissued common stock at the rate of one share for each 10 shares of common stock held. The cash dividends declared on the preferred stock and on the common stock are payable August 1 to stockholders of record July 25, and the stock dividend is to be distributed on September 1 to stockholders of record August 25. The cash dividends are paid by drawing an individual check against the regular checking account of the corporation in The Petroleum National Bank for the amount due each stockholder. The market value of the common stock is $15.50 per share.

REQUIRED: As the accountant for The Cherokee Oil Co., record the declaration of the cash dividends and the stock dividend, the payment of the cash dividends, and the distribution of the stock dividend.

Problem 24-A

July 1. Pierson Brothers, Inc. received $495,000, representing the proceeds from the sale of $500,000 of 5½% first mortgage bonds. The issue matures 25 years from this date. Interest is payable semiannually on January 1 and July 1.

Dec. 31. Bond interest accrued to December 31 is to be recorded.

31. The proper amount of bond discount is to be amortized.

31. The bond interest expense account is to be closed into Expense and Revenue Summary.

Jan. 1. Reverse the adjusting entry for bond interest expense accrued December 31.

REQUIRED: (1) Prepare the entries in general journal form to record the foregoing. (2) Show calculations to prove that the balance of the bond interest expense account (before closing) is the proper interest expense for the first year.

Problem 24-B

As of December 31, 19--, certain accounts in the general ledger of the Jameson Manufacturing Corporation had the following balances:

Bonds payable...	$164,000
Premium on Bonds Payable....................................	2,460
Accrued Interest on Bonds Payable...........................	4,100
Bond Sinking Fund..	4,000

The foregoing accounts relate to an issue of bonds that has been outstanding for ten years (less one day). Originally, bonds with a face value of $200,000 were sold at a price of 103. Interest at the rate of 5% per year is payable semiannually on January 1 and July 1. The bonds mature 20 years after the date of original issue. Under the terms of the bond indenture, the corporation must pay to the trustee (a bank) $4,000 by December 15 of each year. The trustee must use the money to redeem, by purchase in the open market or by exercising a call provision, bonds with a face value of $4,000. This has been done for nine years ($36,000 of the bonds have been redeemed and canceled). The trustee has not yet reported on the disposition of the $4,000 paid in two weeks' earlier.

The proper premium-amortization entry has been made in each of the ten years that bonds have been outstanding.

Early the next year, the following events occurred:

Jan. 1. Semiannual interest was paid, $4,100.
10. The trustee reported that on January 5 four $1,000 bonds were purchased at a price of 98 plus accrued interest of $2.22 — a total of $3,922.22.

REQUIRED: Prepare the entries in general journal form to record (1) the reversal of the interest expense accrual as of January 1, (2) the payment of the semiannual interest expense, and (3) the sinking fund transaction.

656

Problem 24-C

W. S. Watson had been operating The Watson Manufacturing Co. as a sole proprietor. He decided to form a new company which was to be incorporated under the name of The Superior Manufacturing Co. The corporation took over The Watson Manufacturing Co. acquiring all the assets, except cash, and assuming the existing liabilities. Mr. Watson was allowed a price equal to the worth of The Watson Manufacturing Co. (after deducting cash), with no allowance for goodwill or other assets.

The Superior Manufacturing Co. was incorporated January 1, with an authorized capital stock of $10,000,000, consisting of 20,000 shares of 7% cumulative preferred stock, par value $100 a share, and 80,000 shares of common stock, par value $100 a share.

Following is a summary of the operations of the corporation for the year ending December 31, after incorporation:

(a) Subscriptions to the capital stock were as follows:

W. S. Watson — 12,000 shares common and 10,000 shares preferred stock
J. P. Busch — 6,000 shares common and 2,000 shares preferred stock
R. J. Brooks — 2,000 shares preferred stock
A. G. McGraw — 12,000 shares common stock
Evelyn West — 5,000 shares common and 3,000 shares preferred stock
Mary Blasberg — 6,000 shares common and 3,000 shares preferred stock
M. M. Perkins — 12,000 shares common stock
R. B. Johnson — 13,000 shares common stock

The stock was subscribed for at par, remittance to be made upon demand. Certificates of stock are not to be issued until subscriptions are remitted in full.

(b) A firm of certified public accountants was engaged to audit the books of The Watson Manufacturing Co. and to prepare a balance sheet showing the amount of Mr. Watson's equity in the business. The accountants submitted the following balance sheet which reveals an equity of $5,342,000:

THE WATSON MANUFACTURING CO.
Balance Sheet
December 31, 19 --

Assets			Liabilities		
Cash..............		$ 138,660	Notes payable, bank.	$1,180,000	
Notes receivable..... $	48,680		Notes payable, trade.	114,000	
Accounts receivable..	196,362		Accounts payable....	832,688	
	$ 245,042		Total liabilities.......		$2,126,688
Less allow. for bad debts.........	17,850	227,192			
Merchandise inventory.		446,516			
Furniture & fixtures... $	17,952		**Owner's Equity**		
Less accumd. deprec.	1,632	16,320	W. S. Watson, capital		5,342,000
Machinery, tools, and equipment........	$2,712,000				
Less accumd. deprec.	452,000	2,260,000			
Buildings...........		3,380,000			
Land.............		1,000,000	Total liabilities and		
Total assets........		$7,468,688	owner's equity.....		$7,468,688

After deducting cash, Mr. Watson's equity amounted to $5,203,340. In view of the fact that Mr. Watson decided to purchase bonds to be issued by the corporation, it was agreed that any amount due him, after crediting his subscription account with the amount he owes the corporation on account of subscriptions to common and preferred stock, would be credited to his personal account until the details of the bond issue could be completed. Stock certificates were issued to Mr. Watson immediately.

(c) A. G. McGraw and M. M. Perkins paid their subscriptions to the capital stock by conveying to the company title to patents valued at $2,400,000. Stock certificates were issued.

(d) Following the organization of The Superior Manufacturing Co., it was decided to issue bonds as follows (maturity value, $1,000 each):

First mortgage bonds, 5%, 20 years, $1,240,000.
Second mortgage bonds, 6%, 15 years, $1,196,000.
Debenture bonds, 5%, 10 years, $706,000.
W. S. Watson purchased the entire bond issue at par, thereby canceling his account against the company, and paid the difference, $138,660, in cash.

(e) Upon demand, the following subscribers to the capital stock remitted their subscriptions in full in cash and stock certificates were issued:

J. P. Busch...	$ 800,000
R. J. Brooks...	200,000
Evelyn West...	800,000
Mary Blasberg...	900,000
R. B. Johnson...	1,300,000

REQUIRED: Record the foregoing transactions in general journal form.

Problem 25-A

Truesdell Fur Co., a manufacturer of fur garments, occasionally invests surplus cash in corporation bonds and stocks. Following is a narrative of such transactions that were completed during the current year:

Feb. 1. Issued a check for $5,200 in payment of 100 shares of Anaconda Copper Co. common stock purchased at $52 a share, including the broker's commission.

      15. Issued a check for $942.50 in payment of a $1,000, 6% Ford Motor Corporation bond, including broker's commission and $7.50 accrued interest. Interest is payable January 1 and July 1.

Apr. 3. Purchased a $1,000, 5% Sylvania Electric Co. bond for $1,000 on the interest date, including broker's commission.

May 15. Issued a check for $1,050 in payment of a $1,000 Columbus Electric Co. 6% bond due in 1980, including the broker's commission (no interest accrued).

July 3. Received a check for $30 for the semiannual interest on the bond purchased February 15, above.

      3. Redeemed a $1,000, 4% Westinghouse Electric Co. bond that matured July 1. Original cost $940. (Assume that it is a ten-year bond, and make the last discount amortization entry, as well as the entry for the cash receipt of one-half year's interest *before* making the entry for the redemption.)

Oct. 2. Cashed a $25 coupon on a $1,000, 5% Sylvania Electric Co. bond due yesterday.

Nov. 15. Received a check for $30 for the semiannual interest on a $1,000, 6%, bond of the Columbus Electric Co.

Dec. 15. Received a check for $250 as a dividend of $2.50 a share on 100 shares of common stock of the Anaconda Copper Co.

REQUIRED: Record the foregoing transactions on a sheet of two-column general journal paper and foot the amount columns to prove the equality of the debits and credits.

Problem 25-B

Rath Packing Co. owns a $20,000 Consolidated Utilities Co. bond which was purchased at a premium several years ago. The bond pays interest at the annual rate of 5% in semiannual installments on April 1 and October 1. If the premium is to be fully amortized by the date the bond matures, $49.92 must be written off each year. The Rath Co. keeps its records on a calendar-year basis.

REQUIRED: Prepare the general journal entries, as of December 31, to:

(a) Record the interest accrued on the bond at the end of the year.

(b) Record the amortization of premium for the year.

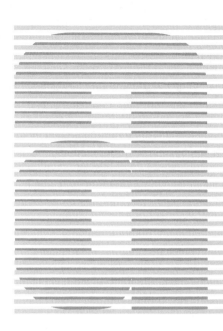

chapter 26

accounting for branch operations

In an effort to sell more goods or services and thus to increase its profits, a business organization sometimes establishes one or more branches. The term *branch* covers a variety of different arrangements. Sometimes such units have many of the characteristics of complete and independent businesses. A branch may have its own bank account, receivables, merchandise inventory, long-lived assets, and various liabilities. The manager of a branch may have wide authority in the management of all phases of his unit's operations. In other cases, a branch may be nothing more than a sales office. The branch manager may confine his activities to soliciting orders for goods that will be shipped from the main plant or home office. He may not have the authority to bind the company in any but sales contracts.

The size of a branch, the nature of its operations, and various other factors will determine what type of records it will keep. In some cases, the branch keeps no permanent formal records. Daily or weekly summaries of branch activities are sent to the home office where all formal records are maintained. The branch may have a revolving cash fund to use in making such disbursements as are not made by the home office. This fund may be accounted for and reimbursed periodically by the home office in a manner similar to the procedure followed in the case of petty cash funds. In other cases, the branch may maintain a complete set of records of its operations. From an accounting standpoint the branch may be a separate entity, keeping its own books of original entry and at least a general ledger, and preparing its own periodic financial statements.

Reciprocal accounts and recording procedure

When formal records are kept at a branch office, it is common practice to follow a procedure that causes the general ledger of the branch and the general ledger of the home office to be *interlocking* or *reciprocal* to each other. In the ledger of the home office there is an account entitled "Branch Office." This account has a debit balance and shows the amount for which the branch must account. In the ledger of the branch there is an account entitled "Home Office." This account has a credit balance that shows the amount for which the branch is accountable to the home office. The balances of these two accounts are equal, but opposite; the debit balance in the one account offsets the credit balance in the other account. The two accounts are reciprocal. The relationship is illustrated by the following diagram:

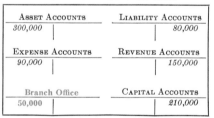

BRANCH LEDGER		HOME OFFICE LEDGER	
ASSET ACCOUNTS	LIABILITY ACCOUNTS	ASSET ACCOUNTS	LIABILITY ACCOUNTS
60,000	5,000	300,000	80,000
EXPENSE ACCOUNTS	REVENUE ACCOUNTS	EXPENSE ACCOUNTS	REVENUE ACCOUNTS
20,000	25,000	90,000	150,000
	Home Office	Branch Office	CAPITAL ACCOUNTS
	50,000	50,000	210,000

Transactions between the home office and the branch require entries in both ledgers, and involve the reciprocal accounts. If, for example, the home office remits $5,000 to the branch, the entry in the home office ledger is a debit to Branch Office and a credit to Bank. In the branch ledger, Bank is debited and Home Office is credited. At the end of the period the branch adjusts its accounts and closes the revenue and the expense accounts into Expense and Revenue Summary. The balance of Expense and Revenue Summary is closed to Home Office, a debit indicating a loss or a credit indicating a profit. When the branch income statement reaches the home office, the home office accountant makes an entry debiting Branch Office and crediting Branch Profit if there was a profit, or debiting Branch Loss and crediting Branch Office if there was a loss.

If the business is engaged in selling merchandise, there probably will be another pair of reciprocal accounts: *Shipments to Branch* in the home office ledger and *Shipments from Home Office* in the branch ledger. When the home office sends goods to the branch, the home office accountant debits Branch Office and credits Shipments to Branch. The branch accountant records the receipt of the goods by a debit to Shipments from Home Office and a credit to Home Office. If the branch gets all of its merchandise from the home office, the shipments from home office account replaces a purchases account in the branch records. It must be understood, however, that branches sometimes purchase goods from outsiders, and in such cases they may have a purchases account in addition to, or in place of, a shipments from home office account.

Branch accounting procedure

In most respects the usual accounting procedures are followed by both the home office and the branch. Each uses books of original entry, each has its general ledger, and each may have as many subsidiary ledgers as circumstances warrant. It has been indicated that the peculiarities of branch accounting arise in connection with transactions or events that affect both home office and branch office accounts (the reciprocal accounts that have been described). The following example is presented to illustrate branch accounting procedure. In each instance, the transaction or event is given first, followed by the entries (all in general journal form) that should be made in the books of the branch and in the books of the home office. It will be observed that each transaction is recorded simultaneously in the books of both the home office and the branch office without regard to dates; whereas in actual practice there usually would be some lapse of time between the dates on which the transactions are recorded in the books of each office.

(1) On January 1, the general ledger accounts of The Barton Sales Co. had the balances as shown below:

Bank.	$ 20,000	
Accounts Receivable.	32,000	
Allowance for Bad Debts.		$ 700
Merchandise Inventory.	28,000	
Prepaid Insurance.	640	
Furniture and Fixtures.	8,000	
Accumulated Depreciation — Furniture and Fixtures.		3,400
Building.	60,000	
Accumulated Depreciation — Building.		28,000
Land.	7,000	
Accounts Payable.		31,000
Capital Stock.		50,000
Retained Earnings.		42,540
	$155,640	$155,640

On January 2, the corporation established a branch in the town of Redfield and turned over to the manager of the branch $8,000 in cash, furniture and fixtures that had just been purchased at a cost of $2,000, and merchandise that cost $7,000. (The long-lived assets used at a branch can be recorded either in the branch ledger or in the home office ledger. In this illustration the long-lived assets used at the branch are recorded in the branch ledger.)

BRANCH OFFICE BOOKS:			HOME OFFICE BOOKS:		
Bank.................	8,000		Branch Office..........	17,000	
Furniture and Fixtures..	2,000		Bank................		8,000
Ship. from Home Office	7,000		Furniture and Fixtures		2,000
Home Office........		17,000	Shipments to Branch..		7,000

(2) The branch manager purchased for cash additional furniture and fixtures for $5,000, paid $400 rent on the branch store, and paid a premium of $180 on a three-year fire insurance policy.

BRANCH OFFICE BOOKS:			HOME OFFICE BOOKS:
Furniture and Fixtures..	5,000		No entry.
Operating Expenses[1]....	400		
Prepaid Insurance.......	180		
Bank..............		5,580	

(3) The home office purchased goods on account for $95,000 and incurred operating expenses in the amount of $32,000.

662

BRANCH OFFICE BOOKS:	HOME OFFICE BOOKS:		
No entry.	Purchases.............	95,000	
	Operating Expenses.....	32,000	
	Accounts Payable.......		127,000

(4) The home office shipped goods costing $45,000 to the branch.

BRANCH OFFICE BOOKS:			HOME OFFICE BOOKS:		
Ship. from Home Office.	45,000		Branch Office..........	45,000	
Home Office........		45,000	Shipments to Branch.		45,000

(5) During the year the branch had cash sales of $5,200 and sales on account of $48,000.

BRANCH OFFICE BOOKS:			HOME OFFICE BOOKS:
Bank.................	5,200		No entry.
Accounts Receivable....	48,000		
Sales..............		53,200	

(6) During the year the home office had cash sales of $22,000 and sales on account of $105,000.

BRANCH OFFICE BOOKS:	HOME OFFICE BOOKS:		
No entry.	Bank.................	22,000	
	Accounts Receivable....	105,000	
	Sales..............		127,000

---

[1]For the sake of brevity in this example, all expenses are charged to the single account, Operating Expenses.

(7) The branch incurred additional operating expenses during the year (rent, wages, light, telephone, advertising, etc.) in the amount of $18,700. Total payments were $16,500.

BRANCH OFFICE BOOKS:			HOME OFFICE BOOKS:
Operating Expenses.....	18,700		No entry.
Accounts Payable.....		18,700	
Accounts Payable.......	16,500		
Bank..............		16,500	

(8) Cash collections on the branch accounts receivable were $26,000.

BRANCH OFFICE BOOKS:			HOME OFFICE BOOKS:
Bank..............	26,000		No entry.
Accounts Receivable..		26,000	

(9) Cash collections on the home office accounts receivable were $86,000, and accounts having balances in the amount of $500 were determined to be worthless.

BRANCH OFFICE BOOKS:	HOME OFFICE BOOKS:		
No entry.	Bank..............	86,000	
	Allow. for Bad Debts....	500	
	Accounts Receivable..		86,500

(10) Home office payments to creditors were $102,000.

BRANCH OFFICE BOOKS:	HOME OFFICE BOOKS:		
No entry.	Accounts Payable.......	102,000	
	Bank..............		102,000

663

(11) The branch office borrowed $5,000 at its bank giving a 90-day note at 6½ percent interest.

BRANCH OFFICE BOOKS:			HOME OFFICE BOOKS:
Bank..............	5,000		No entry.
Notes Payable........		5,000	

(12) The branch returned to the home office for credit, goods costing $400.

BRANCH OFFICE BOOKS:			HOME OFFICE BOOKS:		
Home Office..........	400		Shipments to Branch....	400	
Ship. from Home Office		400	Branch Office........		400

(13) Branch accepted notes from customers in temporary settlement of their accounts, $4,000.

BRANCH OFFICE BOOKS:			HOME OFFICE BOOKS:
Notes Receivable.......	4,000		No entry.
Accounts Receivable..		4,000	

(14) Home office accepted notes from customers in temporary settlement of their accounts, $6,500.

BRANCH OFFICE BOOKS:	HOME OFFICE BOOKS:	
No entry.	Notes Receivable.......	6,500
	Accounts Receivable..	6,500

After posting the foregoing transactions, the branch office accounts appeared as shown in the following "T" accounts:

BRANCH OFFICE ACCOUNTS

BANK

(1)	8,000	(2)	5,580
(5)	5,200	(7)	16,500
(8)	26,000		22,080
(11)	5,000		
22,120	44,200		

NOTES PAYABLE

	(11)	5,000

ACCOUNTS PAYABLE

(7)	16,500	(7)	18,700
		2,200	

NOTES RECEIVABLE

(13)	4,000

HOME OFFICE

(12)	400	(1)	17,000
		(4)	45,000
	61,600	62,000	

ACCOUNTS RECEIVABLE

(5)	48,000	(8)	26,000
18,000		(13)	4,000
		30,000	

SALES

	(5)	53,200

PREPAID INSURANCE

(2)	180

SHIPMENTS FROM HOME OFFICE

(1)	7,000	(12)	400
(4)	45,000		
51,600	52,000		

FURNITURE AND FIXTURES

(1)	2,000
(2)	5,000
	7,000

OPERATING EXPENSES

(2)	400
(7)	18,700
	19,100

After posting the transactions, the home office accounts appeared as shown in the following "T" accounts:

HOME OFFICE ACCOUNTS

BANK

Bal.	20,000	(1)	8,000
(6)	22,000	(10)	102,000
(9)	86,000		110,000
18,000	128,000		

ALLOWANCE FOR BAD DEBTS

(9)	500	Bal.	700
		200	

NOTES RECEIVABLE

(14)	6,500

MERCHANDISE INVENTORY

Bal.	28,000

ACCOUNTS RECEIVABLE

Bal.	32,000	(9)	86,500
(6)	105,000	(14)	6,500
44,000	137,000	93,000	

PREPAID INSURANCE

Bal.	640

FURNITURE AND FIXTURES			
Bal.	8,000	(1)	2,000
6,000			

ACCOUNTS PAYABLE			
(10)	102,000	Bal.	31,000
		(3)	127,000
		56,000	158,000

ACCUMULATED DEPRECIATION — FURNITURE and FIXTURES			
		Bal.	3,400

CAPITAL STOCK			
		Bal.	50,000

BUILDING			
Bal.	60,000		

RETAINED EARNINGS			
		Bal.	42,540

ACCUMULATED DEPRECIATION — BUILDING			
		Bal.	28,000

SHIPMENTS TO BRANCH			
(12)	400	(1)	7,000
		(4)	45,000
		51,600	52,000

LAND			
Bal.	7,000		

SALES			
		(6)	127,000

PURCHASES			
(3)	95,000		

BRANCH OFFICE			
(1)	17,000	(12)	400
(4)	45,000		
61,600	62,000		

OPERATING EXPENSES			
(3)	32,000		

The following trial balance of the branch office accounts was taken at the end of the year:

THE BARTON SALES CO. — REDFIELD BRANCH
Trial Balance
December 31, 19--

Account	Dr. Balance	Cr. Balance
Bank.	22,120	
Notes Receivable	4,000	
Accounts Receivable	18,000	
Prepaid Insurance	180	
Furniture and Fixtures	7,000	
Notes Payable		5,000
Accounts Payable		2,200
Home Office		61,600
Sales		53,200
Shipments from Home Office	51,600	
Operating Expenses	19,100	
	122,000	122,000

The following trial balance of the home office accounts was taken at the end of the year:

THE BARTON SALES CO. — HOME OFFICE
Trial Balance
December 31, 19--

Account	Dr. Balance	Cr. Balance
Bank..................................	18,000	
Notes Receivable...........................	6,500	
Accounts Receivable........................	44,000	
Allowance for Bad Debts....................		200
Merchandise Inventory......................	28,000	
Prepaid Insurance.........................	640	
Furniture and Fixtures.....................	6,000	
Accumulated Depreciation — Furniture and Fixtures		3,400
Building..................................	60,000	
Accumulated Depreciation — Building.........		28,000
Land.....................................	7,000	
Branch Office.............................	61,600	
Accounts Payable..........................		56,000
Capital Stock.............................		50,000
Retained Earnings.........................		42,540
Shipments to Branch.......................		51,600
Sales....................................		127,000
Purchases................................	95,000	
Operating Expenses.......................	32,000	
	358,740	358,740

666

Report No. 26-1

Complete Report No. 26-1 in the workbook. Do not submit the report at this time. Since Reports Nos. 26-1 and 26-2 are related, you should retain the working papers until you have completed both reports. Continue with the next study assignment until Report No. 26-2 is required.

Procedure at close of fiscal year

The books of the home office and of the branch office should be closed in the usual manner at the end of each fiscal year.

Accounting procedure in closing branch office books

Following is a step-by-step analysis of the usual procedure in closing the books of a branch office:

(1) Prepare a work sheet as a means of compiling and classifying the data needed in the preparation of financial statements. In preparing the work sheet it will be necessary to make the usual adjustments to record (a) the merchandise inventory at end of year, (b) the portion of any prepaid expenses consumed or expired during the year, (c) any provision for bad debts, (d) the depreciation of long-lived assets, and (e) any accruals. The adjusted trial balance figures appearing on the work sheet will then provide the proper amounts to be used in preparing an income statement and a balance sheet for the Redfield Branch of The Barton Sales Co.

The data for adjusting the accounts of the Redfield Branch at the end of the year are as follows:

Merchandise inventory, end of year, $21,000
Insurance expired, $60
Provision for bad debts, $400
Depreciation of furniture and fixtures (10%), $700
Accrued interest on notes receivable, $24
Accrued interest on notes payable, $30

The work sheet prepared for the Redfield Branch of The Barton Sales Co. is reproduced on pages 668 and 669. The merchandise inventory at end of year amounting to $21,000 was recorded in the Adjustments columns of the work sheet by debiting Merchandise Inventory and by crediting Shipments from Home Office. After making this adjustment the balance of the account with Shipments from Home Office represented the cost of goods sold by the branch. Under this procedure there is no need for keeping a summary account with Cost of Goods Sold in the branch office ledger. (The other required adjustments were made on the work sheet.)

(2) Prepare an income statement showing the results of operating the branch during the year and send a copy to the home office. The Income Statement columns of the work sheet are the source of the information

Account	Trial Balance	
	Debit	Credit
Bank	22 120	
Notes Receivable	4 000	
Accrued Interest Receivable		
Accounts Receivable	18 000	
Allowance for Bad Debts		
Merchandise Inventory		
Prepaid Insurance	180	
Furniture and Fixtures	7 000	
Accumulated Depreciation — Furniture and Fixtures		
Notes Payable		5 000
Accrued Interest Payable		
Accounts Payable		2 200
Home Office		61 600
Sales		53 200
Shipments from Home Office	51 600	
Operating Expenses	19 100	
Interest Earned		
Interest Expense		
	122 000	122 000
Net Income		

The Barton Sales Co. —

needed in preparing this statement. The income statement of the Redfield
Branch of The Barton Sales Co. is reproduced below:

THE BARTON SALES CO. — REDFIELD BRANCH
Income Statement
For the Year Ended December 31, 19--

Sales....................................		$53,200
Less cost of goods sold:		
Shipments from home office.................	$51,600	
Less inventory, December 31..............	21,000	30,600
Gross margin on sales........................		$22,600
Operating expenses...........................		20,260
Net operating income.........................		$ 2,340
Other revenue:		
Interest earned............................		24
		$ 2,364
Other expense:		
Interest expense...........................		30
Net income.................................		$ 2,334

REDFIELD BRANCH

Sheet

December 31, 19--

	Adjustments Debit		Adjustments Credit	Adj. Trial Balance Debit	Adj. Trial Balance Credit	Income Statement Debit	Income Statement Credit	Balance Sheet Debit	Balance Sheet Credit
				22 120				22 120	
				4 000				4 000	
(c)	24			24				24	
				18 000				18 000	
		(b)	400		400				400
(a)	21 000			21 000				21 000	
		(b)	60	120				120	
				7 000				7 000	
		(b)	700		700				700
					5 000				5 000
		(d)	30		30				30
					2 200				2 200
					61 600				61 600
					53 200		53 200		
(a)	21 000			30 600		30 600			
(b)	1 160	(c)	24	20 260	24	20 260	24		
(d)	30			30		30			
	22 214		22 214	123 154	123 154	50 890	53 224	72 264	69 930
						2 334			2 334
						53 224	53 224	72 264	72 264

669

Redfield Branch Work Sheet

(3) Prepare a balance sheet showing the financial status of the branch at the end of the year and send a copy to the home office. The balance sheet of the Redfield Branch is reproduced below.

(4) Journalize and post the entries required to adjust the accounts of the branch. The Adjustments columns of the work sheet are the source of the information needed in preparing the adjusting journal entries. The

THE BARTON SALES CO. — REDFIELD BRANCH
Balance Sheet
December 31, 19 --

Assets			Liabilities		
Bank.....................		$22,120	Notes payable...........		$ 5,000
Notes receivable..........	$ 4,000		Accrued interest payable....		30
Accrued interest receivable ..	24		Accounts payable..........		2,200
Accounts receivable........	18,000		Home office.............	$61,600	
	$22,024		Plus net income..........	2,334	63,934
Less allow. for bad debts..	400	21,624			
Merchandise inventory......		21,000			
Prepaid insurance.........		120			
Furniture and fixtures......	$ 7,000				
Less accumd. depr........	700	6,300			
Total assets..............		$71,164	Total liabilities............		$71,164

journal entries required to adjust the accounts of the Redfield Branch of The Barton Sales Co. are as follows:

```
Merchandise Inventory......................................  21,000
  Shipments from Home Office.............................            21,000
Operating Expenses.........................................   1,160
  Prepaid Insurance......................................                60
  Allowance for Bad Debts................................               400
  Accumulated Depreciation — Furniture and Fixtures...........        700
Accrued Interest Receivable................................      24
  Interest Earned........................................                24
Interest Expense...........................................      30
  Accrued Interest Payable................................               30
```

(5) Journalize and post the entries required to close the temporary accounts in the branch books. The journal entries required to close the temporary accounts of the Redfield Branch of The Barton Sales Co. are as follows:

```
Sales......................................................  53,200
Interest Earned............................................      24
  Expense and Revenue Summary.............................            53,224
Expense and Revenue Summary................................  50,890
  Shipments from Home Office..............................            30,600
  Operating Expenses......................................            20,260
  Interest Expense........................................                30
Expense and Revenue Summary................................   2,334
  Home Office.............................................             2,334
```

The last journal entry was made to close the expense and revenue summary account and to transfer the net income to the home office account.

(6) Prepare a post-closing trial balance of the branch ledger accounts. The post-closing trial balance of the Redfield Branch of The Barton Sales Co. is reproduced below:

THE BARTON SALES CO. — REDFIELD BRANCH
Post-Closing Trial Balance
December 31, 19--

Account	Dr. Balance	Cr. Balance
Bank.....................................	22,120	
Notes Receivable............................	4,000	
Accrued Interest Receivable....................	24	
Accounts Receivable..........................	18,000	
Allowance for Bad Debts......................		400
Merchandise Inventory......................	21,000	
Prepaid Insurance..........................	120	
Furniture and Fixtures......................	7,000	
Accumulated Depreciation — Furniture and Fixtures..		700
Notes Payable..............................		5,000
Accrued Interest Payable.....................		30
Accounts Payable............................		2,200
Home Office		63,934
	72,264	72,264

(7) Journalize and post the entries required to reverse the adjusting entries for accruals. The entries required to reverse the entries for accruals in the books of the Redfield Branch of The Barton Sales Co. are as follows:

Interest Earned...	24	
Accrued Interest Receivable.......................................		24
Accrued Interest Payable...	30	
Interest Expense...		30

Accounting procedure in closing home office books

Following is a step-by-step analysis of the usual procedure in closing the books of the home office:

(1) Prepare a work sheet as a means of compiling and classifying the data needed in the preparation of financial statements. In preparing the work sheet it will be necessary to make the usual adjustments to record any changes in the account balances resulting from the transactions that have not been entered in the accounts in the routine recording of the business activities completed during the year.

The data for adjusting the accounts of the home office of The Barton Sales Co. at the end of the year are as follows:

Merchandise inventory, $15,000
Insurance expired, $420
Provision for bad debts, $950
Depreciation of furniture and fixtures (10%), $600
Depreciation of building (4%), $2,400
Accrued interest on notes receivable, $45
Branch office profit, $2,334
Corporation income tax, estimated, $12,421

671

The income statement received from the branch office is the source of the information as to the amount of the branch office profit.

It is necessary to adjust the accounts for the amount of the branch office profit in order to bring the account with Branch Office in the home office books into agreement with the account with Home Office in the books of the branch office. After making these adjustments, the home office accounts reflect the total income of the enterprise for the year.

The work sheet prepared for the home office of The Barton Sales Co. is reproduced on pages 672 and 673. A summary account with Cost of Goods Sold was kept in the home office ledger. This account was debited for (a) the beginning inventory amounting to $28,000 and (b) purchases amounting to $95,000, and was credited for (c) shipments to branch amounting to $51,600 and (d) the ending inventory amounting to $15,000. After making these adjustments the balance of the account amounted to $56,400.

(2) Prepare an income statement showing the results of operating the home office during the year. The Income Statement columns of the work

Account	Trial Balance	
	Debit	Credit
Bank	18 000	
Notes Receivable	6 500	
Accrued Interest Receivable		
Accounts Receivable	44 000	
Allowance for Bad Debts		200
Merchandise Inventory	28 000	
Prepaid Insurance	640	
Furniture and Fixtures	6 000	
Accumulated Depreciation — Furniture and Fixtures		3 400
Building	60 000	
Accumulated Depreciation — Building		28 000
Land	7 000	
Branch Office	61 600	
Accounts Payable		56 000
Corporation Income Tax Payable		
Capital Stock		50 000
Retained Earnings		42 540
Shipments to Branch		51 600
Sales		127 000
Purchases	95 000	
Operating Expenses	32 000	
Interest Earned		
Branch Office Profit		
Corporation Income Tax Expense		
Cost of Goods Sold		
	358 740	358 740
Net Income		

672

sheet are the source of the information needed in preparing this statement. The income statement of the home office of The Barton Sales Co. is reproduced on page 674.

(3) Prepare a balance sheet showing the financial status of the home office at the end of the year. The balance sheet of the home office of The Barton Sales Co. is reproduced on page 674.

(4) Journalize and post the entries required to adjust the home office accounts. The Adjustments columns of the work sheet are the source of the information needed in drafting the adjusting entries. The journal entries required to adjust the home office accounts of The Barton Sales Co. are as shown at the bottom of the next page.

Adjustments Debit	Adjustments Credit	Adj. Trial Balance Debit	Adj. Trial Balance Credit	Income Statement Debit	Income Statement Credit	Balance Sheet Debit	Balance Sheet Credit
		18 000				18 000	
		6 500				6 500	
(f) 45		45				45	
		44 000				44 000	
	(e) 950		1 150				1 150
(d) 15 000	(a) 28 000	15 000				15 000	
	(e) 420	220				220	
		6 000				6 000	
	(e) 600		4 000				4 000
		60 000				60 000	
	(e) 2 400		30 400				30 400
		7 000				7 000	
(g) 2 334		63 934				63 934	
			56 000				56 000
	(h) 12 421		12 421				12 421
			50 000				50 000
			42 540				42 540
(c) 51 600			127 000		127 000		
	(b) 95 000						
(e) 4 370		36 370		36 370			
	(f) 45		45		45		
	(g) 2 334		2 334		2 334		
(h) 12 421		12 421		12 421			
(a) 28 000	(c) 51 600	28 000	51 600	28 000	51 600		
(b) 95 000	(d) 15 000	95 000	15 000	95 000	15 000		
208 770	208 770	392 490	392 490	171 791	195 979	220 699	196 511
				24 188			24 188
				195 979	195 979	220 699	220 699

Home Office Work Sheet

673

Cost of Goods Sold..	28,000	
Merchandise Inventory.....................................		28,000
Cost of Goods Sold..	95,000	
Purchases...		95,000
Shipments to Branch.......................................	51,600	
Cost of Goods Sold..		51,600
Merchandise Inventory.....................................	15,000	
Cost of Goods Sold..		15,000
Operating Expenses..	4,370	
Prepaid Insurance...		420
Allowance for Bad Debts...................................		950
Accumulated Depreciation — Furniture and Fixtures..........		600
Accumulated Depreciation — Building.......................		2,400
Accrued Interest Receivable...............................	45	
Interest Earned...		45
Branch Office...	2,334	
Branch Office Profit......................................		2,334
Corporation Income Tax Expense............................	12,421	
Corporation Income Tax Payable............................		12,421

THE BARTON SALES CO. — HOME OFFICE
Income Statement
For the Year Ended December 31, 19--

Sales..		$127,000
Less cost of goods sold:		
Inventory, beginning of year..............	$ 28,000	
Purchases...........................	95,000	
	$123,000	
Less shipments to branch..............	51,600	
Merchandise available for sale..............	$ 71,400	
Less inventory end of year..............	15,000	56,400
Gross margin on sales......................		$ 70,600
Operating expenses........................		36,370
Net operating income......................		$ 34,230
Other revenue:		
Interest earned.........................		45
Net income — home office		$ 34,275
Branch office profit.......................		2,334
Total net income before provision for income tax ..		$ 36,609
Less corporation income tax expense		12,421
Net income after provision for income tax.....		$ 24,188

674

THE BARTON SALES CO. — HOME OFFICE
Balance Sheet
December 31, 19--

Assets			Liabilities		
Bank...................		$ 18,000	Accounts payable.........	$56,000	
Notes receivable..........	$ 6,500		Corp. income tax payable	12,421	
Accrued interest receivable .	45		Total liabilities............		$ 68,421
Accounts receivable.......	44,000				
	$50,545		Stockholders' Equity		
Less allow. for bad debts.	1,150	49,395	Capital stock.............	$50,000	
Merchandise inventory.....		15,000	Retained earnings.........	66,728	
Prepaid insurance........		220	Total stockholders' equity...		116,728
Furniture and fixtures......	$ 6,000				
Less accumd. depreciation.	4,000	2,000			
Building.................	$60,000				
Less accumd. depreciation.	30,400	29,600			
Land...................		7,000			
Branch office		63,934	Total liabilities and stock-		
Total assets.............		$185,149	holders' equity		$185,149

(5) Journalize and post the entries required to close the temporary accounts in the home office books. The journal entries required to close the temporary accounts of the home office of The Barton Sales Co. are shown at the top of the next page.

```
Sales................................................  127,000
Interest Earned.....................................       45
Branch Office Profit................................    2,334
    Expense and Revenue Summary.....................            129,379
Expense and Revenue Summary.........................  105,191
    Cost of Goods Sold..............................             56,400
    Operating Expenses..............................             36,370
    Corporation Income Tax Expense..................             12,421
Expense and Revenue Summary.........................   24,188
    Retained Earnings...............................             24,188
```

(6) After posting the closing entries, a post-closing trial balance should be taken. The post-closing trial balance for The Barton Sales Co. follows:

THE BARTON SALES CO. — HOME OFFICE
Post-Closing Trial Balance
December 31, 19--

Account	Dr. Balance	Cr. Balance
Bank.....................................	18,000	
Notes Receivable.........................	6,500	
Accrued Interest Receivable..............	45	
Accounts Receivable......................	44,000	
Allowance for Bad Debts..................		1,150
Merchandise Inventory....................	15,000	
Prepaid Insurance........................	220	
Furniture and Fixtures...................	6,000	
Accumulated Depreciation — Furniture and Fixtures		4,000
Building.................................	60,000	
Accumulated Depreciation — Building......		30,400
Land.....................................	7,000	
Branch Office............................	63,934	
Accounts Payable.........................		56,000
Corporation Income Tax Payable...........		12,421
Capital Stock............................		50,000
Retained Earnings........................		66,728
	220,699	220,699

(7) After taking a post-closing trial balance, any adjusting entries for accruals should be reversed. The following journal entry is required to reverse the adjusting entry for accrued interest receivable in the home office books of The Barton Sales Co.:

```
Interest Earned.......................................................  45
    Accrued Interest Receivable.......................................      45
```

Combined financial statements of home office and branch

While separate financial statements of the home office and the branch office provide useful information for the separate managements, *combined*

	Home Office	
	Debit	*Credit*
Sales		127 000
Cost of goods sold:		
Merchandise inventory, January 1	28 000	
Purchases	95 000	
Shipments from home office		
Shipments to branch		51 600
Merchandise available for sale	71 400	
Merchandise inventory, December 31		15 000
Cost of goods sold	56 400	
Gross margin on sales		70 600
Operating expenses	36 370	
Net operating income		34 230
Add interest earned		45
		34 275
Less interest expense		
Net income before tax		34 275
Branch profit transferred to home office		2 334
Total net income before tax		36 609
Income tax expense	12 421	
Net income after tax		24 188

676

The Barton Sales Co. — Home Office and Redfield

statements, in which the results of operations and the financial data of both entities are combined, provide more complete information regarding the business as a whole. The preparation of combined statements is facilitated by the use of special work sheets. The work sheet that was used in preparing a combined income statement for The Barton Sales Co. and its Redfield Branch is reproduced above and on the opposite page. The data in the first pair of columns were obtained from the income statement of the home office. The data in the second pair of columns were obtained from the income statement of the branch office. The columns headed "Eliminations" are used to cancel the reciprocal accounts. The only reciprocal accounts are Shipments from Home Office and Shipments to Branch.

The combined income statement for The Barton Sales Co. and its Redfield Branch as reproduced on page 680 was prepared from the information provided in the last pair of columns of the work sheet.

The work sheet that was used in the preparation of the combined balance sheet of The Barton Sales Co. and its Redfield Branch is reproduced on pages 678 and 679. The data in the first pair of columns were obtained from the balance sheet of the home office. The data in the second pair of columns were obtained from the balance sheet of the branch office.

SALES CO.
REDFIELD BRANCH
Income Statement
December 31, 19--

Redfield Branch		Eliminations		Combined Income Statement	
Debit	*Credit*	*Debit*	*Credit*	*Debit*	*Credit*
	53 200				180 200
				28 000	
				95 000	
51 600			51 600		
		51 600			
51 600				123 000	
	21 000				36 000
30 600				87 000	
	22 600				93 200
20 260				56 630	
	2 340				36 570
	24				69
	2 364				36 639
30				30	
	2 334				36 609
2 334					
				12 421	
					24 188

Branch Combined Income Statement Work Sheet

The pair of columns headed "Eliminations" is used to cancel the reciprocal accounts. In this case the only reciprocal accounts are Home Office and Branch Office.

The combined balance sheet for The Barton Sales Co. and its Redfield Branch as reproduced on page 680 was prepared from the information provided in the last pair of columns of the work sheet on pages 678 and 679.

Accounting for merchandise billed to branch in excess of cost

Sometimes a home office bills its branch for an amount greater than the cost of the merchandise shipped to the branch. This practice may be followed in order to keep the branch manager and others from knowing the actual costs and therefore the actual branch profit or loss. In some cases the branch is billed at the selling price of the goods. This practice will not only conceal the cost, but it may facilitate control of the stock at the branch. When the count of goods is made at the end of the period, usually it is easier to value them at sales prices. Furthermore, the sum of the prices

Chapter 26 / Accounting for Branch Operations

	Home Office	
	Debit	Credit
Cash	18 000	
Notes Receivable	6 500	
Accrued Interest Receivable	45	
Accounts Receivable	44 000	
Allowance for Bad Debts		1 150
Merchandise Inventory	15 000	
Prepaid Insurance	220	
Furniture and Fixtures	6 000	
Accumulated Depreciation — Furniture and Fixtures		4 000
Building	60 000	
Accumulated Depreciation — Building		30 400
Land	7 000	
Branch Office	63 934	
Income Tax Payable		12 421
Notes Payable		
Accrued Interest Payable		
Accounts Payable		56 000
Home Office		
Capital Stock		50 000
Retained Earnings		66 728
	220 699	220 699

The Barton Sales Co. — Home Office and Redfield

of goods on hand in the branch plus the amount of sales during the period should equal the opening inventory of goods at selling price plus the total amount of shipments from the home office during the period (assuming no changes in selling prices). Any discrepancy for reasons other than changes in selling prices after the goods are received indicates the need for investigation and closer control of stock.

If the branch is billed for the sales price of goods shipped, the home office may credit an account entitled *Provision for Overvaluation of Branch Inventory* for the difference between the cost and the sales price of the goods sent to the branch. For example, assume that the home office ships goods costing $40,000 to the branch and bills the branch for $60,000, the sales price of the merchandise. This shipment could be recorded in the home office books as follows:

```
Branch Office.............................................  60,000
    Shipments to Branch....................................           40,000
    Provision for Overvaluation of Branch Inventory.............           20,000
        Goods shipped to branch:
        Sales price $60,000, cost $40,000.
```

The branch would record the shipment by a debit to Shipments from Home Office and a credit to Home Office in the amount of $60,000.

SALES CO.

REDFIELD BRANCH

Balance Sheet

31, 19--

	Redfield Branch		Eliminations		Combined Balance Sheet	
	Debit	Credit	Debit	Credit	Debit	Credit
	22 120				40 120	
	4 000				10 500	
	24				69	
	18 000				62 000	
		400				1 550
	21 000				36 000	
	120				340	
	7 000				13 000	
		700				4 700
					60 000	
						30 400
					7 000	
				63 934		
						12 421
		5 000				5 000
		30				30
		2 200				58 200
		63 934	63 934			
						50 000
						66 728
	72 264	72 264	63 934	63 934	229 029	229 029

Branch Combined Balance Sheet Work Sheet

Under such circumstances the branch will never show a profit on its records since its sales and reported cost of goods sold will be equal. It will report a loss equal to the amount of its expenses. Assume that the branch in the case cited had no beginning inventory, received only the one shipment, and sold 70 percent of those goods. Assume also that the operating expenses of the branch were $10,000. The branch would report sales and cost of goods sold of $42,000, expenses of $10,000, and a loss of $10,000. Its balance sheet would show an $18,000 merchandise inventory.

Actually the branch had a net profit of $4,000. (Sales, $42,000, less actual cost of goods sold, $28,000, less expenses, $10,000, equals net profit, $4,000.) The actual cost of the inventory at the branch is $12,000 (66⅔ percent of $18,000). Since the branch debited $10,000 to Home Office when it closed its Expense and Revenue Summary, the home office must credit that amount to Branch Office in its ledger. At the same time the home office will want to record the actual branch profit of $4,000 and reduce the Provision for Overvaluation of Branch Inventory from $20,000 to $6,000 (the overvaluation of the goods now on hand at the branch). This can be accomplished if the home office makes the journal entry shown at the top of the next page to record the loss reported by the branch.

Provision for Overvaluation of Branch Inventory............... 14,000
    Branch Office... 10,000
    Branch Profit... 4,000
      Reported loss of branch, $10,000 (caused by $14,000 over-
      statement of cost of goods sold).

THE BARTON SALES CO.
HOME OFFICE AND REDFIELD BRANCH
Combined Income Statement
For the Year Ended December 31, 19--

Sales..................................		$180,200
Less cost of goods sold:		
Merchandise inventory, January 1..........	$ 28,000	
Purchases.............................	95,000	
Merchandise available for sale.............	$123,000	
Less merchandise inventory, December 31...	36,000	87,000
Gross margin on sales......................		$ 93,200
Less operating expenses..................		56,630
Net operating income......................		$ 36,570
Other revenue:		
Interest earned........................		69
		$ 36,639
Other expense:		
Interest expense.......................		30
Net income before provision for income tax......		$ 36,609
Less corporation income tax expense........		12,421
Net income after provision for income tax......		$ 24,188

680

THE BARTON SALES CO.
HOME OFFICE AND REDFIELD BRANCH
Combined Balance Sheet
December 31, 19--

Assets			Liabilities		
Cash...................		$ 40,120	Notes payable..........	$ 5,000	
Notes receivable.........	$10,500		Accrued interest payable...	30	
Accrued interest receivable .	69		Accounts payable........	58,200	
Accounts receivable.......	62,000		Corp. income tax payable	12,421	
	$72,569		Total liabilities...........		$ 75,651
Less allow. for bad debts.	1,550	71,019			
			Stockholders' Equity		
Merchandise inventory.....		36,000			
Prepaid insurance.........		340	Capital stock............	$50,000	
Furniture and fixtures......	$13,000		Retained earnings........	66,728	
Less accumd. depr.......	4,700	8,300	Total stockholders' equity...		116,728
Building................	$60,000				
Less accumd. depr.......	30,400	29,600			
Land...................		7,000	Total liab. and stockholders'		
Total assets.............		$192,379	equity...............		$192,379

In the process of preparing combined statements for the home office and the branch, the overvaluations in the accounts can be eliminated or canceled so that the combined statements will show actual costs and profit.

In some cases a home office may bill its branch at an amount in excess of cost, though not as high as the selling price of the goods shipped. This procedure may not be any help in keeping control of the branch inventory, but it will keep the true results of the branch operations secret from the manager and others at the branch. The branch may show a profit, but such profit will be understated to the extent that the recorded cost of goods sold is overstated. The mechanics of accounting for shipments and the handling of statement combination in such situations are similar to the procedures used when the goods are billed at selling price.

Several branches

Frequently a company has more than one branch. If each branch has its own ledger, the home office ledger will contain an account for each branch. Preferably the branches will not have accounts with each other. Any transaction between two or more branches will be recorded as though each of them dealt with the home office. For example, suppose that the home office decides to transfer $3,000 from Branch Office No. 1 to Branch Office No. 2. To record this transfer of cash the following journal entries should be made in the books indicated:

BOOKS OF BRANCH OFFICE No. 1:

Home Office...	3,000	
Bank...		3,000
$3,000 transferred to Branch No. 2.		

BOOKS OF BRANCH OFFICE No. 2:

Bank...	3,000	
Home Office..		3,000
$3,000 received from Branch No. 1.		

HOME OFFICE BOOKS:

Branch Office No. 2..	3,000	
Branch Office No. 1..		3,000
$3,000 transferred to Branch No. 2 by Branch No. 1.		

Reconciliation of the reciprocal accounts

While the branch office account in the home office ledger and the home office account in the branch office ledger will have balances of the same amount after all transactions between the units have been recorded properly, it is probable that the balances of the two accounts will not be exactly equal at all times. Apart from discrepancies because of errors, one or more of four situations may result in temporary differences between the balances of these accounts. These situations are as shown on the next page.

(1) The home office has charged the branch, but the branch has not yet credited the home office. For example, a discrepancy of this type could exist during the interval between the date that goods were shipped by the home office and the date that the goods were received by the branch.

(2) The branch has credited the home office, but the home office has not yet charged the branch. For example, a discrepancy of this type could exist just after the branch had transferred a credit balance from its expense and revenue summary account to the home office account, but before the home office recorded the branch profit.

(3) The home office has credited the branch, but the branch has not yet charged the home office. For example, suppose a customer of the branch sent the home office a check in payment of his debt to the branch. The home office deposited the money in its own bank account and sent a letter (or a credit memo) to the branch instructing it to credit the account of the customer and to debit the home office. The balances of the reciprocal accounts would be unequal until the branch made the proper entry upon receipt of the letter or memo.

(4) The branch office has charged the home office, but the home office has not yet credited the branch. For example, suppose the branch has recorded a remittance to the home office, but the home office has not yet received it and therefore has not recorded it.

682

Any difference in the balances of the reciprocal accounts must be accounted for before the statements of the home office and the branch can be combined. When the reasons for any differences are known, any needed correcting or adjusting entries can be made on the combined statement work sheets and, if needed, in the books of the home office, the branch, or both. Sometimes the reciprocal accounts are reconciled at frequent intervals in order to cross-check the accuracy of the branch office and the home office records.

Report No. 26-2

Complete Report No. 26-2 in the workbook and submit your working papers for Reports Nos. 26-1 and 26-2. Continue with the next study assignment in Chapter 27 until Report No. 27-1 is required.

chapter 27

the voucher system of accounting

Many business organizations use a system for controlling expenditures known as the *voucher system*. This method is useful for handling cash disbursements. Under this system written authorization is required for each cash payment. For example, certain officers of a corporation may be authorized to approve expenditures, while the cashier is authorized to issue the checks. Such a system usually involves the use of vouchers, a voucher register, a vouchers payable account in the general ledger, voucher checks, and a check register, although in some cases ordinary checks are used and are recorded in a simple cashbook or in a cash payments journal. There are several accounting procedures applicable to the voucher system. Like most bookkeeping and accounting processes, the voucher system is flexible and readily adaptable to various situations.

The use of the voucher system of accounting is not advisable under all conditions, but it usually may be used to advantage when one or more of the following circumstances exist:

    (a) When the volume of transactions is large enough to require a system of control over expenditures.
    (b) When the nature of the business is such that it is desirable to record invoices at the time that they are received rather than when payment is made.
    (c) When it is the custom of the firm to pay all invoices in full at maturity instead of making partial or installment payments.

Verification of invoices

All invoices received, whether they represent the cost of goods, materials, or other assets purchased or the cost of services rendered, are verified by the proper parties. The receiving clerk usually verifies the receipt of all assets purchased as to quantity and quality. The purchasing agent usually verifies prices, grades, sizes, and terms of payment. Clerks in the accounting department usually verify the mathematical accuracy of the extensions and the amounts. The accountant or auditor may indicate the accounts to be charged. Invoices for services usually are checked by the department receiving the service or incurring the expense.

An invoice received by The B. J. Patrick Manufacturing Co. from Simplex Stationers, Inc., is shown below. This invoice represents the purchase of office supplies on account. The receipt of the supplies has been verified by the receiving clerk, the prices have been verified by the purchasing agent, the extensions and the amount of the invoice have been verified by an accounting clerk, and the accountant has indicated that Account No. 181 should be charged for the amount of the invoice.

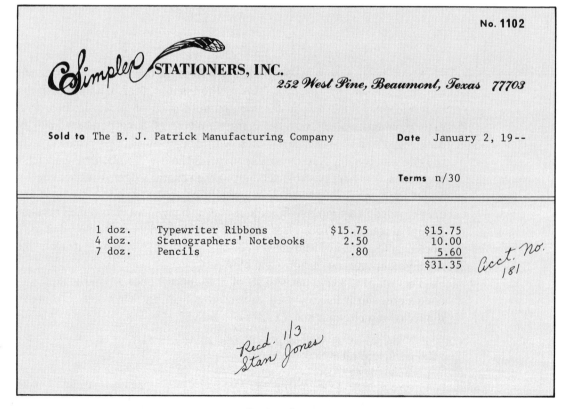

No. 1102

684

Simplex STATIONERS, INC.
252 West Pine, Beaumont, Texas 77703

Sold to The B. J. Patrick Manufacturing Company   **Date** January 2, 19--

Terms n/30

1 doz.	Typewriter Ribbons	$15.75	$15.75
4 doz.	Stenographers' Notebooks	2.50	10.00
7 doz.	Pencils	.80	5.60
			$31.35

Acct. No. 181

Recd. 1/3 Stan Jones

Purchase Invoice

Preparation of vouchers

As used in this connection, the term *voucher* refers to a business paper or document that provides space in which to record information relating to goods or services purchased, accounts to be charged, and authorization for payment. There is also space in which to record the date of payment and the number of the check issued.

A voucher should be prepared for each invoice received except those representing minor expense items that may be paid out of a petty cash fund. There is no standard form of voucher; the form varies depending upon the nature of the business, the classification of accounts, and the distribution desired. The vouchers are usually prepared by a voucher clerk to whom the invoices are referred after they have been verified.

A voucher that was prepared by the voucher clerk for The B. J. Patrick Manufacturing Co. is shown on page 686. The information recorded on this voucher was obtained from the invoice shown on page 684. After the voucher was prepared, the invoice was attached to it and both were referred to the accounting department to be recorded. When the voucher was paid, the date of payment, the check number, and the amount of the check were recorded in the spaces provided for this information on the back of the voucher form.

685

Recording of vouchers

After the invoices have been properly verified and vouchers have been prepared for them, the vouchers should be recorded in a *voucher register*. This register can best be described as an expanded purchases journal; it is used to record the purchases of all types of assets and services. It is similar in many respects to the invoice register previously described.

The ruling and the columnar headings of a voucher register depend upon the nature of the business and the desired classification of purchases and expenses. One form of voucher register is shown on pages 688 and 689. Reference to that illustration will show that voucher No. 101, which is reproduced on page 686, was recorded by debiting Office Supplies, Account No. 181, and by crediting Vouchers Payable for $31.35.

Following is a description of the vouchers that are shown recorded in the voucher register:

Jan. 4. No. 101, Simplex Stationers, Inc., 252 West Pine Street; office supplies, Account No. 181, $31.35; terms, January 2 — n/30.

    4. No. 102, Stuart Truck Co., 3134 S. Grand; factory lift truck, $293.75; terms, January 2 — n/30. (Charge to Factory Equipment, Account No. 231.)

VOUCHER

the b.j. Patrick manufacturing co.

No. __101__ Date Issued __January 4__ 19 -- Terms __n/30__ Due __February 1__ 19--

To __Simplex Stationers, Inc.__

Address __252 West Pine__

__Beaumont, Texas   77703__

INVOICE DATE	DESCRIPTION	AMOUNT	
Jan. 2	Office Supplies	31	35

Authorized By

B. J. Patrick

Prepared By

Jean Coash
Voucher Clerk

(Front of Voucher)

686

DISTRIBUTION

MATERIALS	FACTORY OVERHEAD		OPERATING EXPENSES		SUNDRY ACCOUNTS		
	ACCT. NO.	AMOUNT	ACCT. NO.	AMOUNT	ACCT. NO.	AMOUNT	
					181	31	35

PAYMENT

Date of Payment __February 1,__ 19 --   Check No. __104__   Amount $ __31.35__

CERTIFICATION

This voucher has been audited carefully and is correct in every respect.

Harry H. Osborn
Accountant

(Back of Voucher)

Voucher

4. No. 103, Corn Products Refining Co., Kansas City; materials, $3,600; terms, January 2 — 2/10, n/30.

4. No. 104, B. C. McDonald, 1265 Spruce; factory supplies, Account No. 183, $85.20; terms, January 2 — n/30.

4. No. 105, Morris Machine Co., 1420 N. Sarah St., repairs on machinery, Account No. 7407, $124.50; terms, cash.

15. No. 106, Payroll, January 1–15, $3,264.88. Distribution: Direct Labor, Account No. 731, $702.83; Indirect Labor, Account No. 7401, $706.20; Office Salaries Expense, Account No. 8201, $500; Officers' Salaries Expense, Account No. 8202, $1,450; Sales Salaries Expense, Account No. 8231, $800. Taxes withheld: FICA Tax Payable, Account No. 311, $228.75; Employees Income Tax Payable, Account No. 314, $665.40.

Voucher No. 106 was based on a report of the payroll clerk. The amount payable is the net amount of the payroll after deducting the taxes withheld. The total wages and salaries earned during the pay period ended January 15 amounted to $4,159.03 represented by:

Direct labor	$ 702.83
Indirect labor	706.20
Office salaries	500.00
Officers' salaries	1,450.00
Sales salaries	800.00
Total	$4,159.03

It should be noted that three lines were required to record this transaction in the voucher register. This was because of the three entries in the Operating Expenses Dr. column.

It was also necessary to record the payroll taxes imposed on the employer. The entry to record these taxes was made in the general journal as follows:

Factory Overhead	122.59[1]	
Operating Expenses	239.25[2]	
FICA Tax Payable		228.75
FUTA Tax Payable		20.80
State Unemployment Tax Payable		112.29

When the voucher system includes a voucher register and a check register having columnar arrangements similar to those illustrated on pages 688–689 and 692, the procedure in recording wages may be as follows:

(a) The gross earnings of each employee for the pay period is taken from the time record of the employee. A summary report is then prepared by the payroll clerk showing: (1) a proper classification of the wages earned and the titles or numbers of the accounts to be charged; (2) the amount of the

687

---

[1]This amount was debited to Payroll Taxes — Factory, Account No. 7411, in the subsidiary factory overhead ledger used by The B. J. Patrick Manufacturing Co.

[2]In the subsidiary operating expense ledger used by The B. J. Patrick Manufacturing Co., $169.65 was debited to Payroll Taxes — Administrative, Account No. 8207, and $69.60 was debited to Payroll Taxes — Sales, Account No. 8241. A special form of general journal designed to accommodate entries in subsidiary ledgers (as well as in the general ledger) is used. This journal is illustrated and explained in the following chapter.

MATERIALS PURCHASES DR.	FACTORY OVERHEAD DR.			OPERATING EXPENSES DR.			SUNDRY ACCOUNTS DR.		
	ACCOUNT NO.	AMOUNT	v	ACCOUNT NO.	AMOUNT	v	ACCOUNT NO.	AMOUNT	v
										1
							181	3135	v	2
							231	29375	v	3
360000										4
							183	8520	v	5
	7407	12450	v							6
	7401	70620	v	8201	50000	v	731	70283	v	7
				8202	145000					8
				8231	80000					9
360000		83070			275000			1111313		10
										11

The B. J. Patrick Manufacturing Co. — Voucher Register (Left Page)

total earnings to be charged to each account; (3) the total deductions to be made for taxes withheld, and for any other purposes; and (4) the net amount of wages payable.

(b) A voucher is prepared for the payroll and is recorded in the voucher register by debiting the proper labor accounts and by crediting the proper liability accounts for the taxes withheld, and by crediting Vouchers Payable for the net amount payable.

(c) A check is issued in payment of the payroll voucher. This check is usually made payable to Payroll. The check may be cashed at the bank on which it is drawn to obtain the funds needed to meet the payroll, or it may be deposited in a special payroll checking account and an individual paycheck may then be issued to each employee. The check issued for the net amount of the payroll should be recorded in the check register by debiting Vouchers Payable and by crediting the proper bank account.

(d) An entry is made in the general journal to record the employer's liability for payroll taxes. Sometimes the payroll taxes imposed on the employer are recorded at the end of each month instead of each payday.

When the payroll taxes become due, vouchers should be prepared authorizing the payment of such taxes. These vouchers should be recorded in the voucher register by debiting the proper liability accounts and by crediting Vouchers Payable. When checks are issued to pay the taxes, the checks should be recorded in the check register by debiting Vouchers Payable and by crediting the proper bank account.

In a manufacturing enterprise, separate expense accounts may be kept to record the payroll taxes related to factory wages, administrative salaries, and sales salaries. In recording such taxes, it will be necessary to debit the proper expense accounts.

DAY	VOUCHER NO.	TO WHOM ISSUED	SUNDRY ACCOUNTS CR.			VOUCHERS PAYABLE CR.	DISPOSITION	
			ACCOUNT NO.	AMOUNT	√		DATE	CK. NO.
		AMOUNTS FORWARDED						
4	101	Simplex Stationers, Inc.				31 35		
4	102	Stuart Truck Co.				293 75	1/17	87
4	103	Corn Products Refining Co.				3600 00	1/14	85
4	104	B.C. McDonald				85 20		
4	105	Morris Machine Co.				124 50	1/4	84
15	106	Payroll	311	2288 75	√	3264 88	1/15	86
			314	665 40	√			
				2954 15		7399 68		

The B. J. Patrick Manufacturing Co. — Voucher Register (Right Page)

To prove the voucher register, it is only necessary to determine that the sum of the debit footings is equal to the sum of the credit footings. The footings should be proved before the totals are forwarded and before the summary posting is completed.

689

Posting from the voucher register

Both individual posting and summary posting from the voucher register are required. The individual posting involves (1) posting each item entered in the Factory Overhead Dr. Amount column to the proper account in the factory overhead subsidiary ledger, (2) posting each item entered in the Operating Expenses Dr. Amount column to the proper account in the operating expense subsidiary ledger, and (3) posting each item entered in the Sundry Accounts Dr. and Cr. Amount columns to the proper accounts in the general ledger. As each item is posted, a check mark should be placed beside it in the Check (√) column of the voucher register. The page number of the voucher register should also be entered in the Posting Reference column of the ledger account to which the amount is posted.

The summary posting of the voucher register required each month involves the following procedure:

(a) The total of the column headed Materials Purchases Dr. should be posted as a debit to the materials purchases account in the general ledger.

(b) The total of the column headed Factory Overhead Dr. should be posted as a debit to the factory overhead account in the general ledger.

(c) The total of the column headed Operating Expenses Dr. should be posted as a debit to the operating expenses account in the general ledger.

(d) The total of the column headed Vouchers Payable Cr. should be posted as a credit to the vouchers payable account in the general ledger.

As the total of each column is posted from the voucher register, the account number should be written in parentheses immediately below the total. The page number of the voucher register should also be written in the Posting Reference column of the ledger account to which the amount is posted. Check marks should be placed in parentheses below the totals of the Sundry Accounts Dr. and Cr. Amount columns in the voucher register to indicate that these totals should not be posted.

Filing unpaid vouchers

After the vouchers are recorded in the voucher register, they may be filed numerically according to due date, or they may be filed alphabetically in an unpaid vouchers file. If the vouchers are not filed according to due date, it may be advisable to use a tickler file as an aid in determining which vouchers need to be paid on certain dates. Invoices should be paid according to their terms. Delay in payment may result in discounts being lost or in the loss of credit standing.

Paying vouchers

At or before maturity, the vouchers should be approved by the person authorized to approve expenditures and should be presented to the proper disbursing officer for payment. Ordinary checks may be used. In some cases, however, a special form of *voucher check* is used that provides suitable space for copying data from the invoice or other information concerning the voucher to which the check relates. In the illustration on page 691, a voucher check issued to Simplex Stationers, Inc., in payment of its invoice of January 2 is reproduced. The form of the check is the same as an ordinary check. The statement attached to it provides space for a description of the invoice, including its date, number, description, amount, deductions, if any, and net amount. The information given on the statement attached to the check is for identification purposes and is given for the benefit of the payee of the check.

Recording checks

All checks issued in payment of vouchers may be recorded in a *check register*. When the charges pertaining to each voucher have been recorded

86-1809								No. 104

Beaumont, Texas_____February 1,____19 --

Pay to the order of__Simplex Stationers, Inc._____$ 31.35

Thirty-one 35/100--- Dollars

1st ST FIRST NATIONAL BANK

the b.j. Patrick manufacturing co.

L. A. McNeill

Treasurer

⑆ 1131 ⑈ 1809⑈ 406 ⑈ 56 500 ⑈

— —

DETACH THIS STATEMENT BEFORE DEPOSITING CHECK

the b. j. patrick manufacturing co.

ATTACHED VOUCHER CHECK IS FULL SETTLEMENT OF THE FOLLOWING

DATE_____February 1, 19--

INVOICE		DESCRIPTION	INVOICE AMOUNT		DEDUCTIONS		NET AMOUNT	
DATE	NUMBER				FOR	AMOUNT		
1/2	1102	Office Supplies	31	35			31	35

Voucher Check

in the voucher register, it is not necessary to make provision for distribution of charges in the check register. It is not unusual, however, to find that columns are provided in the check register to record deductions that may be made at the time of payment. The form of check register shown on page 692 has a column for purchases discount deductions. When checks are recorded in the check register, an entry should also be made in the Disposition columns of the voucher register to show that the voucher has been paid. This entry serves the same purpose as a debit entry in a creditor's ledger account.

Following is a description of the checks that are shown recorded in the check register reproduced on page 692.

Jan. 4. No. 84, Morris Machine Co., $124.50, in payment of Voucher No. 105.

14. No. 85, Corn Products Refining Co., $3,528, in payment of Voucher No. 103 for $3,600, less 2% discount.

15. No. 86, Payroll, $3,264.88, in payment of Voucher No. 106.

17. No. 87, Stuart Truck Co., $293.75, in payment of Voucher No. 102.

	VOUCHERS PAY. DR.		DAY	DRAWN TO THE ORDER OF	PURCHASES DISCOUNT CR.	BANK CR.		
	NO.	AMOUNT				CK. NO.	AMOUNT	
1	105	12450	4	Morris Machine Co.		84	12450	1
2	103	360000	14	Corn Products Refining Co.	7200	85	352800	2
3	106	326488	15	Payroll		86	326488	3
4	102	29375	17	Stuart Truck Co.		87	29375	4
5		728313			7200		721113	5
6								6
7								7
8								8
9								9
10								10

The B. J. Patrick Manufacturing Co. — Check Register

To prove the check register, it is only necessary to determine that the sum of the credit footings is equal to the footing of the Vouchers Payable Dr. column. The footings should be proved before the totals are forwarded and before the summary posting is completed.

692   Posting from the check register

No individual posting from the check register is required. It is only necessary to complete the summary posting at the end of each month.

The summary posting procedure is as follows:

(a) The total of the column headed Vouchers Payable Dr. should be posted as a debit to the vouchers payable account in the general ledger.

(b) The total of the column headed Purchases Discount Cr. should be posted as a credit to the purchases discount account in the general ledger.

(c) The total of the column headed Bank Cr. Amount should be posted as a credit to the bank account in the general ledger.

As the total of each column is posted from the check register, the account number should be written in parentheses immediately below the total. The page of the check register should also be written in the Posting Reference column of the ledger account to which the amount is posted.

Filing paid vouchers

It is customary to file vouchers that have been paid. They may be filed either in numerical order, or alphabetically by creditor. Sometimes the canceled check is filed with the voucher.

Proving vouchers payable

When a trial balance is prepared, the balance of the vouchers payable account should be verified by preparing a list of the unpaid vouchers. The total of this list should be equal to the balance of the account.

Purchases returns and allowances

When the voucher system of accounting is used, purchases returns and allowances must be recorded in such a way that the accounts will show correctly the effect of such transactions and that the voucher register will show the proper amounts payable. When credit is received for a return or for an allowance, the amount of the affected unpaid voucher is reduced.

There are several different ways of recording a return or an allowance. If the item relates to an invoice that was vouchered and recorded during the current month, a correcting entry can be interlined in the voucher register. The amount of the allowance can be written in just above the amount in the Materials Purchases Dr. column and just above the amount in the Vouchers Payable Cr. column that relate to the vouchered invoice that is being reduced. Some accountants use red ink to indicate that these amounts are offsets. Instead of using red ink, the amounts interlined can be written in the regularly used color of ink and circled. A notation of the reduction is made on the affected voucher and the credit memo is attached. Such offset items are totaled separately in each column of the register. The sum of any such items in the Materials Purchases Dr. column is posted as a credit to the purchases returns and allowances account. The sum of such negative items in the Vouchers Payable Cr. column should be posted as a debit to Vouchers Payable.

If the return or the allowance relates to an invoice that was vouchered and recorded during a prior month, the foregoing procedure would not be feasible. Some accountants do not favor it in any case. Instead, a general journal entry can be made to cancel the old voucher and to record the return or the allowance. A new voucher for the adjusted amount is prepared and recorded in the voucher register. A notation of the cancellation is made in the Disposition columns of the voucher register.

Another procedure that is often quite satisfactory is (1) to make a notation of the return or the allowance on the voucher that is affected and to attach the credit memo to the voucher; (2) to make a notation of the reduction in the voucher register beside the amount of the voucher that is being reduced; and (3) to record the transaction formally by means of a general journal entry. A return of, or an allowance relating to, a merchandise or materials purchase would require a debit to Vouchers Payable and a credit

693

to Purchases Returns and Allowances. If the return or the allowance related to the purchase of a long-lived asset or to some expense that had been incurred, the credit in the entry would be to the asset or expense account.

Corrected invoices

Sometimes a corrected invoice is received after the original invoice has been recorded in the voucher register. The corrected invoice may involve either an increase or a decrease in the amount of the original voucher. An entry should be made in the general journal to record the change in the amount of the original voucher. If the amount is increased, the entry will involve a debit to the account that was charged for the amount of the original invoice and a credit to Vouchers Payable. If the amount is decreased, the entry will involve a debit to Vouchers Payable and a credit to the account that was charged for the amount of the original invoice. The corrected invoice should then be attached to the original invoice and voucher, and a notation should be made in the voucher register to indicate that this amount has been changed. As in the case of returns and allowances, some accountants would cancel the original voucher and issue a new voucher for 694 the proper amount, while others would interline the correction in the voucher register if that book had not been posted.

Partial payments

The voucher system is not generally used when it is the custom of a business to make partial or installment payments on invoices. When such situations do arise in a company using the voucher system, special handling is required. If it is known at the outset that an invoice will be paid in installments, a separate voucher for each installment should be prepared in the first place. If it is decided to make a partial payment on an invoice already vouchered and recorded, it is recommended that the original voucher be canceled and that two or more new ones be issued. The total amount of the new vouchers should be equal to that of the old voucher. The debit may be to Vouchers Payable on the new vouchers. When they are recorded in the voucher register, the debits to Vouchers Payable will offset the credit to that account recorded from the old voucher. The original debit to the proper account will stand from the old voucher. A note should be made in the Disposition columns indicating that the old voucher has been canceled and showing the numbers of the new vouchers issued. Payments of the vouchers should be recorded in the usual manner.

Notes payable

When a note is given in temporary settlement of a voucher that is due, the note may be recorded in the general journal as a debit to Vouchers Payable and a credit to Notes Payable. At the same time, a notation should be made on the original voucher to show that it has been settled temporarily by means of a note. An entry should also be made in the voucher register to indicate the settlement of the voucher. When the note becomes due, a new voucher should then be issued authorizing the payment of the note and accrued interest. The new voucher should be recorded in the voucher register, and the check issued in payment of the voucher should be recorded in the check register. The entry in the voucher register will involve a debit to Notes Payable for the face of the note, a debit to Interest Expense for the amount of the interest on the note, and a credit to Vouchers Payable for the amount of the check to be issued. The entry in the check register will involve a debit to Vouchers Payable and a credit to the bank account for the amount of the check issued.

If a new note is issued in settlement of an old note plus the accrued interest, the entry may be made in the general journal debiting Notes Payable for the face of the old note, debiting Interest Expense for the amount of the interest on the old note, and crediting Notes Payable for the amount of the new note. A voucher will not be prepared until it is time to pay the new note and any accrued interest.

If a check is issued in payment of the interest and in partial payment of the principal of an outstanding note payable and a new note is issued for the balance, a voucher should be prepared authorizing the amount to be paid in cash. This voucher should be recorded in the voucher register by debiting Interest Expense for the amount of the interest, debiting Notes Payable for the amount to be paid on the principal, and crediting Vouchers Payable for the total. A check should then be drawn in payment of the voucher, and it should be recorded in the check register in the usual manner. The new note issued for the balance should be recorded in the general journal by debiting Notes Payable and also crediting Notes Payable for the amount of the new note. The debit entry cancels the unpaid portion of the old note, and the credit entry records the liability for the new note.

The unpaid vouchers file as a subsidiary ledger

When the voucher system is used, it is possible to dispense with a subsidiary accounts payable ledger. The file of unpaid vouchers serves as the detail to support the balance of the vouchers payable account after all posting has been completed. The voucher register itself partially performs this function. Every blank in the Disposition columns of the register shows that the indicated voucher is unpaid. The unpaid vouchers file can be consulted if more detail about any item is needed.

If a subsidiary accounts payable ledger is not maintained and if unpaid vouchers are filed according to due date, there is no way of quickly finding out how much is owed to a particular creditor. This may not be considered important. Businessmen using the voucher system tend to think in terms of unpaid invoices rather than being primarily concerned with the total amount owed to each of their creditors. However, if the latter information is needed, copies of the vouchers can be filed according to the names of the creditors. A subsidiary creditors' ledger can be maintained if one is desired. It may be wanted to furnish a detailed history of dealings with each creditor.

Petty cash fund

The maintenance of a petty cash fund eliminates the need for writing checks for small amounts. There are two methods of handling such a fund: one is known as the imprest method and the other as the journal method. Under the *imprest method* (which was discussed in some detail in Chapter 3, pages 54 and 55), disbursements from the petty cash fund are recorded in a petty cash record, which is treated as an auxiliary record. The entries in this book are not posted directly. When the fund is replenished, a check is issued for the necessary amount and, when this check is recorded in the check register, the proper expense accounts are debited for the amounts that have been paid out of the fund. Under this plan, the amount of money in the petty cash fund plus the sum of the receipts for the various expenditures should always be equal to the balance in the petty cash fund account in the general ledger.

Under the *journal method*, amounts paid from the petty cash fund are recorded in a petty cash disbursements journal. Each payment is recorded as a debit to the proper account and as a credit to Petty Cash. Special columns may be provided in this journal for the desired classification of expenditures. If special columns are not provided, each item must be posted separately; if special columns are provided, summary posting of the totals will be possible. When the fund is exhausted, additional money is obtained by issuing another check. Each check issued for the petty cash fund should be recorded in the check register as a debit to Petty Cash and a credit to the proper bank account.

The use of the voucher system of accounting does not affect the handling of a petty cash fund, except that a voucher must be prepared for the check issued to create the fund and for each check issued thereafter to replenish the fund. These vouchers must be recorded in the voucher register. If the imprest method is used, the voucher issued to create the fund is recorded in the voucher register by debiting Petty Cash Fund and by crediting Vouchers Payable. At the same time, the check is recorded in the check register by debiting Vouchers Payable and by crediting the proper bank account. Each voucher issued subsequently to replenish the fund is recorded in the voucher register by debiting the proper accounts and by crediting Vouchers Payable.

If the journal method is used, each voucher issued for the petty cash fund is recorded in the voucher register as a debit to Petty Cash and a credit to Vouchers Payable. Checks issued in payment of petty cash vouchers under this method should be recorded in the same manner as when the imprest method is used, that is, by debiting Vouchers Payable and by crediting the proper bank account.

Report No. 27-1

Complete Report No. 27-1 in the workbook and submit your working papers for approval. Continue with the next study assignment in Chapter 28 until Report No. 28-1 is required.

697

chapter 28

accounting for a manufacturing business

A manufacturing business makes articles for sale, rather than purchasing them in finished form as is the case in a merchandising business. Because of this the business operations of a manufacturing enterprise are more complex and, in consequence, its accounting processes are more elaborate. Records must be kept relating to the cost of materials acquired, labor costs incurred, and various other costs that arise in the operation of the factory. Normally, the end of an accounting period finds some unused materials, some unfinished goods, and some finished but unsold goods on hand. The various elements of manufacturing cost must be allocated in an equitable manner to the several types of inventory and to the goods that were sold.

Manufacturing cost; inventories of a manufacturing business

   The elements of manufacturing cost are **(1)** materials, **(2)** labor, and **(3)** factory overhead. The nature of each of these elements is discussed in the paragraphs that follow.

Materials

Certain materials are needed in the manufacture of a product. A manufacturer of automobiles requires sheet metal, bar steel, fabric, tires, and scores of other articles. A manufacturer of candy requires dextrose, citric acid, colors and flavors. The only distinction between materials and finished goods, in many instances, is their relationship to a particular manufacturer. The finished goods of one manufacturer may be the materials of another. Thus, flour is finished goods to a miller but materials to a baker; silver may be the finished product of a mining company but may constitute materials to a manufacturer of silverware. Materials used in manufacturing may be classified as:

(a) Direct materials.
(b) Indirect materials.

Direct materials normally include those that enter into and become a part of the finished product. Thus, the leather trimmings and the linings used in the manufacture of shoes are direct materials. Similarly, the sheet metal, bar steel, fabric, and many other materials used in the manufacture of an automobile are direct materials.

Indirect materials include those used in the manufacturing process that do not become a part of the finished product. Thus, oil and grease used in the operation of machinery are indirect materials. Such materials are often referred to as *factory supplies*. Indirect materials also may include inexpensive items that may become a part of the finished product, but whose small cost is most easily accounted for as a part of factory overhead. Nails, screws, washers, and glue sometimes are treated as indirect materials.

699

Labor

Wages paid to factory workers constitute a part of the cost of the finished product. The employees of a factory may be divided into two classes:

(a) Those who devote their time to converting the materials into finished goods. Such workers may do assembly work or may operate factory machinery. The wages paid to such workers are directly chargeable to the cost of the products being manufactured. This type of labor usually is referred to as *direct labor*.
(b) Those who devote their time to supervision or to work of a general nature. Such workers may include superintendents, foremen, inspectors, timekeepers, engineers, repairmen, receiving clerks, and janitors. The wages paid to such workers cannot be charged directly to the cost of the products being manufactured, but must be included in the indirect costs of the factory operation. This type of labor usually is referred to as *indirect labor*.

While there are many different methods employed in the handling of payrolls, the final results are much the same. Separate ledger accounts should be used for direct factory labor, indirect factory labor, sales salaries, office salaries, and administrative salaries. The payroll should be classified to facilitate the distribution of labor charges. When labor cost is properly analyzed and recorded so as to distinguish between direct and indirect labor, and between labor employed in the factory and in other departments, the accounts will provide better information for preparing manufacturing and income statements.

Factory overhead

It is impossible to operate a factory without incurring a variety of additional costs, often called *factory overhead*. (This group of costs is sometimes described as *manufacturing expenses*, *indirect manufacturing expense*, or *factory burden*.) Factory overhead may be classified as:

(a) Indirect materials.
(b) Indirect labor.
(c) Other factory overhead.

Indirect materials and indirect labor have already been discussed. Other factory overhead includes a variety of things such as:

(a) Depreciation of factory buildings and equipment.
(b) Repairs to factory buildings and equipment.
(c) Insurance on factory buildings and equipment.
(d) Property taxes applicable to factory buildings and equipment.
(e) Payroll taxes applicable to factory wages.
(f) Factory supplies used.
(g) Heat, light, and power consumed.

The accounts kept to record the factory overhead of different firms vary extensively. The information desired in the manufacturing statement, in a separate schedule of factory overhead, or in such other reports as may be required determine what accounts should be kept. Each distinct type of any cost sizable in amount should be recorded in a separate account.

As factory overhead costs are incurred, they should be recorded as debits to the proper accounts. Costs that are wholly chargeable to manufacturing should be recorded in separate accounts. Repairs to factory buildings and equipment is an example of this type of cost. There are certain other costs of a general overhead nature that cannot be charged wholly either to manufacturing or to any other single department. Each of these must be prorated or apportioned on some equitable basis. Power cost, for example, may be distributed on the basis of the amount of power consumed by various departments. Property taxes on land and buildings may be allocated in relation to the departmental space occupied in the buildings. Property taxes on furniture, fixtures, machinery, and equipment may be apportioned in relation to the value of the property in each department. A reasonable basis of distribution must be found for each cost of this type.

Inventories of a manufacturing business

The inventory of a merchant consists of finished goods only. In contrast to this, a manufacturer usually has three inventories: (1) materials, (2) work in process, and (3) finished goods. It is necessary to know the amounts of the inventories of materials and of work in process at the beginning and at the end of the period in order to determine the cost of goods manufactured. The beginning and the ending inventories of finished goods must be known in order to calculate the cost of goods sold. The relationship between these elements is as follows:

COST OF MATERIALS USED
$$\begin{cases} & \text{Beginning inventory of materials} \\ + & \text{Materials purchases (plus freight in, less returns and discounts)} \\ = & \text{Total cost of materials available} \\ - & \text{Ending inventory of materials} \\ = & \text{COST OF MATERIALS USED} \end{cases}$$

COST OF GOODS MANUFACTURED
$$\begin{cases} & \text{Beginning inventory of work in process} \\ + & \text{Cost of materials used} \\ + & \text{Direct labor} \\ + & \text{Factory overhead} \\ = & \text{Total factory costs} \\ - & \text{Ending inventory of work in process} \\ = & \text{COST OF GOODS MANUFACTURED} \end{cases}$$

COST OF GOODS SOLD
$$\begin{cases} & \text{Beginning inventory of finished goods} \\ + & \text{Cost of goods manufactured} \\ = & \text{Cost of finished goods available for sale} \\ - & \text{Ending inventory of finished goods} \\ = & \text{COST OF GOODS SOLD} \end{cases}$$

Assigning cost to inventories

In assigning cost to goods on hand at a certain time, one of the bases listed below must be used:

(a) Cost basis
   (1) First-in, first-out (fifo) cost
   (2) Average cost
   (3) Last-in, first-out (lifo) cost
(b) The lower of cost (fifo or average) or market (cost to replace)

These methods of allocating cost between goods sold and goods on hand in their application to a merchandising business were discussed and illustrated in Chapter 14. Any of these methods can be used by a manufacturing business in allocating the cost of materials purchased between the materials used and those which are still on hand at the end of the period. In the cases of inventories of work in process and of finished goods, cost includes **(1)** materials cost, **(2)** direct labor cost, and **(3)** factory overhead associated with the production of the goods.

Without the use of cost accounting procedures, it may be difficult to determine the costs that relate to the work that is in process. The difficulty may be insurmountable if the company has a large number of different products in various stages of completion at the end of the period. There usually is little difficulty in determining the total cost of materials and direct labor used, as well as the total factory overhead incurred during the period. The problem is to allocate or apportion these costs between the goods completed during the period and the work in process at the end of the period. Often the assignment of costs involves a considerable element of estimation, especially in the determination of the degree of completion of partly finished products.

Considerable accuracy is attainable in some cases, however. The nature of the product and the method of manufacture or processing may make it possible to compute the cost of the materials and the direct labor that have gone into the goods that have been finished and into those that are incomplete at the end of the period. The factory overhead may be apportioned on some reasonable basis. Sometimes it is allocated in proportion to direct labor. For example, suppose that the accounts of a manufacturer disclose the following information relative to a year just ended:

Cost of work in process, first of year................................	$ 18,000
Cost of materials used during year.................................	60,000
Direct labor for year...	100,000
Factory overhead for year..	70,000

Factory overhead amounted to 70 percent of direct labor ($70,000 ÷ $100,000). If it was determined that $12,000 was the cost of direct labor in the work in process at the end of the year, it might be reasonable to consider that $8,400 (70 percent of $12,000) of the factory overhead related to those goods. If $13,500 was determined to be the cost of materials in the incomplete goods, the allocation of all of these costs between finished and unfinished goods would be as follows:

		Cost Apportioned To	
	Total	Goods Finished During Year	Ending Inventory of Work in Process
Opening inventory of work in process..	$ 18,000	$ 18,000	......
Materials used.....................	60,000	46,500	$13,500
Direct labor.......................	100,000	88,000	12,000
Factory overhead	70,000	61,600(1)	8,400(2)
	$248,000	$214,100	$33,900

(1) 70% of $88,000
(2) 70% of $12,000

Inventories at cost or market, whichever is lower

Under most circumstances, the term "market," as used in relation to inventories, means the replacement cost at the date of the inventory for the particular merchandise in the volume in which it is usually purchased. If the lower-of-cost-or-market procedure is used, the market value of each article on hand should be compared with the cost of the article and the lower of the two should be taken as the inventory value of the article. In certain situations it is proper to use the lower of either the total cost of all the items or the total market value of all the items in the inventory.

Because the "cost or market, whichever is lower" rule often is applied to both the work in process and finished goods inventories of a manufacturer, the term "market" has to be specially interpreted. Usually there is no market in which either partly or wholly finished goods exactly like those manufactured could be purchased. The rule effectively becomes "cost or cost to replace, whichever is lower." Cost to replace may have to be estimated. Sometimes the cost of the latest lot of goods finished can be used as a measure. If there has been no change in any of the cost elements since such goods were completed, their unit cost may be considered as the unit cost to replace.

To illustrate the application of the rule, assume that a manufacturer has 3,000 units of Product A on hand at the end of the period. On the basis of first-in, first-out, 1,200 of the items cost $1 each and 1,800 units just completed cost 90 cents each. Further assume that there has been no change in the prices of materials, rates of labor, or other cost elements since the last lot of goods was completed. Thus, it would be proper to consider that the replacement cost is 90 cents per unit or $2,700 for the 3,000 units. The cost of this inventory was $2,820 (1,200 items at $1 plus 1,800 at 90 cents). The manufacturer would consider $2,700 to be the amount of the inventory if the "cost or cost to replace, whichever is lower" rule were followed. If replacement cost had been higher, it would have been ignored. If there had been a recent change in the prices of materials, the rates of labor, or the items of factory overhead, the latest incurred costs could not have been used as a measure of replacement cost. The manufacturer would have to estimate what the cost to replace would be after giving effect to the new conditions.

703

Perpetual inventories

A *perpetual inventory*, sometimes called a *book* or *running inventory*, is a continuous record of the amount of materials or goods on hand. This type of record is a useful device for control. Merchants and manufacturers like to know the quantities and the costs of goods on hand at all times without the delay incident to taking stock. If they believe that such information is worth the extra bookkeeping time and cost that it entails, they will maintain perpetual inventories.

When a perpetual inventory of materials is kept, there is no materials purchases account in the ledger. Instead, all such purchases are debited to the materials inventory account. Under this system, a record must be kept of the quantity and the cost of all materials used or returned. This amount is credited to the materials inventory account. After all posting has been completed, the balance of the account shows the cost of the goods that are presumed to be on hand.

Usually the materials inventory account controls a subsidiary ledger, called a *stores ledger*. This ledger has an account (frequently in the form of a card) for each item in inventory. The card shows the quantity and the cost of materials received, the quantity and the cost of materials issued, and the resulting balance. The postings to these accounts are kept up-to-date so that reference to each stores ledger card will show the quantity and the cost of the item on hand at any time. Often the form of the stores ledger cards (accounts) includes a memorandum column in which to record the quantity of goods ordered but not yet received.

Unless a manufacturer has a suitable cost accounting system, it is not likely that a perpetual inventory of work in process will be maintained. Without cost accounting it usually is difficult to keep an accurate perpetual inventory of finished goods, though this may be possible under certain circumstances. In some cases, records of materials, work in process, and finished goods are kept in terms of quantities alone. When the record is in this form, it is purely supplementary and there is no control account. Nevertheless, this type of record may be helpful in inventory control.

The use of perpetual inventories does not eliminate the necessity for periodically making a count of the materials or goods on hand. The perpetual inventory shows what should be on hand. The record may be wrong to the extent that errors may have been made or goods may have been lost, destroyed, or stolen. Some types of goods are subject to physical shrinkage. At least once a year a physical inventory should be taken. If the quantity of goods on hand is found to be more or less than the quantity shown by the inventory records, an adjustment of the accounts is needed. For example, if the balance of the materials inventory account showed the cost of goods on hand to be $8,000 but a costing of the goods found to be on hand by physical count totaled only $7,500, an adjusting entry would be needed debiting Manufacturing Summary and crediting Materials Inventory for $500. The discovery of an overage or a shortage of finished goods would require an adjustment to the expense and revenue summary account.

When perpetual inventories are maintained, it is not necessary to take an inventory of everything at the same time. One particular type of goods can be counted and the finding compared with the stores or stock card for that item. Another type can be inventoried at a different time. Adjustments can be made as shortages or overages are discovered. In such cases, inventory short and over accounts can be used that are closed at the end of the period. Some large companies are taking physical inventory of some type of goods each working day.

Report No. 28-1

Complete Report No. 28-1 in the workbook and submit your working papers for approval. Continue with the following study assignment until Report No. 28-2 is required.

The charts of accounts and records of a manufacturing business

To illustrate the accounting for a manufacturing business, the case of The B. J. Patrick Manufacturing Co. is presented. The company is a small manufacturing concern whose operations are confined to manufacturing and selling a single product — candy. No merchandise is purchased for resale in its original form. The company does not have a cost accounting system nor does it keep perpetual inventories. The costs assigned to the inventories of materials and finished goods are on the basis of a physical count made at the end of each accounting period. The cost of the inventory of work in process is estimated.

Charts of accounts

The charts of accounts of The B. J. Patrick Manufacturing Co. are reproduced on pages 706 and 707.

There is a similarity in the titles of certain factory overhead, administrative expense, and selling expense accounts. For example, there are three depreciation accounts, including Depreciation of Factory Building and Equipment, Account No. 7405, Depreciation of Office Equipment, Account No. 8204, and Depreciation of Delivery Equipment, Account No. 8235. It is necessary to classify such charges by recording them in appropriate accounts so that the proper information may be set forth in the annual reports. Depreciation of factory building and equipment is factory overhead, while depreciation of office equipment is an administrative expense, and depreciation of delivery equipment is a selling expense. Property taxes and insurance also must be apportioned among the proper cost and expense accounts.

THE B. J. PATRICK MANUFACTURING CO.
CHART OF GENERAL LEDGER ACCOUNTS

Current Assets

Cash
111 First National Bank
112 Petty Cash Fund

Temporary Investments
121 Government Bonds

Receivables
131 Notes Receivable
132 Accrued Interest Receivable
133 Accounts Receivable
    013 Allowance for Bad Debts

Inventories
161 Materials Inventory
162 Work in Process Inventory
163 Finished Goods Inventory

Supplies and Prepayments
181 Office Supplies
182 Advertising Supplies
183 Factory Supplies
184 Prepaid Insurance

Long-Lived Assets
211 Office Equipment
    021 Accumulated Depreciation —
    Office Equipment
221 Delivery Equipment
    022 Accumulated Depreciation —
    Delivery Equipment
231 Factory Equipment
    023 Accumulated Depreciation —
    Factory Equipment
241 Building
    024 Accumulated Depreciation —
    Building
251 Land
261 Patents

Current Liabilities
311 FICA Tax Payable
312 FUTA Tax Payable
313 State Unemployment Tax Payable
314 Employees Income Tax Payable
315 Corporation Income Tax Payable
316 Notes Payable
317 Accrued Interest Payable
318 Vouchers Payable
319 Dividends Payable

Long-Term Liabilities
421 Bonds Payable

Stockholders' Equity
511 Capital Stock
521 Retained Earnings
531 Expense and Revenue Summary

Revenue
611 Sales
    061 Sales Returns and Allowances
    062 Sales Discount
631 Interest Earned

Manufacturing Costs
711 Materials Purchases
    071 Materials Purchases Returns
    and Allowances
    072 Purchases Discount
721 Freight In
731 Direct Labor
741 Factory Overhead
751 Manufacturing Summary

Cost of Goods Sold and Expenses
811 Cost of Goods Sold
821 Operating Expenses
831 Interest Expense
841 Charitable Contributions Expense
851 Income Tax Expense

THE B. J. PATRICK MANUFACTURING CO.

THE B. J. PATRICK MANUFACTURING CO.

CHART OF FACTORY OVERHEAD LEDGER ACCOUNTS

7401 Indirect Labor
7402 Utilities Consumed
7403 Factory Supplies Consumed
7404 Factory Building Maintenance
7405 Depreciation of Factory Building and Equipment
7406 Expired Insurance on Factory Building and Equipment
7407 Factory Repairs
7408 Patent Amortization
7409 Taxes on Factory Building and Equipment
7411 Payroll Taxes — Factory
7412 Miscellaneous Factory Overhead

THE B. J. PATRICK MANUFACTURING CO.

CHART OF OPERATING EXPENSE LEDGER ACCOUNTS

Administrative Expenses

8201 Office Salaries Expense
8202 Officers' Salaries Expense
8203 Office Supplies Expense
8204 Depreciation of Office Equipment
8205 Office Equipment Insurance Expense
8206 Property Tax Expense — Office Equipment
8207 Payroll Taxes — Administrative
8208 Miscellaneous Office Expense

Selling Expenses

8231 Sales Salaries Expense
8232 Traveling Expense
8233 Advertising Expense
8234 Delivery Expense
8235 Depreciation of Delivery Equipment
8236 Delivery Equipment Insurance Expense
8237 Bad Debts Expense
8238 Finished Goods Insurance Expense
8239 Property Tax Expense — Delivery Equipment
8241 Payroll Taxes — Sales
8242 Miscellaneous Selling Expense

707

Ledgers

While all of the accounts shown in the charts of accounts of The B. J. Patrick Manufacturing Co. might be kept in one general ledger, it has been found advantageous to keep the accounts with customers, the accounts for factory overhead, the accounts for operating expenses, and the accounts with stockholders in subsidiary ledgers with control accounts in the general ledger. Following are the names of the subsidiary ledgers and the titles of the control accounts that are kept in the general ledger:

SUBSIDIARY LEDGERS	CONTROL ACCOUNTS
Accounts Receivable Ledger	133 Accounts Receivable
Factory Overhead Ledger	741 Factory Overhead
Operating Expense Ledger	821 Operating Expenses
Stockholders Ledger	511 Capital Stock

The B. J. Patrick Manufacturing Co. uses a four-column account form in the general ledger. This account form differs slightly from those previously introduced in this textbook. It is illustrated on page 708. A few items have already been posted to illustrate the proper use of the form. This account form is especially well suited for general ledger use because it provides a precise means of showing whether the balance of each account

ACCOUNT   *Accounts Receivable*   ACCOUNT NO. *133*

DATE		ITEM	POST. REF.	DEBIT	CREDIT	BALANCE	
						DEBIT	CREDIT
19- - Jan.	1	Balance	✓			24 772 19	
	12		G31		23 50		
	12		G31		357 15		
	22		G32		8 25		
	27	90-day note	G36		1 000 00		
	31		SR44	15 576 09			
	31		CR47		14 771 96	24 187 42	
					16 160 86		

is a debit or a credit. This is important because some general ledger accounts normally have debit balances, while other accounts normally have credit balances. The Item column is seldom used; however, it may be used for writing an explanation of the entry for any unusual transaction.

708 For example, in the illustration the word "Balance" is inserted in the Item column to explain that the entry on January 1 represents the balance of the account which has been brought forward from another page. The notation "90-day note" is an explanation of the entry of January 27, indicating that a customer has been given credit for a note presented in order to obtain an extension of time on his account.

A three-column account form (illustrated on page 203) is used in the accounts receivable ledger, factory overhead ledger, and operating expense ledger. Inasmuch as the balances in these ledgers are normally debits, it is not necessary to provide columns for both debit and credit balance entries. It is customary to extend the balance following each entry in a customers ledger; this is done because of the need for credit information in handling current sales on account. When this account form is used in a factory overhead ledger or an operating expense ledger, the balance need be extended only at the end of each month or when taking a trial balance. The procedure is as follows:

(a) Foot the Debit and Credit amount columns.
(b) Compute the new balance.
(c) Enter the new balance in the Balance column.

After all posting has been completed, the balance of the control account for Accounts Receivable, Account No. 133, may be proved by preparing a schedule of accounts receivable from the data in the subsidiary ledger. The balances of the control accounts for Factory Overhead, Account No. 741, and Operating Expenses, Account No. 821, also may be proved by preparing schedules of their respective subsidiary ledgers.

The form of the account in the stockholders ledger used by The B. J. Patrick Manufacturing Co. is of the same design as the account illustrated on page 578. This account differs from other account forms in that it does not provide any information as to the dollar amount of the shares owned by each stockholder; instead, it provides information only as to the number of shares owned. The control account for the stockholders ledger is Capital Stock, Account No. 511. The control account shows the total par value or stated value of the stock issued. The balance of the control account may be proved by preparing a schedule of the shares issued to stockholders from the information provided in the stockholders ledger and multiplying the total number of shares issued by the par value or stated value of each share.

Since The B. J. Patrick Manufacturing Co. uses the voucher system of accounting, a subsidiary accounts payable ledger is not maintained. The voucher register not only serves as an invoice register, but it also provides information regarding vouchered liabilities. Further detail can be secured by reference to the files of unpaid and paid vouchers. The management of the company feels that the voucher register and these two files provide all of the information needed with respect to transactions with creditors.

709

Journals

The number, the nature, and the variety of the transactions of The B. J. Patrick Manufacturing Co. warrant the use of the following books of original entry:

(a) Voucher register
(b) Sales register
(c) Record of cash receipts
(d) Check register
(e) General journal

The forms of the voucher register and the check register used by this company are similar to those illustrated on pages 688, 689, and 692. A sales register with the following amount columns is used:

General Ledger Dr.
Accounts Receivable Dr.
Sales Cr.
Operating Expenses (Delivery Expense) Cr.
General Ledger Cr.

It is not necessary to provide for the recording of sales taxes since all of the sales of The B. J. Patrick Manufacturing Co. are made to wholesalers and various other distributors. All merchandise sold is "intended for resale." There is no need to provide for a departmental distribution of sales.

A cash receipts record with the following amount columns is used:

General Ledger Dr.
Sales Discount Dr.
Bank Dr.
Accounts Receivable Cr.
Cash Sales Cr.
General Ledger Cr.

The company uses a general journal with three amount columns. The first of these columns is used to record amounts to be posted to subsidiary ledger accounts. The second and the third columns are used to record amounts to be debited and credited to general ledger accounts. The use of this form of journal is discussed on page 720 and illustrated on pages 722 to 725.

The types and the forms of journals and subsidiary ledgers used in keeping the financial records of a business are determined by such factors as the nature of the undertaking, the volume of business done, the amount of information required by the management, and the number of employees required to keep the records. It is important to keep in mind that all transactions should be recorded in some book of original entry or journal. The use of special columns facilitates the classification of the desired information and saves time in posting. Timesaving is important, for accounting is one of the operating expenses of a business that can be unduly expensive if the accounting department is not efficiently organized and if a sound accounting system is not maintained.

Auxiliary records

It has been noted at several points that various auxiliary records are usually kept by businesses. These are supplementary to the journals and ledgers. Such auxiliary records may include the following:

(a) Petty cash disbursements record
(b) Long-lived assets record
(c) Insurance policy register
(d) Notes receivable register
(e) Notes payable register
(f) Payroll record
(g) Employee's earnings record

The purpose of auxiliary records is to supply the detailed information needed in the operations of an enterprise. For example, the long-lived assets record should provide a detailed record of office equipment, delivery equipment, factory equipment, and buildings owned; showing date acquired, cost, rate of depreciation, and total amount of accumulated depreciation. The insurance policy register should provide a detailed record of all insurance policies carried, with provision for distributing the premium uniformly over the life of each policy. This information will facilitate the recording of the expired insurance with a proper classification of the insurance expense. The preparation and maintenance of formal payrolls and employees' earnings records is mandatory for companies subject to the requirements of the Federal Fair Labor Standards Act (the wages and hours law) and the social security acts.

It may be assumed that The B. J. Patrick Manufacturing Co. keeps most, if not all, of the auxiliary records listed. Since this company does not keep any type of perpetual inventories, it does not have formal subsidiary stores and stock ledgers, or even auxiliary records that show only the physical quantities of the materials and goods on hand.

Computer-based accounting in manufacturing businesses

In earlier chapters, reference has been made to the use of computer-based accounting systems. In each instance, it was pointed out that some variety of these systems becomes feasible when there is a large volume of transactions. Inasmuch as the operation of a manufacturing business is more complex than that of a merchandising concern or a personal service enterprise, a manufacturer has a greater variety of transactions and events that must be recorded. If, in addition, a variety of products are manufactured and there is a large volume of business, the accounting and record keeping task may be considerable. It is for this reason that many computer-based accounting systems are found in manufacturing businesses. In the case of The B. J. Patrick Manufacturing Co. however, only one product is involved and the volume of business is relatively small. For these reasons, manually kept records are the most economical for this company.

Report No. 28-2

Complete Report No. 28-2 in the workbook and submit your working papers for approval. Continue with the following study assignment until Report No. 28-3 is required.

Accounting procedure
at end of year

The end-of-year accounting procedure for a corporation engaged in manufacturing is similar to that for a merchandising enterprise. Most accountants use work sheets as a means of summarizing and classifying the information needed to produce certain financial statements, and to assist in the process of formally adjusting and closing the books.

The work sheets of a manufacturing business

The work sheets prepared for The B. J. Patrick Manufacturing Co. for the year ended December 31, 19B[1] are shown on pages 714-716. Since the necessary adjustments affect accounts both in the factory overhead and in the operating expense ledgers as well as accounts in the general ledger, two supplementary work sheets are prepared. Note that the third pair of columns in the summary work sheet is headed "Manufacturing." This pair of columns is used to assemble all of the elements that enter into the calculation of the cost of goods manufactured for the year. The annual report of the company includes a *manufacturing statement* prepared from the information assembled in the manufacturing columns of the summary work sheet. Because of space limitations, this work sheet omits the pair of Adjusted Trial Balance columns that normally follow the Adjustments columns.

Following is a discussion of the steps that were involved in completing the work sheets.

Trial Balance. The first pair of amount columns of the summary work sheet contains the general ledger trial balance. The first amount column of each of the supplementary work sheets contains the trial balance of the indicated subsidiary ledger. If the general ledger trial balance totals had not been the same or if the totals of the account balances in the subsidiary ledgers had not agreed with the related general ledger control accounts (Nos. 741 and 821), the reasons for any discrepancies would have needed to have been discovered and corrected before the preparation of the work sheets could proceed.

---

[1]In the next chapter, several of the financial statements and schedules are presented in *comparative* form. That is, the amounts for the most recent year or date are followed by the amounts for the preceding year or date in that year. To distinguish between the years, the most recent year is identified as "19B" and the year before as "19A."

Adjusting Entries. The second pair of amount columns in the summary work sheet and the second amount column in each of the supplementary work sheets contain the entries required to adjust the account balances.

THE B. J. PATRICK MANUFACTURING CO.
DATA FOR ADJUSTING THE ACCOUNTS
DECEMBER 31, 19B

Inventories:

Materials........................		$16,732.59
Work in process..................		1,083.36
Finished goods...................		77,690.98

Interest Accruals:

Interest receivable..............		82.31
Interest payable.................		934.13
Provision for bad debts, ¼ of 1% of net sales....		488.64
Office supplies consumed..........		287.63
Advertising supplies consumed.....		285.20
Factory supplies consumed.........		430.95

Insurance expired:

On factory building and equipment......	$270.95	
On office equipment...................	81.61	
On delivery equipment.................	108.91	
On finished goods.....................	61.79	523.26

Depreciation:

Office equipment, 10%.................		244.14
Delivery equipment, 25%...............		934.88
Factory equipment, 10%...............		3,451.60

(Factory equipment costing $4,210.98 was purchased on June 28, 19B. It was depreciated for ½ year only.)

Building, 2%:

7/8 charged to factory................	$920.50	
1/8 charged to office.................	131.50	1,052.00
Amortization of patents...............		437.50
Provision for corporation income tax..............		$ 7,517.32

The quantities of materials and finished goods on hand at the end of the year were determined by actual count and their cost was calculated on a first-in, first-out basis. Since a cost accounting system was not maintained, the cost of the work in process at the end of the year was estimated.

Before recording the new or year-end inventories on the summary work sheet, the old or beginning inventories were transferred to the proper summary accounts. The old inventories of materials, $17,578.33, and work in process, $976.57, were transferred to Manufacturing Summary, Account No. 751 (adjustments *a* and *b*). The old inventory of finished goods, $79,102.48, was transferred to Cost of Goods Sold, Account No. 811 (adjustment *c*). The new inventories of materials, $16,732.59, and work in process, $1,083.36, were recorded by debiting the proper inventory accounts and by crediting Manufacturing Summary (adjustments *d* and *e*). The new inventory of finished goods, $77,690.98, was recorded by debiting Finished Goods Inventory, Account No. 163, and by crediting Cost of Goods Sold (adjustment *f*).

The accrued interest receivable, amounting to $82.31 at the end of the year, was determined by computing the interest accrued on notes receivable

713

714

Account	Acct. No.	Trial Balance Debit	Trial Balance Credit
First National Bank	111	2 395 65	
Petty Cash Fund	112	100 00	
Government Bonds	121	6 000 00	
Notes Receivable	131	8 136 11	
Accrued Interest Receivable	132		
Accounts Receivable	133	40 692 57	
Allowance for Bad Debts	013		122 07
Materials Inventory	161	17 578 33	
Work in Process Inventory	162	976 57	
Finished Goods Inventory	163	79 102 48	
Office Supplies	181	363 70	
Advertising Supplies	182	328 25	
Factory Supplies	183	549 30	
Prepaid Insurance	184	828 36	
Office Equipment	211	2 441 43	
Accumulated Depreciation — Office Equipment	021		976 20
Delivery Equipment	221	3 739 50	
Accumulated Depreciation — Delivery Equipment	022		622 64
Factory Equipment	231	36 621 51	
Accumulated Depreciation — Factory Equipment	023		7 324 30
Building	241	52 600 00	
Accumulated Depreciation — Building	024		10 580 00
Land	251	10 000 00	
Patents	261	1 750 00	
FICA Tax Payable	311		965 47
FUTA Tax Payable	312		51 04
State Unemployment Tax Payable	313		275 60
Employees Income Tax Payable	314		1 952 30
Corporation Income Tax Payable	315		
Notes Payable	316		10 200 00
Accrued Interest Payable	317		
Vouchers Payable	318		20 111 24
Dividends Payable	319		1 250 00
Bonds Payable	421		70 000 00
Capital Stock	511		50 000 00
Retained Earnings	521		48 865 75
Sales	611		198 967 60
Sales Returns and Allowances	061	918 62	
Sales Discount	062	2 593 90	
Interest Earned	631		95 80
Materials Purchases	711	57 046 74	
Materials Purchases Returns and Allowances	071		343 26
Purchases Discount	072		2 003 38
Freight In	721	8 669 17	
Direct Labor	731	16 450 25	
Factory Overhead	741	23 975 04	
Manufacturing Summary	751		
Cost of Goods Sold	811		
Operating Expenses	821	48 863 77	
Interest Expense	831	1 725 40	
Charitable Contributions Expense	841	260 00	
Income Tax Expense	851		
		424 706 65	424 706 65
Cost of Goods Manufactured			
Net Income			

MANUFACTURING CO.
Work Sheet
Ended December 31, 19B

Adjustments Debit	Adjustments Credit	Manufacturing Debit	Manufacturing Credit	Income Statement Debit	Income Statement Credit	Balance Sheet Debit	Balance Sheet Credit
						2 395 65	
						100 00	
						6 000 00	
						8 136 11	
(g) 82 31						82 31	
						40 692 57	
(d) 16 732 59	(i) 488 64						610 71
	(a) 17 578 33					16 732 59	
(e) 1 083 36	(b) 976 57					1 083 36	
(f) 77 690 98	(c) 79 102 48					77 690 98	
	(j) 287 63					76 07	
	(k) 285 20					43 05	
	(l) 430 95					118 35	
	(m) 523 26					305 10	
						2 441 43	
	(n) 244 14						1 220 34
						3 739 50	
	(o) 934 88						1 557 52
						36 621 51	
	(p) 3 451 60						10 775 90
						52 600 00	
	(q) 1 052 00						11 632 00
						10 000 00	
	(r) 437 50					1 312 50	
							965 47
							51 04
							275 60
							1 952 30
	(s) 7 517 32						7 517 32
							10 200 00
	(h) 934 13						934 13
							20 111 24
							1 250 00
							70 000 00
							50 000 00
							48 865 75
				918 62	198 967 60		
				2 593 90			
	(g) 82 31				178 11		
		57 046 74					
			343 26				
			2 003 38				
		8 669 17					
		16 450 25					
(y) 5 511 50		29 486 54					
(a) 17 578 33	(d) 16 732 59	17 578 33	16 732 59				
(b) 976 57	(e) 1 083 36	976 57	1 083 36				
(c) 79 102 48	(f) 77 690 98			79 102 48	77 690 98		
(z) 2 624 30				51 488 07			
(h) 934 13				2 659 53			
				260 00			
(s) 7 517 32				7 517 32			
209 833 87	209 833 87	130 207 60	20 162 59	144 539 92	276 836 69	260 171 08	237 919 32
			110 045 01	110 045 01			
		130 207 60	130 207 60	254 584 93			
				22 251 76			22 251 76
				276 836 69	276 836 69	260 171 08	260 171 08

THE B. J. PATRICK MANUFACTURING CO.
FACTORY OVERHEAD WORK SHEET
FOR THE YEAR ENDED DECEMBER 31, 19B

Account	Acct. No.	Trial Balance Debit	Adjustments Debit		Adj. Trial Balance Debit
Indirect Labor	7401	15 820 79			15 820 79
Utilities	7402	2 377 12			2 377 12
Factory Supplies Consumed	7403		(l)	430 95	430 95
Factory Building Maintenance	7404	832 81			832 81
Depr. of Factory Bldg. and Equip.	7405		(p) 3 451 60 (q) 920 50		4 372 10
Expired Insurance—Fac. Bldg. and Eq.	7406		(m) 270 95		270 95
Factory Repairs	7407	639 59			639 59
Patent Amortization	7408		(r) 437 50		437 50
Taxes on Factory Bldg. and Equip.	7409	1 392 64			1 392 64
Payroll Taxes — Factory	7411	2 354 00			2 354 00
Miscellaneous Factory Overhead	7412	558 09			558 09
		23 975 04	(y) 5 511 50		29 486 54

The B. J. Patrick Manufacturing Co. — Factory Overhead Work Sheet

THE B. J. PATRICK MANUFACTURING CO.
OPERATING EXPENSES WORK SHEET
FOR THE YEAR ENDED DECEMBER 31, 19B

716

Account	Acct. No.	Trial Balance Debit	Adjustments Debit		Adj. Trial Balance Debit
Office Salaries Expense	8201	7 238 26			7 238 26
Officers' Salaries Expense	8202	22 400 00			22 400 00
Office Supplies Expense	8203		(j)	287 63	287 63
Depreciation of Office Equipment	8204		(n)	244 14	244 14
Office Equipment Insurance Expense	8205		(m)	81 61	81 61
Prop. Tax Exp.—Office Equipment	8206	184 40			184 40
Payroll Taxes — Administrative	8207	1 846 31			1 846 31
Miscellaneous Office Expense	8208	528 04	(q)	131 50	659 54
Sales Salaries Expense	8231	12 096 69			12 096 69
Traveling Expense	8232	668 80			668 80
Advertising Expense	8233	1 109 60	(k)	285 20	1 394 80
Delivery Expense	8234	1 991 77			1 991 77
Depr. of Delivery Equipment	8235		(o)	934 88	934 88
Delivery Equipment Ins. Expense	8236		(m)	108 91	108 91
Bad Debts Expense	8237		(i)	488 64	488 64
Finished Goods Insurance Expense	8238		(m)	61 79	61 79
Prop. Tax. Exp.—Del. Equipment	8239	38 20			38 20
Payroll Taxes — Sales	8241	370 31			370 31
Miscellaneous Selling Expense	8242	391 39			391 39
		48 863 77	(z) 2 624 30		51 488 07

The B. J. Patrick Manufacturing Co. — Operating Expenses Work Sheet

and government bonds owned. The amount accrued was entered on the summary work sheet by debiting Accrued Interest Receivable, Account No. 132, and by crediting Interest Earned, Account No. 631 (adjustment *g*).

The accrued interest payable, amounting to $934.13 at the end of the year, was determined by computing the interest accrued on notes payable and bonds payable. The amount accrued was entered on the summary work sheet by debiting Interest Expense, Account No. 831, and by crediting Accrued Interest Payable, Account No. 317 (adjustment *h*).

The estimated amount of bad debt losses for the year, $488.64 (¼ of 1% of net sales), was recorded on the operating expenses work sheet by debiting Bad Debts Expense, Account No. 8237, with the credit to Allowance for Bad Debts, Account No. 013, on the summary work sheet (adjustment *i*). (At a later time, after all of the adjustments that affected accounts in the factory overhead and operating expenses work sheets had been recorded, debit entries were made on the summary work sheet to adjust the Factory Overhead and Operating Expenses control accounts.)

The costs of office, advertising, and factory supplies consumed during the year were calculated by making a physical count of the supplies of each type that were on hand at the end of the year, determining their cost, and subtracting the amounts of these inventories from the balances of the accounts for Office Supplies, Account No. 181, Advertising Supplies, Account No. 182, and Factory Supplies, Account No. 183. On the operating expenses work sheet, Office Supplies Expense, Account No. 8203, was debited for $287.63, and Advertising Expense, Account No. 8233, was debited for $285.20. On the factory overhead work sheet, Factory Supplies Consumed, Account No. 7403, was debited for $430.95. The proper supplies account on the summary work sheet was credited in each case (adjustments *j*, *k*, and *l*).

The amounts of expired insurance on various types of property were determined from information provided by the insurance policy register. The entry required was a debit of $270.95 to Expired Insurance — Factory Building and Equipment, Account No. 7406, on the factory overhead work sheet, debits of $81.61 to Office Equipment Insurance Expense, Account No. 8205, $108.91 to Delivery Equipment Insurance Expense, Account No. 8236, and $61.79 to Finished Goods Insurance Expense, Account No. 8238, on the operating expenses work sheet, with a credit of $523.26 to Prepaid Insurance, Account No. 184, on the summary work sheet (adjustment *m*).

Five debits were made to record the depreciation for the year on the four classes of long-lived assets. On the operating expenses work sheet, Depreciation of Office Equipment, Account No. 8204, was debited for $244.14, Depreciation of Delivery Equipment, Account No. 8235, was debited for $934.88, and Miscellaneous Office Expense, Account No. 8208, was debited for $131.50 (representing 1/8 of the year's depreciation of the building). On the factory overhead work sheet, Depreciation of Factory Building and Equipment, Account No. 7405, received two debits: one for $3,451.60, depreciation of factory equipment, and one for $920.50, 7/8 of the year's depreciation of the building. On the summary work sheet, there were proper credits to each of the four accumulated depreciation accounts (adjustments *n*, *o*, *p*, and *q*).

The patents were acquired five years before at a cost of $3,500. At the time of purchase, the patents had a remaining life of eight years. Accordingly, 1/8 of the cost or $437.50 is being written off each year. This amount was recorded by a debit to Patent Amortization, Account No. 7408, on the factory overhead work sheet, with the credit to Patents, Account No. 261, on the summary work sheet (adjustment *r*).

Since the foregoing was the last adjustment that affected the supplementary work sheets, each of these was completed by **(1)** adding any amount in the first column to any amount in the second column and entering the total in the third column, **(2)** totaling the second and third columns and, as a means of proof, checking to be sure that the sum of the totals of column one and column two equal to the total of column three, and **(3)** making the rulings. The total of the Adjustments column of the factory overhead work sheet, $5,511.50, was entered on the summary work sheet as a debit to Factory Overhead, Account No. 741. For purpose of identification, the entry was designated as "y." The total of the Adjustments column of the operating expenses work sheet, $2,624.30, was entered on the summary work sheet as a debit to Operating Expenses, Account No. 821. For the purpose of identification, this entry was designated as "z."

The income tax for the year just ended was estimated to be $7,517.32 on the basis of the prevailing rates. This amount was recorded on the summary work sheet by debiting Income Tax Expense, Account No. 851, and crediting Corporation Income Tax Payable, Account No. 315 (adjustment *s*).

Completing the Summary Work Sheet. The Adjustments columns were totaled. With two exceptions, the amounts in the Trial Balance columns were modified by amounts in the Adjustments columns and extended into the Adjusted Trial Balance columns (not included in the illustration on pages 714 and 715 because of space limitations). The exceptions referred to are the cases of Manufacturing Summary, Account No. 751, and Cost of Goods Sold, Account No. 811. In each of these cases, the amounts in the Adjustments columns were not summarized into a net amount to be shown in the Adjusted Trial Balance columns, but the debits and credits were extended intact. In the case of the debits and credits to the manufacturing summary account (which were the amounts of the beginning and ending inventories of materials and work in process), each of the four amounts was needed in preparing the manufacturing statement. For this reason the two debits and the two credits were extended to the Adjusted Trial Balance columns (not shown) and on to the pair of Manufacturing columns. The debit and the credit to the cost of goods sold account were the opening and closing inventories of finished goods. Since both of these amounts were needed in preparing the income statement, both were extended to the Adjusted Trial Balance columns, and on to the Income Statement columns. The Adjusted Trial Balance columns were totaled.

The amounts of materials purchases, materials purchases returns and allowances, purchases discount, freight in, direct labor, and factory overhead were extended into the Manufacturing columns. All of these amounts, together with the amounts of the opening and closing inventories of materials and work in process, caused the total of the Debit column to exceed the total of the Credit column by $110,045.01 — the cost of goods manufactured during the year. To balance the Manufacturing columns, that amount was placed in the Credit column and was extended to the Income Statement Debit column on the Cost of Goods Manufactured line.

The amounts of sales, sales returns and allowances, sales discount, interest earned, operating expenses, interest expense, charitable contributions expense, and income tax expense were extended into the Income Statement columns. All of these amounts, together with the amounts of the opening and closing inventories of finished goods and the cost of goods manufactured, caused the total of the Credit column to exceed the total of the Debit column by $22,251.76 — the net income for the year. To balance the Income Statement columns, this amount was placed in the Debit column and was extended to the Balance Sheet Credit column.

The next step was to extend the amounts of all asset, contra-asset, liability, and stockholders' equity accounts to the Balance Sheet columns. Finally, all column totals were entered and the proper rulings were made.

Preparing the financial statements

The summary and supplementary work sheets provided all the data needed for preparing an income statement with a supporting schedule of operating expenses for the year 19B, a manufacturing statement for that year, and a year-end balance sheet for The B. J. Patrick Manufacturing Co. These statements and certain others were prepared next. However, for the purpose of better organization of the subject matter in this textbook, the financial statements are illustrated and discussed in the following chapter. The remainder of this chapter will be devoted to illustration and discussion of the formal adjusting and closing procedure of the company at the end of the year.

Adjusting the accounts

The adjustments shown in the Adjustments columns of the work sheets are recorded in the general journal and posted to the proper general ledger and subsidiary ledger accounts. The B. J. Patrick Manufacturing Co. uses a general journal with three amount columns. The second and the third amount columns are used to record debits and credits to general ledger accounts. The first amount column is headed "Detail" and is used to record amounts that are to be posted to subsidiary ledger accounts. The names of the subsidiary ledger accounts to be debited are placed immediately below the name of the general ledger control account to be debited. The names of subsidiary ledger accounts to be credited are placed just below the name of the general ledger control account to be credited.

The journal entries to record the adjustments as of December 31 are reproduced on pages 722 and 723. When these entries are posted, the balances in the general ledger accounts will be the same as those shown in the Adjusted Trial Balance columns of the work sheet. The total of the balances of the accounts in the factory overhead subsidiary ledger will be equal to the adjusted balance of the factory overhead control account, and the total of the balances of the accounts in the operating expense subsidiary ledger will be equal to the adjusted balance of the operating expenses control account.

Closing the temporary accounts

The preparation of closing entries is facilitated by the use of work sheets. There are four steps involved in closing the temporary accounts:

(a) The balances of the accounts that enter into the calculation of the cost of goods manufactured are transferred to Manufacturing Summary, Account No. 751. The beginning and the ending inventories of materials and work in process were entered in this account when the adjusting entries were posted. In closing, it is necessary to transfer the balances of Materials Purchases, Account No. 711; Materials Purchases Returns and Allowances, Account No. 071; Purchases Discount, Account No. 072; Freight In, Account No. 721; Direct Labor, Account No. 731; and Factory Overhead, Account No. 741, to the manufacturing summary account.

(b) The balance of the manufacturing summary account, which is the cost of goods manufactured, is transferred to Cost of Goods Sold, Account No. 811. Since the beginning and the ending inventories of finished goods have already been posted to this account, its balance will be the cost of goods sold during the year.

(c) The balance of the cost of goods sold account and the balances of all of the other accounts that enter into the calculation of net income are transferred to Expense and Revenue Summary, Account No. 531.

(d) The balance of the expense and revenue summary account is transferred to Retained Earnings, Account No. 521.

ACCOUNT *Expense and Revenue Summary*   ACCOUNT NO. *531*

DATE		ITEM	POST. REF.	DEBIT	CREDIT	BALANCE DEBIT	BALANCE CREDIT
19B							
Dec.	*31*	*Sales*	*G15*		*198 967 60*		
	31	*Interest Earned*	*G15*		*178 11*		
	31	*Sales Ret. and Allw.*	*G15*	*918 62*	*199 145 71*		
	31	*Sales Discount*	*G15*	*2 593 90*			
	31	*Cost of Goods Sold*	*G15*	*111 456 51*			
	31	*Operating Expenses*	*G15*	*51 488 07*			
	31	*Interest Expense*	*G15*	*2 659 53*			
	31	*Charit. Contr. Exp.*	*G15*	*260 00*			
	31	*Income Tax Exp.*	*G15*	*7 517 32*			*22 251 76*
				176 893 95			
	31	*Retained Earnings*	*G15*	*22 251 76*		—0—	—0—

ACCOUNT *Manufacturing Summary*   ACCOUNT NO. *751*

DATE		ITEM	POST. REF.	DEBIT	CREDIT	BALANCE DEBIT	BALANCE CREDIT
19B							
Dec.	*31*	*Materials Inv., beg.*	*G14*	*17 578 33*			
	31	*Work in Proc. Inv., beg.*	*G14*	*976 57*			
	31	*Materials Inv., end.*	*G14*		*16 732 59*		
	31	*Work in Proc. Inv., end.*	*G14*		*1 083 36*		
	31	*Materials Purchases*	*G15*	*57 046 74*			
	31	*Freight In*	*G15*	*8 669 17*			
	31	*Direct Labor*	*G15*	*16 450 25*			
	31	*Factory Overhead*	*G15*	*29 486 54*			
				130 207 60			
	31	*Mats. Pur. Ret. and Allow.*	*G15*		*343 26*		
	31	*Purchases Discount*	*G15*		*2 003 38*	*110 045 01*	
					20 162 59		
	31	*Cost of Goods Sold*	*G15*		*110 045 01*	—0—	—0—

721

ACCOUNT *Cost of Goods Sold*   ACCOUNT NO. *811*

DATE		ITEM	POST. REF.	DEBIT	CREDIT	BALANCE DEBIT	BALANCE CREDIT
19B							
Dec.	*31*	*Fin. Goods Inv., beg.*	*G14*	*79 102 48*			
	31	*Fin. Goods Inv., end.*	*G14*		*77 690 98*		
	31	*Manufacturing Sum.*	*G15*	*110 045 01*			
				189 147 49		*111 456 51*	
	31	*Exp. and Rev. Sum.*	*G15*		*111 456 51*	—0—	—0—

GENERAL JOURNAL

DATE	DESCRIPTION	ACCT. NO.	DETAIL	✓	DEBIT	✓	CREDIT	✓
19B Dec. 31	*Adjusting Entries*							
	Manufacturing Summary	751			17578.33	✓		
	Materials Inventory	161					17578.33	✓
	Manufacturing Summary	751			976.57	✓		
	Work in Process Inventory	162					976.57	✓
	Cost of Goods Sold	811			79102.48	✓		
	Finished Goods Inventory	163					79102.48	✓
	Materials Inventory	161			16732.59	✓		
	Manufacturing Summary	751					16732.59	✓
	Work in Process Inventory	162			1083.36	✓		
	Manufacturing Summary	751					1083.36	✓
	Finished Goods Inventory	163			77690.98	✓		
	Cost of Goods Sold	811					77690.98	✓
	Accrued Interest Receivable	132			82.31	✓		
	Interest Earned	631					82.31	✓
	Interest Expense	831			934.13	✓		
	Accrued Interest Payable	317					934.13	✓
	Operating Expenses	821			488.64	✓		
	Bad Debts Expense	8237	488.64	✓				
	Allowance for Bad Debts	013					488.64	✓
	Operating Expenses	821			287.63	✓		
	Office Supplies Expense	8203	287.63	✓				
	Office Supplies	181					287.63	✓
	Operating Expenses	821			285.20	✓		
	Advertising Expense	8233	285.20	✓				
	Advertising Supplies	182					285.20	✓
	Factory Overhead	741			430.95	✓		
	Factory Supplies Consumed	7403	430.95	✓				
	Factory Supplies	183					430.95	✓

722

Account Title	Acct. No.	Debit (Subsidiary)	Debit (Control)	Credit
Factory Overhead	741		270 95 ✓	
Expired Insurance — Factory Building and Equipment	7406	270 95 ✓		
Operating Expenses	821		252 31 ✓	
Office Equipment Insurance Expense	8205	81 61 ✓		
Delivery Equipment Insurance Expense	8236	108 91 ✓		
Finished Goods Insurance Expense	8238	61 79 ✓		
Prepaid Insurance	184			523 26 ✓
Operating Expenses	821		244 14 ✓	
Depreciation of Office Equipment	8204	244 14 ✓		
Accumulated Depreciation — Office Equipment	021			244 14 ✓
Operating Expenses	821		934 88 ✓	
Depreciation of Delivery Equipment	8235	934 88 ✓		
Accumulated Depreciation — Delivery Equipment	022			934 88 ✓
Factory Overhead	741		3 451 60 ✓	
Depreciation of Factory Building and Equipment	7405	3 451 60 ✓		
Accumulated Depreciation — Factory Equipment	023			3 451 60 ✓
Factory Overhead	741		920 50 ✓	
Depreciation of Factory Building and Equipment	7405	920 50 ✓		
Operating Expenses	821		131 50 ✓	
Miscellaneous Office Expense	8208	131 50 ✓		
Accumulated Depreciation — Building	024			1 052 00 ✓
Factory Overhead	741		437 50 ✓	
Patent Amortization	7408	437 50 ✓		
Patents	261			437 50 ✓
Income Tax Expense	851		7 517 32 ✓	
Corporation Income Tax Payable	315			7 517 32 ✓

The B. J. Patrick Manufacturing Co. — Adjusting Entries

724

GENERAL JOURNAL

DATE	DESCRIPTION	ACCT. NO.	DETAIL	✓	DEBIT	✓	CREDIT	✓
19B Dec. 31	Closing Entries							
	Manufacturing Summary	751			111652 70	✓		
	Materials Purchases	711					57046 74	✓
	Freight In	721					8669 17	✓
	Direct Labor	731					16450 25	✓
	Factory Overhead	741					29486 54	✓
	Indirect Labor	7401	15820 79	✓				
	Utilities Consumed	7402	2377 12	✓				
	Factory Supplies Consumed	7403	430 95	✓				
	Factory Building Maintenance	7404	832 81	✓				
	Depreciation of Factory Building and Equipment	7405	4372 10	✓				
	Expired Insurance — Factory Building and Equipment	7406	270 95	✓				
	Factory Repairs	7407	639 59	✓				
	Patent Amortization	7408	437 50	✓				
	Taxes on Factory Building and Equipment	7409	1392 64	✓				
	Payroll Taxes — Factory	7411	2354 00	✓				
	Miscellaneous Factory Overhead	7412	558 09	✓				
	Materials Purchases Returns and Allowances	071			343 26	✓		
	Purchases Discount	072			2003 38	✓		
	Manufacturing Summary	751					2346 64	✓
	Cost of Goods Sold	811			110045 01	✓		
	Manufacturing Summary	751					110045 01	✓
	Sales	611			198967 60	✓		
	Interest Earned	631			178 11	✓		
	Expense and Revenue Summary	531					199145 71	✓
	Expense and Revenue Summary	531			176893 95	✓		
	Sales Returns and Allowances	061					918 62	✓
	Sales Discount	062					2593 90	✓
	Cost of Goods Sold	811					111456 51	✓
	Operating Expenses	821					51488 07	✓

GENERAL JOURNAL

DESCRIPTION	ACCT. NO.	✓	DETAIL	✓	DEBIT	✓	CREDIT	✓
Office Salaries Expense	8201	✓	7 238 26					
Officers' Salaries Expense	8202	✓	22 400 00					
Office Supplies Expense	8203	✓	287 63					
Depreciation of Office Equipment	8204	✓	244 14					
Office Equipment Insurance Expense	8205	✓	81 61					
Property Tax Expense — Office Equipment	8206	✓	184 40					
Payroll Taxes — Administrative	8207	✓	1 846 31					
Miscellaneous Office Expense	8208	✓	659 54					
Sales Salaries Expense	8231	✓	12 096 69					
Traveling Expense	8232	✓	668 80					
Advertising Expense	8233	✓	1 394 80					
Delivery Expense	8234	✓	1 991 77					
Depreciation of Delivery Equipment	8235	✓	934 88					
Delivery Equipment Insurance Expense	8236	✓	108 91					
Bad Debts Expense	8237	✓	488 64					
Finished Goods Insurance Expense	8238	✓	61 79					
Property Tax Expense — Delivery Equipment	8239	✓	38 20					
Payroll Taxes — Sales	8241	✓	370 31					
Miscellaneous Selling Expense	8242	✓	391 39					
Interest Expense	831	✓					2 659 53	✓
Charitable Contributions Expense	841						260 00	✓
Income Tax Expense	851						7 517 32	✓
Expense and Revenue Summary	531				22 251 76	✓		
Retained Earnings	521						22 251 76	✓

GENERAL JOURNAL

DATE	DESCRIPTION	ACCT. NO.	✓	DETAIL	✓	DEBIT	✓	CREDIT	✓
19C Jan. 1	Reversing Entries								
	Interest Earned	631				82 31	✓		
	Accrued Interest Receivable	132						82 31	✓
	Accrued Interest Payable	317				934 13	✓		
	Interest Expense	831						934 13	✓

The B. J. Patrick Manufacturing Co. — Closing and Reversing Entries

The general journal entries to close the temporary accounts of The B. J. Patrick Manufacturing Co. are reproduced on pages 724 and 725. In posting to the summary accounts many accountants follow the practice of *posting in detail*. This means that they make separate debits and credits for each item that is being transferred to the summary account, rather than posting the total of several debits or credits as shown in the journal entry. Each item is labeled in the Description column of the account. This practice makes these summary accounts more informative. The expense and revenue summary, manufacturing summary, and cost of goods sold accounts are reproduced on page 721 with the postings in detail.

Post-closing trial balance

After all of the closing entries are posted, the accounts in the subsidiary factory overhead ledger, the operating expense ledger and all of the temporary and summary accounts in the general ledger will be in balance. It is customary to take a trial balance of the open accounts in the general ledger at this point. If all the work has been done correctly, it will be found that the accounts have the same balances as those shown in the Balance Sheet columns of the summary work sheet except that the balance of the retained earnings account will reflect the net income (or net loss) for the accounting period. A post-closing trial balance is, in substance, an unclassified balance sheet.

Reversing entries

The accountant for The B. J. Patrick Manufacturing Co. follows the usual practice of reversing the adjusting entries for accruals after closing the books at the end of each year. This practice facilitates the recording of the transactions of the succeeding fiscal year in a routine manner. The reversing entries are journalized in the manner shown on page 725.

Report No. 28-3

Complete Report No. 28-3 in the workbook and submit your working papers for approval. Continue with the next study assignment in Chapter 29 until Report No. 29-1 is required.

chapter 29

the annual report; analysis of financial statements

It has been mentioned that the usual sequence of end-of-period accounting procedure is to **(1)** prepare a work sheet (or work sheets), **(2)** prepare the financial statements that comprise the annual report, using the data assembled on the work sheets, and **(3)** journalize and post the adjusting entries, closing entries, and any needed reversing entries.   Solely for purposes of better textbook presentation, the order of steps **(2)** and **(3)** has been reversed in the discussion and illustration of The B. J. Patrick Manufacturing Co. example.   Adjusting, closing, and reversing entries were included in the preceding chapter.   The financial statements that comprise the annual report of this company are presented in the following section. Some of these statements are used as a basis for the discussion of financial statement analysis in the latter part of this chapter.

The annual report of a manufacturing business

The annual report of a corporation always includes an income statement and a balance sheet.   A statement of retained earnings is usually included.   It is becoming the prevailing practice to include a statement of changes in financial position.   If a corporation is engaged in manufacturing, it is probable that there will be a manufacturing statement also. Such other supporting schedules as are considered necessary may be included. The prime purpose of the annual report is to provide the officers and stockholders of the corporation with information as to the results of operations for the year and the financial position of the company at the end of the year. The company's bondholders, general creditors, banks, and certain taxing authorities also may be interested in the annual report. The form of the statements comprising the annual report of a corporation should conform to accepted accounting practice. The nature of the business conducted and the volume of business done by the corporation may have little or no effect upon the form of the statements.

In order to make the financial statements more informative, two practices are widely followed: **(1)** certain of the statements are shown in *comparative* form, and **(2)** in all of the statements, cents are omitted. In looking at an income statement, the reader is almost certain to want to know how the results of the most recent year compare with the results of the year before. In looking at the most recent balance sheet, it is likely that the reader would also like to see similar data for the end of the previous fiscal year. In order to provide maximum information, accountants frequently prepare income statements and balance sheets (and, often, supplementary statements and schedules) in comparative form. It is the nearly universal practice to place the amounts for the latest year to the left of the amounts for the preceding year; that is, to show the most recent year first.

Since little or no meaningful information is provided by carrying all amounts to the last penny, a common practice is to "round" to the nearest dollar. This is accomplished by dropping any amount less than 50 cents, and by raising by 1 the amount in the first dollar position if the amount in the cents column is 50 or more. Usually the cents dropped and the cents added offset each other, though sometimes a total must be altered by one dollar to compensate for the "rounding." In the published annual reports of some very large corporations, the amounts are rounded to the nearest thousand dollars. If this is done, there usually is a notation on the statement, "in thousands" or "000 omitted."

Following is a discussion of the statements comprising the annual report of The B. J. Patrick Manufacturing Co. Most of the data relating to the year 19B (the year just ended) came from the work sheets reproduced on pages 714 and 715. The data relating to 19A came from the annual report prepared for the previous year (not reproduced).

Income statement

Comparative income statements of The B. J. Patrick Manufacturing Co. for the years ended December 31, 19B and 19A, are shown on page 729.

THE B. J. PATRICK MANUFACTURING CO.
Income Statements
For the Years Ended December 31, 19B and 19A

	19B	19A
Sales........................	$198,968	$190,832
Less: Sales returns and allowances	(919)	(895)
Sales discounts............	(2,594)	(2,487)
Net sales......................	$195,455	$187,450
Less cost of goods sold:		
Finished goods inv., Jan. 1..... $ 79,102		$ 80,657
Add: Cost of goods manufac-		
tured................. 110,045		105,329
Goods available for sale...... $189,147		$185,986
Less finished goods inv., Dec. 31 77,691		79,102
Cost of goods sold............	111,456	106,884
Gross margin on sales............	$ 83,999	$ 80,566
Operating expenses............	51,488	49,299
Net operating income.............	$ 32,511	$ 31,267
Other revenue:		
Interest earned................	178	170
	$ 32,689	$ 31,437
Other expenses:		
Interest expense............... $ 2,660		$ 3,819
Charitable contributions......... 260		250
Total other expenses.........	2,920	4,069
Net income before provision for in-		
come tax.....................	$ 29,769	$ 27,368
Less corporation income tax......	7,517	6,637
Net income after provision for income		
tax.........................	$ 22,252	$ 20,731

The B. J. Patrick Manufacturing Co. — Income Statements

The data for 19B came from the Income Statement columns of the summary work sheet for 19B. The amounts for 19A were copied from the income statement of the preceding year. Note that only the total of the operating expenses for each year is shown. These totals are explained by a comparative schedule of operating expenses reproduced at the top of page 730. The data for 19B came from the operating expenses work sheet reproduced at the bottom of page 716. The data for 19A were copied from the statement for the preceding year. The income statements are analyzed in the latter part of this chapter.

THE B. J. PATRICK MANUFACTURING CO.
Schedules of Operating Expenses
For the Years Ended December 31, 19B and 19A

	19B	19A
Administrative expenses:		
Office salaries expense..........................	$ 7,238	$ 6,935
Officers' salaries expense.......................	22,400	21,800
Office supplies expense..........................	288	253
Depreciation of office equipment......................	244	244
Office equipment insurance expense..................	82	82
Property tax expense — office equipment.............	184	165
Payroll taxes — administrative.....................	1,846	1,672
Miscellaneous office expense.......................	659	587
Total administrative expenses....................	$32,941	$31,738
Selling expenses:		
Sales salaries expense...........................	$12,097	$11,628
Traveling expense................................	669	564
Advertising expense..............................	1,395	1,182
Delivery expense................................	1,992	1,765
Depreciation of delivery equipment..................	935	935
Delivery equipment insurance expense...............	109	109
Bad debts expense...............................	489	473
Finished goods insurance expense....................	62	62
Property tax expense — delivery equipment...........	38	42
Payroll taxes — sales.............................	370	348
Miscellaneous selling expense......................	391	453
Total selling expenses...........................	$18,547	$17,561
Total operating expenses.........................	$51,488	$49,299

The B. J. Patrick Manufacturing Co. — Schedules of Operating Expenses

Manufacturing statement

Comparative manufacturing statements of The B. J. Patrick Manufacturing Co. for the years ended December 31, 19B and 19A, are reproduced on page 731. The statement for 19B was prepared from information provided in the Manufacturing columns of the summary work sheet for 19B reproduced on pages 714 and 715, and the factory overhead work sheet on page 716. The data for 19A were copied from the manufacturing statement of the year before. The manufacturing statement supplements the income statement, and is arranged to show the three elements of manufacturing cost: **(1)** direct materials, **(2)** direct labor, and **(3)** factory overhead. For the year 19B, the total of these amounts, $110,152, was the *manufacturing cost* for that year. Of this sum, the cost of materials placed in process was $64,215, or 58.3 percent of the total cost; direct labor was

730

THE B. J. PATRICK MANUFACTURING CO.
Manufacturing Statements
For the Years Ended December 31, 19B and 19A

	19B		19A	
Direct materials:				
Inventory, January 1...............	$17,578		$18,257	
Purchases......................	57,047		54,181	
Freight in......................	8,669		8,278	
	$83,294		$80,716	
Less: Returns and allowances......	(343)		(253)	
Purchases discount..........	(2,003)		(1,835)	
Total cost of available materials.....	$80,948		$78,628	
Less inventory, December 31......	16,733		17,578	
Cost of materials placed in process..		$ 64,215		$ 61,050
Direct labor......................		16,450		15,965
Factory overhead:				
Indirect labor....................	$15,821		$14,982	
Utilities........................	2,377		2,295	
Factory supplies consumed..........	431		387	
Factory building maintenance.......	833		814	
Depreciation of factory bldg. and equip.......................	4,372		4,326	
Expired ins. on factory bldg. and equip.......................	271		260	
Factory repairs...................	640		653	
Patent amortization..............	437		437	
Property taxes on fact. bldg. and equip.......................	1,393		1,329	
Payroll taxes — factory...........	2,354		2,276	
Miscellaneous factory overhead.....	558		539	
Total factory overhead..........		29,487		28,298
Total manufacturing costs incurred during year.......................		$110,152		$105,313
Add: Work in process inventory, Jan. 1		976		992
		$111,128		$106,305
Less work in process inventory, Dec. 31		1,083		976
Cost of goods manufactured during year		$110,045		$105,329

The B. J. Patrick Manufacturing Co. — Manufacturing Statements

$16,450, or 14.9 percent of the total cost; and factory overhead was $29,487, or 26.8 percent of the total. When the amount of the beginning inventory of work in process was added and the amount of the ending inventory of work in process was subtracted, the result was the cost of the goods completed (manufactured) during the year, $110,045. These manufacturing statements are further analyzed in the latter part of the chapter.

731

Balance sheet

Comparative balance sheets of The B. J. Patrick Manufacturing Co. as of December 31, 19B and 19A, are reproduced below and on page 733. The statement for 19B was prepared from information found in the last

THE B. J. PATRICK MANUFACTURING CO.
Balance Sheets
December 31, 19B and 19A

Assets

	December 31, 19B		December 31, 19A	
Current assets:				
Cash..........................		$ 2,496		$ 6,804
Government bonds................		6,000		—
Notes receivable.................	$ 8,136		$ 6,046	
Accrued interest receivable.........	82		73	
Accounts receivable..............	40,693		36,901	
	$48,911		$43,020	
Less allowance for bad debts.....	611	48,300	549	42,471
Inventories:				
Materials.....................	$16,733		$17,578	
Work in process...............	1,083		976	
Finished goods................	77,691	95,507	79,102	97,656
Supplies and prepayments:				
Office supplies.................	$ 76		$ 87	
Advertising supplies.............	43		28	
Factory supplies................	118		101	
Prepaid insurance..............	305	542	234	450
Total current assets..........		$152,845		$147,381
Long-lived assets:				
Office equipment................	$ 2,441		$ 2,441	
Less accumulated depreciation....	1,220	$ 1,221	976	$ 1,465
Delivery equipment..............	$ 3,739		$ 3,739	
Less accumulated depreciation....	1,558	2,181	623	3,116
Factory equipment...............	$36,622		$32,411	
Less accumulated depreciation....	10,776	25,846	7,324	25,087
Building......................	$52,600		$52,600	
Less accumulated depreciation....	11,632	40,968	10,580	42,020
Land.........................		10,000		10,000
Patents.......................		1,312		1,750
Total long-lived assets..........		$ 81,528		$ 83,438
Total assets....................		$234,373		$230,819

The B. J. Patrick Manufacturing Co. — Balance Sheets
(*continued on next page*)

Liabilities

Current liabilities:

FICA tax payable................	$ 965	$ 921
FUTA tax payable................	51	53
State unemployment tax payable....	275	269
Employees income tax payable.....	1,952	1,896
Corporation income tax payable....	7,517	7,122
Notes payable...................	10,200	5,000
Accrued interest payable..........	934	618
Vouchers payable...............	20,111	18,574
Dividends payable...............	1,250	2,500
Total current liabilities...........	$ 43,255	$ 36,953

Long-term liabilities:

Bonds payable..................	70,000	90,000
Total liabilities....................	$113,255	$126,953

Stockholders' Equity

Capital stock (1,000 shares authorized, 500 shares issued)...............	$50,000	$50,000
Retained earnings.................	71,118	53,866
Total stockholders' equity........	121,118	103,866
Total liabilities and stockholders' equity.	$234,373	$230,819

The B. J. Patrick Manufacturing Co. — Balance Sheets (*concluded*)

two columns of the summary work sheet on pages 714 and 715. (Remember that the amount shown for retained earnings is the sum of the balance shown for the retained earnings account plus the net income for the year.) The data for 19A were copied from the balance sheet in the annual report of the preceding year. The balance sheets are arranged in report form. Both assets and liabilities are classified as to current and long-term items. These statements are further analyzed in the latter part of the chapter.

Statement of retained earnings

A statement of retained earnings of The B. J. Patrick Manufacturing Co. for the year ended December 31, 19B, is reproduced on page 734. While a similar statement for the year 19A could have been included, a major reason for such a statement is to reconcile the retained earnings amounts at the start and at the close of the year to which the annual report primarily relates, and a retained earnings statement for the preceding year was not considered necessary. The amount of retained earnings at December 31, 19A, was $53,866. The amount at December 31, 19B, was $71,118. The increase of $17,252 ($71,118 − $53,866) was due to the 19B net income of $22,252, less $5,000 of cash dividends paid or declared.

THE B. J. PATRICK MANUFACTURING CO.
Statement of Retained Earnings
For the Year Ended December 31, 19B

Balance, January 1, 19B...............................	$53,866
Add: Net income for the year (after provision for income taxes in the amount of $7,517).......................	22,252
	$76,118
Less: Cash dividends paid or declared during the year ($10 per share).....................................	5,000
Balance, December 31, 19B...........................	$71,118

The B. J. Patrick Manufacturing Co. — Statement of Retained Earnings

Statement of changes in financial position

The statement of changes in financial position of The B. J. Patrick Manufacturing Co. for the year ended December 31, 19B, together with a schedule of changes in working capital, is reproduced below and on page 735. As in the case of the statement of retained earnings, a statement of changes in financial position for the year 19A could have been included, but since a major purpose of the statement of changes in financial position is to reconcile the amounts of working capital at the start and at the close of the year to which the annual report primarily relates, such a statement for the preceding year was not considered to be necessary. The amount of working capital at December 31, 19A, was $110,428 (current

THE B. J. PATRICK MANUFACTURING CO.
Statement of Changes in Financial Position
For the Year Ended December 31, 19B

Sources of funds:		
Funds provided by operations:		
Net income (per income statement).................	$22,252	
Add expenses not requiring funds:		
Depreciation.....................................	5,683	
Patent amortization...........................	438	
Total funds provided........................		$28,373
Applications of funds:		
Cash dividends paid or declared....................	$ 5,000	
Purchase of factory equipment.......................	4,211	
Retirement of bonds................................	20,000	
Total funds applied..........................		29,211
Decrease in working capital..........................		$ 838

The B. J. Patrick Manufacturing Co. — Statement of Changes in Financial Position

THE B. J. PATRICK MANUFACTURING CO.
Schedule of Changes in Working Capital
For the Year Ended December 31, 19B

	December 31, 19B	December 31, 19A	Working Capital Increase	Working Capital Decrease
Cash............................	$ 2,496	$ 6,804		$4,308
Government bonds....................	6,000		$ 6,000	
Receivables (net).....................	48,300	42,471	5,829	
Inventories.........................	95,507	97,656		2,149
Supplies and prepayments..............	542	450	92	
Payroll taxes payable.................	3,243	3,139		104
Corporation income tax payable........	7,517	7,122		395
Notes and interest payable.............	11,134	5,618		5,516
Vouchers payable....................	20,111	18,574		1,537
Dividends payable...................	1,250	2,500	1,250	
			$13,171	$14,009
Decrease in working capital..........			838	
			$14,009	$14,009

The B. J. Patrick Manufacturing Co. — Schedule of Changes in Working Capital

assets, $147,381, less current liabilities, $36,953). The amount of working capital at December 31, 19B, was $109,590 (current assets, $152,845, less current liabilities, $43,255). The statement of changes in financial position explains the $838 decrease.

735

In preparing the statement of changes in financial position, the accountant for The B. J. Patrick Manufacturing Co. considered all of the possible sources, and all of the possible applications of funds. As explained in Chapter 19, the possible sources are (1) investments by owners, (2) profitable operations (including the adjustment of the calculated net income by the amount of any expenses that did not reduce working capital), (3) long-term borrowing, and (4) sale of long-lived assets. The possible applications of funds are (1) withdrawals by the owners (which, in the case of corporations, normally means cash dividends paid or declared), (2) unprofitable operations (if this amount exceeds the amount of any expenses that did not reduce working capital), (3) repayment of long-term borrowing, and (4) purchase of long-lived assets.

Using the foregoing as a guide, or "check list," each possible source and possible application of funds was considered separately to determine whether it applied to The B. J. Patrick Manufacturing Co. for the year 19B. This item-by-item analysis revealed the following:

Possible sources:

(a) Investments by owners. None. Reference to the balance sheets on page 733 showed that there was no change in the balance of the capital stock account during the year.

(b) Profitable operations. Yes. The income statement for 19B showed an after-tax net income for the year of $22,252. For purposes of the statement of changes in financial position, this amount had to be increased by the amount of any expenses that did not reduce working capital. There were two types of such expenses: depreciation and patent amortization. Reference to the balance sheets on page 732 shows that the four accumulated depreciation accounts increased, in total, $5,683. A check of these accounts in the general ledger showed no debits to any of them (which would have been found if any depreciated assets had been disposed of). Since there were no reductions in any of the accumulated depreciation accounts, the sum of the changes, $5,683, was the total depreciation write-off for the year. The patents account had been reduced $438 when that amount was debited to the patent amortization account (and to Factory Overhead in the general ledger). Accordingly, the increase in funds due to regular operations was $28,373 ($22,252 + $5,683 + $438).

(c) Long-term borrowing. None. The balance sheets on page 733 show that bonds payable, the only type of long-term liability, was decreased — not increased.

(d) Sale of long-lived assets. None. The balance sheets on page 732 show that, except in the case of patents mentioned above, none of the balances of the long-lived asset accounts was reduced during the year. A check of the general ledger accounts confirmed this. (This check of the actual accounts was made to be sure that any decreases in the accounts had not been partly or wholly offset by additions.)

736

As a result of the foregoing analysis, it was determined that regular operations was the only source of funds during the year 19B.

Possible applications:

(a) Withdrawals by owners. Yes. The statement of retained earnings on page 734 shows that cash dividends paid or declared during the year amounted to $5,000.

(b) Unprofitable operations. Not considered since there had been after-tax net income.

(c) Repayment of long-term borrowing. Yes. The balance sheets on page 733 show that bonds payable decreased $20,000. Since the income statement for 19B didn't include any mention of gain or loss on bond retirement, and evidently no premium or discount had ever been involved in connection with these bonds, it is evident that these bonds were reacquired at face value, $20,000.

(d) Purchase of long-lived assets. Yes. The balance sheets show that the amount of factory equipment increased $4,211. (Mention was made of this purchase in connection with the adjustment data given on page 713.)

This analysis showed that there were three types of applications of funds during the year 19B. Together, they amounted to $29,211. Since this amount exceeded the only source of funds by $838 ($29,211 − $28,373), the decrease in working capital was fully accounted for.

Comparative analysis of financial statements

Any fact, by itself, has limited significance. There must be other related facts to give the first one meaning. The validity of this observation is easily demonstrated in the case of information about a business. For example, to learn the one fact that last year's net income of a certain corporation was $78,416 is to learn very little. Does that amount of earnings indicate a successful year or a poor one? Does the amount represent an improvement over or a decline from the year before? Is the amount large or small in relation to sales? — to assets? — to stockholders' equity? How does it compare with the net income of others in the industry? Other facts must be known if the information about last year's income is to have any real meaning. The same can be said of any other single bit of information about a business.

737

Types of comparison

The financial statements of a business are intended to supply information to several interested parties — the management, present and prospective owners, present and prospective creditors, employees and their unions, government agencies, and, sometimes, the general public. Normally, interest centers about three aspects of the business: **(1)** its profitability, **(2)** its solvency (ability to pay its debts on or before their maturity), and **(3)** its stability in these respects. The financial statements can be much more informative and meaningful if they are analyzed on a comparative basis. Four types of comparison may be possible:

(a) Comparison of the latest financial statements and relationships between various elements with the statements and relationships of one or more previous periods.

(b) Comparison of the statements and financial relationships of the business with data for others in the industry.

(c) Comparison of statements and financial relationships of two or more divisions or branches of the same business.

(d) Comparison of information in the statements with pre-set plans or goals (normally in the form of budgets).

Comparisons of the second and third types are not possible if data regarding others in the industry are not available or if the business does not have divisions or branches. Comparisons of the fourth type depend upon some sort of budgeting procedure. Not all businesses have formal budgets, although the practice is growing. Comparisons of the first type, however, are possible for all businesses that keep accounts and prepare periodic statements. This type of comparative analysis will be illustrated. The examples presented relate to The B. J. Patrick Manufacturing Co. The financial statements of this company for the calendar year 19B were reproduced in the preceding section. In the case of the income statement, schedule of operating expenses, manufacturing statement, and balance sheet, comparable data for the preceding year, 19A, were included. These statements and certain relationships that they reveal will be compared in various ways. To facilitate the comparison, certain of the statements for both years are condensed or summarized.

738

Horizontal analysis

A comparison of the amounts for the same item in the financial statements of two or more periods is called *horizontal analysis*. The comparison is facilitated if the amount of any change and its relative size are shown. A condensed comparative income statement of The B. J. Patrick Manufacturing Co. for the two years under review, showing the amount and the percentage of change in each item, is shown on page 739. (In calculating the percent of change, the amount for the earlier year serves as the base.)

In general, the percentage of change is of greater interest than the actual amounts. A study of the percentage of change of amounts in the two income statements shows that gross sales and sales discounts of 19B were 4.3 percent greater than 19A. Sales returns and allowances showed a smaller percent increase, but since the amount was relatively minor, net sales also increased 4.3 percent. Cost of goods sold also increased 4.3 percent. (This is rather surprising since many of the costs of producing goods in a factory remain fairly constant from year to year regardless of the level of activity.) As a result, the percent increase in gross margin likewise was 4.3 percent. Operating expenses did not increase in direct proportion to the growth of sales. These expenses advanced 4.4 percent. This combination of events (an increase in gross margin less than proportional

THE B. J. PATRICK MANUFACTURING CO.
Condensed Comparative Income Statements
For the Years Ended December 31, 19B and 19A

	19B	19A	Increase or Decrease* Amount	Increase or Decrease* Percent
Sales..........................	$198,968	$190,832	$8,136	4.3
Sales returns and allowances........	$ 919	$ 895	$ 24	2.7
Sales discounts...................	2,594	2,487	107	4.3
Net sales.......................	$195,455	$187,450	$8,005	4.3
Cost of goods sold...............	111,456	106,884	4,572	4.3
Gross margin on sales.............	$ 83,999	$ 80,566	$3,433	4.3
Operating expenses...............	51,488	49,299	2,189	4.4
Net operating income.............	$ 32,511	$ 31,267	$1,244	4.0
Other revenue...................	178	170	8	4.7
	$ 32,689	$ 31,437	$1,252	4.0
Other expenses...................	2,920	4,069	1,149*	28.2*
Net income before income tax.......	$ 29,769	$ 27,368	$2,401	8.8
Provision for income tax............	7,517	6,637	880	13.3
Net income after income tax........	$ 22,252	$ 20,731	$1,521	7.3

The B. J. Patrick Manufacturing Co. — Condensed Comparative Income Statements

to the increase in operating expenses) had an undesirable effect upon net operating income — an increase of only 4 percent. The amount of other revenue was too small in both years to make much difference. A 28.2 percent reduction in other expenses (largely the result of less interest expense because some of the bonds were redeemed early in the year) was enough to cause net income before taxes to be 8.8 percent greater. The increase in the relative amount of income tax caused the increase in net income after income tax to be 7.3 percent.

Condensed comparative schedules of cost of goods sold and cost of goods manufactured are shown on page 740. The cost of goods sold schedule shows that since the change in the finished goods inventory was small, the relative change in cost of goods manufactured was approximately the same as the relative change in cost of goods sold. The first four lines of the comparative schedule of cost of goods manufactured are of most interest. While all the elements of manufacturing cost increased because of larger production, the greatest relative increase was in cost of materials used, 5.2 percent. The increase in direct labor was 3.0 percent, and factory overhead, 4.2 percent.

If desired, the horizontal analysis technique could be applied to the comparative schedule of operating expenses and to the individual items that comprise factory overhead.

THE B. J. PATRICK MANUFACTURING CO.
Comparative Schedule of Cost of Goods Sold
For the Years Ended December 31, 19B and 19A

	19B	19A	Increase or Decrease* Amount	Percent
Finished goods inventory, Jan. 1......	$ 79,102	$ 80,657	$1,555*	1.9*
Cost of goods manufactured.........	110,045	105,329	4,716	4.5
Goods available for sale...........	$189,147	$185,986	$3,161	1.7
Less finished goods inv., Dec. 31.....	77,691	79,102	1,411*	1.8*
Cost of goods sold...............	$111,456	$106,884	$4,572	4.3

The B. J. Patrick Manufacturing Co. — Comparative Schedule of Cost of Goods Sold

THE B. J. PATRICK MANUFACTURING CO.
Condensed Comparative Schedule of Cost of Goods Manufactured
For the Years Ended December 31, 19B and 19A

	19B	19A	Increase or Decrease* Amount	Percent
Materials used....................	$ 64,215	$ 61,050	$3,165	5.2
Direct labor.....................	16,450	15,965	485	3.0
Factory overhead................	29,487	28,298	1,189	4.2
Total manufacturing cost............	$110,152	$105,313	$4,839	4.6
Add work in process inv., Jan. 1......	976	992	16*	1.6*
	$111,128	$106,305	$4,823	
Less work in process inv., Dec. 31.....	1,083	976	107	11.0
Cost of goods manufactured.........	$110,045	$105,329	$4,716	4.5

740

The B. J. Patrick Manufacturing Co. — Condensed Comparative Schedule of Cost of Goods
Manufactured

Condensed comparative balance sheets as of December 31 of each of the two years under review, and a comparative schedule of current assets are presented on page 741. The most significant changes in the balance sheets are **(1)** the modest (3.7 percent) increase in current assets and a much greater (17.1 percent) increase in current liabilities, **(2)** the 22.2 percent reduction in bonds payable, and **(3)** the 32 percent increase in retained earnings. The latter was due to substantial earnings in 19B ($22,252) and the small amount ($5,000) of dividends paid or declared. (See the statement of retained earnings on page 734.) It is to be presumed that the modest dividends were due, at least in part, to the fact that a large amount ($20,000) of cash was used to redeem some of the bonds. (See the statement of changes in financial position on page 734.) It will be noted that the changes in the long-lived assets were very minor. In terms of percentages, there were large reductions in the undepreciated costs of office

THE B. J. PATRICK MANUFACTURING CO.
Condensed Comparative Balance Sheets
December 31, 19B and 19A

	December 31, 19B	December 31, 19A	Increase or Decrease* Amount	Increase or Decrease* Percent
Assets				
Current assets....................	$152,845	$147,381	$ 5,464	3.7
Office and delivery equip. (net)......	3,402	4,581	1,179*	25.7*
Factory equipment (net)...........	25,846	25,087	759	3.0
Building (net).....................	40,968	42,020	1,052*	2.5*
Land............................	10,000	10,000	—	—
Patents.........................	1,312	1,750	438*	25.0*
Total assets.....................	$234,373	$230,819	$ 3,554	1.5
Liabilities				
Current liabilities.................	$ 43,255	$ 36,953	$ 6,302	17.1
Bonds payable..................	70,000	90,000	20,000*	22.2*
Total liabilities...................	$113,255	$126,953	$13,698*	10.8*
Stockholders' Equity				
Capital stock....................	$ 50,000	$ 50,000	—	—
Retained earnings................	71,118	53,866	$17,252	32.0
Total stockholders' equity..........	$121,118	$103,866	$17,252	16.6
Total liabilities and stockholders' equity	$234,373	$230,819	$ 3,554	1.5

The B. J. Patrick Manufacturing Co. — Condensed Comparative Balance Sheets

741

THE B. J. PATRICK MANUFACTURING CO.
Comparative Schedule of Current Assets
December 31, 19B and 19A

	December 31, 19B	December 31, 19A	Increase or Decrease* Amount	Increase or Decrease* Percent
Cash...........................	$ 2,496	$ 6,804	$4,308*	63.3*
Government bonds...............	6,000	—	6,000	—
Receivables (net)..................	48,300	42,471	5,829	13.7
Materials inventory..............	16,733	17,578	845*	4.8*
Work in process inventory..........	1,083	976	107	11.0
Finished goods inventory...........	77,691	79,102	1,411*	1.8*
Supplies and prepayments.........	542	450	92	20.4
Total current assets..............	$152,845	$147,381	$5,464	3.7

The B. J. Patrick Manufacturing Co. — Comparative Schedule of Current Assets

and delivery equipment and patents, but the amounts of these assets were small. The reductions (of 25.7 and 25 percent) were due entirely to depreciation and amortization — no assets of either type were sold or discarded.

The comparative schedule of current assets reveals nothing startling. The substantial (63.3 percent) decrease in cash was more than offset by the addition of the temporary investment, government bonds. The 13.7 percent increase in net receivables is slightly out of line with the 4.3 percent increase in net sales noted earlier, but this might have been due to a larger proportion of credit sales near the very end of 19B. The 11.0 percent increase in the work in process inventory means very little since the amount involved is so small. The same can be said for the 20.4 percent increase in supplies and prepayments.

A comparative schedule of current liabilities could be prepared and analyzed in the same fashion. However, since the current liabilities of The B. J. Patrick Manufacturing Co. are much alike in that all of the obligations must be paid in a short time, changes in the components are not of great interest. The fact that the current liabilities, in total, increased 17.1 percent is the significant matter.

Vertical analysis

The amount of each item in a statement can be expressed as a percentage of the total. This is termed *vertical analysis*. A maximum of information is provided if statements relating to two or more periods are vertically analyzed and the results compared or contrasted. Condensed comparative income statements of The B. J. Patrick Manufacturing Co. for the years 19B and 19A, with each item shown as a percent of the net sales for the year, are presented on page 743. These statements reveal that there was very little difference between the two years under review in the proportionate relationship of the items.

Vertical analysis of income statements automatically provides several important ratios relating to each statement. The analysis gives the cost of goods sold ratio (cost of goods sold to net sales), the gross margin ratio (gross margin to net sales), the operating expense ratio (operating expenses to net sales), the operating income ratio (net operating income to net sales), and the net-income-to-net-sales ratio.

The vertical-analysis technique can be used in connection with schedules that supplement the condensed income statements. For example, each item in a schedule of operating expenses can be shown as a percent of total operating expenses. Each item that goes to make up the total of manufacturing cost can be shown as a percent of that total. Factory overhead can be analyzed in a similar fashion.

Balance sheets can be vertically analyzed and compared. On the asset side, each item is shown as a percent of the total assets. On the equity side, each item is shown as a percent of the total of liabilities and owners' equity.

THE B. J. PATRICK MANUFACTURING CO.
Condensed Comparative Income Statements
For the Years Ended December 31, 19B and 19A

	19B Amount	19B Percent	19A Amount	19A Percent
Sales...............................	$198,968	101.8	$190,832	101.8
Sales returns and allowances...........	$ 919	0.5	895	0.5
Sales discounts......................	2,594	1.3	2,487	1.3
Net sales...........................	$195,455	100.0	$187,450	100.0
Cost of goods sold...................	111,456	57.0	106,884	57.0
Gross margin on sales................	$ 83,999	43.0	$ 80,566	43.0
Operating expenses..................	51,488	26.3	49,299	26.3
Net operating income.................	$ 32,511	16.7	$ 31,267	16.7
Other revenue......................	178	0.1	170	0.1
	$ 32,689	16.8	$ 31,437	16.8
Other expenses.....................	2,920	1.5	4,069	2.2
Net income before income tax..........	$ 29,769	15.3	$ 27,368	14.6
Provision for income tax..............	7,517	3.9	6,637	3.5
Net income after income tax...........	$ 22,252	11.4	$ 20,731	11.1

The B. J. Patrick Manufacturing Co. — Condensed Comparative Income Statements

The condensed comparative balance sheets of The B. J. Patrick Manufacturing Co. with vertical analysis are shown on page 744. Comparison of the balance sheets reveals that current assets were a slightly larger share of the total assets at the end of 19B. As a share of the total equities, current liabilities increased slightly and bonds payable were considerably less. As a result, total liabilities were a noticeably smaller share of the total. Retained earnings, in amount and proportion, increased significantly.

If supporting schedules are prepared for current assets or current liabilities, either the total of the items in the schedule or the balance sheet total may be used as the base (100 percent).

Comparative ratio analysis

The use of ratios to assess operating results, debt-paying ability, and other aspects of business activity has been mentioned and illustrated in earlier chapters. While ratios are only a means to an end, they can be a real aid in interpreting financial statements — particularly in making comparative analyses. Any ratio by itself does not mean much, but comparisons reveal trends. To illustrate their use in comparative analysis, several of the most widely used ratios will be calculated for The B. J. Patrick Manufacturing Co. for the two years under review. (The ratios of certain items

THE B. J. PATRICK MANUFACTURING CO.
Condensed Comparative Balance Sheets
December 31, 19B and 19A

	December 31, 19B		December 31, 19A	
	Amount	Percent	Amount	Percent
Assets				
Current assets.......................	$152,845	65.2	$147,381	63.8
Office and delivery equipment (net).....	3,402	1.5	4,581	2.0
Factory equipment (net)...............	25,846	11.0	25,087	10.9
Building (net).......................	40,968	17.5	42,020	18.2
Land.............................	10,000	4.3	10,000	4.3
Patents...........................	1,312	0.5	1,750	0.8
Total assets.......................	$234,373	100.0	$230,819	100.0
Liabilities				
Current liabilities....................	$ 43,255	18.5	$ 36,953	16.0
Bonds payable......................	70,000	29.9	90,000	39.0
Total liabilities.....................	$113,255	48.4	$126,953	55.0
Stockholders' Equity				
Capital stock.......................	$ 50,000	21.3	$ 50,000	21.7
Retained earnings...................	71,118	30.3	53,866	23.3
Total stockholders' equity.............	$121,118	51.6	$103,866	45.0
Total liabilities and stockholders' equity..	$234,373	100.0	$230,819	100.0

744

The B. J. Patrick Manufacturing Co. — Condensed Comparative Balance Sheets

to net sales were determined in making the vertical analysis of the income statements. Those ratios are not repeated.)

Rate earned on total assets

This ratio relates earnings to the total assets of the business. The base for the calculation can be either assets at the beginning of the year or the average assets for the year. When the latter is used in the case of The B. J. Patrick Manufacturing Co., the ratio for each year would be computed as follows:

	19B	19A
Net income after taxes................................	$ 22,252	$ 20,731
Total assets:		
Beginning of year.....................................	$230,819	$232,925
End of year..	234,373	230,819
Average..	$232,596	$231,872
Rate of earnings on average assets.........................	9.6%	8.9%

A major aim of the owners or managers of most businesses is to realize large earnings in relation to the resources of their firms. The rate earned on total assets is a measure of the attainment of this objective. The 8.9 percent return in 19A probably was considered to be barely satisfactory by the management of The B. J. Patrick Manufacturing Co. The 9.6 percent return in 19B was slightly better.

Rate earned on owners' equity

From the standpoint of the owners of a business, the rate earned in relation to their interest or equity is of major interest. The base for the calculation can be either total capital at the start of the year or the average capital during the year. When the latter is used in the case of The B. J. Patrick Manufacturing Co., the ratio for each year would be computed as follows:

	19B	19A
Net income after taxes	$ 22,252	$ 20,731
Total stockholders' equity:		
Beginning of year	$103,866	$100,214
End of year	121,118	103,866
Average	$112,492	$102,040
Rate of earnings on average stockholders' equity	19.8%	20.3%

Because net income for 19B was only 7.3 percent greater than 19A, while the average stockholders' equity increased about 10 percent, the rate of return on the stockholders' equity declined.

745

Earnings per share of common stock

From the standpoint of an individual stockholder, the most meaningful measurement of earnings is the amount of net income per share. The B. J. Patrick Manufacturing Co. has only common stock. During each of the two years in question, 500 shares were outstanding. Thus, the net earnings per share for 19A were $41.46 ($20,731 ÷ 500) and, for 19B, $44.50 ($22,252 ÷ 500). An increasing amount of net earnings per share is considered to be an indication of overall operating improvement.

If there are preferred shares outstanding, the calculation of net earnings per share of common must take into account the amount required to cover preferred dividend requirements. For example, suppose a corporation has 1,000 shares of $100 par, 7 percent preferred stock, and 2,000 shares of common stock outstanding. If the net income for the year was $23,000, the net earnings per share of common stock would be computed as follows:

Net income after taxes	$23,000
Less preferred dividend requirements (1,000 × $7)	7,000
Remainder — applicable to common stock	$16,000
Earnings per share of common stock ($16,000 ÷ 2,000 shares)	$8.00

"Times earned" ratio

When a business has long-term liabilities in the form of bonds payable or a mortgage payable, the interest on such obligations must be paid each year. The holder (or holders) of the bonds or mortgage is interested in the amount of earnings exclusive of the interest and before income tax. While the corporation is obligated to pay the interest whether or not there is net income, the size of the earnings before interest and taxes is one measure of the security behind the obligation. If the bond interest requirement was $6,000 and the net income before this interest and before income tax was $24,000, the interest is said to have been "four times earned" ($24,000 ÷ $6,000 = 4).

During 19A, The B. J. Patrick Manufacturing Co. had bonds payable outstanding in the amount of $90,000. Early in January of 19B, $20,000 of these were redeemed, leaving $70,000 still outstanding. The bonds bear interest at the rate of 4 percent per annum. Thus, the interest expense was $3,600 in 19A (4 percent of $90,000), and $2,800 in 19B (4 percent of $70,000). The "times earned" ratio for each year may be calculated as follows:

	19B	19A
Net income after taxes	$ 22,252	$ 20,731
Add back: Income tax	7,517	6,637
Bond interest	2,800	3,600
Net income before bond interest and income tax	$ 32,569	$ 30,968
Bond interest	$ 2,800	$ 3,600
Number of times bond interest was earned	11.6	8.6

These high times-earned ratios would be very satisfactory to the bondholders. (In many businesses, a ratio of 2 or 3 is considered adequate.)

The same type of computation can be made relative to dividend requirements on preferred stock. The payment of dividends depends upon both earnings and the availability of cash. The present holder or prospective purchaser of preferred shares is very much interested in the earnings in relation to dividend requirements. If there were 1,000 shares of $100 par, 7 percent preferred stock outstanding, the annual dividend requirement on these shares would be $7,000. If net income (after income tax) was $23,000, the preferred dividends would have been about 3.3 times earned.

Current ratio

The *current ratio* (sometimes called "working capital ratio") compares current assets to current liabilities. In the case of The B. J. Patrick Manufacturing Co., the ratio at the end of each year would be computed as shown at the top of the next page.

	DECEMBER 31	
	19B	19A
Current assets..	$152,845	$147,381
Current liabilities...	43,255	36,953
Current ratio..	3.6 to 1	4.0 to 1

This analysis indicates that the current position of The B. J. Patrick Manufacturing Co. worsened slightly in 19B, but it continued to be satisfactory. There is a general rule that anything less than a 2-to-1 current ratio is unsatisfactory, but this rule is subject to modification.

Acid-test ratio

A refinement of the current ratio is termed the *acid test*. It is a comparison of the so-called "quick" current assets — meaning cash, temporary investments (if any), and receivables—to current liabilities. As a general rule, the ratio should be no less than 1 to 1. The acid-test ratio for The B. J. Patrick Manufacturing Co. at the end of each year is as follows:

	DECEMBER 31	
	19B	19A
Quick assets:		
Cash..	$ 2,496	$ 6,804
Temporary investments................................	6,000	—
Receivables (net).....................................	48,300	42,471
Total...	$ 56,796	$ 49,275
Current liabilities......................................	$ 43,255	$ 36,953
Acid-test ratio..	1.3 to 1	1.3 to 1

747

This analysis indicates that The B. J. Patrick Manufacturing Co. "passed" the acid test both times.

While it is generally desirable that both the current ratio and the acid-test ratio be high and improving, it is possible for both of them to be too high for the good of the business. Cash and most receivables are not earning assets and the return on most temporary investments is not large. Inventories are expensive to hold. They take up costly space, tie up money, and are subject to loss of value from various causes. Neither too little nor too much working capital is desirable. Business management must determine and maintain the ideal amount of each type of asset.

Ratio of owners' equity to liabilities

One measure of the margin of safety of the creditors is the ratio between the amount of the equity of the owners and the total amount of the claims of the creditors. If the ratio is high, it indicates that there is plenty of owners' equity to absorb possible losses without jeopardizing the creditors' claims. The ratio for The B. J. Patrick Manufacturing Co. at the end of each year may be calculated as shown at the top of the next page.

	DECEMBER 31	
	19B	19A
Total stockholders' equity..................................	$121,118	$103,866
Total liabilities..	113,255	126,953
Ratio of owners' equity to liabilities.......................	1.1 to 1	.8 to 1

A ratio of 3 to 1 or 4 to 1 would be considered high in some businesses, about average in others, and unusually low in still others. The nature of the individual assets and liabilities is the determining consideration. For example, most of the assets of commercial banks are of a type that can be liquidated quickly without much danger of loss. Even though most of the banks' liabilities are very current, an owners' equity-to-total-liabilities ratio of 1 to 8 (or more) is not unusual. Ratios in the 1 to 1 and 2 to 1 range are acceptable for The B. J. Patrick Manufacturing Co.

Ratio of mortgaged assets to long-term liabilities

Holders or potential holders of the mortgage or mortgage-secured bonds of a company are interested in the market values of the assets pledged in relation to the amount of the liability. This information cannot be secured from balance sheets because the statements do not show the market values of long-lived assets. Rather, the amounts shown are original cost less depreciation (if any) taken to date. However, a contrast of the book value of the mortgaged assets with the amount of the obligation they secure gives a rough measure of the margin of safety of the mortgage holder or bondholders.

A mortgage on the land, factory building, and factory equipment is the security behind the bonds-payable liability of The B. J. Patrick Manufacturing Co. The ratio of the book values of these assets to the bond liability at the end of each year would be calculated as follows:

	DECEMBER 31	
	19B	19A
Assets mortgaged:		
Factory equipment (net)................................	$ 25,846	$ 25,087
Building (net)...	40,968	42,020
Land..	10,000	10,000
Total...	$ 76,814	$ 77,107
Bonds Payable...	$ 70,000	$ 90,000
Ratio of book value of mortgaged assets to long-term debt.....	1.1 to 1	.8 to 1

Since during 19B a small amount of factory equipment was acquired and a substantial amount of the bonds were redeemed, the ratio was considerably improved. The ratio at the end of 19A probably was regarded as inadequate, and the ratio at the end of 19B as barely acceptable.

Book value per share of common stock

If a corporation has only one class of common stock outstanding, a measure of the ownership equity represented by each share can be determined by dividing the total owners' equity (i. e., assets minus liabilities) by the number of shares. During both of the years under review, The B. J. Patrick Manufacturing Co. had 500 shares of common stock outstanding. As of December 31, 19B, the total stockholders' equity was $121,118; one year earlier it was $103,866. Accordingly, the book value per share of stock at the two dates was, respectively, $242.24 and $207.73.

When there are preferred shares outstanding, the calculation of book value per share of common stock must first take into consideration the claims or equity of the senior stock (that stock having first claim upon the assets of the business). For example, suppose that a corporation has 1,000 shares of $100 par value, preferred stock with a liquidation preference of $103 per share, and 2,000 shares of common stock outstanding. There are no dividends in arrears on the preferred stock. The total stockholders' equity of the company is $700,000. The book value per share of common stock would be calculated as follows:

Total stockholders' equity	$700,000
Less liquidation claim of preferred stock ($103 × 1,000)	103,000
Balance — applicable to common stock	$597,000
Book value per share of common stock ($597,000 ÷ 2,000 shares)	$298.50

Book value means nothing more than what it says: value per books. The amount does not indicate what the stockholders would get for their shares in the event of the liquidation of the company. They might get more than book value; they probably would get less. From the stockholder's standpoint, it is generally considered desirable for the book value per share of stock to increase. However, if the major reason for the increase is because dividends are small or nonexistent, some shareholders may be dissatisfied.

In the calculation of book value of shares of capital stock and of certain ratios, some analysts reduce the total stockholders' equity figure by the amount of any intangible assets shown on the balance sheet. The result is called "tangible net worth." This treatment gives a more conservative book-value figure. The B. J. Patrick Manufacturing Co. has only one intangible asset, patents, in an amount too small to have an appreciable effect upon the book value of shares of stock or upon other calculations.

Receivables turnover

It is desirable to have as little as possible invested in accounts receivable since they do not earn any income. Often, any notes receivable in the possession of a merchandising or manufacturing business were acquired because customers wanted an extension of time to pay their debts. The notes may earn interest but, unless the effective rate is high, it is probable that the company would rather have collected the accounts. Carrying notes and accounts receivable is an unavoidable consequence of selling on account, but because the total result may be larger net income, the disadvantage of owning receivables is accepted.

In a well-managed company, constant effort is made to see that receivables are collected promptly. A measure of the success of this effort is the rate of turnover of receivables. It is calculated by dividing net sales by the average amount of receivables. The calculations for The B. J. Patrick Manufacturing Co. are as follows:

	19B	19A
Net sales..	$195,455	$187,450
Receivables (net):		
Beginning of year....................................	$ 42,471	$ 37,268
End of year...	48,300	42,471
Average...	$ 45,386	$ 39,870
Receivables turnover.................................	4.3	4.7

Another way of expressing the result is to divide 365 (days) by the turnover figure to get the average number of days that the receivables were "on the books." In the foregoing case, the result is 85 days and 78 days, respectively, for 19B and 19A. Unless the calculation is distorted because an unusually large amount of sales on account were made in the last few weeks of 19B, a slowdown occurred during the most recent year. Both of these rates of collection should be of concern to the management. In both years the figures fell well outside the general rule that the average collection period (i.e., the average number of days that receivables are on the books) should not be greater than $1\frac{1}{3}$ times the regular credit period allowed. Since this company regularly offers 30 days' credit, the average collection period should not exceed 40 days. B. J. Patrick's management should attempt to speed up the collection process.

Finished goods turnover

The desirability of keeping the inventory of merchandise as small as possible has already been mentioned. Every seller of goods would like to have maximum sales and a minimum inventory. A measure of the relation between sales and inventory is the inventory turnover. It is calculated by dividing cost of goods sold by the average inventory. (Cost of goods sold rather than sales is used, since the latter includes the gross margin.) The result is more accurate if an average of inventories at the end of each month is used. Lacking that, the average of the beginning-of-year and end-of-year inventories is used. In the case of The B. J. Patrick Manufacturing Co., the finished goods inventory turnover for each year would be:

	19B	19A
Cost of goods sold	$111,456	$106,884
Finished goods inventory:		
Beginning of year	$ 79,102	$ 80,657
End of year	77,691	79,102
Average	$ 78,397	$ 79,880
Finished goods turnover	1.4	1.3

The calculations indicate that, during 19B, the goods remained in stock an average of 261 days (365 ÷ 1.4); in 19A, the average was 281 days (365 ÷ 1.3).

While the turnover increased slightly from 19A to 19B, it is probable that the management of The B. J. Patrick Manufacturing Co. is dissatisfied. Slow turnover may be expected when an inventory includes a wide variety of items and, unless the merchandise is perishable, when the business is very seasonal. (For example, turnover is slow when goods are produced during many months and stored in readiness for large sales just before Christmas.) Since The B. J. Patrick Manufacturing Co. produces only one product and its business is not unusually seasonal, the turnover of 1 or 2 must be regarded as very slow. It will be noted that the finished goods inventory at the end of 19B is less than that at the start of that year, and that the latter, in turn, is smaller than the amount at the beginning of 19A. This reduction is a favorable change.

Other turnover ratios

The *materials turnover* in a manufacturing business can be calculated by dividing the cost of materials put into process during the year by the average inventory of materials. The size of a materials inventory may fluctuate considerably during the year. If this is the case, an average of the end-of-month inventories should be used in the calculation. Unless storage space is abundant and there are substantial price advantages from large-lot buying, it is desirable to have a rapid turnover (6 to 12 times a year).

The activity of a business (in terms of net sales) can be related to the amount of any of several types of resources in order to provide a measure of the utilization of these resources. The result of such a calculation is often described as the "turnover" of the resources in question, although this designation is merely one of convenience. For example, net sales divided by average total assets gives a quotient that is sometimes described as the *total asset turnover*. In the case of The B. J. Patrick Manufacturing Co., the calculation of total asset turnover for each year would be as shown at the top of the next page.

751

	19B	19A
Net sales	$195,455	$187,450
Total assets:		
Beginning of year	$230,819	$232,925
End of year	234,373	230,819
Average	$232,596	$231,872
Total asset turnover	.84	.81

The *plant and equipment turnover* may be calculated by dividing net sales for the year by the average book value of plant and equipment during the year. The calculation of plant and equipment turnover of The B. J. Patrick Manufacturing Co. for each year would be as follows:

	19B	19A
Net sales	$195,455	$187,450
Plant and equipment (factory equipment, building, and land — net):		
Beginning of year	$ 77,107	$ 81,562
End of year	76,814	77,107
Average	$ 76,961	$ 79,335
Turnover of plant and equipment	2.5	2.4

The *working capital turnover* may be calculated by dividing the net sales for the year by the average working capital (current assets less current liabilities) for the year. The working capital turnover for The B. J. Patrick Manufacturing Co. for each year may be found as follows:

	19B	19A
Net sales	$195,455	$187,450
Working capital:		
Beginning of year	$110,428	$108,864
End of year	109,590	110,428
Average	$110,009	$109,646
Turnover of working capital	1.8	1.7

Note that there was a very small improvement in each of the four preceding turnover ratios (finished goods, total assets, plant and equipment, and working capital) for 19B in relation to 19A. This suggests that there had been a slightly more effective utilization of the resources of the business in the latter year.

Report No. 29-2

Complete Report No. 29-2 in the workbook and submit your working papers for approval. Continue with the next study assignment in Chapter 30 until Report No. 30-1 is required.

chapter 30

cost accounting

The term *cost accounting* has come to refer to a considerable variety of activities concerned with the assignment of incurred cost to various business operations, including the design and operation of systems that will generate information to help control costs. However, this chapter will be confined to a discussion of the major practices followed in order to assign factory costs in a reasonable manner to units produced. Product cost information is needed for two reasons:

753

(a) To assist in setting selling prices or, in many cases, to determine whether the prices that are being charged to customers are high enough to provide a gross margin that will help cover nonmanufacturing costs and expenses and contribute to net income. Even though the overall result seems to be satisfactory, the management of a multiproduct manufacturing business wants to know whether (and how much) each product or "product line" is adding to (or subtracting from) the net result.

(b) To assist in the determination of the net income (or net loss) of each period. When goods are manufactured rather than purchased, there must be some means of assigning a reasonable share of incurred costs to (1) products finished but unsold at the end of the accounting period — the *finished goods inventory*, and (2) products that are unfinished at the end of the period — the *work in process inventory*.

While many cost accounting systems may be described as somewhat "hybrid," there are two basic types: (1) job order and (2) process. The major characteristics of each of these types will be discussed.

Job order cost accounting

If the product is made to customers' orders or specifications, or if products are made in separately identifiable "lots" or "batches," a *job order* cost accounting system will be suitable. Such a system would be well suited to such enterprises as a printing shop, a cabinet shop, or a shipbuilder. The heart or core of this type of system is a record on which is entered **(1)** the cost of materials that can be clearly identified with the job — the *direct materials*, **(2)** the labor cost that can be clearly identified with the job — the *direct labor*, and **(3)** a share of the *factory overhead* cost that may reasonably be assigned to the job. The form of record used is commonly called a *job cost sheet* or sometimes just *job sheet* or *job card*. An illustration of one form of job cost sheet is reproduced below. This form is in common use, but the record may take a different from. Sometimes, an ordinary ledger account form is used. Whatever form the record takes and by whatever name it is called, its function is to serve as a place to bring together the three elements of the cost of each job — direct materials, direct labor, and a share of factory overhead.

754

Job. No._____					
Item _____			Date _____		
Quantity _____			Date Wanted _____		
For _____			Date Completed _____		

DIRECT MATERIALS		DIRECT LABOR			FACTORY OVERHEAD
Req. No.	Amount	Date	Hours	Amount	Direct Labor _____
					Overhead Rate _____
					Overhead Applied _____
					SUMMARY
					Direct Materials _____
					Direct Labor _____
					Factory Overhead _____
					Total Cost _____
					Cost per Unit _____

Job Cost Sheet

Collectively, the job cost sheets comprise the *job ledger* or *cost ledger*. This job (cost) ledger is subsidiary to the general ledger account *work in process* (sometimes called *goods in process* or *jobs in process*).

Accounting for materials

The subject of accounting for materials, including mention of the distinction between "direct" and "indirect" materials, was considered in Chapter 28. In a cost accounting system it is common practice to keep *perpetual inventories* (mentioned in Chapters 14 and 28). Except in cases where only a few different materials are used, it is quite likely that there will be a *materials ledger* or *stores ledger*. This materials ledger is subsidiary to the general ledger account *Materials*.

It is probable that a form called a *materials requisition* or *stores requisition* will be used in connection with the movement of and accounting for materials. One form of materials requisition is illustrated below. This form serves both as an authorization (when properly approved) to the storekeeper to issue materials, and as a source document for recording the movement of materials. After the costs of the requisitioned materials have been entered on the form, it can be used as the basis for credits in the stores ledger and debits in the job ledger (for direct materials put into production) and for debits in the factory overhead ledger (for indirect materials used in the factory). A summary of the requisitions provides the amounts to be credited to the control account for materials, with debits to the control accounts for work in process and for factory overhead in the general ledger.

755

Deliver To		Date	Requisition No.			
Requested By			Approved By			
Charge To						

ITEM	QTY. REQD.	NUMBER	DESCRIPTION	QTY. ISSUED	UNIT COST	TOTAL COST

Filled By	Priced By	Entered By	Received By	Date Received

Materials Requisition

Accounting for labor

The practices followed in accounting for the earnings, payroll deductions, and the payment of wages and salaries to employees have been described and illustrated at several earlier points in the textbook. Fundamentally the same procedures are involved in the case of a factory with a job order cost accounting system, except that more detail is involved in accounting for labor cost. The earnings of workers whose services are considered to be *indirect labor* (defined on page 699 in Chapter 28) must be charged to the proper factory overhead accounts. The earnings of workers whose services are considered to be *direct labor* must be charged to the jobs on which they worked. This requires that some procedure must be followed for keeping a record of the time worked and labor cost incurred on each job. A wide variety of practices designed to provide this information are in use. One such practice is to require the (direct labor) employees to complete a *daily time ticket* similar to the one reproduced below. This form may be prepared manually, or it may be completed as a printout from a computerized timekeeping system. The tickets of all such workers may be summarized by days, weeks, or months, to provide the direct labor cost of each of the jobs involved.

JOB NO. OR TYPE OF WORK	TIME STARTED	TIME STOPPED	TIME ELAPSED		RATE		AMOUNT EARNED
			REG.	O.T.	REG.	O.T.	

Name _____ Employee No. _____
Dept. _____ Date _____

Signed _____ Approved _____
Employee · Foreman

Daily Time Ticket

A special problem may arise if overtime pay is involved. Under certain circumstances, the total labor cost — including overtime premium — is properly chargeable to the jobs on which the overtime was worked. In certain other cases, overtime may have been necessary because of a heavy production schedule, but it may not be reasonable to charge the particular jobs involved with the extra cost incurred because overtime hours were required. (Note that it is only the premium part of the pay that is at issue here. Each job normally would be charged for the total hours at the straight-time rate.) In such cases the overtime premium portion of the labor cost may be charged to factory overhead.

It is rather common practice to charge factory overhead for the portion of the employer's payroll taxes that relates to all types of factory labor. Factory overhead usually is charged for the cost of any "fringe benefits" (vacation pay, for example) that relate to factory workers.

Accounting for factory overhead

The nature of factory overhead and the entries involved in recording factory overhead were discussed in Chapter 28. In connection with job order cost accounting systems, the major problem is the assignment of a reasonable amount of the factory overhead to each job. When more than one type of product is manufactured (the usual case), a method of factory overhead apportionment that is sensible and equitable must be used. The practice of assigning factory overhead in proportion to the direct labor cost on each job has been widely followed, though other bases — such as direct labor hours or machine hours — sometimes are used. The assignment problem is complicated by the nature of many of the costs that comprise factory overhead. Most of these costs do not vary directly with the volume of production (depreciation of factory building and equipment, for example). Some types of factory overhead are incurred irregularly throughout the year, but the cost does not entirely apply to the month in which it is recorded (vacation pay and repairs and maintenance of machinery, for example).

The foregoing considerations have led to the practice of calculating a so-called *predetermined factory overhead rate* to be used in assigning factory overhead cost to the jobs worked on during a year. Suppose, for example, that the intention is to assign all of the factory overhead cost for each year to the jobs worked on during that year, and it is decided that a direct-labor-cost basis of assignment will give reasonable results. The rate to be used each year is calculated by using the following formula:

$$\frac{\text{Estimated Factory Overhead Cost for the Coming Year}}{\text{Estimated Direct Labor Cost for the Coming Year}} = \begin{array}{l}\text{Factory Overhead}\\ \text{as a Percent of}\\ \text{Direct Labor Cost}\end{array}$$

Suppose it is estimated that, during the coming year, factory overhead cost will be $212,500 and direct labor cost will be $250,000. The predetermined rate for that year then will be 85 percent ($212,500 divided by

$250,000). As each job is completed during the year, an amount equal to 85 percent of the direct labor cost incurred on the job during that year will be added as the job's share of factory overhead cost. At the end of that year, 85 percent of the direct labor cost thus far incurred will be added as a part of the cost of the unfinished jobs (work in process).

It is likely that there will be a control account for factory overhead in the general ledger and a related factory overhead subsidiary ledger. So as not to disturb this relationship, the total amount of factory overhead added to the job cost records may be recorded in the general ledger by a debit to Work in Process and a credit to *Factory Overhead Applied* (a contra account to the control account for factory overhead).

It would be too much to expect that both the estimate of factory overhead cost and the estimate of total direct labor cost would turn out to be exactly correct. Either estimate may turn out to have been too high or too low. Any errors of estimation may partially offset each other, but it is to be expected that there will be some difference between the amount of factory overhead cost incurred and the total amount assigned to the jobs worked on during the year. The difference between the balance of Factory Overhead and the balance of Factory Overhead Applied is described as *overabsorbed* or *underabsorbed* factory overhead. Sometimes the terms *overapplied* and *underapplied* are used. If the amount of such difference is relatively small, it is common practice to close the amount of any over- or underabsorption to Cost of Goods Sold, rather than to go back and recalculate the cost of every job. If there is a large difference, a number of recalculations may be required.

Throughout the foregoing discussion it has been assumed that neither direct labor nor factory overhead is being accounted for on a departmental basis. If the accounting is departmentalized (which may be the case, depending upon a variety of circumstances), the record keeping is certain to be more complicated. It may be that a direct-labor-cost basis of assigning departmental overhead is suitable for certain departments, while a direct-labor-hour basis or a machine-hour basis is more suitable for other departments. If departmentalized cost accounting records are maintained, it will be necessary to allocate costs that are common to all departments (such as factory administration costs and occupancy costs). It is not unlikely that there may be certain *service departments* (personnel and factory maintenance, for example) whose costs must be allocated to the producing departments prior to the assignment of factory overhead to jobs.

It should be mentioned that the policy of attempting to assign all of the factory overhead cost incurred during a given year to the production of that year is not always followed. Many manufacturing businesses use what is known as a *normal capacity* or *average activity* basis of assigning factory overhead. The idea is to assign factory overhead in such a way that, on the

758

average, over several years all factory overhead incurred will be assigned to jobs. However, in any single year it is unlikely that the amount incurred and the amount assigned will be substantially the same. This method is intended to avoid marked changes in unit costs because of fluctuation in the level of production. Another practice that is growing in popularity, though it is not yet an "accepted" method of accounting, is to assign only so-called *variable* factory overhead to the units produced. "Fixed" factory overhead costs, described as *period costs* (in contrast to *product costs* which vary in relation to output), are treated as expenses each year — not as a part of the total cost of units produced. This method is called *direct costing*. Some think that its numerous advantages will cause direct costing to become the most widely followed method of cost accounting.

Flow of costs through job order cost accounts

To illustrate the flow of costs through the accounts of a manufacturing company using job order cost accounting, a summary of the entries made to record costs incurred, jobs completed, and the cost of finished goods sold is presented. The illustration relates to the Duncan Manufacturing Company for the month of January. The accounts of the company are kept on a calendar-year basis. Only transactions involving manufacturing costs are summarized and only six general ledger accounts are shown. Because of space limitations, each of the four subsidiary ledgers illustrated includes only a few accounts. The company uses a voucher system and maintains appropriate books of original entry and auxiliary records. As of January 1, the inventory accounts had the following balances:

GENERAL LEDGER ACCOUNTS		SUBSIDIARY LEDGER ACCOUNTS	
		Stores Ledger:	
Materials..............	$ 9,500	Material A............	$ 4,000
		Material B............	3,000
		Material C............	2,500
		Cost Ledger:	
Work in Process.........	7,000	Job No. 406...........	7,000
		Finished Goods Ledger:	
Finished Goods..........	13,000	Product X............	8,000
		Product Y............	5,000

For purposes of illustration, all of the transactions summarized are presented in the form of general journal entries. Postings to certain accounts in both the general ledger and the subsidiary ledgers are shown on pages 762 and 763. (The accounts are positioned to indicate the flow of costs.) Note that the ending balances in the general ledger control accounts on page 762 agree with the totals of the subsidiary ledger account balances on page 763.

The transactions and journal entries are shown below and on page 761.

(a) Materials (direct and indirect) purchased during the month, $14,000.

Materials..	14,000	
In stores ledger:		
Material A.....................................	8,000	
Material B.....................................	4,000	
Material C.....................................	2,000	
Vouchers Payable.............................		14,000

(b) Materials requisitioned from stores during month, $17,000 (direct materials, $14,000; indirect materials, $3,000).

Work in Process....................................	14,000	
In cost ledger:		
Job No. 407.....................................	6,000	
Job No. 408.....................................	5,000	
Job No. 409.....................................	3,000	
Factory Overhead..................................	3,000	
In factory overhead ledger:		
Misc. Factory Expense...........................	3,000	
Materials......................................		17,000
In stores ledger:		
Material A..............................	9,000	
Material B..............................	5,000	
Material C..............................	3,000	

(c) Factory labor cost for the month, $18,600 (direct labor, $15,000; indirect labor, $3,600).

Work in Process....................................	15,000	
In cost ledger:		
Job No. 406.....................................	2,000	
Job No. 407.....................................	4,000	
Job No. 408.....................................	6,000	
Job No. 409.....................................	3,000	
Factory Overhead..................................	3,600	
In factory overhead ledger:		
Indirect Labor..................................	3,600	
Vouchers Payable, FICA Tax Payable, etc.......		18,600

(d) Other factory overhead cost incurred during month, $5,500.

Factory Overhead..................................	5,500	
In factory overhead ledger:		
Depreciation Expense............................	500	
Misc. Factory Expense...........................	5,000	
Accumulated Depreciation — Factory Building and Equipment, Vouchers Payable, Prepaid Insurance, etc..		5,500

760

(e) Factory overhead applied during month, $12,000 (80 percent of direct labor on jobs).

Work in Process.....................................	12,000	
In cost ledger:		
Job No. 406....................................	1,600	
Job No. 407....................................	3,200	
Job No. 408....................................	4,800	
Job No. 409....................................	2,400	
Factory Overhead Applied......................		12,000

(f) Job No. 408 completed and immediately shipped directly to customer (cost, $15,800).

Cost of Goods Sold.................................	15,800	
Work in Process.................................		15,800
In cost ledger:		
Job No. 408	15,800	

(g) Jobs Nos. 406 and 407 completed and placed in stock, $23,800.

Finished Goods	23,800	
In finished goods ledger:		
Product X......................................	10,600	
Product Y......................................	13,200	
Work in Process..............................		23,800
In cost ledger:		
Job No. 406............................	10,600	
Job No. 407............................	13,200	

(h) Cost of Products X and Y sold during month, $22,000.

Cost of Goods Sold.................................	22,000	
Finished Goods.................................		22,000
In finished goods ledger:		
Product X......................................	10,000	
Product Y......................................	12,000	

761

Report No. 30-1

Complete Report No. 30-1 in the workbook and submit your working papers for approval. Continue with the following study assignment until Report No. 30-2 is required.

762

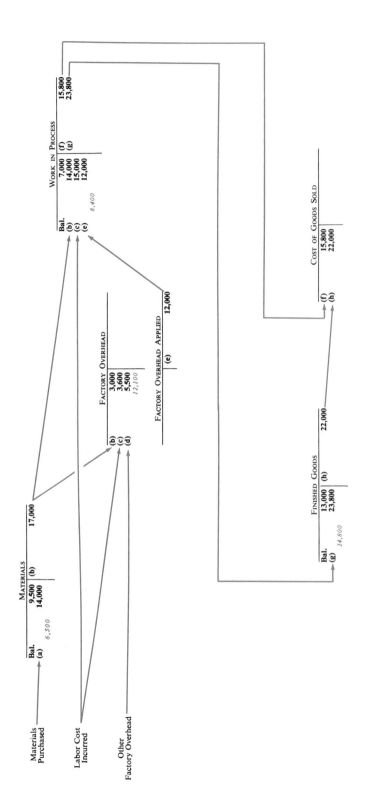

Flow of Costs Through Job Order Cost Accounts
(General Ledger)

FINISHED GOODS LEDGER

COST LEDGER

STORES LEDGER

FACTORY OVERHEAD LEDGER

Flow of Costs Through Job Order Cost Accounts
(Subsidiary Ledgers)

763

Process cost accounting

If a manufacturing business is engaged in the continuous, or nearly continuous, production of a homogeneous product (cement, many chemicals, flour, and certain other foodstuffs, for example) it may not be possible to assemble costs by jobs, lots, or batches. In such cases, the most feasible means of associating costs with units produced may be to gather costs by processes (sometimes constituting separate departments) and to assign a share of the cost to each unit passing through that process during a certain period of time — often a month. This procedure for arriving at unit costs is described as *process cost accounting*. It is an averaging device. If, for example, the costs associated with operating the Mixing Process for a certain month totaled $60,000 (the sum of the cost of materials put into process, the cost of labor connected with that operation, and a reasonable share of the factory overhead) and, during that month, 40,000 units (perhaps pounds, gallons, or barrels) passed through the process, the average cost was $1.50 per unit ($60,000 ÷ 40,000 units). (This calculation assumes that there were no partially processed units either at the start or at the end of the month.) The 40,000 units might pass through one or more other processes which would add to the unit cost at each stage.

764   If (as is sometimes the case) more than one product is manufactured, it is possible that every product does not pass through every process. All may go through the same early processing, but follow different paths for the later stages. There are instances where the manufacture of two or more different products does not involve any of the same processing steps. This situation has been described as *parallel processing*.

In an accounting sense, the heart or core of a process cost system is the account or accounts that summarize the costs associated with each process. These accounts have titles such as *Work in Process — Finishing Department* or just *Finishing Department*. Sometimes titles such as *Process 32* or *Work in Process — Department 28* are found. By whatever name used, such accounts are the focal points for assembling costs. These accounts will be kept in the general ledger unless there are so many of them that a subsidiary ledger must be used.

Accounting for materials

As in job order cost accounting, it is likely that perpetual inventories will be used in a process cost system. If there are many different types of materials, it is probable that a subsidiary materials or stores ledger will be used. The requisition procedure may be followed, particularly if all materials do not enter into production at the same stage. In process cost accounting, the distinction between direct and indirect materials is of little or no consequence. The records kept must provide the amounts to be charged to each process for the cost of materials issued to that process. Usually this is done by means of a summary entry at the end of each month.

Accounting for labor

Under a process cost accounting system, the accounting for factory labor cost may be less complicated than in the case of a job order system. This is because so many of the workers are likely to devote all of their time to a single process. As in the case of materials, the direct-indirect distinction is of minimal importance. If a worker spends all of his time in activities concerned with one process, it doesn't matter whether he is a manager, a foreman, or a "line worker" — he is direct labor with respect to that process. The complication that may result from overtime pay under a job order system doesn't arise under a process cost system.

The payroll records must provide sufficient information to make it possible to charge the proper amount of gross earnings to each process. There will be some labor costs that are not clearly associated with the individual processes — the salaries of the plant manager, his staff, and custodians, for example. Labor costs such as these will have to be apportioned among the processes in some reasonable manner. The procedure followed may involve treating such labor as factory overhead to be allocated along with other costs of an indirect nature.

Accounting for factory overhead

While a larger share of total manufacturing cost can be directly associated with processes and, thus, with products under a process cost system than is likely to be possible under a job order system, there are certain to be some costs that are common to the entire factory or that have a seasonal variation largely unrelated to monthly production. Some procedure must be adopted that results in an equitable allocation of these costs to processes. If (1) general factory overhead is relatively small, (2) several products are not produced simultaneously, and (3) production is relatively stable throughout the year, it may be satisfactory to allocate the "common" costs on some basis that is reasonable with respect to each cost. For example, what are termed *occupancy costs* (factory rent or, instead, depreciation, insurance, and property taxes and the costs of heating or cooling, lighting, cleaning, and repairing the premises) may be apportioned on the basis of the relative amount of space occupied by each processing operation. Supervision and the cost of labor fringe benefits may be apportioned

765

in relation to the number of workers, the hours worked, or the total labor cost of each process. Sometimes what is called an *expense distribution sheet* (a form of work sheet or working paper) is used to assemble the data in developing the monthly summary entries to allocate the various types of costs — both labor costs and general factory overhead costs.

Some factories — particularly large ones — have several *service departments*. Examples include departments such as personnel, maintenance, accounting, production engineering and, sometimes, a power plant. In the primary assignment of all factory costs (materials and labor as well as general overhead costs), the service departments as well as the producing (process) departments are charged with costs clearly identifiable with their respective activities. Then, the costs of the service departments have to be assigned — ideally in proportion to the amount of service rendered to the other departments. This assignment and reassignment is carried out until all of the charges reach the producing departments. Predetermined rates will probably be used to provide a more reasonable monthly allocation.

The general ledger and subsidiary ledger accounts that will be used will depend upon the nature and variety of products, the nature of the production processes, the volume and stability of operations, and the amount of detailed information desired.

Calculation of unit costs

On page 764 a simple example of the calculation of average cost per unit was given. The example was simple both because it related to total cost and because it was assumed that there was neither a beginning nor an ending inventory of work in process. Often such inventories do exist and the calculation of average unit costs must consider the quantities and the degrees of completion of such inventories. To illustrate, assume the following circumstances relative to the first process in a factory:

In process, beginning of month: 800 units, complete as to material content and 50% complete as to processing cost — i.e., labor and factory overhead. Total cost so far assigned to the units..................	$ 1,360
Material put into process during the month: 5,400 units @ $1.20 each (In this example, the material is all put into process at the start — not gradually or at various stages.)	6,480
Processing costs for the month:	
Labor..	2,940
Factory overhead assigned to the process.......................	2,450
Total cost to be accounted for...............................	$13,230
Completed and transferred to next process during month.............	5,000 units
In process, end of month (complete as to materials and 25% complete as to processing costs)..	1,200 units

To be calculated: **(a)** The cost to be assigned to the 5,000 units completed and transferred to the next process.

(b) The cost to be assigned to the 1,200 incomplete units.

The first step in making the calculations is to compute what is called the *equivalent units* (or *equivalent production*) with respect to the labor and factory overhead — which together are called *processing costs*. There are three components involved in the calculation: **(1)** To complete the beginning inventory of 800 units, work equivalent to fully processing 400 units was required since these 800 units were one-half finished last month. **(2)** 4,200 units must have been *started and finished* this month, since a total of 5,000 units were completed during the month, and these units must have included the 800 units started the month before. **(3)** Since the 1,200 incomplete units are each one-fourth processed, the work done on them was the equivalent of fully processing 300 units. Thus, the equivalent production during the month was 4,900 units (400 + 4,200 + 300).

When the number of equivalent units has been determined, the per-unit processing cost can be calculated as follows:

Labor, $2,940 ÷ 4,900 units	=	$ .60 per unit
Factory overhead, $2,450 ÷ 4,900 units =		.50 per unit
Total	=	$1.10 per unit

The foregoing calculation can then be used to arrive at the following cost summary:

	TOTAL	PER UNIT
Cost of beginning inventory of work in process (800 units)...	$ 1,360	
Cost to complete beginning inventory of work in process:		
Equivalent to 400 units @ $1.10 per unit................	440	
Total...	$ 1,800	$2.25
Cost to start and finish 4,200 units:		
Materials..	$ 5,040	$1.20
Labor...	2,520	.60
Factory overhead.................................	2,100	.50
Total...	$ 9,660	$2.30
Total cost of 5,000 units completed and transferred........	$11,460	
Cost of 1,200 units incomplete at end of month:		
Materials..	$ 1,440	
Processing cost (equivalent to 300 units @ $1.10 each).....	330	
Total...	$ 1,770	
Total cost accounted for...........................	$13,230	

767

Flow of costs through process cost accounts

To illustrate the flow of costs through the accounts of a manufacturing company using a process cost accounting system, a summary of the entries made to record costs incurred, units transferred from one process to the next, units completed, and the cost of finished products sold is presented. The illustration relates to the Warner Processing Company for October, the first month of the company's fiscal (accounting) year. Only transactions involving manufacturing costs are summarized and only six general ledger accounts are shown. None of these is a control account. Since only two materials enter into the manufacture of the single product produced, neither a subsidiary ledger for materials nor a subsidiary ledger for finished goods is needed. All items that comprise factory overhead are charged to the two process accounts. In the case of several of these costs, it is necessary to prorate the amount between the two processes. While a subsidiary factory overhead ledger could be used, the accountant for the company thinks that the nature and size of the business does not make that record necessary. The company uses a voucher system and maintains appropriate books of original entry and auxiliary records. As of October 1, the inventory accounts had the following balances:

Material R..	$1,200
Material S..	2,000
Process 2..	6,040
(2,000 units complete as to material content and 60% complete as to processing cost.)	
Finished Goods (1,350 units @ $4.00)................	5,400

It will be noted that there is no inventory of work in process in Process 1. The nature of this process is such that any work started must be finished by the end of the same day.

For purposes of illustration, all of the transactions summarized are presented in general journal form. Posting to certain accounts is shown on page 769. (The accounts are positioned to indicate the flow of costs.) The transactions and entries follow:

(a) Materials purchases: Material R, $1,700; Material S, $4,200.

Material R..	1,700	
Material S..	4,200	
Vouchers Payable..		5,900

(b) Materials put into process: Material R, $1,600; Material S, $5,200.

Process 1...	6,800	
Material R..		1,600
Material S..		5,200

(c) Factory labor cost for the year, $20,080. ($6,000 relates to Process 1 and $14,080 to Process 2. These amounts include the proration of the gross earnings of the plant manager, cost accountant, janitors, watchman, etc.)

Process 1...	6,000	
Process 2...	14,080	
Vouchers Payable, FICA Tax Payable, etc.................		20,080

(d) Factory overhead cost (other than labor) for the month, $10,860. ($4,700 assigned to Process 1 and $6,160 to Process 2. Some of the cost such as supplies used, depreciation of equipment used by each department, and factory payroll taxes could be clearly identified with the separate processes; various other costs such as depreciation, insurance, and property taxes on the factory building, utilities, and miscellaneous factory expense had to be prorated.)

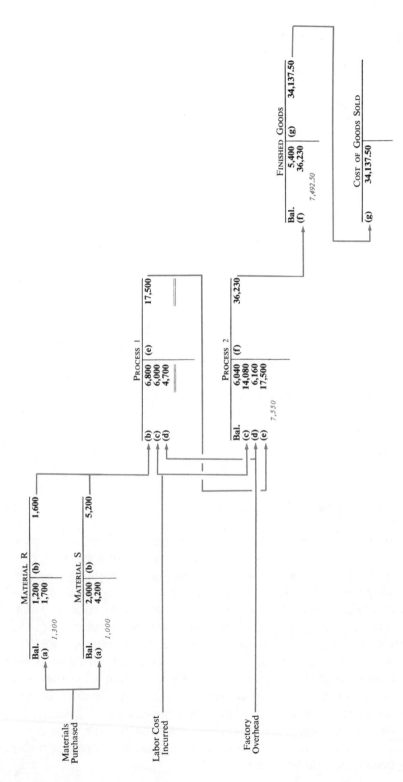

Flow of Costs Through Process Cost Accounts

769

Process 1	4,700	
Process 2	6,160	
Accumulated Depreciation — Factory Building and Equipment, Prepaid Insurance, Factory Supplies, Vouchers Payable, FICA Tax Payable, etc.		10,860

(e) Cost of 10,000 units transferred from Process 1 to Process 2, $17,500. (Reference to the three preceding entries, or to the Process 1 account on page 769, shows that the total was the sum of: materials put into Process 1, $6,800; labor in Process 1, $6,000; and factory overhead assigned to Process 1, $4,700.)

| Process 2 | 17,500 | |
| Process 1 | | 17,500 |

(f) Cost of 9,000 units completed in Process 2 and transferred to finished goods stockroom, $36,230 (based upon calculations in the *cost of production summary* reproduced at the top of page 771).

| Finished Goods | 36,230 | |
| Process 2 | | 36,230 |

(g) Cost of goods sold, $34,137.50. (The company uses the first-in, first-out method of accounting. 8,500 units were sold during the month. The unit cost of the 1,350 units in the October 1 inventory was $4.00 [see page 768]. The average cost of the first 2,000 units completed in October was $3.94. The average cost of all other units completed during the month was $4.05. Accordingly, the cost of the 8,500 units sold was calculated as follows: 1,350 units @ $4.00 + 2,000 units @ $3.94 + 5,150 units @ $4.05 = $34,137.50.)

| Cost of Goods Sold | 34,137.50 | |
| Finished Goods | | 34,137.50 |

Joint products and by-products

In connection with many types of processing operations, it is impossible to produce one product without the emergence of something else. The "something else" may be an unwanted — often unsightly and obnoxious — quantity of matter that must be removed or destroyed (perhaps burned or buried). Commonly, the term *waste* is used to describe such matter. However, it may be that the matter has a very nominal value and can be sold. Often, the term *scrap* is applied in this case. If the value is more than nominal, but still minor in relation to the main product, the term *by-product* is used. If the emerging products are not widely different in value, they may be considered *joint products*. These terms (waste, scrap, by-product, and joint product) are loosely used. Their meanings overlap. There is no precise means of deciding when something has enough value to be called a by-product rather than scrap — or when the term joint product rather than by-product should be applied.

WARNER PROCESSING COMPANY
Cost of Production Summary — Process 2
For the Month of October, 19--

Work in process, October 1 (2,000 units. Complete as to Process 1; 60% complete as to Process 2 costs)	$ 6,040
Units received from Process 1 (10,000 @ $1.75)	17,500
Labor	14,080
Factory overhead	6,160
Total costs to be accounted for	$43,780

Equivalent production for month (labor and factory overhead):

To finish units in process, October 1. Equivalent to 40% of 2,000 units	800 units
To start and finish 7,000 units	7,000 "
To start and 33⅓% complete 3,000 units	1,000 "
Total	8,800 "

Processing costs per equivalent unit:

Labor.....................$\dfrac{\$14,080}{8,800} = \$1.60$

Factory overhead...........$\dfrac{\$ 6,160}{8,800} = .70$

Total..................... $2.30

	Total	Per Unit
Cost accounted for as follows:		
Cost of beginning inventory of 2,000 units in process	$ 6,040	
Cost to complete. Equivalent to 800 units @ $2.30	1,840	
Total	$ 7,880	$3.94
Cost to start and finish 7,000 units:		
Previous department cost	$12,250	$1.75
Labor	11,200	1.60
Factory overhead	4,900	.70
Total	$28,350	$4.05
Total cost of units transferred to finished goods	$36,230	
Cost of ending inventory of work in process:		
(3,000 units. Complete as to Process 1 cost; 33⅓% complete as to Process 2 cost.)		
Previous department cost	$ 5,250	
Process 2 cost. Equivalent to 1,000 units @ $2.30	2,300	
Total cost of work in process	$ 7,550	
Total cost accounted for	$43,780	

Cost of Production Summary

If products with very small value are inevitable in the process of production, any revenue from their sale may be accounted for either as **(1)** a reduction of the total cost of production or **(2)** as "other revenue." If the value of a particular product is more than trivial, it may be desirable to assign some of the total cost of production to that product. It is almost certain that the amount of cost assigned will be something less than the *sales value* of the product. (Sales value means sales price per unit times the number of units produced.) In the case of joint products, the cost to be shared may be allocated in proportion to the *relative sales value* of the products. For example, if the process of production inevitably results in the production of twice as many units (perhaps pounds) of product A as units (perhaps gallons) of product B, but the unit price of B is twice as great as the unit price of A, the sales value of all of the A produced will be the same as the sales value of all of the B produced. If this is the case, the total production cost may be equally divided between the products. (Their relative sales values are 1 to 1.) This practice causes the percent of gross margin (gross profit) to be the same when products of either type are sold. Often the matter of joint cost apportionment is complicated by the fact that not all of the cost is joint. One or all of the products may not acquire any value until further processing after the *split-off point* takes place. Any method of joint cost apportionment is arbitrary to some degree.

Standard costs

A well-established and growing practice among manufacturers is to extend their cost accounting procedures (both job order and process cost systems) to embrace *standard costs*. That term has various shades of meaning, since it includes a considerable variety of practices. Fundamentally, standard costing is a type of *budgeting*. An attempt is made to determine what the cost of an operation, process, or product should be under reasonably ideal conditions, and to keep records that will make it possible to determine whether costs are "out of line" and, if so, where. Standard costing is primarily a device to assist management in the control of costs.

It may have been noted that the expression *actual cost* has never been used in this chapter. Considering the variety of methods of assigning cost to materials used, of calculating depreciation, of assigning or allocating factory overhead, and of handling various matters not specifically mentioned, there is a real question as to whether there is such a thing as "actual" cost in most cases. Experienced cost accountants know that their central task is to develop costs that are "meaningful," "useful," "sensible," and "reasonable" in relation to the intended use of their findings. Sometimes when a comparison is made between budgeted costs (or standard costs) and the amounts of costs as recorded, reference may be made to *budgeted versus actual*, or *standard versus actual*, but the accountant recognizes that "actual" is not being used in the literal sense in such cases.

Report No. 30-2

Complete Report No. 30-2 in the workbook and submit your working papers for approval.

chapters 26-30

practical accounting problems

Problem 26-A

The ledger accounts of The Berra Instruments Co. had the following balances on January 1:

Bank...	$ 64,400	
Accounts Receivable.................................	77,600	
Allowance for Bad Debts.............................		$ 2,400
Merchandise Inventory...............................	54,000	
Prepaid Insurance...................................	800	
Furniture and Fixtures...............................	48,000	
Accumulated Depreciation — Furniture and Fixtures........		23,200
Building..	160,000	
Accumulated Depreciation — Building...................		32,000
Land..	20,000	
Accounts Payable....................................		45,200
Capital Stock.......................................		240,000
Retained Earnings...................................		82,000
	$424,800	$424,800

On January 2, the company established two branches, one in the northern part of the state, called the North Branch, and another in the western part of the state, called the West Branch.

The following are transactions completed by the home office and by the two branches (many of the transactions are given in summary form):

(1) Home office sent $20,000 to North Branch.
(2) Home office sent $24,000 to West Branch.
(3) Total purchases of merchandise at home office, $600,000 (on account).
(4) Total shipments of merchandise to North Branch (at cost), $152,000.
(5) Total shipments of merchandise to West Branch (at cost), $184,000.
(6) Furniture and fixtures purchased for cash at North Branch, $16,000; insurance premium paid, $600.
(7) Furniture and fixtures purchased for cash at West Branch, $19,200; insurance premium paid, $640.
(8) Sales at home office: cash, $132,000; on account, $308,000.
(9) Sales at North Branch: cash, $56,000; on account, $124,000.
(10) Sales at West Branch: cash, $40,000; on account, $160,000.
(11) Operating expenses incurred at home office, $73,600.
(12) Operating expenses incurred at North Branch, $35,600.
(13) Operating expenses incurred at West Branch, $38,400.
(14) Collected on accounts receivable at home office, $320,000; accounts written off as worthless, $2,000.
(15) Collected on accounts receivable at North Branch, $100,000.
(16) Collected on accounts receivable at West Branch, $80,000.
(17) Cash sent by North Branch to West Branch, $40,000.
(18) Cash payments on account at North Branch, $32,800.
(19) Cash payments on account at West Branch, $37,200.
(20) Cash sent to home office by North Branch, $72,000.
(21) Cash sent to home office by West Branch, $108,000.
(22) Cash payments on account at home office, $640,000.

774

REQUIRED: (1) Using two-column journal paper, journalize the foregoing transactions as they should be recorded in the books of the home office and both branch offices. Since dates are purposely omitted, it will be advisable to number each journal entry to correspond with the number of the transaction. (2) Using plain paper, 8½″ x 11″, rule 26 "T" account forms (eight to a page arranged in 2 columns) under the heading Home Office Ledger. In addition to the 13 accounts appearing in the trial balance at beginning of year, the following accounts will be needed: North Branch, West Branch, Purchases, Shipments to North Branch, Shipments to West Branch, Sales, Operating Expenses, Cost of Goods Sold, North Branch Income, West Branch Income, Income Tax Expense, Income Tax Payable, and Expense and Revenue Summary. Enter the opening balances. Rule 13 "T" account forms under the heading North Branch Ledger. Also rule 13 "T" account forms under the heading West Branch Ledger. In each case the following accounts are needed: Bank, Accounts Receivable, Allowance for Bad Debts, Merchandise Inventory, Prepaid Insurance, Shipments from Home Office, Furniture and Fixtures, Accumulated Depreciation — Furniture and Fixtures, Accounts Payable, Home Office, Sales, Operating Expenses, and Expense and Revenue Summary. Post the entries of the three journals to the proper "T" accounts in the three ledgers. Number each entry to correspond with the number of the journal entry. (3) Take a trial balance as of December 31 of the accounts kept for each office.

(23) End-of-year adjustments for North Branch:
  (a) Merchandise inventory, $28,000.
  (b) Depreciation of furniture and fixtures, $1,600.
  (c) Insurance expired, $200.
  (d) Provision for bad debts, $3,200.
      (Debit the sum of b, c, and d to Operating Expenses.)

Journalize the adjusting entries and post to the accounts affected.

Also journalize the entries required to close the temporary accounts and to transfer the branch net income to the home office account.

(24) End-of-year adjustments for West Branch:
  (a) Merchandise inventory, $48,000.
  (b) Depreciation of furniture and fixtures, $1,920.
  (c) Insurance expired, $240.
  (d) Provision for bad debts, $4,800.
      (Debit the sum of b, c, and d to Operating Expenses.)

Journalize the adjusting entries and post to the accounts affected.

Also journalize the entries required to close the temporary accounts and to transfer the branch net income to the home office account.

(25) End-of-year adjustments for home office:
  (a) Transfer the opening inventory and the balances of purchases and shipments to branch accounts to Cost of Goods Sold.
  (b) Ending inventory, $56,000.
  (c) Depreciation of furniture and fixtures, $4,800.
  (d) Depreciation of building, $4,000.
  (e) Insurance expired, $680.
  (f) Provision for bad debts, $6,600.
      (Debit the sum of c, d, e, and f to Operating Expenses.)
  (g) Record the net income of the branch offices in the home office books.
  (h) Provision for income taxes, estimated, $41,600.

Journalize the adjusting entries and post to the accounts affected.

Also journalize the entries required to close the temporary accounts and to transfer the net income to Retained Earnings.

Prepare a work sheet for a combined income statement. The form of this work sheet should be similar to that illustrated on pages 676 and 677. Prepare a combined income statement similar to the one illustrated on page 680.

Prepare a work sheet for a combined balance sheet. The form of this work sheet should be similar to that illustrated on pages 678 and 679. Prepare a combined balance sheet similar to the one illustrated on page 680.

Problem 26-B

The Sandweg Company bills its branch at 25% above cost for goods shipped to it. The home office credits the difference between the cost and the billed price to Provision for Overvaluation of Branch Inventory. At the start of the year, the branch inventory (at billed price) was $67,200. Accordingly, the provision account in the home office books had a credit balance of $13,440. During the year the cost of goods shipped to the branch was $500,000; the billed price was $625,000.

At the end of the year the branch submitted an income statement showing cost of goods sold to be $571,200 and net income to be $52,000. The branch balance sheet showed the ending inventory to be $121,000.

REQUIRED: (1) Compute the actual cost of goods sold by the branch office. (2) Compute the actual net income of the branch office. (3) Compute the actual cost of the goods in the branch office inventory at the end of the year. (4) Prepare a journal entry to record on the home office books the actual branch income and to adjust the Provision for Overvaluation of Branch Inventory.

Problem 27-A

The EMR Telemetry Co., a corporation just organized, plans to use a voucher register and a check register similar to those shown on pages 688–689 and 692.

NARRATIVE OF TRANSACTIONS

(Assume that checks were issued in payment of any invoices subject to discount on the day preceding the last day of the discount period.)

Oct. 2. Issued Voucher No. 1 for $100 to establish a petty cash fund, and cashed Check No. 1 for that amount. (Petty Cash Fund, Account No. 112.)

2. Received an invoice for $250 from the Hardesty Real Estate Co., 18 S. Central Ave., for rent. Issued Check No. 2 in payment of the invoice. (Rent Expense, Account No. 814.)

3. Received an invoice for $1,876.50 from the Magnavox Radio-Stereo Manufacturers, Inc., Fort Wayne, Indiana, for materials. Date of invoice, September 29; terms, 1/10, n/30.

5. Received a freight bill for $126.40 from the C & O Railway Company, the charges on the materials shipped by the Magnavox Radio-Stereo Manufacturers, Inc. Paid the bill with Check No. 3. (Freight In, Account No. 721.)

5. Received an invoice for $225 from Fixman Equipment Co., 8160 Stanford, for an office desk purchased. Date of invoice, October 3; terms, net 30 days. (Office Equipment, Account No. 211.)

6. Received a bill for telephone service from the Commonwealth Telephone Co., 212 Spruce St., and issued Check No. 4 for $19.25 in payment. (General Office Expense, Account No. 818.)

7. Received a bill for office supplies from William J. Kennedy & Co., 802 Pine St., and issued Check No. 5 for $48.50 in payment. (Office Supplies, Account No. 181.)

9. Received an invoice for $793.25 from L & S Electronics, Inc., Valley Stream, New York, for a shipment of materials. Of this amount $43.25

represented prepaid freight charges. Date of invoice, October 6; terms, 2/15, n/60.

12. Received an invoice for $76.35 from the Atkinson Advertising Co., 8 Progress Pkwy., for advertising service. Issued Check No. 7 in payment. (Advertising Expense, Account No. 823.)

13. Received an invoice for $54.10 from the Hartford Insurance Co., 2412 Pierce Bldg., for insurance. Issued Check No. 8 in payment. (Prepaid Insurance, Account No. 184.)

14. Received an invoice for $1,855.30 from the Panasonic Radio Manufacturing Co., Kansas City, for a shipment of radio parts. Date of invoice, October 11; terms, 1/10, n/30.

16. Received from the Union Pacific Railway a freight bill for $95.65, the charges on the radios shipped by the Panasonic Radio Manufacturing Co. Paid the bill with Check No. 9.

16. Issued Payroll Voucher No. 13 covering wages earned for the half month as follows:

> Direct labor, $1,040.
> Indirect labor, $122.50.
> Office salaries, $900.
> Sales salaries, $770.

Taxes withheld:

> FICA tax, $155.79.
> Employees' income tax, $509.85.

Issued Check No. 10 in payment of Payroll Voucher No. 13. The following accounts will be affected in recording the payroll: **777**

> 111 Bank
> 311 FICA Tax Payable
> 321 Employees Income Tax Payable
> 361 Vouchers Payable
> 731 Direct Labor
> 741 Indirect Labor
> 811 Office Salaries Expense
> 821 Sales Salaries Expense

17. Issued a voucher for $80 to be used in purchasing stamps for use in the office. Cashed Check No. 11 for this amount and obtained the stamps. (Charge to Office Supplies, Account No. 181.)

19. Received from the First National Bank a notice of the maturity of a $750 note dated September 21 and discounted at the bank. Issued Check No. 12 for that amount. (Notes Payable, Account No. 341.)

20. Received an invoice from the Stuart Repair Shop, 4504 Natural Bridge, for $57.12, the cost of repairs on factory machinery. Issued Check No. 13 in payment. (Factory Repairs, Account No. 747.)

21. Received an invoice for $2,875.10 from Robbins & Myers, Chicago, for a shipment of materials. Of this amount $175.10 represented prepaid freight charges. Date of invoice, October 20; terms, 1/10, n/30.

24. Received an invoice for $238.15 for factory supplies purchased from the Gaylord Container Co., 5300 Bircher Blvd.; terms, on account. (Factory Supplies, Account No. 183.)

26. Received an invoice from Joyce Cridland Lifts, Milwaukee, for $250, the cost of a lift truck for use in the factory. Terms, net 30 days. (Factory Equipment, Account No. 231.)

30. Received an invoice for $921.40 from the General Electric Co., Phoenix, for a shipment of materials. Of this amount $71.40 represented prepaid freight charges. Date of invoice, October 27; terms, 2/10, n/30.

31. Issued Payroll Voucher No. 21 covering wages earned for the half month as follows:

> Direct labor, $1,000.
> Indirect labor, $145.
> Office salaries, $900.
> Sales salaries, $770.

Taxes withheld:

> FICA tax, $154.83.
> Employees' income tax, $506.70.

Issued Check No. 17 in payment of Payroll Voucher No. 21.

REQUIRED: (1) Record the foregoing transactions in the voucher register and check register. (2) Foot and prove the footings of both the voucher register and the check register. (3) Open an account for vouchers payable and post to it the footings of the Vouchers Payable columns in the voucher register and the check register. (4) Prove the balance of the vouchers payable account by preparing a schedule of the unpaid vouchers from the voucher register.

Problem 28-A

The Austin Manufacturing Company uses three materials designated A, B, and C. Data relative to inventories, purchases, and market prices of these materials are as follows:

	MATERIALS		
	A	B	C
Opening inventory................	6,000 @ $ 2.20	20,000 @ $ .18	500 @ $64.00
Purchases (in order)..............	12,000 @ 2.40	80,000 @ .20	1,000 @ 60.00
	20,000 @ 2.50		2,000 @ 68.00
	4,000 @ 2.80		
Ending inventory.................	5,000 units	15,000 units	1,800 units
Market price, end of period........	$2.90	$.19	$68.00

REQUIRED: (1) On a first-in, first-out basis, calculate the total cost of the ending inventory of each of the three items. (2) Compute the market value of the ending inventory of each of the three items. (3) If the "cost or market, whichever is lower" rule is to be followed, what is the total amount to be assigned to the ending inventory of materials?

Problem 28-B

The J. W. Towle Manufacturing Co. keeps its accounts on the calendar year basis, but the accountant prepares monthly statements. Data for adjustment of the accounts are assembled and entered on summary and supplementary work sheets at the end of each month, although adjustments of the general ledger accounts are recorded only at the end of each year. The factory overhead and operating expense accounts, however, are

THE J. W. TOWLE MANUFACTURING CO.
Trial Balance
December 31, 19—

Account	No.	Debit	Credit
Nordic National Bank	111	50,320.00	
Petty Cash Fund	112	200.00	
Notes Receivable	131	6,712.00	
Accrued Interest Receivable	132		
Accounts Receivable	133	42,976.00	
Allowance for Bad Debts	013		592.00
Materials Inventory	161	8,660.00	
Work in Process Inventory	162	6,688.00	
Finished Goods Inventory	163	16,852.00	
Office Supplies	181	1,112.00	
Factory Supplies	182	2,052.00	
Prepaid Insurance	183	2,100.00	
Office Equipment	211	7,800.00	
Accumulated Depreciation — Office Equipment	021		744.00
Delivery Equipment	221	10,000.00	
Accumulated Depreciation — Delivery Equip.	022		2,500.00
Machinery and Equipment	231	100,000.00	
Accumulated Depreciation — Mach. and Equip.	023		31,200.00
Building	241	148,000.00	
Accumulated Depreciation — Building	024		30,000.00
Land	251	16,000.00	
FICA Tax Payable	311		963.98
FUTA Tax Payable	312		121.46
State Unemployment Tax Payable	313		372.76
Employees Income Tax Payable	314		1,363.32
Corporation Income Tax Payable	315		
Notes Payable	316		15,560.00
Accrued Interest Payable	317		
Vouchers Payable	318		41,960.00
Dividends Payable	319		1,900.00
Bonds Payable	421		14,000.00
Capital Stock ($100 par)	511		202,000.00
Retained Earnings	521		48,936.00
Sales	611		368,536.96
Sales Returns and Allowances	061	2,100.00	
Sales Discount	062	3,780.00	
Interest Earned	631		352.00
Materials Purchases	711	85,384.00	
Materials Purchases Returns and Allowances	071		2,148.00
Purchases Discount	072		1,396.00
Freight In	721	7,904.00	
Direct Labor	731	92,552.00	
Factory Overhead	741	47,806.12	
Manufacturing Summary	751		
Cost of Goods Sold	811		
Operating Expenses	821	104,660.36	
Interest Expense	831	988.00	
Income Tax Expense	841		
		764,646.48	764,646.48

THE J. W. TOWLE MANUFACTURING CO.
Trial Balance of Factory Overhead Ledger
December 31, 19- -

Indirect Labor	7401	18,460.00
Utilities	7402	7,200.00
Maintenance and Repairs	7403	1,672.00
Depreciation of Factory Building and Equipment	7404	11,480.00
Expired Insurance on Factory Building and Equipment	7405	1,232.00
Payroll Taxes — Factory	7406	6,678.12
Miscellaneous Factory Overhead	7407	1,084.00
		47,806.12

THE J. W. TOWLE MANUFACTURING CO.
Schedule of Operating Expenses
For the Year Ended December 31, 19—-

Officers' salaries expense	8201	33,200.00
Office salaries expense	8202	24,540.00
Office supplies expense	8203	
Depreciation of office equipment	8204	
Office equipment insurance expense	8205	
Payroll taxes — administrative	8206	3,816.36
Miscellaneous office expense	8207	1,736.00
Total administrative expenses		63,292.36
Sales salaries expense	8231	24,000.00
Advertising expense	8232	7,268.00
Depreciation of delivery equipment	8233	
Delivery equipment insurance expense	8234	
Miscellaneous delivery expense	8235	6,160.00
Bad debts expense	8236	
Finished goods insurance expense	8237	
Payroll taxes — sales	8238	1,400.00
Miscellaneous selling expense	8239	2,540.00
Total selling expenses		41,368.00
Total operating expenses		104,660.36

780

formally adjusted at the end of each month. These groups of accounts are kept in subsidiary ledgers, controlled by the factory overhead and operating expenses accounts in the general ledger. The trial balance on page 779 was taken on December 31 after the factory overhead adjusting entries for the month had been posted. (It will be noted that a few of the accounts have no balances. These accounts are included because they will be affected by the adjusting entries required on the work sheets.)

The trial balance of the factory overhead ledger and the schedule of operating expenses reproduced above were prepared after posting the factory overhead adjusting entries for December. The operating expense adjusting entries had not yet been made or posted.

The following information is provided. (Bear in mind that the factory overhead accounts have already been adjusted.)

DATA FOR YEAR-END ADJUSTMENT OF GENERAL AND
OPERATING EXPENSES LEDGER ACCOUNTS
December 31, 19—

Inventories:

Materials..		$ 7,500.00
Work in process...		5,600.00
Finished goods...		18,040.00

Accruals:

Accrued interest receivable...............................		28.00
Accrued interest payable.................................		104.00
Office supplies expense...................................		900.00
Depreciation of office equipment..........................		1,580.00
Depreciation of delivery equipment........................		2,500.00

Insurance expense:

On office equipment.......................................	$ 88.00	
On delivery equipment.....................................	148.00	
On finished goods...	136.00	372.00
Provision for bad debts...................................		1,800.00
Provision for corporation income taxes....................		5,691.16

REQUIRED: **(1)** Using twelve-column analysis paper, prepare a summary end-of-year work sheet as a means of summarizing and classifying the information needed in preparing financial statements. (Allow two lines for the manufacturing summary account.) Support this summary work sheet with a three-column supplementary operating expenses work sheet. **(2)** Journalize the adjusting and closing entries. **(3)** Using balance-column ledger paper, open the following accounts:

132 Accrued Interest Receivable	631 Interest Earned
317 Accrued Interest Payable	751 Manufacturing Summary
521 Retained Earnings	811 Cost of Goods Sold
531 Expense and Revenue Summary	831 Interest Expense

Post the adjusting and closing entries that affect these accounts. (Be sure to show any balances in these accounts before adjustment. Refer to the trial balance on page 779.) Using balance-column ledger paper, open Accounts Nos. 8203, 8204, 8205, 8233, 8234, 8236, and 8237 as listed in the schedule of operating expenses on page 780, and post the detail to these accounts. **(4)** Journalize the entries required to reverse the adjusting entries for accruals and post to the accounts affected. (Retain the solution to this problem for use in solving Problem 29-A.)

Problem 29-A

The work sheets for The J. W. Towle Manufacturing Company, completed in Problem 28-B, are needed for the solution of this problem.

REQUIRED: **(1)** Prepare an income statement for the year ended December 31. The amounts in this and all following financial statements should be rounded to the nearest dollar. (There will be a difference of $1 on the balance sheet totals due to rounding.) **(2)** Prepare a schedule of operating expenses for the year ended December 31. **(3)** Prepare a manufacturing statement for the year ended December 31. **(4)** Prepare a statement of retained earnings for the year ended December 31. (Dividends declared during the year amount to $7,600.) **(5)** Prepare a balance sheet as of December 31 in the account form. (The difference of $1 between the total assets and the total liabilities and stockholders equity is due to rounding.)

Problem 29-B

The comparative income statement (condensed) for the years 19A and 19B and the comparative balance sheet as of December 31, 19A and 19B, for the Larson-Minnesota Company are presented below.

THE LARSON-MINNESOTA COMPANY
Condensed Comparative Income Statements
For the Years Ended December 31, 19B and 19A

	19B	19A
Sales...	$362,400	$342,800
Less sales returns, allowances, and discounts............	2,400	2,800
Net sales.......................................	$360,000	$340,000
Cost of goods sold...............................	200,000	196,000
Gross margin on sales............................	$160,000	$144,000
Administrative expenses...........................	$ 60,000	$ 56,000
Selling expenses.................................	68,000	64,000
Total operating expenses..........................	$128,000	$120,000
Net operating income.............................	$ 32,000	$ 24,000
Net interest expense.............................	4,000	4,000
Net income before income tax......................	$ 28,000	$ 20,000
Provision for income tax...........................	8,400	6,000
Net income after tax..............................	$ 19,600	$ 14,000

THE LARSON-MINNESOTA COMPANY
Condensed Comparative Balance Sheets
December 31, 19B and 19A

Assets	19B	19A	Liabilities and Stockholders' Equity	19B	19A
Cash.................	$ 38,000	$ 40,000	Vouchers payable........	$ 96,000	$ 84,000
Receivables (net)........	108,000	100,000	Taxes payable..........	9,200	6,400
Inventories.............	156,000	140,000	Bonds payable..........		80,000
Supplies & prepayments..	2,400	2,000	Common stock..........	120,000	120,000
Buildings & equipment....	64,000	40,000	Preferred stock..........	100,000	
Less accumd. deprec......	(16,000)	(12,000)	Retained earnings........	27,200	19,600
	$352,400	$310,000		$352,400	$310,000

REQUIRED: **(1)** Prepare comparative income statements that show the amount of change in each item and the percent of change relative to the first year. (A separate schedule of cost of goods sold is not required.

782

Round off percent calculations to the nearest 1/10 of 1%.) **(2)** Prepare comparative balance sheets that show the amount of change in each item and the percent of change in relation to the amount on December 31, 19A. (The undepreciated cost of buildings and equipment, rather than both cost and accumulated depreciation, may be shown. A separate schedule of current assets is not required.) **(3)** Prepare comparative income statements that show, for both years, each amount as a percent of the net sales of that year. **(4)** Prepare comparative balance sheets that show, for both years, each amount as a percent of the total assets and equities. **(5)** Calculate the following ratios for each of the two years, using the data in the statements and other information that is provided:

(a) Rate earned on average total assets.
(Total assets on January 1, 19A, amounted to $290,000.)
(b) Rate earned on average owners' equity.
(Owners' equity on January 1, 19A, amounted to $132,400.)
(c) Earnings per share of common stock.
(There were 600 shares of common stock outstanding both years. The preferred stock was not sold and issued until late in December, 19B.)
(d) Current ratio.
(e) Acid-test ratio.
(f) Rate of owners' equity to total liabilities.
(g) Book value per share of common stock.
(The par value of the preferred stock is $100 per share. The liquidation preference is $102 per share.)
(h) Receivables turnover.
(The net receivables on January 1, 19A, amounted to $84,000.)
(i) Inventory turnover.
(The inventory on January 1, 19A, amounted to $124,000.)
(j) Total asset turnover.
(Total assets on January 1, 19A, were $290,000.)

783

Problem 30-A

The Landgraf Manufacturing Co. produces a variety of products to customer specification. One of the jobs now underway and about to be completed is Job No. 417.

REQUIRED: Using the following information, prepare a job cost sheet similar to the one illustrated on page 754 of Chapter 30.

(a) Job No. 417; Item — Storage batteries; Quantity — 1,000; For — Century Electric Co.
(b) Date — July 11, 19--; Date wanted — Aug. 14, 19--; Date completed — Aug. 11, 19--.
(c) Materials requisitions:

#61B for	$1,050	#124C for	$ 940
#87D for	960	#158B for	1,060
#94A for	1,020	#173A for	980

(d) Daily time tickets:

July 11 — 118 hrs.	— $472.00		July 27 — 119 hrs.	— $476.00
13 — 120 hrs.	— 480.00		31 — 120 hrs.	— 480.00
17 — 119.5 hrs.	— 478.00		Aug. 2 — 117.5 hrs.	— 470.00
19 — 117 hrs.	— 468.00		4 — 122 hrs.	— 488.00
21 — 121 hrs.	— 484.00		7 — 121 hrs.	— 484.00
25 — 118.5 hrs.	— 474.00		11 — 120.5 hrs.	— 482.00

(e) Factory overhead rate: 150% of direct labor cost.
(Do *not* round cost per unit figure.)

Problem 30-B

The Maxwell Manufacturing Company uses a process cost accounting system. The following information describes what took place with respect to the first process employed in the Maxwell factory during the month of July:

In process beginning of month:	
400 units, complete as to material and 60% complete as to processing cost.	
Total cost so far assigned	$ 1,200
Material put into process during the month:	
3,500 units @ $2.60 each	9,100
Processing costs for the month:	
Labor	4,340
Factory overhead assigned to the process	3,100
Total cost to be accounted for	$17,740
Completed and transferred to next process during month	3,100 units
In process end of month (complete as to materials and 30% complete as to processing costs)	800 units

REQUIRED: Using the foregoing information, prepare a cost of production summary similar to the one illustrated on page 771 of Chapter 30.

Problem 30-C

The Sellers Manufacturing Company uses a process cost accounting system. Following are selected transactions for the year 19--:

(a) Materials purchases: Material F, $7,200; Material G, $18,000.
(b) Materials put into Process 1: Material F, $6,750; Material G, $22,500.
(c) Factory labor cost for the year, $86,400 ($27,000 relates to Process 1 and $59,400 relates to Process 2).
(d) Factory overhead cost (other than labor) for the month, $41,760 ($18,000 assigned to Process 1 and $23,760 to Process 2).
(e) Cost of 10,000 units transferred from Process 1 to Process 2, $74,250.
(f) Cost of 9,000 units completed in Process 2 and transferred to finished goods stockroom, $152,866.
(g) Cost of goods sold, $145,948.

REQUIRED: Using as your guide the "T" accounts illustrated on page 769 of Chapter 30, post each of the foregoing transactions to a similar set of "T" accounts, and trace the flow of costs through the accounts by means of lines and arrows. Enter the following opening account balances:

Material F, $4,800; Material G, $8,000; Process 2, $24,160; Finished Goods, $21,600.

appendix

computer-based accounting systems — design and use

Structure of accounting systems A-1

The design of a system of forms, records, and reports depends in large measure on the nature of the business by which the system is used. The number of transactions to be recorded in a given time period has much to do with the planning and arrangement of the chart of accounts and of the procedures for gathering and processing transaction information. Physical location of factory buildings, warehouses and offices, and the transaction volume at each location also influence the design of an accounting system.

The nature of the business, the kinds of transactions to be recorded and summarized, the transaction volume, and the location of physical facilities together comprise the *structure* of an accounting system. All of these factors together make careful systems planning essential.

The language of computer-based accounting systems

The original or *source documents* for many kinds of business transactions have been presented in this textbook. The source document is always the key record in a computer-based accounting system just as it is in a manual accounting system. Whether a source document is prepared by hand or by machine, the data it contains must be collected and recorded by people.

Some modern businesses are quite large, and this relative size affects their accounting systems. Modern systems for relatively large businesses include computer equipment that operates without human guidance other than the press of one or more buttons. The use of such equipment in an accounting system makes it a *computer-based accounting system.*

Computer-based accounting has brought about the development of a new language as well as new procedures. In computer-based accounting, information such as ledger account titles, dollar amounts, and physical quantities is known as *data.* The use of these data in different ways for different business purposes is known as *data processing.* Accounting involves the processing of data in several different forms. In fact, the original preparation of the source document for a business transaction is a form of data processing. Likewise, the recording of transactions in books of original entry, posting to ledger accounts, taking trial balances, and preparing financial statements are also forms of data processing.

Those who use computer equipment to process accounting records must apply accounting principles to each step. The same principles of debit and credit apply whether the work is done with computer equipment, with conventional accounting machines, or by the manual bookkeeper. Equipment and machines reduce routine manual work, increase the speed of producing records, and permit more accurate financial reporting.

Data processing is usually described in two ways. The processing of business transactions by the use of simple office machines with card punches or tape writers attached is known as *integrated data processing* (IDP). The processing of business transactions by the use of an electronic computer is known as *electronic data processing* (EDP).

Accounting systems design and use

No one can design and install an accounting system for a business that will function properly without a thorough knowledge of the operations of that business. When a business is first established this may not be possible. What is more, expansion of a business into new areas of operation, new personnel, or increased transaction volume may cause its accounting system to become inadequate.

For any one of the foregoing reasons, a business may decide to review its accounting system on an almost continuous basis, and to change one or more parts of the system at frequent intervals. Accounting systems review subdivides into three essential phases: **(1)** systems analysis, **(2)** systems design, and **(3)** systems implementation.

Systems analysis

Systems analysis has three major objectives:

(a) The determination of business needs for information.
(b) The determination of sources for such information.
(c) The shortcomings in the accounting systems and procedures presently in use.

The first step in systems analysis usually is a review of the organizational structure and the job descriptions of the personnel involved. The second step in systems analysis usually is a study of forms, records, and reports, and the processing methods and procedures used by the business. In this connection, a *systems manual*, which details instructions to employees and procedures to be followed, is extremely valuable to the systems analyst if it is available. The third step in systems analysis is to project management's plans for changes in such operational matters as sales volume, products, territories, salesmen, or customers into the near future.

Systems design

Accounting systems design changes are the result of systems analysis. A good systems designer needs to know the relative merits of various types of computer hardware, and be able to evaluate the various alternatives open to the business, which may or may not involve computer hardware.

Creativity and imagination are important attributes of a successful systems designer. The following general principles also are important:

(a) The value of information produced by an accounting system should never be less than the cost of obtaining it, and preferably the value should be greater than the cost.
(b) Any accounting system needs sufficient built-in internal control to safeguard business assets and protect data reliability.
(c) Any accounting system needs to be flexible enough to absorb data volume increases and changes in procedures and data processing techniques without disruption of the system.

Systems implementation

A newly created or revised accounting system is worthless without the ability to carry out, or implement, the recommendations of the systems analyst. The new or revised forms, records, reports, procedures, and hardware recommended by the systems analyst must be installed, and obsolete items must be removed. Each and every employee who will have a hand in operating the system must be thoroughly trained and adequately supervised until the new system is operating smoothly.

A major systems change, such as from a manual accounting system to a computer-based accounting system, usually is spread over a rather long period of time. For a while during the changeover period, the old and new systems must function side by side at least in part, and care must be taken to avoid seriously affecting the reliability of the data produced by the system(s).

Flow charts

One of the major tools of the systems analyst in the design of computer-based accounting systems is called the *flow chart*. In a flow chart, the major steps to be undertaken in processing a particular accounting transaction or series of closely related accounting transactions are shown in graphic form. The symbols most commonly used in preparing flow charts are:

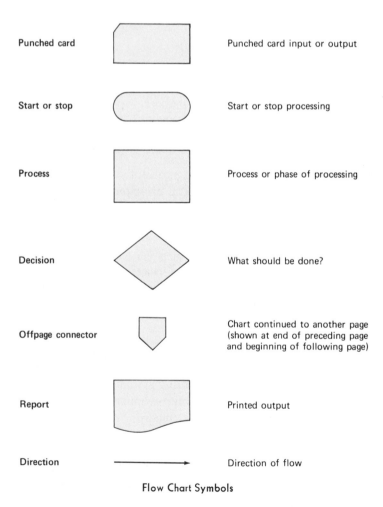

Punched card		Punched card input or output
Start or stop		Start or stop processing
Process		Process or phase of processing
Decision		What should be done?
Offpage connector		Chart continued to another page (shown at end of preceding page and beginning of following page)
Report		Printed output
Direction		Direction of flow

Flow Chart Symbols

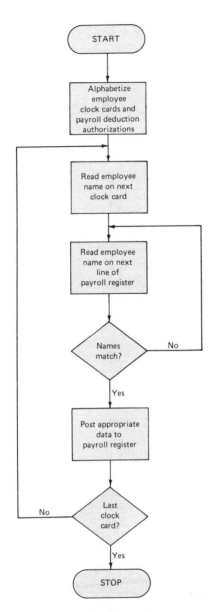

START

Alphabetize
employee
clock cards and
payroll deduction
authorizations

Read employee
name on next
clock card

Read employee
name on next
line of
payroll register

Names
match? — No

Yes

Post appropriate
data to
payroll register

No — Last
clock
card?

Yes

STOP

**Flow Chart—Posting Employee Clock Cards
and Deduction Authorizations
to Payroll Register**

Flow charts usually are prepared to be read from left to right and from top to bottom, with the direction of the flow being shown by lines and arrows. A brief description of each step in processing usually is written inside each flow-chart symbol. When one or more decisions are required at some stage in data processing, the questions to be answered usually are printed inside or next to each decision symbol. Most decisions involve comparison of two data items. If the items match, the decision is to go on with the process; if the two items do not match, the decision usually is to retrace some of the previously completed steps in the process.

The process involved in manually posting information from employee check stubs to a payroll register is shown in the adjacent flow chart.

This flow chart correlates with the discussion on pages 82–84 in Chapter 4. The employee doing the work begins by arranging the completed clock cards and payroll deduction authorization forms in alphabetical order and clipping the related forms together for each employee. (The clock cards were in clock number or social security number order.) He then looks at the name on the first clock card and at the name on the first line of the payroll register. If they match, he proceeds to post the appropriate data to the payroll register. If they do not match, he looks at each succeeding line of the register until he comes to the right one. After posting the appropriate data to the right line, he looks at the name on the next clock card and repeats the process until all clock cards have been posted. This assumes that there is only one clock card and set of related payroll deduction authorization forms per employee, and that each time a new employee is hired, a new clock card is prepared, related payroll deduction authorization forms are completed, and the payroll register listing of employees is revised. Otherwise, the flow chart would have to be extended to include these steps.

A-5

The amount of detail shown in a flow chart depends upon its purpose and the amount of detail desired. In implementing a computerized version of the payroll system illustrated above, information concerning hardware would have to be added, and more detailed information about adding new employees, dropping old employees, etc., would have to be included. The punched card symbol for input or output and the report symbol for printed output would then be pressed into use, as well as the connector symbol for flow charts occupying two or more pages.

The write-it-once principle as a labor-saving device

A source document, such as a purchase invoice or a sales ticket, usually is prepared manually by handwriting or typing on the document at the time of the transaction. The first step in computer-based accounting is the preparation of a punched card or a magnetic tape by a machine operator from a source document. (Equipment is rapidly emerging that can read data from source documents directly into computers.)

If the operator types the source document on an office machine with a card punching or tape encoding attachment, the card or tape is being prepared at the same time that the source document is being typed. If the office machine used is not an integrated data processing machine, the card or tape must be prepared later as a separate operation.

The process of recording the basic information about a business transaction in a form that makes later hand copying unnecessary has been called the *write-it-once principle*. This first step in computer-based accounting makes it possible to save labor in completing the later steps of the accounting cycle. Once a punched card or a magnetic tape has been prepared by a machine operator, the recorded information can be used over and over again when and where needed. The only further human effort needed is to feed the cards or tape into computer equipment. This equipment then performs automatically the functions of journalizing, posting, taking trial balances, preparing financial statements, and adjusting and closing ledger accounts.

Importance of locating errors in the write-it-once operation

If errors in the punching of cards or encoding magnetic tape are not discovered before the cards or tape are fed into computer equipment, such errors will be repeated in each step of the automated accounting cycle.

Designers of computer-based accounting systems have recognized the seriousness of the error problem. Errors in computer-based systems are normally located in either of two ways:

(a) Transaction information is verified as soon as it has been recorded.
(b) Automatic error-locating procedures built into the computer equipment are used later on in the accounting cycle.

A-6

Verifying transaction information already punched into cards is a process of running the cards through manually operated machines a second time. A different machine operator reads the information from the source document and goes through the same punching motions as did the original operator. If each punching stroke hits a hole in the card, the card passes right on through the machine. If a punching stroke hits a solid section of card, an error is indicated, and the machine notches the edge of the card next to the error. Notched cards are set aside and corrected later.

Businesses that find errors very difficult to control may decide not only to verify source document information before cards are processed but also to use automatic error-locating procedures later in the accounting cycle. Computer equipment also may be set up to locate certain errors electronically. When such errors are so located, an error light on the equipment usually goes on, and the equipment stops running.

Basic phases of automated data processing

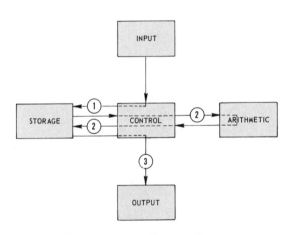

Diagram of Basic Computer System

The automated processing of any data in the completion of the accounting cycle consists of five basic phases. These five phases are common to all computer equipment, regardless of manufacturer. They are: **A-7**

(a) Input   (d) Arithmetic
(b) Control   (e) Output
(c) Storage

A diagram of a basic computer system is shown at the left.

Input. In order that computer equipment may complete the accounting process, the source document may have to be rewritten in a form that the equipment can interpret. Information about a business transaction in a form acceptable for use in automated data processing equipment is known as *input*. Any acceptable means for presenting this information to a computer is known as an *input device*.

Control. *Control* is the nerve center, or "action central" of the computer-based accounting system. It is like the central hall in a home or the lobby of a hotel. People must pass through the lobby of a hotel to get to their rooms. In the same way, transaction information must be routed through control in each step of automated data processing. Transaction information received as input is sent by control to storage, as shown by the flow line labeled "1" in the diagram above.

Storage. Transaction information stops in *storage* to await further use in computer-based accounting. Storage is often called the CPU (central processing unit) by computer people. Because storage holds information for future use just as does the human mind, it is often referred to as "memory." But unlike the human mind, storage must be told in great detail what to do with each item of transaction information that it holds. A detailed list of steps to be followed in completing the computerized accounting cycle is known as a *program*. A person who designs programs is called a *programmer*. The detailed work of arranging transaction information in the most efficient manner for computer processing is called *programming*.

Arithmetic. The primary work of computer-based accounting is done in the *arithmetic* phase. Transaction information is routed from storage through control to arithmetic. In the arithmetic phase, addition, subtraction, multiplication, or division is performed as needed; and the result is returned by control to storage. This round trip is shown by the flow line labeled "2" in the basic computer system diagram. Arithmetic also can compare two numbers and tell whether the first number is smaller than, equal to, or larger than the second number. This feature is useful in controlling inventories and expenses.

A-8

Output. When ledger account balances, financial statement items, or other data are desired, they are obtained from the automated data processing system in the output phase. Business information in a form acceptable for human use is known as *output*. Any acceptable means for converting coded machine information into English is known as an *output device*.

Business information requested by management from the data processing system is routed from storage through control to output, as shown by the flow line labeled "3" in the basic computer system diagram. Output devices are prepared which are used later to print in English the particular business information requested.

Input and output may be and often are handled by the same physical equipment called I-0 equipment by computer people.

The punched card as an input device

At present, the punched card is the most frequently used input device. One form of punched card is the IBM (International Business Machines Corporation) card, illustrated at the top of page A-9.

Utility companies, oil companies, magazine publishers, and mail order houses use punched cards as statements of account. The federal government and many large private companies use punched cards for payroll checks and other remittance checks.

Standard IBM Card

The small figures on the IBM card above show that it has 80 columns, numbered from left to right. The large figures on the card show that it has ten rows, numbered 0 to 9 inclusive from top to bottom. In addition, as the above illustration shows, the blank space at the top of the card provides room for two more rows, called the "twelve row" and the "eleven row."

As shown by the punches in the illustration, a single numerical digit may be formed by punching a small hole in a column at one of the ten positions numbered zero through nine A single letter or symbol may be formed by punching two holes in a column. One of these holes is punched through a position numbered one through nine. The other hole is punched through a position numbered twelve, eleven, or zero, as shown in the illustration above. The three top rows on the card are called the "zone" rows, and a hole punched in one of these rows is called a "zone" punch.

Planning the Use of the Punched Card. The first step in the use of a punched card as an input device is to plan the arrangement of the information on the card. A punched card that is to be used as a statement of account will contain the following information:

(a) Customer's name and address (e) Current sales to the customer
(b) Customer's account number (f) Amount received on account
(c) Billing date (g) Sales returns and allowances
(d) Customer's previous balance (h) Customer's new balance

Each item of information requires that several holes be punched into the card. An estimate is made of the longest group of letters or numbers required for each of the eight items to be placed on any statement of account. The punched card (or cards if two are needed) is then subdivided into eight groups of columns of sufficient size.

A group of columns used for a single item of information on a punched card is known as a *field*. There is a field for the customer's name and address, and a field for each of the other seven items of information.

Punching Information Into the Punched Card. After the information for preparing a customer's statement of account has been provided by the automated accounting system, a machine operator enters this information into a machine which in turn punches information holes into the card. One field on the card is used for each of the eight information items.

A machine used to punch information holes into punched cards from source documents is known as a *key punch*. An IBM key punch machine is illustrated here.

IBM Key Punch

Verifying the Information on the Punched Card. As soon as a batch of cards has been punched, the cards are checked in an attempt to avoid errors. A machine that looks exactly like a key punch and is used to find punching errors is called a *verifier*. As mentioned earlier, another operator reading from the same source document as the key punch operator enters the data into the verifier. The IBM verifier machine "feels" each card electronically to determine whether the correct holes have been punched. Each correct card is notched in a special "verify" position. If the verifier machine "feels" a missing hole or a hole in the wrong position, it notches a special "error" position on the card and the keyboard on the machine locks up.

Printing the Information on a Punched Card. The punched information on each IBM card is printed on a two-part statement card consisting of a statement and a stub. The printing is done by running the punched cards through a special printing machine. An automatic printing machine that lists, totals, and prints information previously punched onto cards is called a *tabulator* or *high-speed printer*. The information may either be printed on the same punched card from which it comes or on a separate sheet of paper.

Completing a Punched Card Statement of Account. After each of the two-part statement cards has been tabulated, the customer's account number and balance due are punched into the stub portion of the card. The statement card is then ready to be mailed to the customer. A completed two-part statement card is illustrated at the top of the next page.

Sorting Customer Remittance Stubs. When the customer receives a statement like the one illustrated on page A-11, he detaches the stub and

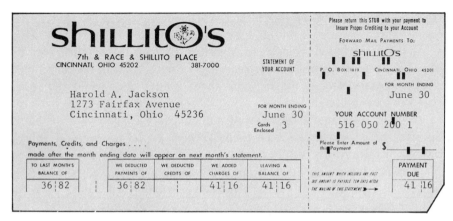

Punched Card Statement of Account

returns it with his remittance. When a remittance arrives, the amount received is keypunched into the stub that comes with the remittance. The stubs are then grouped into piles and run through a machine which sorts them by customer's account number.

A machine that automatically groups all punched cards of a similar kind and arranges them in some order is called a *sorter*. The stubs received from customers are placed in the hopper of the sorter. The sorted stubs drop into pockets. There is a "reject" pocket for cards that the machine is unable to sort.

Posting Customer Remittance Stubs. The final process in accounting for customer remittances is to run the stubs through the printer or tabulator in account number order. This machine process posts the remittances to individual customers' ledger account cards and determines the new account balances.

The same basic operations are followed in processing punched card checks, except that cash payment transactions are involved rather than cash receipt transactions. The transaction information must still be keypunched, verified, printed, sorted, and posted. These are basic data processing operations in computer-based accounting systems.

Magnetic tape as an input device

Magnetic tape usually is used as an input device in EDP systems. It is prepared for input by depositing small magnetized spots on reels of tape. This tape comes from the factory coated with a magnetic metal substance.

The chief advantage of magnetic tape is the speed with which it can be used as input. It is easy to carry and compact to store.

Magnetic ink symbol numbers as input devices

As discussed in Chapter 3, the American Bankers Association recommends the use of symbol numbers printed in magnetic ink on each bank check. The use of these magnetic ink symbol numbers permits the automated processing of checks.

The use of magnetic ink symbol numbers in the processing of bank checks is called *magnetic ink character recognition*. The common abbreviation for this process is *MICR*. A bank check with magnetic ink symbol numbers printed across the bottom of the check is illustrated below:

No. 34   ST. LOUIS *County National* BANK   80-459 / 810

CLAYTON (ST. LOUIS) MO. *April 6, 1972*

PAY TO THE ORDER OF *Edwards Pharmacy* $14.27

Fourteen 27/100 _____ DOLLARS

James K. Roberts

⑆0810⑈0459⑉ 121 077 3⑈

Bank Check with Magnetic Ink Symbol Numbers

Note that the symbol numbers at the bottom of the check use a style that is different from regular Arabic numerals. This is because these numbers are read by a device that "feels" the surface area of each number and recognizes its shape. Regular Arabic numerals, especially 2, 5, 6, and 9, are too much alike to be easily distinguished one from the other by an electronic reading machine.

Encoding Symbol Numbers on Bank Checks. Magnetic ink symbol numbers are printed on checks using special printing machines. A machine for printing magnetic ink characters on checks is called an *encoder*.

Encoding may be done by the company that prints the blank checks, or by the bank that supplies the blank checks to its depositors.

Clearing Encoded Bank Checks Through the Federal Reserve System. The first series of encoded numerals in the check illustration (0810-0459) is adapted from the ABA number in the upper right-hand corner of the check. Notice that the number 80, which represents the State of Missouri, has been dropped from the encoded symbol number. This is because 0810 locates the bank in the Eighth Federal Reserve District (08) and the Greater St. Louis area (10), and the State of Missouri is understood.

The Federal Reserve system sorts checks encoded with magnetic ink symbol numbers as follows:

Step 1. The bank in which the check is deposited forwards it to the Federal Reserve clearing house in its district.

Step 2. The Federal Reserve clearing house sorts the check along with other checks received from banks in its district on special sorting equipment using the first two encoded symbol numbers (08 in the illustration). This results in twelve batches of checks for the twelve Federal Reserve districts.

Step 3. Each Federal Reserve clearing house forwards the checks drawn on banks in other Federal Reserve districts to the proper districts. In this process, the check illustrated on the previous page is forwarded to the Eighth Federal Reserve District clearing house in St. Louis.

Step 4. The clearing house in St. Louis sorts on the next two encoded symbol numbers (10 in the illustration) for distribution of the checks to regional clearing houses. Since the bank on which the illustrated check is drawn is a Greater St. Louis bank, this check is not forwarded to a regional clearing house.

Step 5. Each district or regional clearing house sorts on the next four symbol numbers (0459 in the illustration) for distribution to individual banks. These four symbol numbers are individual bank numbers.

Step 6. Batches of sorted checks are forwarded to the banks on which they were drawn. The illustrated check is sent to St. Louis County National Bank.

Processing Encoded Bank Checks in Individual Banks. The second series of encoded numerals on the illustrated check (121-077-3) is the account number of the individual depositor at his bank. The depositor's bank sorts its own checks by account number. It uses the same type of MICR sorting equipment as that used in the Federal Reserve clearing houses. This equipment can sort as many as 90,000 checks per hour.

In smaller banks, checks sorted by depositor's account number are posted by using conventional bank posting machines. Larger banks having encoders of their own print the amount of each check in magnetic ink under the signature line. Encoding amounts of individual checks makes it possible to sort and post electronically to depositors' ledger accounts in one operation.

The control phase in automated accounting

The control phase of an electronic system receives electronic commands from input devices and sees that they are carried out. Each command refers to some item of transaction information which is in storage. The control phase searches storage locations one by one in carrying out commands from input devices and keeps track of the location of each command as it is carried out. This avoids skipping program steps.

The storage phase in automated accounting

In manual accounting, the journal, the ledger, and the trial balance are methods of temporarily storing transaction information. This information is stored permanently on the financial statements.

In computerized accounting, means of storage must be used which make it possible to complete the accounting cycle automatically. Means of storing journal entries, ledger account balances, and trial balance information must be found. Any means of storing accounting information in between the steps of the computerized accounting cycle is known as a *storage device*.

External Storage Devices. Storage devices physically removed from a computer system that can be fed into the system when desired are known as *external storage devices*. Both punched cards and magnetic tape are able to retain transaction information for long periods of time. For this reason, as well as the fact that they can be physically removed from the system, these input devices are used also as data (external) storage devices.

Externally Stored Journal Entries. External storage devices may be used either for temporary storage or for permanent storage of transaction information. Punched cards are excellent storage devices for journal entries. This is because a separate punched card can be used to record each debit element of a journal entry and a separate punched card can be used to record each credit element of a journal entry. The cards can then be machine sorted by ledger account titles for machine posting.

Journal entries may also be stored on magnetic tape. However, reels of tape cannot be sorted in the same way that punched cards are sorted. Journal entries on reels of tape must be machine posted in the order in which they were recorded. This is the same order in which journal entries would be posted manually. The only advantage of machine posting is that it is faster and relatively free of error.

Internal Storage Devices. The storage phase of a computer system is contained within the machinery. The storage phase receives instructions from control, which have been passed on from input. These instructions are of four types:

(a) Take data from input   (c) Receive data from arithmetic
(b) Send data to arithmetic   (d) Send data to output

Devices for temporarily storing accounting information within a computer are known as *internal storage devices*.

Internally Stored Ledgers. Internal storage devices are used in computerized accounting to keep ledger accounts up-to-date. Each account in the ledger is assigned a storage address. Debits and credits are fed in on punched cards or reels of tape. Control instructs input to transfer a debit or a credit amount into storage from a card or tape reel.

The incoming debit or credit amount must go to a storage address different from the address assigned to the related ledger account. Since this address is needed only for the current posting operation, it is not permanently assigned. However, the accountant must keep a chart of storage addresses (corresponding to a chart of accounts) in order to know at all times which addresses are assigned and which are open.

Automatic Posting. Automatic posting requires the following steps:

Step 1. Control instructs input to read the old balance of the ledger account from a master magnetic ledger tape into its assigned address in storage.

Step 2. Control instructs storage to transfer the old balance of the ledger account from its assigned address to the arithmetic unit.

Step 3. Control instructs storage to transfer the related debit or credit amount, which has just come into storage from a punched card or transaction tape to arithmetic.

Step 4. Control instructs arithmetic either to add the debit amount to or subtract the credit amount from the old balance of the ledger account.

Step 5. Control instructs storage to receive the new ledger account balance from arithmetic and to store it in the assigned storage address for the particular ledger account. This is the same address in which the old ledger account balance was stored.

Step 6. Control instructs storage to transfer the new ledger account balance out to an updated master magnetic ledger tape.

A-15

In a computer-based accounting system, when a new item is stored electronically in the same internal storage address as a previous item, the new item replaces the old item at that address.

To illustrate the automated posting process, suppose that the cash account is assigned storage address number 10. The beginning cash balance, a debit of $1,200, becomes input by means of a punched card and is sent to address number 10 by the control unit. Suppose also that a debit to the cash account, in the amount of $50, is placed in input by means of another punched card and is sent by control to address number 100 for temporary storage.

The posting process will proceed as follows:

Step 1. Control instructs storage to transfer the beginning cash balance of $1,200 from address number 10 to arithmetic.

Step 2. Control instructs storage to transfer the $50 debit to the cash account from address number 100 to arithmetic.

Step 3. Control instructs arithmetic to add the $50 cash debit to the beginning balance of $1,200.

Step 4. Control instructs storage to receive the new cash balance, $1,250, and to store it back in address number 10, the address temporarily assigned to the cash account.

Limitations of Internal Storage. The illustration of automated posting demonstrates that internal storage may be used both for semi-permanent storage of ledger account balances and for temporary storage of debits and credits to ledger accounts. A small business having relatively few ledger accounts could get along with a rather small amount of internal storage. However, a large business having a great many ledger accounts would need a rather large amount of internal storage. Internal storage either must be large enough to handle the ledger accounts and the posting operations of the computer-based accounting system in which it is used, or ledger account balances will have to be stored externally on magnetic tape or punched cards.

The arithmetic phase in automated accounting

The arithmetic phase of an electronic system receives instructions from control to add, subtract, multiply, divide, or to compare two numbers. Arithmetic works with only two numbers at a time, having received them from different storage locations. To avoid returning subtotals or partial products to storage, however, arithmetic has a temporary electronic storage unit of its own. The electronic storage device in the arithmetic phase of a computer system used to store subtotals and partial products for further processing is known as an *accumulator*.

The output phase in automated accounting

In many ways, the output phase in automated accounting is just the reverse of the input phase. Punched cards and magnetic tape have already been described as input devices and as storage devices. Cards and reels of tape may also be used effectively as output devices.

Upon request, control will instruct storage to punch out cards or to write on magnetic tape any information desired. This might be journal entries, ledger account balances, trial balances, or financial statements. The cards or tapes must then be converted to English language information.

The Tabulator as an Output Device. The tabulator has already been discussed in connection with the use of the punched card. As indicated, it can list, total, or print journal entries, ledger account balances, trial balances, or financial statements whenever desired. The tabulator prints a line at a time and can handle up to 90 lines a minute.

The High-Speed Printer as an Output Device. High-speed printing machines are now available into which punched cards, magnetic tape, or electronically readable source documents may be fed. These machines are capable of printing in excess of 900 lines of information per minute.

index

I-1

I

IBM card, A-8; standard, *illustrated*, A-9
IBM key punch, *illustrated*, A-10
Identification number, 93
Imprest method, 55, 696
Improvement bonds, 615
Income, and self-employment taxes, 283; net operating, 252; self-employment, 284
Income and expense statement, 251
Income and retained earnings statement, combined, 605; The Sutton Machinery Company, 606
Income statement, 9, 41, 251, 497, 728; analysis of, 252; branch office, 668; combined home office-branch, 680; comparative, The B. J. Patrick Manufacturing Co., 729; condensed comparative, 743; condensed comparative for The B. J. Patrick Manufacturing Co., 739; for Howard C. Miller, 123; form of the, 251; Holling & Renz, *illustrated*, 498; home office, 674; importance of the, 251; interpreting the, percentage analysis, 500; investment earnings in the, 643; "ladder type," 251; purpose of, 41; The Adams Appliance Store, 253; The Brown Advertising Agency (model), 41; Wilson & Son Wholesale Drug Company, 526, 533
Income statement columns, of ten-column work sheet, 248
Income summary, 268
Income tax, employees income tax payable account, 94; employees' withheld, 78; withholding allowances table, *illustrated*, 80; withholding table, *illustrated*, 80
Incorporating, a partnership, 436; a single proprietorship, 434
Incorporation, articles of, 565, *illustrated*, 567; certificate of, 565; state laws, 564
Incorporators, 426, 565
Increase, in asset offset by decrease in another asset, 8, 15; in asset offset by increase in liability, 7, 14; in asset offset by increase in owner's equity, 7, 14; in asset offset by increase in owner's equity resulting from revenue, 8, 18
Independent contractor, 76
Indirect labor, 699, 756
Indirect manufacturing expense, 700
Indirect materials, 699
Individual posting, 51, 314; sales, 337
Indorsement, 62; accommodation, 185; blank, 185; of notes, 185; of

payment, 185; on note, *illustrated*, 186; restrictive, 62; special, 185
Information desired, 442
Input, in automated data processing, A-7
Input device, A-7; magnetic ink symbol numbers as, A-12; magnetic tape as, A-11; punched card as, A-8
Installment sales, accounting for, 342; account receivable form, *illustrated*, 344; accrual basis, 343; and consignment sales, 341–356; determining gross profit on, 345; installment basis, 343; plan, 341; repossession, 343; sales register, *illustrated*, 342–343
Insurance, accounting for, 371; annual rate, 371; canceled, 374; expired, 371; policy, defined, 371; policy register, *illustrated*, 372–373, 374; premium, defined, 371; term rate, 371
Insurance expense, 484
Intangible asset, 421
Intangible long-lived assets, 378; accounting for, 643
Integrated data processing (IDP), A-2
Interest, accounting for, 174; calculating on notes, 176; formula for computing, 177; 60-day, 6 percent method, 177
Interest, prepaid, 175; accounting for, 374
Interest accounts, adjustment of the, 479
Interest earned, 181
Interest income, 181
Interest payable, accrued, 191, 282
Interest receivable, accrued, 190, 280
Interim financial statements, 451, 518–536; producing with the aid of work sheets, 519
Interim periods, 518
Interim statements, for January, 525; successive periods, 532
Internally stored ledgers, A-14
Internal storage, A-14; limitations of, A-15
Internal storage devices, A-14
Interpretation, of purchase orders, 326
Interpreting, in accounting, 3
Interpreting the balance sheet, 505
Interpreting the income statement: percentage analysis, 500
In transit goods, 359
Inventories, assigning cost to, 701; at cost or market, whichever is lower, 703; of a manufacturing business, 701; perpetual, 703, 755

Inventory, accounting for, 358; book, 703; finished goods, 753; merchandise, 146, 172; perpetual, 491; running, 703; taking a physical, 358; work in process, 753; *see* Merchandise inventory
Inventory turnover, 261
Investment earnings, in the income statement, 643
Investment opportunity, in a corporation, 563
Investments, bond, 637; by owners, 508; corporation stock, 636; permanent, 256; temporary, 255
Invoice, corrected, 694; purchase, 148, 300, *illustrated*, 149, 684; verification of, 684
Invoice method, 150
Invoice of shipment, 348; Mattoon Electric Co., *illustrated*, 349
Invoice register, 300, 309, 443; Holling & Renz, *illustrated*, 310, 464; proving the, 313
Issued stock, 587

J

Job card, 754
Job cost sheet, 754; *illustrated*, 754
Job ledger, 755
Job order cost accounting, 754; *see* Cost accounting
Job order cost accounts, flow of costs through, 759; *illustrated*, 762–763
Job sheet, 754
Jobs in process, 755
Joint products and by-products, 770
Journal, 22; purpose of, 33
Journal, cashbook, 52
Journal, cash disbursements, 52
Journal, cash payments, 52
Journal, cash receipts, 52
Journal, check register, 52
Journal, combined cash, 52, 107, 209; adjusting and closing entries, 125; Howard C. Miller, 112–115; posting from, 166; special columns in, 52; The Adams Appliance Store, 222–225; The Phillips Store, 168–169
Journal, four-column, 47; footing and ruling, 50; *illustrated*, 47; posting from, 51; proving, 49; special columns in, 52, 53; The Brown Advertising Agency, 49
Journal, purchases, 147, 150, 210; *illustrated*, 151; posting from, 152, 166; The Adams Appliance Store, 221; The Phillips Store, 167
Journal, sales, 153, 159, 210; posting